The Gospel to the Nations

Peter T. O'Brien has been Vice-Principal of Moore Theological College, Sydney, since 1985.

In recognition of his contribution to scholarship and life-long commitment to world mission, this wide-ranging collection of essays offers fresh perspectives on the message and mission of the apostle Paul.

In honour of Peter T. O'Brien

The Gospel to the Nations

Perspectives on Paul's Mission

Edited by
Peter Bolt & Mark Thompson

APOLLOS (an imprint of Inter-Varsity Press),
38 De Montfort Street, Leicester LE1 7GP, England

INTERVARSITY PRESS
PO Box 1400, Downers Grove, IL 60515, USA
World Wide Web: www.ivpress.com
Email: mail@ivpress.com

First published 2000

British Library Cataloguing in Publication Data
A catalogue record for this book is available from the British Library.

Library of Congress Cataloging-in-Publication Data has been requested.

16	15	14	13	12	11	10	9	8	7	6	5	4	3	2
12	11	10	09	08	07	06	05	04	03	02	01			

UK ISBN 0-85111-468-7
US ISBN 0-8308-1557-0

Set in Minion Condensed
Typeset in Great Britain by The Midlands Book Typesetting Company, Loughborough.

Printed and bound in the UK by 4edge Limited

Contents

Editors' preface

The mission and message of Paul, apostle to the nations, remain of vital importance as Christians enter the twenty-first century. Paul's burden to proclaim the crucified Christ to a world under judgment and determined in its opposition to the living God remains the burden of all who share with him the salvation accomplished at the cross. His letters to churches and individuals, written with the authority of an apostle of Christ and under the inspiration of the Holy Spirit, expose the depths of the believer's ongoing battle with the flesh, call for clear vision based on what God has done for us through the death and resurrection of his Son, and challenge our preoccupation with lesser matters. The reconciliation won for us at the cross, and the message of reconciliation entrusted to us through that same gracious activity, is meant to transform our life radically in every sphere. It did in Paul's case.

By Paul's own testimony the gospel he was set apart to preach focused on Jesus Christ as the fulfilment of God's promises (Rom. 1:1–3). Modern interpreters of Paul, if they are to be true to the apostle himself, must therefore seek to understand his mission to proclaim the gospel to the nations from the perspective of biblical theology. After an appreciation of the honorand of this volume, the next three essays call us back to this biblical theological perspective, as three Old Testament scholars explore the Old Testament background to Paul's mission. The sweep of the entire Old Testament, the patriarchal narratives and the prophetic hope of Jeremiah provide an important context for Paul's thought and practice. These essays are followed by a series of investigations from within the field of New Testament studies which explore various facets of Paul's mission as developed in his letters and the record of his ministry found in the book of Acts. A further section deals more specifically with the world into which Paul's message was proclaimed. Paul's gospel challenged the life and thought of his time in ways which help us to understand the impact it might have in our own. A final section looks beyond the New Testament to the use of Paul's message in history and in contemporary theological thought. Authentically *Christian* theology has always been shaped by the ministry and message of the apostle to the nations.

A number of people have helped in different ways to bring this project to completion. Peter Jensen, who commissioned the work, has always been enthusiastic and helpful. Successive Theological Books Editors at IVP (UK), Mark Smith and Philip Duce, have provided valuable encouragement and support. Rob Maidment kindly assisted by creating the index. Most of all, thanks are due to Ruby Arthur, who tirelessly worked through one draft after another, and without whom we could not possibly have met the deadlines we had set.

The papers collected in this volume were all produced to honour a man who has made Paul's concerns his own and has helped many to understand those concerns more clearly. As we solicited essays for this volume, we were overcome by the fact that the responses to our invitation uniformly mentioned Peter O'Brien's contribution, not only at the level of academic excellence, but also as a personal godly example and encouragement. Peter's passion for the gospel of Jesus Christ and his care in expounding that gospel and its implications through his own teaching, writing and personal ministry mark him out as a genuine student of the apostle Paul. On his sixty-fifth birthday we would like to thank God for his ministry and pray that his labours to assist God's people in understanding the word of life may continue to bear fruit for many years to come. *Soli Deo gloria.*

November 1999   Peter G. Bolt
                                                               Mark D. Thompson

Abbreviations

AB	Anchor Bible.
ABD	*Anchor Bible Dictionary*, ed. D. N. Freedman et al., 6 vols. (New York: Doubleday, 1992).
ABR	*Australian Biblical Review*.
AC	Augsburg Commentary.
AJJS	*Australian Journal of Jewish Studies*.
AnBib	Analecta Biblica.
ANRW	*Aufsteig und Niedergang der römischen Welt*.
BAGD	W. Baur, *A Greek–English Lexicon of the New Testament and Other Early Christian Literature*, tr. and adapted by W. F. Arndt & F. W. Gingrich, rev. and augmented by F. W. Gingrich & F. W. Denker from Baur's fifth edition (1958) (Chicago: University of Chicago Press, ^{2}1979).
BAR	*Biblical Archaeology Review*.
BBR	*Bulletin for Biblical Research*.
BDF	F. Blass, A. Debrunner and R. W. Funk, *A Greek Grammar of the New Testament and Other Early Christian Literature* (Chicago: University of Chicago Press, 1961).
BECNT	Baker Exegetical Commentary on the New Testament.
BETL	Bibliotheca ephemeridum theologicarum Lovaniensium.
BG	G. Rinaldi, *Biblia Gentium*
BibInt	*Biblical Interpretation*.
BJRL	Bulletin of the John Rylands Library.
BNTC	Black's New Testament Commentaries.
BibTrans	*The Bible Translator*.
BTB	*Biblical Theology Bulletin*.
BZNW	Beiheft, Zeitschrift für die neutestamentliche Wissenschaft.
CQ	*Classical Quarterly*.
CTh	*Codex Theodosianus*
DLNTD	*Dictionary of the Later New Testament and its Developments*, ed. R. P. Martin & P. H. Davids (Downers Grove, IL, and Leicester: IVP, 1997).
DPL	*Dictionary of Paul and his Letters*, ed. G. F. Hawthorne, R. P. Martin & D. G. Reid (Downers Grove, IL, and Leicester: IVP, 1993).
EQ	*Evangelical Quarterly*.
Exp	*Expositor*.
ExpT	*Expository Times*.
FaithMiss	*Faith and Mission*.
GTJ	*Grace Theological Journal*.
HAT	Handbuch zum Alten Testament.
HBT	*Horizons in Biblical Theology*.
HNT	Handbuch zum Neuen Testament.
HTKNT	Herders Theologische Kommentar zum Neuen Testament.
HTR	*Harvard Theological Review*.

ICC	International Critical Commentary.
IDB	*Interpreter's Dictionary of the Bible*, ed. G. A. Buttrick et al., 4 vols. (New York and Nashville: Abingdon, 1962).
IJST	*International Journal of Systematic Theology*
ITC	International Theological Commentary.
JAAR	*Journal of the American Academy of Religion.*
JBL	*Journal of Biblical Literature.*
JECS	*Journal of Early Christian Studies.*
JETS	*Journal of the Evangelical Theological Society.*
JSJ	*Journal for the Study of Judaism in the Persian, Hellenistic and Roman Period.*
JSNT	*Journal for the Study of the New Testament.*
JSOT	*Journal for the Study of the Old Testament.*
JTS	*Journal of Theological Studies.*
KEK	Kritischexegetischer Kommentar über das Neue Testament.
LCL	Loeb Classical Library.
LTJ	*Lutheran Theological Journal*
LXX	The Septuagint
MM	J. H. Moulton & G. Milligan, *The Vocabulary of the Greek New Testament Illustrated from the Papyri and Other Non-Literary Sources* (London: Hodder and Stoughton, 1930).
MSS	Manuscripts.
MT	Masoretic Text.
MusHel	*Museum Helveticum.*
NASB	New American Standard Bible (1963).
NEB	New English Bible (NT 1961, ²1970; OT 1970).
NICNT	New International Commentary on the New Testament.
NIDNTT	*New International Dictionary of New Testament Theology*, ed. C. Brown, 3 vols. (Exeter: Paternoster, 1975–8, rev. 1986).
NIDOTTE	*New International Dictionary of Old Testament Theology and Exegesis*, ed. W. A. van Gemeren, 5 vols. (Carlisle: Paternoster, 1997).
NIGTC	New International Greek Testament Commentary.
NIV	New International Version of the Bible (1973, 1978, 1984).
NovT	*Novum Testamentum.*
NRSV	New Revised Standard Version of the Bible (1989).
NSBT	New Studies in Biblical Theology.
NTS	*New Testament Studies.*
NTTS	*New Testament Tools and Studies.*
OTL	Old Testament Library.
REA	*Real-Encyclopädie der klassischen Altertumswissenschaft*, Pauly-Wissowa.
RTR	*Reformed Theological Review.*
SB	Stuttgarter Bibelstudien.
SBLDS	Society of Biblical Literature Dissertation Series.
SBET	*Scottish Bulletin of Evangelical Theology.*
SBT	Studies in Biblical Theology.
SJT	*Scottish Journal of Theology.*

SNTSMS	Society for New Testament Studies Monograph Series.
StTh	*Studia Theologica.*
SUNT	Studien zur Umwelt des Neuen Testaments.
Sup	Supplementary volume.
SVF	H. von Arnim, *Stoicorum Veterum Fragmenta*
TDNT	*Theological Dictionary of the New Testament*, ed. G. Kittel & G. Friedrich, tr. G. W. Bromiley, 10 vols. (Grand Rapids: Eerdmans, 1964–76).
TDOT	*Theological Dictionary of the Old Testament*, ed. J. G. Botterweck & H. Ringren, tr. J. T. Willis (Grand Rapids: Eerdmans, 1974–).
ThLZ	*Theologische Literaturzeitung.*
ThQ	*Theologische Quartalschrift.*
TJT	*Taiwan Journal of Theology.*
TrinJ	*Trinity Journal.*
TheolToday	*Theology Today.*
TU	*Texte und Untersuchungen zur Geschichte der altchristlichen Literatur.*
TWAT	*Theologisches Wörterbuch zum Alten Testament* (German original of *TDOT*).
TynB	*Tyndale Bulletin.*
USQR	*Union Seminary Quarterly Review.*
VC	*Vigiliae Christianae.*
VoxEv	*Vox Evangelica.*
VT	*Vetus Testamentum.*
WBC	Word Biblical Commentary.
WEC	Wycliffe Exegetical Commentary.
WMANT	Wissenschaftlicher Monographien zum Alten und Neuen Testament.
WTJ	*Westminster Theological Journal.*
WUNT	Wissenschaftlicher Untersuchungen zum Neuen Testament.
WW	*Word and World.*
ZNW	*Zeitschrift für die neutestamentliche Wissenschaft.*
ZThK	*Zeitschrift für Theologie und Kirche.*

1. Peter Thomas O'Brien: an appreciation

Peter F. Jensen

The 'consuming passion' of Peter O'Brien's life is the gospel of the Lord Jesus Christ. He was born in Sydney on 6 November 1935, and educated at the famous Fort St Boys' High School. The family church was St Philip's, Eastwood, and it was in the fellowship of that congregation that he was converted to Christ. His acceptance of the gospel was to be the most significant event of his life. It marked his salvation and his assurance of the grace of God, and it also made him what he essentially is, a missionary.

From the earliest days of his Christian life, Peter preached the gospel. At first he studied accountancy and it seemed that he might find a career in the Commonwealth Bank. But he was deeply involved with Christian ministry through his church, and by the time he was twenty-three he had offered to the Church Missionary Society for service overseas. Entry to Moore College followed and he studied there between 1958 and 1961. During that time he served in the difficult Kings Cross area of Sydney, and evangelized in the open air, a formidable arena for any preacher. Graduation was succeeded by ordination (1961), curacy and a stint as junior tutor at the College. In 1963 he married Mary Elizabeth Beer, whom he had met at St Philip's, Eastwood.

In 1964 Peter and Mary left Sydney for India, where he lectured at the Union Bible Seminary at Yeotmal (now Poona) until 1968. After doctoral work in Manchester, they returned to Yeotmal from 1971 to 1973. Their missionary service was characterized by a remarkable ability to bridge cultural and theological divides. Although Moore College has been his

1

sphere of ministry since 1974, India entered his heart and his speech. To this day Hindi words are made to do duty when an English one will not do. It is always 'as we say in Hindi', not 'as they say'; his identification with India is deep, and in some ways it is as though India is still home. Certainly, cross-cultural mission is at the centre of his thoughts and his ministry. His service of the Church Missionary Society continues unabated, and mission forms one of the key themes of his academic work.

Peter would say (surely with justice) that his commitment to mission is a necessary consequence of being possessed by the gospel of Christ. He does not merely theorize about this. He is quick to commend the gospel in public or in private, in preaching to a crowd or speaking with an individual. He has a great love of teaching the 'ordinary' people in the ordinary circumstances of church life. The goal is that men and women will come to know Christ and be built up in him. He and Mary have joined a Korean congregation, and delight in ministry which crosses the barriers of language and custom. It was natural that when he was invited to give the Moore College Lectures in 1992, his theme should be a missionary one: Paul and the dynamic of the gospel, published as *Consumed by Passion* (1993). It brings together many of the key emphases of Peter's life: mission, Paul, exegesis, biblical theology.

In theology, Peter O'Brien is shaped by his evangelical Anglicanism. His basic commitment is to the One whose greatest work was to save us from the penalty of our sins by dying for us on the cross. Both his piety and his theology (as we should expect) centre at the cross, and reflect an unmistakably deep gratitude and love for Christ. The inspired Scriptures are the infallible revelation of God summed up in Christ, and he sees the Testaments as belonging together, not being willing to divorce them as is the habit of some. He has sought, therefore, to develop a biblical theology, interpreting the parts of the Bible in the light of the development of the whole. In keeping with his belief about the unity and authority of Scripture, he is willing to challenge both the traditions and the speculations of the systematicians. He does not deny the importance of historical and systematic theology – far from it – but he wishes to see the advent of a systematic which is more accountable to exegesis and more truly responsive to biblical theology. At the same time he is interested in the development of Christian lives which are obedient to God's Word.

He is not a controversialist. However, neither does he belong to that school which sees a virtue in spreading out options but not disclosing a conviction. His method is to let students and other scholars know how and why the choices have been made. The 'New Perspective' on Paul receives respectful attention and some praise, but not endorsement. He is a firm supporter of the ministry of women, but his careful exegesis of 1 Timothy 2 prevents him from supporting the ordination of women. Ecclesiology serves the gospel, and is typically congregationally centred and so welcoming of all those who belong to Christ. At every point accurate exegesis is basic to a true understanding of what the Lord has said and is saying, and hence of our obedience to him.

In the last decades a new sort of theological teacher has emerged in some of the seminaries and colleges where students are prepared for ministry. The PhD system has created the self-appointed specialist, whose call to the teaching ministry has not been ratified by the church, and whose expertise is narrow and confessional responsibility muted. It is not surprising that the programme of such institutions has become fragmented and hardly does its job of preparing preachers of God's Word, confident in the Bible and fully committed to preaching its message. The teachers may be highly skilled, but their skill is not integrated with the ministry of the Word of God.

Peter O'Brien's professional skills are also of the first order. His works on the Pauline epistles are treasured contributions to an understanding of the apostle. Their classic character arises from a fundamental reverence for the text, combined with technical expertise and a desire to be faithful to the author and useful to the reader. The result is commentaries which actually enlighten the text and serve the reader. His approach is a model of what the commentator should be, judicious, accurate, unflinching in the face of exegetical problems, pithy. He deeply admired his doctoral supervisor, Professor F. F. Bruce, and it is not surprising to discover much of Bruce's reliability, wisdom and fidelity to the text in what he writes.

The O'Brien skills do not suffer from the comparison with the specialists I have referred to, but he has an utterly different approach to the task of preparing men and women for ministry. His area of expertise is the New Testament, but his interest is the knowledge of God. He is an academic, but not merely an academic. He does not bypass the Bible in seeking to know God, but he acknowledges that the Bible is God's infallible revelation of himself, to be read and understood and trusted and applied in daily life. In Peter O'Brien we see one in whom academic work and the ministry of God's Word are integrated. The aim of theological education as he understands it is to lead students into an ever deeper knowledge of the living God, and to equip them to preach the message of the gospel through the exposition of the Scriptures in all the world. His academic work shows that these convictions do not obscure the truth of the Bible in a doctrinaire way; they actually enhance it, because he listens before he speaks, and prays before he listens.

Missionary service was punctuated by doctoral studies in Manchester. Peter's thesis on the Pauline thanksgivings was published by Brill in 1977. In Manchester Peter and Mary were part of the ministry at St Mary's, Cheadle, and entered associations and friendships which continue to the present. The ministry of the gospel continued to form an essential part of their lives, and research did not suspend it in any way. In 1974, after a third term in India, Peter accepted the invitation of Principal D. B. Knox to join the Faculty of Moore College. In resuming his links with the College, Peter came once more into direct fellowship with those who had most powerfully shaped his theology as a student. From 1959 until 1985, D. B. Knox dominated the scene, with his fertile mind and persuasive speech, a biblical theologian much influenced by the English Reformation. As his Vice-principal until 1974, Donald Robinson introduced a way of studying the New Testament which owed much to Professor C. F. D. Moule, and which set the Scriptures indubitably into their historical context. Both men were invigorating teachers, and both were capable of setting their students on fire with a love for the Bible.

Peter O'Brien's long tenure at the College has been of central significance to its recent history. He is, as has already been observed, first of all a gospel man and a Bible man, and hence a preacher and teacher of God's Word. At every point throughout this long time he has commended the gospel in word and deed. His life at the College has been marked by many obligations and responsibilities which may well have completely diverted his energies from research and teaching. He is punctilious in requiring rigour and integrity, for example, whether in the academic boards, the classroom or the examining process. But there can be no doubt that his main business is to teach the Bible, and so build men and women in their knowledge of God and prepare them to pastor others. From this role he has not deviated. His students are aware that from him they will receive the same reverence for the text, the same integration of theology and practice, the same reliable information, the same acute analysis of current debates as may be found in his writings. Indeed, his colleagues are astonished by the fruit of his industry, since it seems so effortless, given the little time he has available.

In 1985 Peter O'Brien was invited to become Vice-principal of Moore College in succession to Dr W. J. Dumbrell. The College was at a moment of significant transition. Not only had Bill Dumbrell accepted an invitation to serve overseas; the twenty-six-year tenure of Principal Knox, who could be called the founder of the modern College, was coming to an end. The trustees of the College appointed me as Principal from 1 March 1985, and I was relieved and delighted to secure the assent of Peter O'Brien to be the Vice-principal at the same time. From that day, by the Lord's grace, we have served together in the cause of the gospel through the work of the College. There have not been lacking other invitations to Peter to occupy posts which others would regard as more prestigious and more rewarding. To my utter relief, and my undying gratitude, he has declined them all.

More important than my gratitude is the good thus done for the cause of Christ wherever the College's influence may be felt. Peter has provided that wise and godly counsel, support and fidelity which have been absolutely integral to whatever has been achieved. He is trusted by those who have dealings with the College, because his word may be relied on, his judgment is sound and his priorities are godly. Wherever the inner life of the College is understood, his contribution is appreciated for what it is, and there is immediate recognition that his firm and dependable leadership has been essential to the good health of the enterprise. Countless students have received his full attention to their problems, and he has exercised the pastoral gift, whether in public preaching or private counsel, with great skill. I can testify that he has performed the supremely difficult task, where necessary, of correcting those in authority with a fearless yet humble love which has only ever built up!

In all this there has been no neglect of other responsibilities both public and private. Peter has given himself to university lecturing, to editing, to supervision, to preaching, to the necessary work of committees and councils. He has also been a member of Synods and Standing Committees, but the cut and thrust of debates in such bodies are not to his taste, and he has only rarely spoken – though usually to good effect when he does intervene. On the other hand, his membership of the Theological Commission of the World Evangelical Fellowship and of the Doctrine Commission of the Diocese of Sydney have been particularly fruitful. His painstaking exegetical work has been basic to serious reports on such matters as divorce and remarriage, and the ministry of women.

Peter and Mary have four children and five grandchildren. To those who have had the privilege of being their neighbours it is clear that they delight in their family and that the secret of much of Peter's strength in his ministry is in the relationship with Mary. They have served the Lord together, and Mary has made a signal contribution to the ministry and to the Lord's people with the same wholeheartedness and love that have marked Peter's service of the gospel. Peter relaxes with photography, especially avian photography, and they share a love for sport, in which they are both above-average participants. They also share the same quiet joy and infectious humour which make the visitor welcome. The home is a centre of hospitality and kindness. They are 'true yoke-fellows in the Lord'.

This volume is dedicated to Peter O'Brien in his honour. His colleagues and friends take the opportunity to express their gratitude to him as a friend, and as a distinguished scholarly interpreter of the New Testament. We are especially grateful for his faithful witness to the Lord Jesus Christ. We are conscious that, whatever the gifts and graces that others may see in him, he sees himself chiefly as a man in need of redemption. On this ground he has turned in faith to Jesus, who came into the world to save sinners, and he has himself become a preacher of that gospel in all the world. In so doing he confesses that Christ is his only comfort in life and in death. And so we, like him, give all thanks and praise to God.

2. Biblical theology and the shape of Paul's mission

Graeme Goldsworthy

Evangelical biblical theology

Exegesis is the stuff of which biblical theology is made, but it is not of itself a self-evident procedure neutral as to its theological presuppositions. Exegesis is a theological discipline which, with biblical theology, is an integral part of the total process that we have come to refer to as the hermeneutical spiral. An authentically evangelical biblical theology involves a number of key assumptions about the nature of the biblical text. It could be argued that no responsible exegete of the New Testament could be other than a biblical theologian, given the dependence of the New Testament upon the interpretation of the Old Testament texts in the light of Christ. However, an evangelical biblical theology applies certain presuppositions that do not necessarily have universal acceptance in the world of modern scholarship.[1]

An evangelical biblical theology clearly involves certain essential assumptions about the nature and authority of Scripture. First, there is the authority and integrity of the biblical revelation which is understood as the Word of God written. The divine inspiration of Scripture implies both its authority and its essential unity. Part of a coherent theology of revelation is the recognition of the meaning of a text in relation to its author's intention as a valid exegetical pursuit. Secondly, Christology dominates an evangelical biblical theology since the person and work of Jesus Christ are asserted to be the goal of all that has gone before, and the basis of all that is yet to come to pass.

Thirdly, the framework of revelation within the one Word of the one God is that which we speak of as salvation history or redemptive history.

These basic assumptions can be brought to bear upon the treatment of Paul's understanding of his mission.[2] Salvation history is perceived as the context of Paul's understanding of the gospel and of his own mission.

Paul's place within biblical theology

There is a certain scholarly tendency to ascribe the origin of biblical theology to Johann Philip Gabler and his 1787 inaugural address at Altdorf.[3] The myth that Gabler established biblical theology as a distinct discipline rests on the fact that he drew attention to certain contrasts between different ways of doing theology. He was, however, methodologically and philosophically far removed from the establishment of a 'true' biblical theology, despite his stated intention to do so. Evangelical biblical theology claims authenticity from the understanding that it was Jesus and the apostles – including, and perhaps especially, Paul – who were the first biblical theologians, who provided the grounds for the discipline by pointing to the process of revelation in the history of God's people. While involving certain dogmatic presuppositions – divine revelation, theological coherence or unity – the task of the biblical theologian is to discern this process largely through inductive, or descriptive, means.

Various ways have been suggested in Pauline studies of accounting for the shape of Paul's mission. One of the dangers of trying to understand the impact of his conversion experience, for example, is that it can easily go beyond the evidence to become speculative and psychological. If we believe that Paul's mission was a preordained part of the larger plan of God for bringing the gospel to the Gentiles, we in no sense depreciate Paul's personal contribution, his psychology, his biblical theology, or the impact of his Damascus-road experience. We simply ask how Paul and his mission fit into the plan of God revealed in Scripture. While Paul's place in a biblical theology may be thought to overlap to a greater or lesser degree with Paul's biblical theological understanding, the two can be investigated as distinct issues. Yet, if Paul is the human author of inspired Scripture, his understanding of his place in the overall plan of God must constitute a key aspect of the one message of revelation. I want to start with the question of Paul's place in an integrated biblical theology.

There are two aspects to be considered: Paul's place in the larger structure of biblical theology, and Paul as a biblical theologian. Notwithstanding the need to beware of simply reading preconceived notions of the undercurrents of Paul's theology back into the structure of biblical theology, we cannot avoid beginning with the Christological framework that so dominated his thinking. The rationale for a comprehensive biblical theology rests on the consistent recognition of the person and work of Jesus of Nazareth as the goal towards which the whole Old Testament moves. The main reason we have for regarding the theology of the New Testament as a true fulfilment and completion of the Old Testament is the nature of the gospel and the claims of Jesus. The impulse to try to gather up the Old Testament as something more than merely the historical antecedents of the gospel comes from the Christian perspective which we have by virtue of being caught up into the process of salvation history through faith in Jesus Christ.

We can tentatively define biblical theology as the study and description of the progressive revelation of God, his kingdom, and his work of salvation throughout the whole of the Bible.[4] The assumptions involved in such a definition are drawn from the New Testament, specifically from the gospel. The structure of our biblical theology should reflect as accurately as possible the structure of revelation. It should be noted that Jesus and the apostles refer to the testimony of the Scriptures as a whole. They do not appear to make any real distinctions between the theologies of what could be regarded as discrete *corpora* within the Old Testament. Jesus refers to the established parts of the Old Testament canon (Law, Prophets, and Psalms – presumably the Writings) and, in order to locate a particular passage, occasional references are made to various specific books. But there is nothing to suggest that Jesus or the apostolic authors saw any theological discord between the *corpora*. The Scriptures testify to Jesus as the Christ, and it is a unified testimony. An evangelical approach to biblical theology will, for obvious reasons, give great weight to the attitudes of Jesus and the apostles to the unity and authority of the Old Testament.

That a biblical theology is already in existence is shown, for example, by the coherence of that corpus we know as the Deuteronomic history. The disputes about the Tetrateuch versus either the Pentateuch or the Hexateuch serve only to highlight the difficulty faced by those who question the theological unity within the Old Testament. Whatever their differences, the books give a coherent account. Creation, the fall, and the redemptive line through Noah, Shem and finally Abraham form the first stages of redemptive history. A paradigm of redemption and of the kingdom of God is provided from Abraham to David and Solomon, progressing from the promise to the realization of that promise as a historical reality in Israel. The redemptive focus is the exodus, which stands as proof of the faithfulness of

Yahweh to the covenant with Abraham (Exod. 2:23–25; 6:1–8). But Israel's redeemed state also serves a purpose for the nations among whom the people of God are set with a priestly ministry (Exod. 19:4–6). Within this redemptive paradigm, the law given at Sinai functions as the divinely intended structure of the redeemed community in relation to the redeemer. The Deuteronomic history tells the story of the decline, apostasy and final destruction of this earthly and very imperfect manifestation of the kingdom of God in Israel. A biblical theology of mission, which includes Paul's mission, proceeds against the backdrop of the creation and fall narratives, and sees the emerging purpose of God for salvation which is given specific direction in the covenant with Abraham. That the nations of the world will find blessing through the descendants of Abraham is the central missionary motif of the Bible.

The second major epoch of revelation is discernible with the prophets. Alongside the commentary on the decline and fall of Israel, the essence of prophetic eschatology is a recapitulation of the whole structure that was the historical experience from Abraham to Solomon. Two related dimensions emerge in the Scriptures of this period: the actual historical experience of the people of Israel and Judah, and the accompanying prophetic commentary and expressions of hope. The exile and diaspora provided the first real indication that the prophetic eschatology of the nations coming to a restored Jerusalem to share in the blessings, as initially indicated to Abraham, required some reinterpretation. The scattered Jews provided an alternative focus to that of geographical Jerusalem for the dealings of God with his people and the fulfilling of his purposes. For the greater part of Old Testament history, the movements of outsiders into the kingdom were a matter of people coming in to embrace the faith and the national existence of Israel. The same centripetal perspective is found in the eschatology of the prophets, especially as seen in Isaiah 2:2–4 and Zechariah 8:20–23. Zion and the temple constitute the locus of blessing for the nations. On the other hand, both Jeremiah and Ezekiel, as prophets of the exile, contain important seeds of diaspora theology which anticipate the centrifugal momentum of the New Testament mission and especially that of Paul. They do not resile from the basic perspective of the centrality of Jerusalem and the temple, but show that Jews in exile can actually be blessed and be the means of blessing. Thus, on the one hand the prophets point to the ongoing significance of Zion and the temple as the only place where God reconciles people to himself and, on the other hand, the exile experience makes way for the diaspora synagogue as the place from which many will return to the true Zion. The disappointment in the post-exilic restoration only serves to accentuate the distinction between the historical experiences and the future hope. The intertestamental history continues the widening of this gap while the prophetic voice is silent. From the perspective of biblical theology and of the formation of the canon, God has nothing more to say until the fulfilment events are to be announced.

This period saw the development of several different perspectives on the relationship of current events. One of these is the position of the Pharisees. The evidence for the origin and growth of Pharisaism is a matter of history rather than of biblical theology. Not until the New Testament will the clash between Pharisaism and the teaching of Jesus introduce it into the realms of biblical theology as distinct from the theology of Judaism. The evidence of the Gospels and the accounts of Paul himself show the nature of this clash and, in Paul's case, its resolution.

The authors of the four Gospels both accept for themselves and accurately represent the eschatological understanding of Jesus. They also recognize a virtually unbridgeable gap between this understanding and that of the Jewish teachers, the lawyers and the Pharisees. There is, furthermore, a gap between the understanding of Jesus and that of his disciples, which diminishes only with tantalizing slowness. Not until Pentecost do they get it all together. And even this statement has to be qualified by the relatively slow transformation of the mission from Jew to Gentile. If Pentecost marked a new beginning for the history of the gospel, the Gentile 'pentecost' (Acts 10) had to occur before the Jerusalem church was convinced of the implications of the promise to Abraham concerning the nations.

Paul, as a figure in the biblical-theological and salvation-historical progression in the Bible, is introduced to us as a young man who stands by and approves the actions of the Jews while they stone Stephen to death. Although speculative connections must be made with caution, we may wonder what Saul thought of Stephen's dying testimony and his death. Was he able to hear the words which finally drove the Jews to kill Stephen: 'I see the heaven open and the Son of Man standing at the right hand of God'? Luke tells us that Stephen saw Jesus at the right hand of God, but he does not indicate that Stephen identified the Son of Man as Jesus. Why did this stir the religious leaders to such anger? Would Saul have approved of this execution if he had not witnessed this provocative event? It would perhaps help to explain why we next hear of Saul as the vigorous persecutor of the church.

A biblical theologian must ask why this account of Saul is strangely interrupted by two seemingly unrelated incidents in the Acts narrative. The design of Luke would appear to be theological rather than merely chronological. The first incident involves the evangelizing of the Samaritans and the apostolic mission to lay hands on the believers. The second, the account of the Ethiopian eunuch, has some interesting parallels with the visit of the Queen of Sheba to Solomon. When Philip is sent by the angel, he finds this God-fearer reading from the Suffering Servant passage in Isaiah 53, and he uses the opportunity to tell him about Jesus.

Both these accounts express something of the centrifugal momentum of the gospel which conforms to Jesus' instructions to his disciples in reply to their question about the kingdom. It will go from Jerusalem to Judea, to Samaria, and to the uttermost parts of the world. This evangelistic pattern seems strangely at odds with the centripetal pattern of prophetic eschatology concerning the ingathering of the nations. Let us for a moment assume that Paul did hear Stephen claiming to see the Son of Man. Among other things this was a claim to be a party to the fulfilment of the prophecy of Daniel 7. Had Saul also heard that the Nazarene had repeatedly used the title 'Son of Man' of himself? Perhaps he put the two together and recognized the enormity of both claims. His Pharisaic eschatology would presumably not cope with this radical claim that Jesus of Nazareth, put to death by the Romans at the instigation of the Jews, and alleged to have appeared alive again to his friends, is now the Son of Man at the right hand of God.

So Saul sets out with energy to nip this heretical movement in the bud (8:1–3). Acts 9 tells of an event that is so significant that Paul himself is recorded as describing it on two further occasions in the Acts narrative (Acts 22; 26). While journeying to Damascus to arrest any disciples of Jesus that he can lay his hands on, the Lord in heaven identifies himself as Jesus and expresses his oneness with his disciples, so that to persecute them is to persecute him. We cannot avoid the implications of Daniel 7 for this. Stephen's claim is vindicated; Jesus now identifies himself as the exalted Lord, and his unity with his saints echoes the fact that the Son of Man shares his kingdom with the saints of the Most High. That Paul never uses this title of Jesus does not rule out the possibility of this being integral to his understanding of the significance of the resurrection and of the Damascus-road encounter.

Since the miracle of Paul's conversion is hard to come to terms with, the process of the church's acceptance of the converted Paul is exceedingly painful for the disciples (9:21, 26). But Luke's account does not tell us of any delays in Paul's ministry: after his baptism with the Spirit and with water he begins the task of preaching in the synagogues in Damascus. He is so forthright in evangelism that his life is in danger and he is forced to flee. He then goes to Jerusalem where Barnabas vouches for him. Once more his evangelistic zeal brings him into danger and the brethren send him to Tarsus.

Before returning to the matter of Paul's new-found Christian ministry, Luke takes up another aspect of the centrifugal momentum of the gospel (Acts 10). While in Joppa, Peter the apostle finds himself thrown into this movement in a wholly unexpected way. His vision of the net full of unclean creatures, which are then declared to be clean, is clearly a sign to him that a change is afoot. At that point the messengers sent by the Roman soldier Cornelius arrive with the invitation to visit him in Caesarea. Cornelius is open to the gospel and Peter grasps the opportunity to preach the gospel to him and to those with him. These Gentiles embrace the gospel and are filled with the Holy Spirit. The news causes some consternation among the saints in Jerusalem but Peter is able to convince them of the genuineness of the event (Acts 11). Meanwhile, as the believers are dispersed due to persecution, the gospel continues to go to Jews. But some also begin to preach to Hellenists in Antioch (11:19ff.).

Paul the biblical theologian: Luke's account

Some scholars are reticent to accept Luke's version of Paul's preaching and teaching, but it is difficult to see why this hermeneutic of suspicion should be adopted. In fact, Luke's testimony is an important witness to the matter of Paul's theology and his mission. In Acts 13 we have the record of what Paul said on his first missionary journey. Although some may dismiss this sermon in the synagogue in Antioch of Pisidia as Luke's reinterpretation of Paul, there is no reason why it cannot be accepted at face value as an accurate summary of Paul's sermon. The audience consisted of Jews and of Gentiles who are identified as converts to Judaism (vv. 16, 26, 43).

The sermon is a classic expression of a biblical-theological overview of salvation history. It focuses on the activity of God in election and salvation (v. 17), the ingratitude of Israel (v. 18), the gift of the promised land (v. 19), the judges and the request for a king which resulted in Saul's reign (vv. 20–21), and the establishment of David as the king after God's heart (v. 22). The first part of the sermon thus surveys salvation history from Abraham to David. The next move is somewhat surprising. Paul moves from David directly to Jesus as the descendant of David who is the promised Saviour. The reference to the promise may be taken as a reference to the prophetic promise as much as to the original promises to Abraham. Paul then enlarges on the prophetic role in this revelation. The prophets are read every Sabbath, but the Jews did not recognize that they spoke of Jesus. Instead, they unwittingly fulfil the prophecies by putting him to death (vv. 26–29). The resurrection is proclaimed as the event of central significance (vv.

30–39). As he also indicates in his account in 1 Corinthians 15:4–8, Paul understands the resurrection as fully attested by many witnesses. But why this emphasis on the resurrection? Why is the major factor in Paul's proclamation the raising of Jesus from the dead? In 1 Corinthians 15:8 part of the answer might seem to be that Paul is the last of the witnesses, having encountered the risen Christ on the Damascus road.

In the Antioch sermon the reasoning of the apostle is clear. The resurrection of Jesus is the grand climax of salvation history.[5] In this one event the entire scope of promise and prophecy in the Old Testament has reached fulfilment. We note here the Jewishness of the gospel in Paul's preaching, understandable if he is preaching in a synagogue to Jews and God-fearers. 'We bring you the good news that what God promised to our ancestors, he has fulfilled for us the children, by raising Jesus' (vv. 32–33). Significantly, Paul quotes Psalms 2:7; 16:10; and Isaiah 55:3 in support of this assertion, thereby giving these passages a clearly Christological interpretation. It is reasonable to assert that perhaps Stephen's vision of the Son of Man, and almost certainly the Damascus-road encounter, convinced Paul that the resurrection of Jesus was the great eschatological event by which the Messiah comes into his kingdom rule.

The uproar among the Jews resulting from the preaching of Paul and Barnabas on the following Sabbath introduces a significant turning-point in the Acts narrative. Luke records Paul's rationale for the shape of his mission, namely that he should become the apostle to the Gentiles. First, the Jews show themselves unworthy of the privilege given to them as recipients of the fulfilled promises to the fathers. Secondly, Paul takes the words of Isaiah 49:6 as a command to him and Barnabas, that they should be a light for the Gentiles and bring salvation to the ends of the earth. This may seem to be discordant with the Son of Man vision which speaks of the conquest of the kingdoms of the world in judgment. Yet Paul is also driven by the other aspect of prophetic eschatology which reflects the promises to Abraham concerning a blessing to the nations of the world, and Israel's calling to be a priest and a light to the nations. Paul's Christological vision of fulfilment in the resurrection, we can suppose, would mean that he saw the resurrection as the locus of the servant becoming the light to the Gentiles. As the witness to the resurrection, he now can read the servant promise as a command to himself (v. 47).

Luke, as it were, rubs salt into the wounds of the rebellious Jews by telling us of the joy with which the Gentiles heard and received the word of the Lord (v. 48). Further, he speaks of the event as participation by the Gentiles in the eternal predestinating purposes of God, for 'as many as had been destined for eternal life became believers' (v. 48). While Paul continues to speak to Jews when the opportunity is there (Acts 14:1; 17:2, 10; 18:4–6), the emphasis as they proceed through Asia Minor is now on the Gentiles. Indeed, we are reminded in Paul's climactic argument in Romans 9 – 11 that he remains an apostle for the Jews in that he sees his Gentile mission at least in part as a means to an end: the conversion of the Jews. On returning to Syrian Antioch they are able to relate 'how God had opened a door of faith for the Gentiles' (14:27). The way is now open for the kind of tension between Jewish and Gentile believers that results in the Jerusalem assembly (Acts 15).

The shape of Paul's mission: Paul's account

Paul, the biblical theologian, is no mere pragmatist whose Jewish mission backfired, leaving him only the prospect of going to the Gentiles. On the contrary, Paul understands his mission to the Gentiles within the context of his being a Hebrew of the Hebrews. Long after Paul has announced his turning to the Gentiles he continues to make a beeline for the synagogues as he comes to different towns and cities on his missionary journeys. In fact, for one who was convinced that God had commissioned him to be the apostle to the Gentiles, Paul seems to have retained an uncommon attraction for the synagogue! Was he merely an opportunist, or did he rather recognize that mission to the Gentiles and mission to the Jews went hand in hand? If we regard the synagogues as a kind of temporary measure invented by the Jews while separated from the Jerusalem temple, then we are bound to regard the Christian attention to synagogues as merely a strategy driven by pragmatism. If, however, the synagogue functioned as a legitimate expression of the gathering of the people of God, albeit incomplete as to its paraphernalia of reconciliation, since there was no priestly office of sacrifice, then the proclamation to Jew and Gentile at the synagogue would be an extension of the Old Testament view of the ingathering of the Gentiles to precisely the place where God gathered his people Israel.

Peter O'Brien has expounded the significance of certain passages in the epistles for Paul's understanding of his mission.[6] He presents the case for Paul's comprehensive understanding of salvation history and of the continuity of his mission and ministry with the saving work of God revealed in the Old Testament and fulfilled in Christ. In the two works cited, Peter focuses mainly on Galatians 1:11–17; Ephesians 3:1–13; and Romans 15. While I am in substantial agreement with the conclusions drawn, I want to suggest that there are some other passages that reinforce the view, so ably put by Peter O'Brien, that Paul's convictions concerning his own ministry are shaped within the framework of salvation history.

First, Paul's view of the gospel which he sets out at the beginning of Romans is expressed in terms of the link between the gospel, which is God's gospel, and the Old Testament. It is Christologically centred, and Christology, in turn, is defined in terms of the Davidic ancestry of Jesus. His resurrection shows him to be the Son of God, which means that he is the true Israel. The covenant perspective is asserted in the statement that the gospel is the power of God for salvation to everyone who has faith, to the Jew first and also to the Greek.

Secondly, as Oscar Cullman has pointed out, Paul's understanding of Christian existence, life in the Spirit, in Romans 8 is driven by a salvation-history perspective in which we live as the people of the Spirit awaiting the renewal of all things.[7] The idea that Paul inserted chapters 9 – 11 after chapter 8 as a kind of afterthought or parenthesis hardly does justice to this significant part of the epistle. It is integral to the whole business of the relationship of Jew and Gentile in the purposes of God, and Paul works the argument out in terms of salvation history. It is not possible to attempt a full exposition in this brief essay. However, I would suggest that Paul understands this as an essential part of his treatise. I do not think these chapters support some of the views they have been invoked for, such as a premillennial position on the restoration of Israel as a political entity in Palestine. However, it seems to me that Paul does clearly assert that the same confidence that we might have in the election purposes of God as expressed in Romans 8:28–30 should extend to the election purposes of God for Israel.[8] Paul draws on the Old Testament for evidence that a faithless Israel will be moved to jealousy when it observes the outworking of Genesis 12:3 among the Gentiles.

If Paul is the apostle to the Gentiles, this can in no way be taken to mean that he has turned his back on Israel. The shape of his mission is that he perceives himself to be driven by the conviction that his ministry is in direct continuity with the ministry given to Israel to be a light to lighten the Gentiles. He is filled with the sense that this is what his Jewishness means. Furthermore, he knows full well that the gathering of the nations cannot occur without the proclamation of a gospel that is intended for the Jew first. He himself is living proof that God has not cast away his people (Rom. 11:1). Ultimately, Jew and Gentile will inherit the kingdom together. The mystery is the hardening of Israel which has marked its history since the beginning of the nation. Paul sees this as a divine hardening, which in no way removes the responsibility of those who are so hardened, and the purpose is that the double miracle will happen: the full number of the Gentiles will come in, and also all Israel will be saved. These are not the same thing.

Thirdly, Peter O'Brien draws our attention to Ephesians 3 and the mystery of the inclusion of the Gentiles. This surely follows naturally from the previous passage, which deals with the unity that Gentile and Jewish believers have in Christ (Eph. 2:11–22). Here Paul accentuates the relationship by use of temple imagery. The temple was always the place of reconciliation with God and with fellow-believers. Yet Gentiles were restricted in their access. Now the dividing wall is demolished and the two groups become one. The temple made with hands is replaced by the living temple as the dwelling-place of God. There is no suggestion that this is to happen in Jerusalem. It is in Ephesus, or among the churches of the Lycus valley, or anywhere! Wherever Christ's gospel is proclaimed Jews and Gentiles will be gathered into this new temple.

Conclusion

A more comprehensive treatment of the writings of Paul is really demanded by the subject in hand. This brief survey of the testimony in Acts and in some of Paul's epistles is intended to highlight the biblical-theological perspective of Paul. He remains a key exponent of a method of doing theology that should be at the heart of our attempts to understand the total witness of the Bible as Holy Scripture. Paul, the persecutor of Jesus, was stopped in his tracks by his implied victim and converted to be the apostle to the Gentiles. With this self-consciousness of his ministry he could never separate it from the realization that the gathering of the Gentiles was inseparable in the purpose of God from his heart's desire that all Israel should be saved.[9]

Notes

1. See further my 'Dogmatic basis'; 'Viable?', pp. 34–40.
2. See, for example, O'Brien, 'Paul's missionary calling'. The salvation-history dimension is also clear in his *Gospel and Mission*. Peter is, at the time of writing, also engaged in a project concerned with the biblical theology of mission.
3. For a survey of the history of biblical theology, see my 'Viable?', pp. 22–34; See also Robinson, 'Origins', in the same volume (pp. 1–17).
4. Cf. 'Viable?', p. 43.
5. For a biblical-theological consideration of the resurrection see my '"With flesh and bones"'.
6. In *Gospel and Mission* and 'Paul's missionary calling'.
7. Cullman, *Salvation*, pp. 255–256.

8. A point strongly made by Ellison, *The Mystery*.
9. It is well known that Peter O'Brien has devoted most of his energies as an evangelical exegete of the highest integrity to the study of the Pauline literature. His contribution to the discipline of biblical theology may not be as obvious, but his approach to exegetical study clearly reveals the basic evangelical assumptions about the nature and authority of Scripture which are essential to an evangelical biblical theology, and this is especially so in the treatment of Paul's understanding of his mission. It is no surprise that one who has spent a number of years in India with the Church Missionary Society, and who maintains a deep concern for cross-cultural mission, should continue to investigate the biblical theology of mission.

3. Abraham and the Abrahamic covenant in Galatians 3:1–14

William J. Dumbrell

Galatians 3:1–14 majors on who are the true sons of Abraham, i.e. to whom belongs membership of the Abrahamic covenant The section is not concerned with the manner in which covenant entry has been effected. That had been discussed in Galatians 2:14–21. The issue now in these verses and throughout the chapter as a whole is the matter of life within the new relationship. Verses 1–5 constitute Paul's first direct address to the Galatians, and the important question of the Galatians' experience of the faith is taken up. The simple assertion of justification by faith in 2:14–17 is presumed in 3:1–14 and is seen as an experience analogous to God's acceptance of Abraham in Genesis 15:6. If the Galatian Gentile Christians have received the Spirit by faith, then the Abrahamic promises have been fulfilled in them by faith alone. So the argument of the opponents for the place of the Sinai law as an addition to gospel is refuted. Faith in God's provision had been the intended means of salvation for humanity from the beginning of revelation. The law was never planned to be the condition for entering the people of God. Its place was to provide guidelines for those operating within the covenant structure.

Paul's address to them (v. 1) as 'foolish' expresses his deep concern. Their experience should have prevented them from succumbing to the bewitching influence of the Jewish Christian intruders. The implication of the Messiah's crucifixion as a common criminal, clearly proclaimed to them and accepted by them, had led to their reception of the Spirit. God had accepted them, given them entrance into the new covenant (i.e. had justified[1] them), and, as the argument will continue, had adopted them as sons (Gal. 4:6, cf. 28–29). They now belong to the body of Christ without taking upon themselves the yoke of the Torah. There is only one question which Paul needs to ask (v. 2), and all else is implication. Since it was a matter of common agreement that receipt of the Spirit made one a Christian, Paul now asks them whether they had received the Spirit while they were practising the law or whether they had simply heard of and believed in Jesus. The Galatians' reception of the Spirit in 3:1–5 and Abraham's experience of justification in 3:6–9 are parallel. Abraham believed God's promise and was reckoned righteous, i.e. counted as justified (Gen. 15:6). This experience had nothing to do with the law because the Galatians, like Abraham, were outside the law at the time of their initial response to the gospel of Christ preached by Paul.

Likewise, progress in the faith (v. 3) is also a gift of the Spirit. 'Flesh' (*sarx*), probably here 'human nature in its fallenness', is ridiculously presented as the source of strength alternative to the Spirit. Paul, though he raises the question, is convinced that the totality of their experience was not in vain, and he is calling upon the Galatians to choose between alternatives. The 'therefore' (*oun*) of verse 5 builds upon the expected answer to verse 2. Their ground of continued reception of the Spirit (v. 5) must still be the same as their initial acceptance into the covenant.

The Abrahamic connection (vv. 6–9)

Righteousness – i.e. being in the right relationship with God,[2] evidenced by Abraham's faith and expressed in terms of inclusion in a covenant relationship credited to Abraham in Genesis 15:18 – was Abraham's position already in Genesis 15:6. The 'just as' (*kathōs*, Gal. 3:6) marks such covenant inclusion as also the present position of the Galatians.

We may surmise that the Judaizers had used Abraham as a paradigm to advance their views on circumcision and law-keeping. They would have required the Gentiles to accept at least the minimal demands of Jewish law. But Paul makes the point of comparison clear in the conclusion from verse 6 drawn in verse 7. It is a shared faith in God's promises which links Abraham and the Galatians and makes the Galatians his spiritual descendants. God's dealings with Abraham provided the paradigm for all believers. So Paul, in the manner of Romans 4, had gone beyond Abrahamic circumcision in Genesis 17 – perhaps a point of emphasis for the Judaizers – to point to an earlier stage of Abraham's experience. Faith, not circumcision, is evidential of the new-covenant relationship. Those who base themselves on faith in Christ crucified, therefore, are members of the new covenant. As Paul claims the disputed sonship of Abraham for faith, the emphasized and restrictive 'those' (*houtoi*, v. 7) implies (probably contra the Judaizers) that no other criterion for covenant membership (entry or continuance) is required.

Paul then (v. 8) supports the conclusion of verse 7 with particular scriptural authority drawn from an amalgam of Genesis 12:3 and 18:8. Paul argues that Abraham's faith was really an analogous response to the gospel also proclaimed without law. Like the Gentiles, Abraham had believed the divine message conveyed, and had received the promise directed to him and to his spiritual descendants. The Galatians, relying on faith alone (v. 9), and thus now in the covenant, must therefore be descendants of Abraham within the same covenant of promise, enjoying the blessings pronounced on the Abrahamic connection in Genesis 12:3 and 18:8. Paul thus sets up a parallel between the bestowal of the Spirit and the crediting of righteousness (cf. v. 14), for the bestowal of the promised Spirit means the Gentiles' participation in Abraham's blessing. On the question Paul put to the Galatians in verse 2 regarding the receipt of the Spirit, everything else has turned. Moreover, the linkage between verses 1–5 and 6–9 by the common denominator of faith (*pistis*, vv. 5, 6, 7, 8, 9) is clear.

The scriptural argument of 3:10–14 supporting 3:1–9

The 'for' (*gar*) of verse 10 introduces a section designed to underscore by reference to Scripture (perhaps as used by the opponents) the implied dichotomy in verses 6–9 between faith and Mosaic Torah in regard to the continued expression of membership of the new covenant. Paul's reference to 'all who rely on the works of the law' (3:10a) had the continuation of Jewish covenant relationships in mind, for the phrase does not emphasize doing, but a relationship of belonging to the Mosaic covenant.[3] The inclusion of 'all the things written in the book of the law' has in mind narrowly the context of Deuteronomy 27 and the immediate curses for covenant breach, but we may fairly, in the context of Galatians 3, widen it to Torah as a whole. But the point being made in Galatians 3:10a is that the persons referred to in verse 10a will be subject to the curse operating for a violated covenant.[4]

To be cursed (Gal. 3:10) is to be cut off from God, to be outside of the covenant of grace. The curse of the law, argues Paul, has come not merely upon an Israel still in theological exile, but now on individual law-keepers, covenant-keeping Jews and, as we shall see, Christian Jews. The paradox and the Pauline order of the argument in Galatians 3:10 are then clear. Paul is saying that continued obedience to the Mosaic law is in fact disobedience to the will of God. This is an extraordinary assertion which turns out to be a direct Pauline assault upon his opponents, and the implications of this statement must now be examined.

The opponents, assuming the pre-existence of the law, interpreted the faith of Abraham as faithful obedience to the law. But Abraham's total acceptance of God's promise indicates that he placed his confident trust in God to keep his promise about offspring (Gen. 15:5). Abraham's faith had no connection with the law which came 430 years later (Gal. 3:17). The people of faith, Christian believers, Paul argues, are sons of Abraham, since they believe in the same way and they believe the same basic promises. It is to be observed that the blessing for the nations in Abraham is interpreted as justification (Gal. 3:8), while 'in you' (*en soi*, v. 8) is now interchanged with 'with the faith of Abraham' (v. 9). This suggests that to be blessed in Abraham meant to be justified in the same way as believing Abraham was. From the very beginning of the history of redemption, it is clear for Paul that God meant faith, not law, to be the means of justification.

In Galatians 3:10a, by placing a curse on law-keepers, Paul is simply following the unfortunate logic of his opponents. The opponents had stressed, it seems, the continuity of the Mosaic covenant. They seemed to have advocated full obedience to the Mosaic law for covenant membership. They had promoted the law seriously (cf. 2:14–17; 3:1–14; 5:2–4; 6:13a). Perhaps they began their argument with Abraham, since he was the recognized father of God's people, the original recipient of the divine covenant and the promise concerning his descendants in relation to all the nations of the earth (Gal. 3:8). They held that obligations under the Sinai covenant must be fulfilled for living in covenant relationship with God. For them, the Messiah did not come to abrogate the Sinai covenant and law but, as the new Moses, to interpret it (Gal. 6:2; Matt. 5:17). The cross, for them, had led to new possibilities for the fulfilment of the Sinai covenant. The agitators also probably included Jerusalem in the Sarah-Isaac line as the centre for the new messianic community. To come into the covenant, the Gentiles must be circumcised and obey the whole law, for circumcision was a sign of the Abrahamic and Mosaic covenants (Gen. 17:10–14; Josh. 5:2–9).[5] If Paul circumcised Timothy, did he not also preach this? This teaching clearly provoked tension in Galatia (cf. 5:13–14; 6:1–2).

For Paul, the Mosaic law, which was only a parenthesis within the history of salvation, had never possessed the power to save. Its essential purpose within the covenant, as Paul now sees it perhaps in retrospect, was to make sin abound (Rom. 5:20; Gal. 3:19). But now that God had justified believers apart from law (Rom. 3:21), the role of the law as delivered to Israel for covenant continuance had clearly come to an end, so much so that Paul could put the Mosaic law on the same level as paganism (Gal. 4:9).

In Galatians 3:10 Paul is pointing to the situation after the cross and drawing on the reality and logic of the course of salvation history. So Galatians 3:10a says that in the 'now' of the new-covenant age, with Christian mission underway, all Jews and fellow-travellers who rely on obedience to the law to stay in the covenant are under the curse of the law. The Mosaic covenant had ceased in its efficacy with the cross. But why then is the curse operating? Under the normal functioning of the old covenant, atonement for sin through sacrifice, after confession of sin, was available to the individual or nation. With the cessation of the Mosaic covenant there was thus no atonement for sin available to Israel after the cross. This is the point on which Paul is now laying decided emphasis (v. 10b). By Christ's unprecedented saving act he had established a new covenant and new forgiveness. By his ignoble death Jesus appeared as one cut off from the Mosaic covenant by a curse. But God had vindicated the one who was pronounced accursed.

Paul's use of the present tense of his opponents (Gal. 3:10a) thus reflects the changed situation for Israel arising from the death of Christ. The day of the Sinai covenant and of the exclusive role of Israel as the carrier of the Abrahamic covenant promises was over. Paul's implied point in 3:10a is that the curse is operating on Israel and Israelites and on as many as continued to resort to the Mosaic covenant. This was an act of flagrant disobedience, because there could no longer be recourse to a discarded sacrificial system to support a discontinued covenant. The curse, always potential for disobedience, must now automatically and universally apply to adherents of the Sinai covenant. Christ's death was in itself a great Day of Atonement into which all of Israel's yearly Days of Atonement had been incorporated. This seems to be the point that Paul is making in his use of *hilastērion* in Romans 3:25, where his probable conclusion is that Christ's offering of himself was the great and final sin offering (cf. Rom. 8:3 and 2 Cor. 5:21) which brought the institution of sacrifice and its outward appurtenances, priesthood and temple, to an end. The death of Christ legitimated the sacrificial system and validated its entire operation, but also brought it to an end. With the death of Christ the temple in Jerusalem was itself profaned (Mark 15:38). While a sacrificial institution continued in the temple until August AD 70, and was doubtless considered effective by Judaism at large, the reality of the matter was that the death of Christ had brought Israel's institutional system to a conclusive end.

Advocates of the law, who trusted in the keeping of the law for covenant continuance, must now be cursed. In this way Paul points to the illogicality of the Judaizers' position. In acknowledging the need for justification in Christ, but at the same time endeavouring to impose Mosaic covenant law on the Galatians, they were in serious theological confusion. By their demand for the imposition of the Mosaic law they were in fact making a demand for Christian incorporation into the Mosaic and Sinaitic structure. To this extent N. T. Wright's judgment[6] is correct, that the Judaizers' claims were the advocacy of national righteousness. For it is clear that by their imposition of such things as circumcision, food laws and Sabbath-keeping they were doing more than merely making demands for the acceptance of Mosaic law simply in terms of ethical principles. They were assuming the continuance of the Mosaic covenant and demanding that it continue to be recognized. This was not only a category mistake, but it also presumed the continued existence of institutions whose validity had been decisively ended. That is why, in Galatians 3, the Abrahamic connection, and a proper understanding of what Abrahamic sonship involved, was so vital to Paul's argument.

In Galatians 3:10, Paul is reflecting not on the history of Israel generally but on the present constitution of Israel; here, on Christian Jews who have refused to see the work of Jesus Messiah as terminating the Sinai covenant and as determinative of a new covenant relationship. The Judaizers probably saw Christ as a messianic new Moses, affirming the law and strengthening Sinai. But both Judaism and the Christian Jews who were the opponents in Galatia failed to realize that Israel's crucifixion of Jesus irrevocably broke the covenant. Yet Christ, atoning within the old covenant by removing the curse of the law, had established a new covenant with all humankind, and was able indeed to remove national Israel's continued curse. Still attempting to live under the Sinai arrangement but with no arrangements now for the remission of sins, they were all under the curse invoked in Deuteronomy 27:26. The logic of Paul's presentation is thus clear. All who continue to attach themselves to the Mosaic covenant (Gal. 3:10) are under a curse, for inability to keep the law is the reality now, as it always was (v. 10b). However, such a failure now, unlike the situation under the Mosaic covenant, was without any accompanying means of forgiveness.

Paul is himself operating with an implied premiss in Galatians 3:10. Incorporating the premiss 'since the era of the Mosaic covenant has now ended', the thought seems to run naturally that 'all who rely upon the works of the law are under a curse'. For it is written, 'Cursed is everyone who does not observe and obey all the things written in the book of the law.' This premiss, stemming from the exposition in the chapter as a whole, implies the paramount place of the Abrahamic covenant which is now fully operating in this new age of the Spirit. Gentiles had been summoned to enter with Israel into the blessing of the Abrahamic covenant. It is on the new viability of the Abrahamic covenant that Galatians 3:10 proceeds. Since, as a Pauline supposition, the new covenant is operating, all who continue under the old labour under the curse. This state is brought forcibly home by the citation of Deuteronomy 27:26 whereby covenant infringements, unconfessed or unexpiated, brought on the curse stemming from disobedience to the law! Of course, Paul understood, as did Judaism at large, that law under the Mosaic arrangement was easily and readily infringed and that perfection under the law was never attainable so that a covenant life without recourse to atonement of some sort was an impossibility (cf. 1 John 2:2).[7] This was also a Pauline assumption that underlies verse 10b, but one that needs no defence or elaboration. In matters of custom and culture Paul, like Jesus before him, remained a loyal Jew. But Paul also recognized that God had moved further and the new wine had burst the old skins.

Verse 10 finds its direct continuance and logical conclusion in verse 11, which draws general conclusions for covenant membership operative in all areas. Here Paul, probably operating with the same scriptural key texts as his opponents, couples Genesis 15:6 and Habakkuk 2:4. He is at pains to emphasize the point that, just as the curse now rested on law-keepers, the keeping of the law, which was always necessary for continued covenant membership, was ever an exhibition of the obedience of faith (Rom. 1:5; 3:27–31). No-one is (or ever was) justified at covenant entry or continues to be justified in covenant continuance (i.e. in sanctification) before God on the basis of the law. Law-keeping was intended as a response to the relationship concluded on the basis of grace extended by God. Covenant entry and covenant continuance under the new covenant were made possible, as Paul would have put it, through the work of the Spirit in regeneration and ongoing sanctification. It was grace that led to covenant entry, or justification, and also to covenant continuance. If 'the just shall live by faith', then, at least since the advent of eschatological faith in Christ, the just are no longer to be found among those who are from the works of the law, i.e. among the Jews who continue to live under the old covenant.

But once again, Paul must be followed carefully in 3:12. He is not denying the place of law, and the connection between law and faith is rightly differentiated by the citation of Leviticus 18:5. Galatians 3:12 makes clear that the law and faith are different entities and have different roles. Paul uses present tenses, since the relationship was true under Sinai as well as under the new covenant. Paul points to law's role as assuming prominence in covenant maintenance, not in covenant entrance. Faith indicates the fact of covenant membership. Law-keeping through faith indicates the subsequent response to covenant membership. Law is irrelevant to the question of justification, in which faith alone is determinative. If faith presents the onset of the relationship, then law has significance for its continuance. Leviticus 18:5 was addressed to an Israel already in covenant relationship, with life in the Promised Land stretching out before them. Leviticus 18:5 refers not to life in the world to come, but to life in the covenant, i.e. the continued enjoyment of covenant relationships with God.

The asyndeton of verse 13 is noteworthy, since verses 13–14 do not immediately relate to verse 12, but summarize the argument of the whole section, verses 10–14. Galatians 3:13 makes an emphatic statement. Christ redeemed us, says Paul – i.e. redeemed us Jews – from the curse of the law pronounced on covenant reprobates by becoming a covenant reprobate for Israel (those under the law). Yet the Jews served as a representative of all humankind, so that the particular saving act of Christ to redeem the Jews from under the curse of the law also aimed at the Gentiles. It had universal consequences enabling them to share the blessing of Abraham (Gal. 3:14). In this way the universal promise made to Abraham in Genesis 12:3 was fulfilled through the work of Christ. Of course, Abraham's justification by faith meant that through faith in covenant promises (Gal. 3:7–8) a solution to the curse was always available. The problem for Israel after the cross was generated precisely by the death of Christ that annulled the Sinai covenant.

Israel's redemption from the law's curse thus opened the fountain of God's blessing, to stream beyond the bounds of ethnic Israel. The Jew, together with the believing Gentile, now found that Abrahamic sonship was defined by belonging to Christ (3:26–29). As sons of God, Jews and Gentiles were made recipients of the promised Spirit, for, as the Galatians' own experience testified, the Spirit came apart from the law in association with the preaching of the gospel (Gal. 3:2–5).

While the work of the cross availed for all, in terms of the order of the history of salvation, the redemption of Israel was the precondition for the blessing to move out to the Gentiles. Jesus, in his death, vicariously took upon himself the curse of the violated covenant. The act of Christ, interposing himself as the curse, however, did not destroy the curse of the law itself, for it was still imposed on all those who were nomistic members of the old covenant and upon sinners in general (Rom. 6:23). This curse of the law was actually the curse of God, the lawgiver. It involved being cut off from God and his holy community and the forfeiture of the blessing in the covenant.

Paul's question as to how the Gentiles can receive blessing (Gal. 3:8) is answered when he specifies the purpose for which Christ became the bearer of the law's curse for those dwelling under the law (v. 14). He uses two purpose clauses, the second of which is arguably the subordinate of the first (NASB, NIV). Both clauses express the salvation-historical realities to be realized at the Messiah's coming: the blessing of the Gentiles and the arrival of the Spirit (cf. 3:2–5; 4:6). Both effects mentioned in 3:14 are dependent upon the redemption of believing Jews from the curse of the law.

The cross of Christ placed those in Christ within the Abrahamic circle. So the division before the cross between 'us' and 'them' first moved out from 'us' (v. 13) to the Gentiles (v. 14), towards a final inclusive 'we' that makes no distinction between Jew and Gentile (v. 14). The fulfilment of this movement is the gift of the Spirit for all believers. The article before 'faith' is resumptive, pointing back to the type of faith mentioned previously (3:2, 5, 6, 9, 11).

So the joint experience of the Spirit (v. 14) is climactic and the argument by this inclusion has moved in full circle back to 3:1–2 (cf. v. 2). As the Galatians' own experience testified, Jew and Gentile were made recipients of the promised Spirit that came apart from the law in association with the preaching of the gospel. The Jew, together with the believing Gentile, now found Abrahamic sonship defined not by the Sinai arrangement but by belonging to Christ . So ends the argument of 3:1–14 which began with the question, 'How was the Spirit obtained?' The answer has led to a restatement of the Pauline thesis, exploited particularly in Galatians and Romans. The era of the Sinai covenant had now ended and that of the inclusive new covenant had been ushered in.

The implications of a covenant approach to Galatians 3:10 must now be spelled out. Galatians 3:10 provides a major statement of Pauline theology and has rightly attracted considerable attention in recent studies devoted to Galatians 3. It is the logic of the verse in the relationship of its parts which has been seen to raise problems on the initial reading. As noted, the Deuteronomy 27:26 curse of the law, directed in its Old Testament context at lawbreakers, seems in Galatians 3:10 to be applied to law-keepers. What brings the curse is paradoxically both what is done (i.e. works of the law, v. 10a) and what is not done (i.e. all the law, v. 10b). Galatians 3:10a seems to pronounce a curse on potential law-performers, the opposite of what might have been expected. We are not told why the mere attempt to keep the law draws down the curse of the law. Then 3:10b comes to our aid in solving this puzzle by implying that the curse is called down because of failure to keep the whole law. We can understand this, since, in the Old Testament age, failure to obey the law could (but need not) bring down the full covenant curses on Israel (Lev. 26:14; Deut. 28:58). The customary solution has been to supply an implied premiss such as 'no-one keeps everything written in the law'[9] to explain why righteousness could not be obtained through the works of the law. If we accept the need for the implied premiss, the tenor of the exegesis controlling 3:7–12 is then clear. Galatians 3:7–9 has argued that justification is by faith alone and Galatians 3:10–12 then affirms this by emphatically denying that it is by works. The traditional interpretation of verse 10b, then, has been that to fail to do everything that the law commands invokes the curse. Usually it is noted that Paul has included an 'all' here from the LXX of Deuteronomy 27:26 (not in the MT), to indicate in specific detail that perfect obedience was necessary to escape the curse. In this way, it is suggested, Paul makes it thoroughly clear that no-one can obey the whole law perfectly, at all times. But, as previously noted, perfect obedience to the Torah, either nationally or individually by Israel or Israelites, was never contemplated in the Old Testament. Paul himself never indicates that perfect obedience to the law was possible or required. Even on this further side of the cross he is very clear that the entail of sin devolves on all (Rom. 3:20). If he says of himself that as touching the law he was blameless (Phil. 3:6), this is usually exegeted in terms of his own awareness of covenant continuity and his use of the sacrificial system to cover personal sins. Moreover, if Paul is speaking here about the possibility of perfect obedience, then, in his engagement with the Judaizers or Jews or both, he is advancing assumptions that would make further discussion impossible. Apart from that, since Paul argues in this chapter that justification cannot occur on the basis of law, the question of perfect obedience to the law becomes irrelevant to the discussion. Thomas Schreiner suggests that the supposition that Paul would not have demanded perfect obedience fails to perceive the newness in Paul's thought. This not only begs the question, but would have made dialogue on this issue with fellow-Jews impossible.[10]

The approach taken in this essay provides for a natural reading of Galatians 3:10. The assumption of the operation of the Mosaic covenant which forms Paul's thought in Galatians 3:1–9 certainly means that adherents of the Mosaic covenant ('those who rely upon the works of the law', 3:10a) are under the curse. They are still now looking for forgiveness in covenant continuance to a sacrificial system which has been annulled. At the same time Paul recognized (3:10b) that ongoing forgiveness in covenant continuance must be provided, since the obligations required of the covenant member cannot be met. The continued existence of the believer in the flesh with all its weakness means lapses into temptation despite continued commitment to Christ and the presence with the believer of the Spirit. This makes a continued recourse to forgiveness after heartfelt confession of sin necessary (cf. 1 John 2:2). In Galatians 3:10 Paul places before the Galatians the great covenant category error of the Judaizers as the linchpin of his argument.

In recent decades much discussion has been generated about the fundamental problem that Paul is resisting in Galatians. Opinion has been sharply divided as to whether Paul is combating a legalism which espouses a works theology or whether he is making the salvation-history point that justification by faith is now freely open to Gentiles. Both views have had fervent supporters. A rebuttal by Paul of legalism would be supported by the total biblical insistence on salvation by faith alone. My own feeling, as I have indicated in other publications, has been that though such a view is biblically correct it has not done justice to the contextual finesse of Pauline theology. The question will no doubt continue to be debated. And disputants will probably all agree that it must be solved hermeneutically. Scriptural exegesis within a total biblical theology is the way in which interpretive questions must be resolved, but no doubt we will continue to reach different conclusions. We must, however, bear in mind that in Galatians 3 Paul is speaking of life within the covenant, of Christian sanctification, and not salvation. In addressing particular problems involved in Pauline interpretation we must be aware of the totally new situation for Judaism arising as a result of the crucifixion. Something of the dilemma that the Christ event caused for Judaism and Jewish Christianity in particular can be seen from the pull exercised by existing institutions on the audience of the letter to the Hebrews. There the work of Christ is presented as accomplishing a great and final Day of Atonement. My view is that the Pauline clarity of new-covenant perspective is at the heart of Pauline theology. I intend to take this question further, since I feel that the neglect of New Testament new-covenant studies had made it difficult to estimate the many disputes, misunderstandings, confrontations that affected the pre-70 emerging Christian movement. After AD 70 the controversies continued, but by that time, at least, the judgment of God on Jerusalem and the temple, presaged by Jesus, had made it clear to Christians that new-covenant directions had been irrevocably struck. I believe that Galatians 3 particularly admits us, in its own very succinct way, to the Pauline handling of this early, very fundamental Christian problem.[11]

Notes

1. For this association of justification, the anticipation of the verdict of the last judgment, with new-covenant entrance, see my article 'Justification'. Biblically, justification is concerned to point to new status resulting from change, i.e. from regeneration. The work of the Spirit in regeneration creates change; justification recognizes it.
2. Righteousness characteristically in the OT denotes a relationship, not a property. This is always so in Paul except in three doubtful cases in Ephesians, where, in my opinion, a relational view is more likely. See my 'Justification', p. 25.
3. Caneday, 'Redeemed', p. 194, cites BAGD, p. 225, for the expression as meaning 'belonging to the works of the law', i.e. identified with the old covenant.
4. Scott, '"Works of the law"', has argued that the curse of the law in Gal. 3:10 is the curse of continued exile under which Israel labours until final restoration. His general argument on Israel as a nation is correct, but his view on Gal. 3 misses the salvation-history dimension of Paul's logic. Scott's assertion that Paul is arguing nationally in Gal. 3:10 (p. 214, n. 89) may well be correct, since Paul's point in 3:10 is comprehensive. However, the issue in Gal. 3 is not who as a whole is comprehended in the curse but to whom the message is to be applied in this inter-Christian discussion in the chapter, which continues the thought of Gal. 2:14–21. Jewish Christians, not national Israel, are clearly in mind, though the conclusions Paul reaches in Gal. 3:10 can, of course, be more widely applied. Paul is not dialoguing with Judaism in Gal. 3, nor is the issue about any doctrine of merit required for salvation. The issue is whether Paul's converts need to accept the law, or features of it, to continue to be members of the new covenant. We may assume that the rival Christian missionaries (i.e. not Jews or Gentiles, cf. 1:6; 6:12) would not have contested the need for faith in Christ. Peter's position in Gal. 2 seems to have arisen, not from opposition to Paul on basic questions, but from fear of compromising his mission to the Torah community. The Jewish attitude to the admission of Gentiles even in the messianic last days was confused and there was no absolute *halakah* operating within Jewish ranks (Sanders, *Paul, the Law*, p.18), and on my dating of Galatians the Jerusalem Council of Acts 15 still lay ahead. Scott is correct that post-exilic national Israel was labouring under a curse, but we need to remember that until the advent of the new covenant individual Jewish needs continued to be met within Israel by the sacrificial system (cf. Paul and Phil. 3:6). Paul always makes it clear that, while Israel as a whole has been rejected, there has been Christian blessing upon an ethnic remnant of Israel. Paul, here, is pointing to the salvation-historical effect of the cross. For the Jewish audience to whom Paul in Gal. 3 is directing his remarks has obtained the redemption from the curse which is potentially available for the nation, if they turned to Christ. The 'us' addressed in Gal. 3:13 has immediate reference to Jewish Christians who have been recipients of justification by faith (Gal. 2:14–21), but who need to understand its precise implications. On the use of the first-person plural pronoun in Gal. 3:13 see Donaldson, '"Curse of the law"', pp. 105–106; Caneday, 'Redeemed', p. 205; Wright, 'Curse', p. 154.
5. The Abrahamic covenant of Gen. 15:18 legitimated the relationship begun by Abram's call and the basic promise attached to it of Gen. 12:1–3. Alexander, 'Abraham', however, has argued that Gen. 17 represents a second Abrahamic covenant, an eternal covenant of circumcision. As a conditional covenant, this

was different in many ways from the supposedly promissory covenant of Gen. 15. He argues that the new point in Gen. 17 is Abraham constituted to be the father of many nations. Alexander, however, has ignored the careful language of Gen. 17 where 'make a covenant' (v. 2) is Heb. *nāṭan bᵉrîṭ* and not the universal language of initiation in the OT of *kāraṭ bᵉrîṭ*. The sense in chapter 17 is that of 'setting into operation' the earlier covenant promises of Gen. 15. Hence 17:3b–8 is concerned with the promise of descendants, not with a fresh covenant initiation. Particularly the language of 'establish my covenant' of verse 7 refers us back to Gen. 15. See my *Covenant*, pp. 72–77, with pp. 25–26.

6. Wright, 'Curse', p. 154.
7. Cranford, 'Possibility', p. 243.
8. Bonneau, 'Logic', provides a most recent review of opinions.
9. Schreiner, 'The law', pp. 41–45.
10. Schreiner, 'Perfect obedience', p. 158.
11. Finally, it is a great pleasure to be associated with this tribute to the ministry of Peter O'Brien, a friend and colleague of many years.

4. The new covenant and Pauline hermeneutics

Andrew G. Shead

Introduction

Paul's description of the ministry of the new covenant (2 Cor. 3) forms the basis for an extended contrast with the Mosaic ministry of the old covenant. In his discussion of this passage, Richard Hays designates the section beginning 'and not like Moses' (v. 12) a *dissimile*.[1] This label highlights the question why Paul should spend so much time telling us what his ministry is *not* like, in answer to which Hays suggests that

> ... connotations bleed over from the denied images to the entity with which they are discompared ... In the same way, the dissimile in 2 Cor. 3:12 – 4:4 allows Paul to appropriate some of the mythical grandeur associated with the Sinai covenant – particularly the images of glory and transformation – even while he repudiates the linkage of his ministry to that covenant.[2]

The starting-point for the present study is the observation that extended discomparisons are extremely rare in the Bible. And the only comparable example in the Old Testament happens to be Jeremiah 31:32,[3] the very text, as we shall argue, that Paul used in setting up his dissimile in the first place. This raises the possibility that Paul is applying the distinctive mode of argumentation found in Jeremiah 31 to the passage in Exodus 34 as part of an attempt to show how the former provides a hermeneutic for the latter. With this possibility in mind, we turn to the primary focus of the present study, namely, Jeremiah 31. As we do so, we note that the modern background to this study is the increasing tendency to read the new-covenant passage in a way that minimizes or denies any substantive difference between it and the Mosaic covenant, a tendency shown especially by German-speaking[4] and American[5] scholars involved in Christian–Jewish dialogue.

Jeremiah 31:31–34 and the book as a whole

It is impossible, within the constraints of this essay, to do justice to the context of the new-covenant passage. For Jeremiah 31:31–34 is bound tightly into the 'Little Book of Consolation' (Jer. 30 – 31), which in turn has strong links to the rest of the book, not least to the material which sets forth Jeremiah as 'a prophet to the nations' (1:5).

The precise significance of the phrase is debated,[6] but the commission to the nations is reiterated in the programmatic words,

> See, I have appointed you this day over the nations and over the
>   kingdoms,
> To uproot and to break down,
> To destroy and to overthrow,
> To build and to plant.[7]

The following chapters (2:1 – 4:4) provide a sweeping indictment of the unfaithfulness of the people of God, who refuse to return to him (*šwb* is a key word in Jeremiah), yet one in which the precise identity of the terms 'Israel' and 'Judah' is elusive. Clearly, when hope is extended to 'the house of Judah and the house of Israel', it is extended beyond the circle of God's people then extant.[8]

Alongside this idealization of Israel and Judah we find an internationalizing of the hope of return (3:14–18).[9] As a *ba'al* (master or husband), the LORD determines to bring back a remnant to Zion (3:14). In the vision of the future which follows, the disappearance of the ark points to the end of narrowly national pilgrimages and festivals; moreover, the nations are gathering to 'the name of the LORD in Jerusalem', a phrase which, by its reminiscence of the 'name theology' of Deuteronomy (e.g. Deut. 12:11), suggests active participation by the nations in joyful worship. Note, further, that it is not Israel but the nations who will be cured of 'the stubbornness of their evil heart'.[10] This is a vision in which the identity of the covenant partners is no longer exclusively national.

In similar fashion, the book concludes (in the MT) with the 'Oracles against the Nations' (Jer. 46 – 51), culminating in the great Babylon oracle in which the city's fall is both announced and symbolically enacted (51:59–64). The strong correspondences between 50:4–20 and 30 – 31 suggest that chapter 50 is as much about hope for Judah as it is about judgment for Babylon.[11]

Within this overarching frame, the focus is naturally on the citizens of Judah during the reigns of its last kings. Yet the perspective of the frame is never entirely lost. It becomes clear in chapters 1 – 20 that Judah's rebellion has removed any distinction that once existed between her and the nations. Thus the appeal for her to circumcise her heart (4:4) is ignored: 'all the nations are uncircumcised, and all the house of Israel are uncircumcised of heart' (9:26b [Heb., 9:25b]).[12] The climax of this movement is the sign of the potter in 18:1–12. On the other hand, in Jeremiah 21 – 29 we see a shift in the locus of God's plans from Jerusalem to Babylon.

The movements just described suggest a complex relationship between God's people and the nations. The equating of the two groups in 9:25–26 (Heb. 24–25) and 18:5–12 suggests that any hope held out to Israel is also held out in some sense to the nations; by the same token, there is no element of the final judgment of Babylon and the other nations which cannot be applied to Israel and Judah.[13] The ambiguity we feel about Babylon – at once the great oppressor of God's people and the womb of their hope – is no less than what we feel about oxymoronic Israel, God's adulterous wife, his rebellious children. It is thus unsurprising that notes of hope reminiscent of Jeremiah 30 – 31 are to be found in the oracles against the nations. And yet it is equally clear that Judah must come out of Babylon and find her future in the land. At the heart of God's promise lies a return.

Continuity and discontinuity in Jeremiah 30 – 31

The questions of return and discontinuity which pervade the earlier chapters are brought to a head in the 'Book of Consolation', which is built principally around the reversal of earlier themes: terror, labour pains, mortal wounds, lovers, slavery, wilderness, building and planting, the created order, etc. Its six poems are marked by ambiguity, discontinuity and even *non sequitur* (e.g. 'therefore' in 30:16; cf. 32:36); they are framed by a prose introduction (30:1–4) and conclusion (31:23–40).[14] The conclusion is divided into two major sections of similar global structure, verses 23–34 and 35–40. The second section guarantees the promise made in the first, and each section can be further divided into an oracle stressing continuity with the past (vv. 23–26, 35–38) followed by oracles stressing discontinuity (vv. 27–30, 31–34, 39–40, each using *lō"ôd*, 'no longer').[15] The phrase 'behold, days are coming' begins vv. 27, 31, 38, making it a marker for announcements of discontinuity.[16]

The new-covenant passage should thus be read in close conjunction with verses 23–26 and 27–30. In the first oracle, the land will 'once again' ('*ôd*, v. 23) be the locus of God's presence with his people, and people from every part of society will enjoy blessing. In the next, verse 28 conveys a message of stark contrast: God 'watched' (*šqd*) over his people for evil in the past, but will soon watch over them for good. The stress on discontinuity is continued by the 'no longer' of verse 29, which describes a situation of individual responsibility as if brand new.

Note that verse 28 contains a unique reference back to Jeremiah's commissioning, combining the book's fullest reference to 1:10 with the rare word *šqd*, whose punning use introduced 1:11–19 (5:6; 44:27 are the only other occurrences in Jeremiah). In its original context, the almond-tree pun seemed to begin a new section in which the focus had shifted from the nations (vv. 5–10) to Judah. Yet here the two parts of chapter 1 are blended: the object of the uprooting, etc., is Israel and Judah, suggesting that it is as one of the nations that they are being addressed here (cf. 18:7–10).

Exegetical remarks on Jeremiah 31:31–34

'Behold, days are coming', declares the LORD, 'when I will make with the house of Israel and with the house of Judah a new covenant, [32]not like the covenant which I made with their fathers in the day I took them by the hand to bring them out of the land of Egypt, my covenant which they broke, although I was a husband to them,' declares the LORD. [33]But this is the covenant which I will make with the house of Israel after those days,' declares the LORD, 'I will put my law within them, and on their heart I will write it; and I will be their God, and they shall be my people; [34]and no longer they shall teach, each man his neighbour and each man his brother, saying, "Know the LORD," but all of them shall know me, from the least of them to the greatest of them,' declares the LORD. 'For I will forgive their iniquity, and their sin I will remember no more.'

The oracle's formal structure stresses discontinuity. 'Not like the covenant' (v. 32) is opposed by 'But this is the covenant' (v. 33); 'no longer' by 'but all of them' (v. 34).[17] Together with the tone of verses 27–30, this suggests that 'new' in the phrase 'new covenant' indicates radical discontinuity. Nevertheless, given that the only failing mentioned in verse 32 is the people's disobedience, which is not really part of the covenant itself, and given that the solution in verse 33 apparently describes a change not in the substance of the covenant but in the way it reaches the human partners, exegetes have difficulty pinpointing 'just wherein the newness consists'.[18] However, a closer consideration of the rhetoric of verse 32 suggests that its message of newness moves along different lines.

Verse 32

The 'dissimile' of verse 32 is made up of two relative clauses, each of which qualifies 'the covenant', and each of which makes the same general point about God. The striking phrase 'in the day of my taking hold of their hand'[19] uses a verb (*ḥzq*) which is never used of God's bringing Israel out from Egypt, but the cognate adjective often is, for example in the phrase 'with a strong (*ḥᵃzāqâ*) hand and an outstretched arm' (e.g. Jer. 32:21). This reversal, in which the hand is Israel's and not God's, speaks almost hyperbolically (if that were possible) about the compassion of God in the previous covenant, and says that the new covenant will not be like this![20]

The second relative clause draws a strong contrast between the different attitudes towards the covenant of the Israelites of old and God (note the emphatic pronouns 'they ... I'). The unusual redundant object 'my covenant'[21] also heightens the similarity to 11:10, and opens up the possibility that 'they' now refers to Jeremiah's generation, who have done as their fathers did.[22] Either way, God's covenant was made null and void by the people, but for God's part he was a husband to them.[23] Since the only other use of the verb rendered 'I was a husband' (NRSV, NASB) comes in 3:14, the earlier passage is important for us here (see p. 34). Even if we should render 'I was a master' in 3:14 and 31:32,[24] the point of verse 32 would remain unaltered: being a husband (or master) to his people suggests a commitment to them even despite their turning away from him. The logic of 3:14 is that the people can have confidence to return because God, as their husband/master, will take them back with mercy and love.

In short, verse 32 asserts that the new covenant will not be like the covenant in which God's saving initiative was unparalleled in its grace and compassion, and to which he remained utterly faithful in the face of its repeated annulment by Israel. In what way will the new covenant differ from this? And why say so? The point of difference is not the statement that 'they broke it',[25] for this is but a side-light included to illumine the acts and nature of the covenant God. That is, verse 32 leads us to expect a new covenant in which it is God, rather than the people, who acts differently. However, the extended nature of the dissimile means that we have no simple contrast, for, to cite Hays, the connotations of the verse 'bleed over from the denied images to the entity with which they are discompared'.[26] We thus expect the new covenant to be even more glorious than the one described here, to reflect divine deeds of even more breathtaking compassion and faithfulness.

Verse 33

The positive contrast is presented in a syndetic series (*waw* + perfect) of three pairs of clauses and a final, asyndetic pair of clauses which gives the reason for the foregoing. There is therefore a sequence, whether temporal or logical, built into the first three clause pairs: 'I will put my law on their heart; *then/therefore* I will be their God and they my people; *then/therefore* all of them will know me.' The opening word ('I will put') is not so much a *perfectum confidentiae*[27] as a 'report *qatal*', i.e. a verb form reserved for the announcing of information which is new to the hearer/reader.[28] That God is its subject strengthens the conclusion that the newness of this covenant will consist in what God does to surpass his acts of old.

It is often pointed out that Torah on the heart is a feature of the Sinai covenant, whether expressed as circumcision of the heart (Deut. 10:16), or as seeking God with the whole heart (2 Chr. 31:21; 2 Kgs. 10:31). Yet God's promise to do the writing himself is reflected only in Deuteronomy 30:6, speaking of a time after exile.

Therefore, although Torah on the heart was always possible for individuals,[29] Jeremiah makes it plain that in practice the people as a whole were incapable of this (e.g. 2:8; 6:19; 9:26; 16:10–13); indeed, 31:33 is the only positive use of Torah in the book, for their hearts were engraved not with Torah but with sin (17:1).[30] In the new covenant God will not inscribe a tablet; he will produce a palimpsest, over-writing with his words an original sinful text. This writing, moreover, is not on the hearts of scattered individuals; both 'midst' and 'heart' are singular words, for 'it is the corporate will and intention of the people that is at stake'.[31] That is, the law is written not only inwardly, but universally.

Torah on the corporate heart may be new, but the formula which follows is not. It represents continuity with the past. The logic of its positioning, however, suggests newness: law on the heart will enable a relationship (cf. Deut. 30:6; Jer. 24:7). The formula itself reflects formal language of marriage and adoption,[32] making a strong contrast with the end of verse 32, which might in retrospect be paraphrased, 'They were not my people, though I was their God.' Nevertheless, the covenant formula is arranged to put God's action first.[33] The new covenant will be one in which God will take Israel as his wife and she will remain faithful, for his Torah will be on her heart.

Verse 34a–d

One expects verse 34a to follow straight on from the promise of Torah on their heart, and the covenant formula to follow verse 34a. Such a sequence can be found in 24:7: 'I will give them a heart to know me, for I am the LORD; and they shall be my people and I will be their God, for they shall return to me with their whole heart.' Yet the logic of 24:7 is contained entirely within 32:33, suggesting a different function for the promise of knowledge in 32:34.

Since knowledge of the LORD and of his law are closely related in Jeremiah (e.g. 9:3, 6, 24), the separation of verse 34a from the promise of Torah on their heart suggests that knowledge itself is not the main focus here. The opening negation is curious: it is not priests and prophets, but friends and neighbours who will no longer teach one another. In 3:15, shepherds will teach the people knowledge, but this hope is not contradicted here. There may thus be an implicit indictment of the shepherds of the current order, whose failure to teach has thrown the responsibility on to the ordinary people. But this only opens up a further tacit accusation, for there is no sign that such activity ever occurred. All talk of 'neighbour(s)' is of lying, treachery, enslavement and perversion of the LORD's word (e.g. 9:4–8; 23:35–36; 34:15–16). This paradoxical clause has the same rhetorical flavour as the dissimile of verse 32. Positively, however, it sets up the next clause: it is those named who will know the LORD without being taught, not just the elite.[34] In other words, verse 34a is a rhetorical device to show the universality of this unmediated knowledge, rather than a rejection of leadership or teaching *per se*. Note the emphatic position of 'all of them' (*kullām*). In this respect it echoes 31:23–24, in which the universal enjoyment of God's presence is contemplated.

Finally, who are the 'all' who will know God (v. 34)? Who are the house of Israel and the house of Judah (vv. 31, 33)? Most read verse 33 as indicating 'a new total unity'[35] of northern and southern kingdoms, but the terms in the book as a whole with its 'prophet to the nations' orientation point to a reality that goes beyond Israel and Judah as they used to be. Together with the *šqd* reference (v. 28) and the use of 'husband/master' in verse 32, whose echoing of 3:14 prompts thoughts of a future arrangement ('not like' the present one) in which Jerusalem is inhabited by members of many nations, this terminology establishes an undercurrent of universal expectation which, though not the passage's focus, is nevertheless significant.

Verse 34ef

All from verse 33a to this point has been one complex statement. But now the final reason qualifies the entire passage (since the dissimile and counter-assertion are bound together as a dual entity). The sense of the conjunction introducing the final pair of phrases is, 'I will forgive their sins, which is why I will make a new covenant with them.'[36] This is not easy to interpret, and requires careful consideration.

Many identify this with forgiveness under the Mosaic covenant, appealing to Exodus 34:6–7; Psalm 51; Nehemiah 9:26–32 and similar texts.[37] This line of argument, however, ignores the fact that there was no such forgiveness for the Judah of Jeremiah's day. Had God found even one righteous, he might have been able to forgive, but he did not (5:1, 7; 14:10). There was no escape from the covenant curse of exile, and neither inclination nor ability on the people's part to repent (13:23). It follows that if a post-exilic renewed Mosaic covenant is on view, some aspect of that covenant will have to change so that history is not repeated. The people must become faithful, or God's forgiveness must expand. The main weight of our passage lies on the latter aspect.

Alternatively, others identify this with sinlessness under the new covenant. Certainly, verse 33 suggests that God's people will keep the law. This view sees in verse 34ef a forgiveness so comprehensive 'that no further action regarding sin will be necessary ... sin will be foreign to human experience'.[38] One might object that the Mosaic law allows for sacrifice and forgiveness, so that law-keeping need not mean sinlessness. 'Knowledge of God' might boil down to 'the basics of righteousness and kindness',[39] something well within the grasp of a less than perfect new-covenant partner. Yet this objection does not do justice to the argument. Dumbrell, for example, grounds his view in verse 34f itself, maintaining that 'I will not remember their sin' means that 'no action ... *needs* to be taken against sin'.[40] Unfortunately, however, this argument founders on internal contradictions.

Note that two stages are implied. By the logic of verse 34ef, God does not forgive them because they are clean; rather, they are clean because he forgives. Having first been wiped clean of its sin, the people's heart is then written upon afresh. This initial forgiveness is closely linked with the return (33:8; 50:19–20), in the same way that the people's sin is linked with the exile. That actual forgiveness of real sin is in view in the first instance is incontrovertible (hence the phrase 'no further action' in the previous paragraph's first quotation). But when the sinlessness which supposedly results is grounded in the same clause (34f), we are left with a statement which must bear two conflicting meanings – forgiveness necessary; forgiveness unnecessary – depending on which stage is in view.

Either we must restrict verse 34ef to the stage prior to the actions described in verses 33–34d as a once-and-for-all forgiveness, or verse 34ef must mean that forgiveness is an ongoing feature of the new covenant. The lines' final positioning and syntax lend some weight to the latter possibility.[41] Neither possibility can be ruled out, however, which again raises the question of how new the 'new' covenant really is, and so we turn back to the broader context via a comment on this famous expression.

The 'new' covenant

Both verb and adjective in verse 31 are problematic. Dumbrell has argued at length that 'the phrase *kārat berît* is universally used throughout the Old Testament period by biblical writers to describe the [first] point of covenant entry' (Gen. 15:18; Exod. 24:8; Ps. 89:3; etc.), and that for subsequent entry into an extant covenant relationship, other verbs are used.[42] However, there is at least one instance of *krt* being used of an extant covenant, namely Exodus 34:10. Rendtorff maintains that as it is for Exodus 34:10, so it is for Jeremiah 31:31,[43] but Gross has objected that if this were the case, one would expect *berît* to be definite. He is unconvinced that an already cut and established covenant can be cut again.[44] In the same vein, although *ḥadāšîm* probably means 'renewed' in Lamentations 3:23,[45] this is a rare case; the usual sense is of radical newness.[46]

In short, it is more likely on the face of it that this is not a promise to enter into a renewed covenant, but to cut a covenant *de novo*. And the context in Jeremiah 31 bears this out. First, the only comparable use of the word 'new' in Jeremiah occurs in 31:22, a notoriously enigmatic verse, but one which (1) brings to a climax the song cycle which began in 30:5–6, with which verses it forms an *inclusio*, and (2) makes an allusion to Genesis 1:27 by its combination of *neqēbâ* and *bārā'*, thus suggesting the turning of curse into blessing, creation into new creation.[47] In the light of this verse, it is very hard to read Jeremiah 31:31 as describing anything other than a profound newness which leaves nothing untouched. Second, and by contrast with Ezekiel 18, where God's promise not to 'remember' transgression (v. 22) is conditional upon the transgressor's turning away from the old ways to a life of righteousness (v. 31), Jeremiah 31 offers this level of forgiveness as but the first stage in a process of graded reversals (vv. 27–30, 31–34, 38–40). The first reversal ends with a promise that the people will no longer bear the burden of their fathers' sins (31:30), but that individuals will still die for their own iniquity (*ba*ᵃ*wōnô*). Note that verses 27–30 are about the return from exile. It is the return itself which signifies that the sins of the fathers have ceased to weigh with God. But the progression into 31–34 anticipates the problem of the returnees repeating history by promising a new covenant in which God makes all righteous by unconditionally forgiving their iniquity (*la*ᵃ*wōnām*). And in the final, climactic reversal, the irrevocably unclean will be holy to the LORD (v. 40).[48]

It therefore seems safe to conclude that it is more than simply the forgiveness of the Mosaic covenant which is being held out by verse 34. However, this passage, with its focus on God and his actions, seems uninterested in the question whether Torah on the heart means sinlessness. What matters is that, like the flood, the exile will never happen again, and that Israel in days to come will be faithful covenant partners, holy to the LORD. Sinlessness is consistent with this picture, but not the only possibility. Yet whatever the future will look like, it will be radically new and different from anything Israel has known before.

Continuity in Jeremiah 31:23–40

If this is correct, it raises the problem of what to do with the language of continuity which pervades the passage – terms such as 'YHWH', 'covenant', 'Israel', 'Judah', 'Torah' and the covenant formula, not forgetting the implication in verse 32 that, although the Sinai covenant was broken by Israel, YHWH did not break it (cf. Lev. 26:44). In other words, whether the earlier covenant is null and void or not depends on one's point of view.[49] Note, moreover, that the eternal covenant of 32:37–41 involves a return to the land, and that in 33:21 God promises never to break the Davidic covenant. Lastly, two prose sections (vv. 23–26, 35–37) stress continuity as a backdrop to the promises of reversal that have been the focus of this study.

Where verses 23–26 set the scene by looking forward to a land made once more the righteous dwelling of God in the midst of his people, 35–37 guarantee the promise of the new covenant by assuring Israel that their future nationhood (*gôy*, v. 36) will be as permanent as the created order. The simile suggests that the cleansing of Israel will make her the nation of God in the middle of his creation, to which – as the book's frame indicates – the nations will flow, merging into the eschatological nation which is called

Israel but is made up of all peoples. Thus Israel continues, but her continuance is bound up with God's purposes for the whole cosmos. Compare the way in which distinctive imagery of the exodus is used of the creation in 32:17. Similarly, the rebuilt city of Jerusalem (like the new covenant) is fundamentally changed (vv. 39–40). The old categories have changed for ever.

Where does this tension between continuity and discontinuity take us? First, it is always necessary to explain the unknown in terms of the known, and there may be an element of metaphor in the use of the familiar sociopolitical language when used eschatologically. Second, and more significantly, there is a sense in which the earlier covenants are not abrogated by the institution of newer ones: namely, everything they intended to achieve, the new covenant achieves.[50] Finally, the Old Testament does not resolve every suspension. There are significant elements of its picture of the future which remain open, only to be closed off (for Christians) by the life, death and resurrection of Christ.

Paul and the ministry of the new covenant

We pass over the question of whether Paul uses Jeremiah at all in his writings, content to accept, as most do, that 2 Corinthians 3:2 ('you are our letter, *written on our hearts*') alludes specifically to Jeremiah 31:31.[51] The use of the phrase 'new covenant' in verse 6 confirms the connection. Given our contention that Paul uses the new-covenant passage to help him exegete Exodus 34, it is interesting to find that in the Palestinian lectionary cycle Jeremiah 31:31–39 was the *haftarah* accompanying the Torah reading of Exodus 34:27–35.[52] Our reading of Jeremiah 31:31–34 suggests four possible points of contact in 2 Corinthians 3.

First, the reference to 'all men' in 3:2 is interesting in the light of the central emphasis on the universality of God's new initiative in Jeremiah 31. In the shifting metaphor of 2 Corinthians 3:1–3, the letters of recommendation become a letter on Paul's heart 'known and read by all people'.[53] Thus all look at Paul and see the Corinthians – or, more accurately (v. 3), Christ written on the Corinthians' hearts – ministered into place by Paul. Of course, the sense in which 'all' know Christ in the Corinthian believers is different from the sense in which 'all will know me' in Jeremiah 31:34, since 'all people' in 2 Corinthians 3:2 refers to outsiders. Yet could it be that Paul has in mind a transforming knowledge, a knowledge of Christ through the example of the Corinthians' faith that brings outsiders to the same faith when they read Paul's heart? This would certainly be consistent with Paul's self-understanding as an agent of universal gospel mission.[54] Moreover, while 'all people' in Paul might seem to be a far broader category than 'all of them' in Jeremiah, this is just the direction in which we would expect Paul to take Jeremiah, and if our earlier remarks on the openness of the terms 'Israel' and 'Judah' are correct, then the internationalizing of the promise in this way is implicit in the original. Indeed, if it is true that Jeremiah 31 is guiding Paul's thought here, verse 2 inevitably becomes a missionary verse.

Second, the contrast between old and new in 2 Corinthians 3:7–11 reflects the same type of balance between continuity and discontinuity as is displayed in Jeremiah 31.[55] For the ministry of the old covenant was a glorious ministry, and its glory was being abolished[56] only because 'it was done away by the greater glory of the new covenant in Christ'.[57] In precisely the same way, Jeremiah 31:32 points to a new covenant whose dissimilarity from the old consists in the radical increase of love, mercy and faithfulness which God will show. Indeed, the substance of the new covenant and its effects will be just what the Mosaic covenant had had the potential to achieve, though the implementation of the latter for national Israel would never have been possible.[58]

Third, it is not only the fact of the dissimile that links 2 Corinthians 3:12–18 with Jeremiah 31:31–34. The very structure of Paul's argument is closely matched to that of the latter text, and the similarity is even greater to the Greek version (Jer. 38:31–34, LXX). We may tabulate the similarities as follows:

Jeremiah 38:32, LXX	2 Corinthians 3:13–15	
32. not according to the covenant which I made with their fathers ...	13. not as Moses [who] used to put a *veil* over his face so Israel would not gaze at the goal of what was being *abolished*;	for until this day the same *veil* remains at the reading of the old covenant ... because it is *abolished* in Christ
for they abode not in my covenant.	14. *But* their minds were hardened;	15. *But* to this day ... a veil lies over their heart.

Jeremiah's dissimile refers to the making of the Mosaic covenant and to the unfaithfulness of Israel. Each of these points is dealt with twice by Paul, first in its original setting, and then in its present continuation. Each time there is the same movement from grace to condemnation that Jeremiah displays. The protective veil is a sign of grace in verse 13, but after the gracious work of Christ its persistence becomes a sign of condemnation, so that it recurs in verse 15. Note also that the 'minds' of verse 14 have become 'heart' (singular) in verse 15, as if in anticipation of the Torah-filled heart which is about to feature in Jeremiah. Finally, verses 16–18 provide the positive alternative in the same way that verses 33–34 do for Jeremiah 31:32 (LXX 38:32).

Fourth, the way in which Jeremiah 31 transforms Paul's reading of Exodus 34 can be seen in his altered citation:

Exodus 34:34a	**2 Corinthians 3:16**
But when *Moses would go in* before the LORD to speak with him, *he would take off* the veil, until he came out …	But when *one turns* to the Lord, the veil *is removed*.

In this citation, Paul alters (1) 'Moses' to the inclusive '[any]one'; (2) the iterative imperfect 'would go in' (*eiseporeueto*) to the aorist subjunctive 'turns' (*epistrepsē* – a favourite word in Jeremiah (LXX) for rendering *šwb*), signifying not intermittent but constant access; and (3) the action of removing the veil so that God does it. This mirrors the way Jeremiah 31 transforms the Sinai covenant, with its stress on inclusiveness, on permanent relationship, and on God's initiative. And, if we may reverse direction in our final comment, the fact that the unveiled beholding of God's glory results in present and ongoing transformation (v. 18) suggests that, for Paul, at least, the promise of transforming forgiveness found in Jeremiah 31:34ef is to be interpreted as fulfilled in the present, but pointing ultimately to the sinlessness of the people of God in Christ.[59]

Summary

To repeat a frequently asked question: what, then, is new about the new covenant? First, the new covenant is radically new, as new as a new creation. Second, the dissimile of verse 32 conveys the message that God will go immeasurably further than he has done in the past. Third, God will apply the law to the people in such a way that they will not break the covenant, and – this is the main point of verses 33–34d – he will do it inclusively, for every one of his people. Fourth, God will be able to do this because he will forgive his people their sin. This key statement is reserved to the end, creating a climactic 'closure'[60] which maximizes the rhetorical effect of the dissimile.

Fifth, all this newness and discontinuity suggests that it is more than just Sinai-style forgiveness that will be offered, but just what this means is left open. Sixth, the inclusiveness of verses 33–34 resonates with Jeremiah's call to be prophet to the nations and with the associated internationalizing of Israel's hope.

Such a reading of Jeremiah 31 fits very neatly with its use by Paul as a hermeneutical lens for his exegesis of Exodus 34. This hermeneutic operates at three levels simultaneously. At the level of rhetorical method, Paul re-creates the style of argument and flow of thought of Jeremiah 31:31–34, sending the distinctive content of Exodus 34 down a new channel. At the level of promise and fulfilment, he lets Jeremiah's balance between continuity and discontinuity control his own discomparison. And at the level of text and context, he takes what is truly distinctive from his source text and carries it to its conclusion with the tacit approval and assistance of the book of Jeremiah in general. That is to say, the stress on inclusiveness in Jeremiah 31:33–34 becomes, in Paul's treatment, the vehicle for carrying the Sinai covenant into the age of the Gentiles. As the apostle to the nations, Paul did no violence to his Jewishness, but rather brought it along the road to fulfilment that was opened up by the work of Jesus, his master.[61]

Notes

1. *Echoes*, p. 140. We adopt the term without implying that ancient authors ever used the dissimile as a formal rhetorical device.
2. *Echoes*, p. 142. Hays stretches the limits of the dissimile uncomfortably; although images of veiling and glory do appear in 3:18; 4:3–4, there are interruptions at 3:17; 4:1–2.
3. That is, the only extended case in the indicative (*lō'...k*). Imperatival examples are Zech. 1:4; 2 Chr. 30:7 (*'al...k*). In the NT, Rom. 5:15–16 stands out (*ouch hōs*), but is hardly a dissimile.
4. Rendtorff, 'What is New'; Lohfink, *Covenant*; cf. Gross, 'Der neue Bund'; Merklein, 'Der (neue) Bund'. See the discussion of Lohfink and Zenger by Gross, 'Erneuerter', pp. 45–48.
5. Hals, 'Aspects'; Sarason, 'Interpretation'; Holmgren, *Old Testament*.
6. See McKane, *Jeremiah* 1, p. 8; Tomes, 'Reception', p. 240.
7. 1:10; cf. 18:7–10; 24:6; 29:5, 28; 42:10; 45:4. The fact that the phrase is used of Israel suggests that she is viewed as one of the nations; this comes out most clearly in 31:28 (see p. 36).
8. See the discussion by McConville, *Judgment*, pp. 29–33. The formula 'The LORD of hosts, the God of Israel' is frequent in Jeremiah's prose, and covenantal uses of 'Israel' are found in poetry too (10:16; 12:14; 14:8; 17:13; etc.). Cf. Holladay, *Jeremiah* 1, pp. 319–320, on 9:26 (Heb. 9:25).
9. For this division, see Brueggemann, *To Pluck*, pp. 39–48.
10. A phrase everywhere else used of Israel (Deut. 29:18; Jer. 7:24; 9:13; 11:8; 13:10; 16:12; 18:12; 23:17).

11. Cf. Aitken, 'Oracles', pp. 31–36.
12. Note also the refrain equating Judah with the nations (*gôyîm*) in 5:9, 29; 9:9 (Heb. 9:8), and the announcements of salvation for the nations found in 4:1–2; 12:14–17; 16:19; 46:26; 48:47; 49:6, 39. Both motifs contribute to the removal of distinction between the two groups (cf. McConville, *Judgment*, p. 46).
13. Hill, *Friend*, pp. 172–180.
14. Bozak, *Life*, pp. 18–25.
15. The formula *kōh 'amar* is structurally significant, but *nᵉ'um yhwh* simply adds emphasis to the preceding phrase (Parunak, 'Discourse', pp. 508–512).
16. Carroll, *Jeremiah*, p. 608.
17. In both cases, *kî* is to be rendered adversatively ('But this is the covenant ...'; 'but all of them ...'): Gross, 'Erneuerter', p. 50.
18. Hals, 'Aspects', p. 91.
19. Literally; Gen. 19:16; 21:18; Is. 42:6.
20. Compare the similar reversals in 32:40, where God follows after the people, and in 32:41, where we have a unique application to God of the language of covenant obedience. In the future, this implies, the faithfulness expected of the people will be undertaken by God himself.
21. GKC, §138b (1).
22. Cf. Gross, 'Die neue Bund', p. 260. Outside chs. 30 – 33, *prr*, 'to break', is used only in 11:10; 14:21; cf. Deut. 31:16, 20.
23. The LXX reads *emelēsa*, 'I abominated', reflecting *gā'altî* in the LXX *Vorlage*, a reading Becking argues is secondary ('Jeremiah's Book', p. 163).
24. So Holladay, *Jeremiah* 2, p. 198. But see McKane, *Jeremiah* 1, pp. 72–73, for an argument that *bā'altî* in 3:14 is an image from marriage.
25. Against Wolff, 'What is New', pp. 52–53, and many others. The other possibility, argued by Wallis, 'Irony', is that v. 32 is ironic, but one must find no indication at all of newness in order to establish this.
26. *Echoes*, p. 142.
27. Pace Bozak, *Life*, p. 121.
28. Niccacci, *Syntax*, pp. 41–43; cf. Gibson, *Syntax*, §59.
29. The Psalmist can say that God's Torah is 'in my heart' (Pss. 37:31; 40:81; cf. Deut. 30:14).
30. This militates against the use made of these psalms (see previous note) by Lohfink, *Covenant*, p. 56 and Holmgren, *Old Testament*, p. 86. It also negates the claim that Torah on the heart removes human freedom, in that there was no freedom to be removed, but only slavery to sin. See Weippert, 'Das Wort', pp. 339–340.
31. Holladay, *Jeremiah* 2, p. 198.
32. So Sohn, 'I will be'.
33. The emphatic pronoun in the second clause is normal and unmarked for this formula.
34. Note Jer. 6:13, in which greed and lies are predicated of both the masses (using the same clause, 'from the least to the greatest') and the elite ('from the prophet even to the priest').
35. Holladay, *Jeremiah* 2, p. 198.
36. The rendition of *kî* here has been questioned by McKane (*Jeremiah* 2, pp. 822–827). Even he, however, renders it 'for', before going on to argue that 'the logic of the connection is unclear' (p. 822). Gross ('Erneuerter', p. 50) points out

that where the previous *kî* follows *lō'...'ōd* and means 'but', this conjunction precedes *lō'...'ōd* and thus carries a different meaning.

37. So Rendtorff, 'What is new', p. 198; Holmgren, *Old Testament*, p. 88.
38. Dumbrell, *Search*, pp. 101–102; cf. Holladay, *Jeremiah* 2, p. 199; Carroll, *Jeremiah*, p. 612; Keown et al., *Jeremiah*, p. 135; Rudolph, *Jeremia*, p. 203.
39. Holmgren, *Old Testament*, p. 93, commenting on Jer. 22:15–16.
40. *Covenant*, p. 182, emphasis mine. Cf. Gross, 'Der neue Bund', 261; Wolff, 'What is new', pp. 59–60.
41. Imperfect verbs have been used throughout, so that there is no aspectual differentiation between the forgiveness and the consequent acts of writing Torah on the heart, etc. Had the author wanted to say, 'For I will have forgiven their iniquities', he could have done so (hypothetically: *kî 'az sālaḥtî laᵃwōnām*; cf. 2 Sam. 5:24).
42. *Covenant*, p. 25.
43. '*Bundesformel*', p. 87.
44. 'Erneuerter', pp. 51–52 and n. 50; cf. Hasel, '*kāraṯ*', pp. 350–351.
45. Where God's mercies are 'new every morning'. The noun *ḥāḏāš* refers to the cyclical appearance of the new moon (Holmgren, *Old Testament*, p. 77).
46. North, '*ḥāḏāš*', Verhoef, '*ḥḏš*'. Gross would argue that, semantically, *ḥāḏāš* cannot mean 'renewed', there being no scope in Hebrew for expressing gradations of newness, or 'being new' *versus* 'becoming new' ('Erneuerter', p. 51).
47. North, '*ḥāḏāš*', p. 237; Bozak, *Life*, pp. 103–104. For the reasons just given, a link to 31:22 is more likely than that 'new' in 31:31 is being contrasted with 'old' in 11:10, pace Römer, '"Anciens" pères'.
48. See Bozak, *Life*, pp. 127–128.
49. Cf. Williams, '*prr*', 696–697.
50. As a point of method, it is important that we do not pour everything Jeremiah says about the future into each passage about the future, but that we let each text make its distinctive contribution. Jer. 31:31–34 is about newness, discontinuity and the actions of God before it is about human behaviour. Although we may deduce from it that people will not break the future covenant, this is not its main concern (as opposed to 32:37–41). Thus the Mosaic, Davidic and even Levitical (33:21) covenants play a part in Jeremiah's eschatology, for each in its own way provides an image which enriches his total vision.
51. E.g. Barnett, *Second Corinthians*, pp. 164–165. On the broader question of Jeremiah allusions in Paul, note the argument by Rakotoharintsifa ('Jérémie', against claims by Wolff, *Jeremia*, and others) that Jeremiah citations and allusions play a significant, albeit small, role in the argument of 1 Corinthians. On Jer. 1:5 in Gal. 1:15, see O'Brien (*Consumed by Passion*, pp. 6–12).
52. *Encyclopedia Judaica* 15, p. 1387. Note that the earliest evidence of a fixed pattern of *haftarot* is Mishnaic (*m. Meg.* 4:10; see Aageson, 'Lectionary', p. 271; Morris, *Lectionaries*, p. 21).
53. For a defence of the reading *kardiais hēmōn* (v. 2), see Thrall, *Second Corinthians*, p. 223.
54. See esp. O'Brien, *Consumed by Passion*, pp. 36–49, on Rom. 15:18–21; for other uses of 'all men', see Rom. 12:17–18; Phil. 4:5; 1 Tim. 2:1, 4; 4:10; Titus 2:11. Note also 2 Cor. 3:18: 'we *all* ... are being transformed'.
55. We have passed over the undoubted traces of Ezek. 36:26–27 present in v. 3 and in the subsequent references to the Spirit. These allusions support the thrust of

the Jeremiah passage, providing the material about the Spirit which fills out Paul's exegesis. To see the negative contrast between stone tablets and fleshy tablets in v. 3 as acting to disturb what would otherwise be a positive correlation between old and new covenants (so Hays, *Echoes*, p. 128) is to oversimplify the tension between continuity and discontinuity in the Jeremiah text.

56. On the inappropriateness of rendering *to katargoumenon* as 'fading', see Barnett, *Second Corinthians*, p. 187.
57. Hays, *Echoes*, p. 135; cf. v. 10.
58. On this subject, see Dumbrell, 'Paul's Use'.
59. In this respect Dumbrell's unqualified assertion that Jer. 31 only 'points beyond the experience of the Christian believer' (*Search*, p. 102) seems somewhat unbalanced.
60. Watson, *Poetry*, pp. 62–64.
61. This essay is dedicated with gratitude and affection to Peter O'Brien, whom I am privileged to have known as teacher, colleague, friend and example.

5. The truth of the gospel: Paul's mission according to Galatians

Moisés D. Silva

In a document such as Paul's letter to the Galatians, so full of interesting and unexpected details, one particularly intriguing item is the phrase *hē alētheia tou euangeliou*, 'the truth of the gospel,' which occurs twice in chapter 2 (vv. 5 and 14), and nowhere else in the New Testament.[1] What does the phrase mean? And what does it teach us regarding the apostle's understanding of mission?

Any self-respecting exegete would approach the first question by considering the possible uses of the genitive. Do we have here a possessive genitive, as suggested by Burton, who takes the phrase to mean, 'the truth contained in, and so belonging to, the gospel'?[2] Or perhaps a subjective genitive, 'the truth presented in the gospel'?[3] Or do we have a rhetorically expressed attribute, 'the true gospel'?[4] Or an epexegetical genitive, as we probably have in Colossians 1:5, 'the truth, namely, the gospel'?[5]

The problem with this type of question, however, is that it does not correspond to the normal processes of communication. An English speaker using the preposition *of*, for example, does not deliberate about its various uses before uttering phrases like 'that fool *of* a man' (apposition) or 'the fear *of* God' (objective genitive) or 'died *of* thirst' (causal). Nor do the hearers check off a list with all possible functions of the preposition before understanding the phrase.

To be sure, a foreigner whose language makes different use of a comparable preposition, and who therefore is stumped by some of these combinations in English, may well need to check off a list of possibilities. Understandably, then, students of Greek often feel the need to go through a similar process when they come across the genitive. However, it is one thing to categorize grammatical uses for pedagogical purposes, and quite another to make such categorizations the basis of exegesis. Again, when there is a difference of opinion about the force of a genitival construction, scholars may find it convenient to identify the various options by using the standard textbook labels, but this practice can easily degenerate into a debate that is not true to the nature of language.

What needs to be remembered is that the only *grammatical* consideration in these cases is a rather vague one: the genitive links two nouns as having some sort of relationship. What that relationship may be (possessive, subjective, objective, appositional, etc.) can be deduced only on the basis of additional data. Consider, in this very passage, the phrase *to euangelion tēs akrobystias*, literally 'the gospel of the uncircumcision' (Gal. 2:7). If someone should propose that we have here a subjective genitive – or more precisely, a genitive of source – we would readily rule out such an interpretation. Why? Simply because we happen to know that the gospel did not have its origin among the Gentiles. As far as the grammar is concerned, this phrase communicates little more than the fact that the gospel in view has something to do with those who are not circumcised. (Additional, extragrammatical data in this letter make clear that Paul is referring to how the gospel is preached, interpreted and applied to those who are not Jewish.)

Accordingly, all we can say about *hē alētheia tou euangeliou*, grammatically considered, is that Paul is highlighting the relationship that exists between the truth and the gospel.[6] Of course, there are other considerations of a *linguistic* nature that help us understand the force of the expression. Mussner, for example, calls attention to the use of the phrase in verse 14 and perceptively points out that its meaning is context-determined by its linguistic opposition to the clause, 'how do you force [*anagkazeis*] the Gentiles to judaize?'[7] He then logically infers that 'the truth of the gospel' points to Gentile freedom from the Jewish law. Similarly, in verse 5 the phrase stands in opposition to the false brothers' desire to force Titus to be circumcised (v. 3, *oude ... ēnagkasthē peritmēthēnai*), with the intention of enslaving believers (v. 4, *hina hēmas katadoulōsousin*).

We can therefore understand why many commentators interpret the phrase as focusing on purity of doctrine. According to Ellicott, the words contain a 'doctrinal import' that 'is entirely lost' if we explain them as merely equivalent to 'the true gospel' (*to alēthes euangelion*). Echoing this interpretation, Eadie states that by the phrase Paul means 'not simply the true gospel, but truth as a distinctive element of the gospel, – opposed to the false views of its cardinal doctrine which the reactionary Judaists propounded'. And Lightfoot, in words that have been quoted by subsequent commentators, defines the phrase as 'the Gospel in its integrity. This expression in St Paul's language denotes the doctrine of grace, the maintenance of Christian liberty, as opposed to the false teaching of the Judaizers.'[8] Having made the connection clear, Paul can later refer to the same idea by the use of *alētheia* alone (5:7).

The question still remains, however, why the apostle would have chosen to express such a concept with this particular and distinctive phrase. Part of the answer, undoubtedly, is its rhetorical effect. While either 'the truth' or 'the gospel' by itself would have communicated the same basic semantic content, the combination conveys a certain solemnity or emphasis very appropriate to the context.

But could there be more? Martyn thinks so: 'This is an expression that Paul constructs with care, so as to lay more or less equal weight on the two nouns "truth" and "gospel".'[9] While it would be difficult to prove that the apostle was thinking precisely along those lines, Martyn may be on to something with this comment. In expanding what he means, unfortunately, he overinterprets the phrase, being guided more by his emphasis on the theme of apocalyptic antinomies (which he believes characterizes Galatians) than by any clues from the text itself.

> When [Paul] links the nouns 'truth' and 'gospel', he does two things to the former: First, he gives to it a specificity it does not have in common parlance, by saying that the truth *is* the gospel of Jesus Christ. Second, he reflects his perception of a crucial antinomy not really grasped by placing opposite one another truth and falsehood. Were the truth of the gospel not to remain, the result would not be falsehood, but rather disaster in the form of apocalyptic judgment (cf. 2 Cor. 2:14–16 and Gal. 5:21).
>
> We have, then, an instance in which Paul brings to bear the eschatological force of the major Hebrew term for truth (*'emet*). The truth of the gospel is not a thing. Truth is, rather, the end-time *event* of God's redemption in Jesus Christ. For that reason its genuine opposite is not human falsehood, but rather judgment at the hands of God who judges in his truth-event (cf. 1:8–9; 5:10b).[10]

Martyn here appears to mix categories. In fact, the apostle does oppose 'the truth of the gospel' to falsehood in this passage (*pseudadelphous*, v. 4;

elsewhere, cf. *pseudomai*, 1:20, and note Rom. 1:25; 3:7). If we focus on *results* – a distinct category – then the opposition is between freedom and slavery (*eleutheria/katadouloō*, v. 4). Undoubtedly, slavery issues in (apocalyptic) judgment, just as freedom leads to eternal life; moreover, future-eschatological concerns are never far from Paul's mind (cf. 2:2). Still, these are not prominent or even explicit in verses 4–5 and 14. Much less is there anything in the text that would encourage us to think of truth as an 'event' rather than a 'thing' (whatever that means). Evidently, the worn-out distinction between Greek and Hebrew views of truth continues to rear its ugly head.[11]

Whether or not we agree with his understanding of the phrase, however, Martyn is surely on target when he calls attention to the fact that 'the truth of the gospel' is not an ordinary combination of terms and that therefore it probably reflects a deliberate and careful choice on Paul's part. He may also be right in suggesting that the apostle wishes to balance the weight of the two terms. This distinctive phrase likely reflects Paul's twin convictions that there is no (ultimate) truth without the gospel (cf. Rom. 1:16–17) and that a 'gospel' without the truth is no gospel at all (Gal. 1:6–7). If we wish to understand how the apostle himself viewed his mission to the Gentiles, we must give full weight to such a fundamental conception.

The question arises, however, as to why this powerful phrase occurs uniquely in Galatians 2. The two incidents discussed in this chapter – a special meeting in Jerusalem (verses 1–10), and a controversy in Antioch (verses 11–21)[12] – are typically viewed as the last two items in a longer list of events that began earlier. Lightfoot, for example, entitles 1:11 – 2:21 'This Gospel came directly from God', then subdivides it into six sections, the first four of which are covered in the first chapter. We may abbreviate his outline as follows:

1. Paul received the gospel by special revelation (1:11–12).
2. His previous education indeed could not have led up to it (1:13–14).
3. Nor could he have learned it from the other apostles (1:15–17).
4. When at last he visited Jerusalem, he spent little time with them (1:18–24).
5. He visited Jerusalem again, it is true, but he carefully maintained his independence (2:1–10).
6. Nay more: at Antioch he rebuked Peter for his inconsistency (2:11–21).[13]

Most other students of the letter, whatever variations they may introduce into their outlines, follow this basic understanding regarding the connection between chapters 1 and 2. As I have argued elsewhere, however, such an approach does not do justice to the distinctiveness of the material in the second chapter.[14] Lightfoot's words, 'it is true', in the fifth point of his outline alert us to the fact that there is some kind of shift in the argument. The thesis stated in 1:11–12 (Paul did not receive his gospel from men) is fully demonstrated by the time we reach the end of chapter 1; in particular, verses 16–24 have provided all the evidence necessary to prove that during the first fourteen (seventeen?) years of his ministry, Paul had only the briefest of associations with the Twelve.

Why then does the narrative continue? Because Paul finds it necessary to deal with two particular incidents that were most likely brought up by his opponents. The question now is no longer whether Paul had contact with the apostles or even whether the contact was extensive. That question has already been taken care of. By the time Paul travelled to Jerusalem to confer with the 'pillars', his distinctive apostolic ministry had been formed and consolidated, and whatever may have happened at the conference could not affect the *origin* of his gospel. The incidents discussed in Galatians 2, there-fore, must have been special problems that could be interpreted as undermining the independence of his apostleship. To put it differently, the attack that Paul's gospel was formed by early prolonged contact with the apostles now gives way to specific charges regarding his submission to the Three in Jerusalem.

We must not downplay the fact, moreover, that both of the incidents related in this chapter were characterized by some measure of conflict between Paul and the Three. This point is especially obvious in the case of the confrontation with Peter at Antioch, but even the conference in Jeru-salem, in spite of its amicable conclusion, was not without its tensions. No-one has seen this issue more clearly than Lightfoot, who was able to read between the lines of Galatians 2:4, as follows:

> What part was taken in the dispute by the Apostles of the Circumcision?
> ... On the whole it seems probable that they recommended St Paul to
> yield the point, as a charitable concession to the prejudices of the Jewish
> converts: but convinced at length by his representations, that such a
> concession at such a time would be fatal, they withdrew their counsel
> and gave him their support. The sensible undercurrent of feeling, the
> broken grammar of the sentence, the obvious tenor of particular
> phrases, all convey the impression, that though the final victory was
> complete, it was not attained without a struggle, in which St Paul main-
> tained at one time single-handed the cause of Gentile freedom.[15]

If my understanding of Galatians 2 is valid, its implications for the signif-icance of the phrase 'the truth of the gospel' are both intriguing and weighty.

The expression, as it turns out, appears only in the context of conflict, and more specifically, in two passages where the position of the Jerusalem leaders is at best ambiguous (vv. 1–5), and at worst indefensible (vv. 11–14). Is this a coincidence? We would be going much too far to suggest that Paul coined the phrase specifically to distinguish his position from that of the Three, or that the phrase would not have been used by him in other contexts. But the fact that the expression occurs uniquely in Galatians 2 should not be minimized, and if we wish to identify as clearly as possible its force, we surely must take into account this peculiarity.

Now it must be made clear that the question at hand is not whether Paul and the Three operated with different theologies. All the available evidence makes it evident that the apostles were united in preaching a message of grace through faith. Even the vigorous controversy in Antioch reflects their basic agreement in doctrine. Machen expresses the matter well when he argues that 'in the very act of condemning the practice of Peter, Paul approves his principles' (in particular, 'the inadequacy of the Law, and the all-sufficiency of faith in Christ'). Indeed, the conflict at Antioch 'far from establishing a fundamental disagreement between Peter and Paul really furnishes the strongest possible evidence for their fundamental unity'.[16]

It would also be a mistake, however, to minimize the problems faced by the early Christians as they sought to implement the mission of the church. Those problems inevitably gave rise to differences of opinion. With hindsight, it is very easy for us (especially Gentile believers!) to see that circumcision should not have been imposed on non-Jewish converts to Christianity. But such an inference would have been less than obvious to someone who had always been taught to identify God's people with those who embraced the Sinaitic covenant.

The Jerusalem apostles understood well enough – and preached – that salvation could not depend on obedience to the Mosaic law. Yet in the heat of conflict, when the very survival of the church perhaps appeared to be in jeopardy, they may naturally have been willing to acquiesce to the scruples of some of their fellow-Jews in the church. They may well have reasoned that circumcision and other Mosaic regulations could be observed by Christian Gentiles without compromising their faith, if they acted simply out of consideration for Jewish sensibilities.

To Paul, however, 'had been revealed the full implications of the gospel; to him the freedom of the Gentiles was a matter of principle, and when principle was at stake he never kept silent'.[17] To be sure, when Paul affirms in 2:5 that the reason he did not yield for a moment was 'so that the truth of the gospel might not be taken from you',[18] the antagonists in view are clearly the judaizing false brothers rather than the Jerusalem apostles. We cannot, however, overlook the fact that the false brothers had little chance to succeed in their mission unless they could persuade the apostles. In other words, Paul's apprehension that he might have laboured in vain (2:2) was due not merely to the existence of vigorous opponents, but to the possibility that these opponents might influence the behaviour of the Jerusalem leaders. And it was *this distinctive situation* that called forth the apostle's appeal for 'the truth of the gospel'.

The same type of situation is in view when Paul writes about his conflict with Peter in Antioch. In that passage he describes the behaviour of Peter, and of those influenced by him, as a failure to 'follow the right path [using the verb *orthopodeō*, 'walk straight', fig. 'act rightly'] in accordance with the truth of the gospel' (2:14). It is evident that neither Peter nor Barnabas was interested in forcing circumcision on the Gentiles in Antioch so as to rob them of their freedom. Even when Paul accuses Peter of forcing the Gentiles to become Jews (*ta ethnē anagkazeis ioudaizein*), the point is not that Peter is consciously doing such a thing. Rather, Paul wants to make very clear that Peter's inconsistent behaviour could only aid the judaizers' mission: such conduct would surely be interpreted by the Antiochian Christians as further pressure to adopt Jewish ways. (In the absence of a judaizing threat, would not Peter's action have conveyed a somewhat different message from what it did on this occasion?)

It appears, then, that the expression 'the truth of the gospel' points specifically to the need to preserve the gospel of freedom against attack. And the attack in view consists not merely in the direct opposition to the gospel from false brothers, but also and especially in the adverse influence exerted by *true* brothers who may be unduly concerned by the need for moderation.[19] This is undoubtedly dangerous territory. The history of the church – including contemporary history – is full of examples of overzealous Christians who have done little more than create deep and unnecessary pain. But there are not a few examples of well-meaning believers whose passion to preserve peace has done considerable damage to the health of Christ's church.

To help us round out this study of 'the truth of the gospel', we should take careful note of 5:7, where Paul poses this rhetorical question to the Galatians: 'who hindered you so as not to obey the truth?'[20] As suggested earlier, and as recognized by commentators generally, here the word *alētheia* is shorthand for *hē alētheia tou euangeliou*. The use of 'truth' as the direct object of 'obey,' however, is an unpredictable and thus forceful combination.[21] It also raises a question about what Paul means by the word 'truth.' After all, what sense does it make to speak about 'obeying the truth'? What would it mean to *obey* the truth that 2 + 2 = 4, or the truth that Jesus suffered under Pontius Pilate, or even the truth that God is gracious?

It seems remarkable that students of the epistle have not typically remarked on the peculiarity of this expression. That we have something unusual here is reflected in the NEB's attempt to make sense of this combination, namely, through the translation 'from following the truth' (cf. Acts 5:36–37). Dunn, one of the few commentators who pay more than passing attention to the clause, reminds us that the active *peithō* means 'to persuade', and hence renders, 'in not being persuaded regarding the truth'.[22] This approach is defensible, since Galatians bears the marks of persuasive speech (cf. 1:10),[23] and Dunn's rendering has the added advantage of reflecting the play on words with *peismonē*, 'persuasion', in verse 8 and *pepoitha*, 'I am persuaded', in verse 10. But the translation is not fully satisfactory: the English ('to hinder someone in being persuaded') sounds less than natural, and it almost suggests that the Judaizers came in before the Galatians had made a commitment to the gospel.

Happily, at any rate, commentators have refrained from using Paul's language here as evidence of the view that, in essence, truth is not propositional. Of course, while it needs to be affirmed that, according to biblical teaching, truth fundamentally does indeed consist in propositions, we must also insist that it involves much more than that. In so far as 'truth' here is more or less equivalent to 'gospel,' it should be apparent that Paul has in mind not only historical facts and doctrinal teaching, but also biddings and injunctions.[24] On the basis of the *historical* truth that Jesus died and was raised from the dead, and the *theological* truth that this happened for the forgiveness of our sins, Paul proclaimed the *parenetic* truth that God commands everyone everywhere to repent (1 Cor. 15:3–5; Acts 17:30–31).[25]

It becomes apparent, then, that a satisfactory understanding of the phrase 'the truth of the gospel' cannot be achieved unless we take into consideration the concept of obedient response, a concept that Paul expresses in Romans with the rich expression, 'the obedience of faith' (*hē hypakoē pisteōs*, Rom. 1:5; 16:26). In this case too we want to avoid being unduly distracted by the debate regarding the genitival function Paul may have had in mind. At the risk of oversimplifying the problem, we may say that the key notion is his desire to highlight the very close relationship that exists between faith and obedience.

Peter O'Brien, following Don Garlington, wishes to preserve what may be a deliberate ambiguity in the construction. He then adds perceptively:

But even if there is some doubt about the exact nuance of the expression, the immediate context of Romans 1:5, the flow of the argument in chapters 1 – 8, together with other instances in Paul's letters of the language of obedience which refer to Christian behaviour, all indicate that the apostle has in view the believer's total response to the gospel, not simply his or her initial conversion ...

This notion of a total response accords well with the conclusions already reached in relation to the parallel expression of 15:18, 'the obedience of the Gentiles', which focuses not simply on the nations coming to faith or their acceptance of the gospel, but on their initial response *and* constancy in Christian conduct as well.[26]

By the same token, when Paul speaks to the Galatians about 'the truth of the gospel', he is laying before them not only their need to understand his doctrinal teaching (proposition) regarding Gentile freedom, but also their responsibility to respond in obedience and thus finish the course as they began it, by the Spirit and not by the flesh (Gal. 3:3). The Galatians had indeed been brought to faith. The apostle, who does not hesitate to call them 'brothers' (1:11; 3:15; 4:12, 28, 31; 5:11, 13; 6:1, 18), affirms the genuineness of their experience by reminding them that they received the Spirit of God when they believed the message (3:2, 5). Yet he continues to suffer as a woman in labour until Christ is fully formed in them (4:19).

It should be evident that nothing would have been more foreign to Paul's sense of mission than the notion of a brief evangelistic campaign that, aiming at a large number of quick conversions, failed to establish solid and prolonged involvement. Those who respond to the gospel call have begun a race that is anything but straight and smooth. Hindrances and conflicts will meet them at every turn. Accordingly, Paul clearly saw his evangelistic and missionary work as all-encompassing. It was not merely the task of beginning something, but of continuing and completing it as well.[27]

Notes

1. Col. 1:5, at first blush, appears to contain the phrase as well, since it speaks of the Colossians as having heard of the Christian hope *en tō logō tēs alētheias tou euangeliou*, lit., 'in the word of the truth of the gospel,' translated by NIV as 'in the word of truth, the gospel' (similarly NRSV and other translations). The presence of *en tō logō*, however, produces a different syntactical construction, and we should not infer that the semantic force here is the same as in Galatians.
2. Burton, *Galatians*, p. 86. So also Greijdanus, *Galatië*, p. 145.
3. This may be the position of Schlier, *Galater*, p. 73. In his view, Paul wanted the Galatians to hold on to the true implications of the gospel ('Das, was Paulus der

Kirche Galatiens erhalten wissen wollte, ist eben die im Gegensatz zu den Verdrehungen seiner Gegner entfaltete wahre Konsequenz des Evangeliums').

4. Cf. Rom. 6:4, *kainotēs zoēs*, 'newness of life' = 'new life', but with emphasis on the headword, *kainotēs* (this type of expression, attested in classical Greek and Latin, is to be distinguished from the so-called Hebraic or adjectival genitive). Perhaps this understanding is reflected in Bultmann's essay, 'Untersuchungen'. In his view, Gal. 2:5 and 14 point to genuineness and reliability, contrasted to the false gospel mentioned in 1:6 (p. 139).

5. So, apparently, Martyn, *Galatians*, p. 198: 'the truth *is* the gospel of Jesus Christ' (see further below).

6. If the apostle had been asked whether he intended the genitive as subjective or possessive or appositional, he might have appropriately answered, 'What difference would it make?' Not that he would not have been able to distinguish between those meanings, but that those distinctions probably were not particularly relevant for his message here.

7. Mussner, *Galaterbrief*, p. 111. Mussner himself does not use terms like 'context-determined' and 'linguistic opposition,' since his exegesis is not really informed by explicit knowledge of linguistics. Like all good exegetes, however, he is instinctively sensitive to how language functions. Linguistic principles, to a large extent, simply formalize what many would consider common-sense interpretation.

8. Ellicott, *Galatians*, p. 27; Eadie, *Galatians*, p. 117; Lightfoot, *Galatians*, p. 107. Lightfoot is referred to with approval by, among others, Betz, *Galatians*, p. 92, and Longenecker, *Galatians*, p. 53.

9. Martyn, *Galatians*, p. 197.

10. Ibid., p. 198.

11. This is not to say that there is no validity whatever in the distinction, but that a responsible handling of the subject requires careful nuancing. That both *'emet'* and *alētheia* are widely used in contrast to falsehood was long ago well documented by Barr, *Semantics*, pp. 187–205.

12. We do not need to resolve the question whether or to what extent verses 15–21 reflect Paul's response to Peter in Antioch. There is certainly no textual marker separating verse 14 from what follows, so evidently Paul expected his readers to link the two sections, even if in fact the latter part was composed by him for the benefit of the Galatians.

13. Lightfoot, *Galatians*, p. 66.

14. See Silva, *Explorations*, pp. 98–100, 136–138. Some of that material (esp. from p. 138) is reproduced here.

15. Lightfoot, *Galatians*, pp. 105–106. Cf. also Silva, *Explorations*, pp. 150–158.

16. Machen, *Origin*, p. 102.

17. Ibid. Machen wrote these words with specific reference to the Antioch conflict, but they are certainly applicable to the incident in Jerusalem. Presumably he would have agreed with Lightfoot's remark, quoted above, that at the Jerusalem conference Paul was basically alone in maintaining the cause of Gentile freedom, but Machen does not directly comment on that question.

18. My free rendering of *diameinē pros hymas* (lit., 'might remain with you') is based on the clear semantic opposition this phrase has with *katadoulōsousin* in verse 4. To enslave people is to rob them of what they already have, their freedom. But since the *hymas* could easily have a general reference ('you

Gentiles' rather than 'you Galatians'), this statement does not prove that at the time of the Jerusalem conference Paul had already evangelized the Galatian churches. Much less, however, does it support the view that he had *not* evangelized them yet. Martyn (*Galatians*, pp. 198–199), not wanting to resort to 'procrustean linguistics,' and dismissing the fact that the semantic force of a preposition is largely tied to the type of verb it is used with, argues that the most common meaning of *pros* with the accusative is 'toward,' and that therefore Paul acted the way he did in Jerusalem 'so that the gospel might eventually make its way to Galatia in the course of his own labors'. In fact, however, 'toward' is the most common meaning of *pros* with verbs of movement, sending, etc., but *not* when used with verbs of being, staying, etc. I would add, furthermore, that while a rendering such as 'might endure for you' is perhaps possible, taking the phrase that way would still not constitute evidence for inferring whether or not the Galatians were already evangelized.

19. In writing these words, the present writer – for whom moderation is well-nigh the *summum bonum* – condemns himself.

20. *Tis hymas enekopsen [tē] alētheia mē peithesthai?* The NIV tries to capture the force of *enkoptō* and to preserve the foot-race imagery of the verse by translating, 'who cut in on you and kept you from obeying the truth?'

21. Cf. also Rom. 2:8. On the topic of uncertainty and predictability in language, see Silva, *Biblical Words*, p. 160.

22. Dunn, *Galatians*, p. 274.

23. This description would be valid whether we regard the letter as apologetic (judicial) or deliberative – indeed, whether or not we wish to assign the letter to a rhetorical model at all. For a recent and vigorous defence that Galatians exemplifies deliberative rhetoric, see Witherington, *Grace*, pp. 25–36. For a dose of healthy scepticism on this debate, see Dunn, *Galatians*, p. 20; *Theology*, p. 12; and now Philip Kern, *Rhetoric and Galatians*, passim.

24. As E. Molland points out, 'The content of the message and its proclamation are not two distinct meanings of the word [*euangelion*], only two sides of one concept.' *Das paulinische Euangelion*, p. 48. Quoted by O'Brien, *Gospel and Mission*, p. 58.

25. Moreover, although Paul himself does not use language like that of John 14:6 ('I am . . . the truth'), he surely would not have hesitated to affirm that divine truth is at bottom *personal* in nature.

26. O'Brien, *Gospel and Mission*, pp. 59–60.

27. I first met Peter O'Brien in Cheadle, Cheshire, England, in September 1970. Peter was in his last year of doctoral studies at the University of Manchester under F. F. Bruce, and I was barely beginning mine. Unobtrusively and unselfishly taking me under his wing, he made that particular rite of passage much more pleasant than it would have been otherwise. He, his lovely wife Mary, and his beautiful children truly ministered to my family during that year. I am delighted to offer this contribution to him as a token of my gratefulness and respect.

6. Theology and mission in 2 Corinthians

Ralph P. Martin

Setting the stage
Introduction

Commentators note the intensity of Paul's writing in 2 Corinthians, which is often regarded as the most personal and self-revealing of all his correspondence.[1] Noteworthy features include the repeated occurrences of the personal pronoun *egō* (especially in the last four chapters), the broken syntax, grammatical solecisms, emotional language, and plerophoric expressions in several of the autobiographical passages (especially 1:11; 8:4; 10:11–16 and 11:12, 22–29). Such a style of writing does not easily lend itself to the formulation of theological propositions which are, by definition, measured and restrained.

This conclusion stands even if we grant the force of recent studies of Paul's literary method. According to this approach, Paul is seen (in spite of the disclaimer in 11:6) as constructing his letter as an epistolary apologetic, using the literary conventions that belong to the world of the spoken rather than the written word. Training in speech formed a major part of Graeco-Roman education, and the question of what made a person educated in this area were much discussed. Sometimes this was with all seriousness, such as by Quintilian (*Inst.* 2.15.38) who defines rhetoric as *scientia bene dicendi*, 'knowing how to speak well'; sometimes in a more comical vein, such as when Aristophanes, in the *Clouds*, pours ridicule on Socrates and has the philosopher suspended in a basket. When greeting the enquirer Strepsiades with 'What do you want?', Strepsiades replies, 'To learn to speak.'

Rhetorical criticism, and other attempts to place Paul in dialogue with a middle-class, rhetorically trained audience at Corinth, have shown that it is feasible that his letter will adopt some of the literary conventions of the day.[3] Young and Ford[4] have argued that 2 Corinthians falls into four parts, based on the format of Aristotle's *Rhetoric* and Quintilian's *Institutio Oratoria*, and illustrated by Demosthenes (*Ep.* 2: 'About his own Restoration', a speech to the Council and Assembly in Athens composed in exile, 324–322 BCE). This proposal has the merit of simplicity and obvious coherence with the text: (1) introduction, intended to gain attention and win support; (2) narrative, a recital of events and facts on which a case is to be built; (3) proofs, including the evidence of witnesses and refutation of charges brought, and entailing some digression; (4) peroration, contrasting in emotional tenor with the sober exordium yet recapitulating the defence and appealing to the audience directly. This analysis is suggestive, except that Aristotle (*Rhet.* 3.2.1) makes the primary requirement of good oratory the feature of lucidity (*saphēneia*) (cf. Dionysius of Halicarnassus, *Lysias* 4), which hardly characterizes 2 Corinthians.

Adopting such a rhetorical approach, canonical 2 Corinthians looks to be a unity, and, if Paul did not write the letter at one time, this is one possible reason why it may have been so arranged. But, even if 2 Corinthians is designated apologetic speech, there are other major roadblocks in the way of any attempt to compose a theology of Paul based on this document.

Theology shaped by contingencies

The hermeneutical principle stated by J. C. Beker and modified by C. C. Rowland gives us a starting-point in our approach to Paul's thought and comes into its own in 2 Corinthians.[5] Although their choice of terminology varies, both interpreters concur that Paul's theological method is best understood as a bringing together of his basic presuppositions and convictions, called 'coherence' or 'system', and the contextual setting in which Paul expressed himself in the face of pastoral, theological and ethical issues raised by his congregations. The latter factor is dubbed 'contingency' or 'situation'. This principle reminds us how Paul's theological perspectives were both governed by his heritage and his experience (with due recognition of his debt to and use of traditional and liturgical formulations) and shaped by the changing patterns of pastoral and didactic responsibilities laid upon him as he took seriously his 'concern for all the congregations' (2 Cor. 11:28). This interplay between Paul's convictional 'centre' and his responsiveness to given needs and situations, notably at Corinth, makes it difficult to get a fix on his theology at any one time. As our discussion proceeds, we shall have occasion to observe what Paul seems to have regarded as the heart of his gospel. But the scene changes with often bewildering, kaleidoscopic rapidity, and it is not an easy task to tie Paul down in any formulaic statement. Such theological conclusion as we may infer has to be viewed in the light of an emotionally charged and passionately interested manner of writing.

Theology in conflict

A consensus has agreed that much of the letter(s) that make up our canonical 2 Corinthians arises directly out of Paul's engagement (often simultaneously) with two sets of audiences/readers and yields a pastiche of writing that is either defensive or polemical. More than one modern commentator entitles chapters 10 – 13 'a conflict letter', and the exultant tones of parts of chapters 1 – 7 ('a letter of reconciliation') are shot through with reminders of debate, expostulation and persuasion. Once again, such a background, in which Paul is fighting for his life and for his gospel – an *apologia pro vita sua et evangelio suo* – is hardly conducive as a setting for sober theological thinking. The use of a wide variety of rhetorical forms, especially metaphor,[6] irony, parody, diatribe, comparison,[7] invective[8] and, above all, paradox, betrays the intensity of a writer in his engagement with the implied readers (the Corinthians) and with the third-party opponents who are never explicitly named and whose veiled identity has been claimed as a ploy used rhetorically to denounce them.

The place of paradox in 2 Corinthians holds something of special importance (as in the quasi-poetic section of 6:8–10). The more obvious examples are quickly listed: weak/strong (12:10; 13:4–5), treasure/poverty (4:7; 6:10); sowing/reaping (9:6–7); slavery/triumph (2:14).[9] These paradoxical juxtapositions carry a (usually) plain sense, and are part of Paul's overall debating strategy based on the assumption that things are not always what they seem to be (see 4:16–18; 5:7, for the theologically significant axiom of sight/faith in paradoxical relationship). The more significant set of paradoxes comes in the use of reconcile/reconciliation, which is often overlooked. The issue is posed by the parenetic call, 'Be reconciled to God' (5:20). Here Paul employs the language of evangelism side by side with factual statements that represent God's reconciling the world as a past event (5:18–19). The problem is to know how to bring these two types of sentence together. Paul is paradoxically setting in close proximity (1) the indicative statement of reconciliation as an accomplished deed, and (2) the imperative appeal to those at Corinth who were still disaffected with and alienated from his gospel and apostleship and to whom he directs the appeal of 6:1, 'Do not receive God's grace in vain.' Thus, in Paul's dialectical thinking, reconciliation can embrace what is true of God and his saving deed (God has achieved the world's reconciliation) and also what should be (the Corinthians need to live within that new relationship by reaffirming their loyalty to Paul the apostle and refusing to hold out against his affectionate yet authoritative appeal, 5:20; 6:11–13).

God has reconciled the world in Christ; but the task of proclaiming the reconciliation goes on and, adds Paul, it must be applied to concrete human situations. So sure is he of the rightness of what he is doing in this move to secure full restoration of relationships at Corinth that he can call upon God as his ally (6:1) and build on the fact that God is 'working together' (*synergountes*) with him as he is with God in this endeavour. There are no hard feelings on his side (6:11); there should be no continuing resistance on theirs (6:12; 7:2–4) as he works toward a complete reconciliation.

The situation, then, that stands in the background of the letter is one of conflict and tension, both relieved (e.g. 2:14; 7:4) and unrelieved (chs. 10–13, esp. 13:5, 11). Two issues must be considered: (1) the nature and focus of the conflict, i.e., what may we discern from Paul's writing about the points of debate? and (2) what does the sequential flow of the argument require us to say about the arrangement of the letter as we now have it in its canonical shape? This latter question, for our purposes, can be more easily disposed of, since the emerging consensus – although broken by Young and Ford[10] – is that chapters 1 – 7 are a unity, with or without 6:14 – 7:1 and chapters 8 – 9, while chapters 10 – 13 represent Paul's later response to fresh troubles subsequent to the sending of (the) earlier letter(s).

Paul's debates with the Corinthians

As we are still setting down our presuppositions, it will suffice to state briefly the chief issues of discussion between Paul and his implied readers. It must also be borne in mind that there is a third member in the triangular network of conversation partners and debaters, namely the so-called opponents whom Paul, from time to time, includes in his horizon of address. The summary list of topics under debate runs as follows.

Apostolate

Who is the true apostle and by what tokens (*sēmeia*, 12:12) is the authentic apostolic ministry validated? And what is its authority (see 10:18; 13:10)? This crucial issue between Paul and the Corinthians may well be carried over from 1 Corinthians (chs. 3, 9).

The nub of the discussion which polarized the apostle Paul and his opponents in 2 Corinthians, however, is somewhat different. The locus of the debate has changed. When we move into 2 Corinthians the few hints in 1 Corinthians (e.g. 15:8–9) that Paul's apostleship was under suspicion have taken on – in his eyes – a more ominous cast. His entire mission to Corinth as an 'apostle of Christ Jesus by the will of God' (2 Cor. 1:1) is being seriously questioned and denied. The matter under consideration turns on the 'principle of legitimation' (*Traditionsprinzip*, in Käsemann's term) by which the claims of the true apostle are certified to the congregation. This argument over 'criteria of legitimacy' is plain in 13:1–6 and, according to Käsemann, is central to the apologetic argument in 2 Corinthians 10 – 13. Georgi[11] put a sharper point on this, while Betz[12] has given it an even clearer definition with his setting of the issue of *dokimē* (testing, proof, or perhaps validation) in the framework of the philosopher–sophist encounter. The opponents' appeal to their charismatic powers and their claim to be the mouthpiece of divine revelation are the central matters underlying Paul's response as he seeks to defend himself and his ministry against the charge that it is ineffectual (10:10; 11:6) and (ironically) lacking in the very gifts on which they prided themselves (12:11–12).

This is the major theme in the lengthy section 2:14 – 7:4, with central discussions in 2:16–17; 3:1–18; 5:13; 6:3–10. The rhetorical questions, 'Who is adequate for this [kind of ministry]?' (2:16) is answered (at least obliquely) in 3:4–6, 'Our adequacy comes from God, who indeed gave us our adequacy to be servants of a new covenant.'

Territoriality

By this term is denoted the controversy outlined in 10:12–16 as to whether Corinth lay within the missionary sphere of Paul and/or the preachers whose appearance on the scene is not indicated until 11:4 and their presence, influence and opposition to Paul may surely be seen in 11:13–15. The heart of his debate is found in Paul's claim registered in 11:10, which counters those who disputed the legitimacy of his apostolic/mission preaching in Corinth and cast doubt on his service in all its forms (10:7), even perhaps insinuating that he had no Christian standing at all.

The most plausible interpretation of the phrase *to metron tou kanonos* (10:13) is that Paul is defending his 'sphere of service' demarcated by the decision of Galatians 2:7–10.[13] He is insisting that he has every right to be in Corinth, which was the *Missionsgebiet* (sphere of mission) of his 'preaching to the Gentiles'. But while Paul is on the defensive and is resisting the charge that he is no genuine apostle, he is content to grant that there is a proper sphere of service which 'another' (10:16) may rightfully occupy, and he will respect that allocation. That 'division of labour', again reflecting the working agreement in Galatians 2, is important for Paul because only as his mission at Corinth is seen to be valid and its competency *hikanotēs*, 3:5; cf. 2:14 – 3:6) respected can he plan to venture out in further missionary work to the Gentiles (10:16).

We may trace here Paul's awareness of the strategic importance of Corinth as a power base from which to launch a westward extension of the Gentile mission as prelude to the end-time. The obverse side of this missionary strategy is the fact that he had become alienated from Antioch and had lost the support of fellow-believers in both the Syrian province and the holy land of Israel. His energy devoted to raising the 'collection for the saints' (chs. 8 – 9) may be understood on this basis, namely as a fervent effort on his part to cement relations between his congregations and the mother church, and a plea for his acceptance by the Jewish wing of early Christianity, as he came to Jerusalem bearing gifts (8:12–15; Rom. 15:25–33).

Christology

Closely linked with 'apostolate' and 'territoriality' is the matter of Christological emphasis. The arrival of some kind of delegation (heralded in 11:4) brought with it a proclamation of 'a rival Jesus, whom we did not proclaim … a different spirit, which you did not welcome [in our message …] a different gospel, which you did not accept [as our gospel]'. This text is set in a quasi-versified form as three *cola*, with a rhythmical, rhetorical, and climactic appeal. The precise nature of this message introduced to Corinth is hard to determine but several items stand out. (1) There was a serious Christological dispute which Paul had to engage and which led to the fierce denunciations of these intruders in 11:13–15. (2) The presence of the intruders represents an actual, not hypothetical, case, since Paul is not likely to have expressed himself so vehemently over imaginary opponents and in 11:19–20 he remarks on the surprising but nonetheless real way in which the Corinthians have given hospitality to these men. (3) The main terms in the list – Jesus, spirit, gospel – are all interconnected; and if this is the case, it is less likely that Paul is opposing a strictly doctrinal Christology (whether

gnosticizing, docetic, Ebionite or nationalistic) and it is more probable that
the allusion to *pneuma* is not to the Holy Spirit as a person (as if their pneumatology were bizarre: e.g. *Gospel of the Hebrews*, frag. 3) and the rival
message is not a Judaizing tendency (since the word *nomos* is conspicuously
absent from 2 Corinthians). Rather, the gravamen of Paul's charge against
the preachers is that their version of the kerygma put forth a lordly figure
(typified in Moses? – ch. 3) as setting a norm for Christian existence and a
justification for their attitude to the congregation (11:20). That was the
'spirit' they displayed, in contradiction of Paul's strength-in-weakness
teaching and practice. Their 'gospel' is self-condemned in Paul's eyes as a
misnomer and more like a *dysangelion* (to coin a term). In sum, it is a Christological distinction (as Georgi noted) separating Paul and the opponents.
But it is not speculative Christology, but applied.

Eschatology

The mention of some dispute over *pneuma* brings to light the discrepancy in
eschatological perspectives that marked off Paul's teaching from the position debated in 4:18 – 5:10. The polemical centre lies in 5:7: 'for we live by
faith, not by sight', with key terms representing two attitudes to life. The
issue is less concerned (in 5:1–10) with the right way of conceiving a future
existence, and more with relating the kerygma to present experience. *Pistis*
('faith') and *eidos* ('sight') mark the distinction between living out of a
trustful obedience to God in life and death and the opponents' evident claim
that their hope rested on what they saw in ecstatic vision, dubbed by Paul
the outward, 'what is seen and not what is in the heart' (5:12). They failed to
grasp the provisional nature of the present, in which the Spirit is (but) a first
instalment, 'a pledge' (5:5). With an eschatological outlook that is content to
await the future consummation denied, they based their pretension to
power (12:12) on what they saw now (contrast 4:18). For them, the present
and the visible offered the form (*eidos*) of reality. Paul contradicts this, since
faith is not yet realized in vision (cf. 1 Cor. 13:12). He thereby relativizes the
value of their ecstatic experiences and unifies the human person (as in 12:2,
3), refusing to separate the 'pure' soul from the 'imperfect' body. For Paul
the human person is one and indivisible, and dualistic separation into body
and soul is no part of his anthropology. His teaching on the Spirit is, as we
shall see, designed expressly to preserve the eschatological proviso that
holds in tension what is true now and what will be true only in the future.
But once again the essentially practical and pastoral dimension of this
distinction is to be seen. The visionary experiences and knowledge of

mystical secrets (12:1–10) support their apostolic claims to a present 'glory', modelled on Moses' role as a larger-than-life figure in 3:7–17 and which, taking their cue from the present possession, they have no compunction in imposing on the congregation. Paul views 'glory' as a kerygmatic quality, i.e. entirely consonant with his message of strength expressed in weakness (4:7) and essentially provisional (3:18) against the day of its full realization (4:17). So his colleagues reflect Christ's glory now (8:23) as a character reference when their lives proclaim not themselves but Christ Jesus in whom God's glory shines out in the servant Lord (8:9, 13:4).[14]

The contribution of history

Our perception of Paul's theological responses in the letter will, at least in part, be influenced by the way we view the setting of that letter. Only a sketch of this topic is possible here, but it is a needful, if tentative, first step, since it is axiomatic that Paul's epistles did not appear *in vacuo* and need to be set in a historical frame, as best as we may judge. This procedure stands at odds with Hickling's negative response to the question in the title of his essay, 'Is the second epistle to the Corinthians a source of early church history?'[15] He is willing to grant the influence of 'personal factors that emerge strongly in the confrontation' between Paul and the Corinthians. But when he denies the force of 'doctrinal' issues separating Paul and his readers, with the opponents forming a third member of the triangle of relations, he cuts himself off from a valuable source of information. He does not allow the setting of the letter to come to the aid of exegesis. We may concede that Hickling's caution in refusing to get caught in an 'exegetical circle' is praiseworthy. Nonetheless, when he concludes that 'we must remain largely in ignorance of the doctrinal position or tendencies of Paul's rivals [... and that Paul's] magnificent theological assertions are enumerated not principally as polemic but as a positive support for his exposition of the meaning of his apostleship', he is correct in his affirmation, but wrong in his unnecessary denials. Paul's personal history and chiefly his self-understanding as apostle cannot be separated from the ongoing theological debate with his detractors. His self-identity and its theological undergirding were sharpened and refined precisely because he was called on to defend it in the face of his opponents' attacks, notably at Corinth.

A starting-point is the encounter at Antioch (Gal. 2:11–14), pitting Paul against the Jewish Christian mission and its influence on Peter. The modern consensus is that Paul lost his case, with the result that he had to come to terms with alienation from Antioch. The consequences of his defeat after this confrontation may be stated in summary form.

1. It sharpened the focus of his gospel to the point where justification apart from the works of the law became a pivotal issue.

2. Paul's stance set him in inevitable opposition to the 'pillar' apostles, whose authority he then proceeded to challenge, partly in pursuance of his loyalty to the 'truth of the gospel' which he felt they had betrayed and partly in response to the insinuation that began to appear from this segment of Jewish Christianity that he was in fact no true apostle; indeed, that he was no apostle at all. This denial sets the agenda for his *apologia* in 2 Corinthians 3 – 7, 10 – 13. They demonstrate what he came to regard as his valid credentials over against the opponents who sought to base their apostolate on the figure of Moses and who appealed to their self-styled 'superapostles' (11:5; 12:11) as authorities to justify their standing as 'servants of Christ' (11:13).

3. Paul's isolation from Jerusalem at this point of his life put him in an ambivalent position. He still professed concern for national Israel, and was willing to reach out in compassion and in practical ways to aid the 'poor saints' in the holy city (chs. 8 – 9). Nevertheless he soon felt the cool winds of suspicion and hostility, blowing not only from the *Urgemeinde* ('original community') in the person of James (Acts 21:18–25) but also from Antioch. For the church centre at Antioch favoured Barnabas (Acts 15:36–41) and moved increasingly in the direction of a rapprochement with Jewish Christianity in its acceptance of the primacy of Peter (according to Matthew's Gospel) with its openness to Christian nomism and particularism (cf. the epistle of James).

Paul's disaffection with regard to Antioch as a base of missionary operations meant that he was temporarily without a spiritual *Heimat* ('home', or 'place of belonging') and thus vulnerable, since he could be regarded by his detractors as an itinerant preacher doing solo work and without benefit of a legitimating 'home' base. The 'letters of recommendation' (3:1–3) carried to Corinth by his rivals have to be seen in this light. 'Thus they always represented some specific Christian community. Paul did not.'[16] Paul therefore had to interiorize his credentials, seeking them in the lives of his Corinthian converts (cf. 1 Cor. 9:1–2).

4. So by this circuitous route, we reach the occasion of 2 Corinthians and its origin in relation to Paul's missionary career. Not the least consequence of the train of events which led to his stand against Jewish Christians, and especially his confrontation with the emissaries he opposes in chapters 10 – 13, was a new expression of his confidence in his own apostleship and a new definition as he reformulated it in a surprisingly novel way. The pressure of

events which intervened between the composing of 1 Corinthians and the writing of the pieces of correspondence forming 2 Corinthians – the so-called 'intermediate visit' and 'tearful letter' – served further to polarize Paul and the Jewish Christian preachers who claimed authority in Corinth and brought him under a cloud of suspicion, with the result that he was virtually ousted from his place as apostle in that community. It became inevitable that he would define his role as a suffering apostle whose authority is seen in his frailty and inherent weakness (4:7–12; 12:9–10; 13:3, 4, 9). He appeals to the inner reality rather than the tangible and evidential (3:1–18; 4:16–18; 5:7, 12; 13:3). This self-evaluation is the natural corollary of Paul's new insights into soteriology with the cross taking on a new dimension as the place of divine humiliation and self-giving expressed in Christ's surrender of all he had or could be (8:9; Phil. 2:6–11).

The genesis of Paul's teaching on Christ's cross as the locus of divine strength-in-weakness and of his own ministry as 'weak in him' (13:4) may go far to explain the phenomenon of his abundant use of *astheneia* ('weakness'). Of a total of 44 occurrences of this word in Paul, 29 are in 2 Corinthians, with 14 occurrences in chapters 10 – 13. The contingent factors of Paul's isolation, the nature of the Corinthian crisis which took on a more menacing character once the emissaries arrived at Corinth (11:4), and his need to redefine the gospel in terms of a clear distinction from Judaism and Jewish Christian ideology (see in 3:1–18) are all there in the setting of the letter.

A 'theology of the cross', as Paul came to understand it at this stage in his missionary life, became the *esse* (essence) of Christian existence (5:14–21; 13:1–4) and the decisive criterion of the issue, 'What does it mean to be Christ's person?' (10:7). Jesus' death is seen not as a mere fact of past history or an episode that was soon to be swallowed up in the glory of the risen one. It was the hallmark of all that characterized Jesus' historical person and saving significance. To proclaim him is to proclaim the cross – a dictum that is carried over from 1 Corinthians (1:18 – 2:5). Now, in the new situation behind 2 Corinthians, the practical application of this cross-kerygma is made to the church's nature and the apostolic ministry. It is seen – for the first time by any Christian leader of whom we have record – that the *esse* (essence) of the church is its role as a suffering people and that the title to service is written in Paul's own self-designation as 'dying with Christ' (4:10–11; 5:14–15; 13:4). 'The past dying with Christ and the present dying with Christ in suffering are not two unrelated things, but the same thing taking place on two different levels.'[17] When the application is made to the apostolic ministry, the effect of the cross-kerygma is to redefine the nature of authority. The latter still carried weight (10:8; 13:10), but it is viewed as power harnessed to the service of love in seeking to build up, not pull down, and enlisted to encourage people to grow in the maturity of faith (1:24).[18]

The character of God as clue to Paul's theology of ministry

A key to viewing Paul's perspectives on the divine action and purpose is seen in the observation – to anticipate our conclusion – that Paul reasons from who/what God is and what he has done to how his people and servants should respond and act. We shall meet the same connection in regard to Christology and soteriology. Here we focus on theology in its strict meaning of 'discourse about God'.

Using the term *doxa* to mean both 'glory' and 'reputation', Young argues that 'the letter is about two closely related things. One of these is the glory of God, the other is the reputation of Paul. Crucial to the whole is the relationship between these two themes.'[19] This intimate link between God's character and the way his servants are to reflect it gives the clue to the heart of Paul's theological thinking in this letter. The linkage is seen in three ways.

Encouragement

Paul's God is, by definition, the God of Hebrew Scripture and the Jewish-Pharisaic belief. He is to be praised as eminently worshipful (11:31). Hence the exordium of the letter opens on the note of exultation (1:3). 'Blessed (be) the God and Father of our Lord Jesus Christ, the Father of mercies and the God of all encouragement.'[20] The appellations bring together the liturgical tradition of the synagogue and its worship with Paul's distinctively Christian name of God made known in Jesus Christ as his image (4:4–6). 'Father of mercies' is patterned on the synagogue prayer, 'O our Father, merciful Father' spoken to introduce the *Shema*, and the liturgy at Qumran. The acknowledgment centres on God who is the source of mercy/compassion, and the giver of divine 'encouragement' (*paraklēsis*. In the opening period this noun and its verb occur ten times in five verses). The appropriateness of paracletic help (whether as comfort or strength) is apparent in view of Paul's recent trials in Asia (1:3–7), but it also serves a rhetorical function, namely to clear the ground of misunderstanding, to lift prejudice from the readers' minds, and to call attention to what is to be developed later. The style, however, is dictated by the eulogistic form drawn from the Old Testament-Jewish liturgical tradition, employing the standard forms of *liturgica*, e.g. participial clauses and fullness of expression. The introductory thanksgiving, moreover, states the epistolary theme and quickly moves into the way God's acts spill over into the authors' and readers' lives and enable them to reproduce the same beneficial effects. The bridge term is *koinōnoi* (v. 7), implying that sharing in apostolic sufferings leads to a share in the *paraklēsis* Paul and his associates have already known.

The divine character acts as an impetus to both author and readers to reciprocate. This becomes clear in 7:6–16, which is a period of *narratio* designed to persuade the readers to come over to the author's side, with the rehearsal of events, the calling of witnesses (in this case, Titus) and the assurance of Paul's personal interest. He had been wronged at Corinth (2:2–5), but that episode is in the past, since he has forgiven the wrongdoer and the church has acted in discipline (2:7–8). It is time to forgive (2:10; 7:12) and to retell the story of God's dealings, which are in character with his action in encouraging and raising up the downcast (7:6). Titus becomes the mouthpiece of the divine consolation, as Paul hears from his colleague the account of how the 'tearful letter' (2:4) has worked effectively and produced a desirable result (7:7–13a). In addition Titus himself has been encouraged and Paul's own confidence in the Corinthians is vindicated (7:13b–16). The point is established that God's work of *paraklēsis* is extended and made visible in the lives of his human co-workers, who not only receive his beneficence but embody it in dealing with others. Paul and Titus are encouraged so that they might encourage each other and the congregation.

Generosity

The same nexus is clear in the matter of giving and receiving (chs. 8 – 9), a topic which is patterned on the Hellenistic model of benefaction and reciprocity (8:14),[21] but equally supported by Hebrew Scripture (8:15; 9:9–10) and current business practices.[22] The divine character is expressed in 9:8,15 as one of unmeasured generosity and self-giving, a biblical axiom reinforced for Paul the Christian by an incarnational buttress (8:9). In the light of such an understanding of the divine, the corollary as it touches on human responsibility to give is natural (9:11). This kind of giving is more than just reciprocal and perfunctory; it shares in God's bounty and extravagance (cf. the example of the Macedonians, 8:1–5) with illustrations drawn from the farmer's labours (9:6,10) and, possibly, the eschatological motif (8:14, if Israel's 'surplus' looks ahead to Paul's hope of a future outlined in Rom. 9 – 11).

The divine standards set the pattern for others to follow. The Corinthians are urged not only to emulate the Macedonian churches but to rise to even greater heights. The glory of God is the master motive in the apostolic service (8:19); and it is seen reflected in his servants such as Titus who bring 'honour' (*doxa*) to him as they are people of integrity, probity and concern to represent a generous congregation, as Paul hopes his readers will be. Christ's heavenly splendour (3:18: 4:4–6) is seen displayed in human vessels like Paul and Titus (4:7) who are his faithful agents (12:16–18), unlike the servants of 11:13–15 who are dominated by self-seeking and avarice (11:20).

Faithfulness

The characterization of God in the letter is rooted in the belief that the God of both testament ages is faithful and trustworthy. He is eminently known as the God of resurrection and new life out of death (1:9–10), seen *par excellence* in raising his Son (4:14). He will raise his people by the same power (4:14). He is to be relied on and his covenant promise is sure (1:18–20). He is the creator (4:6) who brought light out of darkness (Gen. 1:3) and the Lord of the harvest field (8:10) whose promise of seedtime and harvest (Gen. 8:22) stands.

Paul summons God's faithfulness as a witness (1:23) in the defence he makes of his decision to change travel plans. He finds it needful to rehearse the reasons why he altered his plan to visit Corinth (1:15–22). The charge levelled at him was that he was not to be trusted, since he had acted with 'fickleness'. The implication is that he acted either out of expediency or (if Young's reconstruction is preferred)[23] as a person who made plans and changed them purely on a human level, as if the decision rested with him alone as a worldly person (interpreting *kata sarka* in the light of 10:1–6 with A. J. Malherbe).[24] In reply, Paul responds to the allegation of his vacillating attitude that he is a single-minded apostle, intent on following God's plans. As always, his appeal is to the divine character which is the bedrock of his faith and calling. Paul's 'yes' is validated by the divine affirmation in the message he brought to Corinth and certified by the baptismal actions veiled in the verbs of 1:21: guaranteeing, anointing and sealing with the Spirit. The single point is the one he needed to make, namely that behind his ministry and its fruit in the Corinthians' response to the message (alleged to be as unreliable as the messenger who brought it) is the character of God who is utterly reliable. As God is trustworthy, so Paul's work is defended as sharing in the same 'firmness' (based on the Semitic root *'mn*) that he finds in the divine character.

Kerygma and ministry

In an epistle rich in metaphor the example in 4:7 is highly revealing: 'but we have this treasure in clay pots'. The saying comes after a statement (2:14–17) of the claim that Paul's ministry is marked off from its rivals, a theme to which he returns in 4:1–6. The literary device is that of 'ring-composition', that is, his author's exposition reverts to an earlier statement and so completes the circle, as the links in terminology indicate (cf. 2:14–17 and 4:1–6). Paul's ministry is marked by 'confidence' (3:4) which leads to the forthright speaking out of the message of God (3:12). He is different from the teachers who corrupt the message (2:17) and whose activities are exposed in 4:2. On the contrary, his ministry (4:1) looks back to 3:8–9, as a ministry of the Spirit that leads to righteousness and is sanctioned by Christ's commission (2:17b; 3:4). But there is a shadow side to this claim that could be dismissed as effrontery. Two sets of circumstances presented Paul with a challenge so that his bold stance of confidence (akin to Rom. 1:16) might well be shaken and lead to his discouragement. One is the strength of the opposition, traced to satanic sources (4:3–4; cf. 6:14–15; 11:13–15); the other is the recognition of his own feebleness and exposure to danger and death (1:8–11) especially at this time in his life (1 Cor. 15:32). He is led to a recital of his woes in the rhetorical device of listing *peristaseis* (4:8–10) which are brought in to make clear what his self-evaluation in 4:7 really means.

The backgrounds to 4:7 are various. 'Clay pots' are either vessels or lamps known to be cheap, fragile and expendable, or instruments taken up into the divine service (based on Jer. 18:1–11). The metaphor combines the ideas that the apostolic ministry has no inherent and impressive credentials but that, equally, it is the vehicle by which God's action in human life may be displayed, 'to show that the pre-eminent power belongs to God, not us'. Its value derives from the 'treasure' it holds, explained as God's glory made visible in the person of Jesus Christ (4:4–6). Paul proclaims, therefore, not himself but Christ as Lord with the messengers seen as Jesus' servants – and the congregation's slaves (*douloi*). We may contrast 11:20 which uses the verb 'enslave' (*katadouloō*). The 'treasure' – a term which unites both the message and the messenger, since both God's Messiah (3:18; 4:4) and his servants (3:19, 23; 8:23) are his glory – consists in the manifold ways Paul understood the kerygma he proclaimed in concert with his colleagues in his initial evangelism at Corinth (1:19). These ways may be listed.

Incarnation

Its theme centred in Jesus Christ as Son of God (implying his sent-ness as messianic agent and filial redeemer) and incarnate presence (8:9) come to earth. Such condescension revealed his 'meekness and gentleness' (10:1) as well as his 'grace' (13:13), which in turn becomes an incentive to Christian giving (8:7; 9:12–14). The 'signs and wonders and mighty works' (12:12) may be an allusion, capitalized by Paul's charismatic opponents from Palestinian Christianity, to Jesus' ministry with the attendant 'signs of the kingdom' appealed to as a legitimating factor in their credentials. If so, the way they apparently co-opted the role of Jesus as wonder-worker for their own interests may explain why Paul passed over the earthly ministry in any detail, to express instead the total impact of his messianic ministry from the standpoint of the risen 'life of Jesus' (4:10–14; 5:15; 13:4). But that ministerial life is clearly known by Paul to be one of self-effacing humility and service to others.

Crucifixion

The phrase 'crucified in weakness' (13:4) seems to reflect an acquaintance with the lowly submission of the Lord in his death. It is complemented by the traditional statement that 'he died … and was raised' (5:15), and so 'lives by the power of God' (13:4). Paul sees in this event a sign of Christ's love (5:14) which motivates him for service. But at a deeper level it is the story of the passion and triumph that becomes the believer's story as the summons of 'dying to live' is heard and responded to (5:14–15). The cross not only sets the pattern for Christian living but marks out the boundaries of Christian-apostolic service. That ministry carries the hallmarks of Jesus' dying (4:10–12), implying that the vocation to apostleship is a hard road, with the 'catalogue of crises' (6:4–10; 11:21b–33 in the 'Fool's Speech') becoming its most obvious feature. The weakness of Christ is paradigmatic for the weakness of his messengers as Paul turns the *topos* of self-praise on its head and in his 'comparison' section climaxes the *cursus honorum* in a surprising narrative parody, namely, by celebrating his unceremonious exit down from the city wall in a humble fish-basket.

Living the cross

The Pauline kerygma focused not only on the cross and resurrection seen as 'events' to be proclaimed and re-enacted in explication of the apostolic ministry (cf. Schlatter's dictum, 'The apostle not only proclaimed the passion story; he also lived it').[25] This epistle provides a theological rationale, one of the fullest Paul has left on record (5:18–21). The pericope explains how the new aeon entered history (5:17; 6:2) at the behest of God (v.18). Its key word is 'reconciliation', which is accomplished both 'in' and 'through' Christ. If the prepositions are not synonymous, the difference will be that Christ was both the divine agent through whom God acted and his personal presence in earthly form (v. 19). The background is traced to the human condition as sinful and (in consequence) estranged from God. The divine response is outlined (perhaps by borrowing traditional soteriological categories) as 'God appointed him (who was without acquaintance with sin) to be a sin-offering on our behalf, that in him we might become the righteousness of God' (v. 21).

Paul is moved into this disquisition by pastoral and polemical needs at Corinth. He opens with a statement which lies at the centre of this correspondence: things are not what they seem to be (v. 16). Outward appearances (going back to the debate in 5:1–10) are misleading when what we 'see' ousts the function of faith (4:16–18; 5:7). Christian vision is to be adjusted to the new age which has brought with it a new epistemology and a new network of relationships in the Christian community. Unhappily these relationships are strained at Corinth, with Paul having to defend his apostolate, and with some of his 'children' estranged from him. Hence the soteriology of reconciliation exactly meets the case. In rehearsing the message in these terms (by an appeal to common ground in the catechetical materials) Paul draws out both the role he sees for himself as a 'messenger of reconciliation' (v. 20) and a statement of ministry in precisely those terms (v. 18). Then he launches into an impassioned plea to his alienated 'children' (6:11–13) to come back, for all is forgiven (2:7–10; 7:8–16). There is no barrier on his side; nor on God's side, whose representative he is. To receive the grace in vain (6:1) is to remain obdurate and to range oneself with the unbelieving, satanically dominated world (4:4) and to deny the exclusive claims of Christ and his apostle in the new-temple community (6:14 – 7:1). Paul strives to prevent this outcome in his bid for complete reconciliation at Corinth in the 'day of salvation' (6:2). In this role God as reconciler and Paul his agent are linked (6:1).

God at work

The close identity between God's cause and Paul's apostolic person (to be more fully delineated in the last four chapters, in the face of a new threat at

11:4) leads him to one of his most remarkable utterances on the apostolic ministry. The 'message of reconciliation' is what Paul proclaims as God's ambassador (he uses *presbeuō*, whose only other New Testament use is in Eph. 6:20), 'with God making his appeal through us' (5:20). It is not only that Paul voices God's word as his mouthpiece and messenger; the sentence is turned around to claim that God is present in Paul's words. Not that Paul is acting and speaking for God, but that God himself is the chief actor, working and speaking through Paul. The exigencies of the situation drove Paul to this audacious claim, given the seriousness of the opposition at Corinth, the vulnerability of his own standing, and the sense of isolation from human support he felt at this juncture in his apostolic career.

At a later phase in the relationship between Paul and Corinth this self-understanding will assume a yet more pointed significance. When other preachers arrive on the scene with evident 'missionary awareness' as having been sent (by James? or claiming his authority? 10:13–16), Paul debates with renewed vigour his apostolic calling and how he interpreted it. And he will set his message over against a rival version of the kerygma in starker terms (11:4, 13–15).

Apostolic service in contention

The grounds on which Paul's *apologia* took on a new configuration are clear in chapters 10 – 13. The identity of the preachers who came in the (postulated) interval between chapters 1 – 7 and 10 – 13 is still a matter of debate. However, there is no need to decide whether Paul's rivals were the Twelve themselves as 'pillar' apostles, 'Judaizers' with or without an attachment to Peter as one of the 'highest-ranking apostles', or 'Hellenists' with whom Paul finds it expedient to debate on rhetorical grounds and who may have taken their model from itinerant 'holy men' in Graeco-Roman society or fashioned their role in imitation of Old Testament worthies such as Moses or, nearer to the data presented in the New Testament, early Christian leaders like Stephen and a Hellenistic circle around him. This widely canvassed field is discussed elsewhere.[26] What apparently they did have in common was a sense of mission. They claimed to be sent by some external authority, the Jerusalem Twelve. The one item Paul can invoke in self-defence of his ministry is the territorial agreement in Galatians 2:7–9 which he invokes tacitly in 10:12–18. But in a deeper sense he is precluded from any appeal to external authority because he has no sending church and could well be regarded as a maverick 'apostle'. So he invokes the interior evidence of the Spirit at work in his ministry (3:1–18) and the credentials of his care for the congregation (11:28).

The issue turns then on the question of what kind of ministry produces what sort of results. Under that rubric his opponents are painted in the darkest hues: their rhetorical finesse serves only to promote themselves in a high-minded fashion (10:5), whereas Paul does not proclaim himself, only Jesus Christ the Lord (4:5); their charismatic gifts, inferred from his counter-charges in 11:6, 18, and their exalted status as domineering over the congregation (11:20) and imposing financial pressures for their own ends (11:7) are offset by the role he assumed as a plain speaker (10:10; 11:6 – if *idiōtēs* means non-charismatic and/or non-obscure, as proposed)[27] – and a failed healer who could not cure himself (12:1–10). He ran risks and was not protected from peril, as his 'litany of trials' (11:23–28) makes clear; and their Christology chimes in with their lifestyle, for Paul's counter-arguments in 13:1–4 would lack pertinence unless they were directed at a picture of Jesus who was viewed as an all-glorious figure.

The ultimate test of valid ministry lies in the role assigned to the Spirit. Both sets of disputants claimed to be *pneumatikoi*. The issue to be determined was: to what effect, in understanding and behaviour as well as claims to status-seeking, is the power of the Spirit being applied?

The function of the Spirit

This section can be brief since I have already discussed the passages relevant to the Spirit elsewhere.[28] Such exegetical soundings as are possible in an extended treatment yield a consistent result regarding the role of the Spirit in 2 Corinthians. Whether the theme is Paul's claim to valid ministry, or his insertion of the eschatological proviso to oppose a false dichotomy of soul and body, or the activity of the Spirit as actualizing the power of the new age in Christ, or the opposition to an alien gospel, Paul invokes the Holy Spirit with one chief aim in view. He is seeking to establish the presence of the Spirit as the authentic sign of the new aeon, already begun but not yet realized in its fullness; and he is building his case on the readers' participation in the Spirit as the hallmark of their share in both the new world of God's righteousness (5:17 – 6:2) and the Pauline apostolate that represents it (2:17 – 3:18).

Indeed, we may say that these twin and related statements sum up the chief theological and ministerial emphases of the pastoral-polemical letter of 2 Corinthians. The arrival of the new age, at least in proleptic form, rests upon God's gracious activity in securing the world's reconciliation in Christ, with the promise of its completion at the end-time. The present reality of the Spirit of Jesus in human lives is a token of the character of that new age, as exemplified in the incarnate Lord and in Paul and his team, whose way of life and apostolic service mirror the gospel they proclaim in word and action. Persons showing a 'different spirit' (11:4) serve as a foil so that Paul's own claim to authentic team ministry, it is said, reflects God's glory (8:23) made visible pre-eminently in the person of the Lord (4:4–6) who became poor (8:9) to enrich others, just as Paul's work was designed to do (6:3–10).

These summarizing statements of the Pauline ministry and its theological and pneumatological underpinnings may well be seen as imposing a 'tall order' on the church's ministry today. So our final word is one of encouragement, given the sense of inadequacy that Paul the apostle himself knew. 'Who is adequate for these tasks?' (2 Cor. 2:16). To that rhetorical query, the answer comes back: 'Not that we are adequate to claim this for ourselves, but our adequacy comes from God. He has made us adequate as ministers of a new covenant' (3:5–6).[29]

Notes

1. Hengel, *Between Jesus*, p. 69. My footnotes include reference to works appearing subsequent to, or overlooked in, my *2 Corinthians*.
2. See Kennedy, *New Testament Interpretation*; Lyons, *Pauline Autobiography*; Talbert, *Reading Corinthians*.
3. Marshall, *Enmity*, has the fullest discussion of such conventions in relation to 2 Corinthians.
4. Young and Ford, *Meaning*, pp. 36–40. Cf. Lyons, *Pauline Autobiography*, pp. 24–27.
5. Beker, 'Contingency', pp. 141–150; Rowland, *Christian Origins*, pp. 203–207.
6. Young and Ford, *Meaning*, ch. 6.
7. Forbes, 'Comparison', pp. 1–30.
8. Marshall, 'Invective', pp. 359–373.
9. On 2:14 see Hafemann, *Suffering*, pp. 18–39. Barnett, *Second Corinthians*, pp. 147–148, considers other options, himself seeing both a triumphal and an anti-triumphal motif. See too Thrall, *II Corinthians*, pp. 191–196.
10. Young and Ford, *Meaning*, pp. 28–36.
11. Georgi, *Opponents*.
12. Betz, 'Paul's apology'.
13. Martin, 'Setting', pp. 3–19. See Barnett, *Second Corinthians*, pp. 479–494.
14. On *doxa* in 2 Corinthians, see Wright, 'Reflected glory', pp. 139–150. This sense of *eidos* ('sight') would be reinforced if Thrall's interpretation (on 5:7) were acceptable (*II Corinthians*, pp. 387–388), but it is rightly refused by Barnett (*Second Corinthians*, p. 270, n. 20).
15. Hickling, 'Second Epistle'.
16. Theissen, *Social Setting*, p. 50.
17. Tannehill, *Dying*, p. 77.
18. Other reconstructions of the effect of historical development on Paul's thought are possible. Judge, 'Cultural conformity', for example, pinpoints 'two fault-lines

that run through the Corinthian correspondence: 1. Paul's rejection of rhetorical style (cf. 10:10; 11:6; 11:21–29). This caused him distress (12:11), since it repudiated one of the fundamental principles of the Greek status system, 'the belief that fine form is congruent with truth' and a means of legitimating one's social standing. Moreover, it was seized upon by his opponents as another way to denigrate his apostolate, and his public speaking was disdained (10:10) as unprofessional and that of an amateur (*idiōtēs*, 11:6). 2. Paul's refusal to accept monetary support was tantamount to a decline of friendship, and was seen as a hostile disposition and act. Here Paul offended against a system of the Roman patron–client nexus which entailed giving and receiving as a species of reciprocity. In refusing the patronal system, Paul opted in favour of a new construction of social values by which he accepted the protection of well-connected households at Corinth, especially women, yet reinterpreted those values by his teaching on the congregation as a body.

19. Young and Ford, *Meaning*, p. 12.
20. Cf. Peter O'Brien's pioneering study, *Introductory Thanksgivings*.
21. Danker, *Benefactor*, pp. 363–364, 437–438; also Danker, *II Corinthians*, ad loc. Mott, 'Power', pp. 60–72.
22. Betz, *2 Corinthians 8 and 9*.
23. Young, 'Note', pp. 404–415.
24. Malherbe, 'Antithenes', pp. 91–119.
25. Cited in Friedrich, 'Die Gegner', p. 189.
26. Martin, 'Opponents', pp. 279–289.
27. Forbes, 'Early Christian inspired speech', pp. 257–268.
28. Martin, 'Spirit', pp. 113–128. The principal passages are 1:21–22; 5:5; 3:1–18; 13:13, along with some texts where the allusions are either doubtful (6:6; 12:18) or applicable to an alien spirit (11:4).
29. The aim of this piece, in recognition of the distinguished honorand Peter O'Brien, pays respect to the various aspects of biblical study to which he has made a significant contribution: the Pauline literature, both in regard to its literary shape and (more importantly) its theological thrust; as well as his passionate commitment to the gospel, as to both its Pauline shape and its task as God's truth to be proclaimed and lived out which stands at the forefront of his academic and pastoral work. With these lofty themes in mind, I have turned to a part of the Pauline corpus which, it seems to me, embraces just these areas of study; and I offer this essay in recognition of Peter's long-standing service to the theological understanding of Paul's mission, and a tribute to our equally long-enduring friendship since those far-off days when I greeted him as a postgraduate student at the University of Manchester in 1965.

7. From Jesus to Paul – via Luke

David Wenham

One of the questions periodically discussed by New Testament teachers is whether students should be introduced to the New Testament via the Gospels or via the Epistles. In favour of the former it is argued that Jesus started it all, and that it is logical to start with the accounts we have of his life and teaching. In favour of the latter it is argued that the Epistles are a simpler starting-point, with fewer critical problems, and that in any case the Epistles were written before the Gospels.

I doubt if it matters hugely to students which way round they are taught. But the argument that the Epistles were written first and so that they should be studied first is not entirely persuasive. Even if the few scholars who have dated the Gospels very early are wrong,[1] the Gospels still purport to be describing events that took place and teaching that was given in the lifetime of Jesus, that is, before the writing of the Epistles. Admittedly, critical study of the Gospels, notably form criticism, has raised serious questions about the historicity of the Gospel accounts, and has led many scholars to view the Gospels as reflecting the ideas and situation of the church rather than the ideas and situation of Jesus. However, the radical scepticism of such critics is itself highly questionable, and, if a more moderate critical position is taken, the Gospels are perhaps less complicated than scholars have made them out to be, and they do have a claim to priority.

It is the specific argument of this article that Paul's preaching of the gospel included telling people the story of Jesus' life and ministry , and that, however we today choose to teach the New Testament, we should reckon with the fact that Paul in his letters was building on a knowledge of the stories and sayings of Jesus such as we find in the gospels. To establish this argument, the main witness that I wish to call in this article is the author of Luke-Acts.

The 'we' passages and the authorship of Luke-Acts

The author of this important two-volume work, which takes us through the story of Jesus and much of the story of Paul, claims that he was a companion of Paul. This claim is implicit – or should we say explicit? – in the 'we' passages of Acts (16:10ff., etc.). The use of the first person may be otherwise explained, e.g. in terms of the author's use of someone else's diary or as a literary device; but such explanations do not have the plausibility of the more common-sense view, and they would have little appeal, were it not that some scholars find it difficult to believe that the author could have been an eyewitness.

The main problem scholars have had with the traditional view is that they find the portrait of Paul in Acts to be seriously at odds with the portrait of Paul we find in Paul's own letters. There are supposed to be chronological, historical and theological disagreements.[2] We will look at two examples of this.

1. The *Jerusalem Council* described in Acts 15 is frequently identified with the meeting of Paul and Barnabas with the 'pillars' of the Jerusalem church described in Galatians 2:1–10. This identification raises a host of problems for the historicity of Acts. For example, according to Acts, the council of Acts 15 was the third visit of Paul to Jerusalem after his conversion (the second being the famine-relief visit of Acts 11:29–30; 12:25), whereas in Galatians it is made very clear that the meeting with the pillars was the second visit after the conversion. Furthermore, the visit in Galatians seems a private visit, whereas the council in Jerusalem was a formal council ending in a public agreement and the promulgation of some decrees to be sent to the churches. The conclusion of many scholars is that Acts is a very muddled account, with different visits and meetings getting confused.

2. The speech of Paul to the *Areopagus Council* in Athens in Acts 17 is widely seen as representing a philosophical approach and a creational theology that is at odds with the gospel of the cross Paul preached (cf. 1 Cor. 2:1). Many conclude that the author of Acts, following a common practice among ancient historians, has put on the lips of Paul an appropriate speech of his own devising: the speech reflects the author's tendency to portray his

hero Paul out to have been a reasonable and eloquent man, rather than Paul's own more radical gospel. On the basis of such evidence, and much more,[3] the Paul of Acts is found to be a romantic figure created by the author of Acts, not to be the historical Paul as described by a well-informed companion.

I cannot discuss this view of Acts in any detail here. But I would argue that there is another way of looking at the two examples quoted and also at the whole question of Paul in Acts.

1. With regard to *the Jerusalem Council* there are indeed difficulties for the historicity of Acts if Acts 15 is identified with Galatians 2. But, if the famine-relief visit of Acts 11:27–30 is identified with the visit of Galatians 2, then the picture changes completely, and Acts turns out to make good sense historically.

Admittedly, Acts 11 describes Paul and Barnabas delivering material aid to the 'elders' in Jerusalem, not discussing with Peter, James and John questions to do with the Gentile mission and Paul's apostleship. However, it is quite impossible to read the Acts account of the famine-relief visit and to imagine that the visit did not include substantive discussion of the things referred to in Galatians 2.

Acts describes Paul and Barnabas bringing famine relief to Jerusalem from Antioch, at a time when (1) the Gentile church of Antioch has grown enormously, (2) Paul, the former Pharisaic persecutor of the church, who had hardly been seen in Jerusalem since his conversion, was taking an increasingly leading part in Antioch church, and (3) the Christians in Jerusalem were under pressure of persecution.[4] It may well be that these three things were all related to each other: the Christians in Jerusalem may have been under attack from the Jews (via Herod, who wished to ingratiate himself with the Jews) precisely because of the Christian goings-on in Antioch. Antioch was a very important place, with a large Jewish community, just up the main road from Jerusalem; and it is likely that the Jews of Jerusalem will have been upset by news (1) of the splits produced within the Jewish community in Antioch by the new Christian movement; (2) of the way Christian Jews (like Barnabas) were defiling themselves by association with Christian Gentiles; and (3) of the increasing involvement in the new movement of the ex-Pharisee and Jewish turncoat, Paul. To the fervent Jews of Jerusalem these things will have been infuriating; and to the Jewish Christians in Jerusalem, who were on the receiving end of the Jews' fury, the situation will have been perplexing and uncomfortable, to say the least.[5]

Given this sort of situation in Antioch and Jerusalem – which is what Acts suggests to us – it is absolutely inevitable that Paul and Barnabas will have discussed with the leaders of the church in Jerusalem the question of the Gentile mission and in particular the question of Paul's position. In other words it is inevitable that they will have had the sort of discussions described in Galatians 2, which led to the 'pillars' in Jerusalem recognizing Paul and extending the right hand of fellowship to Paul and Barnabas in their mission to the Gentiles. It seems in fact quite likely that the famine-relief visit was in part motivated on Paul's and Barnabas's side by a desire to discuss matters and to build bridges between Antioch and Jerusalem – because of the tensions and because of the pressures that the Jerusalem Christians were experiencing, not least in a time of famine.[6]

Identifying the famine-relief visit with Galatians 2 eliminates most of the problems that arise from identifying Acts 15 and Galatians 2: thus (1) the second post-conversion visit in Acts is the second post-conversion visit in Galatians; (2) the discussions described in Galatians 2 at the time of the famine-relief visit were private discussions with the apostolic leaders in Jerusalem, and did not lead to any public decrees; and (3) the following sequence of events, including Acts 15, makes good sense.

What followed the discussions of Galatians 2, where the Gentile mission of Paul and Barnabas was recognized by the Jerusalem apostles, was that Paul and Barnabas now extended their Gentile mission out from Antioch to other parts of the Gentile world (13:1–3), starting with their own home areas of Cyprus, where Barnabas came from, and what we would call Turkey, where Paul came from. This Gentile mission was highly successful in places like Galatia, but caused fresh unhappiness in Jewish circles and in Jerusalem, since the Jewish communities of the Mediterranean world were being disturbed and divided by the new Christian movement. The Gentiles were not being required to be circumcised, and Jews were having table fellowship with them. The upshot was further interventions from Jerusalem, with the Gentile converts to Christianity being pressed by Christians from Jerusalem to accept circumcision and with Jewish Christians in places like Antioch being pressed not to eat unclean food. To Paul's horror, even Peter (who according to Acts had been sent by divine command to the house of the 'unclean' Cornelius) and Barnabas abandoned their previous policy of eating with Gentiles: clearly the arguments used must have had considerable force, and it seems likely that the issue was more to do with Jewish Christians making themselves unclean – their abandonment of Judaism, as it would have been seen, may have been causing particular offence among the Jews of Jerusalem[7] – than over whether Gentiles needed to become Jews, though the two questions were arguably interrelated.[8] Peter, perhaps out of a genuine concern for the Jerusalem Christians who were under so much pressure, along with Barnabas, fell out with Paul over the issue, leading to the 'Antioch incident' of Galatians 2. All three of them, together with James, were then involved in the Jerusalem Council of Acts 15, which addressed the painful issues and ended up with an affirmation of Gentile freedom from the law and circumcision, along with a requirement that there be some concessions from the Gentiles, particularly in matters of food, to enable Jewish Christians both to maintain their Jewish customs and to have table fellowship with their Gentile brothers and sisters.

This historical reconstruction of events is not a naïve harmonization of biblical texts, but is the most historically plausible account of the divergent accounts. And it not only leaves Acts historically intact, but shows that, far from being muddled, Luke has very good information about this early period of Paul's life.

2. As for Paul's speech to *the Areopagus court* in Acts 17, it is naïve to read 1 Corinthians 1 – 2 assuming that, when Paul speaks of preaching nothing but Christ and him crucified, he means that he never preached about anything except the crucifixion! Paul's rhetorical purpose in 1 Corinthians 1 – 2 is to affirm the centrality of the cross in Christian theology, not to suggest that a subject index of his sermons would have had only one entry. It is similarly naïve to take it that, when Paul abjures worldly rhetoric or philosophy, he did not preach persuasively, or to conclude that he could not have started to address a body like the Areopagus with references to their religion, philosophy or poetry. Paul has sharp things to say about idolatry when writing to Christians in Romans 1, but it does not follow that he would have felt obliged to start his evangelistic preaching to Gentiles by an explicit condemnation of their false religion as devilish and hellish. Luke suggests that Paul approached Jews evangelistically through the Old Testament and Gentiles through references to creation. There is nothing implausible about this.

But it is not just that Acts is plausible enough in this respect; after all, any author might be expected to paint a plausible picture. There is, in fact, significant evidence that Paul did preach in places like Athens in the way Acts describes. The most striking evidence is in 1 Thessalonians 1:9–10, where Paul describes how the Thessalonians 'turned to God from idols to serve the living and true God, and to wait for his Son from heaven, whom he raised from the dead – Jesus, who rescues us from the coming wrath'. The summary that Paul gives here of the conversion of the Thessalonians is strikingly like the contents of the Areopagus speech – starting with the question of idols, going on to refer to the living creator God, concluding with a reference to coming judgment, and to Jesus' resurrection. It is possible to make light of the similarity and to say that this is typical Jewish-Christian preaching to Greeks (though even to say that leaves us with the conclusion that Paul used such a typical approach, and that therefore Acts 17 makes good sense historically). However, what makes the similarity most striking is the historical context of 1 Thessalonians *vis-à-vis* the Acts narrative. In Acts, Paul's second missionary journey takes him from Philippi to Thessalonica, then via Berea on to Athens (where the Areopagus speech takes place), and then on to Corinth. 1 Thessalonians, as is widely agreed, was written during that missionary journey, just after Paul has left Athens and come to Corinth. So Acts has Paul preach in this way, very shortly after the conversion of the Thessalonians described in 1 Thessalonians 1:9–10 and just before he actually wrote those very verses in 1 Thessalonians. Given this evidence, the conclusion must be that it is unnecessary, if not obtuse, to ascribe to the author of Acts the Areopagus speech, which he ascribes to Paul.[9] It is preferable to conclude that the author of Acts had good sources of information.

That conclusion is supported by other well-known evidence for the topographical and historical accuracy of Acts, noted by William Ramsay and others: the author gets the routes of the Roman roads right, and the names of the local officials.[10] All of this evidence suggests a well-informed author, which is, of course, what the 'we' passages suggest: namely that the author was a companion of Paul, and therefore had very good sources of information about Paul's life and ministry. He had his own perspectives on Paul, indeed, and he was a fan of Paul's; but his declared interest in his subject does not mean that he sits light to history. Indeed, it leads him to tell the historical story.

How Luke describes Paul's preaching – as in continuity with Jesus

Having shown that there is a good case for taking Luke's portrayal of Paul seriously, we may now return to the question of Paul's gospel and Jesus, and call Luke as witness to the view being propounded in this article: namely, that Paul's preaching of the gospel included passing on traditions of Jesus' life and ministry, such as we find in the Gospels.[11] Acts makes it abundantly clear that the apostolic preaching was about Jesus. At first sight it may seem as though this preaching of Jesus focused narrowly on his death and especially his resurrection. However, it is important to recognize that what we have in the sermons in Acts, as also in Paul's references to his 'gospel' in his Epistles, are only summary accounts, often the briefest of summaries. And there are very clear hints that the preaching of Jesus was more wide-ranging than might at first appear, including the sorts of traditions of Jesus that we find in the Gospels.

The evidence for this is fourfold. First, in Acts there are several references to Paul preaching 'the kingdom of God'. Notable is the last verse of Acts, where Paul is described as 'preaching the kingdom of God and teaching the things concerning the Lord Jesus Christ' (28:31). Acts 20:25 is also significant, where Paul reminds the Ephesian elders how he went about among them 'preaching the kingdom' (20:25; cf. 19:8, 28:23).[12] What is clear from this is that for Luke there is continuity between Jesus' message and Paul's preaching. Jesus proclaimed the kingdom; in his ministry he sent out his disciples to do the same; after his resurrection he also talked about the kingdom (1:3), and after his ascension the preaching of the kingdom is taken forward by the church (8:12).[13] Luke does not explain the idea of the kingdom in Acts, but he does not need to do so, because his readers know the Gospel stories of Jesus, where the message of the kingdom is set forth. The implication is that Paul is like one of the Twelve or of the Seventy, who took Jesus' kingdom-message out to people and proclaimed it to them (Luke 9 – 10), even though, of course, Paul ministers from a post-Easter perspective and preaches the kingdom *and* the things concerning the crucified and risen Jesus.[14]

The second piece of evidence hinting that Paul's preaching and that of the other early Christians included passing on the stories and sayings of Jesus is in some of the sermons of Acts, where the summary of the gospel includes references to the life, death and resurrection of Jesus. Most striking is Peter's speech to Cornelius and his family, where Peter speaks of 'the good news (gospel) of peace through Jesus Christ; he is lord of all. You know what happened through all Judea, starting from Galilee after the baptism which John proclaimed: Jesus of Nazareth, how God anointed him with Holy Spirit and power, who went around doing good and healing all who were under the power of the devil, for God was with him. And we are witnesses . . .' (10:36–38). Peter goes on to discuss the death and resurrection of Jesus. Of course, Peter is not Paul, and indeed had big advantages when it came to knowledge of Jesus' ministry! But Acts portrays Paul also as telling the story of Jesus in a similar way – from John's baptism onwards (13:23–31).[15]

We may infer that extensive teaching about Jesus was an integral part of preaching the gospel, thirdly, from the opening of the book of Acts, where Matthias is chosen to succeed Judas, and where the qualification of the new apostle is that he should have been 'with us' from the baptism of John until the ascension (1:21, 22). The new appointee is, like the other apostles, to be a witness to the resurrection, but it is evidently not enough solely to have witnessed the resurrection. Although this appointee is to be primarily a witness to the risen Jesus, he will also be witness to the life of Jesus from the baptism of John onwards (cf. 10:36–38).

The importance of the apostles' teaching is quite clear in Luke's narrative as it proceeds. The earliest church is described before anything else as 'devoting themselves to the apostles' teaching' (2:42), and this teaching is later seen as having top priority, even over the important ministry of food distribution (6:2). The phrase used in that context is 'ministry of the word', the word being 'the word of God', a key Lukan phrase used of Jesus' ministry and of the church's ministry. At the heart of the apostles' ministry of the word is evidently telling the story of Jesus.[16]

We may, fourthly, infer the importance of telling the story of Jesus in the preaching of the gospel, as Luke perceived it, from his own first volume. Although he is not an apostle himself and does not make that claim, it is clear from the prologue to the Gospel that he has been careful to consult with eyewitnesses and 'ministers of the word' (a different Greek word from that used in Acts 6, but semantically similar)[17] and that his Gospel is offered to us as the testimony of such people.

We may conclude that Luke intends us to see his Gospel as representing the sort of picture of Jesus that was preached by the apostles, and by Paul and his companions.[18] Paul did not preach theological abstractions or credal formulae, but the story of Jesus.[19]

Is this Luke's perspective rather than Paul's own?

The evidence we have noticed indicates that Luke would have us think of Paul's missionary preaching as focused on the history of Jesus. Of course, it could be Luke's own interests that have led him to portray Paul thus, and his portrayal could be misleading. However, against that various points are relevant.

First, we have seen that in the case of the visits to Jerusalem and of Paul's speech in Athens Luke was very well informed, and that he has not been as 'creative' historically as scholars have sometimes supposed. We should therefore not readily assume that he gives a misleading impression of what Paul preached.

Second, if he was a companion of Paul, then that in itself is evidence of someone in Paul's ministry team who was very interested in the historical Jesus. It is theoretically possible that Luke had this interest and Paul did not, but it is more likely that Luke was influenced by his hero in this as in other ways.[20] It is theoretically possible that Luke developed this interest in the history of Jesus after the period when he was associated with Paul and that it was not a feature of Paul's own ministry. But to argue this is gratuitous speculation, which goes against the evidence that Luke himself presents to us,[21] and it seems much more likely that Luke's Gospel is precisely a clue to the sort of teaching about Jesus that was an important part of the missionary preaching of Paul and his party.

Third, this is confirmed by the evidence of Paul himself. Although it is not easy to deduce from his letters what his 'gospel' preaching covered, two of the key summaries of his gospel are 1 Corinthians 15:1–4 and Romans 1:1–4.

In 1 Corinthians 15:1–14 Paul is explicitly referring to 'the gospel which I preached (gospelled) to you', and this 'gospel'[22] is that 'Christ died for our sins according to the Scriptures and that he was buried and that he was raised on the third day according to the Scriptures …' What is important to note about this is: (1) that the gospel is all to do with the story of Jesus, and, (2) that what we have in this text is only the briefest summary of Paul's gospel. Sometimes the impression given by scholars is that this was the whole of the gospel Paul preached – in which case his sermons must have been marvellously brief (or highly repetitive, if he said exactly the same thing over and over again!). But in fact it is clearly a summary, and furthermore a selective summary, focusing on the issue at hand in 1 Corinthians 15, namely the question of the resurrection of the dead. Just as we should not take his words about preaching only the cross in 1 Corinthians 1 literalistically, as though he never preached the resurrection, so with 1 Corinthians 15, we should not suppose that his gospel described only the death, burial and resurrection of Jesus.[23]

That point is confirmed by Romans 1:1–4, where Paul refers to the 'gospel of God', and then goes on to say what the gospel is about, namely

his Son,
who was born of the seed of David according to the flesh,
designated Son of God in power according to the Spirit of holiness by
    resurrection of the dead,
Jesus Christ our Lord …

In this different summary of the good news we start with the birth (literally 'becoming') of God's Son and then move on to the resurrection. The Lord's death is not mentioned this time, which is not a proof of the non-Pauline origins of Romans 1:1–4 (though some scholars have argued for that view), but is simply because we have again the briefest of summaries, and in Romans 1:1–4 Paul summarizes the gospel not in order to deal with the question of the resurrection of the dead, but in terms of Jesus' life from the beginning (his birth) to the end (his resurrection). What is common to Romans 1:1–4 and to 1 Corinthians 15 is that 'the gospel' centres on the story of Jesus.[24]

Admittedly, these two passages give us a tantalizingly tiny glimpse into how Paul might have preached the story of Jesus. But that tiny glimpse is sufficient to lend credence to what Luke suggests, namely that Paul's 'evangelism' included telling the story of Jesus in something like the way the story is told in Luke's Gospel, and indeed in the other Gospels.

Scholars tend to make a sharp distinction between the word 'gospel' as used to describe the content of the preaching of people like Paul and the word as used to describe the literary productions of Mark, Matthew, Luke and John. But it may be misleading to make such a sharp distinction: it may be that what we have in Mark and the others is much more like the 'gospel' Paul preached than is often realized. It is intriguing, if nothing more, that Romans 1:1–4, having introduced the theme of the gospel of God, goes on (1) to refer to the fact that it was 'promised beforehand through the prophets in the holy Scriptures', then (2) to the story of Jesus from birth to resurrection, and then (3) to Paul's commission to go to the Gentiles. This corresponds interestingly to the shape of both Matthew's Gospel and Luke's, which in the early chapters especially put the story of Jesus into an Old Testament prophetic context, then describe the story of Jesus from his birth to his resurrection, and finally have the risen Jesus commissioning the disciples to go to the Gentiles. This structural similarity between Paul's 'gospel' as he refers to it and the canonical Gospels proves little by itself, but, given the other evidence we have been examining, it may be more than coincidence.

In addition to the evidence of the two Pauline summaries of his 'gospel', there is a wider body of evidence which suggests that Paul was familiar with much of the story of Jesus as it is attested in the Gospels, including in Luke's Gospel, as the following four examples show.

First, Galatians 4:4: Paul's reference to God sending his Son 'born of a woman, born under the law' reminds us of the Lukan infancy narratives with their stress on Jesus as the divine Son, born of Mary, and brought according to the law to Jerusalem.

Secondly, 1 Corinthians 7:32–35: the language used here is strangely reminiscent of the Lukan story of Mary and Martha in Luke 10:38–42, where the distracted and anxious Martha is contrasted with the devoted Mary: scholars have plausibly speculated that some of the Corinthian women were quoting this story to justify their abandonment of the domestic life in favour of a spiritual life and their slogan that 'it is good for a man not to touch a woman'. They may also have been influenced by the sayings of Jesus about the future resurrection life in Luke 20:27–38, where the Lukan wording, more than that of Matthew and Mark, could well have given rise to the view among the Corinthian charismatics that they had arrived in the resurrection as children of God, who would not die in future (cf. 1 Cor. 15) and for whom marriage was inappropriate.

Thirdly, there are Paul's eschatological teaching and Last Supper traditions: there are interesting echoes of Luke 21:22–24, with its references to wrath coming on Jerusalem and to the times of the Gentiles, in 1 Thessalonians 2:16 and Romans 11:25, and of Luke 21:34–36 in 1 Thessalonians 5:4–7, where we also find an echo of Jesus' parable of the thief. The eager expectation of the Pauline churches of the Lord's return (e.g. 1 Cor. 16:22, also much of 1 Thess.) most likely derives from the Gospel traditions about the master going away, not to mention the Last Supper story which in Luke has a particularly strong sense of looking forward to the coming kingdom (Luke 22:16, 18, 29; cf. Paul's 'until he comes' in 1 Cor. 11:26). In the narrative of institution the Pauline wording of the saying about the cup is famously similar to the longer text of Luke 22:20.

Lastly, we can refer to Paul's resurrection traditions. Paul and Luke agree on the first appearance of the risen Jesus being to Peter, this being followed by an appearance to the Twelve (Luke 24:34–36; 1 Cor. 15:5).[25]

The case for Paul's gospel having a lot in common with Luke's Gospel is a good one.[26] If Paul did know and teach the story of Jesus in his evangelism, then we need to read his letters with this firmly in mind. Scholars, even conservative scholars, typically do not to read Paul in this way – whether because of over-simple assumptions about the relative dating of the documents,[27] or because of the critics' assaults on the veracity of the Gospels, or because of a nervousness about being accused of parallelomania. I believe we should think a lot more in these terms, if only because it is a hypothesis that deserves further thought and testing, but also because, if the hypothesis is true, then it must be important for our reading of Paul.

Reading Paul in the light of Jesus: an example

We conclude this article with one example. Suppose we assume that Paul did know and teach all or most of the eschatological teaching of Jesus that we find in Luke (and the other Gospels), then this will have an immediate impact on our interpretation of a passage like 2 Thessalonians 2 (assuming this to be Pauline). We are bound to read it in the light of the synoptic eschatological discourse, and to connect the Pauline 'man of lawlessness' with the synoptic 'desolating sacrilege' (both having a background in the events of 167 BC and Antiochus Epiphanes); Luke makes clear that his understanding of the desolation has to do with the destruction of Jerusalem at the hand of Gentiles – it is 'wrath' coming on the Jews of Jerusalem.

If Paul was familiar with this prophecy of Jesus, then it throws light on various other passages in Paul. Notable is 1 Thessalonians 2:16, where Paul perplexes commentators greatly by saying that 'the wrath has come upon them [the Jews] finally'. Scholars have found the idea incomprehensible and the language un-Pauline, with some therefore suggesting that it is a gloss. However, there is a good case for saying that, if the language is un-Pauline, this is because Paul is here drawing on traditions of Jesus, such as Luke 21:23, which speaks precisely of wrath coming on the Jews.[28] Furthermore, the idea makes very good sense in the historical context of AD 49 when Paul was writing 1 Thessalonians, because disaster had struck Jerusalem and the Jews at that very time. The disaster was twofold: first, Claudius had expelled the Jews from Rome, which the historian Suetonius tells us was because they were 'rioting at the instigation of Chrestus' (*Cl.* 25.4). The probability is that there had been major trouble within the Jewish community of Rome, because of the arrival of the fast-growing Christian heresy, as the Jews no doubt saw it; the traditional Jews wanted to stop this Gentile-embracing and defiling heresy spreading, and acted violently against the Christians. Paul will certainly have known about this, since Acts 18:1–3 describes Paul staying in Corinth with Aquila and Priscilla following the expulsion, and this is exactly the context for Paul's writing of 1 Thessalonians – he wrote from Corinth in AD 49. Paul in 1 Thessalonians 2:16 speaks of the 'wrath' coming on the Jews because of their attempts to stop the evangelization of Gentiles, and it makes entirely good sense that he sees in what has happened in Rome part of the divine wrath of which Jesus had spoken.

Not that there were just the events in Rome. In the same year there was a catastrophe for the Jews in Palestine, as Josephus tells us: a Roman soldier in Jerusalem acted indecently in the temple area, in such a way as to infuriate the Jews, who protested *en masse*. When the Roman governor responded to their protest with violent force, there was mayhem, and Josephus tells us that twenty or thirty thousand people were killed as a result.[29] Even allowing for some exaggeration, it was a terrible disaster. And it seems quite likely that Paul saw the double disaster striking the Jews in Rome and in Jerusalem as the beginning of the end for the Jews, or, rather, as the beginning of what Jesus had predicted – namely the desolation of the city of Jerusalem at the hands of Gentiles.

There is a further respect in which Paul's knowledge of Jesus' eschatological teaching may illuminate Paul. It has plausibly been suggested by various scholars that one of Paul's main purposes in writing Romans was to get the Jewish and Gentile Christians to work together and to 'welcome one another' (15:7). There may well have been difficulties between the two groups, provoked in part by the expulsion of Jews in AD 49: the Jewish-Christian leaders of the church, such as Aquila and Priscilla, will probably have been expelled too, leaving the Gentiles in charge of the church for some years; but then on the death of Claudius in AD 54 Aquila and Priscilla and other Jewish Christians will have come back to Rome, and it is not hard to imagine the tensions between the old guard and the new guard, with some of the Gentile Christians looking on the Jewish Christians dismissively – after all, were the Jews not under the 'wrath' of God?! Paul writes to encourage unity between the divisive communities. N. T. Wright has taken the argument a stage further, and suggests that Paul was particularly anxious about the unity of the Roman church, because he knew from the teaching of Jesus that Jerusalem was going to be destroyed and he supposed (not without reason) that Rome would then become the centre of the Christian church. It was particularly important to him that, when this happened, the Jewish Christians should not be marginalized or thrown out of the church, so he wrote Romans.[30] At first sight Wright's theory sounds utterly speculative, but if the thesis of this article is correct and if Paul did know very well the teaching of Jesus about coming wrath on the Jews, then Wright's hypothesis has a lot going for it after all.

Reading Paul in the light of the Jesus of the Gospels has all sorts of other possible spin-offs, which we will raise here only as questions. Has Paul's Christology been influenced and even formed in part by his knowledge of the massively significant stories of Jesus' virgin birth, baptism and transfiguration? Has his teaching on justification, the atonement and the Jews been influenced by the parable of the prodigal son (with its picture of the person who was far off and 'dead' being brought back) and by the parable of the Pharisee and the tax-collector in the temple (with the language of justification and propitiation)?[31] Has his teaching on Jesus as the servant who is humble but then highly exalted been influenced by Luke's Last Supper narrative, with the dialogue there about Jesus as the one who serves, and by Luke's emphasis on Jesus' subsequent exaltation and ascension?[32]

We cannot attempt to answer these questions here, or to go into other examples. The evidence is not always straightforward: after all, if Luke was Paul's companion, the relationship might sometimes be in the direction from Paul to Luke's Jesus, rather than from Jesus to Paul. However, there is good reason for believing that the direction is often, if not usually, from Jesus to Paul. And there is good reason for teaching our students that Jesus and Paul have much in common, but that Jesus has priority![33]

Notes

1. E.g. J. W. Wenham, *Redating*.
2. So Barrett, *Acts* (1998), pp. xxviii–xxix.
3. Acts is thought to make Paul out to be much more conformist in regard to the Jewish law than he actually was. For further discussion of this matter and bibliography see my 'Acts and the Pauline corpus'.
4. The description of Herod attacking the church in Acts 12 comes in the middle of the description of the famine-relief visit in Acts 11:27–30; 12:25.
5. Barnabas was their appointed delegate; but they may have had questions about Paul, who was very much an outsider, as well as about the policies being pursued in the Antioch church.
6. Compare the later visit as described in Rom. 15:23–32.
7. Cf. Acts 21:21, 24.
8. Both Paul and the Judaizers took this view.
9. There was no universal convention that ancient historians should invent speeches for the participants in their narratives, and the author of Luke-Acts clearly does not do this in his first volume, since he is regularly drawing there on sources (at least on Mark).
10. A classic modern statement of this sort of view is that by Colin Hemer (a colleague of Peter O'Brien's at Manchester University): *Book of Acts*. See also Brian Rapske's writings, including *Roman Custody*.
11. We may now dare to call the author of Acts Luke!
12. Paul's letters have few references to the kingdom of God, even if those that exist are significant.
13. Acts 1:1 with its reference to what Jesus 'began to do' during his ministry is significant.
14. On the continuity between Paul's preaching in Acts and Jesus' teaching in Luke, see Walton's recent thesis, 'Paul in Acts', which argues that a comparison of the Miletus speech of Acts 20 with 1 Thessalonians shows the speech to be authentically Pauline, and that the speech very much reflects teaching of Jesus as found in Luke's Gospel. Interestingly, the Miletus speech ends with a reference to 'the word the Lord Jesus himself said, "It is more blessed to give than to receive ..."' (20:35). The fact that this particular saying is not found in Luke's Gospel does not change the fact that the Pauline speech ends on that note of remembering Jesus' teaching.
15. W. Barclay, 'Comparison', pp. 168–170, argues forcefully that Acts implies that missionary preaching included teaching about Jesus' life and ministry.
16. See Squires, 'Plan', p. 21.
17. Compare the remarks of Nolland, *Luke 1 – 9:20*, pp. 7–8.
18. Of course, Luke's Gospel reflects Luke's own perspective and it may have been written with particular church contexts in mind (not primarily evangelistically). It is, however, still telling of the good news of Jesus rather than being, in the

first instance, a response to particular pastoral issues. Compare Bauckham's observations in his article 'For whom'.

19. The description of Paul in Acts 28:31 as 'proclaiming the kingdom of God and teaching the things concerning the Lord Jèsus' could almost be seen as describing Luke's own purpose in writing his Gospel!

20. That is not to say that Luke may not have been the person in Paul's group who had a special interest in this direction. A tradition strongly supported in the early church, equated Luke with the 'brother' 'whose praise is in the gospel' (2 Cor. 8:18). This is not impossible; see my father's *Redating*, pp. 230–237. Compare Barclay's comments about Mark in 'Comparison', pp. 169–170.

21. It seems quite likely that Luke will have done all sorts of interesting 'research' in the period of Paul's imprisonment at Caesarea (Acts 27:1), but there is no good reason to think that it was boredom that first inclined Luke to develop an interest in the history of Jesus!

22. I wish we could stop translating *euangelion* with the Old English 'gospel', which now has largely religious connotations; 'good news' conveys much more of the semantic flavour of the Greek word and of the OT Hebrew equivalent.

23. The same point is relevant to his listing of witnesses to the resurrection in 15:5–9, which is not a complete list, but a highly selective one focusing on the apostles and leaders of the church, with the 500 brothers thrown in for good measure.

24. In both the story is set within the context of OT Scripture.

25. Paul has no equivalent of the story of the walk to Emmaus, but this would have been of subsidiary importance compared to the appearances to Peter and the Twelve.

26. Not that Paul's connections are only with Luke. Paul seems familiar with Matthean and other traditions; see my fuller discussion in *Paul*.

27. But, of course, even those who date the Gospels late often date their sources (e.g. 'Q') as early as Paul – the traditions were around!

28. Also the 'Q' tradition of Matt. 23:29–36 // Luke 11:47–51.

29. Josephus, *BJ* 11.223–231; *AJ* 20.105–117.

30. Wright, 'Jerusalem', pp. 64–70.

31. Luke is sometimes accused of having no doctrine of the atonement, but arguably his narrative of the cross (including Jesus' words, 'Father forgive them', and his dialogue with the repentant robber; 23:34, 39–43) has a very powerful theology of the cross implicit in it.

32. Luke's Last Supper has something in common with John's. If Paul knew the story of the footwashing as found in John 13, then this would surely be important background to Philippians 2. It is tempting to connect other Johannine passages with Paul: thus the vine of John 15 could be important background for Paul's 'in Christ' concept; the teaching of John 6:51 about the believer who eats the bread of life living for ever could help to explain some of the early Christians' apparent expectation that they would never die. See further my 'Enigma'.

33. I owe Peter O'Brien a particular debt of gratitude, since he was responsible for my going to teach at Union Biblical Seminary in India; whether the students there noticed a great difference in having me as a Gospels specialist following Peter as an epistles specialist I don't know!

© David Wenham 2000

8. Luke's portrait of the Pauline mission

I. Howard Marshall

Whatever else it is, the book of Acts is a book about mission.[1] Its theme in broad terms is the way in which the small group of disciples of Jesus received the power of the Holy Spirit to be his witnesses and evangelized successively in Jerusalem, in Judea and Samaria and to the ends of the earth (Acts 1:8). People came to believe in the Lord Jesus, received salvation and formed new groups of believers which included both Jews and Gentiles. The story of the mission is at the same time the story of how these two groups were able to form one people of God without the Gentiles having to submit to circumcision and in effect become Jews in order to become Christians. Although the book is rightly understood as 'the Acts of [some of] the Apostles', it is no exaggeration to say that Paul has the major part in this story. It follows that Luke pictures Paul as a missionary.

Story and pattern

Recent criticism of the New Testament tends to examine the various writings from a literary point of view and to attempt to explain the shape and content of any given book on a literary level, i.e. in terms of what the implied author appears to be doing for his implied readers. The danger of this approach is to explain everything on this level, without bearing in mind that the authors of narratives are (or should be) constrained by what happened (or their understanding of what happened) and therefore are by no means free agents, able to mould their materials at will. Acts is a historical narrative and must be evaluated as such. It is true that tensions have been found with the evidence of the Pauline epistles as regards the 'facts' of Paul's career, but a by-product of this essay will be the claim that these tensions do not affect the broad picture.[2]

Luke had the difficult task of covering a complex period of Christian history and, like any writer, he has had to impose some sort of system or pattern on the story. He has constructed a storyline which leads from Jerusalem to Rome, and he has ignored other material, such as the local expansion of Christian groups in Judea and Samaria in detail and the progress of the Christian mission in Egypt and North Africa. He knows that the gospel reached Rome long before Paul arrived there (Acts 28:15), but he has made Paul's arrival and evangelism in Rome the climax of his book, which runs the risk of making Paul's arrival appear to be the 'real' arrival of the gospel in that city. But without making any suggestion that the existing church in Rome differed theologically from Paul, he may be implying that the advent of the Pauline gospel at Rome was a significant matter. The evidence of Romans suggests both that at the time of the letter the church was not unanimous in its understanding of the gospel and its implications (cf. the groups in Rom. 14 – 15) and that Paul was in fact concerned that the Roman Christians should have a clear understanding of his gospel.

The pattern of Acts is not simple, but it is clear that the story falls broadly into two parts, centred respectively on Peter (but including the activity of Stephen and Philip) and on Paul (along with Barnabas and then Silas). These two parts overlap, with Saul/Paul being introduced in Acts 9, and Peter continuing to be an actor until Acts 15. There is good reason to see some deliberate parallelism between the accounts of Peter and Paul, but this remains fairly general and no effort is made to force precise parallels between them. The crucial factor for our purpose is that both of them are presented primarily as missionaries. Both itinerate, the principal activity of both is talking about Jesus to audiences of Jews and Gentiles; both have the power to work miracles of healing (like Jesus) and also to inflict God's judgment on opponents of the work of the Spirit; and both suffer imprisonment on account of their witness. These parallels arise out of the historical facts, but Luke's narrative highlights them, with the effect of putting Peter and Paul alongside one another as the two principal evangelists. This agrees with Paul's own perception of the situation when he thinks of himself as being commissioned as the apostle to the Gentiles and Peter as the apostle to the Jews (Gal. 2:6–10). It may also be noted in passing that the picture of Paul so far is fully in agreement with that gained from the epistles, where he is a traveller for the gospel, preaches a message, does 'the signs of an apostle' (2 Cor 12:12), executes judgment (1 Cor. 5:1–5), and is imprisoned.

The divine and human aspects

Luke's thrice-recorded account of Paul's calling indicates its twofold nature. His calling to be a missionary comes directly from God through a revelation of Jesus Christ to him (cf. Gal. 1:15–17). The initial picture of Paul is accordingly of an individual agent, responsible to God/Christ.[3]

Yet Paul is invited by Barnabas to share in the task of teaching in the church at Antioch (Acts 11:25, 26), and the calling to undertake the first 'mission' recorded in Acts is addressed not to Barnabas and Paul themselves as free individuals, but rather to the church at Antioch, which is commanded to send them out on God's work (Acts 13:1–3). In practice, a missionary could not work without some relationship to other Christians, and we know that different, existing congregations gave practical support to missionaries. Although Paul himself could insist that he received his gospel not from human beings but from Jesus Christ (Gal. 1:12), he can nevertheless refer in 1 Corinthians 15:1–5 to the main points in his message as something which he had 'received' as a piece of Christian tradition. The Lord communicates with his missionaries both directly and through the agency of the congregations. There need be no tension between Paul's insistence that he in effect received the gospel directly from Christ and his acceptance of what he was taught by other Christians; it is the priority of the divine calling to preach to the Gentiles which is crucial for him.

There is perhaps a parallel to this combination of the divine and the human in the way in which the mission progresses. On the one hand, the mission is conducted under divine guidance. God gives directions and encouragement to the missionaries by various agents and agencies (Christ, an angel, the Holy Spirit, and other human beings); he uses a variety of means (heavenly visions, dreams, and prophecies). Paul stands out by reason of the number of ways and times in which this happens. Direct divine instructions and guidance are mediated through such events as the conversion vision; the activity of Ananias; the summons by Barnabas; the guidance at the Antioch prayer meeting; another vision in the temple; the dream of the man of Macedonia; the prophecies by Agabus and others; the vision in Corinth: and the vision on the ship. They are conveyed by a variety of divine agents: the Lord (Acts 18:9–10; 22:17–21; 23:11); the Spirit (13:2, 4; 16:6–7; 20:22); an angel (27:23).[4]

On the other hand, over against these frequent direct indications of God's will we also have the many cases where the missionaries respond to circumstances and, as we say, use their intelligence. Thus the actual itinerary of the first tour is not ascribed to divine guidance. The instigation of the second tour lies with a desire by Paul to follow up the groups established on the first tour. Although there is a case (see below) that Luke sometimes relates an initial incident in such a way that it can be assumed that subsequent, similar incidents follow the same pattern without the need to describe this in detail (e.g. the synagogue sermon in Acts 13 is typical for later preaching in synagogues), there is no reason to believe that, where direct divine guidance is not mentioned, it must be assumed to have taken place. It appears to happen rather in exceptional circumstances such as new ventures or in face of strong temptations to discouragement. Luke mentions it in order to emphasize that the mission takes place with divine encouragement and guidance, but the stress on Paul's obedience to heavenly visions does not imply that these are an exclusive form of guidance, and the story itself shows the missionaries using their own minds to decide what to do in specific circumstances.

The pattern of campaigns

Luke presents the story of Paul the missionary in the form of successive tours. There are three of these, punctuated by periods back on home ground (which stretches from Jerusalem to Antioch), and in the second and third there is a pattern of going over some of the same territory but also engaging in further evangelism. There is a temptation to oversimplify the narrative by speaking of a pattern of ever-increasing circles, but this is to be resisted. The first tour embraces Cyprus and Galatia. The second takes in Galatia (a follow-up visit) but then moves further west across Asia into Macedonia and Achaia with a brief, anticipatory visit to Ephesus. The third tour takes Paul again through Galatia to Ephesus, which becomes the main focus of this trip, but then comes a follow-up trip to Macedonia and Achaia. (The description of the third tour does not in fact include any fresh territory that was not already visited on the second tour, although some of the routes followed are different, and Ephesus had in effect been visited previously only 'in passing'.)

From this summary of the narrative it is easy to see why Bible maps regularly depict Paul's three 'missionary journeys'. Nevertheless, an important point should be noted that has the effect of seriously altering the traditional schematic presentation. Although Luke's narrative does indicate that there are three identifiable trips in which Paul moves from place to place, the 'journey' motif needs considerable qualification. It is frequently misinterpreted to indicate that Paul did a kind of whistle-stop tour, stopping in each place only long enough to establish a small group of believers and then dashing on to the next place. The chronological information provided by Luke should have been sufficient to nip this misapprehension in the bud, in that lengthy periods are spent in Corinth (over eighteen months) and Ephesus (over two years), and in other cases hasty departures were due to circumstances outside the missionaries' control. After the first journey, which may have had something of an exploratory character, Paul and his companions normally made extended stays.

As Luke has presented the matter, we already see indications that some kind of plan was being worked out. In this context a further point becomes significant. The evangelism was conducted for the most part in major centres of population, and was certainly not carried out in the manner of Jesus, who itinerated around villages in a very limited area of country. There were a number of major cities in the Roman Empire: Rome, Alexandria, Antioch, Ephesus and Corinth, together with other, smaller towns which were the major centres of population in their regions. Is it sheer coincidence that Paul visited four of these five major cities?[5] He also stopped in other major towns that were on the main Roman lines of communication in Asia and Macedonia – Philippi and Thessalonica, Athens, Pisidian Antioch.

This would suggest that Paul saw the strategic importance of establishing churches in the major provincial centres. Luke comments that during Paul's time in Ephesus 'everybody' in Asia heard the word of God (Acts 19:10; cf. 19:20). This comment could presumably be applied to the other cities which he visited. If so, we have a strategy for reaching as wide an area as possible in a short time. These points raise the question whether there was a deliberate strategy on the part of Paul or whether Luke has detected (or imposed) a pattern.

Was something like this, then, Paul's vision, or was it imposed on the material by Luke? At this point the evidence of Romans 15:14–33 is crucial. Here Paul comments that he has fully preached the gospel round from Jerusalem to Illyricum and is now setting his sights on Spain (via Rome). He has no more work to do in this area. This indicates that Paul was looking back on the completion of a specific task. The task may of course have been begun without at first realizing its full extent and character, but at some point there dawned on Paul what he had done or was in course of doing. But what was it?[6]

There is a case (based to some extent on a specific interpretation of 2 Thess. 2:6–8) that Paul saw himself as entrusted with at least part of the major task of proclaiming the gospel to all nations as the necessary condition for the parousia of the Lord Jesus. His aim therefore was to hasten that coming by getting round the world as quickly as possible. It was sufficient for this purpose that he preached the gospel 'representatively' in each area of the world rather than that he literally reached every person. By the second/third century we find Christian writers stating that the twelve apostles had in fact reached every nation with the gospel, although how they reconciled this belief with the facts is not clear (Hermas, *Sim.* 9.17; *Apol. Aristides* 2; Justin, *Apol.* 1.31).[7]

However, it has to be said that there is nothing of this consciousness in Romans 15. On the contrary, Paul's mood in the *Hauptbriefe* is one of desire to bring the gospel to both Jews and Gentiles as widely as possible, and to go to places not reached by other Christian missionaries. Evangelism for its own sake, or rather for the sake of the peoples to whom he is conscious of being a debtor (Rom. 1:14–15), appears rather to be the task. Therefore, it is preferable to take Romans 15 in the sense of a strategic endeavour to found churches as centres of continuing Christian work (cf. Eusebius, *HE* 3.37.2–3). Moreover, it is clear that Paul recognized the activity of other missionaries: the mission to the Jews by James, Peter and John (Gal. 2:9) and the missions of other, unknown workers in other areas (2 Cor. 10:16).

If so, the reflections of Paul and the picture in Acts cohere remarkably well. We can accordingly conclude that the strategy which can be deduced from Acts and which Luke had evidently detected was in fact Paul's own strategy and that it has been correctly assessed by Luke.

Evangelism and follow-up

From our summary of the three missionary campaigns, we have already noted the clear pattern of initial missionary activity followed by further contacts to strengthen and encourage the infant groups of believers. This pattern is not peculiar to Paul, but is something to be expected. The initial visit to Samaria by Philip is followed up immediately by Peter and John; they go purely on a basis of goodwill, and it is only when they arrive that they learn of problems that need to be tackled. The trip by Peter and John includes further evangelism in Samaria. The Ethiopian eunuch is an exception to all the rules, in that he suddenly appears in the narrative and then disappears without trace. Peter travels to visit existing 'saints' in Lydda and Joppa. Nothing is said about a return visit to Caesarea after the conversion of Cornelius. The Jerusalem church sends Barnabas to follow up the work in Antioch.

The first missionary campaign by Barnabas and Paul includes return visits to the towns evangelized on the outward journey (and later by Barnabas to Cyprus), and then the first parts of the second campaign and the third campaign take Paul over some of the same ground. (The first campaign probably retraced its steps because of the opposition that the believers in Lystra, Iconium and Antioch were facing.). The towns visited in the second campaign, Philippi, Berea, Thessalonica and Corinth, are implicitly revisited at the end of the third campaign (Acts 19:21; 20:2–3), and then the final part of that campaign sees a follow-up of the work in the west of Asia. It emerges that in virtually every case Paul revisits the congregations which he founds, sometimes more than once. Acts says nothing about the letters which he sent to them,[8] but it does record that he sent his colleagues to visit some of them (Acts 19:22). The picture of a warm, loving relationship emerges.

Once again this picture agrees with that in the letters where there is a continuing relationship between the missionaries and the new congregations, characterized by love and concern for their spiritual growth and their stability despite attacks of whatever kind.

Paul and his companions

The Pauline mission in Acts is carried out by missionaries working in groups. This contrasts with the activity of Peter and Philip, who each travelled on their own, although we do read also of Peter and John's joint activities, especially their follow-up visit to Samaria. The first missionary campaign is carried out by Barnabas and Paul with John (Mark) as their initial helper; but it is Paul who quickly becomes the main actor (Acts 14:9, 13, 16) and the order of naming the principals changes at Acts 14:23. When Paul suggested a return visit to Barnabas, the latter was unhappy with the decision by Paul not to take John Mark with them, and so they separated. Each of them then went off with a partner, Barnabas with John, and Paul with Silas. Silas was a Jerusalem Christian who would help to demonstrate the unanimity between Jerusalem and Antioch in the matter of the 'apostolic decree'.[9] It was not long before a junior member was added to the Pauline group, Timothy. The fact that Paul was able to leave Silas and Timothy in Berea while he alone went on to Athens does not significantly alter the picture. In fact, he was accompanied by Macedonian believers that far. His fellow-missionaries returned to join him by the time he reached Corinth (although 1 Thessalonians may suggest a more complicated set of comings and goings).

At this point Silas disappears from the story, although Timothy remains in it (Acts 19:22; 20:3); there is no need to read anything sinister into this. One suggestion is that Silas replaced Mark rather than Barnabas, i.e. as junior helper rather than equal partner.[10] But this is unlikely in view of the description of Silas as a leading member of the Jerusalem church.

In any case, from this point onwards the narrative refers to Paul by himself without a colleague of equal standing; he is accompanied on occasion by Priscilla and Aquila, and by Acts 19:22 he has a number of helpers; on his return to Jerusalem he has something of an entourage (Acts 20:4), including Luke, who apparently joins the party at Philippi. The significant factor for our study is that the third missionary campaign is apparently the work of Paul with helpers rather than with a colleague. And this is confirmed by the omission of any co-authors in Romans and 2 Corinthians. This omission stands out in view of the contrast with other letters from this period. Both 1 and 2 Thessalonians are co-authored, as is 1 Corinthians (but with a Corinthian Christian, Timothy being away at the time). Galatians is anomalous in that it has neither co-author nor greetings from fellow-believers; the omissions may be due to the intensely personal nature of the letter and perhaps quite simply to the fact that Paul was genuinely on his own when he wrote it.

The problem of Paul's companions may have significance for his relationships with the churches in Antioch and Jerusalem. The change in companionship from Barnabas to Silas may suggest that on the second campaign Paul felt that he was the emissary of both the Antioch and the Jerusalem churches.[11] So far as the former is concerned, the missionaries were again commended to the Lord by Antioch.[12] However, it is not clear whether the church in Jerusalem had anything to do with the initiation of Paul's second campaign, although the implied outcome of the Jerusalem 'council' is that the church in Jerusalem gave its blessing to the ongoing work of enabling the Gentiles to turn to God (cf. Acts 15:19). In any case, at the end of the campaign Paul goes up and visits 'the church' (Acts 18:22); this must be the church in Jerusalem, since Acts 18:18 implies a visit to Jerusalem to terminate his vow. Nevertheless, he spends 'some time' in Antioch, which seems to imply a longer period there than in Jerusalem.

Towards the end of the third campaign, Paul sets his face to visit Jerusalem (Acts 19:21), and his hurry means that there was no question of visiting Antioch on the way.[13] There is thus some sort of relationship with Jerusalem, but the language of commendation and 'spending some time' is not used of Jerusalem. Does it look as though Paul sought recognition and backing from Jerusalem, but did not get it, despite the very warm reception in Acts 15:4? The indications appear to be that Paul worked increasingly on his own initiative and not as the agent of a church, although he strove to maintain good relationships with the churches in Antioch and Jerusalem and to have their backing and support for his work.

We encounter here, as often in Acts, the tantalizing nature of Luke's narrative, which leaves itself open to different interpretations and does not answer some of the questions that we would like to raise.[14]

It must be noted that there does not appear to be any reflection of these problems of the relationship with the churches in Paul's letters. Only in Galatians 2 do we get the leaders in Jerusalem giving their cordial backing to the work of Paul and Barnabas among the Gentiles. This must have been at a time before Paul and Barnabas separated. For the rest, Paul presents himself as an agent responsible only to God (1 Cor. 4:1–5). Nevertheless, there is some kind of relationship with the church in Jerusalem signified by his 'collection for the poor'. This point is not mentioned in Acts, except casually in Acts 24:17, and there is certainly an unresolved tension here, although it may be that the gift was ill-received (cf. Paul's apprehensions in Rom. 15:31) and that Luke has therefore drawn as little attention as possible to it.

Outreach to Jews and Gentiles

The missionary task is witness to all people (Acts 22:15) but Paul is to be sent 'far away' to the Gentiles (Acts 22:21; similarly 26:17), although his mission is also to take place 'before the people of Israel' (Acts 9:15). The task is fulfilled by preaching in Damascus, Jerusalem and Judea and then to the Gentiles also (26:20).

A pattern emerges in Acts according to which, when he comes to a new town, Paul initially visits the Jewish synagogue or makes contact with a Jewish group. This is true of Salamis and of Pisidian Antioch; the story of Paul's visit here (Acts 13:13–52) is told at length so as to serve as an implicit pattern for subsequent towns. Consequently, when Paul follows the same pattern in Iconium, it can be qualified by the phrase 'as usual' (Acts 14:1). The pattern is expressly repeated at Philippi, at Thessalonica (where we have the comment 'as his custom was', Acts 17:2); Berea; Athens; Corinth and Ephesus. The only places where the pattern is not said to be followed are Lystra (where the evangelism affects the non-Jewish population) Derbe and Perga. It is not clear whether the pattern established at Salamis was followed on the journey through Cyprus to Paphos.

The evidence shows that Luke laid particular stress on this feature. Different conclusions have been drawn from the narrative. W. Schmithals could conclude: 'It is almost impossible to imagine Paul beginning his preaching in the synagogues.'[15] Schmithals bases his view on a strict interpretation of the division of missions in Galatians 2, according to which Paul relinquished any mission to the Jews; he may have longed for their salvation (Rom. 9 – 11), but his share in bringing it about was his mission to the Gentiles, designed to make the Jews jealous. His churches were Gentile in composition. But Luke gives a different picture because, for whatever reason, he is presenting Christianity as the true Judaism. Paul did make contact with God-fearers, and his first churches consisted largely of them.

Schmithals' case has the merit of giving a neat solution to the problems raised by Galatians 2. Nevertheless, it cannot be right. There are limits to what a narrator can get away with if there are people around who remember what happened, and so striking a misrepresentation would not be credible. The view that there were no, or next to no, Jewish Christians in Paul's churches is also incorrect; it cannot explain the conflicts that went on within the congregations and not simply between the congregations and outside visitors. If Paul wished to reach the God-fearers, the place to begin was the synagogue.

A very different proposal is offered by J. Jervell: that Paul's missionary work according to Luke was directed to proselytes and God-fearers and scarcely touched Gentiles who were not in contact with Judaism.[16] Where Schmithals is concerned with what actually happened, Jervell is attempting to interpret correctly what Luke is saying, regardless of whether it is historically accurate. But Jervell's interpretation is also questionable, in that it does not do justice to the scenes in Lystra and Athens, which are not to be seen as isolated exceptions to a general rule.

Robert Tannehill also considers the material from the point of view of what it tells us about Luke's understanding. He notes that Paul's procedure follows the lines laid down in Luke 9:5 and 10:11, where the instructions apply to each individual city that is visited. Paul's preaching begins in the synagogue (or, in Rome, with Jewish visitors) to whom the promises of the Messiah are made. Even at the end of Acts Paul is still endeavouring to reach Jews with the gospel. Thus Acts reflects the tension between (1) the need to continue to proclaim the promises to the Jewish people and (2) the rejection of the promises which takes place time and again.[17]

Paul's own letters emphasize that salvation was 'first for Jews and also for the Gentiles' (Rom. 1:16). This is not the same thing as saying that in any given town the mission should begin with the Jews (if there are any), but is probably meant to indicate the historical order in which Jesus came as a Jew and only later was proclaimed as a saviour to the Gentiles also. So is Luke's presentation simply a symbolical expression of this truth, or perhaps even a misunderstanding of it? This also is highly unlikely. For Schmithals, Paul does not preach to Jews at all, but simply longs that they will be saved through envy of the Gentiles; but 1 Corinthians 9:20 clearly excludes this interpretation, and the composition of his churches indicates that Jews had been reached with the gospel. As has often been observed, the synagogue would have been a good strategic place for beginning a mission; however, Luke's narrative implies that it was a matter of principle with Paul to give the Jews in the synagogue the first opportunity to respond to the gospel and only then to go the Gentiles.[18]

Support for missionaries

How did Paul and his companions maintain themselves during their missionary work? In 1 Corinthians 9 Paul is emphatic that missionaries have a right to the provision of food and drink and a right to be accompanied by their wives. The implications are that these rights are due to them from the congregations (that is, from existing congregations on whose behalf they work, but apparently including those which have arisen through their church-planting), and it is founded on an appeal to the words of Jesus and of Scripture. In Galatians 6 he establishes that those who are taught should share material things with their teachers. The right to food and drink may be taken to include the provision of lodging also. There will also have been incidental costs: travel by ship entailed the payment of a fare (Jonah 1:3) and other forms of transport required the same. Some missionaries apparently did live in this way. Paul claims that he and Barnabas worked for their living (so also in 1 Thess. 2) and made it a point of honour to do so, even if this led to misunderstanding at Corinth. We know that Paul did receive financial support from other churches (Phil. 4:14–18), and maybe this contributed to the misunderstanding. (The implication must be that they saved up part of the money to provide for their needs when travelling in new areas.) Self-support was possible only when they were settled in an area long enough to find work, but in the less formal setting of the pre-industrial ancient world it may have been easier to find work than in the present world with its massive unemployment. How easy was it for, say, a tailor to sit down in the street and do instant repairs or make simple clothes for passers-by, such as still happens in some areas of the world today? Would it not have been equally simple for a worker in leather, making shoes or clothing?

The picture in Acts corresponds with this one. It is to be assumed that the church in Antioch gave its material backing to the missionaries whom it sent out (Acts 13:3). In Philippi the convert Lydia provided hospitality. They stayed with Jason in Thessalonica. In Corinth he stayed with Priscilla and Aquila, who appear to have been already believers; here he certainly worked at a trade for part of the time (did part of the proceeds go to his hosts to cover his lengthy stay?), although when Silas and Timothy arrived he devoted himself entirely to missionary work. In Ephesus Priscilla and Aquila welcomed Apollos into their home for teaching, but surely also for hospitality. It is not Luke's purpose to tell us about the daily regimen of missionaries, but the hints he gives are quite sufficient to enable us to generalize from them and see the mixture of hospitality provided by believers and the missionaries' own manual work to earn money.

The missionary and the prisoner

The publication of Brian Rapske's lengthy study of Paul as a prisoner in Acts should have put paid once and for all to the illusion that the second part of Acts is devoted simply to Paul as a travelling missionary.[19] While Paul is a free agent in Acts 9 – 20, nearly all of the last eight chapters of Acts are concerned with Paul under arrest, in prison, appearing before different courts, and finally journeying to Rome in hope of an appeal to Caesar. If he travels, it is now under duress.[20]

The imprisonment of Paul does not alter his role as a missionary, however, but merely the way in which it is carried out. The story is utilized by Luke to allow Paul to provide an apologia for himself, in which the basis for his mission is expounded more than once. It illustrates how Paul was able to use his captivity as a means of witness to the gospel, both in court settings but also in the course of his daily life under various forms of captivity and imprisonment. Agrippa rightly recognized what Paul was trying to do (Acts 26:28), and Paul's activity in Rome, both to the Jews and to all who came to his house, was evangelistic.

It is not surprising, then, that the picture of Paul as a missionary in Acts is the picture of a suffering missionary, and he is a prime example of his own comment that 'we must go through many hardships to enter the kingdom of God' (Acts 14:22). This is especially true of those who are in the forefront of witness for the gospel, although attacks against them would inevitably endanger the converts as well, and Luke records several incidents directed against the latter (Acts 8:1–3; 9:1–2, 21; 11:19; 14:2; 17:1–9, 13). Certainly persecution is not continuous and does not in fact affect everybody, but it can occur at any time, and the story of Paul illustrates this possibility at considerable length, so that he (like Stephen, James and Peter) is presented as a paradigm of what may happen and how to respond positively to it as an opportunity for witness (Luke 21:12-13).

The missionary and the apostle

The three accounts of Paul's initial encounter with Jesus vary in detail and emphasis, so much so that scholars have some grounds for arguing whether it constituted a conversion experience or a missionary calling (like the calling of the prophets). This wooden antithesis is, to be sure, a false one, since the event clearly contains both elements and is conversion and calling in one. The calling element is particularly obvious in Acts 22:10, 14-15; 26:15-18, but is not absent from Acts 9:6, 15-16. In Galatians 1 the persecuting zeal of Paul and his enthusiasm for Judaism are placed in striking contrast with his calling to preach about Jesus; a conversion is clearly part of the calling (cf. Phil. 3:4-10), but here too the calling to missionary work is emphatic (Gal. 1:15-16). Paul is converted for a purpose. There is thus something special about his conversion, since the conversion of other people is not explicitly accompanied by a calling to a new way of life, but they apparently carry on with their normal activities. There is, then, a special calling of certain people to specific tasks.

But to what is Paul called? It is well known that Luke does not use the term 'apostle' for Paul, except in Acts 14:4, 14, where it is applied to both Paul and Barnabas in a rather casual manner. For Luke it is the reconstituted Twelve who are the apostles. It is not obvious how this fact is to be explained and evaluated.

J. Dupont[21] has drawn an interesting comparison between Christ's commission to the Twelve (Luke 24:44-49; Acts 1:8) and Paul's account of his own mission (Acts 26:16-23), establishing a fourfold pattern (which is repeated three times over in Paul's statement): there is a heavenly vision or divine empowering; the call is to be witnesses to Jesus and to declare the message; the message is to go to all nations; the message is based on Scripture and is intended to bring people to conversion. The task of reaching all nations is in fact carried out by Paul rather than by the Twelve, who remain in Jerusalem and then disappear from view.

Dupont's analysis is convincing in showing that Luke sees Paul as engaged in the same work in the same kind of way as the Twelve and reinforces what was said above about the parallelism in activity between Peter and Paul in particular. Even if Paul is not called an apostle, nevertheless he does the same work as the apostles and in fact it is he who completes the part of their calling relating to going to the ends of the earth and preaching repentance and forgiveness of sin to all the nations. (Philip also does the same kind of work, although he is not an apostle and does not have an initiatory vision.)

It is also the case that although the term 'apostle' is not used of Paul, the verb 'to send' is used (Acts 22:21; 26:16–17). In other words, Luke knows that Paul fulfils all the requirements of an apostle, yet he uses the noun for him only twice in this casual way. There is evidence that Luke can under-emphasize things that he does not want to bring too much into the light. His restriction of the term 'apostle' to the Twelve and his general denial of it to Paul falls into this category. The puzzle is why he has acted in this way, especially since he must have known that Paul's self-understanding was bound up with his apostleship.

Barrett argues that in Acts 14 Luke was using a source in which Paul and Barnabas were originally named as apostles of the church (at Antioch), but that he himself expressly restricted the term to those who had been with Jesus during his earthly life (Acts 1:21–22).[22] But *why* did Luke so restrict the term, especially if he was writing at a point when Paul's letters were in existence? If we treat what he writes as history, then the problem goes back to Peter's definition of membership of the apostles, by which Luke felt bound. One possible explanation, then, is that Luke was writing for a church which accepted this definition, and that he wrote in such a way to show that Paul was entitled to the title, but without taking the step of using it, except in this marginal way. He made his case not by claiming the title for Paul, but by demonstrating that in every respect except having been a companion of the earthly Jesus he more than fulfilled the job specification. This would fit in with the hypothesis that one of the purposes of Acts (certainly not its only or main purpose) was to offer some kind of commendation for Paul over against criticisms of his mission to the Gentiles.

In any case, what emerges with complete clarity is that the twelve apostles were in Luke's eyes first and foremost evangelists bearing witness to the risen Lord. But there were others who shared in this task, and there can be little doubt that the story of Paul as a missionary is told in order to give the church a pattern to follow in its continuing life. Luke teaches in Acts by the example of what missionaries did as well as by the exhortation which they gave.[23]

Notes

1. Penney, *Missionary Emphasis*; Marshall and Peterson, *Witness*.
2. Cf. Wenham, 'Acts', pp. 215–258.

3. Most recently: Dunn, 'Paul's conversion', pp. 77–93.
4. Acts provides no clear rationale as to why a particular agent is responsible for any given example.
5. Presumably Alexandria was evangelized by other missionaries, and/or Alexandrian Jews brought the gospel back home from Jerusalem, just as Roman Jews fairly certainly did.
6. In 'Who were the evangelists?' I have explored whether Paul saw his task as simply preaching the gospel representatively in the main areas of the Eastern Mediterranean world, or as planting congregations which would in turn evangelize the areas surrounding them.
7. See Skarsaune, 'Mission'.
8. Aejmelaeus, *Die Rezeption*, has challenged the view that Luke did not know the Pauline epistles.
9. Cf. Kaye, 'Acts' portrait', pp. 16–18.
10. Nixon, 'Silas', p. 1101.
11. Pesch, *Die Apostelgeschichte*, p. 94.
12. This is the natural reading of Acts 15:40, which leaves readers to assume that Silas had returned to Antioch after his departure in Acts 15:33.
13. It is unusual that in Acts 20:3 Paul's destination is given as 'Syria'. Does this imply that his ultimate destination was Antioch? However, according to Pesch, *Apostelgeschichte*, p. 185, from Corinth Jerusalem would be regarded as being in Syria.
14. See especially Taylor, *Paul*.
15. *Paul*, p. 60.
16. *Theology of the Acts*, p. 39; 'The church', pp. 11–20. Jervell has to postulate that when Luke uses the term 'Greeks', it always refers to God-fearers. He claims that the message is rejected by 'pure' Gentiles, and then has to say that a few exceptions do not alter the picture.
17. Rejection', pp. 83–101. Both of Tannehill's points are disputed by Cook, 'Mission', pp. 102–123.
18. Barrett, *Acts* 1, pp. 611, 625, suggests that what for Paul was a theological principle was for Luke a matter of missionary tactics.
19. Rapske, *Paul*.
20. Acts has little to say about the perils in the manner of 2 Cor. 11, but it does mention one flogging by the Romans, some imprisonments and (on the journey to Rome) one shipwreck with the attendant privations.
21. Dupont, 'La Mission'.
22. *Acts* 1, pp. 666–667, 671–672.
23. It is a joy to contribute these thoughts to a volume in honour of one who is both a missionary and a teacher; may he continue to witness to the gospel by his life, teaching and writings *in multos annos*.

9. The story of Jesus and the missionary strategy of Paul

David Seccombe

The Old Testament strains forward to a greater king than David, a greater revelation than Moses', a better priesthood than Aaron's, a more effective atonement than the temple's, a better covenant than Sinai, and a mission to embrace all the nations of the earth. The Gospels give us a fourfold portrait of the man whose mission brought these promises to their victorious 'yes'. Acts tells the story of how the salvation achieved by Jesus pushed out into the world, and the rest of the New Testament reflects upon and interprets his person and work. Is it not curious, then, that there is so little of the life of Jesus in Acts and the letters of Paul?

The account of Jesus' messianic ministry forms the centre-point of the biblical revelation, and the multi-form gospel is the focus of our canon of Holy Scripture. The Old Testament looks forward to it, and the rest of the New Testament interprets and looks back to it. Yet the scarcity of reference to the gospel story in Paul creates a superficial impression, at least, that he was interested only in the salvation-bringing events of Jesus' death, resurrection and glorification, not in his teaching and life story.

It is important that this apparent absence be addressed, for unless a substantial connection can be established, the continuity of biblical theology is threatened at a vital point. Paul devotes much effort to establishing the continuity of the death, resurrection and glorification of Jesus with Old Testament faith and expectation. He would be horrified, I suspect, at the idea that the continuity of his own mission with Jesus might be questioned.

115

But it was, even in his own time, and the once common notion, now coming back into currency in certain scholarly circles, that Jesus was a loyal Jew with a simple-minded faith in the fatherhood of a loving God, and that Paul was the inventor of Christianity, demands that the problem be faced.[1]

F. C. Baur tied Paul's apparent lack of interest in the life of Jesus into his theory of a fundamental conflict between Pauline and Petrine Christianity. H. H. Wendt put it down to Paul's Pharisaic tendency which caused him to transform the simple religion of Jesus into an involved theology. W. Wrede argued that Paul had substituted a theology of redemption for Jesus' straightforward ethical teaching, and W. Heitmüller that Paul was influenced by the Hellenistic Christian community which itself was distant from the history of Jesus. R. Bultmann drew a radical distinction between the Jesus of history and the Christ of faith and maintained that Paul saw the former as of little account. It was of little account to Bultmann, who saw it as a mere prolegomena to the apostolic proclamation. All these views except, arguably, the last imply a deep misunderstanding of Jesus' mission on the part of Paul, and consequently gouge a deep chasm through the biblical theological landscape.

S. G. Wilson, to whom I am indebted for the foregoing historical summary,[2] candidly admits that most traditional forms of Christianity necessarily maintain a close connection between Paul and Jesus; they are driven to it by the logic of their belief that in Jesus, God became a human being. It empties the incarnation of any point if his chief expositor misunderstood him. Nevertheless, Wilson, siding with what he regards as majority scholarly opinion, uses his own spade to deepen the chasm: inevitably we would like to know more about Jesus, but, given the problems of Paul on the one side and the Gospels on the other, we are denied real historical knowledge, and must therefore be content with a proclaimed Christ who may have little in common with the real Jesus.

Before surrendering to the scholarly juggernaut, it is worth considering lines of defence for the consensus of the past two thousand years.[3] A common approach has been to seek to demonstrate that Paul and Jesus teach the same fundamental truths.[4] But this approach has been bedevilled by the insistence of many scholars on an exact identity of outlook, when there is an observable dynamic development of the divine plan through the various stages of Old Testament history, and then from Jesus to Paul. An additional method, therefore, must be to work towards an understanding of the Jesus event on the one hand and of Paul's mission and teaching on the other to see if the one flows naturally from the other. This is the true business of biblical theology. Because my own studies of both Jesus and Paul have again and again uncovered both development and continuity, I propose in this essay to examine the issue from yet another standpoint, that of mission history.

Luke and Acts

What significance shall we draw from the fact that Luke authored both a portrait of Jesus and an account of the early church majoring on the Pauline mission? Luke apparently thought the Christian mission could best be furthered at the point at which he wrote by a clear telling of the Jesus story and the story of the apostolic mission. Was this a new idea?

There are three elements to be considered here: the story of Jesus, the account of the apostolic mission, and the apostolic sermons embedded in Acts. Luke clearly intended that all three should be persuasive. The sermons were not new, though it may be that Luke was the first to see their potential as a literary evangelistic tool. Nor was the Jesus story new. Luke says he is following in the footsteps of others (Luke 1:1). It may be, then, that his only big innovation was to utilize the apostolic story as an evangelistic and theological tool.

If, then, the apostolic gospel and the Jesus story both existed prior to Luke's record, what was their relationship? Three possibilities suggest themselves:

1. They were *different instruments* utilized for evangelism by different parties. The Jesus story (stories) such as we find it in the Gospels was not used by Paul.

2. The accounts of Paul's preaching found in Acts are *severely abbreviated*. In fact, much use was made of the Jesus story in his preaching.

3. The apostolic preaching went *side by side* with the telling of the Jesus story.

The remainder of this essay will show the untenability of the first suggestion and the probability that the answer lies in a combination of (2) and (3).

The necessity of the Jesus story

> If you confess with your mouth that Jesus is Lord and believe in your heart that God raised him from the dead, you will be saved (Rom. 10:9).

The minimum content of saving faith, according to Paul, is recognition of Jesus as the risen Lord. This requires some understanding of what he meant by 'Lord', on the one hand, and on the other sufficient information about Jesus to make it meaningful to affirm *him* as Lord, in contrast to anyone else. The former demands some understanding of the Old Testament's messianic doctrine – God's plan to rescue the world and place it in the hands of a human being, son of Eve, son of David – and further, the acceptance that this Saviour, human though he must be, is also in some manner God. For it is clear from the Old Testament allusion in Romans 10:9 (Is. 45:23; cf. Phil. 2:11) and 10:13 (Joel 2:32) that by 'Lord' Paul means no less than the Lord God Almighty.

Gentiles (and moderns) may have needed instruction in the messianic doctrine, but it would hardly have been necessary for Jews and God-fearers. Most believed, or were familiar with the belief, that someday someone would come to save Israel and rule the world. Believing this did not save anyone or make them Christian. It was the affirmation that Jesus and no other had come to fulfil this role that was all important. Thus, leaving the divinity aspect of Christ's identity to one side, the new element of belief for Jews and God-fearers was some real content to the name of Jesus. Even for Gentiles it was half of the equation.

This was no problem for those close enough temporally and geograph- ically to have a first- or second-hand knowledge of Jesus' ministry, but would it have worked if Paul's missionary proclamation contained no more information about Jesus than that he existed, died and rose again, as a superficial reading of Acts and the letters might suggest? I do not think so. 'So and so died for our sins, and God raised him from the dead and enthroned him as Lord and Christ' raises the question, 'Who?', and 'Jesus' (a common first-century Jewish name) was not a sufficient answer. More information was needed about his life, work and words, which, if it was not part of the initial proclamation, would have been demanded by the listeners as a supplement. This is even more obvious when we consider that what Paul required of his hearers was faith in this Jesus.

Thus when Paul proceeds in Romans 10 to ask how people are to 'believe in him of whom they have never heard' (verse 14), he surely indicates the availability of substantial information within his missionary organization about Jesus' life and work, as well as his messianic role. 'The word of Christ' (*hē rhēma Christou*, v. 17) must have comprised both a doctrinal and a life component.

The face of Jesus Christ

In 2 Corinthians Paul again describes his ministry in terms of preaching 'Jesus Christ as Lord' (*Iēsoun Christon kyrion*, 2 Cor. 4:5). He explains this with imagery suggestive of God's creation of light at creation: 'it is the God who said, "From darkness light shall shine", who has shone in our hearts to bring about the illumination of the knowledge of the glory of God in the face of [Jesus] Christ' (4:6). Conversion is thus explained in terms of the Spirit of God combining with the message about Jesus to bring about a vision of the glory of God.

What level of knowledge of Jesus is required for such an enlightenment? I am not here wishing to discuss how little a person might know and yet be brought to faith by God's supernatural enlightenment, but rather what Paul would have wished to impart to facilitate such a conversion. The answer is surely as much information about the earthly Jesus as was available. If Jesus is the image (*eikōn*) of God (2 Cor. 4:4) such that God's glory becomes visible in him, a display of his words and work, as well as of his death, resurrection and ascension, is demanded. Is this not implied in Paul's reference to Jesus' face? If the glory of God was visible to the Spirit-minded person 'in the face of Christ' (4:6), he would surely ask where he might see that face, and the only sensible answer is in the extant stories of his earthly career.

The sanctifying power

Having noted that Paul locates faith-awakening power in 'the face' of Jesus – that is, in the memory of his mission and not just in the theological explanation of his work – we should also observe that he understands the driving (or drawing) force of sanctification in a similar way.

> We all with unveiled face beholding the glory of the Lord are being transformed into the same image, from glory to glory, which is from the Lord, the Spirit (2 Cor. 3:18).

The same confluence of enlightening Spirit and knowledge of Jesus is found here as we have already seen occurs a few verses later. Paul has in mind Moses' vision of God. His time on Sinai in the presence of God caused his face to shine. In an analogous manner the believer who gazes on the glory of the Lord is transformed inwardly. But how does one behold the glory of the Lord? Only by looking at Jesus. It does not matter whether *katoptrizomenoi* is translated 'beholding (directly)' or 'beholding (as in a mirror)', for the point is the same either way. In seeing Jesus we see God and the vision transforms. It follows that if Paul wished his converts to experience this transformation of life he would have wanted them to see more of Jesus. His own doctrine demands more than explanation of his work and declaration of his heavenly office. If he is the perfect human image of God to which all his people are gradually to be conformed (Rom 8:29), it stands to reason that his humanity must be seen.

The image of Jesus in Paul

Consideration of Romans 10 and 2 Corinthians 3 – 4 leads to the conclusion that the superficial impression of a Paul who was uninterested in the Jesus story is erroneous. The theological explanation found in his letters, and the summaries of his preaching in Acts, present only one side of what must have been a fuller presentation of the Jesus dimension of Christ. Before seeking possible explanations of this omission, it is worth rehearsing what others have done before and pointing out some tell-tale signs of this less visible part of the Pauline mission.

1. In Acts there are numerous descriptions of *Paul's activity* which one would assume included reference to the human story of Jesus. Luke's description of him in Damascus: 'he proclaimed Jesus – that this man is the Son of God' (9:20), sounds like a double-sided message. Some profile of Jesus of Nazareth was necessary for those who did not already know. It cannot be doubted that he had considerable knowledge of the one whose memory he was attempting to wipe from human minds. In Cyprus he presented to the proconsul 'the teaching of the Lord' (13:12). In Thessalonica Paul spent three weeks preaching from the Scriptures that the Christ needed to suffer and rise from the dead, saying, 'This Jesus, whom I proclaim to you, is the Christ' (17:3–4). The same double-sidedness is again indicated. In Corinth Paul was occupied with 'testifying to the Jews that the Christ was Jesus' (18:5). In Rome he testified to the Jews about the kingdom of God, 'trying to convince them about Jesus from Moses and the prophets' (28:23). For the two years following he preached 'the kingdom of God and taught about the Lord Jesus' (28:31). Precision as to the content of Paul's teaching in all these cases is not possible. One must say, however, that it would be strange if all this Jesus-centred ministry did not in some way entail the telling of his story.

2. In the account of Paul's evangelistic sermon in the synagogue in *Pisidian Antioch* Paul rehearses the biblical theological context for Messiah's coming, taking the story as far as God's promise of posterity to David. He then jumps directly to Jesus: 'Of this man's [David's] seed God has brought to Israel a Saviour, Jesus.' At this point he recalls the ministry of John the Baptist and his witness to the Coming One. This part of the sermon sounds very like a shortened version of the John the Baptist story in the Gospels. What then does he mean by the comment that follows: 'Brothers . . . to us

has been sent the word (*logos*, cf. Acts 10:36) of this salvation'? Does there not appear to be a hiatus here? Was Paul more interested in the career of John the Baptist than in that of Jesus? Is it not rather that Luke shortened a longer address by omitting the account of Jesus' ministry up to his trial? He could do this because he knew he had already provided it, both in summary form in Acts (10:36–43; cf. 2:22–24) and in detail in his Gospel. The sermon goes on to describe Jesus' trial, appearance before Pilate, crucifixion, burial, resurrection and appearances, again in a way that recalls the accounts of the Gospels. It appears then that however else the Jesus story may have been handled within his mission, Paul was not unable to tell the story himself when it was appropriate.

3. In at least four places Paul makes *direct references* to the gospel story or to Jesus' teaching: Jesus' teaching about remarriage (1 Cor. 7:10, 25), his instructions about financial support of missionaries (1 Cor. 9:14), the account of the Lord's Supper (1 Cor. 11:23–25) and Jesus' appearance before Pontius Pilate (1 Tim. 6:13).[5]

4. There are numerous phrases, expressions and allusions in the letters which probably rest on *dominical tradition*. Examples are: 'You yourselves know accurately (*akribōs*) that the day of the Lord comes like a thief in the night' (1 Thess. 5:2; cf. Matt. 24:43–44); 'Therefore then do not sleep as the rest, but keep watch and be sober' (1 Thess. 5:6; cf Mark 13:33–37), and similarly 1 Thessalonians 5:15; and Romans 12:19 / Matthew 5:38–39; 2 Thessalonians 1:7 / Matthew 13:41–43; Galatians 5:9 / Mark 8:15; 1 Corinthians 3:9 / Matthew 13:38 and 16:18; 2 Corinthians 11:1 / Mark 2:19–20; Romans 13:8 / John 13:34–35; Colossians 1:6 / Mark 4:8, 20; Colossians 3:13 / Matthew 6:14–15; 1 Timothy 5:18 / Luke 10:7. In citing parallels I am not wishing to argue that Paul was dependent on these exact Gospel sayings, but that he is clearly leaning on tradition that originated with Jesus. Some scholars have discerned vastly more parallels than these; others, noting the illusory nature of the parallels, are more doubtful. D. L. Dungan concluded from a detailed study of two cases where Paul is explicit about his dependence on sayings of Jesus, that allusion was his normal method of citing Jesus' teaching, possible because of the familiarity of the churches with the tradition.[6]

5. There are two places where Paul expresses himself in a way which probably implies *a shared knowledge* of the Jesus story between himself and his readers: 'I Paul exhort you through the meekness and gentleness of Christ' (2 Cor. 10:1); 'for God is my witness how I yearn for all of you with the compassion of Christ Jesus' (Phil. 1:8).

6. Paul uses certain expressions which suggest or imply extensive *instruction about the earthly Jesus* and his teachings. For example: 'You did

not so learn Christ, if indeed you heard and were instructed in him, just as the truth is in Jesus' (Eph. 4:20–21); 'in whom [Christ] all the treasures of wisdom and knowledge are hidden' (Col. 2:3).

7. In 1 Timothy 5:18 Paul actually quotes *a saying of Jesus as Scripture* ('the labourer deserves his wages'), indicating the existence of a written form of the Jesus tradition. This could mean that his exhortation to Timothy to give himself to (public) reading, exhortations and teaching (4:13) included the reading of some form of a Gospel.

These traces are sufficient indication of Paul's knowledge of and concern for the story of Jesus' ministry and teaching, although they still leave us wondering why he makes such little explicit reference compared with his frequent citing of the Old Testament. When the allusions are listed as above, they constitute a considerable number. Spread over all Paul's writing, however, they are sparse, especially references to events in Jesus' career. Some draw the simple conclusion that the Gospels did not exist at the time of Paul's ministry and therefore could not be referred to in the same way as the Old Testament. Possibly the tradition had not evolved to a sufficiently fixed written form to allow citation, but one would have thought he might still have referred to parables, miracles, controversies and so on. His manner may rather betoken a man who knew the Gospel tradition, but did not envisage himself as a 'repeater'. Possibly his consciousness of himself as a prophetic recipient of fresh revelation influenced his teaching style, or there may be other reasons. One possibility worth exploring is that the gospel story was very much part of Paul's missionary method, but it was the ministry of others in his team to impart it, rather than his own.

Was a written gospel a novelty?

In considering this last proposal we return to Luke, who, as a member of Paul's missionary team, wrote a Gospel presumably to assist the missionary enterprise. Part of his objective is stated in his preface: 'in order that you [Theophilus] might know the certainty of the words in which you have been instructed'. Luke assumes a readership which already has some knowledge of Jesus, and wishes to strengthen this by means of a carefully researched, accurate and well-presented account of his ministry. It is reasonable to suppose that such people as were represented by Theophilus were those whom Luke had encountered within the ambit of the mission. They have encountered the Jesus story already, albeit not in the sophisticated form of Luke's narrative.

A second question suggests itself: was the production of a written Gospel a novelty 'within the Pauline circle'? Luke tells us in his preface that 'many have turned their hands to putting in order an account of the things that have been fulfilled among us'. Orderly accounts in this context mean written accounts. Were these accounts part of a methodology foreign to Paul? Was Luke importing a missionary tool that was novel to Paul and his team, or were written accounts of the Jesus story already part of their strategy? The way Luke speaks of the things which were fulfilled 'among us', which were handed down 'to us' by eyewitnesses and servants of the word, creates the impression that the efforts to create orderly accounts were also to some extent an in-house activity. Can anything more be said?

Mark

One of Luke's sources was Mark. Could the Gospel of Mark have arisen in relation to the Pauline mission? Papias says that 'Mark was Peter's interpreter', and for this reason his Gospel is generally associated with Peter. However, Luke informs us that Paul and Barnabas took Mark with them as 'servant' (*hypēretēs*) on their first missionary journey. Is it accidental that in the preface to the Gospel he also refers to 'servants' (*hypēretai*) of the word who handed down the Jesus story? The question whether Mark's role as *hypēretēs* was more than a bag-carrier has been frequently discussed. Rengstorf is no doubt correct to insist that no specific role can be inferred from the word on its own.[7] Yet his survey of the use of the word also makes clear that a *hypēretēs* was no ordinary servant (*doulos, diakonos*); he was the personal assistant of a master or an office bearer of an institution. When, as was often the case, the principal was someone of high authority, the *hypēretēs* was himself a person of some importance. Thus *hypēretai* were sometimes military officers, public officials, or officers of court and temple. Josephus describes Moses as God's *hypēretēs* when he led Israel from Egypt and gave them God's commands (*AJ* V 3.16; 4.317).

To say that Barnabas and Saul took Mark as *hypēretēs* could mean that he was personal assistant to one or other or both, or that he had some recognizable function in relation to the whole expedition. Given Luke's other uses of *hypēretēs* to describe those who handed down the Jesus story, and in Luke 4:20 of the synagogue attendant with responsibility for the scrolls, it would be unwise to rule out the latter possibility, especially when it is observed that he introduces Mark, not where one would expect if he was a general assistant, as they set out from Antioch, but in relation to their activity in the synagogues: 'And arriving in Salamis they proclaimed the word of God in the synagogues of the Jews. And they had John [Mark]as *hypēretēs*' (Acts 13:5). The suggestion of C. S. C. Williams that Mark had a special role in relation to the Old Testament Scriptures, or of T. Boman and A. Wright that Mark was some sort of catechist, or of G. Salmon that Mark's role had to do with his eyewitness reminiscences of the Jesus story, or even of B. T. Holmes that he carried a written Gospel, should not lightly be pushed aside.[8]

Papias' description of Mark's involvement with Peter is generally referred to a time they spent together in Rome, whenever that may have been. However, there is nothing in his description to suggest that his role as interpreter (*hermēneutēs*) did not go back much further. J. Kürzinger explains this term from the background of ancient rhetoric: Mark was the person authorized to pass on Peter's teachings in a particular format.[9] The association of Peter and Mark can be traced to the time when part of the Jerusalem church met in the house of John Mark's mother, and probably goes further (Acts 12:12). Mark would have become familiar with Peter's stories then, even if he did not have his own eyewitness memories of Jesus. Arthur Wright pictures him as a bilingual catechist who had sat at Peter's feet and learned his stories by heart. As the son of a wealthy family he may already have received the scribal training which is evidenced by his later activities. In this case he may have written some things down at a very early stage. Rainer Riesner thinks it is not unlikely that notes were made of Jesus' teaching even prior to Easter.[10]

Mark could therefore have been an indispensable member of the first missionary team, able to tell the Jesus story and even repeat it for the memorization of others. For we must ask ourselves how long a fledgling Christian congregation with all of several weeks' instruction would have lasted with just the Old Testament and the memory of Paul's explanations. There would have been an urgent need for Christian material that could be recited or read in congregational meetings. This accounts for what a serious blow it was to the mission when Mark withdrew and went home.

When did Mark put his Gospel in writing? I would concur with those who date Acts about AD 61–62.[11] Luke's Gospel was probably written during Paul's Caesarean imprisonment (AD 57–59). Mark will then have been earlier. Luke's reference to the 'many' who had produced orderly accounts of the Jesus story implies that such writing had been going on for some time. The early fathers connect the writing of Mark with a period when both Peter and Mark were together in Rome. This could have been in AD 42–44 prior to the first Pauline mission (Robinson),[12] some time in the 50s, or in the early 60s prior to Peter's death. If the Gospel was in writing as early as the first mission (as Robinson suggests is possible), it is puzzling why Mark's defection was such a serious thing. Even if he acted as a scribe and copied the 'Gospel' for each new church, his role could easily have been substituted by someone in the receiving churches. It is more likely that the gospel was in his head, but the needs of the new churches, particularly the knowledge that the missionaries would be moving on in a short time, must have suggested to some of the hearers the wisdom of at least making notes. There seems no reason then not to follow Eusebius and his sources and accept that Mark himself put his Gospel in writing at the request of Christians in Rome when he was there with Peter some time in the reign of Claudius (AD 41–54).[13] If it were not for the Romans, it must have arisen out of a similar situation.

The telling of the gospel story, therefore, belonged to Paul's missionary strategy from the earliest days, even though it was probably often someone other than Paul who did the task. After all, Paul was not an eyewitness of the Jesus events.[14] Nor had he been attentive in any positive way in the early days to those who were. It was natural that he should lean on others for this ministry. Acts frequently describes the missionary preaching as a combined effort. In Iconium, for example, '*they* spoke so that a great company believed' (14:1).[15] When the Paul–Barnabas team split, Silas (Silvanus) replaced Mark for Paul's second journey (Acts 15:37–41). Mark renewed his ministry with Barnabas, and later joined up with Peter and put his Gospel into writing. It is interesting to find both Mark and Silas in company with Peter in Rome when 1 Peter was composed, and Paul requesting Mark's assistance at the time of his last imprisonment (1 Pet. 5:13; 2 Tim. 4:11). It is evidence of co-operation between the missions of Paul and Peter that contradicts any attempt to establish radically opposed forms of Christianity and different missionary strategies. Mark was a bridge between Peter and Paul in both the early and late missionary periods.

Luke

Could Luke have exercised a ministry similar to Mark's after he joined Paul for the journey to Macedonia? Ancient authors (Origen, Ephraem, Eusebius, Ambrose, Jerome, Pseudo-Clement) identified 'the brother whose praise in the gospel is in all the churches', whom Paul sent to Corinth with Titus in connection with the collection for the poor in Jerusalem (2 Cor. 8:18), with Luke, whether by inference or from tradition we know not.[16] Certainly Luke is a likely contender, being a member of the group which accompanied Paul to Jerusalem with the collection. Commentators are quick to point out that the reference cannot be to Luke's written Gospel, which certainly did not exist in AD 55. But 'gospel' may refer to the yet unwritten story. In this context it surely refers to something more specialized than the ordinary Christian proclamation that was engaging many in the Pauline circle. Paul assumes that this brother will be distinguishable from his description. What if Luke was already active in the Pauline churches in a similar role to what I have suggested was Mark's? We cannot be certain, but it is possible to infer from Acts that he remained behind in Philippi when Paul was ejected after only a few weeks of ministry, since it was here that he disappears from Paul's party, and two years later reappears (Acts 16:11–12; 40; 20:1–6). Someone nurtured the church in Philippi from its interrupted infancy to being a mature, generous, mission-minded congregation. Suppose Luke received from Silas the substance of Mark's Gospel (perhaps even a written copy) and that he utilized this to nurture this church and others in the vicinity.[17] If he did, he would surely have felt the paucity of Jesus' teaching in that Gospel, and also wished for an account of Jesus' birth and resurrection. He may well have begun supplementing Mark with such dominical materials as he could obtain. Such activity would account both for Paul's assumption that 'the brother whose praise in the gospel is in all the churches' would be easily identified, and for the later appearance of his written Gospel.

When later Luke accompanied Paul to Jerusalem and had contact with Jesus' brother and some of the early disciples, he was in a perfect position to expand his Gospel even further (Acts 21:8, 16, 18). He was at liberty for the whole of Paul's imprisonment in Caesarea, only two days' journey from Jerusalem and one from Galilee. None of this can be proved, but the probability that something like this was the case shows how dangerous are far-reaching conclusions about the unimportance to Paul of the Jesus story. If Luke was not the brother, some other brother's praise in the gospel was in all the Pauline churches.

Before Antioch

Mark also bridges the gap from Paul to the first days of the Jerusalem church and makes it clear that the use of the Jesus story was not something original to the Pauline enterprise. It came to Antioch from Jerusalem. The daily teaching of Peter and the other apostles must have had a sizable component of Jesus' story and teachings. After all, they were Jesus' *talmidim*. It was expected of them that they would recite the teachings of their rabbi, as well as tell the stories of his significant actions; for these were as important to establishing his *halakah* as his words. We may guess that in the excitement of the early post-Easter expansion there were many garbled and confusing recollections of what Jesus did and said. Even at his trial there were false and conflicting accounts of his words (Mark 14:56–59). This would have highlighted the role of the twelve premier disciples as a kind of living canon of authentic doctrine, the foundation of which were the words and acts of Jesus. Those who were able to memorize the apostolic testimony and carried some form of apostolic authorization would have been much in demand once the number of Christians exceeded the ministering ability of the apostles, and even more in need when the gospel moved beyond the region where Jesus operated and where many knew the stories.

For those who could tell the story in Greek a whole new world of opportunity was about to open up. Philip answered the request of the African eunuch to help him understand Isaiah by 'evangelizing Jesus' to him (Acts 8:35). When Peter was called to speak to the centurion Cornelius, he related the story of Jesus from the baptism of John, through his ministry in Galilee and Jerusalem and up to his death and resurrection, before going on to draw conclusions of a theological and interpretative nature (Acts 10:36–43). As C. H. Dodd observed, this is a skeleton outline of the synoptic Gospels.[18] It establishes a firm bridge between Luke's own telling of the gospel and the apostolic mission.

Why is there so little of the Jesus story in Paul?

Finally, some explanation of why Paul refers so little to the Jesus story must be attempted. I have already suggested two factors. First, Paul's ministry may have lain more on the side of direct theological instruction, in a movement which nonetheless had a double focus. Secondly, as a primary recipient of revelation he may have been naturally inclined to a direct style of teaching, in contrast to exposition of the revelation of others. To the obvious objection that he frequently expounds the Old Testament Scriptures, it should be said that it was a necessary part of his ministry to demonstrate to Jews that Christianity was in direct continuity with their Scriptures; there was not the same problem with his relationship to Jesus.

C. F. D. Moule makes a further suggestion. He regards the demand that Paul should display evidences in his letters of a genuine interest in the gospel story as 'a major blunder in classification':

> There is no reason why Paul should have shown interest in the story of Jesus (however much he felt it) in letters written, for highly specialized purposes, to persons who were already Christians … If the epistles represented Paul's evangelistic gospel and the substance of his primary proclamation, then of course we should be justified in deducing that the story of Jesus did not interest him. But they simply

do not represent anything of the sort. All the prolegomena are assumed in them, because he is addressing Christian congregations.[19]

One more thing might be said. As heirs to two thousand years of spiritualizing and moralizing of the Gospel stories, we are disposed to seek something similar in the New Testament letters. May it not be that this way of handling the Gospels simply had not developed then? Where the modern preacher makes an existential application of the story of Jesus stilling the storm, to 'the storms in our lives', the Gospels tell it to demonstrate Jesus' power to still literal storms – or rather to show his messianic authority through the medium of his many mighty acts. Nor is this spiritualizing hermeneutic prominent elsewhere in the New Testament. The unexpectedly small degree of 'contamination' of the letters to Christians with material from the Gospel narratives may be in part a consequence of this.

Conclusion

Our present Bible consists of a forward-looking, promise-rich collection of law, prophets and writings, a fourfold account of the ministry and teaching of Jesus, an account of the early Christian mission, and a body of forward- and backward-looking writings which interpret the ministry of Jesus, look forward to the consummation of his kingdom, and instruct his followers for life and mission in the interim. Some have inferred from the scarcity of Jesus-story material in Acts and Paul lack of interest on the part of Paul and the non-use of the Gospel tradition in his mission. But this is not the case. Two of the Gospel writers belonged to Paul's circle and their work grew out of a need in new churches for the Jesus story, first in oral form and later in writing. The confession 'Jesus is Lord' requires on the one hand a strong understanding of and commitment to the doctrine of a human-divine saviour-King, and on the other a familiarity with the human person and life of the crucified Jesus of Nazareth. It is Jesus of Nazareth who is now worshipped as the risen Lord. God is known and his glory beheld in the face of the human Jesus. Christian mission then as now must combine theological explanation of the person and work of the crucified, risen, ascended Christ along with narration of the story, works and words of the man from Nazareth.

Notes

1. The writings of G. Vermes may be taken as an example: *Jesus the Jew; Jesus and the World of Judaism; The Religion of Jesus the Jew.*
2. Wilson, 'From Jesus to Paul'. See also Furnish, 'Jesus–Paul debate'.
3. For a recent counter to the notion that there were separate 'Gospel'- and 'Epistle'-using communities see Schweizer, 'Testimony'.
4. Wenham, *Paul*, makes a thorough examination of the teachings of Jesus and Paul and the connections between them. Wenham concludes that Paul was a follower of Jesus, not the founder of a different religion.
5. Perhaps also 1 Thess. 4:2, 15.
6. Dungan, *Sayings*. Holtz, 'Paul', agrees that the amount of allusion is extensive and concludes there were two traditions of transmission of the dominical teaching, the one precise as in the Gospels, the other varied in form to suit the need of the early church.
7. Rengstorf, '*hyperetes*', p. 541.
8. Wright, *Composition*. For other references see Bruce, *Acts*, p. 247; Moule, *Essays*, p. 47.
9. See Riesner, *Lehrer*, pp. 20–24.
10. Riesner, 'Preacher', p. 196.
11. I have argued this in some detail in my *Jesus and the New Age.*
12. Robinson, *Redating*, pp. 11–114.
13. Eusebius, *HE* 2.15.
14. This point is made by Paul Barnett, *Is the New Testament History?*, ch. 11, and *Jesus*, esp. pp. 57–58, but passim, who argues that, although there is much to be learned about the historical Jesus from Paul's letters (see *Jesus*), the paucity of Jesus material in Paul is an endorsement of Paul's reliability as an historical witness: he did not pretend a knowledge he did not have at first hand. Barnett points out that, when compared to the Gospels, it 'is clear that Paul did not manufacture details about Jesus, or exaggerate what details he had. Paul's use of historical evidence was, it appears, both careful and sober.' *Is the New Testament History?*, p. 135.
15. Compare Acts 14:21; 16:32.
16. See Hughes, *Second Corinthians*, p. 312.
17. We do not need to imagine Luke confined to one church; he could have been active in Macedonia, around Troas, where he joined Paul, and perhaps further afield. Paul's description of the brother need not be pressed to mean that he was known beyond the churches known to the Corinthians.
18. Dodd, *New Testament Studies*, pp. 1–11.
19. Moule, *Essays*, p. 41.

10. 'Because of weakness' (Galatians 4:13): the role of suffering in the mission of Paul

Scott Hafemann

The starting-point of this presentation is the claim which I once read: 'Paul was no theologian; he was a missionary' – a claim that is false both in principle and in fact. In principle false, because there is no Christian theology which is not in the broad sense kerygmatic theology; factually false, because the historical Paul wrote as a theologian and worked as a missionary.[1]

C. K. Barrett's starting-point is my own. Indeed, the unity between Paul's kerygmatically driven theology and his missionary endeavours is nowhere more apparent than in those key passages where Paul delineates the significance of his suffering for his proclamation of the gospel. And nowhere is this significance more striking than in Paul's sudden shift from his direct theological arguments in Galatians 2:15 – 4:10, to the implications of his suffering as an apostle in 4:12–20, and then back again to theology in 4:21 – 5:26. It is surprising, therefore, as Ernst Baasland pointed out sixteen years ago, that Paul's recounting of his suffering in Galatians 4:13–14 and the argument he builds from it in 4:12–20, as well as his passing references to his persecution in 5:11; 6:12, 17, have long been a neglected feature of his apologetic in this letter.[2] Though understandable in view of the law/gospel contrast that has dominated the church's engagement with this letter ever since the Reformation, this lack of attention is especially striking in regard to 4:13–14. For within Paul's overall argument this reference to Paul's suffering functions to support Paul's first direct command in the letter

131

(4:12a), which rhetorically marks out a (*the*?) key turning-point in the epistle. The letter's other commands can all be seen to be specific explications of Paul's general admonition in 4:12a (cf. Gal. 5:1, 13, 16, 25–26). Far from being simply an emotional aside in Paul's argument,[3] Paul's reference to his suffering in 4:13–14 provides the immediate, evidential support for his leading appeal to the Galatians. In doing so, it presupposes a theological perspective and follows an apologetic pattern that is pervasive throughout Paul's letters. Thus, rather than rendering it *less* important than the more overtly 'theological' arguments that surround it, the distinct personal nature of this 'highly enigmatic paragraph' (4:12–20)[4] actually calls *more* attention to its importance.

The Pauline gospel: become like Paul!

The personal nature of Paul's argument in 4:12–20 is manifest already in the imperative of 4:12a, which is the main point of Paul's argument in this paragraph: Paul begs the Galatians to become *like him* because *he* also has become like them (the tenses of the implied verbs of the two clauses are naturally present and past respectively). Within the larger context of Paul's argument, this is best taken as a reference to Paul's own conversion-call (Gal. 1:13–24) and its consequence: 'The one who was once persecuting us is now preaching (*euangelizetai*) the faith which he was once trying to destroy' (Gal. 1:23; cf. 4:13). This faith is the gospel which Paul received 'through a revelation of Jesus Christ' (Gal. 1:12) and preached to the Galatians (Gal. 1:8). And it is the same gospel that was now being called into question by the 'Judaizers', who argued that one had to keep the stipulations of both the old *and* new covenants in order to be a fully fledged, Spirit-filled member of God's eschatological people (Gal. 1:6–9; 2:21; 5:2–4). For this reason, Paul begs the Galatians in 4:12 to resist the Judaizers by becoming like him in his freedom from the 'works of the law' as Israel had encountered them in slavery to this world while under the old covenant (Gal. 4:1–7; 5:1). Paul's desire is that they continue to join him in the Spirit-empowered obedience that now truly fulfils the law (5:13–26; 6:8), since, like Paul, God has freed the Gentiles as well from this same slavery (Gal. 4:8–11). In other words, in 4:12, Paul is calling the Galatians to the freedom in Christ that characterizes his own life because of Jesus' death on the cross (2:20; 3:13–14; 6:14). Thus, the cross of Christ that initially caused Paul to persecute the church had now become the centre-piece of his own life and ministry as an apostle. As a result, the persecutor had now joined the ranks of those being persecuted for their faith in the crucified Messiah (cf. 5:11; 6:17).

The role of Paul's suffering in support of his gospel

This brings us to the specific question of how Paul's suffering relates to the gospel he now preached, since in Galatians 4:13 Paul reminds the Galatians that it was *'because* of a weakness of the flesh' (*di'* [6] *astheneian tēs sarkos*) that he first preached the gospel (cf. *euēngelisamēn*[7]) to them. As David Black has argued, the general consensus is correct that here *astheneia* 'refers to a physical condition of the apostle, and not to an unimpressive appearance, timidity, the emotional scars from persecution, sexual desires, human frailty in general, or some other figurative meaning'.[8] Paul's 'weakness' in 4:13 is best seen as a sickness, with the genitive *tēs sarkos* most likely descriptive, i.e., a 'bodily infirmity'. As such, Paul coined a phrase that would locate his weakness in his 'body' (*sarx*), while at the same time creating a play on his own theological concept of the 'flesh' (*sarx*).[9] He did so in order to call special attention to the fact that he was sick *with regard to* his 'flesh', rather than being sick *because of* his 'flesh' (cf. Gal. 3:3; 4:29; 5:13, 16–17, 19–21, 24; 6:8). Attempts to interpret it as a reference to Paul's persecutions (cf. Acts 13:50; 14:19; 2 Tim. 3:11) fail to account adequately for this descriptive use of *sarx* and for the fact that Paul's being persecuted was a result of his preaching, not its underlying cause (cf. 5:11; 6:12, 17).[10] In Galatians Paul's weakness grounds his preaching, whereas persecution is its *consequence*. In addition, Ulrich Heckel has convincingly demonstrated that Paul's parallel reference to his 'thorn in the flesh' (*skolops tē sarki*) or 'weakness' (*astheneia*) in 2 Corinthians 12:7, 9–10 is also best understood not as a reference to his own inner temptations (as in the Latin tradition) or to persecution by his opponents (first found among the Fathers beginning in the fourth century AD), but to Paul's personal sickness.[11] Moreover, Heckel has argued that Paul's silence concerning the nature of his sickness in 2 Corinthians 12:7 is intentional. Paul is not interested in the diagnosis of his weakness in a medical sense, but in its theological origin, cause and purpose.[12] So too, Paul's silence in Galatians 4:13–14 concerning the nature of his suffering demonstrates that the focus is not on the nature of his 'weakness of the flesh' as such, but on its very existence and function. Indeed, the front-loading of *di' astheneian tēs sarkos* in 4:13 is most likely not merely stylistic, but emphatic (cf. the corresponding front-loaded position of *ton peirasmon hymōn en tē sarki mou* in 4:14).

However, in spite of Paul's theological evaluation of his 'weakness' in 2 Corinthians 12:7 and the corresponding development of this theme elsewhere in his letters (see below), most have argued that Galatians 4:13 is a reference only to the occasion that led to Paul's being in Galatia. The assumption is that Paul's suffering had either forced Paul into Galatia or caused him to remain in this region longer than planned, during which time he preached the gospel to the Galatians.[13] In this view, Paul's 'weakness' was merely the circumstantial means by which God, in his providence, brought the gospel to the Galatians logistically. Black even speaks of Paul's 'physical condition which stranded him in Galatia', but 'proved to be a blessing in disguise ... thus accomplishing more than he had originally set out to'.[14]

But to my knowledge there is no evidence in Paul's letters or Acts that Paul's sickness or personal suffering ever influenced his chronology or travel plans. When Paul's plans change it is due either to the needs of others (cf. 2 Cor. 1:15 – 2:4; 2:12–13; Rom. 15:22–29), to persecution (cf. 2 Cor. 11:32–33; Rom. 15:30–33; 1 Thess. 2:18), or to divine intervention (cf. 1 Cor. 16:9). Moreover, the apologetic function of Paul's suffering elsewhere in his letters speaks against Galatians 4:13 being a reference solely to the providential circumstances of his preaching. Rather, as in 2 Cor. 12:7–10, Paul's suffering in Galatians 4:13 is a matter of theological affirmation and interpretation. But whereas in 2 Corinthians 12:7–10 Paul relates his weakness to his personal character as a means to an end (see the purpose-clause inclusio of 12:7: *hina mē hyperairōmai ... hina mē hyperairōmai*), in Galatians 4:13–14 he relates it to his apostolic mission as a cause to its consequence (*di' astheneian tēs sarkos euēngelisamēn hymin to proteron*). In 2 Corinthians 12:7–10 the focus is on the implication of Paul's weakness for himself, since as an apostle he had been entrusted with private revelations in heaven (cf. 2 Cor. 12:7a). In Galatians 4:13–14 it is on the implication of Paul's weakness for the Galatians, since as an apostle he had been entrusted with a public revelation of Jesus Christ on the road to Damascus (cf. Gal. 1:12, 16). Rather than being an unusual circumstance that occasioned Paul's preaching in Galatia, Paul's 'weakness' was the very basis upon which Paul preached everywhere he was sent by God. While the function of Paul's weakness for himself was a private matter that he discussed only when forced to do so by the circumstances in Corinth, the role his weakness played in his preaching was a public affair well known to the Galatians, as it was everywhere Paul went (cf. 1 Thess. 2:1; 1 Cor. 4:9–13; Phil. 1:12–14, 30; 2 Tim. 1:11; 3:11). Instead of being a recourse to emotional special pleading, Paul's return to his suffering in 4:12–20 is an essential aspect of his polemic.

The contrast established in 4:14 confirms that Paul's weakness was not merely the circumstance that brought the gospel to Galatia, though it may have been that as well. More importantly, Paul's suffering was the divinely ordained means by which the gospel itself was made clear to the Galatians. Given the cultural assumption of Paul's day that a deity's approval meant earthly blessing, and inasmuch as the desire for health, wealth and status was the driving motive for participation in the Graeco-Roman civic cults, Paul's suffering posed an immense barrier to his gospel.[15] Moreover, Ernst Baasland has pointed out the conceptual link between Paul's suffering as a 'temptation' (*peirasmos*) to despise Paul (4:14) and the Old Testament 'curse' tradition that made a link between sin and suffering, of which 'the most convincing evidence is found in the *ārûr* catalogue in Deuteronomy 27:15–26; 28:16–19', based on the use of Deuteronomy 27:26; 28:15.[16] Thus, the allusion to this Old Testament curse tradition in 4:14 no doubt reflects Paul's having taught it to the Galatians in order to explain the role of Christ's suffering in taking upon himself God's curse on sin (cf. 3:10), as well as explaining his own willingness to suffer for the gospel as a display of the sufferings of Christ (4:13–14). Neither Christ nor Paul (in this regard) is suffering for his own sins, but each is willingly taking up the cross for the sake of others. For Christ, this suffering was the centre of his calling as the messianic Son of God who was sent to atone for the sins of God's people. For Paul, it was the centre of his calling as an apostle, through whom the gospel of Christ was being mediated to the Gentiles (see below). In theological hindsight, Paul's reminder in 4:14 therefore takes on great polemic significance within the contemporary context: Paul's reference in 3:10 to Deuteronomy 27:26 (28:15) as an essential aspect of his dispute with the Judaizers points to the likely inference that they were probably now using this same tradition *against* Paul, arguing from Paul's own suffering that *he* was the one who was still under the curse of the law, not they. From their perspective, Paul's suffering was evidence that God's judgment or curse had fallen upon Paul for his failing to keep the Sinai covenant (cf. his fivefold punishment as a transgressor by the synagogue in accordance with Deuteronomy 25:1–3 [2 Cor. 11:24]).[17] As in Corinth, in Galatia too Paul's suffering was being used to question the legitimacy of his ministry and message.

Nevertheless, although both Christ's death on the cross and Paul's weakness had initially posed a cultural and theological temptation to the Galatians, they had not rejected Paul's weakness out of contempt (*exouthenēsate*), nor disdained it (*exeptysate*[18]), but had rather received Paul 'as an angel of God' (Gal. 4:14). Given the contrast between the Galatians' refusal to reject Paul out of contempt and their acceptance of him as an 'angel of God' (*angelos theou*), Paul's use of *exptyō* most likely carries more than simply the transferred metaphorical meaning of 'disdain'.[19] It is best taken as a concrete reference to the practice of 'spitting out' that signalled the repulsion of sickness as a demonic threat.[20] If so, then Paul's point is that when he first came to them the Galatians did not attribute

Paul's weakness to demonic activity (i.e. he was not an *angelos Satanas* disguised as an *angelos phōtos*; cf. 2 Cor. 11:14), but accepted it as the very basis of Paul's ministry as a messenger sent from God. In this light, the contrast between 2 Corinthians 12:7 and Galatians 4:13 is maintained here as well: whereas in 2 Corinthians 12:7 Paul's weakness is explicitly attributed to Satan's 'angel' (*angelos*) and hence may be resisted and prayed against, in Galatians 4:14 Paul's weakness was the ground on which God was speaking through Paul as if he were an 'angel' sent to do God's bidding. Rather than falling prey to the temptation to reject Paul and his message because of his suffering, the Galatians saw the essential link between the two and had accepted Paul's life as an embodiment of the divinely authorized gospel that he preached. To quote Baasland again, 'Paul insists that his sufferings are not the result of a curse, but they show that he belongs to Christ',[21] who redeemed him from that very curse (3:13; 4:5).

The reason for the Galatians' earlier acceptance of Paul, in spite of his weakness, is given in the further appositional designation of verse 14c: *hōs Christon Iēsoun*. When Paul preached the gospel because of his suffering, the Galatians accepted him not only as if he were an angel sent from God, but as if he were Christ Jesus himself! This identification of the suffering Paul with Christ is best explained in view of the *missiological* (not ontological) identity between Paul's own suffering as an apostle and the cross of Christ that made up an essential aspect of Paul's early preaching among the Galatians. Paul's suffering was the instrument by which he 'publicly portrayed' the crucified Christ 'before [the Galatians'] eyes' (Gal. 3:1).[22]

In Galatians 3:1 and 4:14 Paul is therefore alluding to a complex of ideas that he explicates in detail in 1 Corinthians 4:6–16; 2 Corinthians 1:3–11; 2:14–17; 4:7–12; 6:3–10; and 12:1–10. I have argued elsewhere that in these passages Paul portrays his apostolic suffering as the revelatory vehicle through which the knowledge of God as made manifest in the cross of Christ and in the power of the Spirit is being disclosed.[23] The clearest direct statements of this point are found in the thesis-like affirmations of 1 Corinthians 4:9; 2 Corinthians 1:9–10; 4:10–11; 6:3–10; 12:9–10; and, by way of metaphor, 2 Corinthians 2:14.[24] In these passages Paul's suffering, as the corollary to his message of the cross, is the very instrument God uses to display his resurrection power (cf. too 1 Cor. 2:2–5; 1 Thess. 1:5). This revelation takes place either by God's rescuing Paul from adversity when it was too much to bear, as in 2 Corinthians 1:8–11 and Philippians 2:25–30, or by the even more glorious means of God's strengthening Paul in the midst of adversity that he may endure his suffering with thanksgiving to the glory of God (cf. 2 Cor. 4:7–12; 6:3–10; 12:9; 2 Tim. 2:10).

Paul's life of suffering as an embodiment of the gospel

In 2 Corinthians 4:7 Paul unpacks in a vivid way the identity between his suffering and the gospel of Christ affirmed in Galatians 4:13–14 by reminding the Corinthians that he carried his gospel 'treasure', i.e. 'the knowledge of the glory of God in the face of Christ' (2 Cor. 4:6), in a 'jar of clay', namely, in his sick and persecution-plagued body.[25] This is God's design in order to make it evident that the power of the gospel did not reside in Paul, but belonged to the God who was at work in and through Paul to reveal himself and deliver his people (4:7b). The power of the gospel is so great and its glory so profound that it must be carried in a 'pot', lest people put their trust in Paul himself (cf. 1 Cor. 2:1–5). For although the purpose clause in 2 Corinthians 4:7b is often translated with the idea of 'making manifest' or 'demonstrating', formally it reads, 'in order that the all-surpassing power might *be* ($\bar{e}$) from God and not from us'. As Savage points out, if we take the verb 'to be' seriously in this text, then Paul's point is even more striking: 'it is only in weakness that the power may *be* of God, that [Paul's] weakness in some sense actually serves as the *grounds* for divine power'.[26] When understood in this way, the parallels to 2 Corinthians 12:1–10, where this point is applied to Paul himself (Paul's 'earthen vessel' keeps him humble and dependent on God), and to Galatians 4:13, where it is applied to his public ministry (Paul's earthen vessel is a platform for preaching the gospel to others), are clear. Paul therefore uses the categories of Jesus' death and resurrection in 2 Corinthians 4:10–11 to interpret his experience of suffering and sustenance from 2 Corinthians 4:8–9 because he is convinced that his experience mediates to the world the knowledge of God revealed in Christ. Yet 2 Corinthians 4:10–11 also makes clear that Paul's suffering and experience of God's deliverance are always derivative, since Jesus' death and resurrection, not Paul's own love and fortitude, provide the pattern for Paul's experience and the content of what is mediated to others. Paul's endurance of faith in the midst of suffering is not a 'second atonement', but a mediation of the reality and significance of the death (cross) and life (resurrection) of Jesus. In his preaching and suffering, Paul stands between the glory of God and the life of his congregation as an instrument in the hand of God to mediate the life of faith among God's people. As such, Paul's sufferings are not coincidental, but part of the divine plan for the spread of the gospel (cf. the 'divine passive' in 4:11).

Hence, just as Christ suffered and died to atone for the sins of his people in order to deliver them from the power of this present evil age (Gal. 1:4), so too Paul is called as an apostle to 'die every day' (1 Cor. 15:31) as a means by which the significance of the cross is made real to those to whom the gospel is preached (Gal. 4:13–14). Paul's willingness to suffer on behalf of his churches reflects and embodies Christ's willingness to consider the need of God's people for salvation more important than his own position in glory (cf. Phil. 2:3–5 as supported by 2:6–11). The foolishness of Paul's 'weakness' as a Spirit-filled apostle is the platform upon which God portrays the foolishness of the crucified Christ as the Son of God. Conversely, Paul's endurance in the midst of his suffering is the vehicle by which God displays the reality of the power of the resurrection. Thus, as the 'aroma of Christ' (2 Cor. 2:15), Paul's suffering embodies and extends the same twofold effect brought about by the cross of Christ itself. This is confirmed by the parallels between 1 Corinthians 1:17–18 and 2 Corinthians 2:14–16a:

1. Paul is sent to preach in a mode that corresponds to the cross of Christ (1:17)
2. For (*gar*) (18a)
3. the word of the cross (18a)
4. is foolishness to those who are perishing (18a)
5. to us who are being saved it is the power of God (18c)

1. Paul is 'being led to death', which is a mode of existence that reveals the cross of Christ (2:14)
2. For (*hoti*) (15a)
3. we are an aroma of Christ to God (15)
4. among those who are perishing ... to those a fragrance from death to death (15c, 16a)
5. among those who are being saved ... to those a fragrance from life to life (15b, 16a)

Both the manner of Paul's life and the content of his message were thus determined by the cross of Christ. Due to its cruciform nature, Paul's ministry consequently functioned to further the process of salvation ('life') and judgment ('death') in the lives of others. To reject Paul and his message of the cross as 'foolishness' (1 Cor. 1:18) or 'cursed' (Gal. 4:14) confirmed that one was already 'perishing'. To accept Paul and his message demonstrated that the power of God was already at work to save.

The apologetic function of Paul's suffering

We can now see why in Galatians 4:12–20 Paul suddenly shifted from the theological and scriptural arguments in favour of his gospel to the personal circumstances of his suffering. The latter, no less than the former, provided a foundation for his past preaching in Galatia and for his present polemic against those who would preach a different gospel (cf. 1:6–9). Like Christ on the cross, Paul's coming to Galatia in the 'weakness of the flesh' portrayed Christ's own participation in this evil age. But like the 'new creation' inaugurated at Christ's resurrection, Paul's corresponding endurance and giving of himself to the Galatians demonstrated that already in this age the Spirit is powerfully transforming the lives of believers (cf. Gal. 5:2–6, 16–26; 6:8, 15). For this reason the recounting in 4:13–14 of the Galatians' prior positive response to Paul's preaching, in spite of his weakness, serves a bilateral, bridging function between 4:12 and 4:15–16. Looking back, it supports Paul's assertion in 4:12c that the Galatians had done Paul no injustice in the past (*ouden mē ēdikēsate*). Rather, they had accepted his suffering as the ground of his preaching, since it was the means by which the significance of the cross was made evident in their midst. Looking forward, it supports Paul's rhetorical questions in 4:15a–16 concerning the present. Given their past acceptance of him 'as an angel of God' who brought the message of 'Christ Jesus', Paul is perplexed (4:20; cf. 1:6) that their past 'blessing' (*makarismos*), which they received from doing so, has apparently disappeared (4:15a). Instead, he has now become their 'enemy' for telling them the truth about those who are seeking to exclude the Galatians from being fully fledged members of the people of God (4:17). Paul's real goal, however, like a woman in travail, is to make sure that they stay alive to the gospel until they can mature enough in Christ to avoid such temptations (4:19, *teknia mou ... ōdinō*; cf. 1:6–9; 5:7–8).

Thus, the structure of Paul's argument in 4:12–16 makes it apparent that Paul's reference in 4:15b to the Galatians' past willingness to pluck out their own eyes in order to give them to Paul does not reflect the nature of his 'weakness' (i.e. some sort of eye infirmity).[27] It is best taken as a proverbial reference to the Galatians' past willingness to do whatever was necessary to support Paul's ministry. The Galatians had been so convinced of the gospel of the cross, and had so esteemed their consequent participation in the Spirit as *the* mark of the new age of the new creation under the new covenant (cf. Gal. 1:6a; 3:3a, 4a; 4:6–7, 9a; 5:5, 7a), that they would have been willing to give even their most precious possession for it if need be.[28] Conversely, both Paul's preaching on the basis of his suffering and the Galatians' acceptance of it confirmed that the new age has in fact dawned and that the Galatians, like Paul, were indeed participating in it. Nothing else can adequately explain why Paul would suffer as he does, both personally (2 Cor. 12:7) and vocationally (Gal. 4:13, etc.), and why he would be willing to live like a Gentile, all for the sake of the gospel (4:12a; cf. 1 Cor. 9:21). Likewise, the Galatians' willingness to give their all for Paul is an example of precisely that 'faith working itself out in love' which can only be attributed to the Spirit's work of bringing about a new creation (cf. 5:5–6). In other words,

Paul's love for the Galatians, manifested in his suffering, and the Galatians' love for Paul, manifested in their acceptance of his suffering, are both expressions of a Spirit-induced freedom to serve one another as slaves (5:13; cf. Rom. 15:7–9). In stark contrast, the attempt to exclude the Galatians reveals the Judaizers' own rejection of the gospel, lack of participation in the Spirit, and corresponding impure motives (4:17–18; cf. 2:13; 6:12). Hence, if the Galatians capitulate to their demands, they will be denying the reality of their earlier 'blessing' of the Spirit as the children of Abraham (4:15a; cf. 3:1–5; 5:2–5), and Paul's labour will have been in vain (4:11; cf. 2:2).

The glue that united Paul's thought and life with the message he preached and the mission he conducted was his suffering as an apostle of Jesus Christ. Paul's suffering was the vehicle through which the saving power of God, climactically revealed in Christ, was being made known in the world. To reject the suffering Paul was therefore to reject Christ; to identify with Paul in his suffering was a sure sign that one was being saved by the 'foolishness' and 'stumbling-block' of the cross. For as Joel White has recently demonstrated, 'to be baptized on behalf of the dead' (1 Cor. 15:29) is not an *ad hominem* allusion to some long-lost cultic ritual.[29] Rather, it is a reference to the convert's identification with Paul's ministry as an apostle, which is here once again pictured in terms of 'death' as a metonymy for the daily suffering that Paul endures in hope of the resurrection and final reign of God in Christ (cf. 1 Cor. 15:28, 30–32). In Paul's words, 'For what will those do who are being baptized on account of the 'dead' (i.e., in response to the ministry of the apostles who suffer for the sake of the gospel)? If the truly dead are not being raised, why then are people being baptized on account of them (i.e., on account of the apostles, since their gospel offers no hope)?' (1 Cor. 15:29).[30] Paul would not willingly suffer, and the Corinthian believers would not have accepted his suffering as legitimate, having been baptized as a result, were it not for the truth of Paul's gospel. To do so otherwise would be ludicrous. The same is true for the Galatians. Like the Corinthians, they too cannot deny that Paul, in and through his suffering, was indeed their father in the faith (1 Cor. 3:5; 4:15; Gal. 1:6–9; 3:1–2; 4:13). So they should not go back on Paul's gospel now. In short, 1 Corinthians 15:29 represents the same argument found in Galatians 4:13–14.

In the end, therefore, if it is no longer adequate to speak of Paul as *either* a theologian *or* a missionary, it is also not adequate to speak of him as a theologian *and* a missionary. Paul's apostolic ministry of missionary suffering and his gospel theology were an inseparable unity. Hence, our study confirms what Peter O'Brien, himself a missionary-theologian like Paul, has observed: although there has been a 'paradigm shift' since the 1960s and

... the notion that Paul was both a missionary and a theologian has gained ground among biblical scholars ... Yet Paul's theology and mission do not simply relate to each other as 'theory' to 'practice'. It is not as though his mission is the practical outworking of his theology. Rather, his mission is 'integrally related to his identity and thought', and his theology is a missionary theology.[31]

Paul was a theologically driven missionary and a missiologically driven theologian. His theology was missiological and his missionary endeavours were theological. May Paul's gospel of the crucified and risen Christ and his willingness to embody it through his own endurance of suffering on behalf of others be our 'consuming passion' as well.[32]

Notes

1. 'Ausgangspunkt dieses Vortrags ist die Behauptung, die ich einst eine Behauptung, zugleich prinzipiell und sachlich falsch. Prinzipiell falsch, weil es keine christliche Theologie gibt, die nicht im breiten Sinne kerygmatische Theologie ist; sachlich falsch, weil der historische Paulus als Theologe geschrieben und als Missionar gearbeitet hat.' Barrett, 'Paulus', p. 18. This essay is part of a larger paper presented at the 'Symposium on the mission of the Early Church to Jews and Gentiles', 28–29 April, 1998, at the School of Mission and Theology, Stavanger, Norway. I am indebted to the members of the symposium for their helpful interaction with it.
2. Baasland, 'Persecution', pp. 135–150. But see now the major studies of Goddard & Cummings, 'Ill or ill-treated?' and T. W. Martin, 'Whose flesh?'
3. So e.g. Black, 'Weakness', p. 26, who suggests that 'the obscurity of this passage perhaps cannot be explained in a purely logical way; it is possible that Paul was so overwhelmed by emotion at this point in writing that he simply lost his train of thought. For this reason many scholars are of the opinion that Paul has ceased argumentation and has turned to emotional begging and appealing' (referring to Lagrange, A. Oepke, Burton, and Mussner as examples). Black himself rightly cautions that such psychological interpretations fail to recognize the rhetorical character of this passage, pointing to Betz's analysis of the unit as a Hellenistic 'friendship' topos (pp. 26–27). But if Betz's analysis holds, this still means that Paul's appeal is primarily personal, based on earlier bonds of friendship, rather than theological.
4. So Black, 'Weakness', p. 25.
5. For the exegetical support behind this section, see my 'Paul and the exile', pp. 329–371. This present essay expands the basic point made in the sketch of 4:12–20 found on pp. 354–355. Goddard and Cummins, 'Conflict', pp. 97–99, reject this common reading as 'a convoluted and inexplicable shift from that which Paul has in view in the first clause (the Galatians as judaizers or about to Judaize) to that in view in the second clause (the Galatians as Gentiles)' (p. 97). In their view, this shift is impossible, since, according to Gal. 4:8–11, the Galatians' former state was 'a negative existence in pagan enslavement' (p. 98). But as Paul's argument in 4:12–20 itself makes clear, Paul is referring to their

conversion (cf. 4:9!), not to their pre-conversion state. Certainly Paul is not saying that in Christ he became a pagan! Goddard and Cummins argue that we should simply leave the verbs omitted and take the comparison to be a general one to 'the whole history ... of his relationship with the Galatians and to their shared identity within that relationship' (p. 99). But quite apart from the fact that the dependent clauses require verbs (their omission does not signal their actual absence (!); Goddard and Cummins actually presuppose two present-tense verbs), Paul's argument rides on a comparison between the present and the point of their conversion in the past (cf. 4:8–9 with 14–16).

6. The most natural reading of *dia* + accusative here is causal, since purpose cannot fit the context; cf. BDF §222, 223 (3). The meaning 'by force of', suggested for Rev. 12:11; 13:14, may also fit here. Cf. Martin, 'Flesh', pp. 73–74, for a proper rejection of the common attempt to take this prepositional phrase as modal (as if it were *dia* + genitive), which occurs because commentators have recognized that a causal reading makes Paul's suffering the ground of his preaching in Galatia, when they desire a 'more noble reason'. Martin too seeks such a reason, but finds one only by denying that 4:13 refers to Paul at all (see below). But once Paul's suffering is seen to be his missiological corollary to the cross of Christ, this cause for his preaching is certainly 'noble' enough.

7. That Paul's 21 uses of *euangelizomai* usually refer not to preaching in general, but specifically to preaching the *gospel*, even when the cognate noun is not present as in Gal. 4:13, has been argued by O'Brien, *Consumed by Passion*, p. 62.

8. Black, 'Weakness', p. 29; cf. his arguments in favour of this consensus against its few detractors on pp. 29–31. For uses of the *astheneia* word group to refer to physical sickness within the Pauline corpus, he points to Phil. 2:26–27; 1 Tim. 5:23; 2 Tim. 4:20.

9. Following Martin, 'Flesh', p. 69, whose extensive survey of the use of *sarx* in relationship to *astheneia* uncovers the fact that '... the phrase "weakness of the flesh" (*astheneia tou* [sic] *sarkos*) as a reference to illness does not occur in ancient non-Christian Greek authors before the seventh century AD. Nor do these authors refer to sickness with the adjectival construction "weak flesh" (*sarx asthenēs*).' Instead the references all speak of the 'weakness of the flesh', whether in a healthy or sick body, in terms of its 'weak' nature as porous or susceptible to the influences of fluids and temperature, etc. ('Flesh', pp. 67–69). Thus, the evidence points to the fact that Paul probably coined this phrase, throwing us back on Paul's own argument for its meaning. But given its uniqueness, Martin rejects the consensus view that *astheneia tēs sarkos* refers to Paul's illness, taking it instead to be a reference to the *Galatians'* pre-conversion fleshly condition and consequent need for the gospel as that which drove Paul to evangelize them (pp. 78–79, 82–86; pointing to Jerome as an advocate of the view that the Galatians were the referent of the phrase and to Gal. 2:16, 20; 5:24; and Rom. 5:6–8; 6:19; 15:20–21). It is important to keep in mind, however, that in 4:13 the noun being modified is *astheneia*, not *sarx*, and *sarx* carries the adjectival function, not *astheneia*. Thus, Martin's lexicography is helpful, but in itself could be misleading, since in the relevant texts outside of Paul *astheneia* is being used adjectivally, rather than as the lead noun. Thus, in comparing these texts at the conceptual level we are, in fact, comparing apples and oranges. Furthermore, in terms of the evidence itself, the sample is small. Martin observes that only eight non-Christian passages before the seventh century even connect the two nouns, of which only four use *sarx* as a genitive modifier. Here too

one must be careful with the evidence. Of these four, two use the plural of *sarx* (i.e. 'fleshly parts') and another a derivative of *astheneia* (i.e. 'weak thing' [*asthenēs*], pp. 66–68). In the only other use, Eustratius refers to 'the soul's being fettered on account of the weakness of the flesh (*di' astheneian tēs sarkos*) if the soul does not do praiseworthy things' (Martin, 'Flesh', p. 68), also clearly not a parallel to Paul. So even at the linguistic level, these parallels are, in fact, of little relevance for determining the meaning of Paul's phrase one way or the other, and they certainly do not rule out interpreting *astheneia* as illness in 4:13 in accordance with one of its common meanings. It is therefore overstating the case to conclude, as Martin does, (p. 71, n. 25), that 'since no authors before Paul and no non-Christian authors after him use this phrase to refer to illness, exegetes would probably not have either were it not for the link with 2 Cor. 12:7'. Indeed, Martin suggests that if Paul were referring to his illness in 4:13, this new modification 'would have confused the Galatians, who viewed illness as a problem of the body, not of the flesh. They would have found Paul's newly coined phrase a strange and unusual reference to illness ...' (p. 70). But to be 'strange' and 'unusual', or even idiosyncratic, is far from being incomprehensible, especially if Paul is following the common linguistic convention in his use of *astheneia* as a reference to sickness (Martin himself admits that the absolute use of *astheneia* is a frequent way to designate illness, p. 66). Evidently such confusion did not exist in the early church, since from the beginning Christian tradition (Martin finds 154 uses in Christian literature!) readily took Gal. 4:13 as a parallel to 2 Cor. 12:7, and understood both as a reference to Paul's illness (cf. Heckel, 'Dorn', pp. 76–77, 83–85, referring to Tertullian on 2 Cor. 12:7, who relies already on oral tradition available to him, and Jerome on the parallel between 2 Cor. 12:7 and Gal. 4:13)! Hence, while Martin's lexicography demonstrates the unusual nature of Paul's construction, in doing so it merely highlights Paul's idiosyncratic and theologically motivated description of his sickness as that which is located *in his flesh*. For the close parallel between *di' astheneian tēs sarkos* in 4:13 and *en tē sarki mou* in 4:14 makes it difficult to accept Martin's thesis that the former refers to the Galatians, not Paul, with its implication that v. 13 'no longer informs the interpretation of the succeeding phrase "your temptation in my flesh" in v. 14' (p. 86; see below).

10. This is the central problem with the thesis of Goddard & Cummins, 'Conflict', that Paul's 'weakness' is a reference to some kind of 'bodily weakness due to the trauma of persecution' (p. 95), or some kind of 'bodily trauma due to persecution which attended his original ministry in Galatia' (p. 125). In their view, Paul is calling the Galatians once again to follow Paul's example of faithfulness in suffering for the sake of the gospel, in the line of the suffering righteous and as exemplifying the suffering of Christ (pp. 99, 103, 107), rather than join the Judaizers in order to avoid persecution (cf. 6:11). For although they too argue strongly that *dia* + accusative must provide the ground or reason for Paul's preaching, in order to make their thesis work they must posit that it also includes not only attendant circumstances, but even consequences of Paul's preaching (cf. p. 103, n. 29). Though there is no doubt that Paul suffered as a regular *consequence* of his preaching, this is simply not Paul's point here. Moreover, even if Paul's persecution were in view here, Paul's persecution cannot be equated with his weakness itself, but must simply be seen as another source for it. In reality, Goddard and Cummins are not offering another interpretation of 4:13, but another hypothesis for the cause of Paul's weakness, which is hidden in history. In turn, Paul is not calling the Galatians to suffer

persecution (though that might become necessary), but to return to the gospel Paul preached and embodied in his life. Hence, Goddard and Cummins ultimately reject a reference to illness in 4:13 as unconnected to Paul's appeal in 4:12 because they fail to see the significance of Paul's suffering as that which embodies and reveals the gospel (cf. pp. 101, 116; for my view of this significance, see below).

11. Heckel, 'Dorn', pp. 66–77, 83–85. Heckel, p. 84, points out that Paul could have already been suffering under the same illness mentioned in 2 Cor. 12:7 at the time of Paul's preaching in Galatia, since the 'thorn in the flesh' was given to Paul fourteen years earlier, c. AD 42. Contra Martin, 'Flesh', pp. 71–73, who, rejecting that 4:13 refers to Paul's weakness, consequently denies the link between 4:13 and 2 Cor. 12:7. In addition to his view of 4:13, Martin does so because in 2 Cor. 12:7 the messenger of Satan affects Paul, whereas in 4:13 the temptation affects the Galatians; in 2 Cor. 12:7 the explanatory phrase refers to the sickness itself, whereas 4:14 it refers to the effect, and in 2 Cor. 12:7 the sickness is a messenger of Satan, whereas the Galatians accept Paul as a messenger of God. For my own analysis of the reason for these differences, see below.

12. 'Dorn', p. 80. In view of Paul's silence in 2 Cor. 12:7 and elsewhere, all attempts to determine the nature of Paul's sickness remain purely speculative. The main suggestions have been: epilepsy, an eye sickness, a speech impediment, malaria, leprosy, hysteria or depression (cf. 'Dorn', pp. 80–83, for the sources, and pp. 84–92 for his evaluation).

13. Cf. e.g. Schlier, *Galater*, p. 210; Betz, *Galatians*, p. 84; Black, 'Weakness', pp. 29, 35. Surprisingly, Heckel, 'Dorn', pp. 84–85, 91–92, also opts for a circumstantial reading of Gal. 4:13–14 in which Paul's sickness held him up in Galatia.

14. Black, 'Weakness', pp. 35–36.

15. For an investigation of the broad cultural values current in first-century Graeco-Roman society, see Savage, *Power*, pp. 19–53. Contra Martin, 'Flesh', pp. 78, 87–90, in view of Gal. 6:13, construes the temptation in 4:14 to be the fact that Paul himself was circumcised, since Gentiles disdained the practice. Yet it is difficult to see how this could have tempted the Galatians to reject Paul, since a hallmark of his gospel was its explicit exclusion of the necessity of such 'works of the law' (Gal. 2:3–5, 16, 18; 3:2–5; 5:3–6; 6:12–15). Moreover, this reading of 4:14 does not fit as well with the argument of 4:12 and 15: if they were tempted to disdain Paul as a circumcised male, then in what sense are they to become like him (to be circumcised but to ignore its significance)? If what potentially offended the Galatians was Paul's circumcision, was this the stumbling-block with Christ too (rather than the cross?), since Paul equates accepting him with accepting Christ? And would not Paul's emphasis here on their acceptance of Paul and Jesus as circumcised males play into the hands of the Judaizers? Moreover, Martin's position entails viewing the problem in Galatia to be the Galatians' desire to return to paganism rather than submitting to the Judaizers' demand for circumcision (which they now see to be a legitimate part of the Christian message), in contrast to the prevailing view of the problem in which they were being persuaded to join the Judaizers themselves (cf. his 'Apostasy'). Finally, such a reading finds no thematic support in the immediate context, which is based on the curse-tradition from Deuteronomy (see below), not the issue of circumcision.

16. Baasland, 'Persecution', p. 141.

17. So too Baasland, 'Persecution', p. 142. As Baasland points out, Paul's failure to require circumcision of his converts could be taken as 'cursing Abraham', which results in falling under the curse of God (cf. Gen. 12:3).

18. Cf. s.v. *ekptyō*, BAGD, p. 244: literally, '*spit* (out) as a sign of disdain … 2) or to ward off evil spirits … hence *disdain* …', and s.v. *exoutheneō*, BAGD, p. 277, which suggests that, since the meaning 'reject something' is well attested for both *diaptyō* and *periptyō*, Gal. 4:14 may be translated, 'You neither treated me with contempt nor did you turn away from the temptation that my physical appearance might have become to you.'

19. Contra Goddard & Cummins, 'Conflict', pp. 105–107, and Martin, 'Flesh', p. 75, who, in line with their respective views of 4:13, take *ekptyō* and *exoutheneō* simply to be synonyms for scorn and disdain (cf. their use in Mark 9:12; 10:34; 14:65; Matt. 26:27; Luke 18:32; 23:11; Acts 4:11; 1 Cor. 1:28; 6:4; 16:11; Rom 14:3,10; etc.).

20. Cf. Schlier, *ekptyō*, pp. 448–449, who is quite certain that this is its meaning here. So too Heckel, 'Dorn', p. 84: 'Für die Galater muß daher die Versuchung nahegelegen haben, in Paulus wegen seiner Schwäche einen dämonisch Befallenen zu sehen.' Cf. Mark 7:33; 8:23; *T.Sol.* 7:3 and the references in Heckel, pp. 85–86, nn. 121–127.

21. Baasland, 'Persecution', p. 146. The implication of this identification has already been given in the counter-curse of 1:8!

22. Here I am more emphatic than Goddard & Cummins, 'Conflict', p. 110, n. 62, who suggest that 'the vivid and visual (rather than aural) language' of Gal. 3:1 'might possibly suggest that Paul *himself* tangibly represented the crucified Christ before the Galatians – not least in the marks of persecution upon his body (cf. 6:17)' (emphasis theirs).

23. For this thesis, with 2 Cor. 2:14 as its centre-piece, see my *Suffering and the Spirit*, slightly abridged as *Suffering and Ministry*. For the similarities and differences between 1 Cor. 4:8–13 and 2 Cor. 4:7–12 as these reflect the essential difference between the situations behind the two letters, together with the parallels between 1 Cor. 4:9; 2 Cor. 2:14 and 4:11 outlined below, see my *Suffering and Ministry*, pp. 59–71.

24. Though Paul's allusion to the Roman triumphal procession in 2 Cor. 2:14 is widely granted, not all have agreed with me that the metaphor of 'being led in a triumphal procession' (*thriambeuō*) should be decoded to picture Paul as a captured slave of Christ who is being led to *death* in Christ by God as the means by which the knowledge of God is being made known in the world. But the structural and semantic parallels between 1 Cor. 4:9; 2 Cor. 2:14 and 2 Cor. 4:11 continue to convince me of my reading (see below). Furthermore, in the other passages within the Corinthian correspondence in which Paul discusses his experiences as an apostle, it is evident that for Paul 'death' is a metonymy for suffering (1 Cor. 4:8–13 [cf. 4:9]; 2 Cor. 1:3–11 [cf. 1:9]; 4:7–12 [cf. 4:10]; 6:3–10 [cf. 6:9]). For the two most substantive criticisms of my proposal, see Schröter, *Der versöhnte Versöhner*, and Scott, 'Triumph'. But neither Schröter nor Scott deals seriously with the exact parallels between 1 Cor. 4:9; 2 Cor. 2:14 and 2 Cor. 4:11 that support my reading. What is significant about these texts is that in 1 Cor. 4:9 and 2 Cor. 4:11 Paul is explicitly discussing the role of his *suffering* as an apostle in his ministry of the gospel, not merely his role in preaching the gospel per se (*à la* Schröter), nor his mystical experiences (*à la* Scott). Moreover, my view does most justice to its immediate context by explaining the transition from Paul's concern over Titus in 2:12–13 to his praise for God in 2:14. Finally, one must ask what the metaphor contributes materially to the discussion at hand. In Schröter's view the metaphor becomes redundant, since the motif of revelation is already explicitly mentioned in the verse (cf. *phanerounti*). In Scott's view, the metaphor contributes something

unique to the text, since there is no other referent in the context to Paul's visionary experiences as the basis of his revelatory function. In fact, in 2 Cor. 12:1–9 Paul explicitly denies that such personal and ecstatic visions of God's glory are the basis or subject of what we communicate to others. So in the first case, Schröter's view says too little. In the latter case, Scott's view says too much.

25. As Savage has pointed out (*Power through Weakness*, p. 165), the idea of picturing humans as 'jars of clay' ('earthen vessels') was common in the ancient world, including the Qumran writings, as a metaphor for human weakness (cf. the references to clay pots as weak and prone to break in Ps. 30:13, LXX; Is. 30:14, LXX, and in 1QS 11:22; 1QH 1:21–22; 3:20–21; 4:29; etc.). Read in this way, Paul's image points to a contrast between his own suffering and the power of God. Others, however, see it as metaphor of 'cheapness', based on Lam. 4:2, LXX, thus establishing a contrast between Paul's lack of significance or worth and the surpassing value of the treasure. Some argue that both ideas of being 'weak' and 'inferior' are present here (as in Lev. 6:21; 15:12, LXX), so that 4:7 provides a contrast to both the 'treasure' and the 'power of God.' In Savage's words, 'the glorious gospel is borne about by those who are comparatively inferior, the powerful gospel by those who are weak' (p. 66). This reading is possible, but the purpose clause in verse 7b seems to indicate that the point of contrast is God's power, and hence the intention of the image is to highlight the weakness of Paul.

26. *Power through Weakness*, p. 166 (emphasis mine).

27. Cf. already Lightfoot, *Galatians*, p. 301, who followed Theodore of Mopsuestia in arguing that the reference to writing with 'large letters' in Gal. 6:11 is not a consequence of Paul's bad eyesight, but a way of emphasizing 'the force of the apostle's convictions' in that they will 'arrest the attention of his readers in spite of themselves'.

28. For the expression 'to pluck out the eyes' as a reference to making the ultimate sacrifice, see Black, 'Weakness', pp. 32–33, who points e.g. to Deut. 32:10; Ps. 17:8; Prov. 7:2; Zech. 2:8; and Horace, *Sat.* ii.5, 33, following the commentaries of Eadie and André Viard. Cf. Goddard & Cummins, 'Conflict', p. 111, n. 67, who also point to this background. The difficulty of applying this insight to their overall thesis is illustrated by their attempt, pp. 112–113, to go on to argue that this metaphor is an actual reference to the gouging out of the eyes as one of the cruelest tortures inflicted on the persecuted (cf. the experience of the martyrs in 4 Macc. 5:29–30). As such, Paul is speaking of the Corinthians' earlier willingness to suffer with Paul and for the gospel. The problem with this view is that the Galatians were willing to pluck out their own eyes for Paul's sake, which can hardly mean a willingness to persecute themselves.

29. White, '"Baptized"', pp. 488–491.

30. See White, '"Baptized"', pp. 493–499, who argues that *hoi baptizomenoi* is to be taken literally, *hyper* is to be understood in its causal sense, *tōn nekrōn* is to be taken metaphorically as a reference to the apostles, and *nekroi* refers to the literal dead, modified by *holōs* (i.e. 'truly dead persons').

31. O'Brien, *Consumed by Passion*, pp. xi–xii.

32. A passionate heart for God's glory in the mission of the gospel, matched by a keen mind in service of the Scriptures, in a humble spirit submitted to Christ – Professor O'Brien has been an example to me of what it means to worship God in Spirit and truth. It is a gift to know him.

11. 'What does it matter?' Priorities and the *adiaphora* in Paul's dealing with opponents in his mission

Richard N. Longenecker

One of the seemingly strange things about Paul is that while he argued single-mindedly and vigorously – even vehemently and defiantly – for 'the truth of the gospel', he also responded diversely to those who opposed him: sometimes castigating them in caustic and virulent language; at other times pleading with them in a somewhat self-deprecating and humble manner; and at still other times taking a rather relaxed attitude towards them and their preaching. Three situations reflected in his letters come immediately to mind. The first is his response to certain Jewish believers from Jerusalem who followed him throughout Galatia and were confusing his converts; the second, his response to some of the believers at Corinth who opposed him; the third, his response to some Christian leaders at Philippi who were jealous of him and sought to make trouble for him.

But while Paul's reactions in certain conflict situations have often been seen to be a bit strange – even, perhaps, somewhat contradictory – his differing responses in the three cases cited above should most likely be understood as (1) springing from an inner consistency of thought and action in his own life and ministry, and (2) setting a paradigm for the thought, actions and ministries of Christians today. For the apostle's responses in these situations reflect both the central priorities and the *adia-phora* of his mission – that is, both matters of great importance and matters of relative indifference, at least as he saw them. And even though it is often confusing to sort out issues that belong to the one category or the other, a

147

study of Paul's responses in such conflict situations has much to teach us with regard to our own priorities, reactions and activities today.

The situation of Galatians and Paul's response

Galatians is a letter that has been variously dated, variously interpreted and variously applied. Most of the issues regarding provenance and interpretation, however, need not detain us here.[1] All we want to do in this article is to sketch out the situation that Paul faced when writing to his Galatian converts and to highlight certain features of his response.

The situation

Paul's opponents in the Roman province of Galatia were, it seems, Jewish believers in Jesus who came from the Jerusalem church to Paul's churches with a message that called for Gentile believers to be circumcised and to keep the rudiments of the Jewish calendar. Undoubtedly they presented their message as being biblically and theologically based. Furthermore, they evidently claimed to be interested only in Gentile Christians being fully integrated into the chosen people of Israel, and so full recipients of the blessings of the Abrahamic covenant. Probably they asserted that they represented the concerns of James, Peter and the Jerusalem church regarding Jewish–Gentile relations in Christian communities outside of Palestine. And probably, as well, they portrayed themselves as not being in opposition to Paul but as seeking only to complete his message, thereby bringing Galatian believers to perfection.

Paul, however, accuses these 'Judaizers' of wanting Gentile Christians to be circumcised primarily in order 'to avoid being persecuted for the cross of Christ' and so 'that they may boast about your flesh' (Gal. 6:12–13). Such an evaluation of their motives suggests that in the rising tide of Jewish nationalism – which existed during the decades prior to the nation's final conflict with Rome in AD 66–70, with antagonism from Jewish Zealots being directed against any Israelite who had Gentile sympathies or who associated with Gentile sympathizers – these Jewish believers from Jerusalem wanted Gentile Christians to be circumcised so that they might be able to demonstrate to their Jewish compatriots how belief in Jesus brought Gentiles into the fold of Judaism, and so thwart any Jewish purification campaign against the church at Jerusalem.

Paul's response

Paul's response to these Judaizers is direct, forceful and condemnatory –
even, in fact, caustic and crude. Immediately after the letter's salutation, he
denounces the Judaizers' message as being 'no gospel at all' – not a supplement to the Christian gospel (an *allo euangelion*), as they evidently claimed,
but a different kind of message altogether (a *heteron euangelion*) – and
declares that their teaching causes people to depart from 'the one [God] who
called' them and confuses and perverts 'the gospel of Christ' (1:6–7). He
twice pronounces an anathema (*anathema estō*) on them and their
preaching (1:8–9), with the word *anathema* meaning 'delivered over to
divine wrath for destruction' and so 'accursed' (RSV, NRSV) or 'eternally
condemned' by God (NIV). And, in what is surely the crudest of all his extant
statements, he says that his wish for his opponents who wanted to circumcise his Gentile converts is that 'they would go the whole way and
emasculate themselves!' (5:12).

Yet while it is stern in its warnings and admonitions, Paul's response to
the Gentile Christians of Galatia – who had evidently begun to observe the
Jewish cultic calendar (cf. 4:10), but not yet submitted to the rite of circumcision (cf. 4:9, 21) – is nowhere near as vitriolic as it is to those who were
troubling and confusing them. He addresses them as *adelphoi* ('brothers
and sisters') at a number of places in his letter (1:11; 3:15; 4:12; 31; 5:11; 13;
6:1, 18), thereby reminding them of his and their family relationship, even
though they were beginning to forget it. Likewise, he speaks of his fears and
perplexities about them (4:11, 20), reminds them of their former concerns
for him (4:13–15), pleads with them for a present positive response (4:12),
and expresses his confidence in them as to their final commitments (5:10).

But he also cannot bring himself to include an opening thanksgiving
section in his Galatian letter, as he does in all of his other extant letters.
Rather, he (1) expresses astonishment over his converts' proposed acceptance of 'another gospel' (1:6); (2) calls them 'foolish' or 'undiscerning' for
not appreciating the work of the Spirit and the importance of faith in their
lives (3:1–9); (3) warns them quite sternly of the disastrous results of
following the Judaizers' programme (3:10–12; 4:8–9; 5:2–4); (4) exhorts
them to live in love and by the direction of the Spirit (5:22–25), and (5) asks
them to help one another in their Christian lives (6:1–10).

The central priority of Paul's missionary activity was what he calls 'the
truth of the gospel' (2:5 and 14; cf. 2 Cor. 11:10, 'the truth of Christ'; Col. 1:5,
'the word of the truth of the gospel'). He defines this gospel in terms of the
grace of God (1:3, 6, 15, passim), the work of Christ (1:4; 2:16–17; 3:13–14a;

4:5; 6:14; *passim*), the ministry of the Holy Spirit (3:3–5; 5:16, 22–25; *passim*), and the faith of believers (2:16–17; 3:2, 5, 6–9, 14b; 3:26; *passim*). Thus he closes his Galatian letter with the statement: 'May I never boast except in the cross of our Lord Jesus Christ, through which the world has been crucified to me, and I to the world' (6:14). And he contextualizes this central focus of the Christian gospel for his Galatian converts in their situation as follows: 'Neither circumcision nor uncircumcision means anything; what counts is a new creation' (6:15).

So when Paul speaks about those who were detracting from the truth of the gospel and confusing his converts with 'another' teaching that contradicted it, he speaks in language that is both denunciatory and condemnatory. While his opponents may have presented themselves as pious and devout believers in Jesus, used carefully formulated biblical and theological arguments, and expressed personal outrage at any suggestion that their message was motivated by anything other than the best of intentions, Paul views their actions and teachings as perverting the gospel of Christ, undermining his ministry to Gentiles, and being under the condemnation of God. It is therefore, as Paul saw it, to be directly, openly and fervently opposed – just as at Syrian Antioch, in a situation that was somewhat similar, he had previously opposed Peter and other Jewish believers because 'he was clearly wrong' and 'they were not acting in line with the truth of the gospel' (2:11–14).

The situation of 2 Corinthians and Paul's response

2 Corinthians is a difficult writing to analyse, chiefly because of uncertainties regarding its compositional character. There is no external manuscript evidence for any of the partition theories proposed for the letter. Nonetheless, there are a number of internal features that suggest that the work should be seen as a composite of various Pauline letters (or, portions of letters), which have been somehow brought together to form what we now have as 2 Corinthians. These internal matters have to do with (1) changes of tone and rhetorical style in the writing, most obviously between chapters 1 – 7 (or, 1 – 9) and 10 – 13; (2) the seemingly disparate character of some portions of the writing, chiefly that of 6:14–7:1; (3) the separate treatments of Titus and the brothers in chapter 8 and of the collection in chapter 9; and (4) references to events in Paul's life and allusions to relations with his Corinthian converts that seem to suggest various times of writing – principally his statement 'This is the third time I am coming to you' of 13:1; his reference to having written the Corinthians a letter 'out of great distress and

anguish of heart and with many tears' after a 'painful visit' with them in 2:1–4; and various allusions in chapters 10 – 13 to strained relations between the Corinthian Christians and Paul.

A number of competent scholars have argued for the unity of 2 Corinthians, most often positing some type of 'compositional hiatus' between chapters 1 – 7 (or, 1 – 9) and 10 – 13. The major problem with such a view has always been: why, then, did Paul retain that earlier conciliatory section of chapters 1 – 7, which speaks of his joy over his Corinthian converts' repentance, in a letter that he then concludes in chapters 10 – 13 in such a severe, harsh and even sarcastic manner? Most scholars today, therefore, have invoked some type of 'partition theory' and postulated some such order for Paul's Corinthian correspondence as follows: (1) a 'previous letter', which is referred to in 1 Corinthians 5:9 and is either 'lost' or represented (to some extent) by 2 Corinthians 6:14–7:1; (2) our present 1 Corinthians, which is a unified letter; (3) an 'intermediate letter', which is possibly referred to in 2 Corinthians 2:3–4; (4) a 'severe letter', which now appears as 2 Corinthians 10 – 13; and (5) a 'conciliatory letter', which now appears as 2 Corinthians 1 – 7 and was written about AD 57–58 – with, perhaps, chapters 8 and 9 appended to that final letter.

We need not get bogged down here in the current critical debates regarding the composition of 2 Corinthians. The integrity of what is written – that is, that Paul is the author of all that we have in 2 Corinthians – is not in question. Nor is it questioned that what Paul wrote in 2 Corinthians has conditions at Corinth in view. It is, in reality, only the historical order of the 'conciliatory letter' (chs. 1 – 7) and the 'severe letter' (chs. 10 –13) that is of any importance for a discussion of Paul's responses to his detractors at Corinth. But even that issue is not of overwhelming significance for dealing with the fact of opposition to Paul among certain Corinthians Christians and the highlighting of how he responds to them.

The situation

However we relate the various portions of 2 Corinthians to one another, it seems obvious that Paul's relations with his Corinthian converts were often strained and that he had his detractors among the Christians of that city. It is clear from chapters 10 – 13 that there was a breakdown of relations between them. For evidently they were claiming that Paul was timid and unimpressive and that he lacked eloquence when with them in person, but that he wrote bold and forceful letters when away from them (10:1–11), that Paul's ministry, when compared with that of others, was not very significant

(10:12–18), and that Paul in his person was somehow inferior to the more imposing 'apostles' of their acquaintance (11:1 – 12:21). And in chapters 1 – 7, even amid a certain conciliatory tone that exists throughout these chapters, there still reverberates a refrain of difficulty and distrust between Paul and his converts – as, for example, his reference to a former 'painful visit' (2:1), his statements about the distress caused by that visit (2:2–4), his allusions to grief caused by someone in some particular situation at Corinth (2:5–11), and various hints that he was aware of a growing unhappiness among his converts regarding his ministry (e.g. 3:1–3, passim).

Paul's converts at Corinth seem to have wanted an apostle who was forceful and eloquent in his preaching and teaching (more of a 'trained speaker' than he appeared to be); one who was a bold leader about whom they could 'boast' (not one who exhibited weaknesses in his leadership); and one who compared well with the other 'apostles' of their acquaintance (not one who was inferior to them in his person). They seem to have thought of themselves as commendable people who needed an apostle who was also commendable; a strong people who needed strong leadership. And in their debates about how to rank their leaders, their apostle and their 'superapostles,' they seem to have entered into 'quarrelling, jealousy, outbursts of anger, factions, slander, gossip, arrogance and disorder' and to have taken matters of 'impurity, sexual sins, and debauchery' to be rather incidental concerns – not only countenancing such matters but also indulging in them (cf. 12:20–21).

Paul's response

Paul's response to his Corinthian converts in 2 Corinthians is twofold. With respect to 'the truth of Christ' (11:10), his converts' 'sincere and pure devotion to Christ' (11:3), and their lives of holiness (13:2–7), he has a 'godly jealousy' for them (11:2) and admonishes them quite sternly – comparable in many ways to his admonitions to his converts in Galatia (cf. esp. the wording of such passages as 10:11; 11:4; 12:20). Thus, for example, his opening words in chapters 10 – 13 are words of passion and rebuke:

> I beg you that when I come I may not have to be as bold as I expect to be toward some people who think that we live by the standards of this world (10:2).

> What we are in our letters when we are absent we will be in our actions when we are present (10:11).

I am jealous for you with a godly jealousy. I promised you to one husband, to Christ, so that I might present you as a pure virgin to him. But I am afraid that just as Eve was deceived by the serpent's cunning, your minds may somehow be led astray from your sincere and pure devotion to Christ (11:2–3).

And his concluding words of these chapters comprise a series of severe warnings and admonitions:

This will be my third visit to you. 'Every matter must be established by the testimony of two or three witnesses' [quoting Deut. 19:15]. I already gave you a warning when I was with you the second time, and I now repeat it while absent: on my return I will not spare those who sinned earlier or any of the others (13:1–2).

Examine yourselves to see whether you are in the faith; test yourselves. Do you not realize that Christ Jesus is in you – unless, of course, you fail the test? (13:5).

This is why I write these things when I am absent, that when I come I may not have to be harsh in my use of authority – the authority that the Lord gave me for building you up, not for tearing you down (13:10).

With respect to his detractors' accusations against him personally, however, Paul is somewhat self-deprecating and responds more humbly. He speaks of a traumatic personal experience that took place in the province of Asia at some time when he was away from Corinth – probably shortly before writing what he wrote in chapters 1 – 7 and interprets that experience as something brought about by God for his converts' 'comfort and salvation' (1:4–7). It was a time when he was 'under great pressure, far beyond our ability to endure, so that we despaired even of life' – when, in fact, he 'felt the sentence of death' and experienced 'deadly peril' (1:8–11). And he continues to allude to that experience elsewhere in chapters 1 – 7, principally in 1:3–7 and 4:7–12.

In chapters 10 – 13 he couches his response in terms of his love for his detractors (e.g. 11:11; 12:15) and his desire for their perfection (e.g. 10:8–9; 13:11). And in responding to their accusations, he 'boasts' about certain features of his ministry and certain incidents in his life that he believes ought to indicate that their assertions against him are invalid. But he does this, it needs to be noted, in a somewhat self-deprecatory and humble fashion.

One such feature of his ministry was his willingness not to be a financial burden to the believers at Corinth, but to proclaim 'the gospel of God' to them 'free of charge' (11:7–12). Another was the whole set of circumstances related to his Jewish heritage and apostolic experiences, which should authenticate to anyone his claim to be a 'servant of Christ' (11:22–33). Another was his experience of having been 'caught up' in a vision 'to the third heaven' – that is, 'to Paradise' – and hearing 'inexpressible things, things that a person is not permitted to tell' (12:1–6). Another, of being given by God 'a thorn in my flesh, a messenger of Satan, to torment me,' but also being assured by God: 'My grace is sufficient for you, for my power is made perfect in weakness' (12:7–9). And still another was the complex of 'signs, wonders and miracles' expressed in his ministry among the Corinthians themselves, which marked him out as an apostle and should have settled the matter of his authority among them (12:11–13).

In the repetition of these features and incidents from his life and ministry, Paul speaks somewhat sarcastically, rebuking the self-serving pride and blatant impertinence of those who levelled accusations against him. But he also, it needs to be noted, responds to his detractors with self-depreciation and humility, saying that he has been forced by them to make such boasts – or, as he says in 12:11: 'I have made a fool of myself, but you drove me to it.'

The situation of Philippians and Paul's response

Scholars have often taken Philippians to be a composite of two or three letters – for example, a letter of thanks for a monetary gift in 4:10–23; another letter regarding Paul's ministry at Philippi in 1:1 – 3:1 and 4:4–7; and another letter on certain disturbances within the Philippian church in 3:2 – 4:3 and 4:8 – 9. On such a view, one must first determine the respective situations and relative chronologies of the various parts of the writing before dealing with any of its themes. But partition theories for Philippians are usually seen today as being, in the words of W. G. Kümmel, 'totally unconvincing'[2] – and deservedly so.

More serious is the question of the letter's provenance and date. For while 1:12–26 indicates quite clearly that it was written from prison, the question remains: was it written from Ephesian imprisonment (at some time during AD 53–57), from Caesarean imprisonment (about AD 58–59), or from Roman imprisonment (about AD 60–62)? Issues regarding provenance usually have to do with (1) the number and nature of the journeys between Philippi and Rome as reflected in the letter, and (2) the kinship of the contents and rhetoric of the letter to Paul's other letters, particularly to material found in Galatians and 2 Corinthians. Cogent arguments can be mounted in support of each of these postulated situations and times. I personally favour, for reasons long ago set out by C. H. Dodd,[3] the view that Philippians was written from Roman imprisonment, and so after Galatians and 2 Corinthians. Obviously, whatever is accepted with respect to the provenance and date of Philippians has a profound effect on how one relates its themes, rhetoric and language to the other Pauline letters. Yet on this matter of Paul's responses to those who opposed him, the data from Galatians, 2 Corinthians and Philippians bear striking resemblances of tone and content, as well as distinguishable differences of response, and so can be treated together, whatever the exact provenances and dates of the letters themselves and/or pertinent sections within those letters.

The situation

The exact nature of the situation addressed in Philippians is difficult to determine. What can be inferred with confidence from the letter itself, however, whether viewed as a single letter or as a collection of two or three letters, is (1) that Christians at Philippi were experiencing some kind of hostility, which Paul believed called for instruction on his part as to how they should live under such conditions, and (2) that certain Christian teachers were opposing Paul in some manner, which motivated Paul to speak about those teachers and to instruct his converts regarding how to respond to them. These two matters – hostility against Paul's converts and opposition to Paul himself – seem to have been related in some way, for intertwined throughout Philippians are ethical teachings for Christians who find themselves in a hostile environment (cf. 1:27 – 2:18; 3:12 – 4:9) coupled with statements about those who opposed Paul (cf. 1:15–18; probably also 3:2–11).

Paul's response

The exact nature of the situation at Philippi may be difficult to ascertain. Nonetheless, it is clear that when Paul deals with the issues faced by his addressees – whether external hostility or internal division – he does so by using the Christ-hymn of 2:6–11 as the basis for his pastoral instructions and the paradigm for how his converts should think and act.

So in dealing with how his converts should live in the face of hostility, Paul holds up the example of Christ as lauded in 2:6–11. For though Christ possessed equality with God, he willingly humbled himself in the incarnation and became obedient throughout his earthly ministry, even to the extent of death (vv. 6–8) – with that attitude and action being approved by God, who then exalted him to the highest of positions (vv. 9–11).

In the exhortations that immediately precede and follow this Christ-hymn, Paul urges believers at Philippi, who were facing some type of external hostility, to adopt Christ's attitude of humility, steadfast obedience, and concern for others. Thus on the basis of the Christ-hymn of 2:6–11 he exhorts his converts: 'Do nothing out of selfish ambition or vain conceit' (2:3a); be humble and 'consider others better than yourselves' (2:3b); 'look not only to your own interests, but also to the interests of others' (2:4); continue in a life of obedience (2:12a); 'continue to work out your own salvation with fear and trembling' (2:12b); 'do everything without complaining or arguing' (2:14); 'hold on to the word of life' (2:16a), and 'be glad and rejoice with me' (2:18). He also implies on the basis of this confessional portion that God will vindicate them for their steadfast adherence to the gospel in the midst of hostility, for God has set the precedent for such action in his vindication of Christ.

Then Paul goes on to show how this pattern of humility, obedience and concern for others was being exemplified in the ministries of two of his co-workers, who were well-known to his addressees: (1) in the ministry of Timothy, whom he characterizes as one who 'takes a genuine interest in your welfare' and 'has served with me in the work of the gospel' (2:19–24), and (2) in the ministry of Epaphroditus (2:25–30), whom he describes as the one 'you sent to take care of my needs,' who 'almost died for the work of Christ' (2:25–30). Furthermore, he declares his desire to have the pattern of Christ's life reflected in his own life (3:10–11). Then he presents certain features and motivations of his own ministry, which he believes reflect the paradigm given by Christ, as a further example for his converts to follow (3:12–21). And he concludes his letter by reminding the Philippians of how this pattern of humility, obedience and concern was expressed in their repeated financial support of him, for which he thanks them and assures them of God's blessing for their actions (4:10–19).

Likewise, when Paul speaks of the Christian teachers at Philippi who opposed him, he also makes use of the main themes of the Christ-hymn of 2:6–11. For when compared with the attitudes and actions of Christ, the selfish ambitions and feigned sincerity of those teachers (1:15–18) – together with their activities (whether actual or possible) as 'mutilators of the flesh' (3:2–3) – come off quite badly. Implied throughout the Philippian letter, in fact, are requests (1) for the opposing teachers to measure themselves by the attitudes and actions of Christ, not by their envious reactions to Paul, and (2) for the Philippian believers to judge those teachers in terms of how they model Christ's pattern of humility and obedience, not by their pretensions or claims.

It is most significant for our purposes, however, to note that when Paul deals with issues at Philippi his response is twofold, just as it was when responding to conflict situations in his churches in the province of Galatia and at Corinth. For when dealing with 'Judaizing' perversions of the gospel – whether then being actively promulgated at Philippi, or viewed by Paul as a live possibility, or only remembered from his experience with the Judaizers in Galatia – he speaks quite sternly and in denunciatory fashion: 'Watch out for those dogs, those men who do evil, those mutilators of the flesh! For it is we who are the circumcision; we who worship by the Spirit of God, who glory in Christ Jesus and put no confidence in the flesh!' (3:2–3). Yet when he refers to a situation where the gospel is being truly proclaimed, but the motivations of some of those who proclaim it are suspect ('some preach Christ out of envy and rivalry, but others out of good will – the latter do so in love, knowing that I am put here for the defence of the gospel; the former preach Christ out of selfish ambition, not sincerely, supposing that they can stir up trouble for me while I am in chains', 1:15–17), he responds: 'What does it matter? The important thing is that in every way, whether from false motives or true, Christ is preached. And because of this I rejoice' (1:18).

Some observations and conclusions

The important point to observe in these three conflict situations is that Paul was able to distinguish between the priorities of the gospel *and* the *adiaphora* (or, issues of relative indifference). There were in his mind at least two categories of concerns: (1) matters of central significance, which must be proclaimed forthrightly, applied to the lives of people appropriately and defended stoutly; and (2) matters of relative indifference, which were not to be confused with the central issues and about which one could be relatively flexible, even though one may have one's own preferences.

The genius of Paul was that he was able to make distinctions between the central priorities of the Christian gospel and the *adiaphora* in his mission, and to make them for the benefit of the gospel and the good of his converts. This ability does not, of course, provide a full explanation for the success of Paul's Christian mission to the Gentile world, for undoubtedly many other factors – both human and divine – were also at work in his ministry. But such an ability should be seen as one important feature of his mental outlook and mission – an ability, it seems, that not all of his apostolic associates had, at least to the same degree (as suggested by the 'Antioch episode' of Gal. 2:11–14, where, from Paul's perspective, Peter was 'terribly wrong' in not seeing how eating separately with Jewish believers undercut an important principle of the gospel; other Jewish believers of the city 'joined him in his hypocrisy', and 'even Barnabas was led astray').

And this same ability to distinguish between central priorities and the *adiaphora* characterized, in large measure, Martin Luther, the great Protestant Reformer of the first half of the sixteenth century. Admittedly, many of Luther's 'protestant' convictions were developed over a span of time during his early days; and much of what he said and wrote was not particularly unique or even highly important – as he himself, on both counts, frequently acknowledged. Furthermore, Luther was a man of his day, with frequent use of earthy (though not obscene) expressions, coarse (though not bawdy or lascivious) language, and polemical invective – as is amply attested, in particular, in his recorded *Table Talk* in the former Augustinian Black Cloister at Wittenberg, where he lived from his marriage to Katherine von Bora in 1525 to his death in 1546. By today's standards, Luther could hardly be called 'politically correct' in many of his ideas or much of his speech. But Luther was a genius at being able to discern between the central priorities of the Christian gospel and many other matters of relative indifference. And that ability should be credited as going a long way toward the establishment of the Protestant Reformation.

For example, in Part II of his 1539 tractate 'On the Councils and the Church', where he discusses the historical significance of the apostolic council at Jerusalem (Acts 15) and the first four ecumenical councils of Nicea (325), Constantinople (381), Ephesus (431) and Chalcedon (451), Luther makes a number of distinctions between the central priorities of the gospel and the *adiaphora* of those days. One such issue has to do with the date of Easter, which had split Christendom into warring parties – with the eastern church, Anabaptists and other sectarians (the so-called *Rotten*) on one side of the debate, and western Christendom being generally on the other. For while Luther believed that the eastern church, Anabaptists and others were on this matter essentially right, and western Christendom wrong, he also viewed this issue as part of the *adiaphora*, and so insisted:

> Therefore I advise that one let Easter come as it now comes, and keep it as it is kept now, and let the old garment be patched and torn (as

was said); and let Easter wobble back and forth until the Last Day, or until the monarchs, in view of these facts [i.e. astronomical calculations] unanimously and simultaneously change it. For this is not going to kill us, nor will St. Peter's bark suffer distress because of it, since it is neither heresy nor sin ... but only an error or solecism in astronomy, which serves temporal government rather than the church.[4]

Or, again on Acts 15, Luther argues that central to a proper interpretation of the Jerusalem council is the distinction that must be made between the central doctrinal issue that drew the council together (i.e. the necessity of circumcision for the acceptance of Gentile believers) and certain peripheral issues that the council also discussed (i.e. the four ethical issues dealt with in the so-called Jerusalem Decree) – with the former seen as binding on the Christian conscience, but the latter viewed as matters of concern for that day.[5] And in his treatment of the first four ecumenical councils, Luther also distinguishes between the central matters of doctrine at issue in the church's deliberations – that is, the divinity of Christ against Arius (at Nicea), the divinity of the Holy Spirit against Macedonius (at Constantinople), the one person of Christ against Nestorius (at Ephesus), and the two natures in Christ against Eutyches (at Chalcedon), where the councils sought to protect the church from error – and the *adiaphora*, where no new articles of faith were created but only matters relative to that day were considered.[6]

It is in his *Table Talk*, however, which has sometimes been something of an embarrassment to modern admirers of Luther, that such distinctions between the central priorities of the gospel and the *adiaphora* particularly appear. So, for example, when speaking about baptism and its administration (i.e. whether cold or warm water should be used), Luther is quoted as saying in December 1532:

I don't care about the element, whatever one may have. Indeed, it's enough to speak the words. Let the children be committed to our Lord God. The baptism itself is of no concern to me [i.e. it's God's business, not mine]. Besides, the Word is the principal part of baptism. If in an emergency there's no water at hand, it doesn't matter whether water or beer is used.[7]

And when in the spring of 1533 Ignatius Perknowsky, who is referred to in the text as 'our Bohemian', interrupted Luther to say that he still had doubts about baptism, Luther is reported by have replied 'gently':

When you first came here you were not at the stage which you have now attained. Continue to be patient. Give our Lord God time. Let the trees bloom before they bring forth fruit![8]

'What does it matter?' though posed somewhat rhetorically by Paul in Philippians 1:18a (and echoed by Luther in his statement, 'It doesn't matter!'), is a question of great importance for the proclamation of the Christian gospel and the course of the Christian mission. For Paul (and for Luther), some things mattered dearly, for they stem from and express the heart of the Christian message. These are matters that are to be proclaimed forthrightly, applied appropriately and defended stoutly. Many other matters for Paul (and for Luther), however, were *adiaphora* – that is, matters of concern for the day on which one needed to make decisions appropriate for the day, but not issues of eternal significance or of vital importance. Paul as a major apostle in the first century and Luther as a major reformer in the sixteenth century seem to have been able to make such distinctions – perhaps better than most of their associates.

It is probably the ability to distinguish between central priorities and the *adiaphora* that should be credited as one important factor in the successes of the respective missions of Paul and Luther. And it needs to be the prayer of the church collectively and Christians individually today to ask God for such a gift of discernment: 'Lord, teach us to be able to discern between the central priorities of the gospel and the *adiaphora* of contextualizing the gospel in our day – to be forthright in the former and conciliatory in the latter!'[9]

Notes

1. For full treatment of these matters, see my *Galatians*.
2. *Introduction*, p. 333; also pp. 332–335.
3. See his 'Mind of Paul'.
4. Luther, 'Consiliis', in *Luther's Works* 41, p. 66; Weimar Ausgabe 50.558.9–15, 17–18.
5. Cf. 'Consiliis', in *Luther's Works* 41, pp. 68–79; Weimar Ausgabe 50.559.31 – 568.22.
6. Cf. 'Consiliis', in *Luther's Works* 41, pp. 67–68, 79–142; Weimar Ausgabe 50.559.10 – 560.10, 569.6 – 624.3.
7. *Table Talk* no. 394 (recorded by Veit Deitrich), in *Luther's Works* 54, p. 61; Weimar Ausgabe: *Tischreden* 1.171.7–11.
8. *Table Talk* no. 515 (recorded by Veit Deitrich), in *Luther's Works* 54, p. 92; Weimar Ausgabe: *Tischreden* 1.236.4–6. A marginal note appended by a later editor reads: 'Observe with what moderation he [Luther] bore this weakness' (n. 328).
9. An essay in honour of Peter O'Brien, a premier scholar and missiologist.

12. Not boasting over the natural branches: Gentile circumspection in the divine economy

Donald Robinson

In the epistle to the Romans, Paul, having expounded God's purpose of salvation in relation to 'the Jew first and also to the Greek' in the first eight chapters, turns in chapters 9 – 11 to consider the situation and future of those Jews, 'my kinsmen according to the flesh', who have not believed the gospel of God. Here, for the first time in Romans, Paul uses the terms 'Israel' and 'Israelites', which heightens the sense of divine calling and privilege which attaches to the Jews collectively.

The distinction between believing and unbelieving Jews is not new in Romans 9 – 11. It has been made in the earlier chapters (e.g. 3:3; 4:12), but Paul's special concern now is to establish that the 'failure' or 'trespass' of some Jews, even though they may constitute the greater part of Israel, does not mean that God's promise of salvation for Israel has failed.[1]

It is in the course of explicating this paradoxical situation that Paul is moved to raise the question of believing Gentiles *vis-à-vis* unbelieving Jews and the attitude of the former to the latter. He does this both in general terms and also as an admonition to such believing Gentiles as are among the recipients or auditors of his letter. Paul's position, in short, is this: (1) the Gentiles owe their access to salvation to the lapse of Israelites; (2) this does not give believing Gentiles any ground for claiming superiority to these Israelites, whose course is not yet run; and (3) Israel will yet have its 'fullness' in regard to salvation, as will the Gentiles.

It is the purpose of this essay to explore a little further Paul's admonition and the argument on which it rests. We will also enquire into the situation which may have prompted the admonition and ask whether Gentile boasting was peculiar to Rome.

Israel's lapse: the wealth of nations (11:11–12)

In Romans 11:13 Paul addresses Gentile readers explicitly for the first time in this letter.[2] Before examining this explicit address, which continues to 11:32, that is, to the conclusion of Paul's discussion of the 'mystery' of Israel's destiny, let us look at the statement which prompted him to draw in his Gentile readers at this point, namely verses 11 and 12.

First, in verse 11 Paul asks the question whether the ensnaring, the blinding and the humbling of Israel (as the Scriptures quoted in verses 8–10 describe God's treatment of them), or their stumbling and offending (Paul's own terms: *eptaisan* and *paraptōma*), have resulted in their total collapse or fall (*pesōsin*, like the *ptōsis* of the house built on sand in Jesus' parable in Matt. 7:27). This possibility Paul emphatically denies, as he is bound to do. Both God's word and his foreknowledge or election are at stake here. Paul has already affirmed that 'God has not rejected his people whom he fore-knew' (or 'acknowledged as his own', REB, 11:2), and also that the word of God in his promise to Abraham and Israel has not failed (*ouch . . . ekpeptōken*, 9:6). Thus God's word and his election are alike infallible. Further, Paul has already pointed to the 'remnant chosen by grace' (11:5) as evidence that the divine plan has not come to an end. Now, in 11:11–12, Paul offers encouraging signs of how the full design of God's blessing is proceeding or may be expected to proceed. In the first place, Israel's lapse is not a total disaster, since 'through their lapse (*paraptōma*) salvation has come to the Gentiles so as to make them jealous'. Here Paul is referring to what the Lord said concerning Israel in the Song of Moses (Deut. 32:21), which he has just quoted in 10:19: 'I will provoke you to jealousy with that which is no nation'. It would appear that Paul interprets *Egō parazēlōsō hymas ep' ouk ethnei* to mean that God will make Israel envious of the blessing he intends to bestow on a nation which, he says, is not a nation, i.e. 'not my people' (*Lo-ammi*), as in Hosea 1:9–10. Paul apparently infers that such envy on the part of Israel will produce a desire to embrace the blessing once forfeited and now enjoyed by outsiders. This interpretation is supported by what Paul says later about himself, as apostle of the Gentiles, hoping to provoke his own kinsmen to envy and thus save some of them (11:14). It is possible, of course, that Paul is also reading the whole 'no nation' prophecy in the light of the original promise to Abraham that he would be 'a father of many nations' (Gen. 17:5; quoted in Rom. 4:17). In the earlier discussion of this promise Paul was aware of how humanly impossible it seemed: it involved belief in 'God who gives life to the dead and calls into existence things that do not exist' (4:18). But given the character of God and his word, the lapse of Israel and the consequent salvation of the Gentiles producing an envious reaction in Israel was a situation full of hope.

The second encouraging sign noted by Paul has more of a parabolic character: 'Now if their trespass (*paraptōma*) means riches for the Gentiles, how much more will their full inclusion (*plērōma*) mean?' (11:12). If Israel yields such a bonus when it is at a loss, will not the bonus be so much greater when the loss has been retrieved? Paul will expand this point later and invoke other analogies, but for the moment the emphasis is on the 'riches' to be expected from Israel. He uses two words, *paraptōma* and *hēttēma*, to define Israel's deficiency. *Paraptōma* is used in the Gospels in the plural as a general term for offences against both our fellows and our Father in heaven (Mark 11:25, and Matt. 6:12 [cf. 14–15], where 'debts', *opheilēmata*, is a metaphorical equivalent). Paul himself uses the plural *paraptōmata* elsewhere in what sounds like a credal formula: 'Jesus was put to death for our trespasses' (Rom. 4:25), and 'having forgiven us all our trespasses' (Col. 2:13). His use of the singular *paraptōma* to describe the defection of Israel in Romans 11:11–12 is parallel to his use of it in 5:15–20 to describe the transgression (*parabasis*) of Adam including the collective *paraptōma* of Adam's descendants. Indeed, it is not impossible that it was the abounding of grace beyond the abounding of Adam's sin which reinforced Paul's belief that Israel's lapse was likewise to be eclipsed by God's ultimate blessing to the world through Israel.

Hēttēma has been rendered as 'defeat' or 'worsting', a passive rather than an active notion. The root idea is that of 'lessening' or 'diminution', and it is this idea which prepares the way for the *plērōma*, the 'filling up' or 'coming to full strength' (so REB) of Israel.

Israel's salvation: the Gentile mission (11:13–16)

Having briefly affirmed that Israel's failure is not final, but that wealth for the world even greater than has come through its lapse is to be expected when it is restored to its full strength, Paul draws the Gentiles of his audience directly into his argument: *Hymin de legō tois ethnesin*. The *de* connects his *legō* with the preceding words about Israel and salvation for the Gentiles. Paul says in effect: 'This is where you come in – you who are Gentiles among those reading this letter.' Then, as a justification for buttonholing his Gentile readers in this way, he assures them that his own ministry as the Gentiles' apostle is involved in what he has to say to them. As God's instrument in the provocation-to-envy process (see 10:19 and 11:11) he hopes he may save some of those who, after all, are his own kinsmen. So, if he has an admonition for his Gentile friends, at least it is by way of boosting (he uses *doxazō*) his own ministry to the Gentiles, and so presumably it is also in their interest.

It is not altogether easy to see how verse 15 serves as an explanation (*gar*) of the preceding sentence, or how verse 16 arises out of verse 15. However, together these two verses affirm the integrity of Israel despite its vicissitudes and divisions, as well as its final acceptance by God which will be nothing short of a resurrection from the dead (cf. 4:16–17). But it is the last image in this section, 'if the root is holy, so are the branches', which provides the peg on which Paul hangs his subsequent picture of Israel as God's olive tree. This imagery is sustained from verse 17 to verse 24, to be followed by a broader theological statement of God's economy of salvation for the world, in which the disobedience of, and mercy to, both Israel and the nations are intertwined, and God's faithfulness and unfathomable judgments vindicated.

'Do not you Gentiles boast over the branches' (11:17–18)

We shall ask shortly about the identity of the Gentiles whom Paul addresses so pointedly in this section. When he singled out the Jew for special treatment in 2:17–29, he had recourse to the second singular *sy*, a rhetorical feature of the diatribe. So also here in 11:17–32 the plural 'you who are Gentiles' of 11:13 becomes the singular *sy*. The effect is to focus on the character of the class of persons addressed (see also 2:1).

What is the boast or proud claim which the apostle deprecates? In verse 18 it is simply the claim by Gentile believers to superiority over those Jews who have been broken off the olive tree. 'Broken off' (*exeklasthēsan*) here is a metaphor for various terms Paul has used in his earlier discussion to describe the lapse or defection of such Jews, or rather God's response to their lapse. What makes this boasting inappropriate is the fact that such believing Gentiles are of inferior stock, wild olives, and only by being grafted on to the olive have they been able to share with the natural branches in the nourishment of the olive tree (cf. 15:27, '... the Gentiles have been made sharers of their spiritual blessings').[3]

Thus in verse 17 the tree is identified as an olive, which is a figure for Israel in Jeremiah 11:16 and Hosea 14:6. But it is unclear whether or not verse 17 contains a reference to the root of the olive: *tēs rhizēs* is absent from Þ [46] D* G and some Old Latin manuscripts among others, and occupies a variety of syntactical positions in the manuscripts where it does occur. The root is not essential to the first part of Paul's argument; it may be that he introduces it as a further consideration which does indeed put the Gentile in his place: if the Gentile is still inclined to boast despite his inferior origin, let him be aware that he depends on the root, not the root on him. But what does this mean?

In Paul's twin aphorisms of verse 16 – 'if the firstfruit is holy, so is the lump; and if the root is holy, so are the branches' – his point concerned the unbelieving Jews whose rejection was not final since their holiness (i.e. their relation to God, not their righteousness) was inherent in their pedigree. 'Holy' is a term used repeatedly of Israel in Exodus to Deuteronomy, that is, in connection with Israel's encounter with God at Sinai and with the covenant whereby it was constituted by God as 'my people'. This pristine status of Israel, rather than a reference to the patriarchs, seems to be what lies behind the firstfruit/lump and the root/branches sayings. 'Holiness' (*qōḏeš*, *qaḏôš*) is never used in Genesis in connection with the patriarchs, whereas '... in the wilderness ... Israel was holiness unto the LORD, the firstfruits of his increase' (Jer. 2:2–3). In Romans 11 the concept of holiness occurs only in our verse 16, where it denotes the relation of the whole tree and all its branches to God who planted it (cf. Jer. 2:21), not the actual characteristics derived by the branches from their relation to the tree.

Now when Paul, pursuing the branches imagery in verses 17–18, specifies the tree as an olive with three categories of branches for the purpose of explaining the status of believing Gentiles as ingrafted wild-olive branches, he speaks of the root of the olive as 'carrying' the believing Gentiles (he uses *bastazō*). As with the root/branches saying in verse 16, the root here is widely taken to be a reference to the patriarchs.[4] Has not Paul earlier (4:11) called Abraham 'the father of all who believe without being circumcised'? However, as I argued earlier in relation to verse 16, I think the root in verse 18 is more likely to be the people Israel in its covenant relation with God, that is, the people Israel as the seed of Abraham through whom God's blessing of salvation was destined to come to the Gentiles, according to the promise. Even the lopped branches still belong to that Israel; indeed, it is to their lapse, paradoxically, that the Gentile believers owe their salvation. Further, the believing Jews with whom the Gentiles share the nourishment of the olive tree are natural branches of that tree, not unnatural ingrafts like the Gentiles. *It is Israel that carries the Gentiles, not the Gentiles that carry Israel.*

'Do not become proud, but stand in awe' (11:19–24)

Paul continues his diatribe by accepting the truth of the Gentile believer's defence: 'Branches were broken off so that I might be grafted in.' Paul himself has already affirmed this in verses 11 and 17. However, he denies that this gives the Gentile anything to boast about. His argument is similar to that of 1 Corinthians 4:6–7, where he rebukes members of the church at Corinth who are boasting about their adherence to various teachers: 'Who sees anything different in you? What have you that you did not receive? If then you received it, why do you boast as if it were not a gift?' Paul's rejoinder in Romans 11:20 implies the same truth: 'your status is due to your faith', that is, to God's mercy, not to any merit in you. The proper response of the Gentile to his situation is a humble contemplation of God's sovereign goodness and severity in the whole process of salvation. Moreover, the full story is not yet told. Since salvation is received by faith, the Gentiles will be cut off if they do not continue in faith, while God both can and will restore the fallen Jews if they do not persist in their unbelief. In that case, such Jews will be grafted back into their own olive tree, whereas believing Gentiles will always be an exotic graft. Not boasting over the natural branches, but humble perseverance in the kindness of God is the right attitude for the Christian Gentile.

What is going on at Rome?

Who are these Gentiles Paul admonishes so pointedly in verses 17–24? It seems to me that he uses the image of the olive tree and its branches, not as a general picture of the relation of Israel and the Gentiles in the plan of God, but as a particular description or paradigm of the situation in Rome at the time he wrote his letter to the community of believers there. Of course, it is all against the background of the exposition of Israel's destiny in chapters 9 – 11, especially 11:7–12 and 11:25–32, but it may be a mistake to suppose that in the olive-tree metaphor Paul was looking beyond the local scene in Rome.

As long ago as 1925 the learned Wilfred Knox, who on other grounds held the view that 'the message of the new teachers was first proclaimed at one of the synagogues of Rome', was attracted by the possibility that in fact the centre of Christian faith in Rome was, in the first instance, the synagogue of the Olive, and that Paul's rather contrived simile of the olive tree with its natural and grafted (and re-grafted) branches was suggested to him by the name of a synagogue to which both Jewish and Gentile believers adhered. Knox's construction of the situation in Rome is this:

There is a tendency among the Gentiles to look down on the Jews, and St Paul reminds his readers that though they are at the moment the true synagogue of the Olive, yet the old branches of the cultivated tree, i.e. the Jewish members of the synagogue of the Olive, are really their superiors and are not to be despised, as though God had finally rejected them.[5]

A somewhat similar view of the situation in Rome was taken by William Manson in 1949.[6] Contrary to the view favoured by most commentators on Romans at the time, that the Christians in Rome were predominantly Gentile, Manson argued that 'the early Christian community at Rome, to a section of which Hebrews was written, was predominantly Jewish-Christian in composition and character'. Manson arrived at this judgment 'principally on the ground of St Paul's Epistle to the Romans'. Paul's manner of approach 'suggests on every page that he thought of that Church primarily in terms of its Jewish heredity and ethos'. In particular, Manson advanced the view that Paul chose to deal with the question of Israel's destiny – which is not a question he tackles in any other of his letters – not merely 'to give the Romans a fully rounded, systematic summary of his teaching as a whole', but 'through his sense of a particular opportunity or challenge confronting him at his approach to the Roman Church'. Such an opportunity or challenge 'would certainly be present if he had reason to regard that Church as predominantly Jewish-Christian in its heredity or outlook or mentality'. When, then, towards the close of his great discourse on Israel, Paul turns directly to the Gentiles among the Roman Christians and reminds them of their privileged position as grafted into the olive tree of Israel, 'he asks them not to vaunt over the broken-off branches'. The words in which he does this, says Manson, are 'remarkable': 'It is not you that carry the root, but the root carries you.' Manson takes this to mean: 'It is not you Roman-Gentile Christians who constitute the stock of the Church at Rome, but your Jewish-Christian brethren.'

Thus both Knox and Manson suggest that Paul's allegory of the olive tree was meant to apply to the specific situation in Rome at the time that he wrote his letter announcing his intention to visit the believers there.

The view that the Christian community in Rome was still, at the time of Romans, more or less within the ambit of Judaism, is supported by E. A. Judge and G. S. R. Thomas.[7] Their thesis is

. . . that the Christian community in Rome was built up mainly through the migration of converts from the East, without any regular organization or public preaching; that it avoided any conflict with the synagogues, providing such extra religious facilities as it needed on a domestic basis; and that it was only launched as a 'church' in opposition to the synagogues after Paul's arrival.

Paul's career as reflected in his letters and in Acts

> ... shows a regular pattern of working first through the synagogues and, after confronting the regular Jewish community with his message, forming a new organisation as a result of the division which followed. The fact that Paul was given no formal reception by any Christian group at Rome fits in with this familiar procedure, and implies that none was yet formed.

Judge and Thomas further note that James and 1 Peter

> ... are explicitly addressed to Jews in general and although Christian belief is assumed, there is no suggestion that this is incompatible with Judaism, or practised under separate auspices ... It may well be, therefore, that the situation at Rome as we have defined it was the more normal at this stage.

Moreover, so far as our knowledge of the churches outside Palestine goes, 'it was Paul who was principally responsible for organizing them separately from the synagogues'.

What is going on in Paul's churches?

Although the situation in Paul's own churches was not identical with what we have supposed the situation in Rome to have been, it is worth asking whether his letters to those churches reveal anything parallel or similar to the boasting over the branches which we have observed in Romans 11. The language of boasting is certainly anticipated in the Corinthian correspondence, as is the language of 'falling' and of being 'cut off' in both the Galatian and Corinthian letters.

In 1 Corinthians 10 Paul deals with Israelites who 'fell' (*epesan*, v. 8). These were Israelites who had provoked God in various ways and had been appropriately punished. Their 'fall' was literal and physical, but Paul treats it as exemplary (*typikōs*, v. 11) for his own time, and his warning to the Corinthians, including the Gentile members, is: 'Let him who thinks he stands take heed lest he fall' (*mē pesē*, v. 12). This is not very different from his warning in Romans 11:20: 'Be not high-minded, but fear.' These Israelites in 1 Corinthians 10 were, it is true, those of the exodus period ('our fathers') who failed despite their having been partakers of the spiritual food and drink provided by God, indeed partakers of the Christ (10:3–4), but they are also models for the present day. In 2 Corinthians 3:14 Paul speaks of the Israelites of Moses' day as having been 'hardened', and he goes on to say that they – meaning their descendants – are still hardened 'to this day', in their synagogues 'whenever Moses is read'. However, Paul's interpretation of the statement in Exodus 34:34 about Moses turning to the Lord and the veil being removed – cited in 2 Corinthians 3:16 – implies that God was restoring formerly unbelieving Jews in Corinth and elsewhere to their true calling. The lesson of Romans 11:23–24 may already have been absorbed in Corinth.

In both Galatians and 2 Corinthians Paul warns his Gentile converts against Jews who profess to follow Jesus as the Christ but who pervert the gospel of Christ and are in reality servants of Satan (Gal. 1:8–9; 2 Cor. 11:15). Of those described in Galatians Paul says, 'Let him be accursed,' and of those in 2 Corinthians he says, 'Their end will correspond to their deeds.' In Galatians he warns his Gentile converts not to be misled by those Jews who have somehow found entrée into the churches of Galatia, and it is in connection with this warning that he employs the vocabulary of being 'nullified' or 'discharged' from Christ, and of 'falling away' from grace (cf. *tēs charitos exepesate*, 5:4). Later in Romans Paul will speak of those natural branches of Israel who 'fell' (*tous pesontas*) through unbelief, and will warn the Gentile believers that if they do not continue in God's kindness they too will be 'cut off' (cf. *epei kai sy ekkopēsē*, 11:22). 'Nullified/discharged from Christ' in Galatians would seem to mean to cease being of the family of God or 'sons of God' (3:26; 4:5), or 'Abraham's offspring, heirs according to promise' (3:29). Israel had this status first, and as such it is inalienable, though it is surpassed by the larger unity of Jew and Greek in Christ (Rom. 4:11–12, 16–17). Again, the situation in the Galatian churches is not the same as at Rome, although there are elements in common; but in Paul's language of anathema and judgment, and in his imagery of cutting off and falling away, we may have the germ of his thought which is later applied in Romans 11 in the olive-tree paradigm.

A comment may be in order on the use of *apokopsontai* in Galatians 5:12, which could well be part of this language and imagery. The active *apokoptō* with an object is to 'cut off' a part of something, e.g. a hand or foot (Mark 9:43, 45) or an ear (John 18:10, 26) from a body. The middle voice, without an object, basically should mean to 'cut oneself off'. In Euripides (*Troades*,

628) it means to 'cut oneself (for the dead)', i.e. to mourn. In later Greek there are a number of instances of its use absolutely, and somewhat euphemistically, for self-emasculation, as in the LXX of Deuteronomy 23:1. Despite the popularity of this interpretation for Galatians 5:12, it is not without difficulty. In this verse Paul concludes his tirade against 'those who are upsetting you' which he began in 1:7 when he delivered a double anathema upon 'those who trouble you'. It seems unlikely that Paul, having consigned the troublers to (God's) curse and verdict (*krima*, 5:10), would conclude his solemn condemnation by indulging in the vindictiveness of a personal wish that they would castrate themselves, suggested allusions to pagan priests notwithstanding. That is not to say that the language of circumcision may not have been what prompted Paul's choice of verb in this final utterance. 'Cutting off' imagery – based on the literal cutting off of limbs or branches – is very common in the Old Testament for excluding from Israel those whom God has judged (mainly Heb. *krt*). I see no reason why Paul should not have moved from the thought of circumcision to a metaphorical use of the middle *apokoptomai* and have expressed the wish not merely that the wicked would cease from troubling, but that they would remove themselves from the churches of Galatia: the *apokopsontai* of verse 12 reversing the *enekopsen* of verse 7. Thus the perverters of the gospel who would compel the Gentile Galatians to cut off the foreskin in circumcision, should rather (*kai*) cut themselves off from the body of Christ.[8]

What is going on today?

While present-day Gentile Christians may be generally aware of their debt to Israel – in the Scriptures not only of the Old Testament but substantially if not entirely of the New Testament as well, and above all in 'the Christ according to the flesh' (Rom. 9:5) – it is probably true to say that there is next to no actual relationship between Gentiles and Jews, believing or unbelieving, of the kind we have been looking at in the New Testament. There may indeed be a sense of superiority to Jews on the part of many Gentiles, even if the worst of anti-Jewish hostility has diminished, and there is still a lingering theology of 'supersession' which holds that the (Gentile) church has replaced Israel in the purposes of God.[9] This may be a form of 'boasting over the branches', even though there may be little or no personal contact involved. Yet H. L. Ellison, himself a Jewish Christian, could claim in 1954 that 'proportionately the church's proclamation to the Jew in the nineteenth and twentieth centuries has been at least as successful as its proclamation in the average mission field, and indeed much more successful than in some'.

He could also quote Professor Gustav Dalman as claiming: 'If all the Jews who have embraced Christianity had remained a distinct people instead of being absorbed by the nations among whom they dwelt, their descendants would now be counted in millions.'[10] It can be added that Jewish evangelization has increased since Ellison wrote, as has the distinctiveness of Jewish or Hebrew-messianic Christianity. So what should be the Gentile response to the Jewish presence in our own day, in and out of the church? It is not possible to pursue this question here, but we can conclude our brief study by summarizing Paul's theology of Israel, which should provide the foundation of 'Gentile circumspection in the divine economy' in every age.

Conclusion: Paul's theology of Israel

The admonition in Romans 11:13–32 was prompted by the situation in Rome, where Gentile Christians were evidently boasting of superiority to Jews who did not believe. Presumably these Gentiles were in reasonably close contact with such Jews. Paul's admonition to humility is firmly based on his theology of Israel's destiny. God's ancient promise to bless Israel, renewed in the dark days of chastisement in the exile, would be fulfilled. That fulfilment already had an earnest in a remnant who had found salvation in Jesus as the Christ. What Israel lacks now is its 'fullness', the salvation of 'all Israel' as promised. For sure, the body of Christ transcends Israel, for it is a new humanity representing all nations. But Israel retains its primacy: in judgment, but also in believing and in being saved (Rom. 1:16; 2:9–10), and it is the means whereby salvation is transmitted to all nations.

Only in Romans does Paul appear to admonish Gentile Christians not to boast over Jews who have been 'cut off', i.e. Jews who had rejected the gospel preached to them. This is perhaps because Gentiles were less prone to such boasting in the circumstances of Paul's churches, where they may not have been daily confronted by such hostile Jews.

But Paul's theology of Israel was not only for the Romans. He has a lot to say to his own churches about unsatisfactory Jews who cause trouble in his churches. He teaches his Gentile converts how to distinguish a true Jew from one who cannot be trusted and whose practices should not be emulated (see e.g. Phil. 3). Paul teaches the Galatians the password for recognizing those who belong to 'the Israel of God' and who therefore can be cordially greeted (Gal. 6:15–16). Paul also is fully aware that the process which will finally result in the fullness of the Gentiles and the salvation of all Israel is under way, involving both a mission to Jews and a mission to Gentiles (in partnership, Gal. 2:7–9), with Jews as well as Gentiles turning to the Lord. Further, the uniting of Israel and the nations in one body of those being saved – the ultimate purpose of God – as described and enlarged upon in the epistle to the Ephesians, is already being anticipated in local churches.

The key passage is Ephesians 2:19–22, in which God's plan is described as the building of 'a holy temple in the Lord', God's house in which 'the saints' (God's holy people Israel) are joined by Gentile strangers from afar.[11] 'The apostles and prophets', the first recipients of the revelation of the mystery of the unity of Jew and Gentile in one body, are the foundation of the house, with Christ Jesus himself as the cornerstone. In God's house, as we know, are many rooms or dwelling-places, and within the larger temple the Gentiles have their own building or 'dwelling-place for God'. It is the Lord who integrates the whole, and it is seen as *growing* into its perfected form. This is 'the church' in its ultimate and transcendent form (1:22; 3:10, 21; 5:23–33), but it is also the model for each local church where Jew and Gentile are reconciled in Christ.[12]

I venture to suggest (contrary to the usual interpretation of the passage) that the same picture of God's plan for Israel and the Gentiles is what Paul has in view in chapter 4, especially verses 11–13.[13] Here the process of creating the 'one body' of Jews and Gentiles is depicted as having been initiated by the ascended Christ through his giving, as his gifts to humankind, the apostles and prophets (already designated as the foundation of the new temple, 2:20, and as the first recipients of the revelation of God's purpose, 3:4–6), together with the evangelists and pastor-teachers (who put the first churches on their feet, as it were). Christ's purpose in giving his gifts of the apostles and so on is described as for the perfecting or restoration (*katartismon*) of 'the saints', who here, as in chapters 2 and 3, will be the Jewish believers, the firstfruits of the Israel of God, who are at the heart of the new temple, and are the light drawing the Gentiles to God.[14] The two accompanying phrases introduced by *eis* (= *en*?)[15] could then describe the means by which the apostles and so on fulfilled their role: namely, the work of the ministry (appropriate to the four categories given), and the building of the body of Christ, bringing Jews and Gentiles together. This uniting of Gentiles to Jews in the unity of the faith and of the knowledge of the Son of God leads to the final goal, when 'we all' (4:13) come to the perfection of God's 'one new man' measured by the full stature of Christ.[16]

Notes

1. For a study of Paul's language of God's destruction of Israel and her subsequent salvation in Romans 9 – 11, see Harding, 'Salvation'. See also my 'Salvation'.

2. I am assuming that Paul addresses the Christians in Rome in 1:6 as being *among* the Gentiles, i.e. as residing in a Gentile sphere of missionary activity, not as necessarily themselves Gentiles. Likewise in 1:13.

3. For due humility by Gentiles when sharing Israel's blessing, see the Gospel incidents of the centurion at Capernaum (Matt. 8:5–13), and the Canaanite woman (Matt. 15:21–28).

4. See Cranfield, *Romans* 2, p. 565.

5. Knox, *St Paul*, p. 258, also pp. 252–254. The existence of *synagōgē Elaias* is known from two inscriptions, one of them (CIG no. 9904, CIJ no. 509) from the catacomb of Vigna Cimarra off the Via Appia. From the fact that this cemetery also contained epitaphs of the Agrippensians, 'who are hardly likely to have retained their name after the memory of their patron had been forgotten', Knox deduced that the cemetery dated from the first century AD. Noy, *Jewish Inscriptions*, 406, dates this inscription to the '3rd century (?)'. The synagogue was no doubt older than the inscription which related to one of its members. The provenance of the second inscription is unknown.

   Although the most common view is that this synagogue was named after the olive tree – Schürer (2, p. 524, n. 81; 3, p. 84) offering as a parallel the 'Synagogue of the Vine' in Sepphoris – others prefer the view that it was named after some city, probably in the East, from which its members had originally migrated. See Leon, *Jews*, p. 146.

6. Manson, *Hebrews: Reconsideration*, pp. 172–184.

7. 'Origin', pp. 81–94.

8. Ramsay, *Galatians*, pp. 437–440.

9. See Robinson, 'Biblical understanding', pp. 24–29.

10. Ellison, 'The church', p. 143.

11. See Robinson '"The saints"?', pp. 45–53.

12. I have discussed the New Testament notion of 'the church' previously. For further details see '"The churc" revisited', and *Faith's Framework*, pp. 114–115.

13. See further my discussion in 'Ministry-Service', pp. 62–64.

14. *Katartismon*, which occurs only here in the New Testament, could well refer to the restoration or rebuilding of the Jewish believers as part of the house of God, made possible by the ministry of the apostles and prophets and leading to the incorporation of Gentile believers into the same temple. A somewhat parallel picture may be seen in James's exposition of Amos 9:11–12 in Acts 15:16, where the tabernacle of David is rebuilt or set up (its *katartismon*?) 'so that the rest of men may seek the Lord, and all the Gentiles who are called by my name'. The equivalent of all this in Romans 11 – Israel's *plērōma* (11:12), the 'grafting back' of its lopped branches (11:23–24), and the salvation of 'all Israel' (11:26) – could also be described as 'the *katartismon* of the saints'. This too is contingent on the 'coming in' of the fullness of the Gentiles.

15. See Moule, *Idiom*, pp. 67, 69.

16. These reflections are offered, out of long friendship, to Peter O'Brien and in appreciation of his diligent and scholarly teaching of the New Testament in Australia, India, and elsewhere.

13. Paul's mission and prayer

Donald A. Carson

The topic assigned me in this essay combines two themes close to the heart of Peter O'Brien: mission and prayer. In both cases – mission and prayer – Peter has displayed a salutary mix of personal commitment and academic focus. To take the domain of mission first: Peter served for a decade as a missionary in India, and continues an interest both in evangelism and in the mission of the church around the world, exemplified not least in his active participation in study groups sponsored by the World Evangelical Fellowship. Academically, his 1993 volume, the fruit of Moore College Annual Lectures, was in large part an examination of certain mission aspects of Paul's theology.[1] Occasional essays attest his deep interest in the subject[2] and more recently he has co-authored a volume likely to become a standard textbook on the theme of mission in the New Testament.[3] But those of us privileged to know him also recognize in him a man of prayer. Not only have we prayed with him; we have read the published form of his dissertation on the introductory thanksgivings in Paul's letters,[4] and noted his return to the subject in various dictionary articles[5] and in the occasional strategic essay.[6]

Introductory thanksgivings in Paul

In some ways Peter's dissertation built on the seminal work of P. Schubert.[7] But while Schubert focused primary attention on the form of Paul's thanksgiving periods and on their ostensible Hellenistic parallels, Peter modified the formal analysis but little, criticized Schubert for his focus on Hellenistic sources, isolated various Jewish parallels, and, above all, examined the function and purpose of Paul's introductory thanksgivings. He demonstrated that they are carefully wrought theological pieces that introduce themes that would figure in the main body of the letter, emphasizing the apostolic pastoral care displayed in these sections. Judging by the many positive and sometimes penetrating reviews, Peter's work convinced large numbers of scholars.[8] Among the many important points he made is that thanksgiving for Paul is never the primary thing: it is always a response to God's goodness in creation and in the gospel. Indeed, Peter made that the primary point of his 1980 essay,[9] opening it with the much quoted words of Deichgräber: 'The praise of the church is the response to God's act of salvation ... praise is never the first word, but alway occurs in the second place ... It is never *prima actio*, but always *reactio, reactio* to God's saving activity in creation and redemption, to his orderly working in nature and history.'[10] That observation enables us to sidle a little closer to the linked themes of this essay. For if thanksgiving and redemption are linked, surely (we might think) we cannot be far from the twin themes of this essay, namely, prayer and mission.

Yet at a merely formal level of analysis, that is not what we find. Of the petitions in Paul's thanksgiving periods, none is directly related to mission. They have a great deal to do with what might be called the ongoing fruitfulness of the gospel, that is, Christian maturation, but very little to do with what we commonly mean by mission today. The comprehensive survey of Paul's intercessory prayers provided by Wiles a quarter of a century ago[11] comes to similar conclusions. Although there are (as we shall see) occasional exhortations to pray for Paul in the context of his apostolic ministry, and although almost all the prayers are in one fashion or another gospel-related, on first reflection it is surprising that there is little intercession for the lost, little evidence of systematic praying for the conversion of men and women, few examples of what we might call mission praying – that is, praying specifically for the outreach of the gospel, not least in cross-cultural contexts.[12] Paul's own prayer life is extensive and intense. He can pray not only for Christians whom he knows, but for Christians and churches of whom he has only heard, wrestling and agonizing in prayer for them (e.g. Eph. 1:15–19). But so far as the explicit evidence goes, it is hard to find evidence of similar intensity in prayers for the lost, even though Paul understands that God has made him an apostle to the Gentiles. The closest approximation to that sort of intensity for the lost is in Paul's agonized supplication for his fellow-Jews – and here, of course, there are special themes operating.

Discussion did not end with Peter's dissertation, of course. It would be tedious to trace all the subtle developments that have taken place since its publication. In some ways, the most interesting essays on Paul's thanksgivings and intercessions have grappled with the relationships between such units and the epistolary form – whether in fairly formal categories[13] or by trying to tie Paul's prayers to many, many elements, both formal and material, of Paul's letter structures.[14] A recent essay argues that there is no sense in which the introductory thanksgivings in Paul's letters are grounded in the genre of letters contemporaneous with the apostles: they are *sui generis*, and the ostensible parallels are two or three centuries out of date.[15] If this position stands, it means that all the generic studies that find subtle meanings anchored in genre-specific details must be scrapped. But this position has itself come under strenuous criticism. Reed argues that some useful parallels are available, and in any case the attempt (and failure) to find virtually identical parallels is methodologically flawed, owing to the obvious flexibility of epistolary formulae.[16] In other words, Paul's introductory thanksgivings have sufficient formal parallels with thanksgiving formulas in Hellenistic literature that one may usefully speak of epistolary conventions in this regard – even though Paul also has 'an ability to alter convention for his own communicative needs'.[17]

But as interesting as these and other developments are, they do not directly help us to answer this question: why is it that Paul's prayers, of various kinds, are so infrequently linked directly to mission? Or, to put it more concretely, why is it that Jesus can tell his disciples to 'ask the Lord of the harvest to send out workers into his harvest field' (Matt. 9:38), while nothing quite similar surfaces in Paul? Why, on the evidence of Paul's epistles, does the title of my assigned essay seem somewhat anomalous? At one level, of course, such questions demand that we reflect on a silence – always a risky business. But at least a few things may be said.

Paul and missionary prayer

For purposes of organization it may be easiest to reduce these reflections to four points.

1. Countless writers have remarked on the occasional nature of Paul's letters. All sides recognize that his literary remains do not have the form of a well-ordered systematic theology, but of letters – letters which for the most part have been called forth by specific exigencies. This means that their themes and priorities are in substantial measure constrained by the occasions which in God's providence called them forth. At the very least, this

calls for caution and attentive listening. What Dunn says about our efforts to reconstruct in full Paul's evangelistic preaching could be said as well about our efforts to reconstruct in full Paul's missionary praying:

> Paul's allusive taken-for-granted references include much of the faith already common to Paul and his readers. This is why it is so difficult to reconstruct Paul's evangelistic preaching – simply because he did not feel it necessary to repeat it in letters to his converts. Instead he could refer to it briefly or allude to it by using brief formulae – usually summarized as 'kerygmatic tradition'. He did so knowing, we may confidently assume, that even such brief formulations would evoke knowledge of a substantial range of basic teaching which he had passed on, when he preached to his readers the gospel of Jesus Christ and established them as a new church. Such allusions should not be evaluated simply by the brevity of their reference. To reconstruct Paul's theology as measured by the proportions of his explicit treatment would certainly result in a statement whose disproportions would have been pointed out at once by both Paul and the recipients of his letters. We do not 'weigh' Paul's theology simply by counting the number of words he used.[18]

So we may agree that the full place Paul gave to prayer in relation to his mission – indeed, to the Christian mission – cannot be adequately assessed by merely counting up the rather sparse references where he does something like encourage his readers to pray for him in his gospel-preaching apostolic ministry. A more substantive analysis is called for.

Nevertheless, before we reflect on some elements of such an analysis, it is surely fair to conclude that the occasional nature of Paul's letters must not be seen as a disadvantage. We must not succumb to secret resentment that the Pauline deposit did not come down to us in some literary form other than occasional letters. Occasional letters have the power to bring the readers into play, to involve them, to force a kind of interaction with the apostolic writer as if he were present with them – and in few domains is this more important than in the domains of thanksgiving and intercession.[19] More importantly, all Christians recognize the canonical function of Scripture, that is, Scripture as *kanōn*. If Scripture functions as 'canon' for us in our Christian priorities and practices, then although it is right to recognize the occasional nature of Paul's letters, it is wrong to hide behind their occasional nature so that every time our practices do not square with them we attribute the difference to the occasional nature of the apostolic documents and thus leave unchanged whatever it is we are doing (or not doing).

In short, while we recognize that the occasional nature of Paul's writings has a bearing on our subject (in part it accounts for the relative paucity of references that directly link prayer and mission), and while we recognize that Christians bound by Scripture will want to listen attentively to other scriptural voices (e.g. the exhortation to ask the Lord of the harvest to send forth workers), we infer that Paul's relative silence on this subject has something to teach us.

2. Before reflecting on the few passages where Paul directly links prayer and mission, it is critically important to observe three other prayer-related themes in Paul. Their relevance will become obvious in a moment. *First*, the apostle insists that all people everywhere *ought* to give thanks to God continually, and *ought* to offer him the praise that is his due. Our failures in this respect mark not only our wilful rebellion but the measure of our alienation and lostness: 'For although they knew God, they neither glorified him as God nor gave thanks to him, but their thinking became futile and their foolish hearts were darkened. Although they claimed to be wise, they became fools and exchanged the glory of the immortal God for images made to look like mortal man and birds and animals and reptiles' (Rom. 1:21–23). Thanklessness is thus bound up with idolatry. It is a wretched characteristic of the 'last days' (2 Tim. 3:1–5), even though it was already displayed in the murmuring of the rebellious Israelite ancestors (Exod. 15:1–18, 24) and ultimately prevented an entire generation from entering the Promised Land (Num. 14:1–4, 22–23). Small wonder, then, that Paul exhorts the Philippian Christians to do everything without complaining (Phil. 2:14 – i.e. without murmuring: *panta poieite chōris gongysmōn*), and warns the Corinthian believers, 'We should not test the Lord, as some of [the Israelites] did – and were killed by snakes. And do not grumble, as some of them did – and were killed by the destroying angel' (1 Cor. 10:9–10).

Second, Paul provides a converse emphasis on the place of thanksgiving in the life of the Christian. If prayerlessness and ingratitude are linked with idolatry, it cannot be surprising that Paul tells believers to 'pray continually; give thanks in all circumstances, for this is God's will for you in Christ Jesus' (1 Thess. 5:17–18; cf. Col. 3:15–17). 'Speak to one another with psalms, hymns and spiritual songs. Sing and make music in your heart to the Lord, always giving thanks to God the Father for everything, in the name of our Lord Jesus Christ' (Eph. 5:19–20). Over against 'obscenity, foolish talk or coarse joking, which are out of place', there must be 'thanksgiving' (Eph. 5:4).

None of this can be understood apart from the Bible's story-line, the narrative of redemption, the account of the acts of God culminating in the coming and death and resurrection of Jesus, and the response that is both demanded of and (ideally) characteristic of God's redeemed people. As Peter O'Brien has finely put it:

> While the grounds for the giving of thanks in Paul's letters are manifold, the great emphasis falls upon the mighty work of God in Christ bringing salvation through the gospel. God's activity in creation is, on occasion, mentioned as a basis for the expression of gratitude (cf. Rom. 1:21 and note the thanksgivings said over food). But the majority of the Pauline references are in the context of God's grace given in Christ (1 Cor. 1:4; and cf. 2 Cor. 9:15 with 8:9). Even when gratitude is expressed for the faith, love and hope of the Christian readers these are not to be understood as the inherent achievements of the believers but are regularly related to the prior work of God in leading men and women to himself through the gospel. And because Paul's apostolic labours are intimately bound up with that saving activity among Gentiles, he is able to give thanks for his calling as an apostle to them (1 Tim. 1:12).[20]

O'Brien adds that thanksgiving 'was almost a synonym for the Christian life'.[21]

Third, for exactly the same reasons Paul's intercessory prayers – whether the reports of his prayers, or his 'prayer-wishes', or his exhortations to pray – are very largely bound up with the gospel, as even the most cursory study of such passages as Romans 15:30–33; Ephesians 1:15–23; 3:14–21; Philippians 1:9–11; Colossians 1:9–14; and 1 Thessalonians 3:11–13 demonstrates. Moreover, most (though not all: cf. Rom. 15:30–33) of these prayers are for the spiritual maturation of believers, for their growth in love and obedience to the gospel and their perseverance to the end. Gospel concerns shape Paul's priorities in prayer, and their applicability to those reading his letters lies first of all in what *they* need (which returns us to the 'occasional' nature of Paul's correspondence). In the words of Wiles:

> While immediate concerns did shape the prayers, they were grounded in and directed by the gospel of Christ. It was the salvation events of the gospel that lay behind Paul's apostolic commission and guided his ministry. So too his prayers were made possible only because of the love of God revealed in the gospel; by this their contours were guided and their range immeasurably deepened and extended. All his requests must be according to the will of God revealed in Christ.[22]

3. It is within this framework, then, that Paul conceives of his own mission, and encourages prayer for it. What forgives and transforms 'lawbreakers and rebels, the ungodly and sinful, the unholy and irreligious ... those who kill their fathers or mothers ... adulterers and perverts ... slave-traders and liars and perjurers' is 'the glorious gospel of the blessed God, *which he entrusted to me*' (1 Tim. 1:9–11; cf. 1:12). In the passage that provides the most explicit link between mission and prayer, Paul shows he is under no illusion that, apostle or not, he needs prayer and God's answers to such prayer if he is to prove faithful in his mission: 'Pray also for me, that whenever I open my mouth, words may be given me so that I will fearlessly make known the mystery of the gospel, for which I am an ambassador in chains. Pray that I may declare it fearlessly, as I should' (Eph. 6:19–20; cf. 1 Cor. 16:9). But perhaps what is most striking about this prayer is what immediately precedes it. Paul has just told his readers to don 'the full armour of God', ending with the exhortation: 'And pray in the Spirit on all occasions with all kinds of prayers and requests. With this in mind, be alert and always keep on praying for all the saints' (6:18). It is at this point that he adds, 'Pray also for me ...'

From this flow of thought we must infer at least two things.

First, while Paul encourages prayers for himself and his gospel mission, he does not conceive of such prayers as belonging to a separate category, a missionary category. The prayers of Paul's Christian readers should be all of a piece, part of what it means to 'be strong in the Lord and in his mighty power' and to 'stand against the devil's schemes' (Eph. 6:10–11). They are part and parcel of being spiritually alert, of praying constantly for all the saints (6:19). The way that Paul refers to the good news he preaches – he wants to 'make known the mystery of the gospel' – inevitably calls to mind his earlier allusions to 'mystery' in this epistle, especially 1:9 and 3:2–13, the latter of which is profoundly tied to Paul's grasp of the significance of his apostolic and gospel ministry.[23] This is weightier than what some of us mean by 'gospel preaching' or 'mission' or the like. It is so declaring the whole counsel of God that now, at the end of the age, the church comes into existence and discloses 'the manifold wisdom of God' (3:10), making Jews and Gentiles alike one people and one body (3:6), declaring the good news which in certain respects 'was not made known to men in other generations as it has now been revealed by the Spirit to God's apostles and prophets' (3:5) since 'for ages past' it 'was kept hidden in God' (3:9). Paul's ministry is thus 'according to [God's] eternal purpose which he accomplished in Christ Jesus our Lord' (3:11). Thus when Paul thinks about the cross-cultural emphases of his ministry (after all, he sees himself as apostle to the Gentiles,

Gal. 2:8–9), he does not conceive of them as crossing many cultural and racial barriers so much as crossing one particular barrier, namely, that between Jews and Gentiles. The crossing of that particular barrier and the uniting of redeemed men and women into one new body, the church, lies at the heart of the gospel itself, and has already been accomplished, in principle, in Christ. This is the framework in which Paul encourages his readers to pray for him that he may make known the mystery of the gospel 'fearlessly' (6:19–20).

Second, it is not too much of a stretch to detect a reciprocal effect. If praying for Paul along these lines is part and parcel of their praying 'for all the saints' (6:18), it is difficult not to perceive that part of what believers should be praying for when they pray for all the saints is a certain holy boldness in their own witness. If even the apostle Paul, who can insist that he is not ashamed of the gospel (Rom. 1:16), discloses his need for God's help in declaring the mystery of the gospel fearlessly, how much more do the rest of us need such help?

4. Perhaps, then, our initial surprise that Paul has not left us with clearer links between mission and prayer betrays our own faulty views of both mission and prayer – especially the former. There are at least four factors.

First, we have tended to think of mission as a discrete project (or as discrete projects), often of a cross-cultural kind, with the result that special prayer for this isolable function is called for. But quite apart from the special calling on his own life as an apostle (indeed, as the apostle to the Gentiles), Paul sees mission in holistic, even cosmic terms. The glory of God, the reign of Christ, the declaration of the mystery of the gospel, the conversion of men and women, the growth and edification of the church, the defeat of the cosmic powers, the pursuit of holiness, the passion for godly fellowship and unity in the church, the unification of Jews and Gentiles, doing good to all but especially to fellow-believers – these are all woven into a seamless garment. All the elements are held together by a vision in which God is at the centre and Jesus Christ effects the changes for his glory and his people's good. This means that thanksgiving and intercessory prayer, though sweeping in the range of topics touched, are held together by a unified, God-centred, vision. Our more piecemeal approach looks for certain kinds of links which for the apostle are embedded in a comprehensive vision.

Second, the comprehensiveness of Paul's outlook is tied to his understanding of his place in redemptive history. To put it differently, it is tied to his grasp of biblical theology. In the fullness of time, God sent his Son (Gal. 4:4), and this eschatological event – this stunning intertwining of prophecies about kingship and suffering, this fulfilment of centuries of models of priests, sacrifices, forgiveness, temple, the rule of God, the anticipation of rescue by God himself – has imposed its priorities on all that Paul thinks and does, all for which he offers thanks and for which he intercedes.

Third, during the first decades of the church's life the expansion was so rapid that it is difficult to think of Christians sunk in the gloom of defeatest introspection asking the Lord to help missionaries out in Pago Pago – even while little by way of evangelism or outreach was attempted at home. Judging by what evidence the New Testament supplies, Christians did indeed pray for outreach/mission. But so far as the evidence goes, such prayer was radically integrated into broader Christian experience. When the Jerusalem church faced its first whiff of persecution, they responded by praying for boldness (Acts 4:29); again, it was while the prophets and teachers at Antioch were worshipping the Lord and fasting that the Spirit instructed them to set apart Barnabas and Saul for new mission outreach. One does not glean, whether from Acts or elsewhere, that the church would get stuck and then pray for guidance about some new 'mission' project; still less does one sense that the church undertook new mission projects and then asked the Lord to bless them. The church was multiplying so quickly that the apostles could not always keep up: the church in Antioch was not founded by an apostle, and neither was the church in Rome or the church in Colosse. In this sort of environment the intertwining of ministry and prayer was so wholesome and inescapable that our piecemeal approach would seem atomistic, perhaps even bizarre. Moreover, at the practical level this sort of environment meant that the most urgent problems faced by church leaders were often the problems *inside the multiplying fledgling churches.* Small wonder, then, that a large proportion of Paul's recorded prayers are devoted to the spiritual maturation of believers.

Fourth, even if there is no concrete evidence in the Pauline letters of a prayer analogous to that of Jesus that the Lord of the harvest would send forth more workers, there is evidence that Paul sought out such workers himself, and exhorted those he trained to do the same thing: 'And the things you have heard me say in the presence of many witnesses entrust to reliable men who will also be qualified to teach others' (2 Tim. 2:2). The conclusion to be drawn is not that Paul has transmuted a topic for prayer into mere activism but that Paul has so integrated prayer and obedience that these instructions to Timothy reflect all that he holds dear for the gospel's sake – and therefore what he prays for and what he does. There is no embarrassing hiatus between what Paul prays for and how he behaves, between the foci of his intercession and the priorities of his life.

Conclusion

If this brief essay is even approximately right, it follows that Paul integrates mission and prayer in unexpected ways and at deep theological levels. If on a first reading Paul's habits in this regard seem vaguely strange and lacking, on a second reading it is our habits that seem vaguely strange and lacking. Certainly we could do with more models like Peter O'Brien, who integrates prayer and mission not only into his writing but into his life.

Notes

1. O'Brien, *Consumed by Passion*.
2. O'Brien, 'Paul's missionary calling', pp. 131–148.
3. Köstenberger & O'Brien, *Theology of Mission*. He has also edited a volume of essays for the Church Missionary Society (Australia) entitled *God's Mission and Ours*.
4. O'Brien, *Introductory Thanksgivings*.
5. See the indexes in Hawthorne, Martin & Reid, *Dictionary of Paul*.
6. O'Brien, 'Thanksgiving', pp. 50–66.
7. *Form and Function*.
8. See reviews by, inter alia, Boers; Morgan-Wynne; Morris; Thomas Norwood Jr; Schenk.
9. See n. 6, above.
10. Deichgräber, *Gotteshymnus*, p. 201.
11. Wiles, *Paul's Intercessory Prayers*.
12. In my own more popular treatment of seven of Paul's prayers (*Call*), I found similar priorities. Paul occasionally exhorts his readers to pray for him in his ministry, but it is hard to find unambiguous examples of prayer for the conversion of the lost, for the extension of the gospel, for the Lord of the harvest to thrust out more workers into his harvest-fields, or the like.
13. E.g. White, 'Epistolary literature', pp. 1730–1756, esp. pp. 1741–1742.
14. E.g. Dippenaar, 'Prayer and epistolarity', pp. 147–188.
15. Arzt, 'The "Epistolary introductory thanksgiving"', pp. 29–46.
16. Reed, 'Paul's thanksgivings', pp. 87–99.
17. Ibid. p. 98.
18. Dunn, *Theology*, p. 16.
19. A point forcefully made by Schnider & Stenger, *Studien*, esp. ch. 2, 'Die briefliche Danksagung', esp. p. 47.
20. 'Thanksgiving', p. 62.
21. Ibid.
22. *Paul's Intercessory Prayers*, p. 294.
23. See esp. Luz, 'Überlegungen', p. 386 – though he does not think Ephesians was written by the apostle.

14. Maturity: the goal of mission

David G. Peterson

The notion of maturity is variously expressed in the writings of Paul. Nevertheless, it is clear that the apostle's concern is to urge and enable Christians, individually and corporately, to move towards a maturity that is God's will for them in Christ. Paul's teaching on maturity must be understood in relation to his eschatology and viewed as the outworking of his gospel preaching.

'Fulfilling' the gospel

In Romans 15:16–21 there is an important statement by the apostle Paul about the content, goal and scope of his missionary work. The passage climaxes with a tantalizing reference to his having 'fully proclaimed the good news of Christ'. Together with the phrase 'the obedience of faith' (1:5; 16:26), this suggests that, in addition to primary evangelism, Paul's intention was to establish his converts in the way of Christian maturity.

Paul's 'priestly' ministry

The apostle first describes himself as 'a minister of Christ Jesus to the Gentiles in the priestly service of the gospel of God, so that the offering of the Gentiles may be acceptable, sanctified by the Holy Spirit' (v. 16, NRSV). Much debate has taken place over the meaning of the phrase 'the offering of the

185

Gentiles', which expresses the goal of his 'priestly' activity. Peter O'Brien has taken the view that *the apostle presents the Gentiles to God* as an offering which is acceptable because of Paul's ministry to them and that this offering is epitomized by the material gifts brought by their representatives to meet the needs of the Jerusalem believers (15:25–32).[1] My own view is that the preceding appeal to present their bodies 'as a living sacrifice, holy and acceptable to God, which is your spiritual worship' (12:1), must be determinative here. Paul's gospel ministry enables *the Gentiles to present themselves* in a way that is acceptable to God (cf. 6:13, 16, 19). Clearly, however, the sharing of their resources with the poor among the saints in Jerusalem is an important expression of the 'understanding worship' that the apostle encourages and makes possible among the nations.[2] Paul's 'priestly' ministry was the divinely appointed means of uniting Jews and Gentiles in the praise and service of God, thus fulfilling the prophetic promises regarding the end-time (cf. 15:5–12). Since preaching was not regarded as a ritual activity in Paul's world, he clearly gives that ministry a novel significance when he describes it as the means by which he serves God (cf. 1:9–15).

The expression 'sanctified by the Holy Spirit' (*hēgiasmenē en pneumati hagiō*) stands in apposition to 'acceptable' (*euprosdektos*) and suggests that the work of the Spirit in drawing the Gentiles into relationship with God through Jesus is what actually makes them acceptable to God (cf. 1 Cor. 1:2, 30; 6:11; 2 Thess. 2:13). Paul goes on to reinforce the idea that the acceptability of the Gentiles' self-offering to God is directly related to his preaching by asserting that the Spirit is at work through his ministry, in what he says and does (vv. 17–19). The Spirit, who is actively present in both preacher and listener, is a necessary agent of the worship of the new covenant because the Spirit makes possible a saving faith in Christ through the gospel. Another way of expressing the same truth is to say that Christ himself has been at work through the ministry of Paul, drawing the Gentiles into relationship with himself, winning 'obedience from the Gentiles, by word and deed, by the power of signs and wonders, by the power of the Spirit of God'.

The obedience of faith

The assertion that Paul's missionary endeavours were designed to bring about 'obedience from the Gentiles' (*eis hypakoēn ethnōn*) must be related to two key texts, at the beginning and end of Romans. In 1:5 Paul makes it clear that his apostolic calling was 'to bring about the obedience of faith among all the Gentiles' (*eis hypakoēn pisteōs en pasin tois ethnesin*), for the sake of Christ's name. In 16:26 'the obedience of faith' functions as part of his concluding praise of God for establishing the Roman Christians in the gospel he preached. Against those who interpret the obedience of the nations quite narrowly in terms of their coming to faith in Christ, O'Brien sides with Garlington in taking it to include not only the Gentiles' believing acceptance of the gospel but also 'their constancy of Christian conduct'.[3] This conclusion is consistent with the whole tenor of Paul's argument in Romans itself and with the earnest desire expressed elsewhere that his converts will be found holy and blameless, and filled with the fruit of righteousness on the day of the Lord Jesus (Phil. 1:9–11; Col. 1:9–14, 22, 28; 1 Thess. 3:12–13; etc.). So when Paul speaks in a shorthand way of 'the obedience of the Gentiles' (Rom. 15:18), it is likely that he has in view their conversion and the obedient lifestyle that flows from faith in Christ.

The result of Christ's work through the apostle is such that he can say, 'from Jerusalem and as far around as Illyricum I have fully proclaimed the good news of Christ' (Rom. 15:19). In view of the qualification about not proclaiming the gospel where Christ had already been named (v. 20), the claim to have literally 'fulfilled the gospel' (*peplērōmoumenon to euangelion*) cannot simply be understood in geographical terms. Paul had not preached in every town or district in the region he outlines! The verb *plēroō* can mean 'doing something fully' or 'carrying it to completion'.[4] It is so used in Colossians 1:25, in a somewhat similar context, to refer to the divine commission literally to 'fulfil the word of God' (*plērōsai ton logon tou theou*). We shall note in due course how this paragraph leads to a critical statement about maturity as the goal of Paul's ministry (Col. 1:28). Peter O'Brien notes the link between these passages and observes that the noun 'gospel' in Romans 15:19 (*euangelion*) is used in the dynamic sense of 'the act of proclamation or the work of evangelism',[5] with the cognate verb (*euangelizomai*) being used in parallel in verse 20. Paul is saying that he has 'completed the preaching of the gospel' in this region. But in what sense?

After a review of various alternative interpretations, O'Brien concludes that it is not simply a reference to the *manner* in which Paul's mission was effected. He follows Paul Bowers in asserting that it has to do with the *scope* of Paul's work:

From his *practice* of residential missions (at Corinth and Ephesus) and nurture of churches (1 Thess. 2:10–12), from his *priorities* (1 Thess. 2:17 – 3:13; 2 Cor. 2:12–13; 10:13–16), and from his *description of his assignment* (Col. 1:24 – 2:7; Rom. 1:1–15; 15:14–16) in relation to admonition and teaching believers to bring them to full maturity in Christ, it is clear that *the nurture of emerging churches* is understood by Paul to be 'an integral feature of his missionary task'.[6]

Paul's missionary vocation found its sense of fulfilment 'in the presence of firmly established churches',[7] from Jerusalem as far around as Illyricum. He had 'fulfilled the gospel' in strategic centres such as Thessalonica, Corinth and Ephesus. Further evangelistic work in the region remained a possibility for others to pursue, but Paul felt free to go up to Jerusalem and move on to Rome and a new sphere of operation westwards towards Spain.

Preaching to the Romans

The notion that preaching the gospel for Paul meant primary evangelism and strengthening believers in their discipleship is also suggested by the argument in Romans 1:8–15. The gospel had already done its work of creating faith in Christ (1:8) and establishing a number of congregations in Rome (16:3–16) before Paul wrote. His longstanding intention to visit them is first expressed cautiously in terms of sharing with them 'some spiritual gift to strengthen you' (1:11). This is then qualified to allow for the possibility that 'we may be mutually encouraged by each other's faith, both yours and mine' (1:12). At the end of the paragraph, however, Paul indicates that this will happen when he comes 'to proclaim the gospel' (1:15, *euangelisasthai*) 'to you also who are in Rome' (*kai hymin tois en Rhōmē*).

Since it was his ambition to preach the gospel where Christ had not already been named, so that he did not 'build on someone else's foundation' (15:20), it is natural to think that his intention was simply to preach to the unconverted in Rome and to found new churches in that city, before moving west to begin a new sphere of work (15:22–32). But the progress of the argument in the letter itself suggests something more. Paul's intention was also to build up and strengthen the Roman Christians by his gospel ministry in their midst. Peter O'Brien notes that where *euangelizomai* is used by the apostle it does not refer to preaching in a general sense but always has in view the proclamation of the *euangelion*, which Paul begins to expound in Romans 1:16–17. Nevertheless, the word-group is used to cover the whole range of 'evangelistic' work, 'from the initial proclamation of the gospel to the building up of believers and grounding them firmly in the faith'.[8] O'Brien goes on to observe that

> The Christian life is certainly created through the gospel (1 Cor. 4:15; Col. 1:5–6); but it is also lived in the sphere of this dynamic and

authoritative message (cf. Phil. 1:27). It needs therefore to be preached to those who have already received it and have become Christians. Believers do not leave the gospel behind or progress beyond it as they grow and mature in their faith. They stand fast in this kerygma and are being saved through it if they hold firmly to it (1 Cor. 15:1–2), for it is in this authoritative announcement that true hope is held out to them (Col. 1:5, 23).[9]

O'Brien further observes the wide-ranging series of activities subsumed under the notion of preaching the gospel in Ephesians 3:8 and Colossians 1:28. I want to support this argument by proposing that Paul's intention of ministering the gospel to the Christians at Rome is anticipated in the writing of his letter to them. Romans itself is an example of how Paul would lead believers to maturity in Christ.

Romans as an exposition of Paul's gospel

Much scholarly debate continues to take place about the nature of Romans and its purpose. Although the letter appears to be occasional from the wording of its introduction (1:1–15) and conclusion (15:14 – 16:27), and although the section about the 'strong' and the 'weak' (14:1 – 15:13) could be related to specific problems in the Roman church, the main part of the document is more like a general tractate on the gospel and its implications. Nevertheless, it is not a timeless theological treatise nor simply a compendium of Christian doctrine. The larger occasion of Romans is Paul's missionary situation, and a variety of specific concerns also combined to produce the finished product.[10]

With regard to its controlling theme, Douglas Moo has rightly argued that we need a topic as broad as 'the gospel' to encompass the various materials in Romans.[11] The word 'gospel' and the cognate verb 'evangelize' are particularly prominent in the introduction and conclusion, as we have seen. 'The gospel' is also the key concept in 1:16–17, which is usually taken as Paul's statement of the theme of his letter, so that even the important ideas of 'salvation' and 'the righteousness of God' are subordinate to the gospel. The claim that the gospel was 'promised beforehand through his prophets in the holy scriptures' (1:2) is substantiated and developed in various ways throughout the letter. The Christological focus of the gospel, which is highlighted in 1:3–4, is foundational to the argument. The soteriological dimension of the gospel mentioned in 1:16–17 forms the basis of much that follows. The purpose of the gospel, which is 'to bring about the obedience of faith among the Gentiles for the sake of his name' (1:5), is an implicit concern throughout the document, as the apostle applies the message of the gospel to a range of practical situations.

The teaching in this letter is conditioned by Paul's own missionary situation and to some extent by the needs of the Christians in Rome. Yet believers throughout the ages have discerned here an understanding of God's purposes that brings assurance of salvation, motivation for godly living, a sense of responsibility to other Christians and an awareness of being part of God's rescue plan for the whole world. In other words, the study and application of Romans can promote a maturity in Christ that is holistic and God-focused, enabling believers to enjoy by way of anticipation the eschatological blessings secured for them in Christ, as they await the consummation of God's purposes. As we shall see from Colossians 1:25 – 2:7, this is the measure of maturity that Paul seeks for his converts in every aspect of his ministry.

Everyone mature in Christ

In a passage that has some interesting parallels with Romans, the apostle details the strategy that he and his co-workers had for presenting 'everyone mature in Christ'. Paul's divine commission is first presented in terms of literally 'fulfilling the word of God' (Col. 1:25, *plērōsai ton logon tou theou*; 'to make the word of God fully known', NRSV). Peter O'Brien notes the various interpretations of this clause that have been offered and argues for a parallel with Romans 15:19. The word of the gospel is 'fulfilled' not simply when it is preached, but when it is 'dynamically and effectively proclaimed in the power of the Spirit ... throughout the world, and accepted by men in faith'.[12] Since Paul had not personally visited them (2:1), the Colossians had become beneficiaries of his apostolic commission through the ministry of his associate Epaphras (1:7).

Proclaiming 'the mystery'

The message which Paul was to 'fulfil' is defined as 'the mystery that has been hidden throughout the ages and generations but has now been revealed to his saints' (1:26; cf. Rom. 16:25–27; 1 Cor. 2:6–10; Eph. 3:4–7, 8–11). The 'saints' are not some select group of initiates here, but those who have heard and received the word of God through the ministry of Paul and his associates, 'for it is in the effective preaching and teaching of the gospel that the revelation of the mystery takes place (cf. 1 Cor. 2:1, 7; 4:1; Eph. 3:8,

9; 6:19)'.[13] The Old Testament prophets looked forward to the eschatological blessing of the nations along with Israel, but the inclusion of Gentiles on equal footing with Jews in the body of Christ remained a mystery until the time of its fulfilment. Paul's duty and joy had been the task of revealing 'the riches of the glory of this mystery, which is Christ in you, the hope of glory' (1:27). Even though they were Gentiles, as members of Christ's body, the Colossians had his life within them. 'They therefore had a sure hope that they would share in that fullness of glory yet to be displayed on the day of "the revealing of the sons of God" (Rom. 8:19; cf. 5:2; Col. 3:4; 1 Thess. 2:12; 2 Thess. 1:10; 2:14).'[14] This setting of the gospel within the broad framework of biblical theology is again reminiscent of the argument of Romans.

The Christological focus of the mystery is brought out strongly in Colossians 1:28 ('It is he whom we proclaim, warning everyone and teaching everyone in all wisdom, so that we may present everyone mature in Christ'). Three related verbs are used in the plural (suggesting that Paul's co-workers shared in this task) and in the present tense (suggesting that this was their habitual practice). The public proclamation or announcement (*katangellomen*)[15] of Christ as the centre of God's purpose for the nations is carried out in conjunction with warning (*nouthetountes*)[16] and teaching (*didaskontes*). 'Clearly for Paul and his colleagues evangelistic and missionary outreach was not effected by some superficial presentation of the saving message about Christ to the world, but rather it was prosecuted through warning and intensive teaching in pastoral situations.'[17] Moreover, in contrast with the gnostic practice of sharing esoteric knowledge with exclusive groups of initiates, the Christian gospel was to be explained to everyone individually (*panta anthrōpon* occurs three times in the singular in 1:28) and 'in all wisdom' (*en pasē sophia*).

Three allied modes of communication are thus shown to be necessary to 'fulfil the word of God' and to 'present everyone mature in Christ': announcing the good news about Jesus, teaching about its scriptural foundations and deepest implications, and urging people to make the proper response. Acts 20:20–31 illustrates how these activities were combined in the apostle's extensive ministry in Ephesus. In various situations, the balance between them may vary, but any one of these modes of Christian communication is inadequate without the others. For example, warning without teaching and the framework of gospel proclamation may be nothing more than moralizing. Teaching without warning and gospel proclamation may simply be intellectualizing.

Maturity defined

The goal of this Christ-centred pattern of proclamation–warning–teaching is 'so that we may present (*parastēsōmen*) everyone mature in Christ'. Here the work of 'presenting' is clearly that of Paul and his associates, whereas in 1:22 it is Christ himself who, through his reconciling death, is able 'to present (*parastēsai*) you holy and blameless and irreproachable before him'.[18] A comparison between these passages is instructive. The verb 'to present' is probably used in a judicial sense in both contexts, to refer to the final appearance 'before him' (1:22, *katenōpion autou*, cf. 1 Cor. 1:8, 'on the day of our Lord Jesus Christ'). 'As men and women who are forgiven and reconciled they are declared blameless (cf. Rom. 8:33, 34), without fault or stain (the terms "holy" and "blameless" appear to have lost any cultic over-tones at Eph. 1:4; 5:27; Phil. 2:15; Jude 24) on the occasion of the Great Assize.'[19] This is the hope of those who believe that God has 'rescued us from the power of darkness and transferred us into the kingdom of his beloved Son, in whom we have redemption, the forgiveness of sins' (1:13–14). What will finally be declared on the day of judgment can be enjoyed by way of anticipation by those who trust in Christ's saving work.

However, the lengthy conditional sentence in Colossians 1:23 makes it clear that continuance in this confidence is the test of reality. The reconcilia-tion has been achieved and its benefits are available to all who believe the promises of the gospel now. But the challenge is to 'continue securely estab-lished and steadfast in the faith, without shifting from the hope promised by the gospel that you heard'. Those who are drawn away from the apostolic gospel lose the hope of ultimate acceptance that it offers. The ministry of proclamation–warning–teaching described in 1:28 is the fundamental means by which God sustains his people in that saving faith.

The word *teleios* is variously used in Greek literature and could be trans-lated 'whole', 'complete', 'mature' or 'perfect'. In sacrificial contexts it denotes the quality of victims that are entire and without blemish (e.g. Homer, *Iliad* 1,66; Exod. 12:5, LXX, for the Hebrew *tāmîm*) and such over-tones have been suggested in Colossians 1:28.[20] However, the terminology is much more commonly employed in the formal sense of 'full', 'complete' or 'perfect', in a great variety of religious, philosophical and everyday applica-tions.[21] In the LXX there is a particular use in the sense of 'blamelessness' or 'wholeheartedness' in relation to God (e.g. Gen. 6:9; Deut. 18:13; 2 Sam. 22:26, where LXX again uses *teleios* for *tāmîm*).[22] The Old Testament also refers to the heart which is wholly turned to God as 'perfect' (cf. 1 Kgs. 8:61; 11:4, where LXX has *teleios* for Hebrew *šālēm*).

This Hebraic perspective on perfection may well have been in Paul's mind, since he writes of 'walking' worthily of the Lord, so as to please him in every way (Col. 1:10, *peripatēsai*, echoing the use of *hālak* in the Hebrew Bible and Dead Sea Scrolls). The participial clauses which follow in the Greek text spell out more precisely what this Christian 'walk' involves: 'bearing fruit in every good work' (v. 10), 'growing in the knowledge of God' (v. 10), 'being strengthened with all the strength that comes from his glorious power for all endurance and longsuffering' (v. 11), and 'giving thanks with joy' (v. 12) for all the benefits of the gospel.

Paul picks up the note of 'walking' again in Colossians 2:6–7, where he urges, 'As you therefore have received Christ Jesus the Lord, continue to lead your lives (*peripateite*) in him, rooted and built up in him and established in the faith, just as you were taught, abounding in thanksgiving.' The 'perfect' or 'complete' Christian will be the one whom God enables to persevere in this Christ-centred, gospel-based lifestyle, firm to the end. The apostle prays for his converts to be mature in this sense (1:10–12) and makes it the goal of his proclamation, warning and teaching (1:28 – 2:7). The image is one not of sinlessness but of blamelessness, steadfastness, fruitfulness and thankfulness.

Du Plessis insists that perfection in Colossians 1:28 means 'the absolute redemption which is in Christ'.[23] This verse certainly parallels 1:22 in some respects, as I have noted, and Du Plessis is right to conclude that 'redemption is effective from the moment of faith, although it is a dynamic category extending from the *archē* to the *telos*'.[24] But he has missed the balance of Paul's argument here because he is so intent on avoiding the interpretation of *teleios* in terms of Christian spiritual growth. The prospect of being presented 'holy and blameless and irreproachable before him' because of Christ's redemptive work (1:22) is meant to be the motivation for the walk of faith and obedience in the present (1:23). This God-given hope brings forth expressions of a holy, blameless and irreproachable lifestyle in advance of that ultimate encounter with Christ (1:3–5), even in the lives of those who are pressured by false teaching and every temptation to sin (2:1 – 4:6). What is implied by *teleios* in the context of 1:28 is not some vague notion of 'spiritual growth' or 'moral progress', but actualization of the redemption in Christ in personal and corporate Christian living.[25] Paul's idea of maturity or perfection is to be understood in the light of his inaugurated eschatology.

Mature and immature

This last point is argued by W. W. Klein in terms of a two-stage view of perfection in the writings of Paul. There is 'a relative kind of perfection that Christians work to attain in this life, and a final state of absolute sinless perfection realized only in the life to come'.[26] However, in Delling's words, 'one does not find in the NT any understanding of the adjective in terms of a gradual advance of the Christian to moral perfection nor in terms of a two-graded ideal of ethical perfection'.[27] What Klein means is that Paul already regards those who are in Christ as *teleioi* (e.g. 1 Cor. 2:6-13), even if they behave as 'infants' in Christ (1 Cor. 3:1-3, *nēpioi*). Paul's concern in 1 Corinthians is to persuade them to adopt the thinking and behaviour that go along with being 'mature' (cf. 14:20).[28] The perfection that Christians are to 'work to attain in this life' is an actualization of the true status and life that are already theirs in Christ.

In Romans 12:2 the apostle urges his readers not to be conformed to this 'age' and its values but to 'be transformed by the renewing of your minds, so that you may discern what is the will of God – what is good and acceptable and perfect'. The mind must be renewed if it is to recognize and embrace the will of God, which is 'perfect, complete, absolute; for he claims us *wholly* for himself and for our neighbours'.[29] Key aspects of the lifestyle that is required of all who are in Christ are then detailed in Romans 12 – 15.

In Colossians 4:12 there are important links with verses that have been considered already. Just as Paul 'struggles' (1:29, *agōnizomenos*) to 'present everyone mature in Christ' (1:28, *teleion*), so Epaphras 'struggles' (4:12, *agōnizomenos*) in his prayers for his converts, 'so that you may stand mature (*hina stathēte teleioi*) and fully assured in everything that God wills'. The passive (*stathēte*) points to the divine enabling that can make such stability possible (cf. Rom. 14:4). The whole expression implies that they are already *teleioi* and need to be kept that way, not that they need to 'make progress here and now'.[30] In particular, the Colossians have been warned about seeking perfection or maturity through the philosophy of the false teachers (2:8-23), which involved ascetic practices, visionary experiences and special revelations, rather than through Christ. To seek perfection elsewhere is to lose the possibility of actualizing the perfection that is ours in Christ.

The maturity or perfection that is in Christ is defined in a particular way in Colossians 4:12 by the expression, 'fully assured in everything that God wills' (NRSV). Peter O'Brien argues that the participle *peplērophorēmenoi* takes the place of the more frequently used synonym *plēroō* ('fill', 'fulfil'). It is deliberately reminiscent of the teaching on 'fullness' (*plērōma*) which runs through the heresy as well as through Paul's corrective.

Accordingly, the prayer addressed to God recalls the polemic against the 'philosophy'. Christ is the one in whom the whole fullness of the Godhead dwells bodily (2:9). Only in him is fullness to be found. And the readers have been filled in Christ (2:10). Paul's co-worker now prays that they will stand firmly as 'perfect', an eschatological perfection that occurs when they are 'filled with everything that is God's will'.[31]

The corporate dimension

In many passages Paul shows his concern for the corporate life of believers, and in Colossians 3:14 he indicates that the perfection he sets before them is not something narrowly individual. In addition to the graces listed in verses 12–13, the apostle urges the Colossians to clothe themselves with love, which he literally describes as 'the bond of perfection' (*syndesmos tēs teleiotētos*). Some have taken this expression to mean that love is the 'perfect bond' which joins all the other virtues to form an organic unity.[32] But Peter O'Brien disputes the use of extrabiblical parallels in this argument and challenges the suggestion that there was a hierarchy of virtues for Paul, with love at the top. He follows those who read the genitive (*tēs teleiotētos*) as one of purpose or result, meaning that love is 'the bond that leads to perfection' or 'the bond which produces perfection'.[33] This suggests a deliberate verbal link with the perfection/maturity Paul sets before them in 1:28 and 4:12. The new idea is that perfection/maturity is attained or actualized only as Christians in fellowship show love to one another. This perspective is amplified in Ephesians 4:11–16, as we shall see.

Keeping the end in view
Perfection in the age to come

In Philippians 3 the apostle makes no explicit statement about maturity being the goal of his missionary endeavours. Nevertheless, as he warns that the final perfecting will come when we share in the resurrection from the dead, Paul puts himself forward as a model of Christian maturity and urges his readers to imitate him in thinking and behaviour. Whatever others may claim, the apostle affirms that he has not yet reached perfection (v. 12, *ouch ... teteleiōmai*). Instead, he keeps on pursuing his long-cherished ambition of knowing Christ fully and thus finally attaining to the resurrection from the dead (vv. 8–11). He keeps on pursuing this ambition 'with the intention of *laying hold* of it, because the risen Christ powerfully *laid hold* on him on the Damascus road, setting his life in this new direction'.[34]

Although there are eight uses of the adjective *teleios* in the generally acknowledged Pauline epistles (Rom. 12:2; 1 Cor. 2:6; 13:10; 14:20; Eph. 4:13; Phil. 3:15; Col. 1:28; 4:12), Philippians 3:12 is the only verse where the derivative verb *teleioō* is found (*teleō* and its compounds occur in Paul's writings quite often). Most commentators agree that this signifies a taking over of the terminology of his opponents for the purpose of correcting their false views. Peter O'Brien rightly observes that the verb is used in parallel with the preceding expression, 'not that I have already obtained (this)' (*ouch hoti ēdē elabon*). Since it can mean 'complete, bring to an end, finish, accomplish; bring something to its goal or accomplishment', it is 'a further explanation in more literal terms of what was described figuratively of obtaining the goal' in the preceding passage.[35] He reviews various theories about Paul's opponents and their teaching and concludes that they were Jewish-Christian Judaizers, who were propounding 'a doctrine of obtainable perfection based on Judaizing practices'.[36] Although he takes issue with Helmut Koester's position, he agrees that Paul's opponents were claiming to have reached a state of perfection defined in terms of 'the possession of the qualities of salvation in their entirety, the arrival of heaven itself'.[37] Paul is opposed to such over-realized eschatology and any suggestion that the ultimate blessedness can be obtained in the present.

That perfection here refers to eschatological consummation is confirmed by the following verses. Paul does not rest secure in his present experience, imagining that he has already laid hold of all that Christ offers, but constantly sets his sight on 'what lies ahead' (v. 13). 'He will not allow either the achievements of the past (which God has wrought) or, for that matter, his failures as a Christian to prevent his gaze from being fixed firmly on the finish line. In this sense he forgets as he runs.'[38] Like an athlete in a race he presses on towards the goal, which in this case is 'the prize of the heavenly call of God in Christ Jesus' (v. 14). According to this imagery, he runs with the divine calling to salvation ringing in his ears, 'as God summons Paul and other Christians in a heavenward direction and to holiness of life'.[39] The apostle has already indicated that this involves a willingness to share in Christ's sufferings 'by becoming like him in his death' (v. 10). In view of his attack on self-indulgence and lawlessness in verses 17–19, it is certain that pressing on towards the goal (v. 14) and holding fast to 'what we have attained' (v. 16) involves a *moral* responsibility to Christ. Yet perfection here is not essentially a moral concept or something that depends on human effort: 'perfection lies in the hands of God, who will bring to completion that which he has begun in calling me "in Christ Jesus"'.[40]

Maturity in the present

In Philippians 3:15–16 Paul urges as many of his readers as are 'mature' to
follow his example (vv. 12–14). Commentators have often taken Paul's use
of *teleioi* here as ironic, since he has just said that he is 'not yet perfected'
(*teteleiōmai*, v. 12). The apostle is arguing that those who regard themselves
as having already received the fullness of eschatological blessing in Christ
should seek perfection in humbly acknowledging their imperfection!
However, Peter O'Brien argues at some length against this line of interpretation. First, the adjective *teleios* does not have to carry a meaning strictly
analogous with the cognate verb in verse 12. Secondly, since Paul includes
himself among the *teleioi* by his use of the verb 'be of the same mind'
(*phronōmen* in verse 15 is first-person plural), a change of meaning from
verse 12 is required anyway. Thirdly, Paul normally uses the relative
pronoun *hosoi* (v. 15: 'those of us', NRSV) *inclusively*, rather than partitively,
so as to refer to all (potentially, at least) those addressed (e.g. Rom. 6:3; 8:14;
2 Cor. 1:20; Gal. 3:27; 6:16). Fourthly, the apostle employs *teleioi* elsewhere
of those who are actually or potentially mature in the Christian life, as we
have seen. Fifthly, *teleioi* does not appear to be used ironically elsewhere in
Paul or the rest of the New Testament. Finally, the ironical interpretation
makes assumptions about the epistolary situation at Philippi that, though
possible, are not certain.[41]

In short, Paul is not speaking ironically but sincerely. He includes himself
among 'the mature' in much the same way as in Romans 15:1, where he associates himself with 'the strong'. But Philippians 3:15 does not assert that every
believer at Philippi is mature. With such rhetoric, 'Paul is skilfully seeking to
draw all his readers into this group, so that each will identify with the description, for he wishes each of them to be mature and therefore to be characterized
by the same Christ-centred ambition he has'.[42] In connection with Colossians
1:28 and 4:12 I argued that maturity involves actualization of the redemption
in Christ in personal and corporate Christian living, so that Paul's teaching has
to be understood in the light of his inaugurated eschatology. In Philippians
3:15, however, maturity involves forgetting what lies behind and pressing on
so as to lay hold of the final prize offered to us in the gospel. An over-realized
eschatology undermines Christian maturity as much as any spirituality which
denies that fullness of life is to be found in the crucified and exalted Christ. The
context of each letter draws forth a slightly different response on the same
topic. Christian maturity involves right thinking about, and an appropriate
response to, the *balance* of New Testament teaching concerning the enjoyment of end-time blessings in Christ.

It is difficult for many in our experiential age to accept that maturity is so bound up with divinely guided *thinking*, and that this is nurtured by the sort of proclamation, warning and teaching in which the apostle engaged. But we have seen this to be the case in several passages. Paul goes on to say, 'and if you think differently about anything, this too God will reveal to you' (Phil. 3:15).[43] He is clearly concerned that his readers should have the right attitude of mind, even though he knows that not everyone may agree with him on every point. It is the general framework of his thinking that he presses upon them. At the same time, he urges them forward in the sort of behaviour that is consistent with this thinking: 'only let us live up to (*stoichein*) what we have attained' (v. 16). The Greek verb here probably derived from *stoichos* (originally a military term for a 'row') and initially meant 'to stand in line, march in line'.[44] In the New Testament it is used figuratively to mean 'to be in line with, stand beside, hold to, agree with, follow' (Acts 21:24; Rom. 4:12; Gal. 5:25; 6:16). If the connotation of marching in step is present in Philippians 3:16, the readers are being urged to move forward together. But certainly a progression from attitude or orientation (*phroneō*, v. 15), to *practise* is intended. This is reinforced by the use of *peripateō* ('to walk, live') in the following verse 17, where the challenge is to be imitators of Paul in the lifestyle that reflects the attitude he has been outlining.[45]

Meeting Christ

The notion of moving forward together towards maturity has been suggested in several contexts. It is made explicit in Ephesians 4, following another important statement about Paul's missionary calling and God's ultimate purposes. In Ephesians 3:1-13, the apostle shows once more how his apostolic commission was tied up with the revelation of the divine 'mystery' (cf. Col. 1:25-27). As he engaged in preaching to the Gentiles 'the boundless riches of Christ' (v. 8), he was also charged with making everyone see 'what is the plan of the mystery hidden for ages in God who created all things' (v. 9). The way in which Jews and Gentiles would be incorporated together in the body of Christ was revealed 'to his holy apostles and prophets by the Spirit' (vv. 5-6) and it was Paul's privilege to make known the profound implications of that 'mystery', even as his preaching made it a reality. Moreover, God's grand design was that 'through the church the wisdom of God in its rich variety might now be made known to the rulers and authorities in the heavenly places' (v. 10).

Paul saw that, by its very existence as a multiracial community united in Christ, the church could be the manifestation of God's 'open secret' in all its wisdom, the unmistakable testimony to his reconciling work in Christ (cf. 2:11–22).[46] But the prayer that follows suggests 'that if the Church is going to become in history an effective preview of God's purposes for the end of history, then God is going to have to help it in a big way'.[47] The apostle prays for his readers to be empowered by God's Spirit and indwelt by Christ so that, being rooted and grounded in love, 'together with all the saints' they might grasp God's revelation in its 'breadth and length and height and depth', and 'know the love of Christ that surpasses knowledge', so that they might be 'filled with all the knowledge of God' (vv. 14–19). As in Philippians 3:12–16, there is a challenge to seek an ever-deepening knowledge of God in Christ and to experience more fully the benefits of his saving work (cf. Eph. 1:17–19). After the doxology, which seeks for glory to be given to God 'in the church and in Christ Jesus' (Eph. 4:20–21), Paul goes straight on to exhort his readers to lead a life worthy of the calling to which they have been called, challenging them to remove every obstacle to the expression of unity in the church (4:1–6).

Within the unity of Christ's body, however, there is a diversity of gifts from the risen Christ (4:7–11), designed to 'equip the saints for the work of ministry, for building up the body of Christ, until all of us come to the unity of the faith and of the knowledge of the Son of God, to maturity, to the measure of the full stature of Christ' (4:12–13). The gifts in this context turn out to be people whose ministries involve some form of proclamation and teaching (v. 11). Apostles and prophets have already been identified as foundational figures for the building of Christ's church (2:20–22). When they are listed together with evangelists and pastor-teachers, the impression is given that 'building' (cf. *oikodomē*, v. 12) the body of Christ involves both growth in size through evangelism and growth to maturity through teaching and the exercise of love.[48] Although it has been disputed, the best reading of Ephesians 4:12 sees a movement from the specific work of Christian leaders, 'for the equipment of the saints' (*pros ton katartismon tōn hagiōn*), to that of the whole church: 'for the work of ministry' (*eis ergon diakonias*); 'for building up the body of Christ' (*eis oikodomēn tou sōmatos tou Christou*).[49]

This pattern of ministry is to continue 'until' (*mechri*) the goals outlined in 4:13 have been reached. These, however, are not distinct goals. Each of the three prepositional phrases beginning with *eis* refers to Christ and must be seen as drawing out different aspects of God's ultimate purpose for the church in relation to Christ. 'Unity of the faith' and 'knowledge of the Son of God' have already been described as God's gift to the church, but they are still to be appropriated fully. The church has already been described as one new 'person' in Christ (*anthrōpos*, 2:15) and yet God's people collectively must be brought 'to the mature/perfect man' (*eis andra teleion*, 4:13). In Colossians 1:28 the focus was on presenting each individual believer 'mature in Christ', but here it is on the church as a unified entity reaching the goal of maturity. The singular expression *teleios anēr* indicates something of the extraordinary relationship between the church and the person of Christ, 'who makes his people participants in his perfection and riches'.[50] Putting it another way, the church is 'to attain to what in principle it already has in him – maturity and completeness'.[51]

The third expression in 4:13 speaks of attaining 'the measure of the full stature of Christ'. It picks up language from the statement in 1:23 about the church being 'his body, the fullness of him who fills all in all', and from the prayer in 3:19 about being 'filled with all the fullness of God'. There is clearly an eschatological tension here between what is already fact and what is yet to be attained. 'The Church is the dwelling place of Christ's attributes and powers and yet must seek more and more to give room for those very attributes and powers to dwell in it.'[52] But the question remains as to when and how the relationship between Christ and his church is consummated.

Even as mutual ministry takes place in love here and now (vv. 14–16), we may no longer be 'children' (*nēpioi*, v. 14) but, by implication, mature. Nevertheless, the language of verse 13 suggests that a more distant and ultimate attainment of maturity is also in view. The verb *katantaō* means literally 'to come down to a meeting', but normally simply 'to reach a goal'.[53] Since each of the three prepositional phrases in the verse points in some way to the person of Christ, it seems reasonable to suggest that a meeting with Christ at his parousia is implied, when all that is his finally becomes the possession and experience of his people.[54] If this is so, Ephesians 4:13 is conveying in different terms the expectation of glorification or complete conformity to the likeness of Christ found elsewhere in the New Testament (eg. Rom. 8:29–30; 2 Cor. 3:18; 1 John 3:2).

Conclusion

The various passages examined suggest that maturity was a goal of Paul's mission at two different levels. On the one hand, he was concerned that his converts should realize and express the maturity that was potentially already theirs in Christ. On the other hand, he was concerned to move them forwards towards the ultimate encounter with Christ, when the perfection of Christ himself would be fully experienced by his people together. To achieve his goal, the apostle gave himself wholeheartedly to a ministry of proclamation, warning and teaching, that included the writing of his epistles. As he unfolded God's total plan of salvation, he showed Christians how to live appropriately in the light of what is already fact and what is yet to be attained in Christ. Part of his strategy was to establish a pattern of ministry in the churches that would in many respects duplicate his own, enabling God's people to promote 'the body's growth in building itself up in love' (Eph. 4:16) and to move together towards God's ultimate goal for them in Christ.[55]

Notes

1. O'Brien, *Gospel and Mission*, pp. 50–51.
2. Cf. Peterson, *Engaging*, pp. 173–182.
3. O'Brien, *Gospel and Mission*, p. 33, citing Garlington, 'Obedience', p. 222. Although many commentators regard faith and obedience as equivalents in Romans, Garlington and O'Brien insist that there is a distinction. The best rendering of *hypakoē pisteōs* is 'faith's obedience' or 'believing obedience' (O'Brien, *Gospel and Mission*, p. 59). The reference is to 'an obedience which consists in faith and an obedience which finds its source in faith' (Garlington, 'Obedience', p. 224). Cf. Moo, *Romans 1 - 8*, pp. 44–45.
4. BAGD, pp. 670–672, and cf. Delling, '*plēroō*, pp. 286–298.
5. O'Brien, *Gospel and Mission*, pp. 39, 113–114; 'Thanksgiving', pp. 144–155.
6. O'Brien, *Gospel and Mission*, p. 42, citing Bowers, 'Fulfilling the gospel', p. 197.
7. Bowers, 'Fulfilling the gospel', p. 198.
8. O'Brien, *Gospel and Mission*, pp. 62–63.
9. Ibid., p. 63.
10. Moo, *Romans 1 - 8*, pp. 16–22, provides a convenient assessment of various theories about the purpose of Romans before arguing his own case. Cf. Donfried, *Romans*, for a series of helpful essays on the subject.
11. Moo, *Romans 1 - 8*, p. 28.
12. O'Brien, *Colossians*, p. 83. Dunn, *Colossians*, p. 119, n.17, argues that 'this interpretation ignores the apocalyptic eschatological context'. Paul's commission as apostle to the Gentiles was intended as 'a decisive factor in completing the inbringing of the Gentiles and so facilitating the final climax of God's purpose'. O'Brien's exposition of Rom. 15:19 and Col. 1:25 does not ignore this aspect of the context in both cases, but suggests that the peculiar use of *plērōsai* points to the way in which Paul actually achieves this eschatological goal.
13. O'Brien, *Colossians*, p. 85.
14. Ibid., p. 87.
15. Cf. 1 Cor. 2:1; 9:14. The verb *katangellō* is used outside the NT for solemn proclamations or announcements relating to religious or political events (Schniewind, '*angelia*', pp. 70–71). In Col. 1:28 it describes 'not simply the initial apostolic announcement, but draws attention to the ongoing and systematic presentation of Christ as Lord as well' (O'Brien, *Gospel and Mission*, p. 64).
16. *Noutheteō* is not a direct synonym of *didaskō*, though the two are often linked. The verb means 'to impart understanding (a mind for something)', 'to set right', 'to have a corrective influence on someone', describing an effect on the will and disposition, as well as on the mind (Behm, '*noutheteō*', pp. 1019–1020). Paul saw it as an important ministry to be exercised by believers to one another

(Rom. 15:14; Col. 3:16; 1 Thess. 5:12,14; 2 Thess. 3:15). Cf. Malherbe, "'Pastoral Care'", pp. 375–391, especially 383–384.

17. O'Brien, *Colossians, Philemon*, p. 88. Against F. Hahn, *Mission in the New Testament* (tr. F. Clarke, London: SCM; Naperville: Allenson, IL, 1965), p. 146, O'Brien argues that it is unnecessary to see here a sharp dichotomy between evangelistic and church proclamation.

18. The eschatological dimension to this presentation before God is especially clear in Rom. 14:10; 2 Cor. 4:14; 11:2; Eph. 5:27.

19. O'Brien, *Colossians, Philemon*, p. 69. Contra Lightfoot, *Colossians*, p. 163, who argues that God is regarded here 'not as the judge who tries the accused, but as the *mōmoskopos* who examines the victims' put forward for sacrifice in the present. Cf. also n. 23 below.

20. Dunn, *Colossians*, p. 125, based on the argument that similar imagery is used in 1:22. Against this view, cf. O'Brien, *Colossians*, pp. 68–69, 89.

21. Cf. Delling, '*telos*', pp. 67–72; Du Plessis, *TELEIOS*, pp. 73–118.

22. In the Qumran writings, 'the perfect' are those who keep God's law wholly, as interpreted by the community, and so walk perfectly in God's ways (e.g. 1QS 1:8; 2:2; 3:8–11). Cf. Delling, '*telos*', pp. 72–73; Du Plessis, *TELEIOS*, pp. 94–115.

23. Du Plessis, *TELEIOS*, p. 199 (emphasis removed). His argument is forced when he proposes that *parastēsōmen* is an ingressive aorist ('because there is an initial moment where faith incepts'), and concludes that the durative participles which follow 'are concerned with subsistent endeavour and not the act of submission'.

24. Du Plessis, *TELEIOS*, p. 200.

25. Delling, '*telos*', p. 76, writes of the 'complete', 'full-grown' or 'whole' man in Col. 1:28, who lives in the power of, and under the direction of, Christ and his cross and resurrection. On the notion of progress in Paul's thinking, cf. Montague, *Growth*.

26. Klein, 'Perfect', p. 700.

27. Delling, '*telos*', p. 77.

28. Cf. Fee, *First Corinthians*, pp. 98–103.

29. Cranfield, *Romans* 2, pp. 610–611 (capitalization removed).

30. O'Brien, *Colossians*, p. 254.

31. Ibid. Dunn, *Colossians*, p. 281, takes the verb to mean 'fully assured' and argues that the prayer is for 'an emotional depth and balance to their faith' and that it should 'express itself in daily conduct where doing the will of God was the primary objective and yardstick'.

32. Cf. Dunn, *Colossians*, p. 232; Bruce, *Colossians*, pp. 155–156.

33. O'Brien, *Colossians*, p. 204. Cf. Du Plessis, *TELEIOS*, pp. 200–202.

34. O'Brien, *Philippians*, p. 422, drawing attention to the double use of *katalambanō* in Phil. 3:12.

35. Ibid., p. 423.

36. Ibid., pp. 26–35 (34). Hawthorne, *Philippians*, p. 155, disengages vv. 12–16 from the earlier part of the chapter when he proposes that no polemic against false teachers is involved in Paul's gentle exhortation here: 'some of his friends at Philippi misunderstood his teaching about justification by faith alone, and as a consequence believed that they had "arrived" and had ceased from that moral striving so characteristic of and essential to the Christian life'.

37. Koester, 'Purpose', p. 322. A brief critique of Koester is provided in O'Brien, *Philippians*, pp. 29–30. Cf. also Peterson, *Hebrews*, pp. 37–40.

38. O'Brien, *Philippians*, p. 429. Hawthorne, *Philippians*, p. 153, observes how the language in 3:13 pictures 'the ceaseless personal exertion, the intensity of the desire of the Christian participant in the contest if he is to achieve the hoped-for goal, namely the full and complete understanding of the Savior'.
39. O'Brien, *Philippians*, pp. 432–433, takes the 'prize' to be 'the full and complete gaining of Christ for whose sake everything else has been counted loss'. 'The heavenly call of God in Christ Jesus' is the divine calling to salvation, 'particularly the initial summons'.
40. Pfitzner, *Paul*, p. 150. Pfitzner seeks to show that the perfection which is the goal of Paul's striving 'dare not be reduced to moral perfection, but must rather be understood as the culminating point of his apostolic ministry and his life "in Christ"' (p. 139). However, Pfitzner exaggerates the extent to which Paul is countering an attack on his own apostolicity in this chapter.
41. O'Brien, *Philippians*, pp. 435–436. I have found this a persuasive challenge to the position I briefly outlined myself in *Hebrews*, p. 40. The ironical view is propounded by Hawthorne, *Philippians*, p. 156, and others noted by O'Brien, *Philippians*, p. 435, n. 89.
42. O'Brien, *Philippians*, p. 437.
43. O'Brien, *Philippians*, pp. 438–440, argues that *apokalypsei* here refers to a revealing in personal experience (cf. Matt. 16:17; Gal. 1:16; 1 Cor. 2:10). 'Nothing is said about the manner in which this divine disclosure would come to them; it may have occurred in a quiet way as they reflected on the contents of the apostle's letter. But whatever the means, such a growth in spiritual understanding would be due to a divine disclosure, that is, it would be purely of grace.' Cf. Paul's prayer in Eph. 1:17–18.
44. Cf. Delling, *'stoicheō'*, pp. 666–669; Esser, *'stoicheia'*, pp. 451–453.
45. Cf. O'Brien, 'Godly models', pp. 273–284.
46. Cf. O'Brien, *Gospel and Mission*, pp. 18–19. Unfortunately, at the time of writing this article, Peter O'Brien's commentary on Ephesians had not yet been published and I was not able to draw on his exegetical insights.
47. Lincoln, *Ephesians*, p. 218. I am not persuaded by Lincoln's arguments that the author of Ephesians was a later follower of Paul writing in his name (lx–lxxiii), but this is not the place to debate such a complex issue.
48. The process by which growth to maturity takes place by mutual ministry within the body of Christ is set out in Eph. 4:14–16. Cf. Peterson, *Engaging*, pp. 206–211.
49. Against Lincoln, *Ephesians*, pp. 253–255, cf. Best, *Ephesians*, pp. 395–399; Montague, *Growth*, pp. 150–151.
50. Barth, *Ephesians*, p. 487. Cf. Montague, *Growth*, p. 153.
51. Lincoln, *Ephesians*, p. 256. This makes better sense than simply identifying the mature or perfect man with 'the corporate man ... who is the church', Best, *Ephesians*, p. 402.
52. Best, *One Body*, p. 14, n. 2. Best, *Ephesians*, p. 402, says the goal to be attained is 'the measure, probably as in v. 7, the full measure, of the maturity or stature of what Christ fills'. Montague, *Growth*, p. 154, writes of the church attaining 'to the mature proportions that befit Christ's complement'.
53. Cf. Michel, *'katantaō'*, pp. 623–625. The verb can describe a literal journey (e.g. Acts 16:1; 18:19; 21:7) or a spiritual attainment as here (cf. Acts 26:7; Phil. 3:11).

54. Barth, *Ephesians*, pp. 485–487, pushes the imagery too far and has the church meeting Christ as 'the Bridegroom'. But Lincoln, *Ephesians*, p. 255, and Best, *Ephesians*, p. 399, are too quick to dismiss the idea of an ultimate encounter with Christ because of Barth's exaggerated development of the imagery. The church cannot reach its final state of perfection without a transforming encounter with the glorified Christ.

55. It is a great pleasure for me to write in honour of someone who has been both colleague and friend for almost thirty years. I am glad to acknowledge in this celebratory volume Peter O'Brien's immense influence on my own scholarship and ministry. It is a particular delight to write on the theme of maturity, which Peter has identified as such a concern of the apostle Paul and which has clearly been the goal of his own life and teaching. Indeed, this chapter is a development of what Peter himself has written on the subject.

15. Ministry in the wake of Paul's mission

Colin G. Kruse

Introduction

The purpose of this essay is to gather information concerning the nature of ministry in the churches founded by the apostle Paul. It is not Paul's ministry we are interested in, but the ministry that operated in his churches after he had moved on. Paul planted churches in the Roman provinces of Galatia, Macedonia, Achaia, and Asia, as well as on the island of Crete. What was the nature of ongoing ministry in these places? Did it vary from place to place? Did it develop over time? Sources for this investigation comprise Paul's letters, Acts, and the writings of the apostolic fathers.

Ministry in the province of Galatia

Paul's letter to the Galatians provides us with a little information about ministry in the Galatian churches. Clearly they were 'charismatic' communities.[1] In Galatians 3:5 Paul asks, 'Does he who supplies (*ho epichorēgōn*) the Spirit to you and works (*energōn*) miracles (*dynameis*) among you [do so] by the works of the law, or by [the] hearing of faith?' The expected answer is that God was supplying the Spirit and working miracles among them because they had responded in faith to the gospel message, not because they were observing the Mosaic law. Paul's question would have no point unless the presupposition underlying it were true, that is, that God was supplying the Spirit and working miracles among them. The close association of the supply of the Spirit and the working of miracles indicates that the latter should be taken as the manifestation of the former. The word translated 'miracles' is *dynameis*. It is found in Galatians only here, but is found frequently in Paul's other writings (forty-seven times) where it can mean simply power, or, more particularly, miracles (such as exorcisms, healings, etc.), and that is probably its meaning here. Paul acknowledges as a fact the exercise of extraordinary spiritual powers by his converts.[2] This tantalizing scrap of information suggests that in these churches there were people through whom God by his Spirit was performing miracles.[3]

This raises an important question. If the Galatian churches were 'charismatic' communities, was ministry in these communities a purely spontaneous affair occurring as people were inspired by the Spirit, or was there also a place for an 'official' ministry?[4] There are hints that officially recognized and even paid ministry was exercised alongside 'charismatic' ministry. In Galatians 6:6 Paul says: 'Those who are taught the word must share in all good things with their teacher.' Paul's exhortation to supply the needs of the teacher would not relate to the Judaizers who were troubling the Galatians with their teachings. It is also unlikely to be a request for assistance from Paul himself. Such a request would be out of keeping with his policy concerning personal financial support.[5] It is more likely an exhortation that the one who was recognized as a teacher of the churches should be supported by those whom he taught. This suggests that the teacher had been set apart for this task, and that he exercised an 'official' ministry among the 'charismatic' Galatian churches.

According to Acts, Paul and Barnabas appointed elders for the churches they founded in Galatia (Acts 14:23). Acts provides no information about the role of these elders. It is tempting to think that they included the 'teacher' with whom the Galatians were to share their 'good things'; however, there is no evidence to indicate whether or not this was the case.

There are references in 1 Timothy which might throw extra light upon the way ministry developed in Galatia. On his second visit to Lystra Paul recruited a young man called Timothy (Acts 16:1–3). In 1 Timothy 1:18 Paul alludes to prophecies made concerning Timothy's ministry: 'I am giving you these instructions, Timothy, my child, in accordance with the prophecies made earlier about you, so that by following them you may fight the good fight.' In 1 Timothy 4:14 he appears to refer to this again when he says: 'Do not neglect the gift that is in you, which was given to you through prophecy with the laying on of hands by the council of elders.' If this prophetic laying on of hands occurred in Timothy's home church in Lystra (and not, say, in

Ephesus), two additional points could be made about ministry in Galatia: (1) a council of elders functioned in Lystra, thus confirming the evidence of Acts mentioned above, and (2) prophecy was exercised in this church, though whether by the elders or others cannot be determined.

Ministry in the province of Macedonia

In the province of Macedonia Paul founded the churches in Philippi and Thessalonica. We have more information about subsequent ministry in these churches than we have in the case of Galatia.

The Thessalonian church also appears to have been a 'charismatic' community. In 1 Thessalonians 5:19–21 Paul exhorted his readers: 'Do not quench the Spirit; do not despise prophecies (*prophēteias*); but test everything.' Such an exhortation presupposes the existence of a prophetic ministry in Thessalonica. It also suggests there was a propensity on the part of some of the Thessalonian believers to think ill of those who prophesied. The content of prophecy in the New Testament is various. It can deal with a new initiative in mission (Acts 13:1–3), edification of believers (1 Cor. 14:3), future events (Acts 11:27–28; 21:10–11), and eschatological information (1 Thess. 4:15–17). The chances are that what was being despised by some of the Thessalonians included prophecies of this last type. The low regard in which some people held prophecies would be understandable if it was the influence of such prophecies on unstable minds that led some to give up their occupations and become idlers (cf. 1 Thess. 4:11; 2 Thess. 3:6–13). 1 Thessalonians 5:19–21 implies that it was the duty of all members of the church to 'test' the words of the prophets. They were not to despise them, nor were they to accept them unthinkingly. But 1 Thessalonians provides no information about criteria for such testing.

The Thessalonian church, like the churches of Galatia, included within its membership those who exercised an 'official' ministry. In 1 Thessalonians 5:12–13 Paul says: 'Recognize those who labour among you, and have charge of you in the Lord and admonish you; esteem them very highly in love because of their work.' The different sort of exhortations in relation to prophecies ('do not despise' them) and those who had charge over the Thessalonians (recognize and esteem them) suggests that different people were involved in these two ministries. It appears that 'charismatic' and 'official' ministries existed alongside one another in this church.

Paul's letter to the Philippians is addressed 'to all the saints in Christ Jesus who are in Philippi, with the bishops and deacons' (Phil. 1:1). Thus it is clear that from the earliest days the church in Philippi had bishops (*episkopoi*) and deacons (*diakonoi*).[6] The letter gives no indication concerning the role of these functionaries.

Towards the end of Philippians Paul pleads with two of his female fellow-workers, Euodia and Syntyche, to agree with one another in the Lord. He describes them as those who 'have struggled beside me in the work of the gospel, together with Clement and the rest of my co-workers' (Phil. 4:2–3). This is a reminder that women laboured alongside Paul in the ministry of the gospel, and in the case of Euodia and Syntyche they appear to have subsequently exercised a settled ministry in the church at Philippi.

Polycarp, bishop of Smyrna, was martyred in about AD 155. He wrote several letters, only one of which is extant (*Philippians*). In this letter he urged the deacons to be blameless in their conduct (*Phil.* 5.2). He exhorted believers to be subject to their presbyters/elders and deacons as to God and Christ respectively (*Phil.* 5.3). Presbyters were to be compassionate to all, restoring those who wander, and caring for the weak, in particular widows and orphans (*Phil.* 6.1). Polycarp's letter was written a long time after the church in Philippi was founded, and a long time after Paul wrote his letter to the church there. It is interesting to note, however, that while he makes no reference to bishops, he does speak of elders (not mentioned in Paul's letter to the Philippians). Possibly Polycarp's elders are the same as Paul's bishops. It is noteworthy that Polycarp's exhortation that people should be subject to presbyters as to God is reminiscent of Ignatius' exhortation to churches in Asia that they should be subject to their bishop as to God. Polycarp provides some hints concerning the nature of the responsibilities of elders: they were to show compassion to all, to restore those who wandered from the faith, and to care for the disadvantaged in the church.

Ministry in the province of Achaia

According to Acts Paul won some converts in Athens, but there is no mention in the New Testament of a Christian community there, or any indication of what ministries were exercised in it after the apostle left. From Athens Paul moved to Corinth. We know more about the church of Corinth than about any other mentioned in the New Testament, thanks to the letters written by Paul and Clement of Rome to that church.

The church at Corinth was particularly blessed with 'charismatic' gifts. In 1 Corinthians 1:4–7 Paul says: 'I give thanks to my God always for you because of the grace of God that has been given you in Christ Jesus, for in every way you have been enriched in him, in speech and knowledge of every kind – just as the testimony of Christ has been strengthened among you – so that you are not lacking in any spiritual gift as you wait for the revealing of our Lord Jesus Christ' (NRSV). Members exercised ministries of instruction, revelation, prophecy, tongues and interpretation (1 Cor. 14:26-29). Prophecy and tongues-speaking in Corinth were singled out by the apostle for special attention. Tongues-speaking by some clearly led to abuses in the Christian assembly. There was an unhealthy obsession with this gift which led the apostle to stress the greater worth of prophecy, both for the edification of church members (1 Cor. 14:6-20) and for its benefits to outsiders who might come to one of their meetings (1 Cor. 14:23-25). In the church meetings numerous people wished to speak in tongues and prophesy. Paul provided guidelines concerning the number of tongues-speakers who should be allowed to exercise their gift (but only when interpretation was available) (1 Cor. 14:26-28). As for prophets, the apostle advised that only two or three be allowed to prophesy, and the others were to 'weigh' what was being said. If while one was prophesying a revelation came to another sitting by, the first was to give place to the second. From this it may be inferred that the nature of prophecy in Corinth, as the apostle comprehended it, was that of a spontaneous revelation from God to one of the community, intended for the instruction of all. It can also be inferred that prophets were in control of their prophesying, for, as Paul insisted, 'the spirits of the prophets are subject to the prophets'. This stemmed from the fact that 'God is a God not of disorder but of peace' (1 Cor. 14:29-33).

The 'charismatic' exuberance of the Corinthian church created all sorts of problems, and put the church at loggerheads with Paul, who, some of the Corinthians thought, lacked the spiritual gifts they possessed (cf. 1 Cor. 4:18-21; 7:40b; 14:18; 2 Cor. 12:1-6, 11-13; 13:2b-4). Nevertheless, Paul tried only to regulate the expression of their 'charismatic' experience, not to quench it.

Paul told his Corinthian converts that all believers had received one of a variety of manifestations of the Spirit to be used for the common good. These manifestations are variously described as 'gifts' (*charismata*) of the same Spirit, 'services/ministries' (*diakoniai*) of the same Lord or 'activities/ workings' (*energēmata*) of the same God. Paul regarded the various ministries of the Corinthians as Spirit-inspired and bestowed according to his will (1 Cor. 12:11). Such ministries included the utterance of wisdom, the utterance of knowledge, faith, gifts of healing, working of miracles, prophecy, discerning of spirits, various kinds of tongues and the interpretation of tongues (1 Cor. 12:4-10). Among those who exercised these gifts, Paul intimates, were certain ones who had been divinely appointed to have precedence in the church. Thus in 1 Corinthians 12:28 he says that God appointed in the church 'first apostles, second prophets, third teachers' (and 'then deeds of power, then gifts of healing', etc.).[7]

There are indications that women were involved in the ongoing ministry in the province of Achaia. In 1 Corinthians 11:2–16 Paul argues that women should wear a head-covering when they pray and prophesy, which implies that women exercised these ministries in the congregation. Although it is possible to pray in private, it is not possible to prophesy in private because prophecy is communication directed to other human beings, unlike tongues which is directed towards God (1 Cor. 14:2–4). According to Acts 18, Paul linked up with Priscilla and her husband Aquila in practising their common trade and, it would appear, in the ministry of the gospel in Corinth as well.[8] While Paul affirmed women's ministries, texts such as 1 Corinthians 11:2–16; 14:33b–35 suggest that he expected them to operate in ways that did not undermine the headship of their husbands.[9] In Romans 16:1–2 Paul commends Phoebe to the Roman Christians, describing her as 'a deacon of the church at Cenchreae' (the eastern port town of Corinth) and 'a bene-factor of many and of myself as well'. This statement contains the first known use of the word 'deacon' (*diakonos*) in the history of early Christianity,[10] and its use here appears to imply that Phoebe occupied some 'official' position in the church. Paul described Phoebe as a 'benefactor' (*prostatis*), using a word found only here in the New Testament. Its masculine equivalent, *prostatēs*, is used in Jewish and pagan religious circles to denote a protector or patron of particular groups.[11] It would seem then that she was a person of significant standing who provided protection and support for Paul and others in Achaia.

There appears to have existed in Corinth an 'official' ministry alongside the 'charismatic' ministries. In 1 Corinthians 16:15–16 reference is made to the devoted service of Stephanas and members of his household, to whom the Corinthians were told to subject themselves, suggesting that they had some 'official' position in the church. Gaius is described as 'host to the whole church' (Rom. 16:23), and this may imply oversight as well as the provision of hospitality. Finally, there is included in the lists of gifts in 1 Corinthians a reference to the ministry of leadership (1 Cor. 12:28). That this gift is listed among others of a more 'charismatic' nature suggests that Paul saw no antipathy between 'charismatic' and 'official' ministries.[12]

Clement, bishop of Rome, wrote a letter to the Corinthians (*1 Clement*) in the name of the Roman church around AD 95. This letter reveals that 'on account of one or two persons the steadfast and ancient church of the Corinthians is being disloyal to the presbyters' (*1 Clem.* 47.6). Clement urged church members, who had previously been obedient to their rulers and paid fitting honour to the elders (*presbyteroi*) among them (*1 Clem.* 1.3), to respect those who ruled over them (*1 Clem.* 21.6). He referred to the apostles' practice of appointing their first converts to be bishops (*episkopoi*) and deacons (*diakonoi*) for future believers, having tested them by the Spirit. This practice, Clement said, was no new thing, but something foreshadowed in the Scriptures: 'many years before had bishops and deacons been written of; for the scripture says thus in one place "I will establish their bishops in righteousness, and their deacons in faith"' (*1 Clem.* 42.4–5; cf. Is. 60:17). Clement said that, because the apostles had foreknowledge of the strife which would arise concerning the title of bishop, they 'afterwards added the codicil that if they should fall asleep, other approved men should succeed to their ministry', and therefore 'it is not just to remove from their ministry those who were appointed by them, or later on by other eminent men, with the consent of the whole church, and have ministered to the flock of Christ without blame, humbly, peaceably, and disinterestedly' (*1 Clem.* 44.1–3). Clement insisted that it was a sin to remove from the episcopate those appointed by the apostles, or those appointed by other eminent men (*1 Clem.* 44.3–4). Applying all this to the situation in Corinth, he stressed that it was shameful that the Corinthians were being disloyal to their presbyters (*1 Clem.* 47.6) and urged those who instigated the sedition to repent and submit themselves to the presbyters (*1 Clem.* 54.1–2; 57.1).

According to Clement, then, ministry in the church at Corinth had from apostolic times involved bishops, elders and deacons, even though Paul makes no mention of these functionaries in his letters to Corinth. *1 Clement* 44:4–5 seems to imply that bishops and elders were synonymous terms, representing the same office. He speaks of the sin of ejecting faithful people from the *episcopate*, and contrasts the lot of such people with the blessedness of *presbyters* who have finished their course and so need not fear removal from office:

> For our sin is not small, if we eject from the episcopate (*episkopēn*) those who have blamelessly and holily offered its sacrifices. Blessed are those presbyters (*presbyteroi*) who finished their course before now, and have obtained a fruitful and perfect release in the ripeness of completed work, for they have now no fear that any shall move them from the place appointed to them.

Ministry in the province of Asia

According to Acts 19:10 Paul continued his ministry in Ephesus for two years, during which time 'all the residents of Asia, both Jews and Greeks, heard the word of the Lord'. In Ephesians 4:7 Paul[13] reminded his readers that 'each of us was given grace according to the measure of Christ's gift', adding that these gifts 'were that some would be apostles, some prophets, some evangelists, some pastors and teachers' (Eph. 4:11). The function of these 'gifted' individuals was to 'equip the saints for the work of ministry (*ergon diakonias*), for building up the body of Christ, until all of us come to the unity of faith and of the knowledge of the Son of God, to maturity, to the measure of the full stature of Christ' (Eph. 4:12–13). This growth was derived through connection with Christ the head of the body, the church, and mediated from him through the 'ligaments' with which the body is equipped. The word 'ligaments' is a metaphor which may be interpreted as a reference to either the apostles, prophets, etc., whom Christ gave to his church, or to members of the church generally. The latter alternative is preferable because the apostle goes on to say that the body's growth is promoted 'as each part is working properly', a reference to each member of the church (Eph. 4:15–16).[14] This is in line with the statement Paul made that the function of apostles, prophets, evangelists, pastors and teachers was to equip the saints for their ministry. Ministry was a function of the whole people of God. The apostle addressed the Christians in Colosse in similar vein (Col. 2:18–19). That he could write in this way to these churches and expect to be understood suggests that ministry in these churches was accomplished through all members as each mediated to the other the power for growth which came from Christ the head.

While what was said above implies a 'charismatic' understanding of ministry, in which each member receives grace and power for growth from Christ and mediates it to others, this does not mean that 'official' ministry was unknown in Ephesus. In Acts 20 Paul addresses the Ephesian elders (*presbyteroi*, v. 17) as those who had been appointed by the Holy Spirit to function as overseers (*episkopoi*, v. 28) of the flock, and who were responsible for guarding it against those who sought to lead people astray. They were to shepherd the church of God (vv. 28–31). That Acts says the elders had been appointed as overseers/bishops of the flock suggests that the terms 'elder' and 'bishop' were being used synonymously.[15]

Paul's letters to Timothy reflect a structured form of ministry in Ephesus. Paul gave Timothy detailed instructions concerning the qualifications of those to be appointed as bishops and deacons in the church (1 Tim. 3:1–13). The bishop had to be 'skilful in teaching' (*didaktikos*) (1 Tim. 3:2), and able to manage the church well (1 Tim. 3:4–5). Teaching and managing constituted the primary functions of the bishop. No information is given in these letters concerning the function of deacons.

Elders were to be considered 'worthy of double honour' if they ruled well, and especially so if they also laboured 'in preaching and teaching'. In 1 Timothy 4:14 Paul says Timothy received his gift for teaching 'through prophecy with the laying on of hands by the council of elders'. If this is a reference to a council of elders in Ephesus (and not, as suggested earlier, in Lystra where Timothy was first recruited by Paul), then the picture of a developed and structured form of ministry in Ephesus is enhanced (cf. Acts 20:28–31). However, this formal ministry structure would not exclude the exercise of prophetic gifts. Timothy's gift for teaching was given 'through prophecy with the laying on of hands'.

Timothy functioned as Paul's delegate in Ephesus after the apostle left (1 Tim. 1:3). He had to counteract erroneous teaching (1 Tim. 1:3–11), order public worship (1 Tim. 2:1–15), appoint bishops and deacons (1 Tim. 3:1–13), provide good teaching and engage in the public reading of Scripture, while at the same time providing an example for the believers in speech and conduct (1 Tim. 4: 6–16; 2 Tim. 4:1–5). He had to regulate the enrolment of widows for financial support (1 Tim. 5:9–16) and ordain elders, but not hastily (1 Tim. 5:22). He was to ensure that they were properly remunerated and that no flippant charges were brought against them (1 Tim. 5:17–21). Timothy's overall responsibilities are summed up in the instruction: 'What you have heard from me through many witnesses, these things entrust to faithful people who will be able to teach others as well' (2 Tim. 2:2). In other words, he was responsible to ensure the faithful handing on of apostolic tradition to the next generation.

Women featured in ministry in the church at Ephesus. Priscilla and her husband Aquila accompanied Paul on his journey to Ephesus and remained there after the apostle left (Acts 18:18–22). Paul described them as his 'fellow-workers in Christ Jesus', people who had 'risked their lives' for him (Rom. 16:3–4). In Ephesus they provided the venue for church meetings (1 Cor. 16:19). They also provided hospitality for Apollos and instructed him in the way of God before he crossed over to Corinth (Acts 18:24–28). While Paul affirmed Priscilla's ministry in Ephesus, instructions given to Timothy suggest that he expected women to exercise their ministries in ways that did not undermine the headship of their husbands (1 Tim. 2:11–15).

Ignatius, third bishop of Antioch, wrote a number of letters to churches in the province of Asia while being escorted to Rome, where he was martyred in AD 108.[16] Because of their early date these letters provide important information concerning ministry. They include many references to bishops, presbyters and deacons. Some of those who held these offices are mentioned by name (cf. *Eph.* 1.3; 2.1; *Magn.* 2.1; 15.1; *Trall.* 1.1; *Philad.* 11.1; *Smyrn.* 10.1). Ignatius' main concern appears to be to ensure that believers submitted themselves to these leaders.

The bishop appears as the leader of the Christian community in a given city. Polycarp, for instance, is referred to as 'the bishop of the Smyrneans' (*Magn.* 15.1). Believers are exhorted to live in harmony with their bishops, and bishops are to provide an example for them to follow (*Eph.* 1.3). Believers are to be subject to the bishop as to God because, Ignatius says, the bishop presides in the place of God (*Eph.* 2.2; 6.1; 20.3; *Magn.* 2.1; 3.1; 6.1–2; 13.2; *Trall.* 2.1–2; 13.2; *Philad.* 7.1; *Smyrn.* 8.1; *Pol.* 6.1). Believers are to remain loyal to the bishop and 'do nothing' without him (*Magn.* 7.1; *Trall.* 7.1–2; *Philad.* 7.2; *Smyrn.* 9.1). When a bishop is youthful, people should not take advantage of that, but submit to him, yet not to him but to the Father of Jesus Christ who is the bishop of all (*Magn.* 3.1). Those who honour the bishop are honoured by God (*Smyrn.* 9.1). The prayer of the bishop and the whole church (in the eucharist) is very powerful (*Eph.* 5.2). Ignatius gives little information about the function of bishops, except that he presides at the eucharist and his prayers have great effect.

Presbyters were closely associated with the bishop. While there is one bishop in each place, presbyters are spoken of in plural form (*presbyteroi*) or as a collective (*presbyterion*). Presbyters were to be attuned to the bishop 'as strings to a harp' (*Eph.* 4.1), to be subject to him (*Magn.* 3.1) and to 'refresh' him (*Trall.* 12.2). While it is said that the bishop presides in the place of God, presbyters are said to preside in the place of the council of the apostles (*Eph.* 20.3; *Magn.* 6.1–2; *Trall.* 2.2; *Smyrn.* 8.1). Believers must 'do nothing' without the presbyters and be subject to them (*Eph.* 2.2; *Magn.* 7.1; 13.2; *Trall.* 7.1–2; 13.2; *Philad.* 7.1; *Pol.* 6.1). Ignatius says little about the function of elders, apart from their role in supporting their bishop.

Deacons must be in every way pleasing to all, for they are not (only) ministers of food and drink, but servants of the church of God (*Trall.* 2.3). They are entrusted with the service of Jesus Christ (*Magn.* 6.1) and must be respected as Jesus Christ (*Trall.* 3.1) and as the command of God (*Smyrn.* 8.1). Deacons could be sent as ambassadors from one church to another (*Philad.* 10.1).

Ignatius' letters lay far greater emphasis upon the status of bishops, elders and deacons than do the New Testament documents, probably because Ignatius was obsessed with the need to increase respect for leaders in the churches to which he wrote. Nevertheless, what we see in Ignatius' letters does have its roots in the New Testament. The threefold ministry of bishops, elders and deacons of Ignatius' letters is foreshadowed in the reference to the Ephesian elders and Paul's charge to them (Acts 20:17–35) and in the instructions to Timothy to appoint bishops and deacons in Ephesus (1 Tim. 3:1–13).

Ministry on Crete

According to Paul's letter to Titus, after missionary work on the island of Crete, Paul left Titus there to carry out work still needing to be done after his departure (Titus 1:5a). As with Timothy in Ephesus, Titus functioned as a delegate of Paul on Crete. He was to exhort members of the Christian community to behave in ways that adorned the doctrine of God our Saviour, to be devoted to good works and to avoid dissensions (2:3 – 3:11). Titus was to model what he taught (2:7–8).

Titus had to appoint as elders people who were 'blameless, married only once, whose children are believers, not accused of debauchery and not rebellious' (1:5–6). Paul explained why such a person (he uses *episkopos*, not *presbyteros*) must be blameless: because he acts as 'God's steward' (*oikonomos*) (1:7). The *oikonomos* was a manager, typically of a household or of his master's property, which suggests that the bishop exercised a supervisory role over a local church. Paul provided Titus with a full description of the qualifications of 'God's steward': he 'must be blameless; he must not be arrogant or quick-tempered or addicted to wine or violent or greedy for gain; but he must be hospitable, a lover of goodness, prudent, upright, devout, and self-controlled. He must have a firm grasp of the word that is trustworthy in accordance with the teaching, so that he may be able both to preach with sound doctrine and to refute those who contradict it' (1:7–9). From this it is clear that the primary function of the elder/bishop was to teach sound doctrine.

The way in which Paul uses the words 'elder' and 'bishop' in Titus 1:5–9 suggests that the two words were synonymous, and it has generally been thought that in the New Testament these were different terms for the same official. However, in recent times this identification has been called into question. Attention has been drawn to the fact that early churches were house churches. Therefore, it has been suggested, the heads of households came to have supervisory responsibilities for the churches which met in their houses, and that these were the bishops of the early church. Further, it has been suggested that, as elders in the Jewish community were not synagogue officials but community leaders, so too early Christian elders were community leaders, not church officials. If we apply this suggestion to the interpretation of references to bishops and elders in 1 Timothy and Titus, elders could be distinguished from bishops. The bishops would be the hosts of the house churches, who exercised a supervisory role over the churches meeting in their houses, while the elders would be leaders in the Christian community. The possibility that one person might act both as an elder (community leader) and a bishop (host of a house church) accounts for the overlapping of descriptions of the tasks of elders and bishops in the Pastoral Letters.[17] If this suggestion proved to be correct, it would throw light upon the references to elders who rule only (community leaders), and elders who also labour in teaching (hosts of house churches as well as community leaders). However, as will be noted in the conclusions below, the results of this study suggest that the matter is complex and the relationship between elders and bishops seems to have varied from place to place and over time.

There are no indications in Titus that ongoing ministry on Crete involved active participation of 'lay people', women, or the exercise of 'charismatic' gifts.

Conclusions

A striking feature of ministry in the wake of Paul's mission is that in nearly all cases the churches he left behind were 'charismatic' communities (Crete being the only possible exception).[18] God supplied his Spirit to the Galatian churches and worked miracles through their members. The Spirit was active in the Thessalonian church, inspiring prophecy, which some were prone to despise. The Corinthian church was blessed with spiritual gifts of speech and knowledge. Spirit-inspired tongues-speaking and prophecy were part of their worship. Paul reminded the church in Ephesus that Christ had gifted 'some as apostles, prophets, evangelists, pastors and teachers', to equip members for ministry. As each member worked properly, the community would be built up as power for growth was mediated from Christ to the church through each of its members. Paul expressed similar sentiments when writing to the church in Colosse.

Equally striking is the fact that these 'charismatic' communities also had an 'official' ministry. In Galatia there was a teacher with whom the Galatians were to share their material goods, and Acts speaks of Paul and Barnabas appointing elders in the churches of this province. Depending upon how 1 Timothy 4:14 is interpreted, it could contain evidence for a council of elders in the Galatian town of Lystra.

In Macedonia the church of Thessalonica included people who had charge of the members and admonished them. The church in Philippi had bishops and deacons from the earliest days, and towards the middle of the second century Polycarp referred to the presbyters and deacons of this church.

In the province of Achaia, in the 'charismatically' gifted church of Corinth, Stephanas and members of his household devoted themselves to the service of the saints, and Paul urged the Corinthians to submit themselves to these people. The apostle Paul listed leadership as one of the gifts of the Spirit in 1 Corinthians, and spoke of Gaius as 'host of the whole church'. Writing about AD 95, Clement of Rome referred to bishops, presbyters and deacons in the church at Corinth, and said that the apostles had appointed bishops to succeed themselves.

Paul's letter to the Ephesians referred to apostles, prophets, evangelists, teachers and pastors given by Christ to equip church members for ministry. Evidently ministry was understood as a function of all members of the church in Ephesus. However, when Paul wrote to Timothy about his work in Ephesus, he referred to bishops, elders and deacons. Bishops were to teach and manage the church, elders to rule, and some of them to preach and teach as well. Acts records Paul's speech to the Ephesian elders, whom he addressed as *episkopoi* appointed by the Holy Spirit to shepherd the flock. Again, depending upon how 1 Timothy 4:14 is interpreted, it could contain evidence for a council of elders in Ephesus. Writing to churches in Asia in the first decade of the second century, Ignatius spoke of their bishops, presbyters and deacons. The bishop was the leader of a Christian community in one city. The elders' primary function was to support the bishop. Deacons, besides their ministry of 'food and drink', were entrusted with 'the service of Christ', and sometimes functioned as ambassadors from one church to another.

On the island of Crete Titus was to appoint elders, from among whom possibly a bishop was to be appointed. The bishop's primary responsibility involved teaching sound doctrine. It is noteworthy that while Paul arranged the appointment of people to the offices of bishop, presbyter and deacon, it was their functions (in the case of bishops/elders: managing/ruling, preaching/teaching), not their status, that he emphasized in his letters.[19] In this respect he differed from both Clement and Ignatius, who were more interested in status than in function.

A rather complex and varied picture of the relationship between bishops, presbyters/elders and deacons emerges from the material surveyed in this essay. Addressing the Macedonian church of Philippi, Paul speaks of bishops and deacons, but makes no mention of elders. However, when Polycarp wrote to the Philippians, admittedly about one hundred years later, he referred to elders and deacons but made no mention of bishops. Paul refers to Phoebe, the deacon in the Achaian church of Cenchreae, in his letter to the Romans, having made no mention of deacons, elders or bishops in his letters to Corinth. Yet Clement, writing to Corinth in about AD 95, refers to all three and writes in such a way as to suggest that 'bishop' and 'elder' were synonymous terms. Acts tells of Paul addressing the elders of the Asian church of Ephesus as bishops whom the Holy Spirit appointed to care for the flock. Here also the terms 'elder' and 'bishop' refer to the same persons. But when Paul wrote to Timothy about his ministry in Ephesus, he spoke separately of bishops (ch. 3) and elders (ch. 5), suggesting that the offices of elders and bishops were distinct. When Ignatius wrote to churches in Asia, some forty to fifty years later, he spoke of the offices of bishop, elder and deacon as quite distinct. The elders' main function was to support the bishop, be attuned to his wishes, and refresh him. The fragmentary information we have, therefore, supports the view neither of those who argue that 'bishop' and 'elder' were synonymous terms, always referring to the same office in the early church, nor of those who hold that they were always used to denote different offices. The evidence, if it supports anything, supports the view that in some places and at some times the terms 'bishop' and 'elder' denoted the same office and function, but at other places and other times they denoted separate offices and functions.

Another result of this study is the recognition of the fairly widespread involvement of women in ministry. In the provinces of Macedonia, Achaia and Asia women were involved in ministry in the early days of the church. In his letter to the Philippians Paul refers to his fellow-workers in the gospel, Euodia and Syntyche, who were then apparently involved in a settled ministry in Philippi. In 1 Corinthians the apostle refers to the women who prayed and prophesied in the meeting of the church, and in Romans he commends Phoebe, who was a deacon of the church of Cenchreae and a benefactor/patron of many. Acts speaks of the ministry of Priscilla and Aquila in Ephesus, in the province of Asia, where they hosted the meeting of the church and instructed Apollos in the way of God. However, the apostolic fathers make no reference to the ministry of women in the places where Paul founded churches.

Finally, it is noteworthy that the almost universal presence of 'charismatic' ministry reflected in the major Pauline letters has no counterpart in those writings of the apostolic fathers which relate to places where the apostle planted churches. Allowing for the fragmentary nature of the evidence, it may still be said that there was a movement over time away from 'charismatic' to 'official' forms of ministry. There is certainly no evidence of movement in the opposite direction.[20]

Notes

1. That is, communities which experienced manifestations of the Spirit in congregational worship.

2. Some have argued that the miracles (*dynameis*) referred to here were those performed by Paul when he first proclaimed the gospel in Galatia (so e.g. Bring, *Galatians*, p. 109), but this is unlikely. Both verbs used, *epichorēgōn* ('supplies') and *energōn* ('works'), are present-tense participial forms more appropriate for depicting an ongoing phenomenon in the churches than for narrating what took place in Paul's pioneer ministry. Also, the whole section, Gal. 3:1–6, constitutes Paul's appeal to the Galatians' own experience of the Spirit to reinforce his argument concerning justification by faith. In such a context the supply of the Spirit to the Galatians and the performance of miracles is best understood in terms of miracles performed by the Galatians themselves, and not by Paul.

3. See my discussion in Kruse, *Foundations*, pp. 83–84.

4. By this is meant ministry exercised by people who had been appointed by human agency and whose position was to be recognized and respected.

5. His policy was not to accept support from churches in which he was currently ministering, although he would accept it from other churches outside the area of his current ministry (cf. 2 Cor. 11:7–11; Phil. 4:15–16).

6. O'Brien, *Philippians*, pp. 46–50, provides a summary of the use of *episkopos* in classical Greek, the LXX and the NT, and of *diakonos* in the NT. He cites H. W. Beyer with approval when he says that 'by the time Philippians was written "there are ... two co-ordinated offices"', adding that 'they have self-evident authority'.

7. Paul's depiction of the charismatic nature of the church in these verses should not be taken as a reflection of how things were in the church at Corinth (where there was an unhealthy obsession with the gift of tongues), but rather as Paul's 'ideal' picture of a church, an ideal to which he appeals in seeking to educate his readers concerning the proper exercise of the *charismata*. Cf. Holmberg, *Structure*, pp. 120–121.

8. According to Acts 18:18, when Paul continued his missionary journey he was accompanied by Priscilla and Aquila, whom he later left in Ephesus, where they instructed Apollos in the faith (Acts 18:19, 26).

9. Cf. my discussion in Kruse, 'Human relationships', pp. 172–174.

10. As Dunn, *Romans* 2, p. 887, observes.

11. BAGD, ad loc. Cf. discussion of patronal relationships in the NT in Marshall, *Enmity*, pp. 143–147. For a more general discussion of benefactors in the ancient world see Winter, *Welfare*.

12. Cf. Holmberg, *Structure*, pp. 120–121; Martin, *Family*, pp. 59–62.

13. Assuming that Ephesians is a genuine letter of Paul. Should it not be so, it would nevertheless reflect Pauline tradition.

14. See discussion in Kruse, *Foundations*, pp. 171–173.

15. Giles, *Patterns*, p. 81, notes that bishops are said to be appointed by the Holy Spirit, but no such statement is made about the appointment of elders in Acts 20. This leads him to question whether Luke equates the offices of elder and bishop. However, the way Luke writes his account in Acts 20 indicates that the elders whom Paul addressed had been appointed bishops by the Holy Spirit, and from this it may be inferred that these two terms refer to the same people and the same office.

16. The date of Ignatius' martyrdom is debated. Corwin, *St Ignatius*, p. 3, gives AD 108–117 as the range in which the date of Ignatius' martyrdom may be placed.
17. Giles, *Patterns*, pp. 71–97.
18. Evidence for the nature of ministry on Crete is restricted to Paul's letter to Titus, in which no mention is made of 'charismatic' ministry. However, in the light of the evidence for charismatic ministry in all other places, we should not place too much weight on arguments from silence.
19. Theissen, *Social Setting*, pp. 42–54, describes three forms of legitimation: charismatic, traditional and functional. Paul was more interested in functional legitimation.
20. It is a pleasure for me to offer this essay to Dr Peter O'Brien in recognition of his substantial contributions to the study of the New Testament, theological teaching, and training men and women for ministry.

16. Women in the Pauline mission

Andreas J. Köstenberger

Paul has been called everything from misogynist to misunderstood with regard to his stance on women in the ministry of the church, and a thorough re-examination of the role women played in the apostle's mission is needed to clear up some confusion. This is especially important since we are not dealing merely with the mission of one important individual, Paul. Ultimately, Paul's mission is *missio Dei*, the mission of God, and the mission of the Holy Spirit *through Paul*. Called and converted by the risen Christ, led by the Spirit, Paul's mission arguably transcends the man and his historical-cultural context. If this is true, it also and especially applies to the role women played in the Pauline mission, and it is here that we can ill afford not to listen and learn from the apostle; for today's churches are in dire need of an authoritative, definitive word on how women (and men) ought to function in the church.

Recent discussions of the role of women in relation to Paul have been plagued by at least three deficiencies.[1] First, primacy has frequently been given, not to Paul's own writings, but contemporary concerns, and Pauline texts have been used to validate the interpreter's own preconceived notions on this issue. Proper hermeneutical procedure, however, demands that Paul's voice be heard first and foremost rather than being drowned out in the clamour of contemporary voices and concerns. Primacy must once again be given to Paul.

Second, studies on women in relation to Paul have frequently focused on

Paul's *teaching* but not on his *practice* (that is, how women actually functioned in churches under Paul's jurisdiction) or, less frequently, vice versa.[2] A comprehensive, balanced apprehension of Paul's stance toward women's roles must take account of both: how women *should* function in the church according to Pauline teaching (didactic passages on women's roles) and how they actually *did* function in the Pauline churches and mission in keeping with the apostle's instructions (narrative passages and references to specific women in Paul's writings).[3] The present essay will start with the latter question in order not to prejudge doctrinal issues and to safeguard a truly inductive approach toward the descriptive passages as much as possible. After this, the treatment of didactic passages in Paul will provide a framework from which to evaluate the first set of references.

The third problem besetting studies of women in relation to Paul is that women are regularly treated in isolation from men. The reason for this may be that the motivation underlying many such discussions is to magnify the contributions made by women to the life of the early church. However, if women are studied in isolation from men, imbalance and loss of perspective are the inevitable result. Women in the Pauline mission should therefore be studied in relation to men.[4]

In investigating descriptive passages in Paul's writings that show how women functioned in the Pauline churches and mission, this discussion will proceed in chronological order of writing. After this, Paul's explicit teaching on women's roles will be surveyed. Because I have previously written on the Pauline teaching on the role of women, this essay will summarize my findings on the didactic passages, and give more detailed attention to providing a thorough treatment of the descriptive references.

Women in the Pauline churches and mission
Data from Paul's letters[5]

A chronological survey of named women in the Pauline corpus yields the following list:[6]

Epistle	Names of women	Information provided
Gal.	none mentioned	
1 Thess.	none mentioned	
2 Thess.	none mentioned	
1 Cor. (2)	Chloe (1:11)	some 'from Chloe'

Epistle	Names of women	Information provided
	Priscilla (16:19)	church at her house
2 Cor.	none mentioned	
Rom. (11)	Phoebe (16:1)	'our sister', servant/deacon (*diakonos*) of church in Cenchrea, benefactress/patroness (*prostatis*)
	Priscilla (16:3)	fellow-worker (*synergos*; with Aquila), church at their house
	Mary (16:6)	'worked very hard for you'
	Junia (?) (16:7)	'outstanding among the apostles' (*episēmoi en tois apostolois*; with Andronicus)
	Tryphena and Tryphosa (16:12)	'women who work hard in the Lord'
	Persis (16:12)	'another woman who has worked very hard in the Lord'
	mother of Rufus (16:13)	'who has been a mother to me, too'
	Julia (16:15)	none
	sister of Nereus (16:15)	none
	Olympas (16:15)	none
Eph.	none mentioned	
Phil. (2)	Euodia and Syntyche (4:2)	co-workers (?), 'contended at my side in the cause of the gospel'
Col. (1)	Nympha (4:15)	church at her house
Philem. (1)	Apphia (2)	'our sister' (cf. Rom. 16:1); church at her house (with Philemon)
1 Tim.	none mentioned	
Titus	none mentioned	
2 Tim. (2)	Priscilla (4:19)	none
	Claudia (4:21)	none

Nineteen passages in Paul's writings refer to a total of seventeen women.[7] Two things are worth observing. First, references to women in Paul's writings are unevenly distributed, with almost two-thirds occurring in Romans 16. Without this chapter, our knowledge of the ways in which women functioned in the early church would be rather minimal, at least as far as the biblical record is concerned. Second, references to women in Paul's remaining letters are either entirely absent or very sporadic. The only women mentioned outside of Romans 16 are Chloe and Priscilla (1 Cor.), Euodia and Syntyche (Phil.), Nympha (Col.), Apphia (Philem.), and Claudia and Priscilla (2 Tim.). Since the references to Chloe and to Euodia and Syntyche are somewhat incidental, and virtually no information is given concerning the other women mentioned outside of Romans 16 (Nympha, Apphia, Claudia), Priscilla alone remains as a woman regarding whom more extensive information is available. We will return to this issue shortly.

Before proceeding with a detailed study of each of the women mentioned in Paul's letters, it may be helpful to compare the references to women in Paul's letters with those to men. Including multiple references, the picture is as follows:

Pauline book	References to women	References to men	Total
Gal.	0	5	5
1 Thess.	0	2	2
2 Thess.	0	2	2
1 Cor.	2	13	15
2 Cor.	0	2	2
Rom.	11	23	34
Eph.	0	1	1
Phil.	2	3	5
Col.	1	10	11
Philem.	1	9	10
1 Tim.	0	1	1
Titus	0	5	5
2 Tim.	2	12	14
Total	19	88	107

Of the persons mentioned in relation to the Pauline mission in the apostle's writings, 82% are men and 18% are women. Once multiple references are eliminated, the Pauline epistles identify about fifty-five men by name as associated with Paul in mission, compared with seventeen women. Of course, this quantitative statistic says nothing about the status of these persons in the early church. Nevertheless, the conclusion can be drawn that, set in perspective, references to women in Paul's letters are rather sparse (especially outside of Rom. 16). This shows that the major weight of responsibility borne for the Pauline mission rested on men, a fact that is frequently obscured in studies on the subject which give exclusive consideration to women.[8]

Discussion of references to women in Paul's letters

Before delving into the references to women in Paul's letters, it will be helpful to address two issues that pertain to the following discussion in general. These issues are, first, the fragmentary and frequently inconclusive nature of the available data, and secondly, the frequent yet fallacious hermeneutical procedure of drawing simplistic conclusions from a designation applied to a given person involved in the Pauline mission (such as 'co-worker') in the assigning of that person's overall status (e.g. of 'leader'). Regarding the first issue, it must frankly be acknowledged that the information provided by Paul regarding women is frequently (if not regularly) inadequate to form firm conclusions regarding the precise nature of their ministry. This is certainly true of Chloe, Junia, Euodia and Syntyche, and a series of other women whose names appear in lists of greetings with virtually no further identification. The following discussion will seek to exercise restraint in creatively filling in these gaps and focus primarily on explicit textual and contextual cues. A survey of the relevant literature indicates that interpreters committed to women's full participation in the church's ministry, including leadership roles, tend to fill in gaps in ways that magnify the contributions of these women in the greatest way possible.[9] The purpose of this procedure is readily apparent: once a certain woman (and all women mentioned in Scripture) have been elevated to the status of prototypical, paradigmatic 'authoritative leaders' in the early church, they can be made models for contemporary egalitarian ministry in the church. But responsible scholarship must distinguish between explicit statements and gaps, and between firm conclusions from explicit data and mere inferences.

The second issue pertains to a fallacious form of argument that is employed with great frequency. It runs as follows: if person *A* is called *X* in one passage, and the same designation X is used for another person (person B; in the present case, a woman) in a different passage, it follows that persons A and B have exactly the same ministry. But the logic of this kind of argument is demonstrably flawed: if the sky can said to be grey, and a cat is grey, does it follow that the sky and the cat are the same in every respect? Of course not.[10] *One* shared characteristic among two objects or persons, whether being grey or being Paul's co-workers, does not establish equality between these persons or objects *in every respect*. To argue thus is to commit the fallacy of focusing exclusively on a certain degree of semantic overlap between two terms while ignoring other aspects of a word's range of meaning that come into play by way of context in one instance but not necessarily in another. Thus the mere fact that both Timothy on the one hand and Euodia and Syntyche on the other are called 'co-workers' of Paul does not necessarily imply that all had identical ministries. All that can be said is that Timothy, Euodia and Syntyche can be called 'co-workers' of Paul in a meaningful sense. But their ministries may very well differ.[11] The strongest piece of evidence for this distinction is the fact that the New Testament calls certain men 'co-workers' *of God*.[12] But it stands to reason that no human being can be a 'co-worker' on equal terms with God. Thus it is possible to link two people by the term 'co-worker' without necessarily implying total equality (or equal authority) between those two persons. Sometimes, the word may refer to lateral 'colleagues'; at other times, there may be genuine collaboration, but not on equal terms. Even in the case of Timothy, who is called a 'co-worker' of Paul, it would be naïve to assume that Paul and Timothy were on an equal footing. Paul frequently takes authority in sending Timothy as his emissary (e.g. Acts 19:22; 1 Cor. 4:17; Phil. 2:19; 1 Thess. 3:2); not once does Timothy send Paul. But Paul can still call Timothy his 'co-worker'. The conclusion is obvious: when the term 'co-worker' (or another term potentially conveying the notion of leadership or authority) is applied to a woman in Paul's writings, we cannot necessarily assume on the basis of this designation that this woman functioned as an equal partner of Paul in his mission. This must be established on further contextual and other grounds. Schreiner says it well: 'All church leaders would be fellow-workers and laborers, but not all fellow-workers and laborers are necessarily church leaders.'[13]

With these preliminary caveats in place, the study of the seventeen women mentioned in Paul's writings may proceed, following the chronological order in which they are mentioned.

Chloe

The first woman referred to in Paul's correspondence is a woman named Chloe (1 Cor. 1:11). In the introduction to 1 Corinthians, Paul says that he had been informed 'by some from Chloe' (*hypo tōn Chloēs*) that there were divisions in the Corinthian church. These people are more likely slaves or freedmen than family members, since in the latter case a father's name would have been used, even if he were deceased.[14] Moreover, in light of the fact that Paul mentions Stephanas, Fortunatus and Achaicus as the Corinthian church's official representatives (16:15–17),[15] it is probable that those 'from Chloe' were people with whom Paul had more informal contact. Perhaps while on business in Corinth, they had become acquainted with the divisions plaguing the Corinthian church and mentioned this to Paul (upon their return?) in Ephesus.[16] The scarcity of evidence does not allow any firm conclusions. All that can be said is that Chloe was presumably a well-to-do (Christian?) woman, perhaps resident in Ephesus or Corinth.

Priscilla[17]

A second reference in the same letter is to Priscilla (1 Cor. 16:19) in connection with her husband Aquila (who is mentioned first here) and the church meeting at their house. Paul, apparently writing from Ephesus (cf. 1 Cor. 16:8), passes on Aquila's and Priscilla's greetings from there to Corinth, where he had first met this couple (cf. Acts 18:2–3). Priscilla, together with her husband Aquila, is mentioned again in Romans 16:3, where both are called Paul's 'fellow-workers in Christ Jesus' who risked their lives for him.[18] Apparently, Priscilla and Aquila had returned to Rome by that time (cf. Acts 18:2). The final reference to Priscilla and Aquila is found in 2 Timothy 4:19, where Paul sends greetings to the couple (back in Ephesus?) from his Roman prison.

In four of the six instances where she is mentioned in the New Testament, Priscilla's name appears before that of her husband (Acts 18:18–19, 26; Rom. 16:3; 2 Tim. 4:19).[19] Scholars have speculated that the reason for this is that Priscilla was converted before her husband, perhaps having led Aquila to faith in Christ, or that she played an even more prominent part in the life and work of the church than her husband.[20] Alternatively, it has been conjectured that 'Prisca was the more dominant of the two or of higher social status, and she may either have provided the financial resources for the business or have been the brains behind it'.[21] But none of this is explicitly stated in the text.

According to Acts 18:26, the couple invited Apollos to their home and explained to him 'the way of God more adequately'. Some have concluded from this that Priscilla serves as a paradigm for a woman teacher or preacher. But this claim is unwarranted. All that can be said is that Priscilla, together with and in the presence of her husband, and in the context of their home, helped to provide corrective instruction to a man, Apollos.[22] Moreover, the genre of the book of Acts is historical narrative, so that care must be taken not to exaggerate the alleged normative character of Priscilla's practice for all women (even though there is no indication that Luke is critical of what Priscilla did).[23]

Nevertheless, according to the book of Acts and Paul's epistles, Priscilla and Aquila were among Paul's most strategic allies in his Gentile mission (cf. *kai pasai hai ekklēsiai tōn ethnōn*; Rom. 16:4), playing important roles in such major centres as Ephesus, Corinth and Rome.[24] Together they hosted house churches in their home wherever they went, instructed others such as Apollos, and even 'risked their necks' for Paul (Rom. 16:4).[25]

Phoebe

Paul's epistle to the Romans contains references to several women.[26] It should be noted that the concluding chapter of Romans includes an unusually large list of people, probably because Paul had not planted or even visited the church before and thus wanted to establish that he knew, either personally or through other means, a significant number of individuals who were now members of the Roman congregation in order to solicit the church's support for his mission to Spain (Rom. 15:24).[27]

The first woman mentioned is Phoebe (Rom. 16:1–2), 'our sister' (that is, a fellow-Christian) and 'a servant (*diakonos*) of the church in Cenchrea'.[28] Paul commends Phoebe to the Roman church, using the technical epistolary expression for introducing a friend to other acquaintances (*synistēmi de hymin*).[29] He asks the believers in Rome to give this woman any help she might need, again using the usual expression in a letter of recommendation, 'in whatever affair she may need [you or your help]' (*parastēte autē en hō an hymōn chrēzē pragmati*).[30] The reason for Paul's request is that the woman so commended 'has been a great help (*prostatis*) to many people, including me', which may refer to the hospitality extended to Paul when he visited Cenchrea at the occasion of his three-month stay in Corinth (cf. Acts 20:2–3).[31] In the present instance, Phoebe may have been the bearer of Paul's letter to Rome, which would explain why Paul mentions her first in his list of greetings in the concluding chapter of Romans.[32]

The designation *diakonos* may be a generic reference to this woman's ministry as a 'servant' (cf. e.g. 2 Cor. 3:6; 11:23; Eph. 6:21; Col. 1:7; 4:7). More likely, in light of 'the official-sounding nature of the phrase by which Paul identifies her' (a *diakonos* of the church at Cenchrea);[33] the use of the masculine term *diakonos*;[34] and perhaps also because of the conjoined term *prostatis*,[35] Phoebe served as a deaconess (cf. esp. 1 Tim. 3:11).[36] Deacons were set apart for 'the practical service of the needy' in the early church (cf. Phil. 1:1; Titus 1:9; 1 Tim. 3:8–13).[37] They were to be of proven Christian character but, unlike overseers, not required to be able to teach (cf. 1 Tim. 3:2 with 1 Tim. 3:8–10,12–13) or to participate in the governing of the church (cf. 1 Tim. 2:12; 5:17). Neuer maintains that the office of deaconess 'certainly did not involve public proclamation of the word, teaching, or leading the church. Perhaps it involved serving the congregation, by bringing material help to the needy (Rom 16:2), in serving women, the sick, and strangers.'[38]

As a wealthy woman, a 'benefactress' or 'patroness' (*prostatis*, the feminine form of *prostatēs*), Phoebe would have used her financial means to come 'to the aid of others, especially foreigners, by providing housing and financial aid and by representing their interests before local authorities'.[39] This would have been a needed ministry in a busy seaport such as Cenchrea. 'Phoebe, then, was probably a woman of high social standing and some wealth, who put her status, resources, and time at the services of traveling Christians, like Paul, who needed help and support.'[40] However, this does not mean, as is alleged with some frequency, that patronesses were leaders of houses.[41] Moreover, to call her 'president', or even 'leader' of the church at Cenchrea, goes beyond the evidence, as does the claim that 'Phoebe held a position of considerable responsibility, prominence, and authority in her congregation'.[42]

Junia

A controversial reference is that to Junia in Romans 16:7, who, together with Andronicus, is called 'notorious among the *apostoloi* (*episēmoi en tois apostolois*).[43] The accusative *Iounian* could derive either from the nominative *Iounia* (accusative accented as *Iounían*), in which case the person referred to would be a woman, or *Iounias* (accusative accented as *Iouniān*), a male name.[44] The name is a Latin one transcribed into Greek.[45] It is taken by some to be a shortened form of *Junianus*, *Junianius*, or *Junilius*.[46] But 'If *Iounias* is indeed a shortened form of the common name *Iounianus*, why then does the name *Iunias* never occur?'[47] Indeed, '(1) the female Latin name Junia occurs more than 250 times in Greek and Latin inscriptions found in Rome alone, whereas the male name Junias is unattested anywhere; and (2) when Greek manuscripts began to be accented, scribes wrote the feminine *Iounían* ("Junia")'.[48] In 1977, B. Brooten could state that 'we do not have a single shred of evidence that the name *Junias* ever existed ... all of the philological evidence points to the feminine *Junia*'.[49] In the past twenty years, no-one has been able to refute these claims, and no further evidence has come to light.[50] In view of these arguments, and the complete lack of evidence for the existence of a male name 'Junias', it must be concluded that, until evidence to the contrary is forthcoming, the person referred to in Romans 16:7 is a woman named Junia.

Andronicus and Junia are identified as Paul's *syngeneis*, which could mean '"fellow-countrymen" [that is, Jews; cf. Rom. 9:3], and not "relations" [that is, relatives]'.[51] In this case it is unclear, however, why Paul, in chapter 16, calls (except for Andronicus and Junia) only Herodion (v. 11), Lucius, Jason and Sosipater (v. 21) Jews, but not Aquila and Priscilla (v. 3), Mary (v. 6), or Rufus and his mother (v. 13).[52] It is therefore more likely that *syngeneis mou* means 'my friends' or 'my close associates' as an expression indicating collaboration in ministry, equivalent to the expression *agapēton mou* in Romans 16:5, 8–9.[53] This would explain why even Lucius, Jason and Sosipater, who are commonly suspected not to have been Jews, can be called *syngeneis mou* by Paul. Andronicus and Junia are further called his 'fellow-prisoners' (*synaichmalōtoi*), a designation elsewhere applied only to Epaphras (Philem. 23) and Aristarchus (Col. 4:10). Nothing is known about the specifics of this imprisonment; it is usually assumed that Paul refers to a literal imprisonment, which appears probable, though a figurative use of the term cannot be ruled out.[54]

Moreover, Andronicus and Junia are identified as *episēmoi en tois apostolois*, 'notorious among the *apostoloi*'.[55] Most commentators see the reference as inclusive, that is, as including Andronicus and Junia among the circle of *apostoloi*, whatever meaning is assigned to this term (see below). However, it is possible that the reference is exclusive, that is, Andronicus and Junia are said to be 'notorious' (i.e. well known) among the circle of *apostoloi* (cf. *Pss. Sol.* 2:6: *epistēmō en tois ethnesin*, 'a spectacle among the Gentiles'). If so, Andronicus and Junia could be church workers or Christians whose ministry is not further specified and who are identified as well known among the apostolic circle (with *apostoloi* perhaps having a more narrow compass).

Alternatively (and perhaps more likely),[56] 'among' may be used in an inclusive sense, in which case this couple would be included among the *apostoloi*, whichever sense the latter term has. In this case, if Junia is indeed a woman, and if she is called 'notorious among the *apostoloi*', does the presence of a woman *apostolos* in the New Testament imply, then, that the early church placed no restrictions on the ministry of women?[57] This depends largely on the question of whether 'apostle' is here used in a narrow or broad sense. Four types of use can be discerned in the writings of the New Testament. First, *apostolos* may refer to the Twelve (e.g. Matt. 10:2). Second, the term is used for someone like Paul who had seen the Lord and was commissioned by him to a special ministry (e.g. 1 Cor. 1:1; 2 Cor. 1:1; Col. 1:1). Third, the expression may denote an emissary sent out to perform a certain task or convey a particular message (1 Cor. 8:23; Phil. 2:25). And fourth, *apostolos* may refer to an itinerant missionary (e.g. Acts 14:4, 14, of Barnabas).[58]

To which of these does the context in Romans 16:7 point in the case of Andronicus and Junia? At the outset, it is highly unlikely that these otherwise unknown figures are said here to stand out among noted apostles such as the Twelve (an impossibility) or Peter, James, or even Paul.[59] The sense 'messenger, emissary' (cf. 2 Cor. 8:23: *apostoloi ekklēsiōn*; Phil. 2:25: *hymōn apostolos*) appears more likely.[60] However, the designation 'outstanding among the messengers' seems a bit awkward, for the role of messenger tends to be rather inconspicuous, and this description is like designating a person as an 'extraordinary usher'. The meaning 'travelling missionary' is therefore most likely, especially in light of 1 Cor. 9:5 (cf. Acts 14:4, 14; 1 Cor. 12:28; 1 Thess. 2:7; Eph. 4:11).[61] In this case, Andronicus and Junia would be identified as 'outstanding among (itinerant) missionaries' (an important office in the early church as well as today), perhaps in part because they were converted before Paul (Rom. 16:7), which means that they must have become believers during the very early days of the church.

If this is the case, Andronicus and Junia were a distinguished senior missionary couple, and the designation *apostolos*, applied to both of them jointly, does not imply that Junia by herself occupied an authoritative leadership position in a local church or in the early Christian movement.[62] Indeed, if Junia is mentioned in the present passage in tandem with Andronicus (who is unquestionably male) *because she is his wife* (note that other husband and wife pairs in Rom. 16 include Priscilla and Aquila in v. 3 and probably Philologus and Julia in v. 15),[63] they would have exercised their travelling ministry jointly rather than independently, similar to Priscilla and Aquila or the pattern mentioned in 1 Corinthians 9:5, so that even in this function Junia should not be elevated to 'apostle' in isolation from (her husband?) Andronicus.[64]

Other women referred to in Romans 16

Several other women referred to in Romans are said to have 'worked (very) hard' (*ekopiasen*) for other believers (Mary; Rom. 16:6) or 'in the Lord' (Tryphena and Tryphosa, Persis; Rom. 16:12). No further information is available for Mary, a common Jewish name in that day. The root underlying the names Tryphena and Tryphosa means 'soft' or 'delicate', and it is possible that Paul was aware of the irony of attributing hard work to two women thus called. Tryphena and Tryphosa may have been (twin) sisters, since it was common to assign children names from the same Greek root;[65] or these two women were grouped together because of the similarity of their names.[66] *Persis* means 'Persian woman' and was a typical Greek slave name.[67] In the case of each of these women, the reference to their hard work may simply pertain to a variety of good works which were to be the hallmark of a godly woman (cf. 1 Tim. 2:10), even though this is not stated explicitly.[68]

Also in Romans, mention is made of Julia (16:15), the (unnamed) sister of Nereus (16:15), and Olympas (16:15). In context, these probably refer to the wife (or, less likely, sister; Julia) and children (Nereus and his sister) of Philologus, who is mentioned first, together with another member of their family or particular house church (Olympas) and others (similarly, v. 14).[69] Because these are common names for slaves and freedmen, it is frequently suggested that they were slaves of the imperial household in Rome.[70] The list of names in Paul's letter to the Romans also includes the (unnamed) mother of Rufus (16:13) 'who has been a mother to me, too'. The Rufus mentioned here may be the person referred to in Mark 15:21, where Simon of Cyrene is identified as 'the father of Alexander and Rufus'; but this identification, while plausible, is less than certain. Paul adds that this woman was *eklecton en kyriō*, 'chosen in (by) the Lord'.

Euodia and Syntyche

The final group of references is found in the prison epistles. In Philippians, Paul makes mention of two women named Euodia and Syntyche, who had contended at his side in the cause of the gospel but who now needed to work out their differences with the help of an arbitrator (Phil. 4:2). The surprising fact that Paul chooses to identify both women by name may indicate that their disagreement threatened the unity of the entire church. Otherwise, it is hard to explain why Paul would embarrass these women by referring to them by name in a letter to be read aloud to the public assembly. Indeed, the book of Acts indicates that ('prominent') women played a significant part in the newly founded churches in Macedonia (16:14–15, 40; 17:4, 12).

Paul mentions that Euodia and Syntyche had contended (the verb is *synathleō*) at his side in the cause of the gospel (4:3).[71] The fact that the same expression is used in 1:27 (the only other New Testament occurrence of this term) with reference to the entire congregation at Philippi suggests that these two women had participated in Paul's own struggle for the advance of the gospel as had the Philippian church as a whole (cf. 1:30).[72] To have contended together with Paul in (the proclamation of) the gospel and to be called his 'co-worker' is a fairly broad designation and does not necessarily imply that Euodia and Syntyche had the same kind of ministry as Paul.[73] Internal evidence suggests that the nature of the Philippians' 'partnership in the gospel' with Paul (Phil. 1:5) centred significantly around their financial support of his ministry (Phil. 4:10–19; cf. 2 Cor. 8 – 9; Rom. 15:25–29) and their willingness to suffer with him for the sake of the gospel (Phil. 1:30).[74]

In particular, the verbal parallel with 1:27 (*synathleō*) indicates that Paul is thinking of Euodia and Syntyche in the same way as he thought of the community as a whole, that is, as believers who bore courageous testimony to their faith and who shared sacrificially of their financial resources in order to advance the cause of the gospel of Jesus Christ. The claim that Euodia and Syntyche were 'important leaders', 'two influential church leaders', 'two women church leaders', or the like, is therefore overblown.[75]

Other women referred to in the prison epistles and the pastorals

In the closing sections of Colossians, Paul includes in his greetings a reference to Nympha and the church meeting at her house (Col. 4:15).[76] No further information is available. In his letter to Philemon, Paul refers to 'our sister' Apphia (Philem. 2), a designation elsewhere in Paul's writings used only with reference to Phoebe in Romans 16:1. Apphia, not a recipient of the letter but merely included in the introductory salutation,[77] has been identified as Philemon's wife from early times.[78] If this is correct, it would explain Paul's mention of her immediately after Philemon, since as Philemon's wife Apphia would wish to know about the situation surrounding the runaway slave Onesimus as well.

Finally, Paul's second letter to Timothy makes mention of a woman named Claudia (4:21). Again, no further information is available.

Evaluation

All of Paul's travel companions were male.[79] This follows the precedent established by Jesus.[80] None of the women mentioned in relation to the Pauline mission serves as pastor-teacher or elder. Phoebe apparently functioned as a deaconess and is also called benefactress. If Junia was a woman (which is highly probable), she probably served as an itinerant missionary or, less likely, as a messenger, together with her presumed husband, Andronicus. Priscilla, together with her husband Aquila, had a church meeting in her house, as did Nympha and Apphia (with Philemon). Priscilla is also shown to have had a (leading?) part in instructing Apollos in her home, again together with her husband.

The positions of Euodia and Syntyche in the Philippian church were apparently significant enough to threaten the unity of the entire congregation. These two women were (in all probability) counted among Paul's co-workers and had contended at his side for the gospel (even though it is unclear precisely which form this partnership had taken). Rufus's mother had been like a mother to Paul, at least on one memorable occasion. Other women had worked very hard for other believers in the Lord (Mary, Tryphena, Tryphosa, Persis). Too little is known about Chloe to ascertain her position in relation to the Corinthian church. Julia (possibly the wife of Philologus), the sister of Nereus (Julia's daughter?), and Claudia are mentioned without specific information about the nature of their ministry.

Overall, the listed data indicate that the influence of women was to a significant extent informal and frequently centred around their home. There are instances of women exercising hospitality, including hosting a house church; devoting themselves to a variety of good works; having a part in raising their children in the faith; and, if wealthy, helping others financially, be it with or without a formal position in the church. Some were engaged in missionary work together with their husbands. What is more, when reading passages such as the sixteenth chapter of Romans, one gets the impression that women were thoroughly integrated in the Pauline churches, having a vital part in the mission and life of the early Christian community and fulfilling roles of significant, albeit not ultimate, responsibility within the church.[81] This included 'missionary work, carrying letters, serving in charitable tasks as deaconesses, providing aid or shelter for traveling apostles, etc.'.[82] In the exercise of their respective roles, they functioned fully within the parameters of their Graeco-Roman surroundings.[83] The roles exercised by them also conformed to the pattern characteristic of the ministry of Jesus. In the ministries of both Jesus and Paul, men bore the ultimate responsibility for the ongoing mission, with women actively supporting and contributing to that mission.

This concludes the survey of women named in the Pauline epistles in relation to their described function in the Pauline mission. We may now turn to a discussion of Paul's explicit *teaching* regarding the role of women in the church.

Pauline teaching on women in the church

The literature on Paul's teaching regarding women is vast indeed, and the issue continues to be hotly debated in the contemporary church and scholarship. Moreover, the New Testament teaching on women is frequently treated as a test case in hermeneutics.[84] Since I have treated the subject in several publications elsewhere, I will limit myself here to a brief summary of the general contours of Paul's teaching on the subject.[85] We begin with a few programmatic comments.

Prolegomena

Several recent studies give short shrift to explicit Pauline teaching on the present subject.[86] Descriptive references are absolutized, while didactic passages such as 1 Timothy 2:9–15 are marginalized as 'difficult' or limited in application. However, the problem with this procedure is that it leaves the interpreter without a proper framework for evaluating the descriptive passages discussed above. There exists, of course, the opposite danger of filtering descriptive passages through a pre-established doctrinal grid derived from didactic passages in Paul's writings.[87] The ideal to strive for is a balanced analysis of both descriptive and didactic passages in Paul, with enough tentativeness in the process to allow for the findings of the analysis of descriptive passages to inform the study of didactic passages and vice versa. Of course, inerrantist interpreters will expect Pauline teaching on women's roles, correctly interpreted, and the way women actually functioned in the Pauline mission and churches, to be found in harmony.[88] Thus, if one starts with an investigation of descriptive passages and ends up with the notion that no clear parameters for women's ministry are evident from these texts, one should be prepared to revisit this issue once Paul's didactic passages have been studied, if such parameters emerge from those texts.[89] But in many instances, this dialectic never takes place.[90]

In fact, didactic passages in Paul deserve to be given full weight, even priority, in the matter. For it would be unreasonable for one to expect to be able to glean a full prescriptive pattern for women's roles in ministry according to Paul from incidental references alone. Moreover, the possibility remains, at least in theory, that descriptive passages depict women functioning in roles not permitted by Paul. Normativity must therefore be established rather than assumed. For these reasons descriptive references should be used primarily to illustrate and provide background for Paul's specific teaching on women's roles in the church. Indeed, as will be seen below, Paul indicates certain parameters within which women were (and are) to function in the church, and there is nothing in the descriptive portions of Paul's letters that actually conflicts with Paul's explicit teaching on the subject. But further discussion of this has to await the conclusion of this essay. We must first provide a brief synthesis of Pauline teaching on the roles of women in the church.

Discussion of didactic passages in Paul regarding women

The major thrust of Pauline teaching on women's roles may be characterized as follows. Paul infers from the creation account in Genesis that God has assigned to the man the ultimate responsibility for the family (cf. Eph. 5:21–33 in conjunction with 1 Cor. 11:3, 7–8).[91] The man's role as 'head' is not a function of the fall; the fall merely led to the man's abuse of his God-given authority in relation to his wife.[92] But even in the church age, Paul affirms that the wife is to submit to her husband, who in turn is exhorted to love his wife as Christ loved the church (Eph. 5:21–33; Col. 3:18–19).

The marriage relationship restored in Christ thus does not lead to a completely 'egalitarian' relationship. Rather, the creation ideal, which included the man's bearing of ultimate responsibility for the married couple (viz. the term 'helper' applied to the woman in Gen. 2:18, esp. in relation to the Pauline statements in 1 Cor. 11:8–9 and 1 Tim. 2:13),[93] is again made possible and freed from the distortions introduced by sin. It is not authority that is sin, but its abuse.[94] And submission does not imply inferiority, since even Christ chose to submit to the Father with whom he is united as equal in the Godhead (1 Cor. 11:3).[95] Paul does not claim to be innovative in this regard; he consistently takes his cue from the foundational narrative of humanity in Genesis 1 – 3.[96]

What does constitute a Pauline innovation, however, is Paul's extension of the biblical teaching regarding marriage to the roles of men and women *in the church*. Since the church is God's 'household' (e.g. 1 Tim. 3:15), it follows that the church, as a 'family of families', functions according to the pattern established for the family and the household in the beginning.[97] And, as argued above, according to this pattern the man has been given ultimate responsibility. Thus, as in the family, so in the church, the man bears ultimate responsibility (cf. the qualification of 'faithful husband' [not 'wife'] for an overseer in 1 Tim. 3:2, esp. in conjunction with 1 Tim. 2:12).

Conversely, Paul does not permit a woman to teach or have authority over a man (1 Tim. 2:12).[98] Why? Because of the man's priority in creation (1 Tim. 2:13) and the woman's 'priority' at the fall, where the creation pattern was reversed (serpent–woman–man–God rather than God–man–woman–serpent; 1 Tim. 2:14). Nevertheless, women have a significant role in managing the household, including childrearing and support of their husband (1 Tim. 2:15),[99] as well as ministry to other women (Titus 2:3–5), children, and a variety of good works.

Regarding the faith, there is no difference between men and women: women, like men, become believers through faith in Christ (Gal. 3:28).[100] As Peter wrote, both are 'fellow-heirs' of grace (1 Pet. 3:7). But equality in worth and dignity does not mean equality in function or role. This seems to be the clear implication from Paul's teaching on the role of women and men in the church.

It is neither possible nor necessary here to discuss all the instances where issues pertaining to women are addressed in Paul's letters, such as his teaching on caring for widows (1 Tim. 5) or singleness (1 Cor. 7), or even the puzzling passage on head-coverings (1 Cor. 11:2–16), since these issues are at best of marginal significance for women's roles in the Pauline mission. We conclude with some pertinent observations tying together our study of descriptive and didactic passages on women in Paul's letters and the book of Acts.

Conclusion

Paul's teaching on the role of women and the way in which women actually functioned in the Pauline churches are consistent.[101] Paul taught that women were not to serve as pastor-teachers or elders, and there is no evidence in Paul's epistles or Acts that women functioned in such roles in the churches established by Paul. Where the principle of the man's bearing of ultimate responsibility for God's household was not jeopardized, Paul allowed women to serve without further limitation. Thus in 1 Timothy 3:11, he lays down qualifications for deaconesses, and in Romans 16:1 we learn that Phoebe apparently functioned in such a role.[102] Women also supported the Pauline mission by exercising numerous other ministries.

The pattern of women's roles in the Pauline mission and churches also coheres with that found in the mission of Jesus. Jesus, too, chose only men for his Twelve; but he ministered to women and was supported by women in a variety of ways. Above all, both Jesus and Paul sought to integrate women fully in the community of believers, treating them with dignity and appreciation for their contribution. But they did so demonstrably and precisely without removing all parameters for women's ministry.[103] Frequently, this is not so much explicitly argued as assumed, for Jesus' and Paul's contemporaries generally were not likely to challenge a pattern of ministry that assigned ultimate responsibility for the community of believers to men. Men, not women, were generally regarded as heads of households, and elders in Jewish synagogues, to give but one example, were regularly men rather than women.

What are the implications of these observations for the practice of the contemporary church? While this has not been the primary focus of the present essay, I would be amiss if I failed to acknowledge the significance of the findings of this investigation for contemporary church practice. While it is not the purpose of the book of Acts or Paul's letters to legislate for every conceivable circumstance, I do find several principles that have abiding significance for the role of women in the church. Negatively, women are not permitted to serve in positions of ultimate responsibility over the entire church, such as pastor-teacher or elder. Positively, women may serve in roles of hospitality, missionary work, benevolence of various kinds, private teaching in conjunction with their husbands, ministry to younger women, responsibility for raising children together with their husbands, and other significant ministries.

As in Old and New Testament times, what is to determine women's roles is not the dictates of contemporary culture but the designs of God. God's plan is consistent from the time of creation to the age of the church, and from his pattern for the family to that for God's 'household'. As the present essay has shown, women made a vital contribution to the Pauline mission; they continue to make an important contribution today.

It is not easy to write on a subject that continues to divide the church. May the present essay help to shed light on this important issue. I conclude with a pertinent observation by E. E. Ellis: 'Paul and his colleagues are not called "teacher" or "leader" although some of them do teach and lead. For they have one teacher, the Messiah, and they are all brothers. Probably in response to their Lord's command, they eschew titles of eminence. With reference to their task they are the workers, the servants, the special messengers, with reference to one another they are the brothers.'[104] We would do well to emulate the example of Paul and the early church. For we who are 'in Christ' are all brothers and sisters in Christ, and together strive to fulfil the mission entrusted to the church today, seeking to hasten the coming of our Lord whom we will soon see face to face.[105]

Notes

1. On these and other hermeneutical issues, see my 'Gender passages'.
2. At the risk of oversimplification it may be said that interpreters advocating limitations on the ministry of women in Scripture tend to focus on the Pauline teaching on women's roles while egalitarian scholars favour descriptive passages.
3. For a helpful general treatment along these lines see Schreiner, 'Valuable ministries'.
4. See Ellis, 'Paul' and 'Coworkers', especially the helpful chart on p. 438 = p. 184 respectively. See also Ollrog, *Paulus*.
5. The only woman mentioned in the book of Acts in relation to Paul's ministry is Priscilla (18:2–3, 18–19, 26). When Kroeger, 'Women', p. 1216, claims that 'No fewer than eleven women are specifically named [in the book of Acts], and five are involved in church-related ministries', she discusses only the involvement of 'Mary the mother of Jesus and her female associates' in 1:14 and Dorcas in 9:36–41. On women's roles in Acts see also Keener, 'Woman', pp. 1206–1207.
6. The order of writing is judged to be: Gal., 1 and 2 Thess., 1 and 2 Cor., Rom., the prison epistles (Eph., Phil., Col., Philem.), and the pastoral epistles (1 Tim., Titus, 2 Tim.). Here, all thirteen are considered as part of the Pauline corpus, and references in them to people and places are taken seriously. Regarding the Pauline authorship of the pastorals, see my 'Ascertaining', pp. 107–108, n. 1. Unnamed women will be considered only if some identifying mark is provided, e.g. 'the mother *of Rufus*' (Rom. 16:13). The reference to Lois and Eunice (2 Tim. 1:5) will not be included in the present study, because these two women had no *direct* involvement in the Pauline mission. Named women *in ancient times*, such as Hagar or Sarah, likewise fall outside the scope of the present investigation.
7. The only multiple reference pertains to Priscilla (three times). Cotter, 'Women's roles', p. 350, n. 2, lists only thirteen women, not mentioning Persis (an oversight?), Junia (considered to be male?), Nympha (Colossians deutero-Pauline? oversight?), and Claudia (pastorals deutero-Pauline?).
8. E.g. Cotter, 'Women's roles'; Witherington, *Women*. A notable exception is Richardson, 'From apostles'.
9. See e.g. Schüssler Fiorenza, 'Missionaries'.
10. For the semantic fallacy of confusing sense and reference, cf. Carson, *Exegetical Fallacies*, pp. 63–64.
11. Cf. Ellis, 'Paul', p. 440: 'Co-workers may be described as equal to one another, as are Paul and Apollos in I Cor. iii. 8f., but this is not implicit in the term.' Contra e.g. Grenz, *Women*, p. 85: 'the terms Paul uses in this text [Rom. 16] suggest the participation of women in all dimensions of the ministry'.
12. Timothy is called 'co-worker of God' in 1 Thess. 3:2 (*synergon tou theou*). The same designation is applied to Paul and his associates in 1 Cor. 3:9 (*theou gar esmen synergoi*). Cf. Ellis, 'Paul', p. 440, who further points out that Philo, with reference to the plagues on Egypt, can call the insects God's *synergoi* (Philo, *de vita Mosis*, 1.110). Ellis provides further examples on p. 440, n. 3.
13. Schreiner, 'Valuable ministries', p. 219.
14. Fee, *First Corinthians*, p. 54, n. 32, referring to Theissen, *Social Setting*, p. 57. See further Theissen's comments on pp. 93–94.
15. Cotter, 'Women's roles', pp. 351–352, fails to address this piece of evidence. She thinks Chloe was a wealthy member of the church at Corinth, primarily because

she believes that the vague reference indicates that Chloe was well known in the community.

16. For a similar view, see Fee, *First Corinthians*, p. 54, n. 34, referring to Ramsay, 'Historical commentary', pp. 103–105.
17. The diminutive 'Prisca' is used in Acts, while 'Priscilla' occurs in the epistles.
18. The term 'fellow-workers' (*synergoi*; used elsewhere in Rom. 16:9, 21; 1 Cor. 3:9; 2 Cor. 1:24; 8:23; Phil. 2:25; 4:3; Col. 4:11; 1 Thess. 3:2; Philem. 24) denotes work in ministry, with the particular kind of ministry not specified. Cf. Moo, *Epistle to Romans*, p. 920. Witherington, *Women*, p. 111, claims on the basis of 1 Cor. 16:16–18 and 1 Thess. 5:12 that the term 'co-worker' implies 'a leadership function involving some form of authoritative speech', whether 'teaching, preaching, or both'. But his argument is fallacious, for even if it were said in certain contexts that certain *synergoi* were in positions of 'authority' or 'leadership' (notoriously slippery terms), it is illegitimate to conclude that this necessarily applies to everyone designated Paul's 'co-worker' in his letters. To argue thus is to confuse meaning and reference. See above.
19. Aquila is mentioned first in Acts 18:2 and 1 Cor. 16:19.
20. Cranfield, *Romans* 2, p. 784.
21. Dunn, *Romans 9 – 16*, p. 892.
22. The wording chosen by Keener, 'Man', p. 589, that 'Luke portrays her [Priscilla] as a *fellow-minister* with her husband, joining him in instructing *another minister*, Apollos (Acts 18:26)', is misleading, because it generally suggests an *ordained* minister in modern parlance, which (as far as we know) neither of those people was. See already the heading in Keener, *Paul*, p. 240: 'Priscilla, a woman minister'.
23. Contra Witherington, *Women*, p. 156, who claims that 'By including this story [Priscilla and Aquila instructing Apollos], Luke reveals the new roles women ought to be assuming in his view in the Christian community', and that 'By the very fact that Luke portrays women performing these various roles, he shows how the Gospel liberates and creates new possibilities for women'. It is hard to escape the conclusion that Witherington's analysis is significantly influenced by contemporary agendas while flowing less from an accurate historical apprehension of the 'first horizon' of Scripture.
24. Cf. Witherington, *Women*, p. 114.
25. Kroeger, 'Women', p. 1218, in a section of considerable length, seeks to revive the suggestion made by von Harnack that Priscilla and Aquila might be the authors of the epistle to the Hebrews, complete with the conspiracy theory that 'if Priscilla were perceived as the primary author, there might be a tendency to suppress this fact'. But this relies on the unconvincing argument that the use of a masculine singular to refer to the writer at Heb. 11:32 (*diēgoumenon*) 'may [merely] indicate male input (!) [rather than male authorship]'.
26. For an analysis of Rom. 16 in light of ancient inscriptional evidence, see esp. Lampe, *Die stadtrömischen Christen*, pp. 135–153.
27. Cf. Fitzmyer, *Romans*, p. 734. For a decisive refutation of the view taken by some that Rom. 16 is not an integral part of Romans, see Cranfield, *Romans* 1, pp. 5–11. Among the most extensive arguments against the 'Ephesian hypothesis' concerning Rom. 16 are Ollrog, 'Die Abfassungsverhältnisse', pp. 221–244, esp. p. 234 (see also Ollrog's comments on Paul's intentions in writing Rom. 16 on pp. 239–242); and Lampe, *Die stadtrömischen Christen*, pp. 124–135.

28. The term *ekklēsia*, as in vv. 4, 5, 16 and 23, probably refers to a local congregation, presumably a house church.
29. Keener, 'Man', p. 589, noting that twice as many women as men are commended in Rom. 16, speculates that this 'may indicate his [Paul's] sensitivity to the opposition women undoubtedly faced for their ministry in some quarters'. Paul may well commend Phoebe, in this instance, for a variety of reasons other than this.
30. Cf. Fitzmyer, *Romans*, pp. 728, 731.
31. Ibid., p. 731.
32. Ibid., p. 729.
33. So Clark, *Man*, p. 119.
34. Schreiner, *Romans*, p. 787.
35. Dunn, *Romans 9 - 16*, pp. 888-889, is probably correct in suggesting that Phoebe's two roles, *diakonos* and *prostasis*, should be seen as linked. He is followed by France, *Women*, p. 88.
36. See esp. Clark, *Man*, pp. 119-123.
37. Cf. Cranfield, *Romans* 2, p. 781; Moo, *Epistle to Romans*, p. 913; Neuer, *Man*, p. 121. See also the comments by Theissen, *Social Setting*, pp. 88-89. Contra Bruce, *Acts*, p. 122, who in his discussion of Acts 6 suggests that 'it might be better to render it [the term *diakonos*] by the more general term "minister"', and is followed by Keener, *Paul*, p. 239; and esp. Ellis, 'Paul', p. 442 (following Georgi, *Opponents*, pp. 27-32), who claims that 'the *diakonoi* appear to be a special class of co-workers, those who are active in preaching and teaching. They appear in Paul's circle not only as itinerant workers but also as workers in local congregations, such as Phoebe (Rom. xvi. I).' Ellis reiterates this claim in 'Coworkers', p. 185: 'It [the term *diakonos*] is probably best rendered "minister" since it refers to workers with special activities in preaching and teaching.' But Ellis fails to address the absence of the requirement 'able to teach' for deacons in 1 Tim. 3:8-13, and the rather general nature of the majority of NT references to *diakonos* just cited. See also the following discussion and note.
38. Neuer, *Man*, p. 121. Contra Arichea, 'Phoebe?', p. 409, who contends, without adducing evidence, that *diakonos* in Rom. 16:1 describes 'a person with special functions in the pastoral and administrative life of the church; and such functions would most probably include pastoral care, teaching, and even missionary work'.
39. So Moo, *Epistle to Romans*, p. 916. The term *prostatis* often refers to the function of 'protection', such as in Appius, *BC* 1.11. Cf. also Cranfield, *Romans* 2, p. 783, who comments that the choice of the expression *prostatis* 'implies that Phoebe was possessed of some social position, wealth and independence'; and Theissen, *Social Setting*. Witherington, *Women*, p. 115, argues, on the strength of the use of *proïstamenos* in Rom. 12:8, that Phoebe may have held the formal position of 'a person in charge of the charitable work of the church', but this is pure conjecture.
40. Moo, *Epistle to Romans*, p. 916.
41. Cf. e.g. Keener, *Paul*, p. 240, and the critique in the following note.
42. Cf. Schulz, 'A case', pp. 124-127; the list of commentators given in Fitzmyer, *Romans*, p. 731; and Keener, *Paul*, p. 239. Schulz, in seeking to make his case for 'president' Phoebe in Rom. 16:2, (1) inappropriately links the verb form *proïstēmi* with the noun *prostatis*; (2) inappropriately equates the meaning of

the feminine *prostatis* with the masculine *prostatēs* (cf. Schreiner, 'Valuable ministries', pp. 219–220; the same flaw can be detected in Keener, *Paul*, p. 240, whose evidence for his suggested meaning of the term *prostatis* consists of an article on *prostatēs* and two references in Epictetus and Marcus Aurelius likewise featuring *prostatēs* [p. 252, n. 26]); (3) unduly minimizes the possible connection between *prostatis* and the verb *paristēmi* (which means 'to help') in the same verse (cf. Schreiner, 'Valuable ministries', p. 219); (4) unduly suggests that *prostatis* must mean 'leader' or 'president' here because it is linked with *diakonos* (which, whether it is used here as a technical term or not, bears the original meaning 'servant' and was in any case not equivalent to the function of overseer in the early church); and (5) adduces tenuous background information regarding the role of priestesses in (goddess) worship in Greek religion. Moreover, it is puzzling how Schulz can claim that *'prostatis* may be the closest NT word we have to "president"': why not terms such as *episkopos* (Acts 20:28; Phil. 1:1; 1 Tim. 3:2; Titus 1:7)?

43. Regarding the latter phrase, see further the comments below.
44. Both UBS 3 and 4 as well as Nestle-Aland 25th and 26th print the masculine accentuation. Note that a few textual witnesses (esp. $\mathfrak{p}^{46}$ [c. AD 200]) read *Ioulian*, which Metzger regards as a 'clerical error' (cf. Rom. 16:15). Cf. Metzger, *Textual Commentary* (1975 ed.), p. 539.
45. So Cervin, 'Note', pp. 464–470.
46. So BAGD, p. 380: *'Iounias, a, ho, Junias* (not found elsewh., prob. short form of the common Junianus; cf. Bl.-D. §125.2; Rob. 172) ... The possibility, fr. a purely lexical point of view, that this is a woman's name *Iounia, as,* "Junia" ... deserves consideration (but s. Ltzm., Hdb. ad loc.).' However, the assertion by Lietzmann, *Die Briefe*, p. 73: *'Iounian* muss wegen der folgenden Aussagen einen Mann bezeichnen, also *Iounias* = Junianus', is sheer dogmatism. Bl.-D. §125, 2 cite as a possible parallel the shortening of *Silouanos* (Paul and 1 Pet. 5:12) to *Silas* (Acts) or *Sileas*; Fàbrega, 'Junia(s)', p. 49, adds the shortening of *Antipas* for *Antipatros* (Rev. 2:13), of *Klōpas* or *Kleopas* for *Kleopatros* (John 19:25; Luke 24:18), and of *Loukas* for the Latin Lucius or Lucanus (Col. 4:14; 2 Tim. 4:11; Philem. 24). See also MM, p. 306, who comment that *'Iounias* is probably a contracted form of *Iounianus*, which is common in the inscrr., e.g. *CIL* III. 4020'.
47. Cervin, 'Note', p. 466. Similarly, Schulz, 'Romans 16:7', p. 109: 'The Junias theory is an argument from silence.'
48. Metzger, *Textual Commentary* (1994 ed.), p. 475. For a survey of patristic exegesis, see esp. Fàbrega, 'Junia(s)?', pp. 54–63, who discusses in particular the references in Chrysostom, Theodoret and Origen.
49. Brooten, 'Junia', pp. 142–143.
50. Reference should be made to Brooten's claim ('Junia', p. 144, n. 4) that Migne's edition of the text of the earliest commentator on Rom. 16:7, Origen of Alexandria (c. 185–253/54), has *Junia* emended to *Junias*, but that the MSS themselves have *Junia* or *Julia*. To date, I have not been able to obtain these MSS to verify Brooten's claim. But see Fàbrega, 'Junia(s)?', p. 59 n. 51, who points out that the name Junia is found in a commentary written by Hraban of Fulda in c. AD 820, which the latter claims to have taken verbatim from Origen's (Rufinus's) commentary (is this the basis for Brooten's claim?). In his extensive discussion (pp. 58–60), Fàbrega also notes that Origen's Romans commentary, written in AD 244, has

been preserved only in a Latin version written by Rufinus in AD 404. In this version, Rufinus frequently condenses Origen's comments or even replaces them with his own. Also, Rufinus's interpretation is based not on the Greek, but the Latin, text of the Roman epistle. With reference to the work of E. von der Goltz and O. Bauernfeind, Fàbrega concludes that it is likely that Origen himself did not comment at all on the list of names in Rom. 16. The implication of this is that Origen should in future discussions of the issue be excluded as evidence for a patristic interpretation of *Iounian* as male (or, of course, female, for that matter).

51. So Cranfield, *Romans* 2, p. 788, referring to Sanday & Headlam, *Romans*, p. 423. Contra Ellis, 'Coworkers', p. 186, who seeks to make a case that *syngeneis* in Paul's writings regularly refers to the apostle's literal relatives. Consequently, Ellis conjectures that Andronicus and Junia 'were very likely Jerusalem relatives who were missionaries from that church to Rome'.

52. Cf. Fàbrega, 'Junia(s)?', p. 49.

53. Fàbrega, 'Junia(s)?', p. 50; following Michaelis, '*syngenēs ktl*', *TDNT* 7, pp. 741–742.

54. Cf. Meeks, *Urban Christians*, p. 57: 'Andronicus and Junia(s) (Rom. 16:7) have also moved from the East, where they were imprisoned with Paul somewhere, sometime, to Rome ...' Possibly Paul does not mean to indicate that Andronicus and Junia were imprisoned with him at the same time or in the same place but simply that they too had been imprisoned for the faith at some point. Cf. Fitzmyer, *Romans*, p. 739. For an argument for a figurative use of this expression, see esp. Kittel, '*aichmalōtos*', in *TDNT* 1, pp. 196–197.

55. This is the almost unanimous view of commentators, including Dunn, *Romans 9 – 16*, p. 894; Cranfield, *Romans* 2, p. 789, referring also to Schnackenburg, 'Apostles', pp. 287–303; and Cervin, 'Note', p. 470, who also notes the Vulgate rendering, 'qui sunt nobiles in [i.e. among] apostolis'. The term *episēmos* is used elsewhere in the NT only in Matt. 27:16 (referring to the 'notorious' prisoner Barabbas) and occurs eight times in the LXX (Gen. 30:42; Est. 5:4; 1 Macc. 11:37; 14:48; 2 Macc. 15:36; 3 Macc. 6:1; Pss. 2:6; 17:30), generally to denote that which is distinguished or conspicuous as over against that which is insignificant, nondescript or otherwise unnoticed.

56. For this inclusive sense, see Lucian, *Merc. Cond.* 28.5: 'he will be conspicuous among the claques' (*episēmos esē en tois epainousi* [2nd cent. AD]); Eusebius, *Praep. Evang.* 10.14: 'This man became most distinguished among the Greeks' (*ho anēr episēmotatos en tois Hellēsi*; 4th cent. AD]); *Concilium Ephesenum* 1.1.7.152.26: 'a man prominent among the *ekklēsiastikoi* (*anēr aei en tois ekklēsiastikois* [5th cent. AD]).

57. The ideological stake in this question is helpfully acknowledged by Moo, *Epistle to Romans*, p. 923. Keener, 'Man', p. 589, may have a point when he comments that the proposal that *Iounian* in Rom. 16:7 represents a shortened form of *Iounianus* or the like 'rests on the assumption that a woman could not be an apostle, rather than on any evidence inherent in the text itself'. Similarly, France, *Women*, pp. 86–87. See also Brooten, 'Junia'; and more recently, Grenz, *Women*, p. 211.

58. Cf. Witherington, *Women*, p. 115, referring to Barrett, *Signs*, pp. 23ff.; and Schnackenburg, 'Apostles', pp. 293–294.

59. So rightly Ellis, 'Coworkers', p. 186. Contra Dunn, *Romans 9 – 16*, p. 894, who exceeds the evidence when he 'firmly' concludes 'that one of the foundation apostles of Christianity [viz. Eph. 2:20] was a woman and a wife'.

60. This view is adopted by Piper & Grudem, 'Overview', p. 81, who ascribe to Andronicus and Junias (sic) 'some kind of itinerant ministry', citing as parallels Phil. 2:25 and 2 Cor. 8:23.

61. Cf. Cranfield, *Romans* 2, p. 789, followed by Witherington, *Women*, p. 115; Moo, *Epistle to Romans*, p. 924; Ellis, 'Coworkers', p. 186; France, *Women*, p. 87; and Lampe, *Die stadtrömischen Christen*, p. 137. Fàbrega, 'Junia(s)?', p. 53, also cites the German commentators Lietzmann, Schmithals, Schnackenburg and Wilkens as holding this view.

62. *Contra* Grenz, *Women*, p. 96, who claims that 'the weight of evidence favors interpreting Junia as an authoritative apostle'.

63. This is called by some the consensus view of ancient commentators until the twelfth or thirteenth century (e.g. Lohfink, p. 328; for a list of references, see Fitzmyer, *Romans*, pp. 737–738). But this is inaccurate, since accented ninth-century minuscule mss (e.g. 33) already bear the masculine form *Iouniãn* and never the feminine form *Iounían* (cf. Lampe, 'Iunia/Iunias', p. 132, n. 1; Fitzmyer, *Romans*, p. 738). Keener, *Paul*, p. 242, appropriately comments that 'If Junia is a woman apostle travelling with Andronicus, a male apostle, certain scandal would result if they were not brother and sister or husband and wife. Since most apostles, unlike Paul, were married (1 Cor. 9:5), the early church was probably right when it understood them as a husband-wife apostolic team' (this does not imply endorsement of Keener's use of the terms 'apostles' and 'apostolic' in this statement). See further Jeremias, 'Paarweise Sendung', p. 139, who calls Andronicus and Junias a 'Sendbotenpaar der Urgemeinde' in keeping with the Jewish pattern, emulated by both Jesus and Paul, of sending out messengers in pairs.

64. Cf. Moo, *Epistle to Romans*, p. 923, who calls Andronicus and Junia 'this husband and wife ministry team'. Similarly, Dunn, *Romans 9 – 16*, p. 894: 'The most natural way to read the two names within the phrase is as husband and wife'. Perriman, *Women*, p. 70, n. 29, cites Clement of Alexandria, who wrote that the apostles took their wives with them as 'fellow ministers' through whom 'the Lord's teaching penetrated into the women's quarters without scandal' (*Stromateis* 3.6.53). Note also Fitzmyer, *Romans*, p. 739: 'They could be considered paired messengers of the gospel, even if husband and wife.'

65. Moo, *Epistle to Romans*, p. 925, n. 54.

66. Cf. Cranfield, *Romans* 2, p. 793.

67. Ibid.; Lampe, *Die stadtrömischen Christen*, p. 145.

68. Cf. Dunn, *Romans 9 – 16*, p. 894, who points out that *kopiaõ* is a general term that does not denote leadership per se. But see von Harnack, '*Kopos*', pp. 1–10, esp. p. 5, who contends that *kopiaõ* was used by Paul to refer to missionary service as well as to service in the church: 'the Christian who works on behalf of others performs "hard labour"' (my translation); and Lampe, *Die stadtrömischen Christen*, p. 137, who calls the term a '*terminus technicus* der Missionssprache'.

69. Cranfield, *Romans* 2, p. 795; Fitzmyer, *Romans*, p. 742.

70. See e.g. Dunn, *Romans 9 – 16*, p. 898.

71. See further *IPol.* 6:1: 'Labour with one another, struggle together, run together, suffer together, rest together, rise up together as God's stewards and assessors and servants' (*synkopiate allēlois, synathleite, syntrechete, synkoimasthe, synegeiresthe hos theou oikonomoi kai paredroi kai hypēretai*), advice which is addressed to the entire Christian community.

72. O'Brien, *Philippians*, pp. 481–482. The suggestion by Cotter, 'Women's roles', p. 353, that Euodia and Syntyche 'belonged to a team of men and women evangelizers' is unduly specific and thus exceeds the evidence.

73. See already the preliminary observations made above. Note also the early variant *kai tōn synergōn mou kai tōn loipōn* ('and my co-workers, and the others'; Codex Sinaiticus, $\mathfrak{P}^{16}$), which, if original, would suggest that the women and Clement are not included in the category of 'co-workers'. Cf. Silva, *Philippians*, p. 223.

74. This is argued persuasively by Malinowski, 'Brave women', pp. 60–64.

75. The references are to Furnish, *Moral Teaching*, p. 105; Koester, 'Philippians', p. 666; and Scroggs, 'Women', p. 966.

76. There is some uncertainty whether this refers to a man or a woman, but on balance a female reference seems to be preferred. Cf. O'Brien, *Colossians*, p. 256; Perriman, *Women*, pp. 71–72. On house churches, see also references to Philemon (Philem. 2; see further next note), Lydia (Acts 16:15, 40), Gaius (Rom. 16:23), and Aquila and Priscilla (1 Cor. 16:19; Rom. 16:5).

77. The reference to the church meeting in 'your' (*sou*) house is singular and refers to Philemon alone; cf. O'Brien, *Colossians*, p. 273. Contra Cotter, 'Women's roles', p. 351, who claims that Apphia is one of 'the main leaders of that otherwise faceless assembly', citing as evidence only that this is the view of Schüssler Fiorenza, *Memory*, p. 177.

78. Cf. Lohse, *Colossians*, p. 190 (followed by O'Brien, *Colossians*, p. 273): 'Since her [Apphia's] name follows immediately after Philemon's, one can assume that she is his wife', referring also to Theodoret: 'Paul … adds the name of the wife … to that of the husband' (*Paulus … marito … jungit uxorem*).

79. Hadorn, 'Die Gefährten', p. 73.

80. Luke 8:1–3 is no real exception, for the thrust of this passage is not that women were among those who were part of Jesus' regular travel companions but that some women who had benefited from his ministry supported him and the Twelve in their itinerant work. See Bock, *Luke 1:1 – 9:50*, p. 713, who notes, with reference to Talbert, *Reading Luke*, pp. 92–93, and Witherington, 'Road', pp. 243–248, that it was unusual for women to travel with a rabbi in Jesus' day.

81. Cf. Schreiner, 'Valuable ministries', p. 222: 'it is clear that Biblical writers consistently ascribe ultimate responsibility to men for the leadership of the church'. Ellis, 'Coworkers', p. 187, may overstate his case when he maintains that a 'remarkable number of women are mentioned as Paul's associates, both in Acts and in his letters. Some are *called ministers* (*diakonoi*) or coworkers (*synergoi*) or missionaries (*apostoloi*), several of whom were *engaged in ministries of teaching and preaching* (Rom. 16:1, 3, 7; Phil. 4:2–3; cf. Acts 18:26)' (emphasis added). See the discussion of *diakonos* as 'minister' and the treatment of Phoebe, Priscilla, Junia, and Euodia and Syntyche, above.

82. Witherington, *Women*, p. 116.

83. The primary focus of the present essay is the study of the relevant biblical passages rather than extensive exploration of the ancient cultural background. For a helpful survey, see e.g. Witherington, *Women*, pp. 5–23. Cf. also Cotter, 'Women's roles', whose study is, however, marred by her ambiguous use of the terms 'authority' and 'leadership' and by her one-sided focus on descriptive Pauline passages at the exclusion of didactic portions (for a fuller critique, see my review in *CBMW News*, p. 14).

84. Cf. most recently France, *Women*. See also Köstenberger, 'Gender passages', pp. 259–283.

85. See esp. Köstenberger, Schreiner & Baldwin, *Women*; Köstenberger, 'Syntactical background'; idem, 'Gender passages'; idem, 'Crux'; idem, 'Ascertaining roles'.

86. Cf. e.g. Grenz, *Women* (see my review).

87. Examples of this are the insistence of complementarian scholars such as Grudem and Piper that Junia(s) is a man, despite the fact that there is virtually no evidence to support such a claim, or the refusal by certain conservative interpreters to entertain seriously the possibility that Phoebe indeed functioned as a deaconess merely because their preconceived doctrinal commitments preclude such a possibility. On the first issue, cf. Piper & Grudem, 'Overview', pp. 79–81; and most recently Grudem, 'Willow Creek', p. 5, where the only two pieces of evidence cited are a debatable reference in Origen (see n. 50 above) and a probably unreliable piece of information from Epiphanius (as Grudem himself points out in a damaging concession, Epiphanius also identified the obvious feminine name 'Prisca' in Rom. 16:3 as a masculine name; p. 479, n. 19). Also, it is methodologically fallacious for Grudem and Piper completely to rule out from consideration relevant evidence from Latin literature (except for the dubious Origen reference) as well as inscriptional evidence. This selective appraisal of the evidence is all the more remarkable as Grudem himself appropriately excoriates egalitarian scholars such as Kroeger for refusing to concede that *kephalē* regularly denotes 'head' with the connotation of authority while maintaining, with evidence that evaporates when checked out, that it means 'source'. See Grudem's devastating critique of Kroeger, 'Head', at the Annual Meeting of the Evangelical Theological Society (21 November 1997) and his article 'The meaning'.

88. Contra France, *Women*, p. 89, who concludes his survey of women in the Pauline churches with the comment that 'This material, together with the evidence we have cited from other Pauline letters and from Acts, is in such striking contrast with the refusal in 1 Timothy 2.11–12 to allow a woman to teach or to have authority, and with the concept of "submission", that it raises sharply the hermeneutical question of where within the varied and apparently conflicting testimony of the New Testament it is right to start to construct our biblical understanding of women's ministry'. France's solution to this 'dilemma' is to follow Bruce, *Galatians*, p. 190, in distinguishing between 'basic principles' such as Galatians 3:28 and 'less basic' texts such as 1 Timothy 2:11–15 (ibid., p. 94). But this procedure is not only highly subjective (as France himself admits, ibid.; what criteria?) but also establishes a 'canon within a canon' (also conceded by France, ibid.) that accentuates preferred texts while marginalizing (or altogether ignoring) unwelcome texts. For a critique, see Köstenberger, 'Gender passages', pp. 273–279.

89. Keener, 'Appendix A', in *Paul*, p. 237, acknowledges the tension he feels when he writes, 'The biggest problem with interpreting 1 Timothy 2:11–15 as excluding women from teaching roles in the church is that Paul clearly commended women for such roles.' But Keener is apparently not prepared to take 1 Tim. 2:11–15 at face value and revisit the narrative sections of Paul's writings to see whether it was appropriate for him to read these as indicating 'that Paul clearly commended women for such roles [of teaching in the church]' in the first place.

90. Cf. e.g. Witherington, *Women*; Cotter, 'Women's roles'.

91. On Eph. 5:21–33, esp. v. 32, see Köstenberger, 'Mystery'.
92. Ortlund, 'Male–female equality'.
93. I am aware of the discussion surrounding the Hebrew term for 'helper' in Gen. 2:18, but remain unconvinced that the expression, in context as well as understood by later Christian interpreters such as the apostle Paul, refers to nothing but the woman's position as equal to the man without connotations of functional subordination. Cf. esp. Ortlund, 'Male–female equality'; and Köstenberger, 'Gender passages', p. 271, n. 45.
94. This seems to be missed by Grenz, *Women*, pp. 216–218, who writes: 'the complementarians' more hierarchical understanding of church structure tends to undermine their good intention to maintain a servant focus. It is difficult to see pastors primarily as servants of God's people when ordination appears to endow a privileged few with power and status' (p. 218).
95. Cf. Cottrell, 'Christ', pp. 7–8.
96. See Köstenberger, 'Gender passages', pp. 267–271.
97. Cf. Poythress, 'Church', pp. 233–247.
98. Witherington, *Women*, pp. 121–122, did not have the benefit of the evidence presented in Köstenberger et al., *Women in the Church*, particularly Köstenberger, 'Complex sentence structure'. He correctly points out that in a (unique) passage by Chrysostom (c. AD 390) the crucial word *authentein* apparently means 'act the despot' or the like; but he fails to consider that the sentence structure of 1 Tim. 2:12 requires *authentein* to have a positive connotation. Thus Paul is shown not merely to correct a local abuse in the Ephesian church but to set abiding parameters for the ministry of women in the church: they are 'not to teach or have authority over a man'.
99. For a recent interpretation of 1 Tim. 2:15, see Köstenberger, 'Ascertaining roles'.
100. On the interpretation of Gal. 3:28 in the context of recent discussions of women's roles, see Köstenberger, 'Gender passages', pp. 273–279.
101. Cf. Moo, *Epistle to Romans*, p. 927.
102. See Schreiner, 'Valuable ministries', pp. 213–214 and 219–220.
103. See esp. Neuer, *Man*, p. 122: 'His [Paul's] attitude is in complete agreement with that of Jesus, who in his teaching and actions recognised the differences between men and women. Jesus and Paul agree that creation and redemption do not conflict with each other; rather they constitute an inseparable unity, since both nature and grace are the work of God. For this reason Jesus and Paul do not abrogate the created order of the sexes in the kingdom of God, or the church, but expressly acknowledge it.'
104. Ellis, 'Paul', p. 451.
105. It is highly fitting that a treatment of women in the Pauline mission be included in this volume and it is both a pleasure and a privilege to present this essay to P. T. O'Brien, a scholarly statesman and Christian gentleman of the highest order.

© Andreas J. Köstenberger 2000

17. Theology and ethics in the letter to the Romans

Michael Hill

It is universally agreed that Paul was not an ethicist. He was a theologian. At no point in his letters did he present his readers with an explicit systematic account of the nature of morality. Nor did he ever try to vindicate his moral judgments in terms of an ethical theory. Paul's focus was not on the task of developing and vindicating an ethical theory but on what God had done in Christ and the consequent salvation offered to people of all nations. Nevertheless, in a number of his letters there is a close connection between the doctrinal and the parenetic portions. Since Bultmann's essay in 1924, the logical structure of the bridge between these parts has been identified as the movement from indicative to imperative.[1] Perhaps it is an overstatement to say that theology is ethics as far as Paul is concerned, but the theological basis for his ethical judgments cannot be denied.[2] The various forms of moral material found in his letters derive their authority and power from their theological underpinning. The purpose of this essay is to examine the logic involved in the movement from theology to ethics in the letter to the Romans in the hope that it might provide some insight into 'the Christian's source for finding the moral will of God'.[3]

Paul had a number of reasons for writing the letter to the Romans.[4] Some of these reasons were clearly primary and others were secondary. His purpose to outline and defend the gospel was fundamental. Contained within this general apologetic purpose was the more specific desire to clarify and correct misunderstandings about his view of the Mosaic law. Central to the defence of the gospel was his delineation of, and, insistence on, the 'righteousness of God' (*dikaiosynē theou*). The first eleven chapters take up God's plan of salvation and carry the reader through the themes of the human predicament created by sin, God's provision for sin in Christ, the eschatological reality of salvation, and the role and place of Israel in God's plan. In chapter 12, Paul's focus shifts from what God has done in Christ (indicative) to exhortations (imperative) about how the community of faith should live in the light of the dawning of the age to come.

The general consensus among commentators seems to be that the *oun* of Romans 12:1 is not taken as a mere transition particle but as indicating a connection with the previous teaching, with the inference that a conclusion is being drawn.[5] The full force of *oun* is supported by the phrase *dia tōn oiktirmōn tou theou*.[6] This phrase, translated 'by the mercies of God' in the NRSV, should most probably be taken to refer 'to the whole of the epistle so far'.[7] Just previously in 11:30–32 Paul has explicitly summarized the mercy of God in terms of God's provision of salvation despite the disobedience of both Gentiles and Jews. The theme of the disobedience of all humankind takes us back to the passage at the beginning of the letter on the universal nature of sin (1:18 – 2:16). This passage includes specific references to both Gentile and Jewish disobedience. While no explicit use is made of the phrase *dia tōn oiktirmōn tou theou* in chapters 1 – 10, the elements of God's mercy are found there.[8] The kindness, patience, love, and grace of God fill out the contours of the salvation history outlined and defended in these chapters.[9] These elements are caught up in the flow of Paul's argument. The climax of Paul's teaching on the righteousness of God is reached in chapter 11, where, following his summary of the mercy of God (11:30–32), he breaks into unbounded praise (11:33–36). It is natural, then, to read the whole text as building up to this point where the concept of mercy is appropriately employed to cover the range of God's activities in salvation history.

While there is a consensus about the relationship between chapters 1 – 11 and chapter 12 there is no agreement about the relationship of the indicative to the imperative. Parsons has sorted the various approaches of Pauline scholars on the relationship between the indicative and the imperative into three loose but distinct categories.[10] One group of scholars maintains that the indicative and imperative are not related. Another group argues that the two are so intimately connected that they cannot be distinguished. A third group affirms that the indicative and imperative are closely connected but in a way that allows them to maintain their distinctiveness. After an exegetical study of four key passages, including Romans 12:1–2, Parsons concludes that the evidence sustains the third approach. The connection between the indicative and imperative is indissoluble and cannot be broken. Neither can they be fused together. Parsons asserts that the connection is to be understood 'in terms of our actions flowing from our being'.[11] Moreover, he contends that the Holy Spirit 'is the link between the indicative and the imperative of Christian reality and existence'. The Holy Spirit 'is at once an element of the former and a constituent part of the latter'. While no exception is taken here to Parsons' conclusion, the matter of the relationship of the indicative to the imperative in Romans can be taken to another level.

It will be argued that there is a natural teleology implicit in the logic of Paul's argument in the body of the letter to the Romans (1:18 –15:13).[12] To understand the nature of this claim, a distinction must be made between natural and historical teleology. O'Donovan has located the core element in the distinction: 'The essential thing to observe about the difference between natural and historical teleology is that natural ends are generic, historical ends are particular.'[13] Before we turn to examine the difference between kinds and particulars, some attention must be given to the notion of teleology.

Teleology is the study ends or goals (cf. *telos*). Some of the ancient philosophers, observing the evidence of design or purpose in nature, developed a doctrine that everything was designed to serve a purpose. Moreover, they held that the nature of a thing, its design or form, enabled it to move towards its appropriate goal. The notion of *telos* was developed in several different ways. From Aristotle we get the traditional example that the *telos* of an acorn is to become an oak tree. In the same way it was thought that the goal of the human being as a rational creature was to think. It was thought that each kind of thing found in the world had its own goal. Aristotle's mentor and teacher, Plato, arranged the various kinds of things in a hierarchical order, linking the goal of one kind to another. The goal of vegetables was to grow luxuriantly in order to serve animals as food. A chain of order was devised. Vegetables were to serve the animal, the animal was to serve the rational, and reason was to serve divine truth.

Careful note ought to be taken that, while the statement 'that the *telos* of an acorn is to become an oak tree' is in the singular, it refers not just to one particular acorn but to all acorns. The reference is generic in that it refers to every seed of the same kind. The reference, then, introduces the concept of generic order or types.[14] It was observed that particular or individual things could be grouped together. One important word used to designate this grouping was *typos*. The imagery conveyed by the word *typos* is that of a stamp or cast. *Typos* meant 'originally the impression made by striking something, and comes thereby, to designate form, pattern, or example'.[15]

Fundamental to this notion is the idea of similarity. There is a similarity between the stamp (the thing that strikes) and the impression made.

Two different kinds of order are now apparent. Things can be ordered on the basis of similarity or goal (purpose). The first kind of ordering is labelled generic order and the second telic order. Telic order can be broken up into two sub-groups. The first kind of telic order involves only one kind of entity. Acorns, for example, are ordered to the goal of becoming oak trees. The second kind of telic order is between entities of different kinds. For example, vegetables are ordered to animals as food.

If individual things are to be recognized, then they must recognized as particulars of a certain kind. Moreover, individual things inhabit the spatio-temporal world in a way that kinds do not. The kind 'human' does not walk around the world in that way that individual humans do. The distinction between natural and historical teleology should now be clear. 'In created order one is destined to some fulfilment because it is the appropriate fulfilment for being of one's kind; but historical destining is a unique and unrepeatable destining of events to a single goal.'[16] Historical teleology has to do with the physical world of the senses. Natural teleology has to do with the intelligible pattern, the design, built into the spatio-temporal world. While historical teleology is concerned with the material level of reality, natural teleology is interested in the second-order issues of metaphysics.

Paul was familiar with the notion of kind or type. He uses it in 5:14 where he reflects on Adam as a type of the one to come – Christ. The particulars, Adam and Christ, are seen as types. Paul trades on this notion of type in several ways in 5:12–21. First, the similarity between Adam and Christ is accented (v. 15b). The similarity he draws attention to is the fact that the individuals, Adam and Christ, influence the many. One through trespass brought death to the many, while the other through a gracious gift brought justification. While there is a similarity between Adam and Christ, there is also a similarity between both Adam and Christ to the many. Both Adam and Christ are seen as moulds that shape, or provide the pattern for, the many. But familiarity with the notion of types or kinds is not enough to establish the thesis that Paul utilizes the notion of natural teleology. The thesis requires that Paul had a concept of natural kinds.

There can be no doubt that Paul was acquainted with the creation narratives of Genesis 1 – 3. His theology operates within a salvation-history framework where the creation and subsequent fall provide the backdrop for his understanding of the redemption and new creation won through the work of Christ. The Genesis accounts present the creation as ordered according to kinds. Among the kinds mentioned in Genesis are plants yielding seeds, fruit trees, birds and sea creatures. No complete list is given, nor is it required. The various kinds of things are subsequently arranged according to purpose (1:28–31). Humankind is given every plant yielding seed and every tree with seed in its fruit for food. Birds, beasts and creeping things are given every green plant for food. Beyond this mundane ordering, humankind is given a general or overall purpose of having dominion over creation. In the context of Genesis there is no doubt that this includes keeping the order which God has given to creation.

In Romans 1:26–27 Paul employs the phrase of *para physin* in the context of a universal indictment against humanity (1:18–32). The purpose of this passage is to show that humankind is without excuse (1:20). The conclusion reached is that although people know God's just decrees, they practise disobedience and applaud others who do likewise (1:32). The passage is part of a history of damnation[17] contained in 1:18 – 3:20 that arrives at the verdict that no human being will be justified by deeds prescribed by the law (3:20). The essence of Paul's argument is simple. No-one does good, therefore no-one will be justified by works. Revisionist attempts to weaken the sense of *para physin* so that it does not have the sense of 'against nature' have not succeeded.[18] A detailed examination of the context will reveal the basis on which Paul is able to evaluate homosexual activity as *para physin* and *aschēmosynē*.

The universal indictment begins with the declaration that the wrath of God is revealed against the ungodliness and wickedness (*asebeian kai adikian*)[19] of those who by their wickedness suppress the truth (1:18). The rebellion against God's majesty expresses itself in violations of God's just order (*en adikia katechontōn*). The consequence of the suppression is that both (a) the truth about God's majesty and (b) a knowledge of his order are kept hidden. The point of 1:18 – 3:20 is that the whole of humanity, both Gentile and Jew, belong to the same type. It is the type categorized as 'those who by their wickedness suppress the truth'. After asserting that God's wrath has been revealed, Paul directs his attention to detailing the nature of the suppression and its consequences. Various allusions indicate that Paul had both the account of Adam's fall and the fall of Israel at Horeb in mind. Added to this, the context demands that every generation of both Jews and Gentiles are included in this fall.[20] The suppression that leaves all without excuse is found in the fact that, though they knew God, they did not honour him as God or give him thanks (1:21). As a consequence, their minds were darkened. In the futile thinking of their darkened minds they exchanged the glory of the immortal God for idols (1:23), the truth about God for a lie (1:25), and natural sexual practices for unnatural (1:26).

The concept of nature is not Hebraic. The word *physis* and its cognates are found in the Septuagint only in the later deuterocanonical books. Paul generally uses these words to describe 'the way things are by reason of their intrinsic state or birth' (see 2:14; 11:21, 24).[21] The use of *chrēsis* (lit. 'function') in 1:26 as a periphrasis for sexual intercourse was well known.[22] In using the antonyms *thēleia* and *arsenes*, Paul stresses the sexual distinction between male and female. As these antonyms are constantly used in association with the creation narratives, the context demands that the phrase *tēn physikēn chrēsin* means something like 'sexual intercourse in accordance with the intention of the Creator'. If this is so, then *para physin* would mean 'contrary to the intention of the Creator'.[23]

Before the meaning of these terms can be settled, another aspect of the context must be examined. Many scholars have thought that the description of the suppression of the knowledge of God in 1:20–21 indicates that Paul espouses a doctrine of natural theology as well as a doctrine of natural revelation. The oxymoron in verse 20 is explained, according to those who hold that Paul espoused a natural theology, by the fact that the metaphysical reality[24] of God's eternal power and deity is manifested to the mind through the created order evident to the senses. If this view is accepted, then the point being made in these verses is that while people have a theoretical or tacit knowledge of God, they fail to acknowledge him and consequently are without excuse.[25] There are, however, many reasons why this view should be rejected. Perhaps the strongest reason is found in the words *gnontes ton theon* in verse 21.[26] These words indicate that God is known, not that something is known about God. Moreover, the natural theology interpretation infers that the solution to the problem lies in the renewal of the will. The text of Romans, however, indicates that what is needed is a transformation of the mind (1:21; 12:2). It is the knowledge of God's will that is missing from human minds. If verse 21 is given its natural sense, then the logic of the argument is, as Bell points out, 'that the knowledge of God is only retained and guaranteed if there is subsequent acknowledgement'.[27]

Given the fact that Paul does not have a natural theology, *physis* and *physikos* can only be referring to the created order prior to the fall and known through the revelation of the Hebrew Scriptures. While it is true that the male/female distinction is still evident after the fall, there can be no doubt that Paul is taking Genesis 1:27 as a normative model. The text of 1:26–27 bears witness to this very fact. If the fallen creation were the normative model for Paul, then homosexual activity would be in accordance with nature. Paul can apply the concept to pre-fall and post-fall creation. But only the pre-fall application provides a knowledge of the will of God.

Genesis 1 – 2 seems to provide a normative model for Paul. In Romans 1:26–27 the point being made is that sinful humanity ignores the generic order established by God. There is a distinction within humankind between male and female (Genesis 1:27) that the participants in homosexual activity treat with disdain. In other places, like 1 Corinthians 6:12–20, Paul uses the telic order of creation to establish an ethical norm. In this case Christians are having liaisons with prostitutes and the generic order of creation is being observed. Paul's objection is based on the telic order revealed in Genesis. He reminds his readers that the purpose of sexual union between male and female was that 'the two shall be one flesh' (Gen. 2:24). The implication is clear. One way the rejection of God expresses itself is in the dismissal of both his generic and his telic order.

Paul's moral evaluation in Romans 1:26–27 is based on the normative model provided by the revelation found in Genesis 1 – 2. The universal indictment (1:18–32) is founded on the fact that all have sinned. The allusion to Adam's fall in 1:23 is taken up and developed in 5:12–21, revealing that an understanding of Genesis 3 plays an essential role in Paul's perception of the history of fallen creation. Within the context of history he can refer to the patterns experienced by all people in this fallen world as natural. For example, he can refer to the normal pattern of growth of an olive tree. But Paul does not use this pattern as an ethical standard. What is natural in the fallen world does not provide ethical standards. Rather, the pristine shape of creation prior to the fall is the pattern Paul appeals to in making basic ethical judgments about sexual behaviour. Looking backwards from and through fallen creation, this pristine pattern cannot be detected in its unity. Paul mentions two reasons for this fact. The first is epistemological. Human minds have been darkened and subjected to futility. They are unable to see how to worship God through maintaining his order in creation. The second is ontological. Both human nature and the subhuman creation have been damaged. The human body awaits redemption, and the inner nature, the thinking, feeling, and willing subject called the self, needs renewing (12:2). The subhuman creation suffers 'from a sense of incompleteness and even frustration' (8:20).[28] The goals set by the will of God in the act of creating are not achievable in an unredeemed world.

These ontological and epistemological aspects of the universal fall must be properly differentiated if confusion is to be avoided. Indeed, it has been the failure to discriminate between the ontological and epistemological elements in Romans 1 that has led to a misunderstanding of Romans 2:14–15. This passage, understood in conjunction with 1:19–20, has often been taken as evidence that Paul had a doctrine of natural law. Since the term 'natural law' has been nuanced in a number of ways, it will be helpful to have a general definition. Dwyer has successfully delineated the general meaning of the term. In a theistic context the term means 'the purposes and goals which are inherent in things because God made them'. In a non-theistic context it means 'the natural goals which are simply part of the reality of things'.[29] Christian doctrines of natural law make three basic claims. These claims are ontological, epistemological and moral.[30] The first is that things and persons have a purposiveness that is part of their very being. This ontological element is foundational to the doctrine. The second is that the purposiveness embedded in reality can be discovered by an intelligent examination of the world. The claim that the pattern or order of reality can be known supplies the epistemological aspect essential to the doctrine. The necessary moral component is given by the assertion that the purposiveness revealed in reality is normative in moral decision-making. That is to say, the goals built into the very nature of things provide the moral criteria for life.

If the understanding of Romans 1 adopted in this essay is correct, then it implies that Paul would agree with only one of the three elements of natural law. He could concede the point in relation to ontology, but only with a serious qualification: that God's original pattern of generic and telic order has been fractured in the fallen world. In the futility of their darkened minds, people have ignored his purposes and established other goals. They have also dismissed his generic order. The consequence has been that the original order is like a jigsaw puzzle that is broken into pieces. Until the overall shape of things is revealed, the bits and pieces have limited significance. The point of 2:14–16 is that when the Gentiles, who do not possess the Mosaic law, are doing *ta tou nomou* (the things that the Mosaic law requires) they show that the inner man is aware of bits and pieces of God's pattern – the ontological reality that lies behind the Mosaic law. This fractured knowledge is enough for the conscience to operate in these cases and accuse or excuse them as the case may be. The bits and pieces will be enough to condemn them on the day of judgment because they have broken God's law even though they did not know it was God's law. This fractured knowledge plus the fact that they also had a knowledge of the principle of retribution (1:32) would show that they were without excuse (1:20) and that God was impartial in his judgment on the basis of the law (2:11).[31] That fact that the Gentiles have a fractured ontology to work with is tantamount to a denial of the ontological claim of natural law. The epistemological aspect of natural law would find no acceptance with the apostle in the light of 1:20–32. But he could agree with the moral assertion.

The outcome of this discussion seems to be that while Paul sees a rational order underlying everyone's experience of the created order, people's minds have been darkened because of sin. The rejection of God is at the centre of this process. Failing to acknowledge God as God, people became futile in their thinking and the rational aspect of their inner being was blocked from seeing the illumination provided by this natural revelation. At this point in the text, no comment is made in relation to the 'natural' order having been defaced or destroyed. Later it will be revealed that not only human minds were affected, but creation itself was subjected to futility and is in bondage to decay (8:20–21). The conclusion drawn from this information must be that Paul distinguishes between fallen creation and nature in the context of Romans 1. Fallen creation is that which is empirically known in history. It includes bits and pieces of God's original plan, but this knowledge is futile, since it is not enough to allow people to understand or attain God's purposes. Nature, for Paul, includes the generic and telic order that accords with the perfect unified will of God and is only known through the revelation. Nature is a metaphysical or theological aspect of reality. As such it is open to the renewed mind (12:2) only by the work of the Spirit (8:1–8). This distinction between nature and creation trades on the subject/object distinction. Creation as object is open to interpretation by the subject. The one reality can be viewed in two different ways. The particular understanding of reality adopted depends on the mind.

Two basic perspectives are delineated in relation to the interpretation of the created order. The first group, those without faith in Christ, can be further divided into Jews and Gentiles. Gentiles without Christ, like the Jew without Christ, have not retained a knowledge of God, and as a consequence their minds have become worthless – useless for their proper purpose (1:22, 25, 28).[32] Even though they lack wisdom, they know that the principle of retribution operates in the world (1:32).[33] Moreover, even though the generic order of fallen creation cannot achieve the purposes of God, it still reflects the order of nature. However, the reflection is fractured, and the knowledge of this order is partial. Gentiles outside of Christ can be faithful in marriage and refrain from murder and robbery, and so on. Bits and pieces of the pattern of God's original demand are evident in their lives (2:14).[34] A partial knowledge of God's order, even though it is not known as God's order, is enough to facilitate the operation of conscience and secure condemnation (2:15).[35] On the day of judgment, this partial knowledge, accusing and excusing them over particular actions through the operation of conscience, will ensure that there is no acquittal on the basis of observing the law (3:20).[36]

Jews outside Christ are in a different position from Gentiles outside Christ. They rely on the Mosaic law for a knowledge of God's will (2:17). This law is the embodiment of knowledge and truth (2:20). This being so, these Jews have a form of wisdom. Within the framework of God's revealed will they are able to discern what is best or essential in life (2:18).[37] Despite this revelation, they fail to keep God's law (2:22–24). They are under the power of sin (3:9). The failure to acknowledge God expressed itself as the rebellion of the creature against the Creator. Because they live in the flesh (7:5) as slaves to sin (6:17), the law provoked sin to express itself (7:7–8). The law, because it was the embodiment of knowledge and truth (2:20), was good (7:13). It did reveal the will of God, and as such it was an expression of the order that God had in mind in creating the world. Jews without Christ, who delighted in the law of God, were caught up in an inner conflict that led only to condemnation (7:14–25). Their actions led to death (6:21). There was to be no acquittal on the day of judgment.

The perspective on reality given to both Jews and Gentiles who have faith in Christ is radically different from those outside of Christ. Those in Christ can 'discern what is the will of God – what is good and acceptable and perfect' (12:2). But this epistemological benefit comes only with an ontological change. This ontological change is brought about by the work of Christ. The promise of God to Abraham (4:13) finds its fulfilment in history in a particular person – Jesus, the Christ. The epistemological benefit is found in the righteousness that comes by faith (4:13–25). For Paul, God's work in Christ is the centre of history. 'The cross and resurrection of Christ are both the fulfilment of the OT and the basis and anticipation of final glory.'[38] Paul's apocalypticism and eschatology re-introduce the topic of teleology. It is important to note that because redemption is part of a historical process constructed and understood within the conceptual framework of promise and fulfilment, we are dealing with historical and not natural teleology. The Christ, a particular man in a particular place in the temporal sequence of things, is the goal of history. The attainment of the historical goal, nevertheless, has ramifications in the domain of natural teleology.

The inauguration of the new age in the work of Christ means that the ontological change in believers comes about in two stages. The present evil age came into being with Adam and it will end on the day when Christ returns in judgment. The new age has come into being with the death, resurrection, and ascension of Christ. Unlike in popular Jewish apocalyptic, the end of the old age did not mark the beginning of the new. The two ages overlapped. In this overlap of the ages the body of the believer is dead (8:10) because it comes under the law of sin and death. Like the rest of creation, it awaits redemption (8:23). Yet through the work of the Spirit the mind is renewed in so far as it is focused on the things of the Spirit (8:5). In this way the inner being of the believer has found life and peace (8:6).

The notion of historical teleology finds its clearest expression in 10:4, where Christ is declared to be the *telos* of the law. This is a particularly difficult verse to interpret. 'The polysemy of *telos* has given rise to an incredible wide spectrum of interpretations.'[39] Despite this fact, a general consensus has emerged in recent scholarship where *telos* is taken to mean 'end' in the sense of 'termination'. Given the context of the verse, there can be little doubt that this is at least one facet of Paul's meaning. Westerholm has convincingly argued that for Paul the law serves a negative function. Since everyone has broken the law, the only sanction still operative is the penalty of death.[40] Hence no righteousness comes by deeds of the law (3:20). So, in salvation-history terms, Christ is the end of the law. However, the thrust of Romans 3:21 – 8:39 demands that a teleological nuance be found in 10:4. It was always God's purpose that the righteous would live by faith. Paul illustrates the point with reference to Abraham (4:1–12). The single Greek word seems to combine the nuances of the English words 'end' and 'goal'.[41] Moo finds the analogy of a racecourse helpful. The finishing-line is both the termination and the goal of the race.

As the historical goal of God's promises, Christ, a particular individual, operates as a stamp or matrix. Christ becomes the type of all those who have faith. While the body awaits redemption (8:23), the inner person is renewed (5:12–6:14). By faith the believer has been united with Christ in his death and resurrection. Justification is not just a declaration of innocence but the work of God's creative word. Those who have died and risen with Christ walk according to the Spirit (8:4) and set their minds on the things of the Spirit (8:5). A commitment to rebellion and disobedience is replaced by a dedication to righteousness. Rebellion has no dominion over the believer (6:14). Believers have a new nature or being. The shape of this new being is found not in Adam but in Christ. This new generic order provides the basis on which Paul can exhort the believer to set new goals (6:13; 12:2). With the new generic order comes the possibility of achieving God's original and unchanging purposes.

If the relationship of the indicative to the imperative parallels the relationship of generic to telic order, then we may place it in the third of Parson's three categories. This is the group that recognizes that the imperative and the indicative are related, but in a way that allows them to maintain their distinctiveness. Clearly, telic order is related to generic order. The shape of human nature, for example, is related to the purposes of God for humankind. Humans, with their ability to think, feel and choose, are in the category of things that can enter into relationship with God and one another. Reason plays an important part in the development of these relationships. It is necessary to understand the character of God and others. Yet nature and goal are distinguishable. The capacity to think, feel and choose is not identical with the achievement of deep personal relationships. Generic order allows the possibility that the goal can be achieved, but nature and goal are different.

The letter to the Romans is thoroughly teleological. Historical teleology informs Paul's eschatology. Natural teleology provides the basis for his moral judgments. In Paul's understanding, history moves towards its goal – Christ. In the movement towards the goal of history, three windows are opened upon the generic and telic order that was part of the original and ultimate purpose of God. These are the windows provided by creation prior to the fall, the Mosaic law and Christ. It is the study of generic and telic order in salvation history that will enable Christians to locate the moral will of God.[42]

Notes

1. Bultmann, 'Das Problem'.
2. For a discussion of the relationship between the indicative and the imperative and consequently between theology and ethics see Parsons, 'Being precedes act'.
3. Moo, *Epistle to Romans*, p. 757.
4. Wedderburn, *Reasons*.
5. See Moo, *Epistle to Romans*, p. 748, nn. 16 and 17; Parsons, 'Being precedes act', p. 234.
6. Cranfield, *Romans 2*, p. 595. Barrett, *Romans*, p. 230.
7. Parsons, 'Being precedes act', p. 234.
8. The words *eleos* and *eleeō* are also missing from these chapters.
9. Parsons, 'Being precedes act', p. 235.
10. Ibid., p. 218.
11. Ibid., p. 247.
12. This claim that natural teleology is implicit in the logic of Paul's argument is tantamount to asserting that Paul was aware of this notion. Specifically the claim is that Paul was tacitly aware of the notion. The fact that he did not make this knowledge explicit does not imply that he was not aware of it. For example, a person can be explicitly aware of another person's face but not explicitly aware of the shape of parts of that face. Concentrating on the face as a unified whole, the person is tacitly aware of the shape of the parts (e.g. the eyes and the nose) and their relationships. The person could refocus and concentrate on a particular part (e.g. the nose) in which case knowledge of the nose would become explicit. The evidence that Paul was tacitly aware of this notion is found in the fact that he uses it. His logic trades on the notion. The reason he did not focus on the notion and make it explicit was that his purposes were not philosophical but

soteriological. He was concerned with God saving his people. When it suits his purposes he clearly is able to undertake the task of analysis and explication.

13. O'Donovan, *Resurrection*, p. 59.

14. Particulars, like acorn seeds, may be ordered or categorized on the basic of similarity. For realists like Aristotle and Paul, this categorization was not just something that went on in the mind of the observer. Things like acorns had a correspondence in objective reality. Paul's doctrine of creation commits him to a realist position.

15. Moo, *Epistle to Romans*, p. 334, n. 85.

16. O'Donovan, *Resurrection*, p. 59.

17. For a detailed study of this passage see Bell, *No One*.

18. See De Young, 'Meaning', and Schmidt, *Straight and Narrow?*, pp. 77–83.

19. A distinction can be made between these two words. *Asebeia* is sin as 'an attack on the majesty of God' while *adikia* highlights the fact that it is also 'a violation of God's just order' (Cranfield, *Romans* 1, p. 112). However, in Paul 'the distinction is not usually maintained' (Moo, *Epistle to Romans*, p. 102, n. 50). It seems here that the two aspects of sin are combined to give 'a more rounded description' (Cranfield) where both elements are included.

20. See Bell, *No One*, pp. 26–27.

21. Moo, *Epistle to Romans*, p. 114. So in 11:21 *kata physin* implies that there has been no human interference with the olive tree, and *para physin* in 11:24 refers to divine intervention.

22. Cranfield, *Romans* 1, p. 125.

23. Ibid.

24. This could read 'theological reality'. In so far as theology goes beyond the empirical data, theology is metaphysics.

25. The notion of tacit knowledge has been included to cover views like that of Cranfield. Cranfield denies that Paul is establishing a natural theology but goes on to claim that people are unwittingly, though objectively, aware of God (*Romans* 1, p. 116).

26. Bell convincingly argues that in the phrase *gnontes tou theou*, the genitive should not be taken as partitive. The phrase refers not to 'what can be known about God' but to 'God in his knowability'. Bell, *No One*, pp. 35–40.

27. Ibid., p. 49.

28. Moo, *Epistle to Romans*, p. 513.

29. Dwyer, *Foundation*, p. 15.

30. Ibid., pp. 15–16.

31. See Bell, *No One*, pp. 90–118, 145–162.

32. See Cranfield, *Romans* 1, p. 128; Moo, *Epistle to Romans*, p. 117.

33. The use of the singular *to dikaiōma tou theou* in 1:32 is significant. In contrast to 8:4, it most probably refers to the principle of retribution – that those who practise such things deserve to die (1:32). Although they claim to be wise (1:22), they could not consistently determine what was best in life (2:18). Even so, they had enough knowledge to leave them without excuse.

34. The exegetical support for this understanding of 2:14–15 is found in Moo, *Epistle to Romans*, pp. 148–153, and Bell, *No One*, pp. 90–102, 145–162.

35. For the evidence that conscience in Paul is judicial and not legislative see Pierce, *Conscience*.

36. The fact that Gentiles are without the Mosaic law but have some knowledge of the law in a generic sense does not necessitate that 3:20 refers to the generic law,

since the reference of both is the metaphysical order of nature expressed by the will of God.

37. For the relationship of law to wisdom in Paul see Schnabel, *Law and Wisdom*.
38. Moo, *Epistle to Romans*, p. 26.
39. Badenas, *Christ the End*, p. 2.
40. Westerholm, *Israel's Law*, ch. 9.
41. See Moo, *Epistle to Romans*, pp. 636ff.
42. Peter O'Brien has been a friend and colleague for nearly twenty-five years. During this time I have valued his quiet, godly manner and his thorough and systematic approach to biblical scholarship. Since I hold him in the highest esteem and regard him with the greatest of affection, it is a privilege to be able to honour him in this way.

© Michael Hill 2000

18. Jewish mission in the era of the New Testament and the apostle Paul

Paul W. Barnett

Definitions

Was there a Jewish mission to Gentiles in the New Testament era? This question has been the subject of extensive enquiry, with no apparent consensus.[1] There is evidence for some Jewish proselytizing of Gentiles, but is it enough to establish the existence of a Jewish mission to Gentiles?

We immediately face the problem of *definition*. Are we to think of such a mission as 'aggressive', polemical against other religions and with missionaries sent to convert all others? Or are we to define such a mission softly, as a mere 'missionary consciousness', with Jews regarding conversion to Judaism as a 'desirable' outcome?

Closely related is the question of the *extent* of such a mission. Does the evidence point to an activity which was universally prosecuted by the Jews, or merely by isolated individuals?

A majority of scholars have argued for the existence of a Jewish mission, including L. Feldman,[2] who contents himself with speaking of Judaism as 'a missionary religion'[3] without closer definition. A minority, including Munck, McKnight and Goodman, dispute the existence of a Jewish mission to Gentiles.[4]

To a significant degree a scholar's verdict depends on the definition of 'mission' adopted. McKnight and Goodman reach their negative conclusion on the basis of maximilist definitions.[5] Paget, however, defining Jewish mission in relatively weak and passive terms, reaches positive conclusions.

In my view, insufficient attention has been given to the critical relationship between becoming a proselyte and being circumcised. There is ample evidence for a large body of Gentile 'God-fearers' within the Roman Empire during the New Testament era. There is also probable evidence of Jewish efforts to encourage Gentiles to become 'God-fearers'. If that was all there was to the question, the existence of a Jewish mission ought to be agreed. It is clear, however, that the 'God-fearer' was and remained a Gentile and was not yet a Jew. Indeed, there were many grades and categories of 'God-fearer', ranging from those at the very fringes of Judaism to those who were about to submit to the initiatory rites of circumcision and baptism.

Until he was circumcised, the 'God-fearer' lived simultaneously in the contradictory worlds of the pagan and the Jew. Someone such as Cornelius, the Roman centurion from Caesarea, would attend the temple of the gods of Greece and Rome one day, and then, on another, the synagogue.

Although it was relatively undemanding for such a man to be a Gentile *and* a Jewish 'sympathizer' or 'God-fearer', this changed when he faced circumcision. The surgical act was painful and medically dangerous. Furthermore, once circumcised, that man became a Jew, and he now inhabited only one world. Indeed, he was now a member of a race despised and vilified by many Gentiles.

In my view, therefore, the definition of a Jewish mission to Gentiles must be couched in terms of circumcision. Was there a Jewish *circumcision* mission to Gentiles? This essay will argue that there is insufficient evidence to establish the existence of a widespread Jewish mission to convert Gentiles to Judaism with the attendant circumcising of males.

Related issues

Several other preliminary issues must be raised. First, was there, as F. Millar[6] has suggested, an 'immense expansion of Judaism' at the time of Jesus which cannot be explained by natural increase alone, but the 'multitude of settlers … throughout the world'[7] must be due to conversions to Judaism?

As late as the Maccabean age the Jewish community in the motherland was quite small, scarcely extending beyond the borders of 'Judea' proper.[8] To be sure, historical distance and absence of statistics leave us with only an impression of such 'expansion'. Yet that impression is strong when we consider the many references to multitudes of Jews in North Africa, Egypt, Syria, Mesopotamia, Anatolia and Italy. Even in the list of nations represented at the Feast of Pentecost, we find 'Jews and *proselytes*' (Acts 2:9–11; cf. 6:9).

Second, if some Jewish missioning occurred – as we will argue it did – how did that affect and influence the missionary activities of Paul the apostle? Were Paul's activities modelled on pre-existing Jewish proselytism?

Proselytes and 'God-fearers'

By New Testament times a proselyte[9] was a person of Gentile race who was converted to Judaism by means of circumcision (in the case of males) and baptism, who kept the law of Moses and who, as opportunity arose, offered sacrifice.[10]

Proselytes must be carefully distinguished from 'God-fearers'.[11] Scholars face two problems in identifying the 'God-fearers'. One is that the book of Acts has no uniform mode of reference to these persons. They are spoken of as 'those who fear God' (*hoi phoboumenoi ton theon*, Acts 10:1–2, 22; 13:16, 26) or 'those who worship God' (*hoi sebomenoi ton theon*, Acts 13:50; 16:14; 18:6–7; cf. 13:43; 17:4, 17). Are these the same people?[12] Another difficulty has been that the epigraphic sources use the term *theosebēs*, which is not found in Acts, and which could mean a 'worshipper of God' or simply a 'pious' Jew. In view of these problems the very existence of the 'God-fearers' has been disputed.[13]

However, recent analysis of the third-century AD inscription at Aphrodisias has put the question beyond reasonable doubt.[14] This inscription has a list of Jews in the synagogue and a *separate* list of *theosebeis*, which must therefore mean 'worshippers of God'. Thus the numerous references to *theosebeis* in other inscriptions, which otherwise might have been understood as 'pious' Jews, are now able to be identified as *Gentile* 'worshippers of God', that is, as belonging to one and the same class of person noted in the Acts of the Apostles.

It is clear, however, that there was no uniformity for this class. No fewer than seven categories have been noticed, from those Gentiles who had minimal interest in Judaism to those who were at the point of full-blooded conversion to Judaism.[15] Serious inconsistencies of behaviour are either known or suspected to have existed. Numbers of Gentiles attended the synagogue *and* participated in the Imperial Cult.[16] Cornelius, who is called 'a devout man who feared God' (Acts 10:2), must in the course of his duties as a centurion also have worshipped the Roman gods. In view of the disparity and diversity within this class it comes as no surprise that its members have been described as 'God-worshippers', or as 'Jewish sympathizers',[17] but their existence is beyond doubt.

Three obstacles blocked the path towards a 'God-fearer' becoming a proselyte. First, there was the universal odium in which Jews were held by Gentiles. At the time of his circumcision the proselyte was warned of oppression by Gentiles ('Israel at the present time are persecuted and oppressed, despised, harassed and overcome by afflictions'). Second, following his circumcision a proselyte faced dire penalties from the synagogue for breaches of the law that he would not previously have faced: for example, stoning for breaking the Sabbath (*b. Yebamoth* 47a, b). Third, submission to circumcision for adult males was a major deterrent on account of the pain involved in the surgical process and the risk of infection.

Since many 'God-fearers' lived simultaneously in the world of idolatry in the temples, and in the imageless worship of the synagogue,[18] a decision to become a proselyte by submission to circumcision, with attendant rites of baptism, must have marked a moment of high moral seriousness. Thus the Mishnah distinguished between 'God-fearers', whom it called 'proselytes of the gate', and genuine proselytes, whom it called 'proselytes of righteousness'.[19]

Juvenal, the Roman satirist of the second century AD, though not using terms like 'proselytes' or 'God-fearers', appears to have 'God-fearers' in mind. He mentions a circumstance of generational transition from 'God-fearer' to proselyte:

> Some who have had a father who revere the Sabbath, worship nothing but the clouds and the divinity of the heavens, and see no difference between eating swine's flesh, from which their father abstained, and that of a man; *and in time they take to circumcision.* Having been wont to flout the laws of Rome, they learn to practise and revere the Jewish law ... (*Sat.* 14.96).

Gentile movements towards Judaism

If narrow definition of Jewish mission is set aside, it is possible to speak more broadly of 'Gentile movements towards Judaism' within the New Testament era, which include individual proselytes, coerced conversions and the 'God-fearer' phenomenon.

Individual proselytes

Individual 'proselytes' are mentioned in the New Testament (Acts 2:11; 13:43), although only one is named (Nicolaos of Antioch, Acts 6:5). Josephus writes of Fulvia, a Roman 'woman of high rank who had become a prose-lyte'.[20] Her more thorough conversion may be noted by comparing Josephus' description of Nero's consort Poppaea as, merely, a 'worshipper of God'.[21]

Coerced conversions: Idumeans and Itureans[22]

The Idumeans were descendants of the Edomites,[23] a desert people occupying the region between the Gulf of Aqaba and the Dead Sea. In the time of the exodus they had blocked the route of the Israelites from Egypt to the promised land (Num. 20:14–21). By the latter part of the Hellenistic era they had migrated from south of the Dead Sea to occupy a tract of land east to west between the Dead Sea and the coastal plain and north to south between Bethlehem almost to Beersheba.

The two great roads – the coastal Via Maris and its desert parallel through Petra – passed sufficiently close to Idumea to provide her major source of prosperity, trading with the considerable volume of travellers on these roads. The major city of Idumea was Marisa,[24] which flourished in the Hellenistic era, becoming a settlement of about ten thousand.

During the rule of the Hasmonean John Hyrcanus (134–104 BC), the Jews conquered the Idumeans (Josephus, *AJ* 13.257–258). This was to have consequences in the coming years. First, it tended to assimilate the Idumeans into the Jewish religion. Previously they had been deeply influenced by Greek deities. But now, whether by force or by more gradual means, the people of Idumea adopted Judaism, though with varying degrees of understanding.[25] Most significant of all, the leading family among the Idumeans became the chief political force in Israel after the Romans arrived with Pompey (63 BC), eventually bringing Herod to the throne.

Herod attempted to hide his proselyte origin, putting about various claims that he was descended from the first Jews to have returned from the exile in Babylon (Josephus, *AJ* 14.9) and that he was a member of the Hasmonean house (*b. B.B.* 3b, 4a). Although he was a proselyte, according to Josephus Herod was no more than a 'half-Jew' in terms of blood and conversion of heart and mind (*AJ* 14.403), and his influence within Judaism deserved criticism: 'Herod ... gradually corrupted the ancient way of life, which had hitherto been inviolable. As a result we suffered considerable harm at a later time as well, because those things were neglected which had formerly induced piety in the masses' (*AJ* 15.257).

It is likely that the effect of Herod's rule, followed by that of his grandson Herod Agrippa I,[26] created a negative attitude to proselytes and proselytism.

Large numbers were added to Judaism through Israel's military and political relationships with the Idumeans. However, this must lie outside the concept of a Jewish mission as ordinarily understood.

The emergence of 'God-fearers'

The role of Jewish apologetics

Jewish propaganda in this era was aimed not so much at converting Gentiles as at offering some reply to their vilification and mockery of Jewish faith and practice. Evidence of this comes from places where there were large concentrations of Jews (Rome, Alexandria and Roman Asia). Roman writers ridiculed the Jews for three matters in particular: their abstention from pork ('kindness bestowing on pigs a ripe old age' [Juvenal, *Sat.* 6.160]), their hypocrisy in observance of the Sabbath ('the charm of indolence beguiled them' [Tacitus, *Hist.* 5.4; Horace, *Sat.* 1.9.60–72]), and their imageless worship (they 'worship nothing but the clouds and the divinity of the heavens' [Juvenal, *Sat.* 14.96]). The Alexandrians made the more serious complaint that Jews were disloyal to the emperor, as expressed in their refusal to worship the statues of the emperor and the gods (Josephus, *Ap.* 2.66–78). Tacitus, the proconsul of Asia early in the second century, writes bitterly of Jewish separation from participation in the life of the Roman world:

> They regard the rest of mankind with all the hatred of enemies. They sit apart at meals, they sleep apart ... they abstain from intercourse with foreign women ... They believe [God] to be supreme and eternal, capable neither of representation nor of decay. They do not allow any statues to stand in their cities, much less in their temples. This flattery is not paid to their kings, nor this honour to our emperors (Tacitus, *Hist.* 5.5).

Antipathy like this, more than a desire to win allegiance of Gentiles to Judaism, appears to have motivated Jewish apologetic.

Extant examples of Jewish apologetic include the works written in Greek by Philo and Josephus. In defending the observance of the Sabbath against the charge of laziness, Philo reflects on the value of attending the synagogue and learning from the teacher:

> Each seventh day there stand wide open in every city thousands of schools of good sense, temperance, courage, justice and other virtues

in which the scholars sit in order quietly with ears alert and with full attention, so much do they thirst for the draught which the teacher's words supply ... (Philo, *Spec. Leg.* 2.60–64).

Josephus' *Against Apion*, written late in the first century, gives useful insight into the anti-Semitism of the times against which it is written. Josephus must answer the accusation that Jews swear an oath to show no goodwill to any non-Jew, especially against the Greeks (2.121). Josephus' reply is, in effect, a eulogy of the law of the Jews, that it is God-given and beneficent (2.174–175, 184–185; especially for family life, 2.199–203), and that it precedes and at certain points has actually been imitated by the philosophers of the Greeks (2.281).

'God-fearers'
In fact, argues Josephus, 'many' Greeks throughout the world have attached themselves to the Jewish communities:

Many of them have agreed to adopt our laws; of whom some have remained faithful, while others lacking the necessary endurance, have again seceded. Of these not one has ever said that he had heard the oath in question pronounced by us (*Contra Ap.* 2.124).

It will be seen that [our legislator – i.e., Moses] took the best of all possible measures at once to secure our own customs from corruption, and to throw open ungrudgingly to any who elect to share them. To all who desire to come and live under the same laws with us, he gives a gracious welcome, holding that it is not family ties alone which constitute relationship, but agreement in the principles of conduct. On the other hand, it was not his pleasure that casual visitors should be admitted to the intimacies of our daily life (*Contra Ap.* 2.210).

The masses have long since shown a keen desire to adopt our religious observances; and there is not one city, Greek or Barbarian, nor single nation, to which our custom of abstaining from work on the seventh day has not spread, and where the fasts and the lighting of lamps and many of our prohibitions in the matter of food are not observed (*Contra Ap.* 2.282).

Although somewhat romantic, Josephus' account of widespread Gentile attraction to Jewish practices and attitudes can scarcely be doubted. At the same time it is difficult to escape the impression that, in his apology for the law of God, Josephus himself is commending that law, its practices and its beliefs to his Gentile readers.

There is some evidence that women proved the more responsive, often those of higher social standing. According to Josephus, the greater part of the female community of Damascus was devoted to Judaism (*BJ* 2.560). Josephus also narrates how Jewish proselytizers penetrated the royal house of Adiabene, teaching the wives of king Monobazus 'to worship God in the manner of the Jewish traditions' (*AJ* 20.34). Among the wives 'brought over to [Jewish] laws' was the king's favourite, Helena. Queen Helena is arguably the most prominent convert to Judaism during the first century (see below), to whom may be added Fulvia the proselyte and Poppaea the 'God-fearer'.[27] Women 'God-fearers' also figure significantly in the ministry of Paul in Galatia, Macedonia and Asia as recorded in the book of Acts (13:50; 16:14; 17:4, ?12).

Confirmation of the effectiveness of Jewish propaganda is provided by Strabo. Although he was not a convert, or uncritical of Jewish 'superstition', Strabo nonetheless expressed some sympathy for Moses and for a view of a God who comprehends all things but is not to be represented by images (Strabo 16.2.35).[28] Others, however, were hostile to any inclination towards Judaism. Tacitus, for example, was antagonistic not only to Judaism (as noted above), but also to those who 'come over to their religion' because they submit to circumcision, 'despise all gods ... disown their country, and set at nought parents, children and brethren' (*Hist.* 5.5).

Notwithstanding the remarkable growth of the 'God-fearers', evidence is lacking that such growth arose from Jewish missioning. Written Jewish apologetic should not be equated with intentional mission activity.

'Light to the Gentiles'

Jewish propaganda may have had the effect of bringing Gentiles into the community of Israel, but it was not necessarily conceived to that end. Its purpose may have been limited to commending the validity of the Jewish viewpoint, under the conviction that the Jews were in some sense the teacher of the peoples of the world in fulfilment of the vocation of Isaiah 49:6: *tetheika se eis phōs ethnōn*. This view certainly emerges from Justin's dialogue with the Jew, Trypho (*Dial. Trypho* 121–122), and Paul's reflections on the role of the Jews supports it: 'and if you are sure that you are a guide to the blind, a light to those who are in darkness, a corrector of the foolish, a teacher of children ...' (Rom. 2:19–20).

Although the zealous presentation of some apologists may have given their work a 'proselytizing' edge and 'converts' may have been won, the

conversion of Gentiles may have been an unsought, perhaps even an unintended, consequence of Jewish apologetic, broadly speaking.

Jewish proselytizing

What, then, is the evidence for direct Jewish missioning in the first part of
the first century? We examine the evidence first through Jewish eyes and
then through Gentile eyes.

Proselytizing from the Jewish perspective

Matthew 23:15: Making proselytes

> 'Woe to you, scribes and Pharisees, hypocrites! for you traverse sea
> and land to make a single proselyte, and when he becomes a pros-
> elyte, you make him twice as much a child of hell as yourselves.'

This is the second of a series of woes from the lips of Jesus addressed to
'scribes and Pharisees'. With no Lucan parallel, the text originates either in
the special 'M' source or is a Matthean redaction of an earlier source. The
stereotypical format ('Woe to you') invites the question whether the whole
saying is dominical or reshaped from an earlier saying.[29] But this text does
not provide a basis for a later scribe's evaluation of missioning. Jesus' woe is
on account not of their proselytizing but of its results. The historicity of the
activity is assumed.

Jesus criticizes the scribes and Pharisees, not because they 'proselytize',
or because they proselytize zealously ('they compass sea and dry land to
make even *one* proselyte'), but because of the hellish effects of their proselytism ('you make him ... a son of Gehenna'). The proselyte is converted to
behaviour which is empty and hypocritical (cf. the other 'woes' pronounced
in this passage).[30] However, Jesus is not speaking merely as a social critic.
The hypocrisy of the scribes and Pharisees blinds them to the presence of
the messianic kingdom in their midst. As the previous 'woe' declared, 'you
neither enter yourselves, nor allow others who would enter to go in'. That
the proselyte is a 'double son' of Gehenna suggests that he, too, now engages
in proselytism, adding more Gehenna-bound persons by his activities.

But who is this 'proselyte' whom the scribes and Pharisees have 'made'?
There are three possibilities: either the scribes and Pharisees travel abroad
to win converts for Judaism from among outright Gentiles; or they attempt
to persuade synagogue-connected 'God-fearers' to become full proselytes;
or they seek to bring Jews of the diaspora into the sect of the Pharisees.[31]

The answer depends on Jesus' use of 'proselyte'.[32] If he spoke of a proselyte in a metaphorical sense of 'convert', broadly understood, it would point to scribes and Pharisees converting fellow-Jews to their own strict sect. But while this word may carry a non-literal usage today, it is unlikely that 'proselyte' was used metaphorically then; this eliminates the third option. The first option may also be discarded. The transition from outright idolator to circumcised proselyte is too large a single step to be easily imaginable. The second option, that of winning a proselyte from among the 'God-fearers', is the most plausible understanding of Jesus' words. The scribes and Pharisees travel beyond Palestine in their search for proselytes from among the existing pool of 'God-fearers', with some, but not very great, success.

However, this proselyte, thus converted, according to Jesus was no ordinary Jew. In winning him the scribes and Pharisees have 'made' him one of their own, that is, a Pharisee, hardened against Jesus and the kingdom. In this case there is a sense in which the specific answer to the question is irrelevant. The end result of the scribes' and Pharisees' proselytism, whether of raw Gentiles (highly improbable), of 'God-fearers' (readily imaginable), or of those who were already Jews (improbable), was that the proselyte became as blind to truth as those who had won his allegiance. The proselyte's acceptance of Pharisaism blinded the convert to the heaven-sent bearer of the messianic kingdom who stood among them.

Naturally, Matthew 23:15 prompts questions about tangential historical evidence for Jewish missioning among Gentiles during the first half of the New Testament era.[33]

Matthew 10:5–6: Going to the Gentiles

In a context of a mission charge to his disciples it is striking that Jesus forbids ministry among Gentiles or Samaritans:

> These twelve Jesus sent out, charging them, 'Go nowhere among the Gentiles, and enter no city of the Samaritans, but go rather to the lost sheep of the house of Israel.'

Jesus' prohibition has been taken to point to an existing programme of proselytism among Gentiles and Samaritans.[34] This is an unnecessary inference, however, for Jesus' restriction is more likely *eschatological*. The time will come for these disciples to 'go' to the nations (Matt. 28:16–20), but it is not yet.

John 7:35: Teaching the Greeks

During an exchange between Jesus and 'officers' sent by the chief priests and

Pharisees to arrest him, an important question was asked:

> The Jews said to one another, 'Where does this man intend to go that we shall not find him? Does he intend to go to the Dispersion among the Greeks and teach the Greeks?

The particle *mē* introduces a rhetorical question expecting a negative answer. Because Jesus was not a recognized member of the Jewish 'academy' of Jerusalem, these 'officers' do not think the 'unlearned' Jesus from Nazareth should travel to the Diaspora to teach the Gentiles. It is possible that the passage points to an established practice of Jews travelling among Gentiles to teach them (the law?).

Proselytizing from the Gentile perspective

As we have seen, significant numbers of Gentiles became 'God-fearers', and some, at least, submitted to circumcision to become proselytes. But the attempt to establish by what means this movement towards Judaism occurred proves difficult. The evidence from the Gentile side that exists, found chiefly in Roman writers, is both limited and ambiguous.

A brief comment from Horace (65–8 BC) is cited as the earliest evidence of Jewish proselytizing zeal: 'We [poets], like the Jews, will compel you to make you one of our throng' (*Sat.* 1.4, 138–142; cf. 1.9, 68–72).

However, the meaning of 'compel' or 'our throng' is far from clear, and other interpretations have been suggested.[35]

Tacitus (c. AD 56–117), in his account of the origins, beliefs and practices of the Jews, disparages them as having a 'passion for propagating of their race' (*Hist.* 5.5).[36] But this could refer to adding to the Jewish race by natural increase rather than by proselytization.

The conversion of Fulvia

As noted previously, the Roman noblewoman Fulvia became a proselyte. According to Josephus, this arose from the activities of a Jew, resident in Rome, who 'played the part of an interpreter of the Mosaic law and its wisdom' (*AJ* 18.81). Joined by three other Jews, this man persuaded Fulvia to send gifts of gold and purple to the temple in Jerusalem, which, however, they kept for themselves. In the subsequent outcry Tiberius expelled the Jewish community from Rome. According to Josephus, this was on account of the rascally behaviour of these Jews. Dio Cassius (c. AD 150–235), however, asserted that the Jews were expelled specifically for proselytizing:

'As the Jews had flocked to Rome in great numbers and were converting many of the natives to their ways, [Tiberius] banished most of them' (Dio Cassius 57.18.5a).

Despite the conflict, or the apparent conflict, between Josephus and Dio Cassius on this point,[37] it is evident that Jews engaged in proselytizing of (a) Gentile(s) among the people of Rome at this time. In the case of Josephus the wicked actions of these men ought not to obscure the intentional and effective missioning of Fulvia. But neither Josephus' reference to the Jew who 'interpret[ed] the Mosaic law', nor Dio's noting of Jews 'converting many of the natives' amounts to evidence of a Jewish mission to Gentiles.

The conversion of Helena and Izates

The best and most detailed example of Jewish proselytism resulted in the conversion of the royal house of Adiabene in Parthia during Claudius' principate. Josephus, with evident pride, makes many references to the house of Adiabene (*AJ* 20.17–96; *BJ* 2.520; 4.567; 5.55, 119, 147, 252; 6.355–356). In the latter years of the aged king Monobazus, his favourite wife, Helena, was instructed by a Jew and converted to Judaism. Her son, Izates, who had by then succeeded Monobazus, also decided to convert to Judaism. However, when he chose to be circumcised, his mother opposed him on the grounds that so manifest a conversion would bring political division to his kingdom.

Another Jew, the merchant Ananias, who had proselytized other wives of the former king, sided with Helena in her viewpoint. Ananias argued that one could be converted to Judaism without circumcision, and indeed that such conversion counted more than circumcision (*AJ* 20.41–42). Another Jew, Eleazar from Galilee, who was evidently of Pharisaic conviction, having 'a reputation for being extremely strict when it came to the ancestral laws' (*AJ* 20.43), convinced Izates, on the basis of the law, to be circumcised. Josephus' narrative and passing comments clearly endorse Eleazar's view (*AJ* 20.44–49).

The conversions of Helena and Izates were to have far-reaching consequences. Izates' brother Monobazus II, who succeeded him as king, also became a proselyte with the rest of his relatives. Many connections were established with Israel.[38] Izates' five sons were educated in Jerusalem. Helena made a pilgrimage to Jerusalem at the time of the famine, bringing food for the people. Helena and Monobazus II built palaces in Jerusalem and made valuable gifts to the temple. Helena and Izates were buried in Jerusalem, almost certainly in the so-called 'tomb of the kings'. During the

66–70 war with the invading Romans, the relations of Monobazus II fought on the side of the Jews.

Later Jewish references

According to the Talmud, the scattering of Jews among the nations was for a missionary purpose: 'The Holy One, blessed be he, did not exile Israel among the nations save in order that the proselytes might join them' (b. *Pes.* 87b). This view is confirmed by a conversation between the Gentile philosopher Celsus and a Jew who said that Isaiah 52:13 – 53:12 referred to the Jewish people as though they were a single person. They were scattered among the Gentiles and smitten so that many among the nations might become proselytes (*Contra Cels.* 1.55).

From the viewpoint of historical precision, these texts must be used with caution, for they are later than the New Testament era by several centuries. Moreover, a new situation was created in the time of Hadrian, who forbade Gentiles to have themselves circumcised. Furthermore, both passages refer to persons becoming proselytes, but are silent about any intentional Jewish mission by which such conversions may have been achieved.

Jewish missioning and Jewish multitudes

The conversion of the house of Adiabene noted above is significant. No fewer than three Jews – Ananias who taught the wives of Monobazus I, an unnamed Jew who influenced Helena, and Eleazar the merchant who persuaded Izates to be circumcised – were involved in ministry to this dynasty. Was this flurry of activity in Adiabene evidence of concerted Jewish missioning among the Gentiles, or was it an isolated case of Jewish missionary zeal?

In my view, the latter alternative is the more likely in face of the fragmentary evidence available to us. To be sure, there can be no doubt that numerous Gentiles were attracted into the broad 'God-fearer' class. The evidence for this is clear enough. Some of these who were drawn into the synagogue communities appear to have taken the further critical step of becoming proselytes through circumcision. But this number was probably relatively small in comparison to the numbers of 'God-fearers'. Individual Jews appear to have proactively missioned Gentiles, as indicated by the proselytizing of Fulvia, the passing comments of the Roman writers Juvenal and Tacitus, Jesus' 'woe' on the scribes and Pharisees, the Jews' question about Jesus going to the Diaspora to teach the Greeks, and the intentional missioning in Adiabene. But it must be added that such actions appear to be uncoordinated and haphazard and quite dependent on the temperament and attitude of individual Jews. There was no mission as such by Jews to convert the Gentiles to Judaism.

But if there was some Jewish missioning of Gentiles, among which groups would it have occurred? Almost certainly it was not directed to outright Gentiles thoroughly enmeshed in the temple culture of the cities which ringed the Mediterranean. Rather, the proselytizers would have worked among the 'God-fearers' on the fringes of the synagogue communities. Had the royal family of Adiabene, for example, been influenced beforehand through the existing Jewish presence in Parthia? Were they already 'God-fearers'?

In my view it is unlikely that the increase of Jews in the Diaspora was attributable to conversions of Gentiles. Although the many Gentiles of anti-Semitic persuasion may have been alarmed by the growth of numbers in the synagogues through the addition of 'God-fearers' to those communities, in Jewish eyes such 'God-fearers' may have been a very uncertain quantity. They lived double lives and their convictions were brittle, even if it was good to have such a group on the periphery of the synagogue for the protection and influence they afforded (cf. Acts 13:50).

The emergence of a 'God-fearer' class of significant proportions, for whatever reason, ought not be equated with a significant number of proselytes.[39] The step from 'God-fearer' to proselyte through circumcision was a giant one, that few Gentiles actively sought and few Jews actively encouraged. Although arguments from silence are always precarious, the relative absence of references to proselytes must be noted.[40]

Instead, the explanation for the growth in Jewish numbers outside Palestine should probably be sought in the stability of family life among these strict law-keepers, their noticeable tendency to raise large families, and their ideological opposition to contraception, abortion and exposing their children (Josephus, *Contra Ap.* 2.199–203; cf. Tacitus, *Hist.* 5.5).

Paul the proselytizer

This sketch of Jewish proselytizing can now form a background to the discussion of Paul's ministry to the Gentiles.

Paul, preacher first of circumcision then of the cross

By his own self-disclosure Paul reveals that he had previously been a

'Pharisee' and 'zealot', a 'persecutor of the church of God' (Phil. 3:6; Gal. 1:13) prior to the Damascus road Christophany. His attitude at that time to Gentiles and their inclusion in the covenant people of Israel may be discerned by his brief rejoinder to misinformation being spread in Galatia: 'But if I, brothers and sisters, still preach circumcision, why am I still persecuted? In that case the stumbling-block of the cross has been removed' (Gal. 5:11–12).

The twice stated *eti*, 'still', most probably indicates that his preaching of circumcision was back to back with his preaching of the cross. Before the Damascus road Christophany he preached circumcision, but after it he preached 'Christ crucified'. He cannot be preaching both together. Apparently, the pre-Christian Paul, Saul the Pharisee and man of 'zeal', had 'preached circumcision' to the Gentiles,[41] and he must now correct the assertion that he is still doing so.

This explanation of Galatians 5:11–12 does not affirm the existence of a thoroughgoing Jewish mission to Gentiles in which Saul had participated. Rather, it is to observe that among strict Pharisees like Saul circumcision was a defensive barrier to Gentiles, preventing them from finding an easy entry into the covenant people. Paul's words suggest that he was a 'zealous' defender of the boundaries separating the covenant people from the Gentiles. Here Paul has been bracketed with Eleazar, mentioned earlier, who insisted against his fellow-Jew Ananias that Izates, king of Adiabene, *must* be circumcised.[42]

Paul, apostle to the uncircumcised

In his earliest extant letter, written about AD 48 to the messianic assemblies in southern Galatia, Paul reflects on the previous decade and a half. While he was a determined would-be destroyer of the church of God in Jerusalem, travelling to Damascus, God revealed his Son to him and called him to preach that Son to the Gentiles (Gal. 1:9–16). This Paul did throughout the intervening fourteen years, in Damascus, 'Arabia', Damascus and Syria-Cilicia (Gal. 1:17–24).

In Galatians 2:7–9 Paul reports on his and Barnabas' meeting in Jerusalem with James, Cephas/Peter and John (c. AD 47). He writes of having been 'entrusted [by God] with the [apostolate of the] gospel to the uncircumcised', which the 'pillars' of the Jerusalem church recognized. At that meeting it is evident that Paul sought the goodwill of James, Peter and John to 'go' more deliberately to the Gentiles, which was agreed to by those leaders of the Jewish apostolate.

To that point Paul had chiefly preached in Syria-Cilicia (including Tarsus, one supposes), where assemblies of Christian believers had been formed, and Antioch on the Orontes, where the church had been established by others beforehand, in the mid to late thirties. But now, as a result of the missionary concordat of c. AD 47, Paul would embark on a westwards, that is, *Rome*-wards, mission, preaching to Gentiles and establishing messianic communities in the Roman provinces of Galatia, Macedonia, Achaia and Asia. Doubtless he would have pressed on to the Eternal City to lay his apostolic foundation there, had Claudius' expulsion of the Jews from Rome in AD 49 not intervened.

The circumcision dispute: Galatians

By the time Paul began his westwards mission he had been preaching to Gentiles for a decade and a half. Through the 'revelation' he received and in the crucible of missioning during those years, he had firmly concluded that the gospel of the Messiah Jesus must be made available to Gentiles on a law-free, circumcision-free basis. Gentiles were called on to put their faith in the Messiah Jesus, who had died for sins and been raised alive from the dead. According to Genesis 15:6, Abraham 'believed the LORD and he reckoned it to him righteousness'. It was critical to Paul's understanding that this 'reckoned … righteousness' occurred *before* Abraham was circumcised. Thus 'righteousness' would now be 'reckoned' to Gentiles *apart* from circumcision, based on their faith in the Messiah, crucified and risen.

The fierce reaction to Paul's preaching of Christ in the synagogues in southern Galatia around AD 48 reverberated to Jerusalem and back again to Galatia. The Gentile members of the new assemblies, who we suppose were chiefly 'God-fearers', were now being urged to submit to the Jewish law, including the circumcision of males. Paul's mission had that unintended and unexpected consequence. This pressure on Gentiles was coming not from local Jews *per se* but ultimately from Christian believers among the Jewish community in faraway Jerusalem through the agency of local non-Christian Jews in southern Galatia (Gal. 1:7; 5:10–11; 6:12–13).[43]

The circumcisers presumably argued that it was impossible to be seen to keep the law apart from circumcision. Most probably they were all too conscious of the equivocation of many 'God-fearers', living as they did simultaneously in the worlds of the Graeco-Roman temple cults *and* the synagogue. Circumcision was so important because it represented the final and irrevocable step into Judaism. The proselyte became a Jew, but the 'God-fearer' remained a Gentile.

Paul's counter-argument, as it is classically stated in Galatians, is based on the premises of 'the truth of the gospel' (2:5, 14; cf. 5:7). That 'truth' is corrupted whenever the principle of 'compulsion' is introduced, whether it is the compulsion to be circumcised explicitly demanded of Titus (2:3) or implicitly required of the Gentile Antiochenes by the action of Peter in withdrawing table fellowship from them, that they 'live like [a] Jew[s]' (2:14). For Paul, circumcision is part of the law (5:3). Yet no-one can find the righteousness of God by observing that law (2:16). Righteousness is reckoned by God not through the keeping of the law, but only by believing in Christ, crucified and risen, who bore in himself the curse of the law-breaker (3:10–13). Those who accept circumcision and the keeping of the law are thereby cut off from Christ (5:4).

The Moses-covenant dispute: 2 Corinthians

In consequence of the disputes in Galatia and Antioch on the Orontes, which arose from 'the circumcision party' in the Jerusalem church, apparently composed of Pharisees (Acts 15:5), a meeting was held in Jerusalem in about AD 49. The president, James the brother of the Lord, decreed that Gentile believers were not to be compelled to submit to circumcision. Nonetheless, for the sake of Jews in the Diaspora the Gentile believers were to abstain from idol-sacrificed food and from fornication, and were to eat only kosher-killed meat (Acts 15:19–21, 28–29; 21:25). These observances appear to arise from the Levitical provisions for resident aliens living within Israel, who were the historical precursors of the latter-day proselytes (Lev. 17 – 19).

Paul returned from the Jerusalem Council to his westwards mission work, which he had left off after his initial visit to Galatia. Having failed to move on to Rome from Macedonia by means of the Egnatian way on account of Claudius' expulsion of Jews from the capital, Paul headed south to the major Roman metropolis, Corinth. As an alternative to reaching Rome, Paul concentrated on building up strong Gentile churches first in Corinth and then in Ephesus, both of which were major Roman settlements. At the same time his churches in the provinces of Galatia, Macedonia, Achaia and Asia formed a block against the power and influence of the Jerusalem church. The collection for Jerusalem from the churches of this group of adjoining provinces was probably intended to lock these churches into an ongoing fellowship with the mother church.

Around AD 55 a group of Jews attempted to subvert the Corinthian assembly against its apostolic founder, Paul. These men came (from

Jerusalem?) with the definite intention of establishing their own leadership in place of Paul's in Corinth, preaching an alternative Christology with a Moses-based righteousness (2 Cor. 11:4, 15). Lack of evidence leaves uncertain precisely what form of Moses-observances they advocated; circumcision finds no mention within this letter. Second Corinthians, written from Macedonia after Paul's eventual reunion with Titus from Corinth (2 Cor. 2:17 – 3:2; 5:11–12; 10:12 – 12:13), was his passionate last-ditch attempt to secure the allegiance of the Corinthians away from these impressive newcomers.

In Galatians Paul had argued that Jews like James, Peter, John and himself would find no righteousness from God based on the law, but only through faith in Christ (Gal. 2:15–16). In that letter Paul pointedly declared that 'the present Jerusalem' is 'in slavery with her children' (Gal. 4:26), but that those who belong to Christ are 'free'. In 2 Corinthians Paul teaches that the old covenant, that is, the 'letter chiselled in stone', has been abolished, eclipsed and de-glorified by the new covenant of the Spirit and righteousness (2 Cor. 3:1–11). In consequence, those who remain under the old covenant are blind to the goal of the old (2 Cor. 3:12–18), that is, righteousness in Christ by faith, to which the law pointed (Rom. 10:4). Thus Paul regarded the old covenant as now 'ended' by the messianic person and the saving work of the Son of God, though he did harbour the passionate hope that the inclusion of the Gentiles would provoke the Jews to turn to their Messiah (Rom. 11:25–36).

Conclusions and corollaries

The missioning by Jews of Gentiles, uncoordinated as it appears to have been, forms a fascinating backdrop to the conversion and ministry of Paul. Such Jewish missioning appears to have been directed to those who had already been drawn into the communities of the synagogues as 'God-fearers'. Circumcision was the objective of such proselytizing, though in our view this probably occurred relatively infrequently. Most probably, Paul's words that he 'preached circumcision' point to his pre-Christian life as Pharisee and 'Zealot', during which he persecuted and tried to destroy the church. His preaching of circumcision, however, was as much as anything to exclude the Gentiles from entry to the people of Abraham.

By contrast, Paul became convinced that God had called him to preach 'Christ crucified' to the nations of the world. The Gentiles were to have ready access to God and to his covenant people apart from the law, apart from circumcision. Paul set about this commission quite *intentionally*, especially after the Jerusalem missionary concordat of c. AD 47 in travels that took him

Rome-wards. This is in contrast with the haphazard and largely negative character of previous Jewish proselytism. It is likely that Paul, too, sought to find Gentile converts among the 'God-fearers', though not exclusively so by any means (cf. 1 Cor. 6:9–11).

Whereas the proselytizing Jews raised the stakes very high for Gentiles, demanding circumcision, Paul's demand was, strikingly, Christological – the confession of adherence by baptism to the Christ, Jesus. This explains why within five or six years of the resurrection adherents of the new movement were called *Christianoi*, 'Messiah people' (Acts 11:26). The constant appeal of Paul, however, was to no outward rite but to the new and inward reality of the Spirit of God in the individual's heart (Gal. 3:1–5; 4:6 [cf. Rom. 8:15]; 2 Cor. 3:1–3) and in the observable life of the community of faith.

Paul was moved by the astonishing stature of the Messiah, the filial (and not merely messianic) Son of God, by whose death and resurrection the world had been reconciled to God (2 Cor. 5:14–15, 16–21). For the Jew the law of Moses was the means of knowing God and of access to God. For Paul, however, that way was only through God's Son, the Messiah Jesus, who had removed sins by his death and given the hope of life to his people by his resurrection. As sinners and law-breakers, the way to God through law was blocked (Rom. 3:19–31), but all who directed their faith towards Christ were true children of Abraham. While Jewish missioners may have been content with just 'one' proselyte (Matt. 23:15), Paul the Jew was seeking nothing less than the reconciliation of humanity (Rom. 11:15).[44]

Notes

1. For a review of major views see Paget, 'Jewish proselytism', pp. 65–103, who argues that there was such a mission, although it needs careful definition. Paget steers a middle course between the maximilists Georgi and Feldman and the minimalists McKnight and Goodman (Paget, p. 76).
2. Feldman, 'Success', pp. 288–341.
3. Ibid., p. 289.
4. Munck, *Paul*; McKnight, *A Light*; Goodman, *Mission*.
5. For a review of the definitions of McKnight and Goodman and for discussion of his own definition, see Paget, 'Jewish proselytism', pp. 76–77.
6. In Schürer, *History* 3, p. 171.
7. Millar, in Schürer, *History* 3, p. 4.
8. Baron, 'Population', estimates that there were 150,000 Jews at the time of the exile, but 8 million by NT times.
9. See Jeremias, *Jerusalem*, pp. 320–334; Schürer, *History* 3, pp. 150–176; Stuehrenberg, 'Proselyte', pp. 503–505.
10. For the conditions of becoming a proselyte see Schürer, *History* 3, p. 173. The Greek *prosēlytos* translates the Heb. *gēr*, a word originally applied to a resident

alien or sojourner in Israel (e.g. Exod. 20:10; 22:21; 23:9,12). LXX uses *prosēlytos* for *gēr* 77 times, though only when a religious context is implied, otherwise using *zenos* or *paroikos*. Later, *prosēlytos* was used of a convert to Judaism (see e.g. Philo, *Somn.* 2.273; *Spec. Leg.* 1.51, 308). Nonetheless, a proselyte, while expected to observe the ordinances of Judaism, was regarded as inferior and lacked the full legal rights of Jews, whether within Palestine or the Diaspora (Jeremias, *Jerusalem*, pp. 320–334).

11. See Levinskaya, *Diaspora Setting*, pp. 51–126 ; Hengel & Schwemer, *Paul*, pp. 61–80.

12. For an affirmative answer see Levinskaya, *Diaspora Setting*, pp. 53–54.

13. For a review of opinions see Levinskaya, *Diaspora Setting*, pp. 53–58.

14. Ibid., pp. 70–80.

15. Ibid., pp. 78–79.

16. Ibid., pp. 123–124.

17. For discussion of these terms see ibid., pp. 52–53.

18. See, too, though from a later era, the comments of Tertullian, *Ad Nat.* 1.13.3–4.

19. Cf. Benediction 13 of the *Shemoneh 'Esreh*. For further references and discussion see Schürer, *History* 3, p. 171.

20. *AJ* 18.82. Note, however, that it is the verb which is used here.

21. Gk. *theosebēs* (*AJ* 20.195). See Smallwood, 'Alleged Jewish tendencies', pp. 329–335; Williams, 'Theosebēs', pp. 97–111.

22. The conversion of Itureans was regarded as enforced by Josephus (*AJ* 13.318–319), but as voluntary by Strabo (16.2.34). I pass over the Itureans without further comment, since they are of minimal importance for subsequent Jewish history, unlike the Idumeans, whose Herodian house dominated Jewish life for decades.

23. The names of the kings of Edom are given in Gen. 36:31–39; they are believed to have descended from Esau (Gen. 36:40; cf. 25:30).

24. See Kloner, 'Underground metropolis', pp. 24ff.

25. Richardson, *Herod*, pp. 52–62, questions the usual view that the Idumeans were forced to adopt Judaism.

26. See Jeremias, *Jerusalem*, pp. 332–335.

27. Cf. Schürer, *History* 3, p. 162, n. 55.

28. See further ibid. 3, p. 154.

29. Davies & Allison, *Matthew*, p. 287, identify a traditional core which has been turned into a woe by the evangelist. However, McKnight, *Light*, pp. 106–109, regards these as fully the words of Jesus.

30. The view of Davies & Allison, *Matthew*, p. 288, that the text refers to 'conversion to Judaism without the Messiah' is not warranted.

31. See e.g. Goodman, *Mission and Conversion*, pp. 69–74, and for a rebuttal Paget, 'Proselytism', pp. 96–97.

32. See above, n. 29.

33. Davies & Allison, p. 288, following Munck, suggest that Matt. 23:15 'reflects competition for adherents in the post-Easter period'.

34. Paget, 'Proselytism', p. 97.

35. Nolland, 'Proselytism', pp. 347–355, argues for a political rather than a proselytizing meaning.

36. This, however, is ambiguous. Tacitus may be referring to procreation rather than to proselytizing.

37. Both Tacitus (*Ann.* 2.85.5) and Suetonius (*Tiberius* 36.1) mention the expulsion, but give no reason for it.
38. For details, with references, see Schürer, *History* 3, pp. 163–164.
39. In my view, Paget, 'Proselytism', p. 83, fails to recognize the significance of the step from 'God-fearer' to proselyte by means of circumcision.
40. The word 'proselyte' is rare on inscriptions. In the 500 funerary inscriptions in Rome, the term occurs only seven times, and in texts from the third century AD. See Noy, *Jewish Inscriptions*, nos. 62, 218, 224, 392, 489, 491, 577.
41. See Donaldson, *Paul*, pp. 273–292.
42. Donaldson, *Paul*, p. 277.
43. It is evident that Paul is replying to misinformation which could only have come from Jerusalem (1:18–19; 2:7–10; 5:11).
44. After forty years of friendship with him, two things, at least, stand out for me about Peter O'Brien: his love for Christ and his careful scholarship. Like St Paul, on whose texts he is a distinguished commentator, Peter is 'consumed by passion' for Christ, to give the title of his important monograph on the labours of the apostle. I thank God for Paul the missionary, for Peter's life-long work of seeking to understand him, and for the service of the Master rendered by both in turn.

19. Dangers and difficulties for the Pauline missions

Bruce W. Winter

Paul's missionary journey and its fruits have rightly earned him the accolade of the greatest missionary of the early Gentile church, if not in the history of Gentile Christianity. He himself did not minimize the enormous effort he expended, and claimed that he 'laboured more abundantly than them all' (i.e. the other apostles), although he was quick to add, 'yet not I, but the grace of God which was with me' (1 Cor. 15:10).

In circumstantial terms the extent of Paul's endeavours has been attributed to the supposedly unprecedented ease of inter-city and inter-provincial travel in the East, for he used the highly sophisticated road system which the Romans developed in the late republic and early empire. Popular piety has sometimes linked this to Galatians 4:4: 'When the fullness of time came, God sent forth his Son.' The time was seen to be 'ripe' for the instant reception of the gospel in major cities in the East. These cities were readily accessible to this apostle to the Gentiles through ease of travel, and the *Pax romana* made this possible.

In the last century Paul's missionary endeavours were popularly seen as unimpeded triumphal advances. This may, in part, have been a legacy of the nineteenth century's tendency to read back into Paul's mission its own unprecedented 'success' in missionary work in the Third World; the latter's own difficulties and setbacks were not to be generally acknowledged until the last decades of the twentieth century, when missiology became an academic discipline.

While much discussion has rightly been devoted to the theology and the

285

strategy of the Pauline mission, little focus has been given to the not inconsiderable complexities and the tremendous challenges which Paul faced in founding Christian work in the major cities in the East of the Roman Empire. The New Testament openly acknowledges them. For example, Luke does not hide the despair that Paul experienced in Corinth and which brought him to the point of wanting to abandon his mission to this sophisticated Roman colony (Acts 18:9–10). Paul himself summarizes many of the dangers he faced in his many travels in 2 Corinthians 11:23–27. He informed the Corinthians that he had suffered three shipwrecks, and spent a day and a night adrift in the sea (2 Cor. 11:25). He later experienced another shipwreck on the way to Rome (Acts 27). In retrospect, this is how he described the dangers he experienced in travelling: 'In journeys often, in dangers from rivers, dangers of robbers, dangers in the wilderness, dangers from my counterymen, dangers from the Gentiles, dangers in the city, dangers in the wilderness, dangers from false brethren' (2 Cor. 11:25–26). Paul uses the term 'danger' (*kindynos*) in the plural eight times in verse 26 for each of the problems he had faced in his frequent travels.[1]

The purpose of this celebratory essay is to examine some of the dangers and difficulties of Paul's missionary activities. In order to do this it is proposed to examine first, the dangers of travel; secondly, the legal dangers facing his early Christian communities; and thirdly, some of the other difficulties and dangers which Paul and the churches he founded had to confront.

The dangers of travel

Travel had never been as easy as it was in the first century. Sea trade had become highly organized, largely brought about by the demands for grain to provide the corn dole for large numbers in Rome. The whole economy was geared to this. Claudius built the new port of Ostia specifically for the grain ships that plied the Mediterranean Sea in order to ensure that the Eternal City would not suffer grain shortages.[2] The late republic and early empire saw the unprecedented construction of a network of road systems. They provided rapid travel not only for Rome's highly mobile armies but also for increased inter-city trade.[3] All this reinforced the propaganda of the *Pax romana* and blessings of almost messianic proportions that the emperors claimed to have brought to their empire.

Paul's own missionary journeys were greatly assisted by the network of roads in Asia Minor and Greece. While the mountainous terrain in the provinces of Asia and Galatia must have tested the stamina of Paul and his coworkers, the Roman road system was of enormous help.

There is, however, an underlying assumption that under the Romans travel was not only easy but also safe. Paul himself presents a very different picture of the journeys he undertook between major cities in the East. D. French, who has undertaken extensive studies on the Roman road systems in Asia Minor while heading the British School of Archaeology in Ankara, has made the interesting observation that, in the latter period of Paul's missionary journeys, he chose less obvious routes rather than main ones. He sees on the part of Paul

> ... a deliberate rejection of major public roads and places in Asia Minor, the extensive travel by ship and at the end of his third journey the final avoidance of Ephesus reflect Paul's conscious awareness of hostile public, civic and official attitudes, an awareness born at Colonia Antiochia and Iconium, cruelly emphasised at Lystra, and finally perhaps hardened by the Diana riots and by his two years' sojourn at Ephesus and Asia.[4]

What were these dangers from 'robbers'? One the main dangers of travel arose as one passed out of a city's legal jurisdiction and safety, especially in the rugged territory Paul travelled across. The existence of a professional robber (*lēstēs*) or a kidnapper (*andrapodistēs*) on the roads is well documented. Some not only took possessions but also robbed travellers of their liberty.[5] Some people simply disappeared altogether, being kidnapped into a lifetime of slavery on a country estate. These unfortunate victims were not afforded the normal seven-year manumission given to household slaves in the empire.[6] In 1 Timothy 1:10 reference is made to the 'slave-dealer' or 'kidnapper'. The term used (*andrapodistēs*) was appropriately applied to both crimes, given that the purpose of kidnapping was normally for enslavement, and for legal purposes robbery.[7]

On three occasions Paul experienced being beaten with rods (2 Cor. 11:25). One incident, which was a beating by the lictors who acted at the direction of the magistrates, is recorded only in Acts 16:22, 37. While the law provided that Roman citizens could not be beaten, this rule was not always observed.[8] Moreover, in that particular case, Paul drew attention to his status only after the event.

The Jews, his 'own countrymen', were in hot pursuit of him. He experienced dangers from them. At their hands thirty-nine stripes were given on five separate occasions (2 Cor. 11:24). The other danger Paul faced as he travelled was the existence of hostile Jews who were ready to murder him if they could. His effective work among some Diaspora Jews and his 'stealing' of proselytes and God-fearers in his contact with their synagogues provided the justification for his death, given that he was responsible for their 'apostasy'. He was later to be the subject of an attempted murder by more than forty Jews while *en route* from Jerusalem to Caesarea Maritima. The provision of such a large armed guard reflected the easy opportunity that travel by road presented to exterminate an enemy of the Jews.[9] Outside the jurisdiction of the city, no protection was provided for travellers, certainly not in the East.

Paul speaks of the dangers he experienced both in the wilderness and in the cities. Of the former we know nothing. In Damascus he records that he escaped over the city wall from the ethnarch who had been directed to apprehend him for the king, Aretas (2 Cor. 11:32–33). There was an attempted stoning in Iconium, which was actually carried out at Lystra at the behest of Jews from Antioch and Iconium (2 Cor. 11:25; cf. Acts 14:5, 19). There were unspecified dangers from the Gentiles, as well as dangers from false brethren.

After outlining the dangers he experienced in his ministry, Paul reveals additional information, i.e. the hardships experienced in travelling.[10] It was 'through many a sleepless night, in hunger and thirst, often without food, in cold and exposure' that he operated (2 Cor. 11:27). Even though inns were provided on some Roman roads, many of those on which Paul travelled passed through inhospitable country.[11]

Paul's specific reference to dangers and difficulties begins with a claim to have experienced more imprisonments, beatings and near mortal incidents than other ministers of Christ. This catalogue was part of his countering the imitation of apostles who made great claims for themselves (2 Cor. 11:13–14). He appears to have been reluctant to disclose all these details, and it would seem that here he is doing so here for the first time with the Corinthians, even though he had worked among them for some eighteen months (2 Cor. 11:23; Acts 18:11). He does so only in response to his opponents' boasts about their successes. By contrast, Paul will boast only of his difficulties and his weaknesses and swears a solemn to that effect (2 Cor. 11:16–31). From the biographical details given in Acts the reader could not have estimated the extent of the dangers and difficulties that Paul experienced in pursuing his missionary calling as the apostle to the Gentiles.

The danger of meeting weekly

Pagan citizens did not normally worship together in a formal service; for them, worship was largely an individual activity. An exception was the worship of civic gods, including the deified reigning and deceased emperors who were honoured at an annual feast day. Because a weekly corporate meeting of adherents was not something that was associated with cultic practices in pagan religion, the Romans were puzzled by a 'religion' that had a regular 'meeting' (*ekklēsia*) of all its members as one of its essential characteristics.[12] They certainly would have been suspicious of the use of the political term *ekklēsia* for a 'gathering' which was not an ordinary association but a religious one, and yet possessed no statue of a divinity.[13]

E. A. Judge has given some idea of how the early Christians were first perceived by the Romans in Syrian Antioch. He discusses the significance of the term 'Christians' (*Christianoi*), which was coined by the Romans: 'they were first named "Christians"' (Acts 11:26):

> [The term] can hardly be invented by orthodox Jews since it concedes the messiahship of Jesus. Its suffix implies the word was coined by speakers of Latin … The suffix *-ianus* constitutes a political comment. It is not used of the followers of a god. It classifies people as partners of a political or military leader, and is mildly contemptuous.[14]

It was not a self-designation but a perception of this messianic movement of Jesus, not by Jews who would not have conceded the title, but by the Roman authorities.

In a recent work, *Criminal Law in Ancient Rome*, O. F. Robinson, a Roman legal historian, draws attention to the legal prohibition forbidding associations from meeting more than once a month. After he had consolidated his power base, one of the first acts of Augustus was to move against associations. Jews had been granted a specific exemption to meet every Sabbath in the very legislation which proscribed associations meeting more than once a month. '*Collegia* represented a threat to public order rather than a standing offence, but they could be repressed severely.'[15]

So what technically was this gathering in the eyes of the Romans? Robinson argues that 'the Christians could hardly have formed a legal *collegium* [association], since they needed to meet weekly'.[16] The weekly Christian gathering might well be seen as the seditious activity of an 'association' (*collegium*) devoted to the memory of a crucified Jew. The meeting could be alleged to be seditious because it broke the monthly rule. If 'Christian' was a somewhat politically derisory designation, then their meetings could be viewed only with a measure of curiosity at best, and suspicion at worst. They had no visible representation of a god and they were followers of a deceased leader, neither a political or military one. Furthermore, their leader had been crucified following what would have been assumed to be the due processes and impartiality of Roman law.

The treason trials under Tiberius had created a permanent fear for every Roman of guilt by association.[17] Besides, it was the duty of citizens to take cognisance of any unusual activities in the city. Augustus singled out associations for urgent and special attention, given that any allegations of sedition against the state could have disastrous consequences for all involved.[18] Rome had long ago banned pagan religions such as Bacchanalism, and had destroyed the temple to Isis in Rome. Only recently, Tiberius had restricted the activities of the Druid priests, and Claudius subsequently abolished that religion all together.[19] How would this 'religion' be judged, and could it survive once it became known by Rome and those who held the *imperium* in the provinces?

In Corinth the noted Roman jurist, the governor of Achaea, Gallio ('the friend of Claudius' who declared that disputes with the Christian movement were an internal 'Jewish' matter), issued a totally unexpected legal decision in favour of the Christian community. Weekly meetings during his governorship could not be condemned as a contravention of the Roman law governing associations, given this decision (Acts 18:12–17).[20] However, this ruling did not mean that, like Caesar's wife, their activities would automatically continue to be seen as above legal reproach. Gallio left Corinth after his brief rule of the province, and each subsequent governor would exercise that all-powerful *imperium* as he himself judged fit.[21] A ruling by a governor did not create a precedent in another province, certainly not in Rome.

How was this movement seen in the eyes of other Roman provincial courts? In a subsequent case before Felix, the Roman governor of Judea (Acts 24–26), Paul stressed the Jewish origins of early Christianity in his defence. Tertullus wished to portray Paul as 'a pestilent fellow, an agitator among all the Jews throughout the world', thus casting him as a seditious Jew, the likes of whom Claudius writes about in his letter to the Alexandrians.[22] In his defence Paul's *exordium* expresses confidence in the expertise of Felix to judge over 'this nation'. He affirms that he worships 'the God of our fathers, believing everything laid down by the law and the prophets' (Acts 24:10, 14). When the case resumes, he is at pains to claim before Festus and Agrippa his Jewish upbringing, and declares that he is on trial for 'hope in the promises made by God to our fathers ... saying nothing but what the prophets and Moses said would come to pass' (Acts 26:4–6, 22). It was the legal opinion of Festus that 'when the accusers stood up, they brought no charge of such evil things as I supposed'. He perceived that the case was, in effect, about 'certain questions against him [Paul] of their own superstition, and of one Jesus who was dead, whom Paul asserted to be alive' (Acts 25:18–19).

What was the attitude of the authorities in Rome towards the movement? At this stage in the history of the early church we have no legal opinion either for or against it. However, Luke's two-volume work concludes with the comment that, although under house detention, Paul was preaching the kingdom of God and teaching 'the things concerning the Lord Jesus' in Rome 'with all boldness' and, Luke adds, 'unhindered' (Acts 28:31); the concluding adverb indicated that there was no legal impediment preventing Paul from engaging in his mission.[23] Luke was clearly concerned to demonstrate that what Roman courts had declared to be legal in the provinces was, by implication, endorsed in its capital; no legal impediment had been placed by the Roman authorities while Paul was under guard. Yet the status of early Christianity would be tested in the appeal to Caesar of the case of the Jews versus Paul. The official proceedings of Paul's defence before the two governors of Judea would have been recorded in shorthand and summarized.[24] These would have been forwarded to Rome along with an accompanying legal memorandum summarizing the case – a document Festus found difficult to compose. Festus had consulted with the legal counsel who sat with him at assizes, and his legal opinion was: 'I found that he had committed nothing worthy of death', an opinion that was backed up by Agrippa, who said, 'This man might have been set at liberty, if he had not appealed to Caesar' (Acts 25:12, 25).[25] Festus confirmed Gallio's view that Christians were a sect within Judaism.

The action of the Jewish converts to Christianity in Galatia may provide some evidence of the anxiety felt concerning the uncertain legal status of their 'association' in this pro-Roman province. Paul says that 'as many as wish to provide a good legal *persona*'[26] by means of the flesh, i.e. circumcision, they themselves compel you [Gentiles] to be circumcised only in order that they may not be persecuted for the cross of Christ' (Gal. 6:12). Creating lookalike Jews out of Gentile Christians by compelling them to be circumcised (a criminal offence under Roman law, as it was equated with castration, but was permitted for Jews and those male converts to what Rome saw as a 'superstition'),[27] and by having Gentiles keep the Mosaic law, was seen to be a way of avoiding persecution for being a Christian by being seen to be Jewish.

Because Gentile Christians had been compelled to become Jews by their Jewish Christian brothers up to the time when Paul wrote Galatians, Christian gatherings there would be lookalike synagogue meetings as its members bore the social marks of being Jewish. There would be, then, no problems with the authorities concerning their meeting weekly, and it would also enable Gentile converts to avoid any obligations towards the imperial cult celebrations in Galatia. The Jews in Pisidian Antioch would have to bring a case against the Christians before the governor of the province in order to show that Christians were in breach of Roman law on associations by meeting weekly, as they did not qualify for their special exemption under the law governing associations.[28]

It is interesting to note that, in the Trajan–Pliny correspondence of the next generation, the former, like Augustus, had banned all gatherings which were judged to be associations because it was the emperor's belief that 'men who banded together for a common end will all the same become a political association (*hetaeriae*)'. This was why the governor took such severe actions against Christians in the province of Bithynia, executing provincials and sending Roman citizens to trial in Rome itself.[29]

Difficulties of the crucifixion, the cult and other Christians

Other difficulties for Paul's missionary endeavours will be dealt with briefly. Those who believe that in the first century the gospel was instantly recognized as 'good news' have failed to understand the difficulties it posed because of the manner of Christ's death. A crucified Messiah as God's means of reconciling a lost world was a bizarre message. Crucifixion was reserved for those who lacked any legal *persona*. This instrument of death, calculated to humiliate its scourged victims by stripping them of their clothes as well as their *dignitas* and to prolong the terminal torture, smacked of the crudest superstition ever. In the early third century the pagan, Caecilius Natalis, said, 'I hear that they adore the head of an ass, the basest of creatures – a worthy and appropriate religion for such manners.' A graffito of a man's body with an ass's head found in the quarters of the imperial pages in Palatine reflects a similar response by Gentiles to 'the folly of what we preach', for they saw it as insulting to their intelligence. Under this graffito was the caption 'Alexamenos worships [his] God'.[30] In response a Christian page wrote, 'Alexamenos is faithful', because he knew that here salvation was to be found. Those who embraced Paul's message did so because of God's calling (1 Cor. 1:22–4), in spite of the enormous difficulties the crucified God posed.

In addition, there existed the problem of the imperial cult, in which every citizen in the time of the Julio-Claudian emperors was required to participate. Its demands on provincials have been seriously underestimated by

New Testament scholars. Religious pluralism was a given, but the fastest-growing religion in the first century was the imperial cult. It was the means of expressing loyalty to emperor and the empire. The Jews were exempt from cultic participation, for they offered up a sacrifice for the emperor, and not to him, in Jerusalem. During the annual feast day for emperor worship, citizens in white festive garments with garlands joined in processions, entrances to houses were decorated, public spectacles took place and individuals burned incense before the imperial statues.[31] These were high-profile occasions and it was not easy to absent oneself from such an important imperial obligation. Dio Cassius records that Roman citizens living in the provinces of Asia and Bithynia had a binding civic obligation to worship 'the Divine Julius (*Divus Iulius*) and Roma', while ordinary provincials were committed to the worship of 'Augustus and Roma'.[32] This applied in the provinces throughout the empire. The widespread evidence of temples erected to Augustus and Roma supports this claim, and includes the one erected by Herod the Great at Caesarea Maritima, the seat of the governor of the province of Judea.[33]

How did the Gentile converts cope with this challenge? As Professor S. Mitchell noted recently in his discussion of the imperial cult in Galatia:

> One cannot avoid the impression that the obstacle which stood in the way of the progress of Christianity, and the force which would have drawn new adherents back to conformity with the prevailing paganism, was the public worship of the emperors ... it was not a change of heat that might win a Christian convert back to paganism, but the overwhelming pressure to conform imposed by the institutions of his city and the activities of his neighbours.[34]

In Corinth Paul draws the sharp distinction for those in the Christian community who participated in the worship of 'gods in heaven or on the earth' and put pressure on other Christians to join them. The former divinities certainly included reigning emperors and at times members of their family. Paul said that 'for us there is only one God and one Lord', and forbade Christians to attend these festive occasions in the temple (1 Cor. 8:4–6; 10:21). For Christians the imperial cult simmered like a volcano, eventually erupting after Paul was dead. It posed a definite problem for converts of his day.

There were other problems, not least of all the attempts by Christians to create further difficulties for Paul's mission; his imprisonment at a time when he was having unprecedented opportunities with the Praetorium guards and the imperial household, i.e. 'the rest' (some were to send their Christian greetings to the church in Philippi, Phil. 1:12–13; 4:22). This disruptive activity was typical in trials where opponents or disaffected persons sought to prejudice the outcome of a trial by stirring up difficulties for the accused before the case was heard. First-century converts were capable of continuing to act like pagans even in the context of apostolic mission,[35] while others were spurred on by Paul's bold witness to preach the Messiah at the centre of government in Rome (Phil. 1:14).

Reflecting on the dangers and personal hardships which Paul experienced should prevent a nostalgic backward look to the early church, especially where it has been assumed that the circumstances were ideal for the spread of Christianity to Syria and Greece. There has also been a tendency to idealize a more recent era of Christianity, that is, Third World missionary endeavours before religious pluralism was on the very doorsteps of the citizens of the First World and the New World. The unique message of salvation based on Christ's work and not on the observation of religious activities by sincere, pious adherents continues to offend, in the same way as it did in Paul's day. There has never been an 'ideal' age where society found the Christian message one that was amenable to its aspirations. The history of Christian missions clearly demonstrates this, from the missionary activities of Paul to this present day. While examining the extraordinary magnitude of Paul's mission and the important theology of missions which can be deduced from both Acts and Paul's letters, this discussion has shown that it would be inappropriate not to record the logistical difficulties, personal dangers and debilitating experiences he encountered in his travels in order to bring the gospel to so many cities in the East.[36]

Notes

1. Murphy-O'Connor, *Paul: A Critical Life*, p. 97, reminds us that 2 Cor. 11:26 refers not to difficulties but to 'dangers'.
2. For a discussion see Rickman, *Corn Supply*.
3. Chevallier, *Roman Roads*, and Casson, *Travel*, ch. 10.
4. French, 'Acts and the Roman roads', pp. 57–58.
5. Suetonius, *Augustus* 32.
6. Bradley, *Slaves and Masters* and Weaver, *Familia Caesaris*, ch. 5.
7. The recent discussion of Harrill, 'Vice', must not be allowed to obscure the fact that travellers were kidnapped into slavery for estate labour by slave-dealers.
8. Sherwin-White, *Roman Society*, pp. 73–74.
9. Acts 23:12–25. Verse 23 speaks of an armed guard of some 470 men.
10. For records of varying degrees of discomfort in travel by sea and on land see Casson, *Travel*, pp. 190–196.

11. For a general discussion of the difficulties see Murphy-O'Connor, *Paul: A Critical Life*, pp. 98–99; Casson, *Travel*, ch. 11.
12. They also had no statues of which they could say, as they did of their deities, 'Here is Apollo', believing that there dwelt the divinity. They were subsequently to be accused of atheism because of this.
13. For a discussion of this widely used secular term, see my 'Problem', ch. 13.
14. Judge, 'Judaism', p. 363.
15. Robinson, *Criminal Law*, p. 80.
16. Ibid.
17. Levick, *Tiberius*, ch. 12.
18. Robinson, *Criminal Law*, ch. 6.
19. Ibid., p. 95.
20. For a discussion of the preliminary hearing of the case of the Jews versus Paul see my 'Gallio's ruling'.
21. Sherwin-White, *Roman Society*, pp. 5ff.
22. *P.Lond.* 1912.
23. For a discussion of this point see my 'Gallio's ruling'.
24. See my 'Role'.
25. See my 'Official proceedings'.
26. For a discussion of the use of *prosōpon* for 'legal status' or identity and *euprosōpos*, 'to have a good legal face', with its cognate *euprosōpeō*, see my *Seek the Welfare*, pp. 137–138. I cite among other evidence: 'I do not know what answer you can make to give you *euprosōpos* before your accusers', because of the impossibility of defending the indefensible (Lucian, *Apology for the Salaried Posts of Great Houses* 3).
27. Robinson, *Criminal Law*, p. 52.
28. Ibid., p. 80.
29. *Letters of Pliny* 10.96.
30. For a reproduction of the graffito see Green, *Evangelism*, p. 174, and the quotation from C. Becker, *Der 'Octavius'* 9.
31. For a helpful discussion which includes specific details of participation in the East as well as the West, see Fishwick, *Imperial Cult* 2.1, ch. 8.
32. Dio Cassius 51.20.6–7.
33. See Sherwin-White, *Roman Citizenship*, pp. 403–408, on the importance the cult of Augustus and Roma assumed in this period.
34. Mitchell, *Anatolia* 2, p. 10.
35. For a detailed discussion see my *Seek the Welfare*, ch. 5.
36. Peter O'Brien has long held together very considerable gifts as a commentator on the Pauline letters with a deep concern for missions. This is reflected not only in his earlier calling as a theological educator in India but also in a course designated 'Bible and missions', which he established some twenty years ago in the college where he now teaches. It reveals his conviction that neither could be properly studied apart from the other, for neither could be fully understood without the other. Nowhere is this more clearly seen than in the life and letters of Paul. It therefore seems an appropriate way of honouring a long-standing friend to turn to one of his great interests, viz. the Pauline mission.

20. The impact of Paul's gospel on ancient society

Edwin A. Judge

This title (offered to me by the editors) was bound to tempt a footloose student of history on to very tricky ground. Our honorand himself has warned that Paul gave no direct instructions covering what we mean by 'impact'.[1] The new life of the churches was indeed revolutionary. But it was designed for fulfilment when the existing 'society' reached the end of its time. In this life it 'remains hidden'.

I know that this should not trouble an ancient historian. The reigning fashion is to insist that the conversion of Rome changed nothing of social consequence.[2] If so, we may as well say the question evaporates. Paul converted the world all right, but since he was not looking for any particular changes in it, we need not bother looking for them either. Yet we know that our own world, the modern one, certainly bears the most profound imprint of biblical thought.[3] We may, then, at least ask why that had not happened already in antiquity, or (if it had) why people have not noticed it.

A further problem in looking for 'impact' is how to distinguish the impress of Paul from that of the New Testament as a whole. And if one were to go only for Pauline distinctives, one might well end up only with marginal issues rather than central ones. I propose therefore to treat as Pauline such positions as I judge basic to his thinking, even though they may be shared in one way or another with comparable positions in the Gospels or other writings. But they will be concepts that he decisively

297

298 The gospel to the nations

develops and which are terminologically identifiable as his.

I propose to find a way around the main impasse by taking both key terms in the broadest sense. By 'gospel' I shall mean the whole body of Paul's teaching (generated presumably from the gospel in its strict sense). By 'society' I shall mean not only the fabric of social relations but the formative ideas or conventions behind them which we might ordinarily refer to as 'culture'. The question being taken this way (and allowing for my further caveat above), I then start with the following proposition: in the modern world the impact of Pauline teaching on our culture may be recognized most clearly at two focal points.

The 'inner man' and the 'one new man' in modern society

The first is our preoccupation with the 'inner man' (Rom. 7:22; Eph. 3:16).[4] In classical culture interest was concentrated upon the individual and his fate, seen in relation to external events. So in Greek tragedy the drama typically centres upon the inability of even the well-meaning to spot the point in time. Their zeal then slips over into the fateful arrogance (*hybris*) that provokes doom (*nemesis*). Or in Stoic (and much other) ethical thinking the aim is to guard one's own integrity unshaken by the emotional shocks of contact with others. Pity (if it lacks moderation, Alcinous 32.4) is as much a vice of the soul as cruelty. The cardinal virtues are generally properties of character: courage (*arête*, 'enterprise'), prudence (*phronēsis*), self-control (*sōphrosynē*). Such qualities are not featured in biblical culture, which focuses rather on constructive responses to others: trust (*pistis*), hope (*elpis*) and care (*agapē*). Justice (*dikaiosynē*), the fourth cardinal virtue, is, however, in Greek inscriptions, to be seen in social action, though it is not featured from that perspective in biblical culture, where it means righteousness (in God's sight).[5] In Pauline thought it is credited to the believer 'without works' (Rom. 4:6). In broad terms one may say that in the Hellenic tradition the problems of life centred upon keeping one's balance, and preserving the good one possessed. Education would train one successfully in this.[6]

It was Paul who most dramatically shattered such self-assurance. Not only did he see the cosmos as itself corrupted from without ('sin entered', Rom. 5:12, a notion unthinkable when the cosmos was by definition complete, perfect and unchanging), but the evil had enslaved even his own will (Rom. 7:14–25). The drama is no longer one of adjustment to fate within a closed system. Its limits explode at the cosmic level, while a microcosm of conflict is exposed within one's own heart.

The distant source of this apocalypse is clear: the serpent in the garden, and the demand of the Shema for total commitment of one's inmost being (Deut. 6:5, 'You shall love the LORD your God with all your heart, and with all your soul, and with all your might'). A phrase similar to Paul's 'inner man' is found in both Plato (*Rep.* 9.589A) and Plotinus (*Enn.* 1.1.10) for the self-mastery of reason. But the Pauline scenario reaches out, from indwelling sin (Rom. 7:20) to the liberating Spirit of life (8:2). Transformed by the renewal of our mind (12:2), we take the body for the temple of the Holy Spirit (1 Cor. 6:19), as we are daily renewed within (2 Cor. 4:16), a new creation (5:17).

Paul's searching of his own heart is, for his time, unparalleled in its candour. It was pursued even more ruthlessly by Augustine.[7] The self-disclosure we now expect in autobiography was not a feature of ancient culture, which concentrated on self-display.[8] Ancient romances waited on their happy ending with all the breathlessness of a soap opera. But modern novels and films are engrossed with our deeper dilemmas of motivation and morality. We look to them for a kind of psychological autobiography. The fact that the modern novel (as its name implies, an innovation) emerged in the period between the hey-days of the Puritans and of the Methodists may tell the tale. It is the cultural imprint, surely, of Paul's inner quest.[9] Similarly, our ideas of individual vocation and gifts are the cultural legacy of Paul's doctrine of the Spirit.

The second focal point of Pauline teaching that has profoundly marked modern culture is his concept of the 'one new man' (Eph. 2:15). This is his answer to the polarization of Jew and Gentile. The 'one new man' is not, however, a new type of individual. The 'one body' of the cross (2:16) reconciles the two, who are now 'of joint body' (*synsōma*, 3:6). The neologism seeks to imply an organic unity that is in fact social. This has already been made clear by the repeated use of metaphors from the civil order. Previously excluded from the 'commonwealth' of Israel as 'foreigners' to the covenants (2:12), the Gentiles have exchanged their status of 'resident aliens' for that of 'joint citizens with the saints', and thus 'members of God's household' (2:19). The figure then shifts again, to one forged for this very purpose. The whole 'construction' (*oikodomē*, elsewhere often ineffectively translated as 'edification', which itself arises from the Latin term for 'building') 'grows' into a 'sacred shrine in the Lord' (2:21). As a metaphor, *oikodomē* seems to have been another innovation of Paul's. It is a favourite way of his expressing the social reconstruction for which the new 'assemblies' meet. Everything is to serve that end (1 Cor. 14:26).[10]

It is not clear to me how Paul expected this to work out in practice, given the continuing synagogue assemblies from which the churches arose. But I have no doubt that the social autonomy asserted in the name of the 'one new man' is the historic source of what we now call 'the open society'. The right to an alternative lifestyle, grudgingly tolerated by 'national values', has been won, with painful slowness, from the blood of the martyrs. Rejection of status consciousness (*prosōpolēmpsia*, a term first attested in Rom. 2:11) no doubt springs from the same source.

Paul in later antiquity

Fragments of all the Pauline letters (except those to Timothy) survive from Egypt prior to Constantine's taking control there. The earliest papyri happen to be from the letters to Titus and Philemon. The survival rate for the subsequent parts of the New Testament, and for the Gospels of Matthew and John, is stronger. From the early fourth century comes a writing exercise based on the opening of Romans. From the end of it there is a bilingual text of Ephesians (Greek and Latin), and an alphabetic acrostic in verse using Pauline terms and themes.[11] This papyrus record shows the Pauline corpus in active use.[12]

The apocryphal *Acts of Paul (and Thecla)*, a second-century romance that also filled in the missing correspondence between Paul and the Corinthians, was probably more popular still.[13] In the year 307, however, the bishop of Thmuis in Egypt, Phileas, was interrogated by the prefect, Culcianus, on the facts about Paul. Two Greek papyrus transcripts of the trial have been published.[14] The governor needed to persuade the bishop, a wealthy community leader, to offer the public sacrifices. The governor himself seems quite familiar with the weak points in the bishop's position, or had been briefed by a well-informed consultant. Several of the gambits use detailed knowledge of Paul to catch the bishop out.

Culcianus asks whether Paul had not sacrificed (alluding perhaps to Acts 21:26). Phileas denies it. Later, on the resurrection of the body, Culcianus asks whether Paul had not rejected it (switching him with those he complains of in 1 Cor. 15:12?). Phileas flatly denies this too. 'Then who did deny it?' 'I'm not telling you', retorts Phileas. After another change of tack, Culcianus asks whether Paul was not a persecutor (as indeed the latter affirms in 1 Cor. 15:9, Gal. 1:13, Phil. 3:6). Another flat denial (is Phileas losing his grip?). Culcianus presses home the advantage: Was Paul not untrained (*idiōtēs*, the very word he cites against himself at 2 Cor. 11:6)? Was he not a Syrian, and did he not lecture in Aramaic? 'No', says Phileas, 'He was a Hebrew. But he also lectured in Greek, and was of the highest distinction, excelling everyone.' They argue about whether Paul was superior to Plato (Phileas offers to teach Paul to Culcianus). 'He was more profound than any man. He convinced all the philosophers.' Later Culcianus comes back for a last attempt. 'Was Paul God?' 'No,' answers Phileas. 'Who was he then?' Phileas replies: 'He was a man like ourselves, but the Spirit of God was in him; and so he performed signs and wonders and acts of virtue in the Spirit.'

The key part assigned to Paul in this cross-questioning demonstrates that he had become far more than a romantic hero. His identity, intellectual standing and integrity are critical to the bishop's resistance. As the champion of orthodoxy, the government has to be able to undercut him. It may not always have been so clear.

For the earliest generations after the New Testament period Paul has been called 'the thorn in the flesh' of the churches.[15] Some of the most popular writings stood outside his influence. This is conspicuously true of the *Shepherd* of Hermas, which rivals Paul's letters in its frequency of papyrus remains. The *Didache*, *Barnabas* and the apologists draw largely upon material from non-Pauline sources. They sought antiquity. Only Marcion is a thoroughgoing Paulinist.[16] Some of the Gnostic traditions took Paul up, especially in his romantic dress. They understood 1 Corinthians 15:46–48 to justify their doctrine of three types of men with fixed natures. Not for nothing did Tertullian call him 'the apostle of the heretics'.[17]

With Irenaeus, Clement of Alexandria, Tertullian and Origen, spanning the second half of the second century and the first of the third, Paul comes into his own as a major authority.[18] But his establishment, and the need to prove the self-consistency of Scripture, have blunted the response to some of his more challenging insights.[19] It could not be admitted, for example, that his soul-searching was an authentic account of his own experience, since he must have been perfect, the model for imitation, as he had imitated Christ, a point he himself had made (1 Cor. 11:1). For Origen he was already 'divine'. So his problems had only been assumed for our instruction.[20]

Neither the 'inner man' nor the 'one new man', so far as I have seen, attracted particular attention from commentators during the first four centuries.[21] Not, at any rate, for their potential social impact. Symptomatic of this is the case of Marius Victorinus.[22] He was ideally placed to answer our question. Professor of Rhetoric at Rome in the time of Julian, he resigned his chair after the ban on Christian teachers (362). We possess quite extensive literary works of his, both as a believer and from the time before his conversion, which happened slowly while he was already a famous man. His baptism was a public sensation, according to Augustine (*Conf.* 8.2). He must have been fully conscious of the cultural significance of what was happening to him and to his age. Yet his Pauline commentaries stick closely to the text.[23] He amplifies it into a copious paraphrase, aiming to spell out the nuances of Paul's thought strictly in Pauline terms. There is no symbolic interpretation such as others had used to escape the hard word. Yet he sometimes misses the point. Observers of our contemporary wave of Bible translators will recognize the problem. One slips too easily into one's own ideas.

Commenting on the 'one new man' (Eph. 2:16) Victorinus says (tr. M. J. Edwards, n. 21 above):

> Their souls have thus been reconciled to the eternal and the spiritual, to all things above. The Savior, through the Spirit, indeed the Holy Spirit, descended into souls. He thereby joined what had been separated, spiritual things and souls, so as to make the souls themselves spiritual. He has established them in himself, as he says, 'in a new person'. What is this new person? The spiritual person, as distinguished from the old person, who was soul struggling against flesh.

Whatever one may think of this as an interpretation of Pauline anthropology (and the English translator has syncopated it somewhat towards the end), it appears completely to miss the point that Paul is talking about the uniting of Jew and Gentile in the 'one new man', a social and not a psychological aim. Nor can one say it is a temporary diversion on the part of Victorinus. When he comes in 2:19 to 'fellow-citizens with the saints' he defines the latter as 'the apostles, prophets and all who formerly experienced God or spoke divinely through the Spirit dwelling within them'. Yet in 2:17 he had recognized that 'those who are near' are 'obviously' Jews.

In addition to the vast corpus of patristic homilists and commentators, there were being circulated at the time substantial critiques of Scripture. Most of these (e.g. Celsus, Porphyry and others that are anonymous) are preserved only by citation in the refutations that its defenders published.[24] Of those that survive in their own right, the most instructive for our purposes are the works of Julian. As the last heir of the house of Constantine, he had been brought up on Scripture, though secretly rejecting it. On coming to power, he set out to reinvigorate the classical cults on the model of the churches. This illusion baffled his supporters, and the reforms would have perished through irrelevance anyway had his premature death not cancelled the question.[25] The central preoccupation of both critics and defenders of Scripture is with its alleged inconsistencies.

Since my assignment, however, concerns 'impact on society', I will take the two most spectacular public manifestations of the gospel, allowing them as possible outworkings of the two Pauline focal points I have named. They are monasticism (for the 'inner man') and martyrdom (for the 'one new man').

The 'inner man' and the *monachoi*

The earliest classical author to take a better than negative notice of 'the school (*diatribe*) of Moses and Christ' was the medical polymath Galen, in the second century. He saw what we call monasticism and martyrdom as the two things Christians sometimes do that align them with true philosophers. We all see for ourselves, he says, that they despise death, and that they shun sex out of a kind of modesty. There are women and men among them who have avoided intercourse throughout their lives. There are also those so far advanced in self-discipline and dedicated study that they yield nothing to true philosophers.[26]

By the fourth century the practice of celibacy had institutionalized itself in the person of the monk (*monachos*, 'solitary' or 'single-minded'). The term is first attested in this sense in a civil petition of 324.[27] Commenting on 1 Corinthians 7:25 and 1 Timothy 4:1, an anonymous critic later asked, 'How is it that certain people boast of their virginity as if it were some great thing, and say that they are filled with the Holy Ghost similarly to her who was the mother of Jesus?' (*BG* 708). In the churches too there were those who judged that the Pauline option had been upstaged by monasticism. We have polemical works by Jerome defending the new discipline against Helvidius (383), Jovinian (393) and Vigilantius (406). In the meantime an influential literature was developing around it, inspired by Athanasius' idealizing *Life* of Antonius, and the latter's published letters.[28]

Asceticism was not itself a distinctive of the Christian tradition.[29] But a Christian practice of 'spirituality' made use of it.[30] At the social level, however, fourth-century monasticism produced reactions of horror or contempt. Julian (himself admired for his asceticism) accused the monks of exploiting their sacrifices for gain, like the Cynics (Loeb ed., 2, p. 122). Their retreat to the desert came from misanthropy (p. 296). Libanius, who revered Julian's memory, called them pale, tomb-living enemies of the gods (*Or.* 62.10). They pack themselves into caves, moderate only in dress (*Or.* 2.32). The black elephants attack the temples, concealing gluttony under artificial pallor, artisans aping philosophy (*Or.* 30.8–31).

In the meantime the Christian Roman government strove to regulate the new craze. Legislation in 370 accused men of taking to the desert to escape civil duties (*CTh* 12.1.63). In 390, however, the monks were obliged to stay in their desert (16.3.1, revoked two years later, 16.3.2). In 390, bishops who admitted tonsured women to the altars were deposed (16.2.27). In 398 bishops were made responsible if monks in their territory gave sanctuary against the law (9.40.16).[31]

The historian Eunapius (fr. 55) complains that the Goths of Alaric had their own tribe of so-called monks, for admission to which one needed only sweep around in dirty cloaks and tunics, and to be evil and plausible. Those who destroyed the Serapeum at Alexandria in 389, he says, were human pigs, who needed only black clothes and public squalor to achieve tyranny, chaining the human race to the dishonest slave-cult of the martyrs (*Lives of the Sophists* 6.11.6). The poet Palladas quipped, 'How can you be solitaries when you go around in crowds?' (*Anth. Pal.* 11.384). Writing of the year 403, the historian Zosimus asserts that the monks were taking over most of the land, impoverishing everyone (*Hist. nov.* 5.23.4).

Can we call this the impact of Paul's problems with the 'inner man'? He would surely have joined the lost voices of those who condemned it. Yet the quest of Antony for a radical victory over the enemy within must owe something to his insights. Should the 'inner man' have been locked away again?

The 'one new man' and the *martyres*

From the official viewpoint, the 'one new man' was a non-starter. Though many Romans were interested in Judaism, going over to it was disgraceful. All the more, to have tried to create a new (potentially universal) citizenship would have seemed superfluous. Rome was already well on the way in practice to achieving that much herself. In the event, the Jews were to be violently suppressed in their main homelands in the late first and early second centuries. But their traditional autonomy of lifestyle was respected, and secured by a place in the tax system. In spite of the fashionable assumption in New Testament studies that the demarcation between Jews and Christians proceeded only by slow and mixed stages, and was not inescapable, the Romans seem never to have seriously linked the two. No-one, Roman, Jew or Christian, across two and a half centuries of baffling repression, appears to have thought of the obvious: let the Christians go their own way and tax them too for the privilege. The whole point was that the Christians owed national loyalty to their own Roman or Greek culture, their birthright, and the law of their fathers. The Christians rejected this. They obeyed a higher law, and for ancestry appealed to Abraham.[32]

On one thing the Romans and the Christians readily agreed. They were treating themselves as a separate nation, a 'third race', as Tertullian put it, between Jews and Romans.[33] In terms of political philosophy the matter was formulated for the Christians by Origen (*Contra Cel.* 1.1): 'It is not wrong to form associations against the law for the sake of truth.' This is the first time in recorded history that the right to self-determination was defined. Would Paul have shrunk from this as the outcome of his 'one new man'? I think not.

But the price was high. Paul understood the cost of witnessing. He had seen Stephen pay it. He paid it himself, no doubt.[34] The Romans could accommodate the perverse will to die, within limits.[35] There came the point, however, where it was, for the government, self-defeating. It risked the neglect of the very gods it was supposed to appease. In his edict of toleration of 311, the dying Galerius, a monster to the Christians, reiterated the unchanging complaint against them. They were creating deviant communities on divergent principles (Lactantius, *De mort. pers.* 34.2: *per diversa varios populos congregarent*). But the time had come when they should at least pray (*orare*, the distinctive Christian term) to their own God for their own safety, and for his. The wall came down. Rome accepted the Christian principle of self-determination.

Three generations later, it was still unclear to Ammianus Marcellinus what the nature of the Christian community was.[36] Ammianus is the last great historian of Rome, the heir of Tacitus. He toyed with various terms: *ritus christianus, christiana lex, cultus christianus, christiana religio.* He has no parallel for such an adjective with any of these nouns, and none of them in his usage relates primarily to what we call 'religion' in antiquity. He is casting about for a way of formulating the cultural phenomenon as a whole. His older contemporary, Marius Victorinus, had already adopted the neologism, *christianitas.*

Ammianus coyly accepts, with apologies to his Latin readers, several Greek terms now making their way into Latin (he is himself a Greek!): *presbyter, diaconus, synodus, martyr.* The latter two are very public phenomena which he carefully explains. He also habitually assimilates the episcopal system to a military command structure. He accepts the professionalism of the Christian calling, and the dedication of virgins and martyrs. He likes the uncontentious, ethically quietist and tolerant elements. He recognizes the drive for orthodoxy, the political independence of bishops, the solidarity of the communities. He recoils from factionalism, brutality, pomp and superstition as he saw it already in the churches.

Yet many crucial aspects escape him. He does not see the connection between doctrinal commitment and political troubles. He does not see the biblical sources of dogmatic controversy. He seems unaware of the influence of women in the churches, of the charitable enterprise, even of monasticism (apart from the virgins). But he fully grasps the impact upon public life of the phenomenon he cannot either clearly perceive or define. He wants to isolate its positive behaviour and assimilate that to the general good. In both his uncertainty and his intentions he is registering, as an instinctively responsible student, the historical novelty of beliefs about God creating an alternative culture, which is what we now mean by 'religion'.

Paul may not exactly have intended this for his 'one new man', but it holds within it still the keys to the higher destiny he had in mind. The social impact has been profound, but mostly very long delayed.[37,38]

Notes

1. O'Brien, 'The church', p. 117. Paul's 'social theory of organization' has been described as 'truly novel and innovative. As a transition strategy, the pattern is emergent rather than imposed': Marshall, 'The enigmatic apostle', p. 174.
2. MacMullen, 'What difference?', p. 341: '... non-Christian moral history runs parallel to Christian. Or the two are one.'
3. Judge, 'Biblical shape'.
4. The use of this translation is now banned by US publishers, but if I say 'inner being' or 'inner self' I lose the strong sense, created by the use of *anthrōpos* ('man'), that the inner self is the definitive person. I also destroy the verbal concurrence with my second focal point, the 'one new man', where *anthrōpos* would have to be translated 'humanity', wiping out the strikingly personal character of the Greek concept here also. Both 'men' are embodied 'in Christ' (Eph 2:13; 3:17). Chamblin, 'Psychology'.
5. *Dikaiosynē* stands for fair dealing in the marketplace, inscribed on weights and deified by magistrates: Robert, *Documents de l'Asie Mineure*, pp. 25–29.
6. Many in antiquity, like Suetonius and Tacitus, appear to have thought character was fixed from birth: Lindsay, 'Characterisation', p. 301; Gill, 'Character development'; Swain, 'Character change'.
7. Grossi, 'Anthropology', p. 45: 'Augustine ... who definitively disjoined anthropology from cosmology, for whom man interrogates himself directly to find out who he is and filters the whole of the reality he encounters, not excluding God, through himself.'
8. Misch, *A History*. On the psychology of the phenomenon, see Hutch, *The Meaning of Lives*.
9. Watt, *The Rise*. For the view that fairytales were driven out of English popular culture by the Puritans and other intellectual moralists, and that 'novels ... are an alternative to Methodism', see Hunter, *Before Novels*, pp. 143, 134. On the ancient romances see Tatum, *Search*.
10. Barclay, 'One new man', pp. 73–81, making the point that 'new' (*kainos*) connotes not repetition but radical innovation.
11. P. Oxy. 2.209 (Rom.); PSI 13.1306 (Eph.); P. Bodmer 47 (acrostic, published by Carlini).
12. For the use of Scripture in church and community see Kaczynski, *Das Wort*.
13. Details of the extant papyri and translations in Schneemelcher, *New Testament Apocrypha*; discussion in Bremmer, *The Apocryphal Acts*.

14. Pietersma, *The Acts of Phileas*; Latin text and translation available in Musurillo, *The Acts of the Christian Martyrs*.
15. Dassmann, *Der Stachel*. Lindemann, 'Der Apostel', pp. 39–67.
16. Hoffmann, *Marcion*.
17. Wiles, *The Divine Apostle*, pp. 29–30, 18 (citing Tertullian, *Adv. Marc.* 3.5.4); Pagels, *The Gnostic Paul*.
18. Noormann, *Irenäus*.
19. Mitchell, '"A variable and many-sided man"', pp. 93–111.
20. Patristic citations of Scripture across the first three centuries are tabulated in Allenbach, *Biblia Patristica* 5, covering Basil and his contemporaries. It emerges from these tallies that in all periods 1 Cor. is cited much more often than Rom. (except in the case of Origen), though the letters are of similar length, and far more often than the somewhat shorter 2 Cor., Eph. always more often than Gal., and Col. than Phil., two pairs also of similar length.
21. Patristic commentaries are catalogued, together with the homilies, in Sieben, *Kirchenväterhomilien*. Extracts from the commentators, in translation, are given in the new series Ancient Christian Commentary, of which I have seen New Testament vol. 8, *Galatians, Ephesians, Philippians*, ed. M. J. Edwards. For evaluation, see Wiles (n. 17 above), and Young, *Biblical Exegesis*.
22. Hadot, *Marius Victorinus*.
23. Locher, *Marii Victorini*. Souter, *The Earliest Latin Commentaries*.
24. The critiques are reproduced with translations in the order of the biblical books in Rinaldi, *Biblia Gentium*. Celsus can be largely reconstructed from the response of Origen; Borrett, 'Celsus', pp. 259–288.
25. Smith, *Julian's Gods*, is more reserved on these issues.
26. This fragment, preserved in Arabic, is reproduced in Latin in W. den Boer, *Scriptorum Paganorum*. In general, see Wilken, *The Christians*.
27. *New Documents Illustrating Early Christianity* 1 (1981), pp. 124–126.
28. Brakke, *Athanasius*; Rubenson, *The Letters of St Antony*.
29. Wimbush, *Ascetic Behaviour*.
30. Ladner, *The Idea of Reform*, entirely devoted to reform of the 'inner man'. For a theological 'deepening' see Williams, *The Wound*.
31. For a complete catalogue of legislation relating to Christian practice or ideals, see Joannou, *La Législation impériale*.
32. Judge, 'Judaism'.
33. Harnack, *Mission*, section II vii, 'The tidings of the New People and of the Third Race', pp. 240–265; Excursus: 'Christians as a Third Race in the judgement of their opponents', pp. 266–278.
34. Tajra, *Martyrdom*.
35. Bowersock, *Martyrdom*.
36. The following remarks are based upon my own reading of Ammianus. Recent studies include Barnes, *Ammianus Marcellinus*; Matthews, *The Roman Empire of Ammianus*; Rike, *Apex Omnium: Religion*; Hunt, 'Christians', pp. 186–200; Neri, *Ammiano*.
37. According to Wilken's review, it is the finding of Kinzig, *Novitas Christiana*, that Christianity did, probably, create the idea of cultural progress.
38. However difficult it may be to trace historical cause and effect, one need have no doubt that in the long run a dominant source of cultural transformation in the West (and now worldwide) has been the churches' repeatedly seeking a fresh

start from Scripture. In Dr Peter O'Brien we salute a master of that fine art, especially now in his searching commentary on the letter to the Ephesians.

21. Paul and the evangelization of the Stoics

Richard J. Gibson

One of the perennial fascinations for students of Christian origins is the possibility of personal contact between the Christian apostle, Paul, and the Roman Stoic, Seneca. Their biographical and literary parallels inclined some church fathers to 'adopt' Seneca. One early writer thought correspondence between them deserved to exist, even if it had to be invented. In each generation somebody places the relationship back on the scholarly agenda.[1] This interest is driven by more than the curiosity of a trivia buff or the romantic appeal of finding two famous figures in the same school photo. Stoicism was 'the most important and influential development in Hellenistic philosophy'.[2] The early Christians came to the Graeco-Roman world with a gospel – 'the power of God for salvation to everyone who has faith for the Jew first and also for the Greek' (Rom. 1:16). What happened when these two movements met? Latent, then, in this fascination with a personal relationship is a thirst for insight into a widespread philosophical, cultural, and missiological phenomenon. It is a phenomenon which inevitably left its mark on Paul's mission and the pages of the New Testament, but in the absence of explicit commentary scholars have been left to read between the lines, with a bewildering array of agendas and results.[3] My agenda is to revisit this age-old question in the light of recent scholarship to see how it might illuminate Paul's distinctive strategy and message in his mission to Stoics.

Seneca and Paul

Somewhere between 5 BC and AD 1, Lucius Annaeus Seneca was born in the Roman colony of Cordoba, Spain.[4] The birth of Saul took place in Tarsus, the principal city of Cilicia, 'in one of the first few years of the Christian era'.[5] Brought to Rome at the age of two, Seneca eventually became tutor to the young Nero, and the emperor's advisor from 54 until 62, when he retired from public life. Paul arrived in that great city in the spring of 61 and spent two years under house arrest 'teaching about the Lord Jesus Christ quite openly' (Acts 28:31). Having fallen out of favour with the emperor, Seneca was forced by Nero to commit suicide in AD 65 (Tacitus, *Ann.* 15.60). Within a few years, even months, according to tradition (Eusebius, *HE* 2.25.5–8), both Paul and Peter died at the hands of the same tyrant. In other words, 'it is evident that Paul and Seneca lived at the same time in the same world'.[6]

To this circumstantial evidence, Luke adds a tantalizing biographical convergence. He records the abortive attempt by Corinthian Jews to bring Paul to trial before a Roman tribunal 'for persuading people to worship God in ways that are contrary to the law' (Acts 18:13).[7] The charges are heard by the proconsul of Achaia, Junius Gallio, alias Marcus Annaeus Novatus, Seneca's brother. Judging it a 'a matter of questions about words and names and your own law' (Acts 18:15), Gallio summarily dismisses the case. On the basis of the narrative, Farrer rejects as absurd the tradition that Gallio sent his brother some of Paul's writings. He also scotches any conjecture 'that Seneca had personal intercourse with St. Paul':

> Probably the nearest opportunity which ever occurred to bring the Christian Apostle into intellectual contact with the Roman philosopher was this occasion when St. Paul was dragged as a prisoner into the presence of Seneca's brother. The utter contempt and indifference with which he was treated, the manner in which he was summarily cut short before he could even open his lips in his own defence, will give us a just estimate of the manner in which Seneca would have been likely to regard St. Paul.[8]

Gallio was clearly anti-Semitic and Farrer feels confident this was an attitude shared by his brother.[9]

However, Bruce construes Acts 18:17 quite differently, as a commendation of the proconsul's impartiality, rather than an accusation of his 'indifference to spiritual matters'. Paul's confidence in appealing to Rome a few years later (Acts 25:11) was encouraged by 'this refusal of Gallio to interfere with Christian preaching'.[10] The incident operated as an important precedent for the extension of Roman protection of the Jewish religion to the Christian mission. Its significance was, no doubt, enhanced by the influence of Gallio's brother at the imperial court.[11] Nevertheless, it does not provide any substantial grounds for positing a meeting between Paul and Seneca.

Many have thought the writings of Paul and Seneca reveal a genuine meeting of minds.[12] As Lightfoot observed, 'the coincidences of thought and even of language between the two are at first sight so striking, that many writers have been at a loss to account for them, except on the supposition of personal intercourse, if not of direct plagiarism'.[13]

The affinity with Paul that most distinguishes Seneca from the sentiments of early and Roman Stoics is the fact that he 'speaks of God in warm, personal ways'.[14] To the question, 'What was God's reason for creating the world?', he replies, 'God is good' (*Ep.* 65.10). Elsewhere he asserts, 'between good men and the gods there exists a friendship – a friendship do I say? nay, rather a relationship and a resemblance'. The relationship is one of a parent to his children, in which God 'most dearly loves the good'. He 'wishes them to become supremely good and virtuous' and 'allots to them a fortune that that will make them struggle' (*De prov.* 2.7). Furthermore, 'God hardens, reviews and disciplines those whom he approves, whom he loves'.[15] In words reminiscent of Paul, Seneca maintains, 'a holy spirit indwells within us, one who marks our good and bad deeds, and is our guardian' and 'God is near you, he is with you, he is within you' (*Ep.* 41.1, 2; cf. 73.16). We might imagine Paul nodding in agreement as the philosopher expounds the universality and depth of human depravity[16], the need for awareness and confession of sin[17] and the goal of living openly before God with a clear conscience.[18] After all, Seneca depicts the soul's 'struggles against this weight of the flesh' (*Ad Marc.* 24.5), and likens life to warfare (*Ep.* 51.6; 96.5; 120.18) and a brief sojourn in a foreign land (*Ep.* 120.14). The philosopher, too, is mindful of his own frailty;[19] remembering that he brought nothing into the world and can take nothing from it;[20] comparing his life to a 'vessel that the slightest shaking, the slightest toss will break' (*Ad Marc.* 11.3).

Apparently, affinities of thought like these led some early Christians to embrace Seneca. Late in the second century, Tertullian called him 'often our own'.[21] Nearly two centuries later, Jerome dropped the qualification, referring to 'our Seneca'.[22] In the meantime, a collection of letters, known to both a credulous Jerome (*De vir. ill.* 12), and a more circumspect Augustine (Augustine, *Ep.* 153.14), had emerged, purporting to be correspondence between Seneca and Paul.[23] Its circulation strengthened Seneca's credentials as a Christian. The hope that it might give access to Seneca–Paul communication is ruled out by the letters' patent spuriousness. 'The poverty of thought and style, the errors in chronology and history and the whole conception of the relative positions of the Stoic philosopher and the Christian Apostle', concludes Lightfoot, 'betray clearly the hand of a forger.'[24] Even the prospect of insight into early speculation about Paul's evangelization of a Stoic is defused in this correspondence by the assumption of Seneca's converted state. 'Paul' counts himself 'fortunate in the approval of a man who is so great' (*Sen. ad Paul, Ep.* 2). When 'Paul' does self-consciously recall the claim 'to be all things to all men' (*Sen. ad Paul, Ep.* 10) it is in the context of sycophantish self-remonstration at not treating Seneca with the deferential courtesy due his senatorial status.[25]

Even the impression of substantial agreement between their genuine writings is dismissed by Lightfoot and Sevenster. Seneca remains a pantheistic materialist; his personal God is 'only illusionary'. The parent–child relationship is simply the resignation of the wise man to the vicissitudes of life. As much as the good man, 'the creator and ruler of the universe' is subject to impersonal fate.[26] For, the Senecan god(s) 'is not better than a good man; he is richer, but riches do not constitute superior goodness; he is longer lived, but greater longevity does not ensure greater happiness'.[27] In the absence of a personal God there cannot be a sense of sin comparable to Paul's:

> With Seneca error or sin is nothing more than the failure in attaining to the ideal of the perfect man which he sets before him, the running counter to the law of the universe in which he finds himself placed. He does not view it as an offence done to the will of an all-holy all-righteous Being, an unfilial act of defiance towards a loving and gracious Father.[28]

If these conclusions are accepted, the Stoic whose sentiments most approximate to those of Paul still falls well short of his radically personal theology and anthropology. Furthermore, this is truly representative of the gulf between apostolic Christianity and Stoic philosophy. However, there are a number of reasons for probing this wider relationship further. Traditionally, Christians have been preoccupied with searching for indications of Seneca's conversion or sympathy to the faith. Recently the pendulum has swung back, with efforts to trace the roots of the Hellenization of Christian thought. Since Lightfoot there has been an explosion of historical and philological studies by classicists and New Testament scholars exploring Stoic sources for Paul's thought. The Middle Stoic historian Posidonius is often mentioned in this regard.[29] In the quarter of a century since Sevenster, a considerable volume of research has sought to place Paul more precisely within his Hellenistic context.[30] In the light of these developments, it is appropriate to consider evidences of Stoic influence in Paul's epistles.

Stoic influences on Paul

The possibility that Paul's thinking was shaped in dialogue with Stoicism is raised initially by his birthplace. In Acts 21:39, Paul declares, 'I am a Jew from Tarsus in Cilicia, a citizen of an important city'. Strabo (14.5.131) depicts Tarsus as a 'university city', renowned for the enthusiasm of its population for philosophy and learning, surpassing even Athens and Alexandria in reputation.[31] It was particularly associated with Stoic philosophy. Chrysippus, the 'second founder' of Stoicism, and the poet Aratus were born in nearby Soli.[32] The Stoic Athenodorus (c. 74 BC–AD 7) was born in Tarsus, went on to become tutor to Augustus and was later commissioned by the emperor to reform the administration of his home city.[33] He was linked so closely to Posidonius that Ramsay is led to say that 'he may confidently be called his pupil'.[34]

Some have concluded that Saul must have been steeped in Greek philosophy.[35] However, Saul himself asserts, 'I am a Jew, born (*gegennēmenos*) in Tarsus in Cilicia, but brought up (*anatethrammenos de*) in this city at the feet of Gamaliel, educated (*pepaideumenos*) strictly according to our ancestral law' (Acts 22:3). On the basis of this sequence of participles (cf. the discussion of Moses in Acts 7:20–22), van Unnik concludes that Saul's parents moved to Jerusalem 'before he could peep round the corner of the door and certainly before he went roaming on the street'. He decries as fable all the 'fine dissertations', which begin Paul's biography with the 'indelible youthful impressions' left by Hellenistic Tarsus. Saul first encountered Hellenism consciously as an adult steeped in Judaism.[36] More recently, Hengel has argued that relocation to Jerusalem occurred during adolescence. Despite the longer exposure to Tarsus, Hengel's Saul grew up in a strictly Jewish family and attended 'a good Greek elementary school which was a *Jewish* school'. Consequently his writings bear the imprint of the Septuagint and Jewish texts, rather than the literature 'from Homer to Euripides'.[37]

Since even judgments about Paul's childhood turn on the presence of Hellenistic ideas in his writings, it is worth examining some passages which cannot be accounted for from Jewish writings alone. With respect to the lists of Galatians 5:16–23, Longenecker notes Easton's half-century-old claim that it is 'generally recognized that the catalogs of virtues and vices in the New Testament are derived ultimately from the ethical teaching of the Stoa'. Longenecker can point to the enormous popularity of such lists among Graeco-Romans, including Seneca (*De brev. vitae* 10.2–4). After canvassing the view that the Jewish 'Two Ways' tradition explains Paul's employment of the form, Longenecker prefers 'to view 5:19–23 as modeled after the Hellenistic "catalog" genre'. Significantly, he adds a qualification: 'However, the distinctive duality of the list is derived from Paul's own flesh–Spirit dualism.'[38]

The distinctive vocabulary of Philippians 4:8–9 draws forth similar verdicts. Paul places before his readers eight virtues. 'Pleasing' (*prosphilēs*) and 'commendable' (*euphēmos*) occur only here in the New Testament. 'Excellence' (*aretē*) is otherwise absent from Paul's writings. 'Honourable' (*semnos*) is paralleled only in 1 Timothy and Titus, while 'just' (*dikaios*) and 'worthy of praise' (*epainos*) are used in a manner unparalleled within the Pauline corpus. Some, like Michaelis and Lohmeyer, have sought to prove the catalogue's dependence on the Septuagint. O'Brien regards their attempt as a failure. The terms are probably Stoic in origin, though their adoption does not imply an endorsement of Stoicism :

> On balance then it is best to conclude that the apostle has taken over terms that were current coin in popular moral philosophy, especially in Stoicism. He wants his Philippian friends to develop those qualities, which are good in themselves and beneficial to others, and so he has pressed these terms into service. His appeal is not to some pagan religious ideal, nor to an acceptance of Stoic presuppositions lying behind the ideas, much less to some wholesale acceptance of the norms and values of the world.[39]

Paul's subsequent reflections on contentment have also been construed as 'a massive Stoicism'.[40] Paul is able to say, 'I have learned to be content (*autarkēs*) with whatever I have' (Phil. 4:11). While *autarkeia* is found elsewhere in Paul (2 Cor. 9:8; 1 Tim. 6:6), Stoics frequently used it to describe the wise man's inner resources to face anything fate might send (DL 7.127; 10.130; cf. Cicero, *De fin.* 5.79). The 'happy man', according to Seneca, 'is content with his present lot, no matter what it is, and is reconciled to his circumstances' (*De vita beata* 6). Other parallels are readily cited by commentators, but just as readily dismissed as merely apparent. In fact, Fee claims a polemical use of the term against the Stoic's misplaced faith in human autonomy. Of 1 Timothy 6:6 he comments, 'Paul has already used this word in an analogous context in Philippians 4:11; there he "turned the tables" on the Stoics by declaring that genuine *autarkeia* is not *self-*sufficiency but *Christ*-sufficiency'.[41]

Many have appealed to a common popular philosophy, yet such a notion has been subjected to serious criticism. Engberg-Pederson warns of a danger inherent in such an appeal:

> ... in Pauline scholarship it is far too often used as legitimation for not taking Paul's use of the various moral terms seriously at all. This is a constant practice in the commentaries – to note the contacts with 'Hellenistic moral philosophy' in the sense of 'popular philosophy' and then rush on to point out the difference (usually in the singular!).[42]

In contrast, Engberg-Pedersen finds Paul in Philippians drawing on Stoic ethics 'as part of his own thinking'. Though Paul remains an apostle of Christ, and not a philosopher, 'the fusion is total', with Stoic terms like *koinōnia, politeuma, prokoptō* and *telos* being woven into a tapestry along with elements alien to Stoic thought. While vocabulary like this is common to both, some of Engberg-Pedersen's own claims are strained and his proposed reading of the letter unconvincing. It is difficult to see how these terms Stoicize the letter once they are cast into such a radically eschatological and Christological framework.[43]

Purportedly Stoic elements are not confined to ethical contexts. Two features of Paul's theological affirmations particularly occasion comment. These are brought into conjunction when Paul declares: 'yet for us there is one God, the Father, from whom are all things and for whom we exist, and one Lord, Jesus Christ, through whom are all things and through whom we exist' (1 Cor. 8:6).

This cascade of prepositions with reference to God and the cosmos is common enough (cf. Rom. 11:36; Col. 1:16–17), but also typically Stoic. Compare the way the Stoic emperor, Marcus Aurelius, addressed nature: 'of you are all things, in you are all things, unto you are all things' (*Med.* 4.23; cf. Seneca, *Ep.* 65.8). Despite the similarity, it is immediately clear from the context that Paul is anything but 'a spokesman for Stoic pantheism'.[44] Besides, such formulae had been domesticated into Jewish monotheism before Paul by Hellenistic Jews like Philo.[45]

Embedded in verses like these (cf. Eph. 1:22–23; 4:6), is the expression 'all things', which Norden identifies as a 'Stoic formula of omnipotence'.[46] In response, Barth points to Old Testament antecedents sufficient to account for the idea (Gen. 1:26; Ps. 8:6; 110:1; Prov. 8:22–31; cf. Wis. Sol. 7:22 – 8:1), and insists that such language 'is essentially distinct from pantheistic and Stoic affirmations of the deity's omnipresence and omnipotence'.[47] According to Fee, such statements are not simply stripped of their Stoic associations, but placed in a wholly different constellation of ideas. Having noted parallel phraseology in Seneca (Seneca, *De benef.* 7.2.5; 3.2; 4.1), he says, of the phrase 'all things are yours' (1 Cor. 3:21), that Paul's '"in Christ" existence so thoroughly transforms everything, even the language he uses, and gives it a new meaning'.[48]

Romans 1:18–32 provides the most promising Pauline context for discerning characteristically Stoic terms and parallels. Paul's teaching is often thought to approximate to the Stoic doctrine of *theologia naturalis*. Moreover, the preceding verses in Romans 1 place Paul's gospel and mission in the foreground. He reminds the Romans of his service of the gospel concerning God's Son (Rom. 1:3, 9) and his unashamed eagerness to proclaim it to them (1:15–16), so that he 'may reap some harvest among you as I have among the rest of the Gentiles' (1:13; cf. 1:5). In analysing human rebellion, Paul employs a series of characteristically Stoic phrases. The antithesis between immortal and mortal (*aphthartos, phthartos*) in 1:23 is 'probably drawn ultimately from Stoic philosophy'.[49] There is no genuine Hebrew antecedent for the concept of 'what is contrary to nature (*physis*)' (1:26). It is a common enough Greek idea, but Paul could hardly have been unaware of the crucial role it played in Stoic and Cynic accounts of virtue.[50] While the exact meaning of the phrase was a matter of discussion, the early Stoics maintained that 'living consistently with nature' was at the heart of the rational, virtuous life (DL 7.87–89; Stob. 2.7.6). It continued to be the way later Stoics formulated the goal of existence (Cicero, *De fin.* 3.31; Epictetus, 2.6.9). The impression that Paul is fully conscious of these connections is further reinforced by the addition in verse 28 of a Stoic technical term for 'what is fitting' (*ta kathēkonta*),[51] followed by the kind of vice list common in Stoic ethical texts (Rom. 1:29–31).

The passage also contains two impressive parallels to Seneca's writings:

They consecrate the holy and immortal and inviolable gods in motionless matter of the vilest kind: they clothe them with the forms of men, and beasts, and fishes (Seneca, *De superstitione*, cited in Augustine, *De civ. Dei* 6.10).

... and they exchanged the glory of the immortal God for images resembling a mortal human being or birds or four-footed animals or reptiles (Rom. 1:23).

... and then is their wretchedness complete, when shameful things not only delight them but are even approved of them (Seneca, *Ep.* 39.6).[52]

... yet they not only do them but even applaud others who practise them (Rom. 1:32).

How should we construe these points of contact? Does Paul seek to commend the intellectual integrity of the message? Does Stoicism provide resources, not found in the Scriptures, for a more trenchant attack on contemporary culture? For Dunn, they reflect Paul's strategy of engagement. The apostle wishes to be 'as meaningful and as widely admitted as possible'.[53] So Paul

... is clearly and deliberately following Hellenistic Judaism in using this kind of language as an apologetic bridge to non-Jewish religious philosophy ... Paul is trading upon, without necessarily committing himself to, the Greek (particularly Stoic) understanding ... And he ensures that his language, however indebted to Stoic thought, should not be understood in terms of Stoicism by giving prominence to the thought of *creation*.[54]

In fact, whatever the provenance of the terms, the language provides a vehicle for conveying a thoroughly Jewish theology. The explicit creation framework and subtle allusions to Adam point back to Genesis 1 – 3. Psalm 106 and Isaiah 44 inform the attack on idols. The benediction of 1:25 is unambiguously Jewish, while the condemnation of homosexuality reflects the Scriptures' abhorrence of the behaviour.

So Paul articulates his thoroughly Jewish theology in a way designed to draw both Jewish and Greek readers into his accusation of universal human culpability. Perhaps this was calculated with the Stoic very much in mind. With their great aspiration to be 'wise' and their self-satisfaction at their own rigour in pursuing it, they represent a fitting target for Paul's attack on those 'claiming to be wise (*sophoi*)' who instead 'became fools' (1:22). Many Stoics would fit the profile of Romans 2 – people who smugly stand in judgment of their immoral and irreligious contemporaries. While Romans

2:9–11 chiefly implies self-righteous Jewish readers, Dunn suggests that the 'phrasing is so general as to include the sophisticated Stoic proud of his living in accord with reason: v. 2 echoes 1:32 in drawing the Stoic recognition of "what is improper" under an explicitly theistic banner'.[55] For all their confidence in *theologia naturalis* and *consensus omnium* as sure guides to the divine will and a life lived in harmony with nature, Stoic rationality has left them in the dark and their philosophy has suppressed the truth. Not even the values shared with biblical morality exempt the Stoic from the wrath of God.[56]

Paul's speech before the Areopagus

Thankfully, the only New Testament context explicitly to mention Stoics places them in evangelistic contact with Paul. Luke records the presence of some Epicurean and Stoic philosophers (*tines de ... tōn ... Stoikōn*) in the marketplace at Athens (Acts 17:16–18). They were debating with (*syneballon*) the apostle; Paul was evangelizing (*euēngelizeto*). This unambiguous instance of Paul discussing the gospel with Stoics may indicate more than their participation. According to Croy, the structure of Luke's account suggests a relatively positive response from them. Luke frequently contrasts two responses (Acts 2:12–13; 14:4; 23:7–8; 28:24). Here some (*kai tines*) belittle the apostle as a gossip-monger (*ho spermologos houtos*);[57] others (*hoi de*) are willing to hear more despite their confusion about Jesus and the resurrection (Acts 17:18). The correlative language used, so closely following mention of the two schools, suggests that one school rejected the message while the other received it, albeit cautiously.[58]

This literary impression is strengthened by historical considerations. Epicurean materialism uniformly regarded death as extinction.[59] Extant Stoic texts present a more complex picture. Cicero's claim, that Stoics 'say that souls will endure for a while; they deny that they will endure for ever' (*Tusc. Disp.* 1.31.7), seems to provide a reasonable summary. Many early and Middle Stoics thought some survival of the soul was likely. However, no soul could survive the periodic conflagration (*ekpyrōsis*). Seneca's own writings are ambiguous. Life on earth is simply the gestation period. Death is birth into a new state (*Ep.* 102.23); to die is to begin eternity (*Ep.* 102.26). Yet elsewhere he speaks of the coming conflagration when they and their loved ones will be changed into their original elements (*Ad Marc.* 26.1–6). He can even speak of death as the cessation of existence (*Ep.* 65.24; cf. 54.4; 63.16; 99.30). Croy concludes that 'no Stoic ever entertained the notion of the resurrection *of the body*'. However, he asks: 'could it be that the Stoic

hope of an afterlife was at its pinnacle at about the time that Paul ...
proclaimed the resurrection of Jesus in Athens?'[60] If this was the case, Acts
17:32 (*hoi men echleuazon, hoi de eipan*) may reveal a desire of at least some
of the Stoics to know more.[61]

Between these two pairs of responses lies Paul's address to the Areopagus. This is not the place to canvas the vast literature, myriad issues and
scholarly divisions generated by this account.[62] For some it is paradigmatic
for Paul's preaching to educated pagan audiences; for others a failed exper-
iment, which he immediately regretted. Perhaps the most fundamental
divide of recent decades separates philosophical and theological approaches
to the speech.[63] The former read it as 'a Hellenistic speech about true knowledge of God', the latter as 'a Judeo-Christian missionary sermon'. However,
more recently, this either/or approach has been set aside in favour of a both/
and reading, noting the speech's extensive use of *doubles entendres*.[64]

Ambiguity is a feature of the speech from the beginning. Paul declares he
can 'see how extremely religious (*deisidaimonesterous*)' the Athenians are
(Acts 17:22). Is this a 'cultured compliment' in keeping with the rhetorical
convention of *captatio benevolentiae*?[65] Or is the Christian reader meant to
understand the adjective in the sense of 'superstitious' (cf. Acts 25:19)?[66]
This accolade/accusation is followed by reference to their 'objects of
worship (*sebasmata*)', which were the cause of Paul's deep distress
(*parōxyneto*; 17:16) earlier.[67] The significant motif (17:23a, 23b, 30) of
'ignorance' (*agnoia*) also points in two directions. Does 'unknowing'
(*agnoountes*) worship imply a 'non-culpable epistemic failure' (Rom. 1:13;
1 Cor. 10:1),[68] or a morally reprehensible dereliction, tantamount to sin
(Eph. 4:18; DL 7.93; Epictetus, 1.26.6)? In the wider context of Acts, Peter's
charge of ignorance against Israelites is based on their execution of 'the
Author of life', and leads to a call to repentance (3:14–19). At Athens Paul's
reference to God's overlooking of 'times of misconception/culpable error'
(Acts 17:30) issues in a similar call.[69]

Nevertheless, even construed as a biting critique, it is unlikely that a
Stoic would be offended by Paul to this point. The sentiments of 17:24–25
appear to be meaningful within a Stoic framework.[70] The use of *kosmos* for
the universe, the assumption of God as its maker (Epictetus, 4.7.6), his independence of human assistance (Clement of Alexandria, *Strom.* 5.76.1) and
humanity's dependence on him, were familiar affirmations. A Stoic audience would find the allusion in verse 26 to the essential unity of humankind
equally agreeable. The universal brotherhood of the race was axiomatic.
Their own literature condemned idolatory,[71] and their founder counselled
against building temples 'because a temple not worth much is also not

sacred, and no work of builders or mechanics is worth much'.[72] However, Plutarch observed that the Stoics remained vulnerable to a critique such as Paul's: 'The Stoics, while applauding this as correct, attend the mysteries in temples, go up to the Acropolis, do reverence to statues, and place wreaths upon the shrines, though these are the works of builders and mechanics.'[73] What a Stoic audience might not realize is the extent to which Paul draws on Old Testament creation and temple theology (Gen. 1:1–25; Exod. 20:11; 1 Kgs. 8:27; Is. 42:5; 57:15–16; Amos 5:12–23).

The divergence between theological and philosophical readings of Paul's speech is most apparent at 17:26. The 'appointed seasons' (*kairoi*) may recall the solstices and annual cycles of Wisdom 7:18 (cf. Acts 14:17; *1 Clem.* 20:4, 9). God's allotment of 'boundaries (*horothesia*) could signify arctic, tropical and temperate geographical zones, the last being ideal for human habitation. Understood in this way, these terms take us within the orbit of discussions of providence markedly influenced by Stoic thought (*1 Clem.* 20; Dio Chrys., *Or.* 40.35–41). In favour of the theological approach, *kairoi* could encapsulate the periods allotted to nations and kingdoms in God's economy (Luke 21:24). Deuteronomy 32:8, from a context foundational to the Old Testament polemic against idols, provides a striking background for the rest of the verse. Most significant is its inclusion of the growth of humankind from one person, a concept alien to Stoicism:

> When the Most High divided the nations (*ethnē*)
> when he separated the sons of Adam,
> he set the bounds of the nations (*horia ethnōn*)
> according to the number of of the angels of God (MT sons of Israel).

It is also possible to read Acts 17:24–6 as a summary treatment of Genesis 1 – 10, with verse 26 corresponding to the table of nations in Genesis 10.[74]

The ambiguity of Paul's speech is sustained by his description of the purpose of God's creative and providential care (Acts 17:27). The goal, for people to seek (*zētein*) God, can imply a dispassionate investigation (Plato, *Apol.* 19b, 23b; *Rep.* 449a), or a turning and cleaving to God in trusting obedience (Deut. 4:29; 2 Sam. 21:1; Hos. 5:15). Likewise, people may 'reach out' (*psēlaphaō*) as they seek to establish the existence of an object or person by physical contact (Luke 24:39; 1 John 1:1), or as they fumble and stumble around in the dark (Plato, *Phaedo* 99b; Is. 59:10; Judg. 16:26; Deut. 28:29; Job 5:13, 14; 12:25). The impression given by English versions that some 'find' God is thoroughly consistent with Stoic confidence in the capacity of human reason.[75] However, the Greek construction (*ei ara ge ... heuroien* –

note the optative) does not necessarily support such optimism. If *kai ge* is understood concessively, the nearness of God need not suggest his accessibility to human endeavour.[76] Further, if these remarks constitute a reflection on the thwarting and scattering of the nations at Babel (Gen. 11:1–9) the assessment must likewise be negative rather than positive.

Paul's accommodation to Stoicism seems most obvious in his reference to 'some of your own poets' and the quotation: 'For we too are his offspring' (Acts 17:28). The latter recalls verse 4 of *Hymn to Zeus*, by Zeno's successor, Cleanthes. However, it resembles even more closely the *Phaenomena* by Aratus, a Stoic poet from Soli, in Paul's native region of Cilicia.[77] Those pursuing the philosophical approach to Paul's speech seize on it as an appeal to Stoic notions of human kinship, happily consonant with biblical assumptions (Ps. 139; Luke 3:38). However, rather than affirming this notion in Aratus, Paul's use of the citation could be interpreted as an 'attack on idolatry and the false conception of God which underlies it'.[78] In contradiction of the anthropomorphic impetus of idolatry (Acts 17:30) and Stoic epistemology, Paul insists that God created humanity and not the other way around.[79]

Having already been sensitized to the ambiguity of 'ignorance', what can we glean from Paul's assurance that 'God has overlooked the times of ignorance'? The verb, *hyperoraō*, is a New Testament *hapax legomenon*. It may carry the meaning, adopted by most versions, of 'to overlook', in the sense of disregarding the past (Jos. 1:5; Ps. 9:22). As divine tolerance of former epistemological limitations, the expression reinforces the philosophical reading. However, Isaiah 58:7 shows that it can also mean 'to despise' or 'disdain'.[80] If this is the case here, Paul's readers are being reminded that God has always been provoked to anger and jealousy by the worship of the idols he abhors (Deut. 32:16).

The 'both/and' approach encourages us to keep two parallel discourses alive for much of Paul's speech. But what does its conclusion disclose about Paul's ultimate intention? Are his remarks gentle and irenic, finding genuine common ground with Stoic natural theology, commending the sincerity of their searching and excusing gaps in their understanding? Does he find in Stoicism 'a legitimate conversation partner in the approach to God' and a suitable helpmate in forging a 'Christianized Hellenistic culture' for which this speech serves as 'both anticipation and symbol'?[81] Or is he using one acceptable tradition within Stoicism, namely the Middle Stoicism of Posidonius, to critique the excesses and complacent idol worship of later, Roman Stoicism?[82]

These interpretations are rendered very unlikely by the closing call to repentance. With it, Paul irrevocably parts company with the theology of his Stoic audience. They stand accountable before God. There is no room for self-congratulation, self-justification or complacency. For all their wisdom, superstition and searching they remain culpably ignorant. Their reflection on nature has never amounted to 'theology'. Despite the immanence of the living God, they have not found him; nor have they known him. There is only one, pressing imperative for them (along with all people): they must repent. This is the essential nature of human solidarity. In declaring a fixed day for universal judgment, entrusted to one man, Paul develops a dual particularity that is without precedent in, and scandalously at odds with, Stoic thought. The providential judgments identified by Posidonius within history do not constitute a meaningful parallel to the eschatological nature of this reckoning.[83] Neither is there anything approaching messianic expectation in the Stoic literature. If those in the Areopagus were to evaluate the truth of this starkly confronting message, they would have to explore the resurrection of that one man from the dead.

The speech's conclusion invites us to review its sustained ambiguity, without collapsing it retrospectively into the monotones of a narrowly theological approach. Rather, the motive for Paul's careful choice of words comes into focus. Paul appears before this partly Stoic audience, determined to gain a hearing for an urgent message. Knowing that his audience is fascinated by novelty (Acts 17:21) and yet responsible for the critical evaluation of his message, Paul adopts a curiously veiled and cryptic strategy.[84] Sandnes notes a striking omission, even if the speech is taken to be a highly edited summary. Jesus' name is not mentioned. Later, despite the apparent call to repentance, there is no record of this response. Instead, people ask for follow-up information.[85] Drawing on his familiarity with Stoic assumptions and themes, Paul crafts a speech which can be heard as a sympathetic acknowledgment of Stoicism's quest, but is a vehicle for his Christian understanding of creation and sin. 'In the heartland of Stoicism and before the Athenian Epicureans', observes Winter, 'Paul tailored his approach to the audiences' needs in order to engage their world views.'[86] Only with the introduction of judgment and repentance does his message radically break with the vocabulary of his audience.[87]

Paul's sermon in the Areopagus is often said to be paradigmatic for evangelization of a Gentile audience, especially a well-educated one. Luke, it is said, includes three representative speeches – one before Jews, one before a Roman governor and this 'exemplary meeting between Jerusalem and Athens'.[88] Consequently, some regard the exclusion of Old Testament quotations, fulfilled prophecy, the cross and atonement as significant and normative for contemporary evangelism. Yet the veiled and cryptic nature of Paul's strategy challenges this view. We are on much firmer ground with the summary that is repeated by Luke often enough to imply a normative status. As Jesus said to his disciples just before he ascended into heaven, 'Thus it is written, that the Messiah is to suffer and to rise from the dead on the third day, and repentance and forgiveness of sins is to be proclaimed in his name to all nations' (Luke 24:46–47).

This refrain runs through Acts (5:30–32; 10:39–43; 13:37–39; 26:20–23) and resembles closely the gospel Paul preached to the Corinthians (1 Cor. 15:1–3). There is too much missing from Paul's address to the Areopagus for it to constitute a definitive evangelistic sermon. At least the marketplace debates raised the name of Jesus. No doubt, those who returned to hear more from Paul were introduced to forgiveness and the sufferings that won it for them.

Paul and the evangelization of the Stoics

Sadly these conclusions highlight our failure to find a definitive example of Paul's evangelization of Stoics. However, the New Testament does offer considerable insight denied by the obscurity of the Seneca–Paul relationship and the spuriousness of the 'Seneca–Paul' correspondence. Paul's writings evince more than a passing acquaintance with Stoic thought, perhaps gleaned from a childhood in Tarsus or regular visits there. At points, the apostle happily endorses Stoic values and virtues that are consistent with life in Christ. Elsewhere, building on the lead of Hellenistic Judaism, he transforms Stoic phrases by his radically monotheistic, Christological and eschatological framework. Both Romans 1 – 2 and Acts 17 witness to Paul's adeptness at incorporating distinctively Stoic vocabulary into thoroughly Jewish and Christian critiques of Greek idolatry, immorality and intellectual pride. Both contexts underline his skill and flexibility in drawing a Stoic audience into his charge of universal culpability before the judgment seat of God. Both remind us that true knowledge of God is found by faith in his Son, not rational investigation of his world. In his encounter with Stoicism we meet the flexibility and single-mindedness of an apostle who willingly 'became all things to all people, that I might by all means save some' (1 Cor. 9:22). And in this we surely have a model to imitate (1 Cor. 10:33 – 11:1).[89]

Notes

1. Sevenster, *Paul*, p. 1; Colish, 'Stoicism', pp. 335–336.
2. Long, *Hellenistic Philosophy*, p. 107.
3. 'Over the centuries, the relations between Stoicism and early Christianity have

been a vehicle for Christian apologists of all kinds, for intra-humanist rivalries, for humanists and anti-humanists, for Enlightenment rationalists and their opponents, for nationalists and internationalists, for ecumenists and the repudiators of antisemitism, as well as for the proponents of academic wrangles and educational reforms of various sorts.' Colish, 'Stoicism', p. 379.

4. Ferguson, *Backgrounds*, p. 342, opts for the later date.
5. Bruce, *New Testament History*, p. 234.
6. Sevenster, *Paul*, pp. 6–7, notes that Tacitus' account of Nero's torture of Christians (*Annals* 15.44) is followed soon after by the conspiracy of Piso (15.48) which led to Seneca's death (15.60).
7. Bruce, *Acts: Greek Text*, p. 347.
8. Farrer, *Seekers*, pp. 17–18.
9. Cf. Seneca, *De superstitione*, cited by Augustine, *De civ. Dei* 6.11, 'the customs of this accursed race (*gens sceleratissima*) have gained such influence that they are now received throughout all the world'. (All extrabiblical quotations are from the LCL unless indicated otherwise.) Cf. Witherington, *The Acts*, p. 551.
10. Bruce, *Acts: Greek Text*, p. 348.
11. Bruce, *Acts*, pp. 375–376; Fitzmyer, *Acts*, p. 630.
12. Ferguson, *Backgrounds*, p. 343.
13. Lightfoot, 'St. Paul', p. 278.
14. Ferguson, *Backgrounds*, p. 342.
15. Seneca, *De prov.* 1.5; 4.7.
16. 'We shall ever be obliged to pronounce the same sentence upon ourselves, that we are evil, that we have been evil, and (I will add it unwillingly), that we shall be evil.' Seneca, *De benef.* 1.10.
17. 'The beginning of safety is the knowledge of sin ... As far as thou canst, accuse thyself, try thyself: discharge the office, first of a prosecutor, then of a judge, lastly of an intercessor.' Seneca, *Ep.* 28.9–10.
18. Seneca, *De benef.* 7.1, describes the good man, who 'has opened out his conscience to the gods, and always lives as if in public, fearing himself more than others'.
19. 'Every day and every hour reveal to us what a nothing we are, and remind us with some fresh evidence that we have forgotten our weakness'. Seneca, *Ep.* 101.1.
20. Seneca, *Ep.* 33.9.
21. Tertullian, *On the Soul*, 20.
22. Jerome, *Adv. Jovin.* I.49.
23. Colish, 'Stoicism', pp. 338–339; Elliot, *Apocryphal New Testament*, p. 547. It is likely that the collection cited by Jerome is substantially the same as modern additions. Letters 11, 13 and 14 are suspected as later additions.
24. Lightfoot, 'St. Paul', p. 271; Cf. Sevenster, *Paul*, pp. 14–15. Given that Lactantius (*Inst. Div.* 6.24.13–14) betrays no knowledge of the letters, a likely period for their composition is between AD 325 and 390.
25. Cf. Epistle 14, which urges Seneca to 'make yourself a new herald of Jesus Christ by displaying with the praises of rhetoric that blameless wisdom which you have almost achieved'.
26. Sevenster, *Paul*, pp. 36–38.
27. Lightfoot, 'St. Paul', p. 295, summarizing Sextius in Seneca, *Ep.* 73.12, 13.
28. Lightfoot, 'St. Paul', p. 296; cf. Sevenster, *Paul*, p. 240, who concludes that any

affinities between Seneca and Paul are merely superficial.
29. Colish, 'Stoicism', pp. 367–373, lists, for example, A. Deissmann, R. Bultmann, R. Liechtenhan and others.
30. Engberg-Pedersen, 'Stoicism', p. 256 n. 1, refers to H. D. Betz, A. J. Malherbe, D. L. Balch, E. Ferguson and W. A. Meeks.
31. Gasque, 'Tarsus', p. 6: 334; Bruce, *Paul*, p. 35.
32. Brownrigg, *Pauline Places*, p. 36.
33. Bruce, *Paul*, p. 34.
34. Ramsay, *Cities*, p. 217.
35. Ibid., pp. 228–235; Gasque, 'Tarsus', p. 334.
36. Van Unnik, *Tarsus*, pp. 52–58.
37. Hengel, *Pre-Christian Paul*, pp. 37–39, points out that Saul may have travelled regularly between Tarsus and Jerusalem (cf. Acts 9:30; 11:25).
38. Longenecker, *Galatians*, pp. 250–252.
39. O'Brien, *Philippians*, pp. 501–503.
40. E. g. Brownrigg, *Pauline Places*, p. 36.
41. Fee, *1 and 2 Timothy*, p. 143; cf. O'Brien, *Philippians*, p. 521; Sevenster, *Paul*, pp. 113–114; Hawthorne, *Philippians*, p. 199.
42. Engberg-Pedersen, 'Stoicism', p. 262, n. 10.
43. For instance, Paul applies the language of 'progress' (*prokopē*) to the gospel in 1:12, rather than moral progress. Engberg-Pedersen, 'Stoicism', pp. 262, 274, claims that the Stoic technical use of *chara* finds 'an obvious correspondence with Paul in Philippians'. In the absence of the other *eupatheia* ('caution' and 'will'), this is very difficult to sustain. See also Nussbaum, *Therapy*, pp. 400–401, on the sternness of Stoic joy in Seneca, *Ep.* 23.4–6.
44. Dunn, *Romans*, p. 702.
45. Ibid., pp. 701–702; Fee, *1 Corinthians*, pp. 373–374.
46. Cited in Barth, *Ephesians*, p. 177.
47. Barth, *Ephesians*, pp. 177–179, 471.
48. Fee, *1 Corinthians*, p. 155.
49. Dunn, *Romans*, p. 62.
50. Sandbach, *Stoics*, pp. 52–55; Long, *Hellenistic Philosophy*, pp. 110–111.
51. DL 7.124, 129; Cicero, *Ad Att.* 16.11, 4; Stobaeus 286.10; *SVF*, III.495.
52. These two quotations from Seneca follow Lightfoot's translation ('St. Paul', p. 289).
53. Dunn, *Romans*, p. 71.
54. Ibid., p. 58; cf. Colish, 'Stoicism', pp. 373–374.
55. Dunn, *Romans*, p. 90.
56. Pohlenz, *Die Stoa* 1, p. 403, points to the offensive nature of 'God's anger' (Rom. 1:18) for the Stoic. However, Balch, 'Areopagus', p. 59, finds parallel notions of the providential wrath of God in history in Posidonius.
57. BAGD: 'lit. *picking up seeds* (of birds) ... *gossip, chatterer, babbler, one who makes his living by picking up scraps, a rag-picker'*. Witherington, *Acts*, p. 515, offers 'dilettante'.
58. Croy, 'Hellenistic philosophies', pp. 21–39.
59. DL 10.63–67;124–125; 10.139; Lucretius, *De rerum natura* 3.624–633; 3.830–1094.
60. Croy, 'Hellenistic philosophies', pp. 36–37.
61. Ibid.; cf. Johnson, *Acts*, p. 318.

62. Witherington, *Acts*, p. 511.
63. Gasque, *History*, pp. 210–214.
64. Given, 'Not either/or', pp. 370–371.
65. Dunn, *Acts*, p. 234; Charles, 'Pagan mind', p. 57; Johnson, *Acts*, p. 314.
66. Fitzmyer, *Acts*, p. 606; Given, 'Not either/or', pp. 364–365; Witherington, *Acts*, p. 520.
67. The verb is used in the LXX for God's intense anger, often at idols or false worship (Deut. 1:34; 9:8, 18; 32:16, 19; Ps. 78:40; 106:29; Lam. 2:6). *Sebasmata* is used pejoratively in Wis. 14:20; 15:17.
68. Given, 'Not either/or', p. 366.
69. Ibid., p. 368.
70. E.g. Witherington, *Acts*, p. 526; Dunn, *Acts*, p. 235; Fitzmyer, *Acts*, p. 608; Charles, 'Pagan mind', p. 57.
71. Strabo, *Geog.* 16.2.35–39, citing Posidonius.
72. Plutarch, *Stoic. Rep.* 1034B.
73. Ibid.; cf. Balch, 'Areopagus', p. 71, who cites Dio Chrysostom's *Olympic Oration* 12.
74. So Scott, 'Luke's geographical horizon', pp. 541–543.
75. DL 7.147; Cicero, *De natura deorum* 1.39, citing Chrysippus.
76. Witherington, *Acts*, pp. 528–529.
77. Edwards, 'Quoting Aratus', p. 267; Fitzmyer, *Acts*, p. 611.
78. Wilson, *Gentiles*, p. 208.
79. Ibid.; Witherington, *Acts*, p. 530.
80. BAGD; Given, 'Not either/or', p. 368.
81. Johnson, *Acts*, pp. 317–320.
82. Balch, 'Areopagus', p. 79.
83. Contra Balch, 'Areopagus', pp. 67, 79.
84. 'There is much to suggest that we are dealing with an informal inquiry before the education commission of the Areopagus court', B. Gärtner, *Areopagus*, p. 59; cf. Winter, 'On introducing gods', p. 88.
85. Sandnes links this to the frequently observed parallels between Paul and Socrates. Sandnes, 'Paul', pp. 13, 20–25; cf. Dunn, *Acts*, p. 233; Fitzmyer, *Acts*, p. 605; Witherington, *Acts*, pp. 515–516; Johnson, *Acts*, pp. 312–314.
86. Winter, 'In public', p. 143.
87. Understood in this way, the speech recalls 1 Thessalonians 1:9, 10. Its message and rhetorical strategy are reminiscent of Rom. 1:18 – 2:15; cf. Winter, 'In public', p. 127; Witherington, pp. 534–535.
88. Johnson, *Acts*, p. 318.
89. Winter, 'In public', pp. 142–143; O'Brien, *Consumed by Passion*, pp. 104–107. It is appropriate to close with a reference to P. T. O'Brien's reflections on this Pauline trait. Like the whole volume, this paper is dedicated to a man whose devotion to preaching, teaching, studying, imparting and imitating Paul's passion for the gospel has been a constant inspiration.

22. The philosopher in the hands of an angry God

Peter G. Bolt

The Pauline mission and Middle Platonism
Rival eschatologies

As the Christian movement advanced across the first-century Graeco-Roman world, the apostle to the Gentiles was pre-eminent among 'those who turned the world upside down' (*hoi tēn oikoumenēn anastatōsantes*, Acts 17:6). Paul's message was profoundly eschatological, but the world in which he proclaimed it was already well supplied with eschatological views.[1] The acceptance of Paul's gospel entailed the rejection of rival eschatological views in favour of those proclaimed by the apostle. In particular, Paul's mission was conducted against the prospect of a coming judgment day on which God would, at least in part, inflict wrath. But how would this aspect of Paul's message fit with the eschatology of his Gentile audience? How would the hearers of Paul's message have responded to the message about an 'angry' God?[2]

Resurrection and judgment

According to Acts, Paul brought a message that was primarily positive: news of salvation, for both Jew and Gentile, through the forgiveness of sins. It was a future-oriented message, for it spoke of the resurrection from the dead, and it was proclaimed with a great confidence arising from the historical reality that God had already raised a man from the dead. The resurrection that Israel had hoped for on the last day (cf. Dan. 12:2; John 11:24) had commenced – in one case – and so it would certainly be completed in due course (26:23; cf. 4:2).[3]

But this positive message of hope was firmly cast against the backdrop of God's judgment.[4] God had raised Jesus from the dead to show that all people everywhere must face him as judge (Acts 17:31). The resurrection of both the just and the unjust (*anastasin ... dikaiōn te kai adikōn*, 24:15; cf. Dan. 12:2) meant that, for some, the resurrection would be a resurrection to judgment. Paul also therefore spoke of righteousness and self-control, and of the coming condemnation (*tou krimatos tou mellontos*, 24:25). This certain future judgment process and the fearful prospect of a condemnatory outcome led Paul to announce that God 'commands all people everywhere to repent' (*parangellei tois anthrōpois pantas pantachou metanoein*, 17:30), and to urge faith in Christ Jesus (*tēs eis Christon Iēsoun pisteōs*, 24:24).[5]

Emergent Middle Platonism

In AD 51, when Paul spoke in Athens before the Areopagus, some Stoic and Epicurean philosophers were among his hearers (*tines ... kai tōn Epikoureiōn kai Stoikōn philosophōn*, 17:18). Given the eschatology of his Greek audience in general, and the presence of representatives of these philosophical schools, each of which had its own eschatological views, it is no surprise that Paul's message of resurrection was greeted with derision (17:32a), albeit with some acceptance (17:32b, 34). Evidence from gravestones suggests that Stoicism and Epicureanism had even seeped down to ordinary people, teaching them not to expect too much, if anything at all, from the afterlife.[6] Paul's message of resurrection was in stark contrast to these groups.

In disputing with these groups, Paul would find a potential ally in any Middle Platonists in the audience. This resurgent Platonism,[7] which would eventually give birth to the Neoplatonism which dominated from Plotinus in the third century AD into the sixth century AD, was united by a common belief in the immortality of the soul,[8] which brought it into conflict with the Stoic and Epicurean eschatology. Evidence for this 'combat' can be gleaned from Plutarch of Chaeronea, who has bequeathed the only surviving corpus of work from this 'school'.[9]

Even though it is highly unlikely that Plutarch and Paul ever crossed paths personally, since both represent abiding streams of thought, it is a fair guess that people of similar persuasion did have contact as time went on.[10]

Plutarch's writings can be examined as a sounding of one stream of thought within the first-century society from which the various Gentile audiences who heard Paul's gospel originated. They can be usefully compared with Paul's letters in an attempt to answer the question: how would Middle Platonists like Plutarch have heard the apostle's message? Such questions could indeed be asked about any aspect of Paul's message, but, by examining the 'emotional' language used to refer to God's 'wrath', this essay will explore the question: how would the philosopher have reacted when Paul spoke of God exercising anger and fury?

God's 'wrath' and the Middle Platonist

What follows is a vocabulary study which adopts a 'sampling' approach. From the wealth of material written by Plutarch,[11] only one essay will be examined, *The Delay of the Divine Vengeances*. It is chosen because, of all the *Moralia*, *Delay* is arguably the essay most directly concerned with eschatology, and because it provides a sample of text roughly equivalent in size to that provided by the undisputed Pauline letters.[12] From the variety of words that could be compared among the eschatological vocabulary of the two, this study selects two 'emotional' terms used by Paul in connection with divine punishment: 'wrath' (*orgē*) and 'fury' (*thymos*). It will show that although this emotional description of God's 'anger' would have currency with some in the Greek world, it would cause difficulty for a Middle Platonist such as Plutarch.

Plutarch's *Delay of the Divine Vengeances*

Probably written in the nineties, *Delay* takes the form of a dialogue in which Plutarch is the main speaker, answering questions and objections put to him by his three friends Patrocleas, Olympichus and Timon. In the preamble, the essay is addressed to *Kynie*, which may indicate that the essay is addressed to a representative Cynic.[13] The preamble also indicates that the essay deals with Epicurean concerns, for it begins with one 'Epicurus' – 'the representative Epicurean'[14] – disappearing from the scene having 'pelted providence' with furious and sundry arguments (548C) which then become the impetus for the discussion between Plutarch and his friends. Given that the Cynics had links with the Stoics,[15] we can conclude that in this essay Plutarch spars with roughly similar opponents to those Paul met in Athens: Epicureans, and Cynic-Stoics.

The essay has two parts. After beginning with the argument (*logos*), it ends rather abruptly, after the style of Plato,[16] with an account of the journey of the soul of 'a man of Soli' (home of Chrysippus, 'the second father of Stoicism'),[17] Thespesius, through the other world. Although this latter section can be labelled 'myth' (*mythos*), we should be aware that Plutarch himself does not clearly identify it as such. When he pre-empts its introduction he calls it an 'account' (*logos*) he had recently heard; he is reluctant at first to introduce this section, because these things may *appear* as myth (i.e. fiction) to his companions, and, when he does provide the details, he adds the rider 'if indeed myth it is' (*ei ge dē mythos estin*). After dying, Thespesius had apparently revived at the time of his funeral three days later (563D). During the interval he had visited the afterlife, and this had so affected him that he underwent a complete renovation of life from that moment on (563C). Plutarch's 'myth' consists of reporting what this man told of his journey to the other world. Although there has been a tendency to suggest that Plutarch's real beliefs can be found in 'the argument', but not in 'the myth', both are probably important to him, acting in a complementary fashion. In Plutarch's view, the contemplation of the other world (as is forced upon the reader by 'the myth') helps to shape the imagination, thus allowing the process of transformation to begin in the soul.[18]

The 'argument' begins by identifying the delay of the divine vengeance as the most serious of Epicurus' attacks on providence.[19] Patrocleas and Olympichus feel that such a delay is not fitting for God, and that it destroys a belief in providence. Timon's 'crowning difficulty' is put on hold while Plutarch answers his first two companions. Drawing on Plato, Plutarch begins by asserting that God's delay is part of his exemplary moderation, and that it springs from his greater discrimination of the needs of individual souls. It also allows time for potential benefits to arise, and for punishment to come at the most fitting time and in the most fitting manner. Plutarch despises human retributive justice which simply requites pain with pain, calling it a 'cur's justice' (551C).[20] Whereas such punishment only manages to bark along behind, by dealing only with the body, not the soul, God directs his justice towards 'the passions of a sick soul' (*psychēs nosousēs ta pathē*, 551D). The argument then takes a major turn (553F) as Plutarch begins to explore Hesiod's opinion that punishment does not follow the injustice, but accompanies it, which means that the delay actually makes the punishment more lasting.

When Timon is permitted to speak he introduces Euripides' difficulty with the gods visiting the sins of the parents on the children, listing numerous absurdities that arise as a result. After dismissing Timon's examples, Plutarch defends the underlying principle by establishing that families are interconnected, and by drawing upon the 'general principle' of punishment, namely, that 'what is helpful is also just' (*to chrēsimon kai dikaion estin*). He then uses the analogy of medical practice to speak of punishment having no other object than the cure of the soul. This principle, and its medical analogy, constitute Plutarch's major understanding of punishment.

This understanding expands the sphere of divine justice beyond the merely temporal 'wraths' and calamities (perceived as divine vengeances) into the afterlife. Plutarch is therefore required to defend the survival of the soul, which he does by building upon the belief in providence that his friends have already espoused (cf. 560F). A belief in the soul's survival, in turn, implies that it is probable that the soul receives its due after death (561A–B), as, he says, the account of Thespesius will show. Before providing it, however, Plutarch returns to the medical analogy, and argues that, if punishment is cure, then it must be just. God is more aware of each person's nature than we are, and so he punishes descendants, not in response to injustice, but to cure them of any vice inherited from their forebears. He charges his friends with inconsistency: they complain when God delays the punishment, and now, in the case of punishment of descendants, they complain when God punishes early! To reiterate the key part of the argument: because God's punishment aims at cure, then it is always just. If this cure is incomplete at death, it will continue (at least for those impure souls not deemed 'incurable') beyond the grave when the soul is given into the hands of Dikē (i.e. 'Justice').

The distinctive vocabulary of punishment in Plutarch and Paul

Before turning to the 'wrath' terms, which are used by both writers, it is worth noting that both Paul and Plutarch use some terms for punishment that are not found in the other. An examination of these distinctive terms reveals the framework in which each of them discusses divine punishment.

Plutarch's distinctive punishment terms

The two most frequently used families among Plutarch's distinctive terms are (1) *kolazō, kolasis*, etc., and (2) *timōreō, timōria, timōros*.[21] Delay maintains an older distinction between these two groups, in which *timōria* implies personal, emotion-inspired revenge, whereas *kolasis* is performed in a disinterested fashion (cf. Aristotle, *Rhet.* 1369[b]). Despite the later movement towards the two word-groups being used interchangeably,[22] there is evidence that these two groups were still distinguished closer to Plutarch's time, with *timōria* 'convey[ing] like the verb the idea of giving an offender his deserts, without the thought of *discipline* which normally attaches to *kolasis*'.[23]

In *Delay*, this distinction is assumed by Plutarch's friends, and by Plutarch himself, even though he wishes to make a correction. In summary, Plutarch attempts a redefinition of these words in line with his view of punishment as cure. He is aware of the prevailing view that equates divine punishment with sudden disaster, which is labelled vengeance (*timōria*). With Hesiod, he suggests (553F) that rather than vengeance (*timōrian*) following the evil deed, 'wickedness engenders pain and punishment for itself' (*hē de ponēria syngennōsa to lypoun eautē kai kolazon*, 554B), which makes it more properly discipline (NB *kolazon*). This sits nicely with Plutarch's preference for divine punishment as chastisement, or correction, or cure. In his view, even the (so-called) 'vengeance' of the afterlife has the function of discipline which aims at cure.

Paul's distinctive punishment terms

Paul has no notion of punishment as cure.[24] Instead, his distinctive terms draw upon the forensic setting of justice, vindication, and punishment (i.e. forensic penalty). They include, most notably, the various words associated with the *krin-* family, used for judgment/condemnation, as well as various retributive terms, such as *antapodidōmi/antapodoma*.[25] Such terms do not suit the 'punishment as cure' ethos of *Delay*, but they do suit the forensic setting which provides the framework against which Paul's doctrine of punishment needs to be read.

Judgment by works is known by Paul and appears to be a common principle of divine justice held by both Jew and Greek.[26] This principle abides for Paul, but he also proclaims a gospel which has revealed a new and different principle, even if it assumes the 'judgment by works' principle as a necessary backdrop (cf. Rom. 3:21–26). Judgment, for Paul, is built upon the righteousness of God, and so his forensic terminology (*krin-*) is closely associated with the *dik-* family, rather than with vocabulary with overtones of vengeance. Since Plutarch also draws upon the *dik-* family, and is intensely interested in divine justice, Paul's framework of justice would have some appeal to him, even if Paul's use of retributive terms may risk God's justice sounding like the 'cur's justice' which Plutarch despises.[27]

'Wrath' terms in Paul

Alongside these terms drawn from a forensic conceptual pool, Paul also introduces the 'emotional' aspect of 'wrath' into God's judgment, using the terms *orgē* and *thymos*. Although Plutarch also uses these terms, an analysis of *Delay* indicates that the philosopher would be none too pleased with such terms being applied to God.

Orgē

Although Paul does not use the verb in his undisputed letters, it occurs once in Ephesians (Eph. 4:26 = Ps. 4:5) to restrict human anger. The noun is also used in disapproval of human *orgē* (Col. 3:8; cf. Eph. 4:31 and 1 Tim. 2:8), as well as occurring twice of the proper exercise of wrath by the God-ordained civil authorities (13:4–5). In the large bulk of the occurrences, however, *hē orgē tou theou* is in view (although this full phrase occurs only in Rom. 1:18; Col. 3:6 [and Eph. 5:6]).

In 1 Thessalonians 1:10 this wrath is future. The Thessalonians await the return of God's Son from heaven, who is described as *ton rhyomenon hēmas ek tēs orgēs tēs erchomenēs*. This should be their confident hope (5:8), because God appointed them to receive salvation, not wrath (5:9, *ouk etheto hēmas ... eis orgēn*).

Some consider that the aorist tense of *ephthasen* suggests that the wrath had already fallen on the Jews (1 Thess. 2:16).[28] However, *ephthasen* may simply mean that the wrath had come very close to the Jews, so that, because of its association with the parousia, it too is imminent indeed.[29] The much discussed final prepositional phrase (*eis telos*), should be taken closely with *hē orgē*, namely, that the wrath Paul talks about is 'the wrath (of God) with a view to the end', i.e. end-time wrath, or even 'eternal wrath'.[30] The sentence therefore talks of the future manifestation of God's wrath, indicating that this final wrath has come very close indeed to the Jewish opponents of the Gentile mission.

In Romans, Paul declares that his gospel is revealing the wrath of God (Rom. 1:18). Manifest corruption provides evidence that the Gentile world is under God's wrath: their behaviour clearly deserves the death sentence (cf. 1:32). But Paul quickly turns to the task of implicating the Jew in the same problem (Rom. 2). There is a future day of wrath (2:5) against which any lack of repentance stores up wrath. The ancient and widespread 'judgment by works' principle teaches that the self-seeking, who reject the truth and follow evil, will receive wrath and anger (*orgē kai thymos*) on that day

(2:8), whether Jew or Gentile. With an eye on this eschatological day, Paul's imaginary objector can even call God 'the one who inflicts wrath' (3:5, *ho epipherōn tēn orgēn*). In discussing the role of faith, Paul introduces a contrast between promise and law: law brings only wrath (4:15). This also has primary reference to eschatological wrath, since Paul has already stated that, at the judgment day, the 'judgment by works' principle condemns all who do not keep the law (ch. 2). However, this also means that the law ensures that even the Jewish people live under wrath in the present, as long as they live under law. Romans 1:18 – 3:20 has argued that all of humanity is liable (3:19, *hypodikos*) to God, i.e. they live under his wrath revealed from heaven.[31] The way of escape is through Christ and his gracious death, which ensures salvation from that future wrath (5:9). Paul talks of those outside his elective purposes as vessels of wrath who are made to display his wrath (9:22). By 12:19 the Romans are instructed to leave any revenge to God's future judgment day, to leave a place for wrath.

In Colossians the wrath of God (*hē orgē tou theou*) is coming because of the evil deeds of humanity (Col. 3:6; cf. v. 5; cf. Eph. 5:6).

Thymos

Paul also speaks against the negative human emotion, *thymos*. It is listed in the plural as one of the obvious 'works of the flesh' (Gal. 5:20), and as one of the undesirable activities he hopes not to find when he visits the Corinthians (2 Cor. 12:20). To the Colossians *thymos* is listed alongside *orgē* as one of the things that ought to be laid aside (Col. 3:8; cf. Eph. 4:31).

However, despite this negative usage in the realm of human relations, on one occasion Paul has no qualms about a divine *thymos* (Rom. 2:8). In this theoretical discussion on the principle of judgment according to works,[32] he states that such a position implies that 'for those who are self-seeking and who reject the truth and follow evil, there will be wrath and anger (*orgē kai thymos*)'. This coupling of *orgē* and *thymos* is then associated with two further terms (v. 9): 'There will be trouble and distress (*thlipsis kai stenochōria*) for every human being who does evil'. These terms are illuminated further by contrast with the opposite outcomes awarded, in the 'judgment by works' scheme, to those with the opposite lifestyle. For, seeking 'glory, honour and immortality' (*doxan kai timēn kai aphtharsian*), they are not only given 'eternal life' (*zōēn aiōnion*, v. 7), but also 'glory, honour, and peace' (*doxa kai timē kai eirēnē*, v. 10).

In summary, like the Septuagint before him, Paul does not balk from using these two words of God, in order to speak of his 'wrath' and 'fury'.[33]

Wrath in Plutarch
Orgē

Orgē appears ten times in Plutarch's essay, and the passive of the cognate verb (*orgizomai*) twice. It is used of Epicurus, who launches the dialogue (548C) by, in Plutarch's words, lashing out at providence 'like someone savagely attacking in anger and abuse' (*hōsper orgē tini kai loidoria sparattōn*). As part of Plutarch's insistence that God delays so that we can imitate his patience (550F) he couples *orgē* with *thymos* (in a quotation),[34] and argues that God is slow in punishment because he 'would teach us not to strike out in anger ... or when in its fiercest fever and convulsion "Our rage o'erleaps our wits"' (*didaskōn mē syn orgē mēd' hoti malista phlegetai kai sphadazei pēdōn ho thymos tōn phrenōn anōterō*). In the same section (551A) he agrees with Socrates against taking vengeance 'while we are turbid and clouded in our judgment with rage and fury (*tholeron onta ... ton logismon orgēs kai manias*), before being settled and becoming clear'. The coupling with *mania*, the resulting effect on the reasoning, and the contrast with 'being settled and becoming clear' indicate Plutarch's negative assessment of this human emotion.[35] He immediately states the same point positively, illustrating from Melanthius, that 'reason likewise achieves justice and moderation only after putting rage and anger out of the way' (*ho logismos ta dikaia prattei kai metria tēn orgēn kai ton thymon ekpodōn themenos*). He then cites the examples of Plato, who delays punishing his slave, and Archytas, who simply says to his insubordinate servants, 'It is your good fortune that I am furious (*orgizomai*) with you' (551B), before making conclusions about the divine delay of justice using an a fortiori argument from the human examples, whose recollection allays 'the harshness and intensity of anger' (*to trachy kai sphodron ... tēs orgēs*). By contrast, 'the gentleness and magnanimity' (*tēn praotēta kai tēn megalopsychian*) which God displays must be held as a 'divine portion of virtue' (*theion morion aretēs*).

In later sections, Timon's mention of Aesop's 'angry dispute' (556F) is of peripheral interest, but the conclusion to his 'crowning difficulty' is of more significance when he asks why 'the wrath(s) of the gods' (*hai tōn theōn orgai*) should disappear only to emerge later (557E). Here the word is in the plural, and Timon shows that these are experienced in 'the direst calamities (*symphora*)'.

As Plutarch answers Timon's 'crowning difficulty' he makes a reference to the unchanging nature of the Athenians' displays of 'favours and angers' (*charites kai orgai*), which reveals that *charis* can be considered an antonym to *orgē* (559B). More substantially, he later goes on (562D) to deny that God has been provoked so as to 'be angry' (*orgizetai*) at the wrongdoer, which is in parallel with 'retaliate' (*amynetai*) and 'hate' (*misei*). Rather, when he punishes (*kolazei*) it is for curative purposes (*iatreias heneka*). This reveals that, in Plutarch's view, responding with anger is not only extremely negative, but is also at loggerheads with the divine reformative purpose. In the 'myth' it is the descendants of the evildoers that respond with anger, as the soul of such a descendant 'flew [at them] in fury' (*prosepipten orgē*, 567D) and great clusters of descendants' souls were 'gibbering shrilly in angry memory (*tetrigyias hypo mnemēs kai orgēs*) of what they had suffered through their fault' (567E).

In summary, *orgē* is a negative human emotion that clouds reason and should not be present in the exercise of human justice. Only Timon directly attributes anger to the gods and he does so only once. Plutarch, however, considers that God does not punish out of anger, but only for the purpose of cure. If anger is experienced in the afterlife, it is that of wronged relatives. On Plutarch's view, on analogy with what is clearly a problematic human emotion, it would be inappropriate to suggest that God was associated with anger.

Thymos

Plutarch first uses *thymos* in an unidentified quotation concerning human rage (550F),[36] to support his contention that God's delay ought to be imitated. Here it is clearly close in sense to *orgē*, and both terms are highly emotive, since the quotation supports the statement '[God] would teach us not to strike out in anger at those who have caused us pain, or when in its fiercest fever and convulsion'. Their opposite is to 'imitate his mildness and delay and resort to chastisement with all due order and propriety, with Time as our counsellor, who will be least likely to involve us in regret'.

By using a quotation from Melanthius, Plutarch pits anger (*thymos*) against the wits (*phrenēs*), and goes on to say that reason (*logismos*) 'acts with justice and moderation, only after putting rage and anger out of the way' (*ho logismos ta dikaia prattei kai metria tēn orgēn kai ton thymon ekpodōn themenos*). Plato is then quoted as saying (551A), in explanation for remaining motionless before punishing his slaves, that he was 'chastening his rage' (*ton thymon kolazōn*).

The data therefore show that Plutarch does not use *thymos* when expressing his own point of view, but only in quotation or explanation of quotation. Where it so appears it is always used of human beings, is closely related to *orgē*,[37] and concerns an emotion that is viewed unfavourably. If the Platonic model is followed, *thymos* should not be part of punishment, but it ought to be 'punished' itself. The significant point for our purposes is that, since he is arguing for this being the divine pattern, it is true to say that Plutarch has no place for a divine *thymos* in the punishment process. Rather than acting from such passions, God acts only for the sake of cure (*iatreias heneka*).

Conclusion

How would a Middle Platonist like Plutarch have heard the apostle's message of a God who showed wrath?

Plutarch and wrath

Plutarch would have applauded Paul's opinion that anger is an inappropriate part of human relations. However, given its evident problems in the human sphere, Plutarch would have been uncomfortable with Paul allowing anger into the divine. Why would Paul act with such apparent inconsistency, by disallowing anger to humans, and then speaking of it as a present and future reality for God?

Plutarch and a modern debate on Paul

Just as familiar as Plutarch and Paul with the excesses of human anger, many a modern interpreter has shared Plutarch's dislike of attributing anger to God and has attempted to rescue the apostle from this inconsistency. God's wrath cannot be 'the irrational passion of anger';[38] nor can it mean that 'God personally reacted against the sinner with explosive ire and "took it out on him" in punishment';[39] nor can it express 'an unbridled and normless exercise of vengeance, which as is to be found in the heathen representations of the wrath of the gods'.[40]

Some talk of Paul using a mere anthropopassism, that is, 'God's attitude to such sinners is described in terms borrowed from the human passion of anger or "wrath"'.[41] Others have tried to rescue Paul from anthropomorphism through proposing an evolutionary history-of-religions schema, in which 'wrath' is a throwback to a more primitive time before a greater rationality took over.[42] Attempts have also been made which propose that the 'wrath' of which Paul speaks is unlike the human wrath he condemns. After all, it is described in terms 'less personal' than those describing his love.[43] Proposing that it is some kind of principle of judgment enables interpreters to downplay the emotional component, so that 'the idea of the working of God's wrath predominates above that of the emotion'.[44] Bultmann speaks against the 'false notion that God's wrath is a quality', arguing that wrath is an occurrence,[45] so that 'the wrath of God there does not so much have the significance of a divine emotion or of a movement within the divine being as indeed of the active divine judgement going forth against sin and the world'.[46]

Thus, 'wrath' becomes an impersonal process, to some degree separable from God himself. So, in Romans 1:18–32, 'the disastrous progress of evil in society is presented as a natural process of cause and effect, and not as the direct act of God'.[47] Or, in Hanson's words, 'for Paul the impersonal character of the wrath was important; it relieved him of the necessity of attributing wrath directly to God, it transformed the wrath from an attribute of God into the name for a process which sinners bring upon themselves'.[48] Or again, MacGregor put it this way: 'Such divine retribution is not to be thought of as something as it were external to the sinning, but is to be found in the tragic fact that the regular result of sin is to create its own punitive consequences.'[49]

The strength of this 'impersonal' view is that it rightly points to the 'cause and effect' fact that sin brings its own judgment. Both Paul and Plutarch agree that this view accurately described reality, albeit in part. There was nothing new in this, for, in the Greek world, it was as old as Hesiod's principle that 'punishment is contemporary with vice' (see *Delay*, 553F), and for the Jewish world, especially in its 'wisdom' traditions, sin led to a foolishness which inevitably caused distress in life. But despite the truth that is found in this view, our study of Plutarch has shown that not only is he aware of this view already, but he also sees it as a thing separate from the attribution of anger to God. For this reason he is happy to incorporate such a view into his own framework. Nevertheless, the fact that he could make this distinction implies that Paul's use of the language of anger would not have automatically been taken to mean some Hesiod-like impersonal process.

Paul on wrath

Why is Paul comfortable with speaking of divine wrath? Perhaps because it, unlike human anger, is restrained by God's justice. In this regard, it is interesting that Paul avoids exactly the terms associated with vengeance,[50] while nevertheless using the emotional language of wrath. When *orgē* and *thymos* occur of God, they are set within a forensic framework in which wrath is expressed in the context of justice. Although human anger does not achieve the righteousness of God (to borrow from Jas. 1:20), God's wrath and righteousness are of a piece (cf. Rom. 1:16–17, 18), and God's wrath is always thoroughly righteous and just (Rom. 2:5; 3:5). This is also the case in the present state of wrath under which the world labours. For this manifest wrath comes as a result of God handing human beings over to the desires of their hearts (Rom. 1:24, 26, 28), which is certainly completely impartial and fair, even though this is a terrible 'grace', because it is impossible to live in God's world without him. In this way, the tragic effects of sin working its own judgment (*à la* Hesiod, and his modern counterparts) are felt in the world at large.

Plutarch hearing Paul

Plutarch appreciated the delay in the divine vengeance because of the opportunity it afforded the soul for further cure. His divine physician was not wrathful, but his justice consisted in patiently working towards reformation. Even in the afterlife there was no divine anger, simply, through reincarnation, a second chance at cure – at least for those not deemed 'incurable'. For Paul, the delay was to allow time for repentance (Rom. 2:5). If the patience of God was despised through lack of repentance, then this delay became a period for storing up wrath which will be poured out on God's great day of wrath in the future. When this was done, it would not be in an irrational pique, but it would be the considered verdict of the one who is the judge of all the earth, justly giving each person what he or she is due.

As someone like Plutarch listened to someone like Paul, he would have heard a radically different message about the God who was personally offended, in fact, justly angry, at this world. He would have heard that God had already fixed a day in which he will judge the world through a man whom he had raised from the dead. This person would have heard the call for repentance. And he would have heard that those who heeded the call to repentance would move out from 'under wrath' and begin to live 'under grace' in the Lord Jesus Christ. For them, the final day would be a day of salvation, not of wrath.

When Paul spoke in Athens, any Middle Platonist in the crowd would agree with him, against the Stoics and the Epicureans, that there was a real hope for the afterlife that clearly provided comfort in the face of death and a drive to a moral life. Both philosopher and apostle could argue for this, using their own particular *logos*. But they also both had a *mythos*, i.e. a vision of another world meant to inspire the imagination and so evoke change in this world. Plutarch, drawing upon his Platonic hearth, spoke of the 'other world', existing alongside our own, which the soul enters at death. Paul, drawing upon the apocalyptic view of history, spoke of the 'next world', entered by resurrection and through judgment. Human life was going somewhere, and human life was therefore important. Whereas Plutarch's God's punishment was directed towards the cure of 'the passions of a sick soul', Paul believed in a resurrection in which people would be recompensed for deeds done in the body (2 Cor. 5:10). Whereas for Plutarch, retribution was a 'cur's justice', suitable for the body but not the soul, Paul's gospel assumed that evil was not simply a soul problem, but it is done 'in the body'. It is therefore entirely suitable that, on that future day of judgment (cf. Rom 2:6–10), it will be recompensed 'in the body'.

The concept of bodily resurrection was known among Greek thinkers, but only to be despised – especially by the Platonists.[51] Upon entering the afterlife, if the soul was still impure (and yet curable), further purification would take place – including experiencing the anger of wronged relatives – before reincarnation. The eventual goal of the curative process was to gain such purity of soul that it enters the upper realms free from the encumbrance of a body. In this curative framework, the attribution of wrath to the divinity was inappropriate, and had no place in the process.

For a Middle Platonist to accept Paul's message he would have to accept a judgment that included the infliction of wrath. This would entail the acceptance of a punishment that is not curative, but retributive, to be received in the body when bodies are raised to judgment. Thus, for the Middle Platonist, one problem was 'solved' by another! However, the demonstration that this future judgment day was already fixed was that a man had already risen from the dead as an event in human history. The resurrection was demonstrated to be true in the case of one man and that man is appointed judge of all the earth.

The good news of Paul's gospel was that, despite the fact that the wrath of God is already being revealed, and despite the fact that future wrath is a certainty, God has also acted to bring about salvation from wrath. In fact, the man who will be judge has absorbed the wrath of God in his own body: Jesus, the one who rose again from the dead.

If the first-century Middle Platonists were to accept Christ after hearing Paul's gospel, it would certainly mean that their eschatology, and so their world, would be 'turned upside down'.[52]

Notes

1. I have discussed the various afterlife views in Bolt, 'Life'.
2. This article is a distillation of some of the material in Bolt, 'Plutarch's *Delay*'. The text of *Delay* can be conveniently consulted in de Lacy & Einarson, *Moralia* VII.
3. Cf. 1 Thess. 4:14; 1 Cor. 15.
4. Bultmann, *Theology* 1, p. 77: 'The preaching of the resurrection from the dead is inseparable from that of God's judgment, for the dead, too, are to be brought to account for their former deeds.'
5. Despite the importance of judgment to Acts, the terms of interest here are not utilized: *orgē* is absent; *thymos* appears only once, when it is a human emotion (19:28).
6. Cf. Bolt, 'Life', p. 68.
7. This resurgence is dated from Antiochus of Ascalon (d. c. 68 BC) to Plotinus (b. AD 205). See Dillon, 'Platonism, Middle'.
8. According to Atticus, in Eusebius *Prep. Ev.* 15.9.2, this was almost the one thing that held them together. Cf. Young, 'Some Middle Platonists'. In *Delay*, Plutarch argues towards a belief in the immortality of the soul from a view of Providence shared with his opponents.
9. 'As a Platonist Plutarch often polemicizes against both the Stoics and the Epicureans' (Einarson & de Lacy, 'Introduction', p. 2). They list ten essays which are specifically directed against Epicureanism, not including *Delay*. It is, however, discussed in relation to Epicureanism by Flacelière, 'Plutarque', and Brenk, 'Imperial heritage', p. 261, also recognizes that it is directed against the Epicureans.
10. Although Plutarch was a student in Athens in AD 66/67, it is unlikely that he was part of Paul's audience in the Areopagus some fifteen years previously. Plutarch was born about AD 40 and died after AD 120; see Jones, 'Plutarch', p. 961. For another useful introduction to Plutarch, see Russell, 'Plutarch'. Plutarch was apparently oblivious to the burgeoning Christian movement: 'He never mentions Christianity', Brenk, 'Imperial heritage', p. 297; cf. Trench, *Plutarch*, pp. 14–17, 112; Russell, *Plutarch*, p. 81; Barrow, *Plutarch*, p. 99. The one possible exception – 'Coniugalia praecepta' – is by no means clear and can be explained otherwise. Barrow also refers to some who have (mistakenly) argued for a knowledge of Christianity from *Delay*, on the basis of similarity of conceptions.
11. 'He is known to have written about 250 works in 300 volumes', two or three of which are now lost; Jones, 'Plutarch', p. 963.
12. Although this essay deals primarily with the nine undisputed letters (Rom., 1 and 2 Cor., Gal., Phil., Philem. and 1 Thess.), references from the rest of the Pauline corpus are also considered.
13. For this conjecture, contra the usual emendation to 'O Quietus', see my 'Plutarch's *Delay*', pp. 1–10.
14. Cherniss & Helmbold, p. 6, who point out that Plutarch similarly uses Aristotle in *De facie quae in orbe lunae apparet* (920F, 928E ff.).
15. Stoicism emerged out of Cynicism, in that Zeno was a disciple of Crates. Not all Stoics accepted Cynicism, however, and there were Stoics (as well as Epicureans) who polemicized against Cynics. Cf. Moles, 'Cynics'.

342 *The gospel to the nations*

16. The myth of Er in *Republic* 10 is most similar, but it is also reminiscent of *Gorgias*; Jones, 'Platonism', p. 43. Vernière, 'Le Léthé' compares Plutarch's myth with his predecessor's.
17. Zeller, *Stoics*, pp. 45–46.
18. Bolt, 'Plutarch's *Delay*', pp. 26, 33–40, 49. The reader thus benefits vicariously from Thespesius' journey.
19. This 'problem' was felt by others, including those within the ambit of the NT (cf. Rom. 2:4; 1 Pet. 3).
20. This may, indeed, be a broadside at a kind of 'vengeance ethic' which had ancient precedent and was praised by the Cynics. Several of the sayings in the 'Delphic Canon' suggest that it may have been a part of the ethic promoted at Delphi, where Plutarch was a priest. See my 'Plutarch's *Delay*', pp. 297–298.
21. Plutarch also has a number of distinctive minor terms; cf. my 'Plutarch's *Delay*', ch. 2.
22. Horsley, 'A prefect's circular', AD 198/9, uses the nouns synonymously, as does P. Ryl. II.62[10] (3rd cent. AD) – pace MM, p. 636.
23. MM, p. 636, citing P. Lond. 1171 *verso (c)*[12] (AD 42), P. Leid. W[vii.28] (2nd/3rd cent. AD) and BGU IV.1024[iv.17] (4th/5th cent. AD).
24. Although he does have one instance of sickness as 'discipline' (1 Cor. 11:30–32), drawing upon the conceptual pool of education (v. 32, *paideuō*; cf. 2 Cor. 6:9; 1 Tim. 1:20; 2 Tim 2:25; Titus 2:12), not medicine. Olympichus (549C) uses *paideuō* in an analogy for divine justice, but Plutarch does not.
25. Paul also has a number of distinctive minor terms, cf. my 'Plutarch's *Delay*', ch. 4.
26. Rom. 2:6, cf. Prov. 24:12, LXX; Ps. 62:12; Eccles. 1:14; Hos. 12:2; *m.* 'Abot 3:15. The Greeks had the principle *drasanti pathein*, 'the doer must suffer'.
27. *Delay* also uses retributive terms, but simply to raise views that Plutarch himself disagrees with. See my 'Plutarch's *Delay*', pp. 79–83.
28. Whether in the fall of Jerusalem or the expulsion of the Jews by Claudius or a massacre in Jerusalem in AD 49; see Bruce, *1 & 2 Thessalonians*, p. 117.
29. Bruce, *1 & 2 Thessalonians*, p. 117, lists Marshall and Best in support of this view. For argument that this verb connotes imminence rather than arrival cf. Martin, 'Messianic age', p. 272; Daube, *Sudden*, pp. 35–36.
30. This would be akin to a common usage in the LXX where *eis telos* means 'for ever'; e.g. Job. 20:7, 23:7; Ps. 9:7; Hab. 1:4.
31. Cf. Eph. 2:3, where the state of humanity, both Jew and Gentile, is that they are 'children by nature' – i.e. in the normal state of affairs – 'of wrath' (*tekna physei orgēs*).
32. Beginning with a quotation regarding the impartiality of God's justice, with which his Jewish readers would no doubt agree (v. 6, cf. Ps. 62:12; Prov. 24:12), Paul's discussion concerns the theoretical implications of this 'judgment according to works' position. That it is theoretical becomes plain as the argument proceeds and Paul provides his view of the actual facts (3:1–20) and the new basis for judgment that God has revealed (3:21–26).
33. E.g. Ps. 77:9; Dan. 3:13; Mic. 5:15. The LXX usage is despite its tendency to downplay the anthropopassisms found in the Hebrew Bible. See Ringgren, *Israelite Religion*, p. 347.
34. Nauck, *Trag. Graec. Frag.*, Adespota, p. 390.
35. Cf. his 'Fragment: On Rage', in Sandbach, *Moralia* XV, pp. 274–277: actions done in anger 'are blind, senseless and entirely miss the mark'; 'It is not possible

to act with calculation (*logismos*) when in a rage, and anything done without calculation is unskilful and distorted. A man ought to make reason (*logon*) his guide'; '… rage (*orge*) or asperity or quick temper' is 'unbecoming to manly hearts'. Practising controlling the temper with one's slaves and wife is the way for a man to be 'the physician of his own soul'.

36. Nauck, *Trag. Graec. Frag.*, Adespota, p. 390.
37. The classical distinction was that *thymos* was the inner emotion, and *orge* its outward expression.
38. Dodd, *Romans*, p. 24.
39. MacGregor, 'Concept', p. 105.
40. Ridderbos, *Paul*, p. 108.
41. MacGregor, 'Concept', p. 101.
42. Dodd, *Romans*, pp. 21–24.
43. Ibid., p. 21; MacGregor, 'Concept', p. 103. Travis, 'Wrath', p. 997, provides some counter-arguments.
44. Ridderbos, *Paul*, p. 108; with Stählin, '*orge*', p. 424.
45. Bultmann, *Theology* 1, p. 288.
46. Ridderbos, *Paul*, p. 108.
47. Dodd, *Romans*, p. 29.
48. Hanson, *Wrath*, p. 69.
49. MacGregor, 'Concept', pp. 105–106.
50. Even when forbidding personal vengeance, in favour of 'leaving room for the wrath of God', his terms for revenge are drawn from the 'justice' root (*ekdikeo*; *ekdikesis*; Rom. 12:19–21, cf. Prov. 25:21).
51. See Bolt, 'Life', pp. 72–75.
52. It gives me a great deal of pleasure to contribute to the honouring of Peter O'Brien, who was instrumental in my entering ministry, and has since filled the various roles of my teacher, chaplain, academic supervisor and colleague. His friendship, teaching, wisdom, and example have all enriched my life.

23. The uniqueness of Christ, 'Chalcedon' and mission

Robert C. Doyle

The creed or definition of the Council of Chalcedon (AD 451), and the creeds of Nicea and Constantinople it sought to protect, continue to attract criticism for their purported rigid and arid ontological interests and consequent, stultifying effect on understanding God's actions in Christ in the contemporary world.[1] Further, the underlying intent of these creeds, to articulate and proclaim the uniqueness of Christ as *God*, also attracts adverse comment in the pluralist world which surrounds us at the start of the third millennium.[2]

For evangelical theology and mission, the most telling criticisms come from Peter O'Brien's own field of endeavour, New Testament studies. If it can be shown that the fathers of the early catholic church have mistaken the teaching of Holy Scripture, then their credal endeavours are cut off at the roots.

What I aim to do in this essay is first of all to look closely at one representative criticism, that of Morna Hooker in her essay, 'Chalcedon and the New Testament'.[3] This promises to be a useful exercise, not only for the obvious reason that Professor Hooker is an eminent New Testament exegete herself, but also because the essay appeared in another *Festschrift*, that for Maurice Wiles, whose own criticism of traditional Christology helped to produce the highly influential volume, *The Myth of God Incarnate*. Secondly, aided by the Scottish patristic expert and eminent theologian, T. F. Torrance, I want to demonstrate the ontological deepening which is

345

offered us by certain conceptualities of Nicea-Constantinople as we continue to think through the nature of evangelical mission in the world.

Morna Hooker on Jesus Christ and Chalcedon

Morna Hooker's case is presented with great clarity, and can be summarized in her own words. It is 'a little disconcerting for a New Testament scholar to find the careful definition of Chalcedon couched in language which is utterly foreign, not simply to the ideas and language with which we are familiar today, but also to those we identify as belonging to the writers of the New Testament: how very different is this description of Christ's person from what the New Testament writers have to say about him!'[4] Indeed, the real concern is that 'the influence of Chalcedon is still a positive hindrance to our understanding of what the New Testament authors were trying to say about Jesus in their very own different times and circumstances'.[5]

What then, did the New Testament authors say about Jesus? Hooker's starting-point is the question: does John 1:14 teach that God was incarnate in Jesus Christ? Making use of Old Testament and intertestamental resources, Hooker then traces motifs used by John and Paul to describe the person and work of Christ.

In Paul's writings, according to Hooker, 'what we become through Christ is what, in the purpose of God, we are meant to be – truly human; men and women are recreated in God's image, they are children of God, enjoying the liberty and privileges of God's children, and reflecting his glory'. She argues that the language and motifs that Paul uses to describe this redemptive activity are 'appropriate to one who is truly what Man is meant to be': Son of God, and as Son, obedient to God; the Man from heaven – standing in contrast to Adam, the man from earth; the image of God, and in the form of God – as Adam was before the fall; like Adam in the Garden of Eden reflecting the glory of God; and again reminiscent of Adam as the one commanded to have dominion over the earth.[6]

Using these motifs and the contrast Paul makes between Christ and the Jewish understanding of the law, Christ is depicted as pre-existent because he more directly represents God's purposes to re-create humanity. He is Son, because he acts in obedience to God. Because 'everything that happens through Christ is the activity of God himself', Christ stands not only as one with humanity, but also in this redemptive work, as one with God. That is, Pauline studies show that Christ is 'divine', in that he is, in the Jewish context at least, uniquely one with the redemptive purposes of God. The range of Pauline texts from which Hooker draws these motifs is impressive.

Her concluding comparison with Nicean theology is telling.

Thus it would seem that statements which appear at first sight to be 'incarnational formulae' are not, strictly speaking, 'incarnational' at all. Rather, for Paul, they refer to the conviction that by sharing our fallen humanity (i.e. life in Adam) Christ enabled men and women to become what he is: but Paul does not, as did Athanasius, understand that as meaning that they become divine (*De Inc.* 54).[7]

Hooker next gathers and interprets prominent redemptive themes in John's Gospel. She argues that from the prologue onward, Jesus is the fulfilment of Judaism. 'The Prologue provides the justification for these claims [in the body of the Gospel] about Jesus. The Word of God, active in the past in creation, in history, in the prophets, was believed by Jews to have been embodied in the Law given to Moses on Mount Sinai. Christians are now claiming that a fuller, more complete embodiment of God's Word, or Logos, has taken place in Jesus Christ.' In 'Hebrew thought a word once spoken had a dynamic life of its own. The Logos is referred to as though a separate being, over against God; but in a similar way, Jewish writers had already spoken of Wisdom as God's master-workman, helping in the work of creation, dwelling among God's people, speaking through the prophets (Prov. 8:22–31; Wis. 7:22 – 10:21; Sir. 24).' 'Since God speaks in him his words are the words of God; his deeds also, are the deeds of God (10:37–8). He comes from above (8:23). He is "from God" (9:33). He is one with the Father (10:30).'[8]

Thus, when understood in this context, neither John 1:14 ('the word became flesh'), nor 1:18 (*monogenēs theos*), nor the confession of Thomas at the end of the Gospel ('my Lord and my God') speak of '*God* incarnate'. In the midst of this frame of reference, which is very different from Chalcedon, John also makes it clear that the Word, or Jesus, stands over and against God. This is especially the case at the 'high' Christological points of 1:1 ('the Word was *with* God') and 1:18 ('No-one has ever seen God'). Further, in contexts in which Jesus appears to ascribe divinity to himself, or divinity appears to be ascribed to him, Jesus identifies himself over against God ('My Father is greater than I', 14:28; he is ascending 'to my Father and your Father, to my God and your God'). Hooker's conclusion follows quite logically:

What John is trying to express is the notion of revelation ... The Revealer God is encountered in his revelation, and when one encounters the revelation, one encounters God. But it is surely more accurate to speak (as John himself does) of the incarnate Word, rather than of the incarnate God.[9]

Hooker exegetes Christ's 'divinity' and 'humanity' in Hebrews in a similar fashion. Thus, she argues, 'Paul, the fourth evangelist, and the author to the Hebrews all declare that God's self-revelation in Christ is final and complete: there is nothing to be known of God which is not known in him. In the language of Colossians, "in him all the fullness of God was pleased to dwell".'[10]

The conclusion of this study draws three comparisons between the world of the New Testament and Chalcedon, and demonstrates how these support the line of argument adopted in Maurice Wiles' paper, 'Does Christology rest on a mistake?'[11] The New Testament authors wrestled with issues very different from those which occupied the Chalcedonian fathers. 'Their concern was to show that it was the same God who had been at work in the past who was now at work in Christ, and that this new work of Christ was the fulfilment of everything that had gone before: hence the importance of showing his superiority to Moses.' The idea of an incarnate God was foreign to Jewish thinking, as the prayer of Solomon in 1 Kings 8:27 shows. When individuals are accorded divine honours, it does not mean that they are themselves 'divine' beings; rather, their authority and honour are manifestations of the fact that God is revealing his power and purpose through them.[12] Maurice Wiles's strength, according to Hooker, is his argument that just as modern knowledge has led us to demythologize the story of Adam's creation and fall, so we must now demythologize Christ.[13] The mythological language of the Old Testament, New Testament, and even Chalcedon, was appropriate in its time. Nevertheless, we may take our cue from Paul, who in part demythologized the Jewish eschatological framework in order to explain a Christian eschatological expectation of a restoration that is not yet a fully accomplished fact.[14] Hooker thus begins to follow Maurice Wiles in insisting that the biblical images depict human, religious experience which speaks of and promotes personal and community transformation, and not any actual historical event.[15]

The outcome of her biblical investigations for the Chalcedonian definition, which affirmed that Jesus as the 'Son of God', the second person of the Trinity, is 'of one substance with the Father', are not unexpected. The 'Chalcedonian definition is not a direct "translation" of what is being said in the New Testament into another set of terms, for the questions its authors addressed were totally different from those which exercised the authors of the New Testament'.[16]

Questions theologians ask

Such a *tour de force* as Morna Hooker has accomplished deserves to be taken with utmost seriousness. My first reaction is to agree with much of her summation of the major Christological themes operating in the fourth Gospel, the Pauline corpus, Hebrews and the Synoptics, together with the force she attributes to them in making sense of the Christ event against the interests apparent in both the Old and New Testaments. Indeed, the 'dynamic' language and conceptualities of the biblical witness were appropriated as such by Irenaeus and Athanasius. But further, the Nicean-Constantinoplian creed, although in some sense written in a 'foreign' language which is at home with Greek philosophy, also speaks of Christ's person and work in the dynamic terms of God's sovereign activity in creation and redemption. It is essentially an exposition of the work of God in Christ 'for us men and for our salvation', stretching from creation to re-creation. But what may we do with Morna Hooker's central observation that the New Testament does not teach that *'God* became incarnate', that Christ was not actually this *God?* Three sorts of questions suggest themselves.

Exegetical questions

First, is the exegesis right? And associated with it, has enough been done? Here we have been well served by Peter O'Brien. After reviewing the background to Colossians 1:15–20 in the Jewish wisdom literature, he asks how it came about that these predicates and activities of Wisdom were applied to Jesus of Nazareth, recently crucified and risen from the dead. This move is not adequately explained by the background itself.[17] O'Brien comes close to Hooker's position when he sees the antecedents of 1:15 ('He is the image of the invisible God') in the wisdom background of the Old Testament and Judaism, but he goes further to argue that as this points to Christ's revealing of the Father and his pre-existence, it has both functional and ontological connotations.[18] On 1:19 ('For in him all the fullness [of deity] was pleased to dwell'), O'Brien argues for the propriety of seeing this fullness as drawing down on three lines old Old Testament thought, which present 'fullness' in terms of the acts and attributes of God.[19] Once again a similar observation was made in Hooker's essay. However, on the parallel statement in 2:9 ('For in him the whole fullness of deity dwells bodily'), O'Brien points out that *hē theotēs* ('deity') is the abstract noun from *ho theos* ('God'). 'Deity' thus means the being of God, the divine essence or Godhead, and is to be distinguished from *hē theiotēs* ('divine nature, quality'), the abstract noun from *theios* ('divine'). He cites Meyer with approval: 'Accordingly, the *essence* of God, undivided and in its whole fullness, dwells in Christ in His exalted state, so that He is the essential and adequate image of God (1:15), which He could not be if He were not possessor of the divine essence.'[20] O'Brien himself urges that the reception of salvation, described in verse 10 as being fulfilled in Christ alone, and on which the fullness imparted to the readers depends, becomes meaningful only if Christ is the one in whom the plenitude of divinity is embodied. Further, he cites Murray Harris's point that a functional Christology presupposes, and finds its ultimate basis in, an ontological Christology.[21]

A similar exegetical service is done for us on Philippians 2:1-11. With respect to the question we are pursuing concerning the 'godness' of Jesus, O'Brien draws two apposite conclusions. First, '*morphē* refers to that "form which truly and fully expresses the being which underlies it." The phrase *en morphē theou* is best interpreted against the background of the glory of God, that shining light in which, according to the OT and intertestamental literature, God was pictured ... The expression does not refer simply to external appearance but pictures the pre-existent Christ as clothed in the garments of divine majesty and splendour.'[22] Secondly, the participial clause that begins verse 6, *hos en morphē theou hyparchōn*, ought be rendered not concessively but causally: 'precisely *because* he was in the form of God he did not regard this equality with God as something to be used for his own advantage'.[23]

Now, as Hooker would point out, although verse 6 is a very important control for the meaning of the verses which follow, O'Brien's conclusion concerning the meaning of 'form' is no knock-down argument for Christ being *God*, because intertestamental literature depicts individuals in their revelatory role accorded divine honours. For example, Philo, elaborating on Exodus 7:1, declared that Moses had been given the name of god and king.[24] However, because texts cannot just be captive to their background, whether the Old Testament, Jewish intertestamentary literature, or the more immediate Hellenistic environment, I would want to maintain that the evidence Peter O'Brien brings forward at least provides us with an inference licence for seeing this passage as the apostle Paul bearing witness to Jesus Christ as *God*. Whether we apply that licence or not is a question I want to return to later in looking at how the Nicean theologians understood 'image' language in its application to Christ.

There are other important exegetical questions. The New Testament contains some sixteen passages where the word *theos* seems to be applied to Jesus. Although direct application is not the only way of explicitly indicating the divinity of Jesus, it is self-evidently a very powerful way. In his book

Jesus as God: The New Testament Use of Theos *in Reference to Jesus*, Murray
Harris has concluded that two of these passages are certain in their application of *theos* to Jesus, four others very probably refer to Jesus as God, while a
seventh probably does. Since an impressive number and range of scholars
recognize between five and ten such ascriptions, and because Harris's
examination is rigorous, we may regard the categorization of the following
seven as conservative: certain, John 1:1; 20:28; very probable, Romans 9:5;
Titus 2:13; Hebrews 1:8; 2 Peter 1:1; probable, John 1:18.[25]

Other questions may be asked about how particular texts are exegeted.
Romans 9:5 ('Christ, who is God over all, blessed for ever') is a case in point.
The United Bible Societies textual commentary on the Greek New Testament
(third edition) points out that structurally, grammatically and syntactically
the Greek ought be punctuated so that *theos* refers to *Christos*. However,
because of a view which the majority of the committee took as to the 'general
tenor of his theology', Paul could not have meant this. One is forced to ask
the editors of the textual commentary whether a construal of theological
development in Paul has greater force than the direct evidence of the text.

I am not here seeking to argue a definitive ruling between disputed interpretations of various Christological texts. Rather, I present the more modest
claim that there appears to be good exegetical ground for observing that in
some places at least, the New Testament directly ascribes full divinity to
Jesus Christ. To use James Dunn's terms, we must reckon with the fact that
while only God may properly be worshipped, in some New Testament
contexts the exalted Christ is not just venerated, but appropriately
worshipped (Rev. 4:1 – 5:14; cf. 19:10; 22:8–9).[26]

What we bring to the text

The second type of question which theologians ask exegetes concerns what
they themselves may bring to the text. Beside the more obvious analytical
tools of New Testament scholarship, what other structures of thought may
be shaping the exegete's approach and conclusions? What is the propriety of
these structures to the text in front of them? Since I have been examining
only a single article by Morna Hooker, any conclusions reached ought to be
seen as very provisional. In what follows I will treat both Hooker's 'Chalcedon and the New Testament' and Wiles's 'Does Christology rest on a
mistake?', since the link between them has been firmly established. Two
observations suggest themselves.

First, how is 'history' evaluated and how does it function? Hooker,
following Wiles, takes it as axiomatic that nowadays most people loose the

biblical teaching on creation and fall from any certain, specific action or actions in history. The argument of both these essays is that the same should be done with the Bible's teaching on the incarnation and 'Godness' of Jesus in particular, and its teaching on redemption in general.[27] In Hooker's essay, this conclusion appears to rely on several assumptions most often associated with 'the Enlightenment'. Paul's teaching is deemed unable to transcend its background, whether that background is clear in the texts or constructed by New Testament scholars on the basis of clues they see in the texts. We are left to ask what, given his background, Paul would have to have written if he wanted to say something *radically* new, in this case that Jesus Christ *is God*. At one level the question is unanswerable, because what we have of Paul is all we have of Paul, and we must make do with that. However, there also seems to be an assumption that God could *not* intervene through specific actions in history to reveal himself in person. This is similar to one of the assumptions behind Hume's radical scepticism, that in coming to a conclusion as to the facticity of Christ's resurrection one is bound on the basis of general historical experience to disbelieve it.[28] But, as Wolfhart Pannenberg has quite rightly insisted, Hume's analogy can only enable us to discern events of a similar kind; it cannot prejudge the historicity of events which are dissimilar.[29] Further, rigorously applied, such use of the analogy destroys all historical work, for history yields its meaning very much from the dissimilarity of events. The biblical accounts purport to be historical, and there are quite clear historical markers around the actual resurrection itself which are open to modern historical investigation, and thus require some assessment of the unique central claim that Jesus Christ rose from the dead.[30] Creation, fall, and redemption in Jesus Christ may be able to rest on certain specific actions in history. We ought not be too quick in using the term 'mythology' to resolve the problem of history.

This brings me to the second observation, the unchallenged 'dualism' which is evident in both these essays. In his work on philosophical theology, T. F. Torrance has extensively criticized the radical dualism which exists in much Enlightenment and post-Enlightenment thought.[31] Particularly relevant is the distinction between *Historie*, the kind of history that is to be interpreted in terms of strict causal connections, and *Geschichte*, the kind of history that is interpreted in terms of how things appear to us, or to the apostle Paul. 'That distinction goes back through Hermann and Kant to Lessing's "ugly big ditch" between the necessary truths of reason and accidental truths of history.'[32] Behind this lies the radical dualism posited by Newton between 'absolute mathematical time' and 'relative apparent time', which issues in a determinist conception of the universe that rules out rational consideration of anything that could not be explained in terms of physical laws.[33] In the same way that the Newtonian conception establishes a radical dualism between empirical events and theoretical constructions of those events, Hooker's appropriation of Wiles's thought establishes an unbridgeable chasm between the New Testament's depiction of the creation and redemption as real *historical* events and their mythological explanation by the Bible writers or ourselves. The use of such a chasm predetermines our evaluation of Christological material.

The problem with this is that it rests, especially in Wiles, on epistemological and cosmological assumptions that have been shown to be deficient. In light of the Einsteinian revolution in physical science, it has been evident that theoretical constructs, the inner rationality of an event or thing, are inherent in the events or things themselves in their appearance towards us. This is now widely accepted. Indeed, Professor Michael Dummest has charged New Testament scholars with a 'fraudulent' handling of the resurrection narratives in the Gospels.[34] However, even before the Einsteinian revolution James Denney made the same point. The theology of the New Testament is no mere epiphenomenon superimposed upon the history (as *Geschichte*), but is part of the chain of cause and effect which prompted all the characters in the story, Jesus too.[35]

This criticism also operates at a deeper level. The Enlightenment dismissal of the possible historicity of the resurrection of Jesus Christ depends on the assumption of a closed instead of an open universe. Yet even David Hume from time to time needed to appeal to an open system;[36] and modern cosmological thought, especially that which takes its rise in physics, is pushed to acknowledge that the universe cannot be adequately explained on the assumption of it being a closed physical system. One must posit a transcendent intelligence.[37] It comes down to whether we believe with Israel that the God who made the heavens and the earth and all that lives therein has, in fact, power over death. If we answer this in the positive, then an incarnation of God is less problematical.

The fathers and the Bible

It is worth pointing out that the early fathers also struggled to overcome dualism, a dualism which was integral to Greek philosophy. They 'struggled' because they saw that the biblical message of God's acts in history, and the nature and being of God it revealed, would be swallowed up or relativized by the dualism which permeated their culture (as had in fact happened in the teaching of Arius). Torrance has pointed out that the 'image' language of the

New Testament in its application to Christ would first of all be understood in the optical terms used by contemporary philosophy to explain their epistemology.[38] It was an explanation of 'image' in terms of the *ho chōrismos* between the real world of 'heavenly ideas' and their unclear earthly counterparts, through which, like the aleatory changes in the shadows of the observers on a cave wall, one can obtain only a very indefinite and fundamentally non-realist knowledge of what was actually true. Words which described the highest form of knowledge or *sapientia* are only signs of signs, *merely* significative.

But in coming to grasp what the New Testament meant by saying that Christ was the very image of God, the fathers departed from their immediate background and fell back on a Hebrew or Old Testament understanding of how God reveals himself. The revelation of God to Moses ('I AM WHO I AM', Exod. 3:14), showed them that only God could name himself, and that such naming was a direct revelation, a first-hand or ostensive sign of the reality it pointed towards. God is in his own being who he says he is. Thus, since God names himself as Father, Son and Holy Spirit, and as Matthew 11:27 makes clear, only God can do this, the person and work of Jesus Christ as 'image' is the first-hand and so personal revelation of God himself. Thus, given that the God of the New Testament is the same as the God of Israel witnessed to in the Old Testament, then not only at Romans 9:5, but also in Colossians 1:15 and Philippians 2:6, one is compelled to exercise the inference licence inherent in these passages in terms of Jesus being not just human, but *God*. In opting to use the Bible in this way, the Nicean theologians were able to operate with fewer, not more, assumptions than was possible from within their Graeco-Roman world. Likewise, it seems to me that in the present day too much contemporary New Testament scholarship has to exercise more assumptions rather than fewer in coming to its conclusions about the meaning of the Christological texts.

The relevance of the Nicean-Constantinoplian proclamation of the uniqueness of Christ for mission today

How may our understanding of the nature of evangelical mission in the world be deepened by Nicean theology?

The scriptural data

The Bible makes it clear that the genesis of our understanding of the doctrines of God and Christ lie in the gospel. Against the idolatry of Israel and her pagan neighbours, God makes himself known in the context of salvation, the coming of his righteous rule (Is. 45:20–23). Further, as promised in the Old Testament, this coming of God's righteous rule which reveals his character is personal: God himself characteristically promises that he himself will come and rescue his people. In Isaiah 40:3–11 (cf. Is. 35:1–10), it is the LORD who is said to be coming, coming with power, and coming to be the shepherd of his flock. The New Testament starts with the observation that it is through and in Jesus Christ, Son of God and Son of David, that this promise and revelation are fulfilled: 'After John was arrested, Jesus came into Galilee, preaching the gospel of God, and saying, "The time is fulfilled, and the kingdom of God is at hand; repent, and believe in the gospel" ' (Mark 1:14–15).

Jesus is characteristically called *ho erchomenos*, the Coming One: 'She said to him, "Yes, Lord, I believe that you are the Messiah, the Son of God, the one coming into the world"' (John 11:27; cf. Matt. 11:3; Luke 7:19–20; Matt. 3:11; Rev. 1:4, 8; 4:8; 11:17). And it was precisely the nature and manner of this fulfilment which led to the Christian confession in the New Testament that (1) 'Jesus is Lord' (Acts 10:36; Rom. 10:9–13; 1 Cor. 12:3; Phil. 2:11; Rev. 17:14; cf. Matt. 12:8; Mark 2:28; Luke 6:5); (2) he is the one who pours out the Spirit (Mark 1:7–8, John 20:19–23; Acts 1:1–5); and (3) he is to be worshipped as God (John 20:11–29; Rom. 9:5; Rev. 4 – 5; cf. 19:10; 22:8–9).

In retrospect, then, four main groups of biblical data lead us to confess with the New Testament church that Jesus Christ, the 'Coming One', is not just pre-eminently messianic Son of God, Son of David, but is himself God:

1. He does the work unique to God: creation, re-creation, judgment and salvation (Mark *passim*; cf. Matt. 1; Eph. 1:20–23; cf. 1 Cor. 15:24–28).

2. He properly bears the ascriptions peculiar to God: 'Wonderful Counsellor', 'Mighty God', 'Everlasting Father', 'Prince of Peace', 'Emmanuel' (Is. 9:6–7; Matt. 1:18–25; Luke 2:8–11); 'the Lord' (Acts 10:36; Rom. 10:9–13; 1 Cor. 12:3; Phil. 2:11; Rev. 17:14; cf. Matt. 12:8; Mark 2:28; Luke 6:5).

3. In the midst of a determinedly monotheistic Jewish culture, where only God can by properly worshipped, he is the object of worship (John 20:11–29; Rom. 9:5; Rev. 4 – 5, cf. 19:10; 22:8–9).

4. At times he is directly designated as God (John 1:1; 20:28; Rom. 9:5; Titus 2:13; Heb. 1:8; 2 Pet. 1:1).[39]

The nature of Christ's uniqueness

Under the impress of this sort of biblical evidence, the ancient catholic church joined with the New Testament in confessing that Jesus Christ, messianic Son of God, Son of David, was himself truly God. Against the pressure of dualism, the mythological and philosophical theism of ancient Greece and Rome, and against the unbelief of the Jews, the creeds of Nicea and Constantinople confessed that Jesus Christ was double *homoousion*, of the same substance with humankind and of the same substance with the Father, truly human and truly God. The eternal and unchanging God himself, the eternal Word of the Father, has entered our space and time, and taken our humanity to himself so that by his incarnation, a life of obedience centred on his death, and by his resurrection and heavenly session, he might redeem us from sin, death, the devil and judgment to be God's own possession, his inheritance, his joy and delight (Eph. 1:14; 1 Pet. 2:9; Deut. 32:9).

That is, our understanding of the uniqueness of Jesus Christ as truly human and truly God – *who he is* – cannot properly be understood apart from *why he came*: to save us poor sinners. Conversely, 'to know *Christ*, is to know his benefits'. On this basis, then, the double *homoousion* and the claim that Jesus is the only way to the Father go together (John 14:6). He who is unique Son of God and truly God is also *inclusively* and *exclusively* the Saviour. In his person and saving work Jesus Christ is *inclusive* of all the creation because he who is the Creator is also the Second Adam, the starting-point of the new humanity, and the Re-creator of the new heavens and the new earth. The scope of the cross and resurrection encompasses the cosmos, so that the apostle Paul can declare that God was in Christ reconciling 'to himself all things, whether on earth or in heaven, making peace by the blood of his cross' (Col. 1:19–20; 2:13–15; 2 Cor. 5:16–21). Further and concomitantly, Jesus Christ is *exclusively* the Saviour, the only way to the Father (John 14:6) because he is God, for it is the constant witness of both the revelation given to Israel and the revelation given to the one new humanity in Christ that *only God* can reveal God and save humanity.

This then is the uniqueness of Jesus Christ, that he is both truly human and truly God, and, as that, he alone is exclusively the Saviour, by an act of sheer grace the saviour of the whole world. Where humankind rebuffs this salvation and this God, and prefers to remain in thrall to sin, death, the devil and ignorance, it is not because Christ in his uniqueness is insufficient, but *because of* that uniqueness; for to reject Christ is to reject God himself and his unconditional grace poured out on us in his Son. To reject such a God and such grace is to choose the impossibly irrational, and to remain self-condemned in our self-referential state (John 3:16–21).

Theological implications of the uniqueness of Christ

The ancient church grasped the biblical insistence that there can be no true knowledge of God without reconciliation. If we who are trapped in our wickedness and sins are to know the Holy One of Israel, we need a reconciling exchange in which our pollution and ignorance are replaced with the righteousness of Christ who is also our light and wisdom (2 Cor. 5:21; John 1:1–18; 1 Cor. 1:30; Col. 2:2–3). In thinking into each other what systematic theology calls 'the person and work of Christ', we come to see that in his uniqueness Jesus Christ gives to all of God's self-revelation its meaning and power.

Three foundational New Testament doctrines thus gain their proper understanding and power on the basis of Christ's uniqueness: the doctrines of the knowledge of God, propitiatory atonement, and the church; all of which impinge directly on mission. Once again, it needs to be emphasized that because 'being' and 'act' are not separated in God, the meaning of these doctrines arises concomitantly with the recognition of who Jesus Christ is and what he has done for us.

Knowledge of God

Against the pressure of Arianism, which asserted that God must be known on the basis of his likely external relations to his creation, the early church reaffirmed that the Son of God is indeed 'of the same substance with the Father'. In doing this they were affirming that God can be properly known *not* on the basis of external relations, but only on the basis of his unique *internal relations*, as Father, Son and Holy Spirit, one God in Trinity. As Hilary of Poitiers was to put it, only God can know God and God can be known only through God. God cannot be known on the basis of human experience and imagining, but only as he sovereignly reveals himself in and through himself, on the basis of the One who is in himself the exact imprint of God's own being (Heb. 1:2–3; 2 Cor. 4:4).

This insight from the nature of the revelation of God in Jesus Christ has enormous consequences. It means that when through the revelation of Jesus Christ we know God as Father, Son and Holy Spirit, we know God as he really is. God really is anteriorly in himself as he is towards us in his Son. When the incarnate Word of God (the 'Revealed God') weeps over Jerusalem (Matt. 23:37–39), God in his eternal majesty ('God concealed') also laments; for whatever Jesus Christ does tells us something of the Father. Further, because Jesus Christ is truly human and truly God, when we 'dwell in him and he in us', then we indeed are partakers of that divine circumincession or perichoresis which constitutes the unity of the three Persons of the Trinity (John 14:8–11; 22–24; 17:20–24). Because Jesus Christ is the unique Son of God who is God, he does indeed lead us to the Father, so that, in the terms of 2 Peter 1:4, while always maintaining our creaturely status, we 'become partakers of the divine nature'. That is, in Duns Scotus' words, we become *fellow-lovers* in the life of the God who is himself love.

However, if Jesus Christ in not unique in that he is both our God and only Saviour, we do not know God as he really is in himself. At best, we can know him only on the basis of some external relation we may posit for him to the world. Theology must then become mythology. At the heart of God would be not the One who is revealed to us in Christ as Father, Son and Spirit, but an absolute mystery. If Jesus Christ is not God, we do not know that God is sovereign in the revelation of himself. Kant and Feuerbach are then correct to claim that all our God-talk is of necessity just talk about ourselves. If Jesus Christ is not 'true God of true God', all our trinitarian talk has lost its rational ground and control. In that way all our talk of perichoresis becomes but an oppressive power-discourse engaged in by religious professionals who will inevitably define perichoresis in our own image and not through the one, true Image of the holy God (cf. 2 Pet. 1:3–9).

Propitiatory atonement

Perhaps at no other place does the fact of the uniqueness of Jesus Christ throw as much light on theology as it does when we think about the meaning of the cross. The uniqueness of Jesus Christ tells us that the propitiatory act of atonement wrought by his incarnation, his life of obedience and especially by his death is in fact an act *in* God himself. The one who 'has borne our sins in his body on a tree' (1 Pet. 2:24–25), and 'become a curse for us' (Gal. 3:13), 'the Judge who has been judged in our place' (to use Karl Barth's felicitous phrase), also reveals by his life and person that the reconciliation wrought by this act of propitiatory atonement not only penetrates to the very depths of *our* being, but also falls within the being and life of God himself.

How is this the case? In what follows I am much indebted to Tom Torrance's extensive treatment of the formula of Nicea-Constantinople and the Bible.[40]

First, because the Father/Son relation subsists eternally within the being and life of God, we must think of the incarnation of the Son as *falling within the being and life of God*. Nevertheless, it is something genuinely 'new' for God.

Secondly, since Jesus Christ is God and human being in one Person, the atoning mediation and redemption which he wrought for us fall *within* his own being and life as the one mediator between God and fallen humankind. The work of atoning salvation does not take place outside of Christ, as something external to him, but takes place *within* him, *within* the incarnate constitution of his person as mediator. Since, to use Athanasius' words, as mediator, Christ acted 'instead of all' (*anti pantōn*) and 'on behalf of all' (*hyper pantōn*), his redemptive work was fully representative and truly universal in its range. The incarnate Logos acts *personally* on our behalf from within the ontological depths of our human existence, which he has penetrated and gathered up into himself. Christ's person and work are inseparably linked. He not only makes our nature his own, but also takes on himself our lost condition subject to condemnation and death, so that he might substitute himself in our place, discharge our debt, take on himself the penalty due to all in death, and offer himself in atoning sacrifice to God on our behalf.

Thirdly, it follows that atonement, as with the incarnation, also falls *within the life and being of God*. In Paul's words, '*God* was in Christ reconciling the world to himself' (2 Cor. 5:19; cf. Phil. 2:5–11; Heb. 5:7; Rom. 8:32). That is, the atoning propitiation which God himself provides in the sacrifice of his incarnate Son occurs *not external* to God, but *within* God. In this way, the *homoousion* of Nicea gives expression to the unbroken relation in being and act between the incarnate Son and God the Father, and likewise between the Holy Spirit and God the Father.

Thus, we can rightly understand the meaning of the atonement as it occurs between God and us poor sinners only in the light of the fact that it is first an act within Christ himself, and thus within God. This theological and ontological priority gives us the ground against which the meaning of our reconciliation becomes clear. To separate our reconciliation from this theological and ontological ground inevitably produces distortions.

Positively, this ontological deepening of our understanding produces several beneficial insights.

1. We are spared a superficial socio-moral or judicial transaction between God and humankind which does not penetrate into the ontological depths of human being and bear savingly on our deep corruption and distortion.

2. Union with God in and through Jesus Christ, who is of one and the same being with God, belongs to the inner heart of the atonement.

3. It overcomes the moral problem of how one person can take the place of another in bearing moral responsibility for the other's actions. The inexplicable fact that God in Christ has taken our place raises questions larger

and deeper than those we often ask. God in Christ acting in redemption helps us to recognize that the *whole moral order itself*, as we know it in this world, needed to be redeemed and set on a new basis. Redemption is indeed of those 'under the law', but it occurs 'apart from the law' (Gal. 4:3–4; Rom. 3:20–21). As Torrance puts is: 'In this interlocking of incarnation and atonement, and indeed of creation and redemption, there took place what might be called "a soteriological suspension of ethics" in order to regroup the whole moral order in God himself.'[41] That is, the forensic elements are held within the doctrine of atonement in a more profound way.

4. The incarnation ensures a more extensive 'substitution' than is usually recognized. 'The whole Christ became a curse for us' (Athanasius). All of Christ's life is atoning. Since atonement was *in* Christ himself and not in some external way, the whole person, body and soul, is delivered from penalty, debt, ignorance, law, death and the devil. In this way, then, the image of God is restored, and we come to know God. In the self-sanctification of the Son of God, we are sanctified (John 17:17–19).

5. Against their internal ontological ground in Jesus Christ, we can view the various aspects of the biblical presentation – deliverance, propitiation and expiation, and advocacy – not only as interrelated concepts speaking of the love of God and the riches and depths of our reconciliation, but also in a way which avoids the intrusion of secular concepts which tend to take over when the atonement is seen primarily as an external transaction. Thus, early fathers such as Irenaeus have no concept of a 'ransom' paid to the devil. By way of contrast, Gregory of Nyssa explained the notion of 'sacrifice' too narrowly as purification, and gave insufficient attention to the gravity of guilt. The moral requirements of God's nature highlight the propitiatory and expiatory nature of the atonement. Given these, Gregory of Nyssa may well have avoided the morally repugnant concept of a ransom being paid to the devil.

6. The notion of the great, atoning exchange (2 Cor. 8:9) is shown to embrace the whole relationship between Christ and ourselves. We are caught up in a transforming consecration into Christ himself and into the immediate presence of the Father. In this, (1) we see that the benefits of the exchange are inexhaustible and eternal. (2) Our passion, hurt and suffering are taken up by God in his measureless love and compassion, and consequently they are exhausted in his divine impassibility. Likewise, our ignorance is transformed by our participating in his wisdom. (3) The atoning exchange means our *theopoiēsis* ('divinization'), in which the ontological differentiation between God and humankind is not confused, but our lost humanity is re-created 'to enjoy a new fullness of human life in a blessed

communion with the divine life'.[42] In this, the Holy Spirit is mediated to us through the humanity of Christ, so that we may be sanctified (John 17; 20:19–23). In the receiving of the Spirit by Christ in his self-sanctification *for* us and in his subsequent giving of the Spirit *to* us, we see the atonement operating in the depths of human being.[43]

However, if Christ is *not* truly human and truly God, the act of atonement he wrought is an act *external* to God. 'Propitiation' will then either be dismissed as mythological language, or it will suffer distortion by being subjected to the unbending strictures of an Aristotelian-Ciceronian definition of human justice. If Christ is not the unique Son of God who is himself God, his sacrifice will dissolve into mere example; representation into mere empathy; victory over sin, death, the devil and alienation into, at best, a pluralism of beliefs and lifestyles in which the Christian church must make the best account of itself it can, or at worst, into mere relativism.

The church

Because Jesus Christ is *homoousion* with us and with God, the church, which is his body and over which he is the head, truly participates in the life of God himself. The assertion at 1 Corinthians 12:27 that 'you are the body of Christ' exists in the context of the declaration in verse 12 that it is not so much that Christ *has* a body as that he *is* a body. As John Calvin puts it, by faith we are so united to him in his body that Christ deems himself, so to speak, as incomplete without us. Further, as head of his own body, Christ takes up the whole church, both the earthly and the heavenly reality, into himself, and thus into a holy and living fellowship with the Father. In this way, in all our churchly existence and activities, the earthly church is rightly a corporate participant in the eternal love of the Father, a society of fellow-lovers with the Father through the Son and in the Spirit (Heb. 12:18–24; cf. 2 Cor. 8:1–9).

However, if Jesus Christ is *not* the unique Son of God who is himself God, then the existence and nature of the church are not an act in God but something *external* to himself. We no longer are the holy fellowship of the firstborn brought to the Father, but are merely another religious society among many, the corporate expression of a religion among the religions.

Conclusion

As I read the writings of the apologists and church fathers, although arguably at times too many concessions are made to their surrounding culture, I am impressed at the sheer boldness and joy of their belief in the uniqueness of Christ as truly human and truly God, the exclusive and universal Saviour. For them the uniqueness of Christ was not in a modern sense a problem to be solved, but a truth to be understood and proclaimed; *the* truth which liberates us from the viciousness of immoral lifestyles as it at the same time peels back the darkness of our minds and brings us into the joyful presence of the living God. Further, they used ontological categories such as the double *homoousion* not as a springboard for arid ontological speculation but to recognize that in God's mission in the world, God in Christ was himself the agent. God is personal in all his works, and for that reason the scope of Christian mission is universal, and the change it brings and promises is quite literally a new creation, not merely a subjective transformation produced in the pious the meaning of which has to be articulated by and limited to the language of religious experience.[44]

Notes

1. E.g. Kaufman, *Systematic Theology*, pp. 187–189; Wiles, 'Christology'. In his own way, Jürgen Moltmann is an appreciative critic who has sought through his eschatological and Hegelian reflection to give a more acceptable understanding of both the intent and content of these creeds; see Moltmann, *The Way*, pp. 4, 46–55. Likewise Macquarie is a critic who seeks to reinterpret Nicene concepts into more contemporary terms; Macquarie, *Jesus Christ*, pp. 165–167, 382–386.
2. There is much written on this, e.g. Knitter & Hick, *Myth*; Vanhoozer, *Trinity*.
3. Hooker, 'Chalcedon', pp. 73–93. In measured fashion, Dunn, *Theology*, pp. 204–206, 252–260, 292–293.
4. Hooker, 'Chalcedon', p. 73.
5. Ibid., p. 74.
6. Ibid., p. 76.
7. Ibid., p. 79.
8. Ibid., pp. 80–81.
9. Ibid., p. 82.
10. Ibid., p. 85.
11. Wiles, 'Christology', pp. 122–131.
12. Hooker, 'Chalcedon', pp. 87–88.
13. Ibid., p. 88.
14. Ibid., p. 89.
15. Wiles, 'Christology', pp. 127–131, where he develops the 'specialness of Jesus' along positive lines.
16. Hooker, 'Chalcedon', p. 99.
17. O'Brien, *Colossians*, p. 40.
18. Ibid., pp. 43–44.
19. Ibid., pp. 51–53.
20. Ibid., pp. 111.
21. Ibid., p. 112.
22. O'Brien, *Philippians*, pp. 210–211.
23. Ibid., p. 216.

24. Hooker, 'Chalcedon', p. 88.
25. Harris, *Jesus*, pp. 271–273, and p. 274, n. 2.
26. Dunn, *Theology*, pp. 257–260.
27. Wiles, 'Christology', pp. 123–126; Hooker, 'Chalcedon', pp. 88–91.
28. Hume can be understood as part of a cycle of 'optimism' and 'scepticism' long existent in western thought; see Ovey, 'Augustine', pp. 134–148.
29. See Pannenberg, *Basic Questions* 1, pp. 44–50; and his *Systematic Theology* 2, pp. 359–363.
30. Doyle, *Eschatology*, pp. 50–51.
31. E.g. Torrance, *Theological Science*, and, more recently, *Preaching Christ*.
32. Torrance, *Preaching Christ*, pp. 4–5.
33. Ibid.
34. Ibid., p. 9.
35. Caird, 'Biblical classics', pp. 196–199.
36. Hume must assume a closed and rational system for his dismissal of miracles, and an open one in order to uphold Newtonian science and human moral experience. At a deeper level though, Hume is acutely aware that if, as he does, we deny that causation is rational or true, then far from having a closed system, we have no 'system'. To give Newtonian science a place he must invoke 'a trivial property of the fancy', a 'trivial property' which, although unsupported by reason, is necessary. That is, he strongly argues on *pragmatic* grounds that we cannot live in the world his philosophy has constructed, acknowledging that 'Nature is always too strong for principle'. Questions of the moral nature of human existence, of ultimate meaning and the reliability of empirical science, i.e. common sense, force Hume to acknowledge the limits of his radical empiricism. See his *Human Nature* 1, pp. 178–179, 252–255; and *Enquiries*, p. 160.
37. For example, Paul Davies argues that the rules of physics 'look *as if* they are the product of intelligent design. I do not see how that can be denied.' However, he is wary of being able rationally to construct a unitary theory of physics and metaphysics which would account for everything in 'a complete and self-consistent explanation'. See his *Mind*, pp. 214, 226, 231. From within a Christian tradition of physicists, Polkinghorne, *Science*, pp. 1–3, points out that quantum theory and the existence and operation of complex dynamical theories quash the notion of a closed mechanistic universe in favour of an open process where the physical and metaphysical are related.
38. T. F. Torrance, *Trinitarian Faith*, pp. 68–75.
39. See Harris, *Jesus*, pp. 271–273, and p. 274, n.2.
40. Torrance, *Trinitarian Faith*, pp. 154–90, and *Mediation*, pp. 109–126.
41. Torrance, *Trinitarian Faith*, p. 160.
42. Ibid., p. 189.
43. Ibid., p. 190.
44. My debt to Peter O'Brien is personal as well as theological, but in the latter at least he has constantly modelled the truth that the pathway through Holy Scripture to its Author is one of patient and careful exegesis. *Deo soli gloria!*

24. The missionary apostle and modern systematic affirmation

Mark D. Thompson

For whatever was written in former days was written for our instruction, that by steadfastness and by the encouragement of the Scriptures we might have hope (Rom. 15:4 RSV).

Paul, the apostle to the Gentiles, formerly known as Saul of Tarsus, is responsible for thirteen epistles in the New Testament.[1] In each case the letter arises from his missionary activity in the eastern Mediterranean in the middle decades of the first century. In a very real sense Paul's epistles are occasional documents, written into specific situations and often in response to particular questions (see e.g. 1 Cor. 7:1; 8:1; 12:1; 16:1). As such, they bear the marks of their historical location, including greeting-lists (e.g. Rom. 16:3–16; Col. 4:10–15; 2 Tim. 4:19–21; Philem. 23–24), references to difficulties in the churches to which they are written (e.g. Rom. 14:1 – 15:7; 16:17–19; 1 Cor. 1:10–17; 4:6–21; 5:1–13; 11:17–22; Phil. 4:2–3) and incidental comments about Paul, his readers, or others known to them (e.g. Rom. 15:15–33; 1 Cor. 2:1–5; 3:1–4; 16:15–18; 2 Cor. 1:15–24; 8:16–24; Gal. 6:11; Eph. 6:21–22; Phil. 4:10–19; Col. 4:7–9; 1 Tim. 1:20; 2 Tim. 4:9–18; Titus 3:12–14; Philem. 22). Though on one celebrated occasion Paul encourages his readers to pass his letter on to others and to read a letter he had addressed to others (Col. 4:16; cf. 1 Thess. 5:27), for the most part his epistles are not self-evidently open-ended in their address.

However, for all of this historicality, modern systematic theology, particularly evangelical systematic theology, makes frequent use of Paul's letters in its statements of Christian belief at the beginning of the third millennium. Indeed, a number of important Christian doctrines have some of their most significant biblical anchors within the pages of the Pauline corpus: for example, the wrath of God (Rom. 1:18–32); justification by faith (Rom. 3:21 – 4:25; Gal. 2:11 – 4.31); the resurrection of the body (1 Cor. 15:1–58; 1 Thess. 4:13 – 5:11); the return of Christ (1 Thess. 4:13 – 5:11; 2 Thess. 1:3 – 2:12); the nature of the pastoral ministry (Eph. 4:1–16; 1 Tim.; 2 Tim.; Titus), and the nature and use of Scripture (2 Tim. 3:1–17). It is not too much to say that Pauline terminology and argument have dominated Protestant theology since Luther made his critical discovery in the midst of exegetical explorations of Romans 1:16–17 around 1518.[2] However, modern Roman Catholic theology also continues to affirm a place for Paul's ideas in the shaping of the Christian tradition.[3]

The question which this paper addresses is that of how, and on what basis, one is able to move from these seemingly occasional documents written by one man in the first century to affirmations of truth for the whole world in the twenty-first. While this is very much an open question for many today,[4] the particularity of the Pauline epistles and the tension it generates in any theology derived from them is not simply a modern preoccupation. A concern to emphasize the 'catholicity' of Paul's letters has characterized Christian exposition of them from the earliest days, as Nils Dahl observed in 1962:

> The particularity of the Pauline Epistles was felt as a problem from a time before the *Corpus Paulinum* was published and until it had been incorporated into a complete canon of New Testament Scriptures. Later on, the problem was no longer felt, but the tendency towards generalizing interpretation has remained, not only when the Epistles were used as dogmatic proof-texts, but also when they served as sources for reconstruction of a general 'biblical theology' or a system of 'paulinism'. Even 'existential interpretation' and the approach of 'Heilsgeschichte' may lead to similar consequences.[5]

However, despite the fact that our question would seem to be a perennial one, it is fair to say that the current debates over the status and function of Scripture in modern theology have given it a new urgency.

In what follows we will deal with two aspects of this question. The first concerns the nature of the Pauline materials themselves. What is it about

Paul's writings that set them apart from other letters in the first century? Are there any clues to what Paul thought he was doing as he wrote to the churches within his missionary orbit? Indeed, how important is this missionary context for understanding his letters? After exploring such questions from the viewpoint of Paul's apostleship, we will turn our attention to the second aspect of the question, the broader issues surrounding the use of any scriptural text in modern systematic theology. This will involve asking just what is the nature and function of Christian doctrine as well as what constraints are to be observed in articulating and defending it. The essay will end by making a series of proposals for the practice of theology at the beginning of a new century.

Paul's apostolic authority

In nine out of the thirteen epistles bearing his name, Paul identifies himself as an *apostolos Christou Iēsou*. His apostleship is critical to his self-understanding and the authority that has attached to his letters ever since they were first written. The use of such a theologically laden term as *apostolos*[6] was meant to emphasize Paul's unique relationship to the *mystērion*, the open secret of God's plan to unite Jew and Gentile in salvation through Christ (Eph. 3:1-7; Rom. 9 – 11).[7] As the risen and ascended Christ made clear to Ananias soon after the Damascus road incident, Paul was 'a chosen instrument (*skeuos eklogēs*) ... to carry [the Lord's] name before the nations and kings and the sons of Israel' (Acts 9:15). His specific mission to the nations, as well as his absence from the earthly ministry of Jesus and his earlier career as a persecutor of the church, certainly marked Paul out as distinct from the Twelve (including Matthias) mentioned in Acts 1:12-26.[8] Questions about his standing as an apostle were pointedly raised from time to time. Nevertheless, Paul vigorously defended his place in the purposes of God, most notably in Galatians:

> Those, I say, who were of repute added nothing to me; but on the contrary, when they saw that I had been entrusted with the gospel to the uncircumcised (*pepisteumai to euangelion tēs akrobystias*), just as Peter had been entrusted with the gospel to the circumcised (for he who worked through Peter for the mission to the circumcised worked through me also for the nations (*energēsen kai emoi eis ta ethnē*), and when they perceived the grace that was given to me, James and Cephas, and John, who were reputed to be pillars, gave to me and Barnabas the right hand of fellowship, that we should go to the nations

and they to the circumcised; only they would have us remember the poor, which very thing I was eager to do (Gal. 2:7–10 rsv).

It is evident that Paul understood his *apostolē* in terms of both authority and responsibility. Its unique authority arose from its origin in a personal commission from the risen Lord Jesus Christ and that commission itself functions within the broader framework of God's eternal purposes.[9] However long it may have taken Paul to put the pieces together after the incident on the Damascus road, by the time he wrote to the Galatians he had come to realize that God had set him apart *ek koilias mētros mou* ('from my mother's womb') for a particular task (Gal. 1:15). The allusion to the Septuagint text of Isaiah 49:5 (*ho plasas me ek kolias doulon eautō*) and Jeremiah 1:5 (*pro tou me plasai se en kolia epistamai se kai pro tou se exelthein ek mētras hēgiaka se*) is both patent and significant.[10] Paul's apostolic commission is to be understood on analogy with the divine commissioning of the great Old Testament prophets. His proclamation of the gospel and its implications is to be understood as authoritative on analogy with their utterances.[11] Paul's ministry as apostle to the nations is as vital for the furtherance of God's purposes under the new covenant as the ministry of the prophets was critical for life under the old covenant (2 Cor. 3 – 4). It cannot be dismissed as merely transitory or contingent. However, there is more. Both Galatians 1:15 and the Old Testament texts to which it alludes speak of the salvation of the nations.[12] As the programmatic appeal to Joel 2 on the day of Pentecost makes clear, this is an activity of the last days. Paul's commission to carry the gospel to the nations thus takes on a decided eschatological flavour. The ultimate meaning of the prophetic hope of *phōs ethnōn* ('a light of the nations') now at last comes into view through Paul's own missionary activity. The gospel of the kingdom must indeed be preached *en holē tē oikoumenē* ('in all the world') as the critical precursor to the end and Paul has a unique role to play.[13] Paul's commission designated him as a key agent in the progress of salvation history. In such a context the urgency and authority of his message becomes apparent.

Yet Paul preached and wrote, not only as a way of exercising his apostolic authority, but as a means of discharging his apostolic responsibility towards the Gentile churches. Nowhere is this sense of responsibility clearer than in the opening chapter of the epistle to the Romans:

I am under obligation (*opheiletēs eimi*) both to Greeks and to barbarians, both to the wise and to the foolish: so I am eager to preach the gospel to you also who are in Rome. For I am not ashamed of the gospel: it is the power of God for salvation to every one who has faith, to the Jew first and also to the Greek (Rom. 1:14–17 RSV).

His commission to preach the gospel, and indeed the content of that gospel itself, puts Paul under an obligation and at the same time gives him the courage to persist against all kinds of opposition. His letters, whether to congregations or to individuals, are part of his discharge of that apostolic obligation, expounding the gospel, pressing home its implications, and defending it against the assault of false teaching.[14] Paul's missionary activity does not simply end when men and women turn from idols to serve the true and living God and as a result Christian congregations are established. His goal is the maturity of those within his missionary orbit. When Paul informs the Roman Christians of his desire that *hē prosfora tōn ethnōn* ('the offering of the Gentiles') might be acceptable and sanctified, he does so as part of his explanation for discharging his apostolic responsibility through the writing of an epistle (Rom. 15:15–16).

This brief discussion of Paul's understanding of his *apostolē* bears directly upon our central question of the use of his missionary writings in modern systematic theology. The appeal of the Pauline epistles to apostolic authorship represents a significant qualification of their occasional character. They are certainly not ahistorical. They self-evidently arise within particular situations, and those situations must be appreciated if we are to deal with the text of Paul's letters responsibly. In particular, the missionary context we have noted above is critical for understanding Paul's priorities, line of argument, and conclusions.[15] Paul's apostolic commission demands that we recognize that his letters derive ultimately from the risen Lord and are thus eschatologically positioned, not just historically located. As Paul wrote or dictated his epistles, he was doing much more than simply sharing his experiences or even using the Old Testament to construct 'an argument in support of what on the basis of his missionary experience he thought was right'.[16] He was fulfilling his commission as a spokesman for the risen Christ, conveying the address of God to men and women in the last days. His epistles to individuals and congregations caught up in the great eschatological ingathering of the nations are part of the final act of divine self-revelation before the end.[17] This is why, for all the incidental and occasional remarks, his words, arguments, and overall theological perspective cannot be confined to the immediate situations he faced in the mid-first century Mediterranean region. The continuing relevance and authority of Paul's epistles are tied to his particular role in the purposes of God.

That is not to say that these implications of the eschatological dimension to Paul's missionary activity have always been appreciated within the Christian church. If they had been, early Christian theologians may not have felt the same need to demonstrate 'the catholicity of the Pauline epistles' in other ways. Some attempted to account for the relevance of the Pauline texts beyond their immediate situation by highlighting the fact that Paul, like John in Revelation 2 – 3, wrote to seven churches and so symbolically to the whole church.[18] Of course, this argument later became problematic when the Epistle to the Hebrews was added to the list of those attributed to Paul. Other early Christians resorted to textual emendation to make the same point. For example, some of the earliest witnesses to the text of Ephesians 1:1 omit the words *en Ephesō*. Was this an early attempt to 'catholicize' that epistle by removing the one feature which tied it to a particular situation? Some modern investigations have pointed to a similar critical omission of the words *en Rhōmē* in Romans 1:7 and *tois en Rhōmē* in Romans 1:15. Perhaps the same concern explains what some see as the insertion of the words *syn pasin tois epikaloumenois to onoma tou kyriou hēmōn Iēsou Christou en panti topō* ('with all those who call on the name of our Lord Jesus Christ in every place') in 1 Corinthians 1:2.[19] It may no longer be possible to establish conclusively the precise circumstances which generated these textual variants. However, together with the evidence of patristic statements about the significance of the number of Pauline epistles, they would seem to suggest that the question of catholicity was an important one even in the early centuries. Dahl has identified 'a marked contrast between the orthodox authors, who stress the catholicity of the Pauline epistles, and the Marcionite prologues, which show much more interest for the historic origin of each letter in Paul's conflict with false apostles'.[20]

It is Paul's apostolic commission which sets his epistles apart from other letters in the first century. As letters of an apostle, indeed the apostle to the nations, they are placed alongside the other apostolic documents and continue to exercise a unique and normative role in the church of Jesus Christ. The Pauline epistles should not be viewed as simply some of the earliest 'unchallengeable instances' of gospel-speaking.[21] In and through their undoubted particularity the risen Christ continues to address his people.

The place of Scripture in systematic theology

In the modern climate such an appeal to the Pauline epistles – indeed to any portion of Scripture – as normative revelation is liable to be regarded as simplistic. Some suspect it implies a doctrine of divine inspiration that is mechanical and superstitious, as well as a hermeneutic that is, frankly, naïve.[22] It is frequently presented as the last refuge of the insecure, who avoid the dynamic and precarious nature of Christian faith and life and seek certainty rather than truth. A recent article has suggested that even the modern shift away from the term 'Christian doctrine' towards the more fashionable 'systematic theology' arises at least partly from concern that the prior term suggests 'a body of teaching conveyed either authoritatively, ahistorically even, as a given and changeless totality'.[23]

Instead of this kind of direct appeal, a less direct one is preferred: Scripture provides us with a starting-point or backdrop to our modern exploration of the truth of the Christian gospel. Robert Jenson makes a similar point in his recent *Systematic Theology*: 'Theology, as we have seen, may be described as the historically continuing discussion and debate internal to the mission of the gospel. Apostolic theology is the founding beginning of this discussion.'[24]

There can be no doubt that Jenson considers Scripture to be important and even that it operates as, in some sense, normative within his theology. However, he insists that 'Scripture becomes theology's norm only mediately'.[25] We must take seriously the fact that the canon of Scripture is a dogmatic decision of the church, implying – indeed requiring – the antecedent authorities of ministry and creed (*regula fidei*). The personal appeal of the earliest Christians to the gospel witness of the apostles was over time translated into a conviction that their literary remains provide access to the authentic message which was constitutive for the Christian mission and so for the churches. Such a perspective insists we recognize the New Testament as a collection of documents 'in which to see how the church spoke the gospel while the church's reliance on the apostles was not yet problematic'.[26] The task of theology is, therefore, to further the continuing practice of articulating that gospel whose beginnings are documented in the apostolic writings. This will not necessarily involve reproducing the words or arguments of the apostles; after all, their writings are not 'the best thought-out instances of gospel-speaking', simply 'the unchallengeable instances'.[27] Indeed, others argue there may be times when we must insist upon the freedom to disagree with the biblical text in the name of the gospel.[28] Modern Christian theology, according to this model, is properly understood as a commitment to the same interpretive conversation begun by the apostles: an exploration of the Jewish biblical and theological traditions in the light of the life, teaching and fate of Jesus of Nazareth, and vice versa.[29]

Here we arrive at the nub of the problem. Modern systematic theology often pits exploration against reiteration, conversation against proclamation.[30] When this is done, the apostolic writings are allowed to operate only as the earliest stages in that exploration and conversation. They may have set the agenda, but they do not necessarily continue to dominate the ensuing discussion.[31] Modern theological formulation has an integrity of its own, with a licence for creative improvization within the overall trajectory suggested by its orthodox antecedents.[32] The reasoning behind this position is simple and straightforward. It is the Enlightenment, we are told, that makes this our only option. Since the Enlightenment it is no longer possible to make a direct appeal to Scripture as divine revelation.[33] Critical study of the Bible has ruled this out by progressively raising questions about the historicity, coherence and relevance of its contents.[34] Much has been written about, for instance, the coherence of thought across the Pauline corpus.[35] Today it is the humanity of the biblical text which is firmly in the foreground, and a charge of docetism is levelled at those who appeal to divine inspiration or the self-revelatory activity of God. The most that can be conceded is what Karl Barth called *die Indirektheit der Identität von Offenbarung und Bibel.*[36]

A more radical approach has been suggested by Maurice Wiles. His ringing endorsement of critical biblical scholarship borders on positivism: 'There are no objective criteria that can justify our treating the scriptural writings as if they were distinctive; to treat them in that way is only possible on the basis of an "as if".'[37] This leads him to suggest that modern theology needs to renounce 'the probative employment of the Bible'. Indeed, the term 'authority' itself must be considered inexpedient. It is far better and will prove far more productive 'to see scripture as an indispensable resource rather than as a binding authority'.[38] Wiles explains what he means by drawing on John Barton's answer to the question 'What is the Bible?':

First, it is the primary and in many cases the only historical evidence for the events that lie at the source of Christian faith. Second, it is a collection of theological reflections from the classic periods in which Jewish and Christian faith were forming, the earliest records we have from that long and unbroken chain of those who have reflected on the God in whom Jews and Christians believe – his actions, his character, and his demands. Third, it is a body of literature whose power to inform the lives of those who read it is amply attested in many ages. These are the positive aspects of the Bible which are lost sight of as soon as debate begins to circle round the small and sterile issue of whether 'biblical teaching' is *binding*, and the Bible begins to be treated as a kind of digest of essential rules, like the Highway Code, in neglect of its true character as literature. These three aspects provide more than enough justification for taking the Bible seriously.[39]

For Barton, Wiles, and many others, contemporary 'resurgent biblicism' is founded on a double misunderstanding: a faulty view of Scripture and a consequently erroneous theological method.[40]

It is evident that neither the proposal of Jenson nor that of Barton and Wiles is capable of doing justice to the place of the apostle Paul in the purposes of God, as briefly outlined in the first section of this paper. In the first place, Paul was most definitely not commissioned to begin a conversation or to provide a resource for future theological reflection.[41] His life was turned around on the Damascus road, and he became an ambassador of the living God, addressing the nations on behalf of God (2 Cor. 5:20). What is more, Paul himself did not see a qualitative difference between his personal teaching ministry and his letters (2 Thess. 2:15). His words, whether spoken or written, carry the authority of the one who had commissioned him, an authority that later theological reflection does not share. Paul's letters have an eschatological context and not simply an historical one. These are the words by which the divinely appointed apostle to the nations addresses men and women in the last days concerning the gospel and its implications. Whatever other particularity may attach to them, they have a unique role in the eschatological ingathering of the nations.

Herein lies a second inadequacy in many modern theologies. They frequently fail to realize that Paul writes to *our* situation. We too are people of the last days, and our common eschatological position with his first readers underlines the truth that these words of Paul are the word of God to us. Of course, the twenty-first century is significantly different from the first. The cultural and intellectual challenges to the gospel in our own time comes from quarters our forebears could hardly have imagined. Conversely, the earliest Christians faced particular struggles that were later resolved in one way or another. Nevertheless, in the later terms of God's eternal purposes we, like they, stand between the ascension and the promised return of the Lord. The context of our Christian thought and life is similarly the eschatological ingathering of the nations. Among other things this means we must test our proclamation of the gospel, our reflection upon its implications, and our lives lived as gospel people against a responsible reading of the words of Scripture, not least among them the words of Christ's apostle.[42] Paul's consuming passion to see men and women saved was not simply a personal matter associated with his peculiar role in the purposes of God; it was something he sought to foster in his readers in view of the age in which we live.[43]

Perhaps it is true that current debates about the function of Scripture in systematic theology arise mostly from a concern to acknowledge both the relevance of Scripture to the task and the need for an interpretation of the teaching of Scripture which is intelligible and credible at our own point within the last days. Certainly only the most extreme proposals suggest that Scripture has no place at all in modern theological formulation. However, many contributions demonstrate a profound inadequacy at this most basic level. Theologians today are often unable to move with ease between the Bible and a current restatement of its teaching because of an a priori commitment to understanding its writers as merely human witnesses to God's revelation. An emphasis on the particularity and humanity of the biblical writings frequently obscures dimensions explicitly affirmed by the Bible writers themselves, including the divine commission which imbues them with authority and their eschatological context.

An agenda for modern systematic theology

In conclusion, and as a contribution to the contemporary discussion on the place of Scripture – in particular the place of the apostle Paul – in modern systematic theology, I offer briefly the following seven observations. None of them is novel or original. Taken together, however, they may well lead to a renaissance of truly biblical systematic theology in this new century.

1. *Modern systematic theology needs a new appreciation of the living God as one who speaks.* Theology is impoverished when it fails to recognize that God has spoken and his speech must take priority over our own. The Christian God is not only *Deus volens* and *Deus agens*, but also *Deus loquens*.[44] In some circles it is almost axiomatic that God reveals himself in action and that this revelation is to be distinguished from the human reflection upon its meaning and significance which we find in the Bible. Scripture might operate as a witness to God's revelation, but its essentially verbal or propositional character (though expressed in a variety of genres) precludes us from speaking of it as itself revelation.[45] Others speak of revelation through symbols, which, though largely found in Scripture, require translation at the hands of theologians.[46] The symbols themselves are 'signs imbued with a plenitude or depth of meaning that surpasses the capacities of conceptual thinking and propositional speech'.[47] In most quarters there is a comprehensive rejection of 'propositional revelation'.[48] However, in its haste to

distance itself from the scholastic theology of the late sixteenth and seventeenth centuries, modern systematic theology may well have thrown out the baby with the bathwater. There is much wisdom in this simple observation by Broughton Knox from 1960:

> What is it then, that makes the tribal migrations of the Israelites pregnant with revelation throughout the Old and New Testaments, while those of their related tribe, the Syrians, reveal only one fact of God's general providence to which Amos alludes (Amos 9:7)? Similarly, why are the invasions of neighbouring countries by the Assyrians, and the fate that overtook the Assyrians, revelational of God's character (Isaiah 10), while the inter-tribal warfare of, say, the Maoris is not? It is not as though God's sovereign control is exercised any the more over the one, or any the less over the other, of these different events; but simply that to the one have been added interpretive propositions and statements, but not to the other. It is the proposition which carries the revelation, giving meaning to the event, to our minds. The event, by itself, reveals nothing. The conclusion is that revelation is essentially propositional.[49]

Perhaps it is time the doctrine of the word of God, so dominant a theme in Barth's theology, was revisited with serious attention to the importance of words and even propositions for personal relationships, the significance of the speaking and hearing dynamic for the nature of God's dealings with his creation, and God's own initiative in giving his word a written form.

2. *Modern systematic theology needs a new appreciation of Scripture as the speech-act of God.* The application of the speech-act philosophy of John Searle and John Langshaw Austin to the question of divine revelation and especially the doctrine of Scripture may prove fruitful in overcoming the antithesis between personal and propositional revelation.[50] A number of important studies have begun to probe the possibilities.[51] The charge of bibliolatry sometimes levelled at those who appeal to the words of Scripture is hard to sustain when one appreciates that Scripture does not exist in isolation or in competition with God's own person or work in the world. To take God's communicative act seriously is to take God himself seriously, not to replace him with a book.[52] Further, this speech-act model allows us to give due recognition to the variety of genres within the Bible. Speech acts come in differing types: promises, commands, descriptions, arguments, expressions of desire, and many others. Differences of genre within the biblical materials do not necessarily suggest different degrees of authority or

different levels of divine involvement with the text. Finally, speech-act theory, with its distinctions between locution, illocution and perlocution, may even allow for a more trinitarian appreciation of Scripture than has characterized some modern treatments.[53]

3. *Modern systematic theology needs a new appreciation of the role of the human authors of the New Testament as uniquely commissioned spokesmen of the risen Christ.* This has been the primary burden of our discussion in this essay. The apostle Paul did not see himself as providing merely human commentary on the events of Jesus' life in the light of the Hebrew Scriptures. Nor was this the understanding of the other apostles who have contributed to the New Testament (2 Pet. 3:14–16; 1 John 4:4–6). Their unique commission invested their writing – as it did their preaching – with a particular authority tied to their distinctive role in the eternal purposes of God. In fact, their writing even enabled the Old Testament to be seen in its proper light as preparation for and predictive of the Christ who has now been identified as Jesus of Nazareth.[54] The eschatological framework into which both Testaments are now properly set ensures that the genuine particularity of each component is respected without insisting that the relevance of each part of Scripture be confined to its original audience. Furthermore, such a perspective will not allow the Scriptures to be treated as simply one early voice among many others. There is a qualitative difference between the Gospels, the epistles of Paul or Peter or John, or the Old Testament canon to which they appeal, and the writing of others through the centuries, no matter how orthodox or how insightful they may have been.

4. *Modern systematic theology needs a new appreciation of its task as proclaiming and explaining the self-revelation of God in Scripture into the context of our contemporary world.* Contrary to some of the suggestions we have canvassed above, it is time to reaffirm that systematic theology is first and foremost a means of preaching the gospel of Jesus Christ. This is not to deny that theology may indeed perform other functions, for instance providing a sense of community identity, transposing the scriptural narrative into concepts, or making sense of Christian experience (in both its individual and corporate forms).[55] However, systematic theology exists to serve the preaching of Christ's gospel in today's world. Reiteration of the biblical material cannot, therefore, be dismissed as unimportant even if it is not all that is to be said about the task of theology. An understanding of those influences which shape the contemporary context into which the gospel word is spoken (among Christians and in the world at large) remains important. So too does a thoughtful engagement with those who have gone before us – after all, we are not the first to open the Scriptures or the first to

seek to explain them to others. An ability to discern the cutting edge of Christian theology, those points at which it most directly challenges and critiques contemporary thinking and living, is particularly valuable. Yet all of these things serve the basic task of proclaiming and explaining the self-revelation of God in Scripture for the edification of God's people and the rescue of men and women in the world.

There is another implication of this basic relationship between theology and preaching which has been best appreciated by some in the Lutheran tradition. If the proclamation of the gospel to the world is the end served by the task of systematic theology, then this end must to some extent shape the task of systematic theology itself. Systematic theology does not exist for its own sake, a kind of intellectual self-indulgence by those who happen to enjoy playing with religious ideas. It needs the focus and discipline which a concern for public proclamation of the Word of God provides. Here is a valuable lesson from the past which we have too often overlooked. Some of the most profound and influential theologians from the last two thousand years – such as Augustine, Luther, Calvin and Barth – have been preachers driven from the pulpit to the study and vice versa. Systematic theology is not in itself the conclusion of the task of thoughtful men and women in the last days, yet it ought to drive its practitioners to that conclusion. When it does not one might suggest there has been a misstep along the way.

> Everyone knows and generally agrees that systematic theology exercises a critical function over against the proclamation of the church. But if there is a genuine correlation the proclamation needs to reflect back on and raise critical questions about systematic theology ... If and when systematic theology looks on itself as the conclusion of the argument – the means by which ultimate persuasion is to take place so that there is no room or place for proclamation – it has overstepped its bounds and falsified itself. That is, the systematic reflection should not only leave room for the proclamation but must make the move inescapable.[56]

5. *Modern systematic theology needs a new appreciation of biblical theology – understood as the unfolding narrative of God's dealings with his creation from Genesis to Revelation – as the interpretive control for its work.* The relation of biblical theology and systematic theology has been the subject of a number of important studies.[57] However, some confusion has resulted from a failure to agree on a definition of the slippery term 'biblical theology'. Among the most helpful definitions is that provided by Graeme Goldsworthy:

Biblical theology is concerned with God's saving acts and his word as these occur within the history of the people of God. It follows the progress of revelation from the first word of God to man through to the unveiling of the full glory of Christ. It examines the several stages of biblical history and their relationship to one another. It thus provides the basis for understanding how texts in one part of the Bible relate to all other texts. A sound interpretation of the Bible is based upon the findings of biblical theology.[58]

The importance of such a discipline for a responsible use of Scripture in modern systematic theology can hardly be overstated. It is a check against a misappropriation of individual texts and the 'proof-texting' methods of the past which have isolated single verses from their context in paragraphs, chapters and books, let alone the most important context of God's over-arching purposes from Genesis to Revelation. It gives the theologian the capacity to judge the relative weight which should be given to different passages in doctrinal formulation.[59] In addition to all this, however, biblical theology provides systematic theology with its most fruitful starting-point, the gospel. The gospel of Jesus Christ is also an appropriate starting-point because it is 'eschatological to its core, and contains within itself the great doctrines of creation, revelation, God, humanity, the Christ and the church which must later be unfolded'.[60] With such a starting-point systematic theology can be demonstrably more dynamic and less open to charges of irrelevant abstraction.

6. *Modern systematic theology needs a new appreciation of the impact of human sin on those who write it as well as on those who read it.* All too frequently in modern theology fallibility is attributed to the biblical text as a matter of empirical certainty while at the same time the theological constructs of the writer are presented without the slightest hesitation or acknowledgment of provisionality. The impression is given that only in the current generation have the practitioners of theology been able to escape the impact of the fall upon the human mind. There is a serious need for those of us who are involved in the discipline to admit that our own formulations are provisional and fallible, liable to be corrupted by our own prejudices and backgrounds as well as a deeply ingrained self-interest. When the gospel unfolded in systematic theology challenges our own commitments and preferences it is all too possible for us to perform hermeneutical and theological gymnastics in order to avoid the response of repentance and faith. This is not to say that we must inevitably be mistaken. It is still possible to speak the truth faithfully. Nevertheless, our own capacity for error and the possibility of

recasting Christian theology in the image of our own belief structures ought to make us reluctant to dismiss too quickly the contributions of others, and especially the prima facie teaching of the biblical text.

7. *Modern systematic theology needs a new appreciation of the fact that all its work is done in the presence of God.* Calvin's great insight that all of life is lived *coram Deo* is no less true in the world of academic theology than in any other sphere. Too often theology speaks of God as if he were someone who has momentarily left the room. This is in stark contrast to the apostle Paul, who regularly moved seamlessly between theology and doxology; perhaps the classic example is Romans 11:33–36. One can only speculate on the difference an awareness of the present Christ would make to much that has been written by systematic theologians in the last two hundred years. Our anthropological preoccupation may have to give way to a renewed determination to honour the one who has spoken his Word to us. Our boldness in making pronouncements about the intra-trinitarian life of God might be somewhat muted. The modern theological agenda might be significantly rewritten, with a new appreciation of the reality of sin and judgment. If God has not only spoken, but is present by his Word and Spirit, then the work of systematic theology takes on a new seriousness. Perhaps we could bring this essay to a conclusion in no better way than to quote one of the giants of late twentieth-century theology:

> The source of all our knowledge of God is his active revelation of himself. We do not know God against his will, or behind his back, as it were, but in accordance with the way in which he has elected to disclose himself and communicate his truth in the historical-theological context of the worshipping people of God, the Church of the Old and New Covenants. That is the immediate empirical fact with which the Holy Scriptures of the Old and New Testaments are bound up. They are composed under the inspiration of the Holy Spirit, and in the providence of God have been handed on to us as the written form of the Word of God.[61, 62]

Notes

1. The disputes about which of the thirteen epistles are genuinely Pauline continue. However, the reasons for doubting Paul's authorship of the Pastorals, or of Col. and Eph., have failed to attract universal support. In particular, arguments relying on the early church's endorsement of the practice of pseudepigraphy have been subjected to sustained critique in recent times. See, for example, Clark, 'Investigation'; Ellis, 'Pseudonymity'; Ellis, *The Making*; Duff, 'Reconsideration'.

2. Luther's own comment on this is found in a preface to a collection of his Latin writings published in 1545. Luther, 'Vorede', in *Luther's Works* 34, pp. 336–337; Weimar Ausgabe 54, 185.12 – 186.21.

3. E.g. Dulles, *The Craft*, p. 15: 'The great masters of theology, such as John and Paul, Origen and Augustine, Aquinas, Luther, Barth, and Rahner, have brilliantly depicted how Christian faith can nourish the quest for understanding. Their output, comparable in many ways to masterpieces of music, painting, and literature, is a brilliant imaginative construction that exhibits the beauty and illuminative power of faith itself. Such theology continues to inspire multitudes of Christians who are influenced by it either directly or indirectly.'

4. 'The question of how we use Paul for today remains as firmly on the table as ever.' Wright, *What Saint Paul*, p. 21.

5. Dahl, 'Particularity', p. 271.

6. Note references to a developed sense of apostleship among the earliest Christians in Mark 3:14 and Acts 1:25–26.

7. Cf. O'Brien, *Consumed by Passion*, p. 21.

8. Best, 'Revelation', p. 26.

9. '... it is clear that for Paul the Christophany on the Damascus Road constituted both his gospel (see also Gal. 1.12) and his apostolic commission for the Gentile mission'. Kim, *Origin*, p. 57.

10. Bruce, *Galatians*, p. 92.

11. Clark, 'Apostleship', p. 51.

12. Munck, *Paul*, pp. 24–26; cf. Bruce, *Paul*, p. 146, who aruges that Paul understood himself as fulfilling that part of the mission of the servant of Yahweh 'which involved the carrying of God's saving light among the Gentiles, near and far'.

13. Matt. 24:14. '[Paul] is a man who has been appointed to a proper place and a peculiar task in the series of events to be accomplished in the final days of this world; those events whose central person is the Messiah, the Christ Jesus, crucified, risen, and returning to judgment and salvation' (Fridrichsen, *Apostle*, p. 3). These observations can be made without inflating Paul's eschatology, a danger Best warns against in 'Revelation', pp. 20–22.

14. Nils Dahl described Paul's intention in Romans as 'preaching the gospel in writing'. Dahl, 'Missionary theology', p. 75. Cf. 2 Thess. 2:15.

15. Dunn, '"A light"', p. 265; O'Brien, 'Paul's missionary calling', pp. 131–148.

16. Morgan, 'Bible', p. 117.

17. O'Brien, 'Paul's missionary calling', p. 133, quoting Bowers, 'Studies', p. 172.

18. Rome, Corinth, Galatia, Ephesus, Philippi, Colosse and Thessalonica. Evidence that such an argument was mounted by early church fathers such as Hippolytus, Cyprian, and Victorinus of Pettau was first gathered by Zahn, *Geschichte* 2, pp. 73–74, n. 2.

19. Dahl, 'Particularity', pp. 267–270.

20. Ibid., p. 263. A classic example is Tertullian's comment when Marcion questioned the address of the epistle to the Ephesians: 'When the apostle writes to a particular church, he writes to all' (*ad omnes apostolus scripserit, dum ad quosdam*). Tertullian, *Adv. Marc.* 5.17 (*Corpus Scriptorum Ecclesiasticorum Latinorum* 47, p. 632).

21. Jenson, *Systematic Theology* 1, p. 32.

22. '... one of the liberating features of the critical inheritance has been its destruction of mechanical and superstitious views of inspiration.' Gunton, *Enlightenment*, p. 143.

23. Gunton, 'A rose', pp. 4–5.
24. Jenson, *Systematic Theology*, p. 32.
25. Ibid., p. 28.
26. Ibid., p. 28.
27. Ibid., p. 32.
28. Morgan, 'Bible', p. 117.
29. Jenson, *Systematic Theology*, p. 30.
30. Is this a danger even for Colin Gunton, who is concerned 'to move beyond a merely didactic conception of Scripture's function and authority' and to locate systematic theology in 'the logical space between the written words of the text and the communal life that is shaped by it'? Gunton, 'Using and being used', pp. 257, 259.
31. Contrast the words of Thomas Oden: 'The only promise I try to make to my readers, however inadequately carried out, is that of *unoriginality*. I hope to present nothing whatever original in these pages.' Oden, *Word*, p. xvi.
32. There have been a number of recent attempts to recast biblical authority in terms of the backdrop and impetus for modern Christian life and thought. The task of biblical interpretation – and indeed systematic theology – is then conceived as 'improvization' or 'performance'. Lash, 'Performing', pp. 37–46; Young, *Art*; Wright, 'How can the Bible', pp. 7–32; Barton, 'New Testament interpretation', pp. 179–208.
33. 'The question of divine revelation became problematic in Protestant theology as a result of the Enlightenment and the Romantic reaction.' Avis, 'Divine revelation', p. 45.
34. 'The result of this analysis is that theology cannot continue as a special science of divine revelation on the basis of Holy Scripture.' Pannenberg, 'The crisis', p. 12; cf. *Systematic Theology* I, p. 26.
35. E.g. Bruce, '"All things"', pp. 82–99; Longenecker, 'Concept', pp. 195–207; Räisänen, *Paul*; Hübner, *Law*; Beker, 'Recasting Pauline theology', pp. 15–24; Silva, 'Systematic theology', pp. 6–12.
36. Barth, *Kirchliche Dogmatik* I/2, p. 545 = *Church Dogmatics* I/2, p. 492; *KD* I/2, pp. 553–554 = *CD* I/2, p. 499. It is unlikely, however, that Barth would have developed this observation in quite the same direction as Jenson.
37. Wiles, 'Scriptural authority', p. 53. Wiles's allusion is to an argument by Charles Wood, which concludes: 'we may nonetheless read scripture *as if it were* a whole, and as if the author of the whole were God.' Wood, *Formation*, p. 70.
38. Wiles, 'Scriptural authority', pp. 50–51.
39. Barton, 'Place', p. 207.
40. Ibid., p. 204. Note the assessment of John Webster: 'Conservative Protestantism has produced an entire armoury of materials on just this point [doctrinal construal of the Bible] – though their relative lack of sophistication, their entanglement in polemics and apologetics, their reliance on scholastic or nineteenth century construals of the nature of the Bible, and their generally rationalistic understanding of theological method, have all contributed to the marginalisation of this strand of Christian thought.' Webster, 'Hermeneutics', pp. 311–312.
41. The stinging words of Gal. 1 are sufficient to establish this fact.
42. For what such a responsible reading of Scripture will entail – attention to grammar, syntax, literary context, historical context, biblical-theological context, and the *analogia fidei* – see Carson, 'Role', pp. 39–76.

43. O'Brien, *Consumed by Passion*, pp. 104–107.
44. A very helpful investigation of the issues surrounding the claim that God speaks has recently been provided by Wolterstorff, *Divine Discourse*.
45. Karl Barth, who gave classic expression to this notion of *die Schrift als Zeugnis von Gottes Offenbarung*, recognized there was more to be said: '*d. h. Zeugnis von der Offenbarung, das selber zu Offenbarung gehört*', Barth, *Kirchliche Dogmatik* I/2, p. 555 = *Church Dogmatics* I/2, p. 501.
46. 'Finally, images, symbols, and kerygma may not be directly translated into theological concepts. Theology rather has the task of "redescribing" what has been expressed biblically in symbolic or mythic language, employing for these theologians [Lionel Thornton, Paul Tillich and Rudolf Bultmann] at least, a philosophical conceptuality (whether process, idealist, or existentialist) and an "imaginative construal" of what Christian faith is all about. Only in that way can it be set forth intelligibly to the modern mind.' Farley & Hodgson, 'Scripture', p. 79.
47. Dulles, *Craft*, p. 18.
48. See the treatment of the objections of G. Lindbeck, S. McFague and G. Downing in Gunton, *Brief Theology*, pp. 7–13.
49. Knox, 'Propositional revelation', pp. 5–6.
50. Searle, *Speech Acts*; Austin, *How to Do Things*.
51. Wolterstorff, *Divine Discourse*; Vanhoozer, 'Speech-acts', pp. 143–181; Vanhoozer, *Meaning*, esp. pp. 201–280.
52. 'Why is it that if we interpret God as telling us, by way of the scriptures, about God's entrance into our history centrally and decisively in Jesus Christ, we have turned the Christian religion into a "religion of the book" – worse yet, into *bibliolatry*?' Wolterstorff, *Divine Discourse*, p. 296.
53. Vanhoozer, 'Speech-acts', pp. 176–178.
54. The sermons recorded in Acts and the critical appeal to the OT made in the course of the argument of the epistles to the Romans and to the Hebrews are clear examples.
55. McGrath, *Genesis*, pp. 35–80.
56. Forde, *Theology*, pp. 4–5.
57. Gaffin, 'Systematic theology', pp. 281–299; Hasel, 'Relationship', pp. 113–127; Vanhoozer, 'Canon', pp. 96–124.
58. Goldsworthy, *According to Plan*, p. 37.
59. Goldsworthy, *Gospel and Kingdom*, p. 40.
60. Jensen, 'Teaching doctrine', p. 81.
61. Torrance, *Divine Meaning*, p. 5.
62. I deem it a great honour to be involved in the production of this *Festschrift* for Peter O'Brien, who, as a beloved teacher and colleague, has modelled both the highest standards of scholarship and a thoroughgoing commitment to Christ and his mission. May he continue to be an instrument of God's blessing to the Christian churches.

Bibliography

Aageson, J. W., 'Lectionary', in *ABD* 4, pp. 270–271.

Aejmelaeus, L., *Die Rezeption der Paulusbriefe in der Miletrede* (Helsinki: Suomalainen Tiedeakademia, 1987).

Aitken, K. T., 'The oracles against Babylon in Jeremiah 50 – 51: structures and perspectives', *TynB* 35 (1984), pp. 25–63.

Alexander, T. D., 'Abraham re-assessed theologically: the Abrahamic narrative and the New Testament understanding of justification by faith', in R. S. Hess, G. J. Wenham & P. E. Satterthwaite (eds.), *He Swore an Oath: Biblical Themes from Gen 12 – 50* (Carlisle: Paternoster; Grand Rapids: Baker, 1994), pp. 7–28.

Allenbach, J., *Biblia Patristica: index des citations et allusions bibliques dans la litterature patristique*, vols. 1–6 (Paris: CNRS, 1975–95).

Arichea, D. C., Jr, 'Who was Phoebe? Translating *diakonos* in Romans 16.1', *BibTrans* 39 (1988), pp. 401–409.

Arzt, P., 'The "epistolary introductory thanksgiving" in the papyri and in Paul', *NovT* 36 (1994), pp. 29–46.

Austin, J. L., *How to Do Things with Words* (Cambridge, MA: Harvard University Press, [2]1975 [1962]).

Avis, P., 'Divine revelation in modern Protestant theology', in P. Avis (ed.), *Divine Revelation* (Grand Rapids and Cambridge: Eerdmans, 1997), pp. 45–66.

Baasland, E., 'Persecution: a neglected feature in the letter to the Galatians', *StTh* 38 (1984), pp. 135–150.

Badenas, R., *Christ the End of the Law: Romans 10:4 in Pauline Perspective* (Sheffield: JSOT, 1985).

Balch, D. L., 'The Areopagus speech: an appeal to the Stoic historian Posidonius against later Stoics and the Epicureans', in D. L. Balch, E. Ferguson & W. A. Meeks (eds.), *Greeks, Romans and Christians: Essays in Honor of Abraham J. Malherbe* (Minneapolis: Fortress, 1990), pp. 52–79.

Barclay, W., 'A comparison of Paul's missionary preaching and preaching to the church', in W. W. Gasque & R. P. Martin (eds.), *Apostolic History and the Gospel: Biblical and Historical Essays Presented to F. F. Bruce* (Exeter: Paternoster; Grand Rapids: Eerdmans, 1970), pp. 165–175.

————, 'The one new man', in R. A. Guelich (ed.), *Unity and Diversity in New Testament Theology: Essays in Honor of G. E. Ladd* (Grand Rapids: Eerdmans, 1978), pp. 73–81.

Barnes, T. D., *Ammianus Marcellinus and the Representation of Historical Reality* (Ithaca: Cornell University Press, 1998).

Barnett, P. W., *Is the New Testament History?* (Sydney and London: Hodder and Stoughton, 1986).

——, *Jesus and the Logic of History* (NSBT 3; Leicester: Apollos, 1997).

——, *The Second Epistle to the Corinthians* (NICNT; Grand Rapids: Eerdmans, 1997).

Baron, S. W., 'Population', in C. Roth (ed.), *Encyclopedia Judaica* 8 (Jerusalem: Keter, 1971), cols. 866–903.

Barr, J., *The Semantics of Biblical Language* (Oxford: Oxford University Press, 1961).

Barrett, C. K., *A Commentary on the Epistle to the Romans* (London: A. and C. Black, 1962).

——, *The Signs of an Apostle* (Philadelphia: Fortress, 1972).

——, 'Paulus als Missionar und Theologe', *ZThK* 86 (1989), pp. 18–32. Now in M. Hengel & U. Heckel (eds.), *Paulus und das antike Judentum: Tübingen-Durham- Symposium im Gedenken an den 50. Todestag Adolf Schlatters (d. 19. Mai 1938)* (Tübingen: Mohr, 1991), pp. 1–15.

——, *The Acts of the Apostles*, 2 vols. (ICC; Edinburgh: T. and T. Clark, 1994, 1998).

Barrow, R. H., *Plutarch and his Times* (London: Chatto and Windus, 1967).

Barth, K., *Die Kirchliche Dogmatik* (Zurich: Zollikon, 1938), I.2. ET: *Church Dogmatics* I.2 (tr. G. T. Thomson & H. Knight; Edinburgh: T. and T. Clark, 1956).

Barth, M., *Ephesians* (AB 34; Garden City, NY: Doubleday, 1974).

Barton, J., 'The place of the Bible in moral debate', *Theology* 88 (1985), pp. 204–209.

Barton, S. C., 'New Testament interpretation as performance', *SJT* 52.2 (1999), pp. 179–208.

Bauckham, R., 'For whom were gospels written?', in R. Bauckham (ed.), *The Gospels for All Christians* (Edinburgh: T. and T. Clark, 1998), pp. 9–48.

Becker, C., *Der 'Octavius' des Minucius Felix: heidnische Philosophie und frühchristliche Apologetik* (München: Verlag der Bayerischen Akademie der Wissenschaften, 1967).

Becking, B.,'Jeremiah's Book of Consolation: a textual comparison. Notes on the Masoretic Text and the Old Greek version of Jeremiah xxx – xxxi', *VT* 44 (1994), pp. 145–169.

Behm, J., '*noutheteō, nouthesia*', *TDNT* 4, pp. 1019–1022.

Beker, J. C., 'Contingency and coherence in the letters of Paul', *USQR* 33 (1978), pp. 141–151.

————, 'Recasting Pauline theology: the coherence-contingency scheme as interpretive model', in J. M. Bassler (ed.), *Pauline Theology* 1: *Thessalonians, Philippians, Galatians, Philemon* (Minneapolis: Fortress, 1991), pp. 15–24.

Bell, R. H., *No One Seeks For God: An Exegetical and Theological Study of Romans 1.18 – 3.20* (WUNT 106; Tübingen: Mohr [Siebeck], 1998).

Best, E., *One Body in Christ* (London: SPCK, 1955).

————, 'The revelation to evangelize the Gentiles', *JTS* 35 (1984), pp. 1–30.

————, *A Critical and Exegetical Commentary on Ephesians* (ICC; Edinburgh: T. and T. Clark, 1998).

Betz, H.-D., 'Paul's apology: II Corinthians 10 – 13 and the Socratic tradition' (The Center for Hermeneutical Studies in Hellenistic and Modern Culture, Colloquy 2, 1970; Berkeley: Center for Hermeneutical Studies, 1975).

————, *Galatians: A Commentary on Paul's Letter to the Churches in Galatia* (Hermeneia; Philadelphia: Fortress, 1979).

————, *2 Corinthians 8 and 9: A Commentary on Two Administrative Letters of the Apostle Paul* (Hermeneia; Philadelphia: Fortress, 1985).

Black, D. A., 'Weakness language in Galatians', *GTJ* 4 (1983), pp. 15–36.

Bock, D., *Luke 1:1 – 9:50* (BECNT; Grand Rapids: Baker, 1994).

den Boer, W., *Scriptorum Paganorum I–IV saec. de Christianis testimonia* (Leiden: Brill, 1948).

Boers, H., Review of P. T. O'Brien, *Introductory Thanksgivings*, *JBL* 98 (1979), pp. 303–304.

Bolt, P. G., *Plutarch's "Delay of the Divine Vengeances" and Pauline Eschatology* (unpublished MA [Hons.] thesis, Macquarie University, 1994).

————, 'Life, death, and the afterlife in the Greco–Roman world', in R. N. Longenecker (ed.), *Life in the Face of Death: The Resurrection Message of the New Testament* (Grand Rapids: Eerdmans, 1998), pp. 51–79.

Bonneau, N., 'The logic of Paul's argument on the curse of the law in Galatians 3:10–14', *NovT* 39 (1997), pp. 60–80.

Borrett, M., 'Celsus: a pagan perspective on Scripture', in P. M. Blowers (ed.), *The Bible in Greek Christian Antiquity* (Notre Dame: University of Notre Dame Press, 1997), pp. 259–288.

Bowers, W. P., *Studies in Paul's Understanding of his Mission* (unpublished PhD dissertation, Cambridge University, 1976).

——————, 'Fulfilling the gospel: the scope of the Pauline mission', *JETS* 30 (1987), pp. 185–198.

Bowersock, G. W., *Martyrdom and Rome* (Cambridge: Cambridge University Press, 1995).

Bozak, B. del A., *Life "Anew": A Literary-Theological Study of Jer. 30 - 31* (AnBib 122; Rome: Biblical Institute, 1991).

Bradley, K. R., 'Manumission', in *Slaves and Masters in the Roman Empire: A Study in Social Control* (Oxford: Oxford University Press, 1987), pp. 81–112.

Brakke, D., *Athanasius and the Politics of Asceticism* (Oxford: Clarendon, 1995).

Bremmer, J. N., *The Apocryphal Acts of Paul and Thecla* (Kampen: Kok Pharos, 1996).

Brenk, F., 'An imperial heritage: the religious spirit of Plutarch of Chaironeia', in W. Haase (ed.), *ANRW* 36.1 (Berlin: de Gruyter, 1987), pp. 248–349.

Bring, R., *Commentary on Galatians* (Philadelphia: Muhlenberg, 1961).

Brooten, B., 'Junia … outstanding among the apostles (Romans 16:7)', in L. & A. Swidler (eds.), *Women Priests: A Catholic Commentary on the Vatican Declaration* (New York: Paulist, 1977), pp. 141–144.

Brownrigg, R., *Pauline Places* (London: Hodder and Stoughton, 1989).

Bruce, F. F., *The Acts of the Apostles: The Greek Text with Introduction and Commentary* (London: Tyndale, 1952; rev. Leicester: Apollos, 1990).

——————, *The Book of the Acts* (NICNT; Grand Rapids: Eerdmans, 1954, rev. 1988).

——————, *Paul: Apostle of the Free Spirit* (Exeter: Paternoster, 1977, rev. 1980).

——————, '"All things to all men": diversity in unity and other Pauline tensions', in R. A. Guelich (ed.), *Unity and Diversity in New Testament Theology: Essays in Honor of George E. Ladd* (Grand Rapids: Eerdmans, 1978), pp. 82–99.

——————, *New Testament History* (New York: Doubleday, 1980).

——————, *Commentary on the Book of Acts* (Grand Rapids: Eerdmans, 1981).

——————, *The Epistle of Paul to the Galatians: A Commentary on the Greek Text* (NIGTC; Exeter: Paternoster, 1982).

——————, *1 & 2 Thessalonians* (WBC 45; Waco: Word, 1982).

——————, *The Epistles to the Colossians, to Philemon, and to the Ephesians* (NICNT; Grand Rapids: Eerdmans, 1984).

Brueggemann, W., *To Pluck Up, To Tear Down: A Commentary on Jeremiah 1 - 25* (ITC; Grand Rapids: Eerdmans; Edinburgh: Handsel, 1988).

Bultmann, R., 'Das Problem der Ethik bei Paulus', *ZNW* 23 (1924), pp. 123-140.

————, *Theology of the New Testament*, 2 vols. (tr. K. Grobel; London: SCM, 1952, 1955).

————, 'Untersuchungen zum Johannesevangelium' (1928), repr. in *Exegetica: Aufsätze zur Erforschung des Neuen Testaments*, ed. E. Dinkler (Tübingen: Mohr [Siebeck], 1967), pp. 124-197.

Burton, E. de W., *A Critical and Exegetical Commentary on the Epistle to the Galatians* (ICC; T. and T. Clark, 1921).

Caird, G. B., 'Biblical classics: VIII. James Denney: *The Death of Christ*', *ExpT* 90 (1979), pp. 196-199.

Caneday, A., 'Redeemed from the curse of the law: the use of Deut. 21:22-23 in Gal. 3:13', *TrinJ* 10 (1989), pp. 185-209.

Carlini, A., 'P.Bodmer XLVII: un acrostico alfabetico tra Susanna-Daniele e Tucidide', *MusHel* 48 (1991), pp. 158-168.

Carroll, R. P., *Jeremiah: A Commentary* (OTL; London: SCM, 1986).

Carson, D. A., *Exegetical Fallacies* (Grand Rapids: Baker, 1984, rev. 1996).

————, 'The role of exegesis in systematic theology', in J. D. Woodbridge & T. E. McComiskey (eds.), *Doing Theology in Today's World: Essays in Honor of Kenneth S. Kantzer* (Grand Rapids: Zondervan, 1991), pp. 39-76.

————, *A Call to Spiritual Reformation: Priorities from Paul and his Prayers* (Grand Rapids: Baker; Leicester: IVP, 1992).

Casson, L., *Travel in the Ancient World* (Baltimore and London: Johns Hopkins University Press, 1994).

Cervin, R. S., 'A note regarding the name "Junia(s)" in Romans 16.7', *NTS* 40 (1994), pp. 464-470.

Chamblin, J. K., 'Psychology', in *DPL*, pp. 765-775.

Charles, J. D., 'Engaging with the (neo)pagan mind: Paul's encounter with Athenian culture as a model for cultural apologetics (Acts 17:16-34)', *TrinJ* 16 (1995), pp. 47-62.

Cherniss, H., & W. Helmbold, *Plutarch's Moralia XII* (LCL; Cambridge, MA: Harvard University Press; London: Heinemann, 1957).

Chevallier, R., *Roman Roads* (Berkeley: University of California Press, 1976).

Clark, A. C., 'Apostleship: evidence from the New Testament and early Christian literature', *VoxEv* 19 (1989), pp. 49-82.

Clark, L. F., 'An investigation of some application of quantitative methods to the Pauline letters with a view to the question of authorship' (unpublished MA thesis, University of Manchester, 1979).

Clark, S. B., *Man and Woman in Christ: An Examination of the Roles of Men and Women in Light of Scripture and the Social Sciences* (Ann Arbor, MI: Servant, 1980).

Colish, M. L., 'Stoicism and the New Testament: an essay in historiography', in W. Haase (ed.), *ANRW* II.26.1 (Berlin: de Gruyter, 1995), pp. 334–379.

Cook, M. J., 'The mission to the Jews in Acts: unraveling Luke's "myth of the myriads"', in J. B. Tyson (ed.), *Luke-Acts and the Jewish People: Eight Critical Perspectives* (Minneapolis: Augsburg, 1988), pp. 102–123.

Corwin, V., *St Ignatius and Christianity in Antioch* (New Haven: Yale University Press, 1960).

Cotter, W., 'Women's authority roles in Paul's churches: countercultural or conventional?', *NovT* 36 (1994), pp. 350–372.

Cottrell, J., 'Christ: a model for headship *and* submission', *CBMW News* 2.4 (1997), pp. 7–8.

Cranfield, C. E. B., *A Critical and Exegetical Commentary on the Epistle to the Romans*, 2 vols. (ICC; Edinburgh: T. and T. Clark, 1979).

Cranford, M., 'The possibility of perfect obedience: Paul and the implied premiss in Galatians 3.10 and 5.3', *NovT* 36 (1994), pp. 242–258.

Croy, N. C., 'Hellenistic philosophies and the preaching of the resurrection (Acts 17:18, 32)', *NovT* 39 (1997), pp. 21–39.

Cullman, O., *Salvation as History* (London: SCM, 1967).

Dahl, N. A., 'The particularity of the Pauline epistles as a problem in the ancient church', in W. C. van Unnik (ed.), *Neotestamentica et Patristica: Eine Freundesgabe, Herrn Professor Dr. Oscar Cullmann zu seinem 60. Geburtstag überreicht* (Leiden: Brill, 1962), pp. 261–271.

————, 'The missionary theology in the epistle to the Romans', *Studies in Paul: Theology for the Early Christian Mission* (Minneapolis: Augsburg, 1977), pp. 70–94.

Danker, F. W., *Benefactor: Epigraphic Study of a Graeco-Roman and New Testament Semantic Field* (St Louis: Clayton, 1982).

————, *II Corinthians* (AC; Minneapolis: Augsburg, 1989).

Dassmann, E., *Der Stachel im Fleisch: Paulus in der frühchristlichen Literatur bis Irenäus* (Münster: Aschendorff, 1979).

Daube, D., *The Sudden in Scripture* (Leiden: Brill, 1964).

Davies, P., *The Mind of God: Science and the Search for Ultimate Meaning* (London: Penguin, 1992).

Davies, W. D., & D. C. Allison, *The Gospel According to Saint Matthew*, 3 vols. (ICC; Edinburgh: T. and T. Clark, 1988–97).

De Young, J. B., 'The meaning of "nature" in Romans 1 and its implications for biblical perspectives of homosexual behavior', *JETS* 31 (1988), pp. 429–447.

Deichgräber, R., *Gotteshymnus und Christushymnus in der frühen Christenheit* (SUNT 5; Göttingen: Vandenhoeck und Ruprecht, 1967).

Delling, G., *'plērēs, plēroō, ktl.*, *TDNT* 6, pp. 283–311.

———, *'stoicheō, systoicheō, stoicheion'*, *TDNT* 7, pp. 666–687.

———, *'telos, teleō, ktl.*, *TDNT* 8, pp. 49–87.

Dillon, J. M., 'Platonism, Middle', in S. Hornblower & A. Spawforth (eds.), *Oxford Classical Dictionary* (Oxford: Oxford University Press, ³1996), p. 1193.

Dippenaar, M. C., 'Prayer and epistolarity: the function of prayer in the Pauline letter structure', *TJT* 16 (1994), pp. 147–188.

Dodd, C. H., *The Epistle of Paul to the Romans* (London: Hodder and Stoughton, 1932).

———, 'The framework of the Gospel narrative', in *New Testament Studies* (Manchester: Manchester University Press, 1953), pp. 1–11.

———, 'The mind of Paul: change and development', *BJRL* 18 (1934), pp. 5–26. Repr. as 'The mind of Paul: II', in *New Testament Studies* (Manchester: Manchester University Press, 1953), pp. 83–128.

Donaldson, T. L., 'The "curse of the law" and the inclusion of the Gentiles: Galatians 3:13–14', *NTS* 32 (1986), pp. 94–112.

———, *Paul and the Gentiles: Remapping the Apostle's Convictional World* (Minneapolis: Fortress, 1997).

Donfried, K. P. (ed.), *The Romans Debate* (Edinburgh: T. and T. Clark; Peabody, MA: Hendrickson, 1977, rev. 1991).

Doyle, R. C., *Eschatology and the Shape of Christian Belief* (Carlisle: Paternoster, 1999).

Du Plessis, P. J., *TELEIOS: The Idea of Perfection in the New Testament* (Kampen: Kok, 1959).

Duff, J., *A Reconsideration of Pseudepigraphy in Early Christianity* (unpublished DPhil thesis; University of Oxford, 1998).

Dulles, A., *The Craft of Theology: From Symbol to System* (New York: Crossroad, 1992, rev. 1995).

Dumbrell, W. J., *Covenant and Creation* (Exeter: Paternoster, 1984).

———, 'Paul's use of Exodus 34 in 2 Corinthians 3', in P. T. O'Brien (ed.), *God Who is Rich in Mercy: Essays Presented to Dr D. B. Knox* (Homebush West, NSW: Lancer, 1986), pp. 179–194.

———, *The Search for Order: Biblical Eschatology in Focus* (Grand Rapids: Baker, 1994).

———, 'Justification and the new covenant', *Churchman* 112 (1998), pp. 17–29.

Dungan, D. L., *The Sayings of Jesus in the Churches of Paul* (Oxford: Blackwell, 1971).

390 *The gospel to the nations*

Dunn, J. D. G., '"A light to the Gentiles": the significance of the Damascus road Christophany for Paul', in L. D. Hurst & N. T. Wright (eds.), *The Glory of Christ in the New Testament: Studies in Christology in Memory of George Bradford Caird* (Oxford: Clarendon, 1987), pp. 251–266.

————, *Romans* (WBC 38; Dallas: Word, 1988).

————, *The Epistle to the Galatians* (BNTC; Peabody, MA: Hendrickson; London: Black, 1993).

————, *The Acts of the Apostles* (Peterborough: Epworth, 1996).

————, *The Epistles to the Colossians and to Philemon* (NIGTC; Grand Rapids: Eerdmans; Carlisle: Paternoster, 1996).

————, 'Paul's conversion – a light to twentieth century disputes', in J. Ådna, S. J. Hafemann & O. Hofius (eds.), *Evangelium Schriftauslegung, Kirche: Festschrift für Peter Stuhlmacher zum 65. Geburtstag* (Göttingen: Vandenhoeck und Ruprecht, 1997), pp. 77–93.

————, *The Theology of Paul the Apostle* (Grand Rapids: Eerdmans, 1998).

Dupont, J., 'La Mission de Paul d'après Actes 26.16–23 et la mission des apôtres d'après Luc 24.44–9 et Actes 1.8', in M. D. Hooker and S. G. Wilson (eds.), *Paul and Paulinism: Essays in Honour of C. K. Barrett* (London: SPCK, 1982), pp. 290–299.

Dwyer, J. C., *Foundations of Christian Ethics* (New York and Mahwah: Paulist, 1987).

Eadie, J., *Commentary on the Epistle of Paul to the Galatians* (1894; Grand Rapids: Zondervan, n.d.).

Edwards, M. J., 'Quoting Aratus: Acts 17,28', *ZNW* 83 (1992), pp. 266–269.

———— (ed.), *Galatians, Ephesians, Philippians* (Ancient Christian Commentary on Scripture: New Testament, vol. 8; gen. ed. T. C. Oden; Downers Grove, IL: IVP, 1998).

Einarson, B., & P. H. de Lacy, 'Introduction to "Non posse suaviter vivi secundum Epicurum"', *Plutarch's Moralia* XIV (LCL; Cambridge, MA: Harvard University Press; London: Heinemann, 1967).

Ellicott, C. J., *St Paul's Epistle to the Galatians* (London: Longmans, 1854).

Elliot, J. K. (ed.), *The Apocryphal New Testament* (Oxford: Clarendon, 1993).

Ellis, E. E., 'Paul and his co-workers', *NTS* 17 (1970–71), pp. 437–452.

————, 'Pseudonymity and canonicity of New Testament documents', in M. J. Wilkins & T. Paige (eds.), *Worship, Theology, and Ministry in the Early Church: Essays in Honor of Ralph P. Martin* (JSNTSup 87; Sheffield: Sheffield Academic Press, 1992), pp. 212–224.

————, 'Coworkers, Paul and his', in *DPL*, pp. 183–189.

————, *The Making of the New Testament Documents* (Biblical Interpretation Series 39; Leiden: Brill, 1999).

Ellison, H. L., 'The church and the Hebrew Christian', in G. Hedenquist (ed.), *The Church and the Jewish People* (London: Edinburgh House, 1954).

————, *The Mystery of Israel* (Exeter: Paternoster, 1966).

Engberg-Pedersen, T., 'Stoicism in Philippians', in T. Engberg-Pedersen (ed.), *Paul in his Hellenistic Context* (Edinburgh: T. and T. Clark, 1994).

Esser, H.-H., '*stoicheia*', in C. Brown (ed.), *NIDNTT* 2, pp. 451–453.

Fàbrega, V., 'War Junia(s), der hervorragende Apostel (Rom. 16,7), eine Frau?', *Jahrbuch für Antike und Christentum* 27.28 (1985), pp. 47–64.

Farley, E., & P. C. Hodgson, 'Scripture and tradition', in P. C. Hodgson & R. H. King (eds.), *Christian Theology: An Introduction to Its Traditions and Tasks* (Philadelphia: Fortress, 1985), pp. 61–87.

Farrer, F. W., *Seekers after God* (London: Macmillan, 1892).

Fee, G. D., *The First Epistle to the Corinthians* (NICNT; Grand Rapids: Eerdmans, 1987).

————, *1 and 2 Timothy, Titus* (Peabody, MA: Hendrickson, 1988).

Feldman, L. H., 'The success of proselytism by Jews in the Hellenistic era and early Roman periods', in L. H. Feldman, *Jew and Gentile in the Ancient World: Attitudes and Interactions from Alexander to Justinian* (Princeton: Princeton University Press, 1993), pp. 288–341.

Ferguson, E., *Backgrounds of Early Christianity* (Grand Rapids: Eerdmans, 1987, rev. 1993).

Fishwick, D., *Studies in the Ruler Cult of the Western Provinces of the Roman Empire* 2.1: *The Imperial Cult in the Latin West* (Leiden: Brill, 1991).

Fitzmyer, J. A., *Romans* (AB 33; New York: Doubleday, 1993).

————, *The Acts of the Apostles: A New Translation with Introduction and Commentary* (New York: Doubleday, 1997).

Flacelière, R., 'Plutarque et l'Epicurisme', *Epicurea in memoriam Hectoris Bignone* (Genoa: Università di Genova, 1959), pp. 197–215.

Forbes, C., 'Comparison, self-praise and irony: Paul's boasting and the conventions of Hellenistic rhetoric', *NTS* 32 (1986), pp. 1–30.

————, 'Early Christian inspired speech and Hellenistic popular religion', *NovT* 28 (1986), pp. 257–270.

Forde, G. O., *Theology is for Proclamation* (Minneapolis: Fortress, 1990).

France, R. T., *Women in the Church's Ministry: A Test Case for Biblical Interpretation* (Grand Rapids: Eerdmans, 1995).

French, D., 'Acts and the Roman roads of Asia Minor', in C. Gempf and D. W. J. Gill (eds.), *The Book of Acts in its First Century Setting* 2: *The*

Book of Acts in its Graeco-Roman Setting (Grand Rapids: Eerdmans; Carlisle: Paternoster, 1994), pp. 49–58.

Fridrichsen, A., *The Apostle and his Message* (Uppsala: Lundequistski, 1947).

Friedrich, G., 'Die Gegner des Paulus in 2 Korintherbrief', in O. Betz, M. Hengel & P. Schmidt (eds.), *Abraham unser Vater (Festschrift* for O. Michel; Leiden andKöln: Brill, 1963), pp. 181–215.

Furnish, V. P., *The Moral Teaching of Paul* (Nashville: Abingdon, 1979).

————, 'The Jesus–Paul debate: from Baur to Bultmann', in A. J. M. Wedderburn (ed.), *Paul and Jesus* (Sheffield: Sheffield Academic Press, 1989).

Gaffin, R. B., 'Systematic theology and biblical theology', *WTJ* 38.3 (1976), pp. 281–299.

Garlington, D.B., 'The obedience of faith in the letter to the Romans. Part I: The meaning of *hypakoē pisteōs*' (Rom. 1:5; 16:26),' *WTJ* 52 (1990), pp. 201–204.

Gärtner, B., *The Areopagus Speech and Natural Revelation* (tr. C. King; Lund: Gleerup, 1955).

Gasque, W. W., *A History of the Interpretation of the Acts of the Apostles* (Peabody, MA: Hendricksen, 1975).

————, 'Tarsus', in D. N. Freedman (ed.), *ABD* 6, pp. 333–334.

Georgi, D., *The Opponents of Paul in Second Corinthians* (tr. H. Attridge, I. and T. Best, and others; Philadelphia: Fortress, 1986 [German: 1964]).

Gibson, J. C. L., *Davidson's Introductory Hebrew Grammar: Syntax* (Edinburgh: T. and T. Clark, 4th edn 1994); revision of A. B. Davidson, *Hebrew Syntax* (3rd edn 1901).

Giles, K., *Patterns of Ministry among the First Christians* (Melbourne: Collins Dove, 1989).

Gill, C., 'The question of character development: Plutarch and Tacitus', *CQ* 33 (1983), pp. 469–487.

Given, M. D., 'Not either/or but both/and in Paul's Areopagus speech', *BibInt* 3 (1995), pp. 356–372.

Goddard, A. J., & S. A. Cummings, 'Ill or ill-treated? Conflict and persecution as the context of Paul's original ministry in Galatia', *JSNT* 52 (1993), pp. 93–126.

Goldsworthy, G. L., *Gospel and Kingdom: A Christian Interpretation of the Old Testament* (Exeter: Paternoster, 1981).

————, '"Thus says the Lord": the dogmatic basis of biblical theology', in P. T. O'Brien & D. G. Peterson (eds.), *God Who is Rich in Mercy: Essays Presented to Dr D. B. Knox* (Homebush West, NSW: Lancer, 1986), pp. 25–40.

————, *According to Plan: The Unfolding Revelation of God in the Bible* (Leicester: IVP, 1991).

————, 'Is biblical theology viable?', in R. J. Gibson (ed.), *Interpreting God's Plan: Biblical Theology and the Pastor* (Explorations 11; Adelaide: Openbook, 1997; Carlisle: Paternoster, 1998), pp. 18–46.

————, '"With flesh and bones": a biblical theology of the bodily resurrection of Christ', *RTR* 57.3 (1998), pp. 121–135.

Goodman, M., *Mission and Conversion: Proselytizing in the Religious History of the Roman Empire* (Oxford: Oxford University Press, 1994).

Green, M., *Evangelism in the Early Church* (London: Hodder and Stoughton, 1970).

Greijdanus, S., *De brief van den apostel Paulus aan de gemeenten in Galatië* (Kommentaar op het Nieuwe Testament 9.1; Amsterdam: H. A. van Bottenburg, 1936).

Grenz, S. J., *Women in the Church: A Biblical Theology of Women in Ministry* (Downers Grove, IL: IVP, 1995).

Gross, W., 'Der neue Bund in Jer 31 und die Suche nach übergreifenden Bundeskonzeptionen im Alten Testament', *ThQ* 176 (1996), pp. 259–272.

————, 'Erneuerter oder Neuer Bund? Wortlaut und Aussageintention in Jer 31,31–34', in F. Avemarie et al. (eds.), *Bund und Tora: Zur Theologischen Begriffsgeschichte in alttestamentlicher, frühjüdischer und urchristlicher Tradition* (WUNT 92; Tübingen: Mohr [Siebeck], 1996), pp. 41–66.

Grossi, V., 'Anthropology', in A. D. Berardino, W. H. C. Frend, Institutum Patristicum Augustinianum (eds.), *Encyclopedia of the Early Church* (New York: Oxford University Press, 1992), pp. 44–46.

Grudem, W., Unpublished critique of C. Kroeger's article 'Head', in *DPL*, presented at the Annual Meeting of the Evangelical Theological Society (21 November 1997).

————, 'The meaning source "does not exist"', *CBMW News* 2.5 (1997), pp. 1, 7–8.

————, 'Willow Creek enforces egalitarianism', *CBMW News* 2.5 (1997), pp. 1, 3–6.

Gunton, C. E., *Enlightenment and Alienation: An Essay towards a Trinitarian Theology* (London: Marshall, Morgan and Scott, 1985).

————, 'Using and being used: Scripture and systematic theology', *TheolToday* 47.3 (1990), pp. 248–259.

————, *A Brief Theology of Revelation* (Edinburgh: T. and T. Clark, 1995).

394 *The gospel to the nations*

—————, 'A rose by any other name? From "Christian doctrine" to "systematic theology"', *IJST* 1.1 (1999), pp. 4–23.

Hadorn, W., 'Die Gefährten und Mitarbeiter des Paulus', in *Aus Schrift und Geschichte: Theologische Abhandlungen Adolf Schlatter zu seinem 70. Geburtstage* (Stuttgart: Calwer Vereinsbuchhandlung, 1922), pp. 65–82.

Hadot, P., *Marius Victorinus: recherches sur sa vie et ses oeuvres* (Paris: Études Augustiniennes, 1971).

Hafemann, S. J., *Suffering and the Spirit: An Exegetical Study of II Cor 2:14–3:3 within the Context of the Corinthian Correspondence* (WUNT 2.19; Tübingen: Mohr, 1986).

—————, *Suffering and Ministry of the Spirit: Paul's Defense of His Ministry in II Corinthians 2:14 – 3:3* (Grand Rapids: Eerdmans, 1990).

—————, 'Paul and the exile of Israel in Galatians 3 – 4', in J. M. Scott, *Exile: Old Testament, Jewish, and Christian Conceptions* (JSJSup 56; Leiden: Brill, 1997), pp. 329–371.

Hahn, F., *Mission in the New Testament* (SBT 47; tr. F. Clarke; London: SCM, 1965).

Hals, R. M., 'Some aspects of the exegesis of Jeremiah 31:31–34', in J. J. Petuchowski (ed.), *When Jews and Christians Meet* (Albany: State University of New York Press, 1988), pp. 87–97.

Hanson, A. T., *The Wrath of the Lamb* (London: SPCK, 1957).

Harding, M., 'The salvation of Israel and the logic of salvation in Romans 9 – 11', *ABR* 46 (1998), pp. 55–69.

von Harnack, A., '*Kopos, kopiaō, hoi kopiōntes* im frühchristlichen Sprachgebrauch', *ZNW* 27 (1928), pp. 1–10.

—————, *The Mission and Expansion of Christianity* (tr. J. Moffatt, 1908; Gloucester, MA: P. Smith, 1972).

Harrill, J. A., 'The vice of slave dealers in Greco-Roman Society: the use of a topos in 1 Timothy 1:10', *JBL* 118.1 (1999), pp. 97–122.

Harris, M. J., *Jesus as God: The New Testament Use of Theos in Reference to Jesus* (Grand Rapids: Baker, 1992).

Hasel, G. F., '*kāraṭ*', in TDOT 7, pp. 339–352 (German: TWAT 4.1–5, pp. 339–352.)

—————, 'The relationship between biblical theology and systematic theology', *TrinJ* 5 (1984), pp. 113–127.

Hawthorne, G. F., *Philippians* (WBC 34; Waco: Word, 1983).

Hays, R. B., *Echoes of Scripture in the Letters of Paul* (New Haven and London: Yale University Press, 1989).

Heckel, U., 'Der Dorn im Fleisch: Die Krankheit des Paulus in 2 Kor 12,7 and Gal 4,13f.', *ZNW* 84 (1993), pp. 65–92.

Hemer, C., *The Book of Acts in the Setting of Hellenistic History* (Tübingen: Mohr, 1989).

Hengel, M., *Between Jesus and Paul: Studies in the Earliest History of Christianity* (tr. J. Bowden; Philadelphia: Fortress, 1983 [German: various dates]).

——————, *The Pre-Christian Paul* (London: SCM, 1991).

Hengel, M., & A. M. Schwemer, *Paul Between Damascus and Antioch: The Unknown Years* (tr. J. Bowden; Louisville: Westminister, 1997 [German: 1998, WUNT]).

Hick, J., *The Myth of God Incarnate* (London: SCM, 1977; with new preface, 1993).

Hickling, C. J. A., 'Is the second epistle to the Corinthians a source of early church history?', *ZNW* 66 (1975), pp. 284–287.

Hill, J., *Friend or Foe? The Figure of Babylon in the Book of Jeremiah* MT (Biblical Interpretation 40; Leiden, Boston and Köln: Brill, 1999).

Hoffmann, R. J., *Marcion: On the Restitution of Christianity. An Essay on the Development of Radical Paulinist Theology in the Second Century* (Chico: Scholars, 1984).

Holladay, W. L., *Jeremiah: A Commentary on the Book of the Prophet Jeremiah*, 2 vols. (Hermeneia; Philadelphia: Fortress, 1986, 1989).

Holmberg, B., *The Structure of Authority in the Primitive Church as Reflected in the Pauline Epistles* (Philadelphia: Fortress, 1980).

Holmgren, F. C., *The Old Testament and the Significance of Jesus: Embracing Change – Maintaining Christian Identity* (Grand Rapids and Cambridge: Eerdmans, 1999).

Holtz, T., 'Paul and the oral gospel tradition', in H. Wansbrough (ed.), *Jesus and the Oral Gospel Tradition* (Sheffield Academic Press, 1991), pp. 380–393.

Hooker, M. D., 'Chalcedon and the New Testament', in S. Coakley & D. A. Pailin (eds.), *The Making and Remaking of Christian Doctrine* (Oxford: Clarendon, 1993), pp. 73–93.

Horsley, G. H. R. (ed.), 'A prefect's circular forbidding magic', in *New Documents Illustrating Early Christianity* 1 (North Ryde, NSW: Ancient History Documentary Research Centre, Macquarie University, 1981), pp. 47–51.

Hübner, H., *Law in Paul's Thought* (Edinburgh: T. and T. Clark, 1984).

Hughes, P. E., *The Second Epistle to the Corinthians* (Grand Rapids: Eerdmans, 1962).

Hume, D., *A Treatise of Human Nature* 1 (3 vols; 1739–40; repr. London: Dent, 1911).

——————, *Enquiries Concerning Human Understanding and Concerning the Principles of Morals* (1748, 1751; Oxford: Clarendon, 1902).

Hunt, E. D., 'Christians and Christianity in Ammianus', *CQ* 35 (1985), pp. 186–200.

Hunter, J. P., *Before Novels: The Cultural Contexts of Eighteenth-Century English Fiction* (New York: Norton, 1990).

Hutch, R. A., *The Meaning of Lives: Biography, Autobiography and the Spiritual Quest* (London: Cassell, 1997).

Jensen P. F., 'Teaching doctrine as part of the pastor's role', in R. J. Gibson (ed.), *Interpreting God's Plan: Biblical Theology and the Pastor* (Explorations 11; Carlisle: Paternoster, 1997), pp. 75–90.

Jenson, R. W., *Systematic Theology 1: The Triune God* (New York: Oxford University Press, 1997).

Jeremias, J., 'Paarweise Sendung im Neuen Testament', in A. J. B. Higgins (ed.), *New Testament Essays: Studies in Memory of Thomas Walter Manson* (Manchester: Manchester University Press, 1959), pp. 136–143.

——————, *Jerusalem in the Time of Jesus: An Investigation into Economic and Social Conditions during the New Testament Period* (tr. F. H. & C. H. Cave; London: SCM, 1969 [German: 1962]).

Jervell, J., 'The church of Jews and Godfearers', in J. B. Tyson (ed.), *Luke-Acts and the Jewish People: Eight Critical Perspectives* (Minneapolis: Augsburg, 1988), pp. 11–20.

——————, *The Theology of the Acts of the Apostles* (Cambridge: Cambridge University Press, 1996).

Joannou, P.-P., *La législation impériale et la christianisation de l'Empire romain (311–476)* (Rome: Pontificium Institutum Orientalium Studiorum, 1972).

Johnson, L. T., *The Acts of the Apostles* (Collegeville: Glazier, 1992).

Jones, C. P., 'Plutarch', in T. J. Luce (ed.), *Ancient Writers: Greece and Rome*, 2 vols. (New York: Scribner's, 1982), 2, pp. 961–983.

Jones, R. M., 'The Platonism of Plutarch (1916)', in *The Platonism of Plutarch and Selected Papers* (New York: Garland, 1980).

Judge, E. A., 'The earliest attested monk', in G. H. R. Horsley (ed.), *New Documents Illustrating Early Christianity* 1 (North Ryde, NSW: Ancient History Documentary Research Centre, Macquarie University, 1981), pp. 124–126.

——————, 'Cultural conformity and innovation in Paul: some clues from contemporary documents', *TynB* 35 (1984), pp. 3–24.

——————, 'Judaism and the rise of Christianity: a Roman perspective', *AJJS* 7.2 (1993) 80–98, repr. with slight adjustments in *TynB* 45.2 (1994), pp. 355–368.

────────, 'The biblical shape of modern culture', *Kategoria* 3 (1996), pp. 9–30.

Judge, E. A., & G. S. R. Thomas, 'The origin of the church at Rome: a new solution?', *RTR* 25.3 (1966), pp. 81–94.

Kaczynski, R., *Das Wort Gottes in Liturgie und Alltag der Gemeinden des Johannes Chrysostomus* (Freiburg: Herder, 1974).

Kaufman, G. D., *Systematic Theology: A Historicist Perspective* (New York: Scribner's, 1968).

Kaye, B. N., 'Acts' portrait of Silas', *NovT* 21 (1979), pp. 13–26.

Keener, C. S., *Paul, Women and Wives: Marriage and Women's Ministry in the Letters of Paul* (Peabody, MA: Hendrickson, 1992).

────────, 'Man and woman', in *DPL*, pp. 583–592.

────────, 'Woman and man', in *DLNTD*, pp. 1205–1215.

Kennedy, G. A., *New Testament Interpretation through Rhetorical Criticism* (Chapel Hill: University of North Carolina Press, 1984).

Keown, G. L., P. J. Scalise & T. G. Smothers, *Jeremiah 26 – 52* (WBC 27; Dallas: Word, 1995).

Kern, P. H., *Rhetoric and Galatians* (SNTSMS 101; Cambridge: Cambridge University Press, 1998).

Kim, S., *The Origin of Paul's Gospel* (Grand Rapids: Eerdmans, 1981).

Kittel, G., '*aichmalōtos, aichmalōtizō, ktl.*, *TDNT* 1, pp. 195–197.

Klein, W. W., 'Perfect, mature', in *DPL*, pp. 699–701.

Kloner, A., 'Underground metropolis: the subterranean world of Maresha', *BAR* 23.2 (1997), pp. 24–35, 67.

Knitter, P. F., & J. Hick (eds.), *The Myth of Christian Uniqueness: Toward a Pluralistic Theology of Religions* (Maryknoll: Orbis, 1987).

Knox, D. B., 'Propositional revelation the only revelation', *RTR* 19.1 (1960), pp. 1–9.

Knox, W. L., *St Paul and the Church of Jerusalem* (Cambridge: Cambridge University Press, 1925).

Koester, H., 'The purpose of the polemic of a Pauline fragment', *NTS* 8 (1961–62), pp. 317–332.

────────, 'Letter to the Philippians', *IDB*Sup (Nashville: Abingdon, 1976), pp. 665–666.

Köstenberger, A. J., 'The mystery of Christ and the church: head and body, "one flesh"', *TrinJ* 12 (1991), pp. 79–94.

────────, 'Gender passages in the NT: hermeneutical fallacies critiqued', *WTJ* 56 (1994), pp. 259–283.

────────, 'A complex sentence structure in 1 Timothy 2:12', in A. J. Köstenberger, T. R. Schreiner & H. S. Baldwin, *Women in the Church: A*

Fresh Analysis of 1 Timothy 2:9–15 (Grand Rapids: Baker, 1995), pp. 81–103.

————, 'Syntactical background studies to 1 Tim. 2.12 in the New Testament and extrabiblical Greek literature', in S. E. Porter and D. A. Carson (eds.), *Discourse Analysis and Other Topics in Biblical Greek* (*JSNT*Sup 113; Sheffield: Sheffield Academic Press, 1995), pp. 156–179.

————, Review of Cotter (vid. sup.), in *CBMW News* 1.4 (1996), p. 14.

————, 'The crux of the matter: Paul's pastoral pronouncements regarding women's roles in 1 Timothy 2:9–15', *FaithMiss* 14 (1996), pp. 24–48.

————, 'Ascertaining women's God-ordained roles: an interpretation of 1 Timothy 2:15', *BBR* 7 (1997), pp. 107–144.

————, Review of Grenz, *Women in the Church*, *JETS* 41 (1998), pp. 516–519.

Köstenberger, A., & P. T. O'Brien, *The Theology of Mission in the New Testament* (NSBT; Leicester: Apollos, 2000 [forthcoming]).

Köstenberger, A. J., T. R. Schreiner, & H. S. Baldwin, *Women in the Church: A Fresh Analysis of 1 Timothy 2:9–15* (Grand Rapids: Baker, 1995).

Kroeger, C. C., 'Head', in *DPL*, pp. 375–377.

————, 'Women in the early church', in *DLNTD*, pp. 1215–1222.

Kruse, C. G., *New Testament Foundations for Ministry* (Basingstoke: Marshall, Morgan and Scott, 1983).

————, 'Human Relationships in the Pauline Corpus', in D. G. Peterson and J. Pryor (eds.), *The Fullness of Time: Biblical Studies in Honour of Archbishop Donald Robinson* (Homebush West: Lancer, NSW, 1992), pp. 167–184.

Kümmel, W. G., *Introduction to the New Testament* (tr. H. C. Kee; Nashville: Abingdon, rev. 1975 [German: 1965]).

de Lacy, P. H., & B. Einarson, 'Introduction to *Delay*', in *Plutarch's Moralia* VII (London: Heinemann; Cambridge, MA: Harvard University Press, 1968).

Ladner, G. B., *The Idea of Reform: Its Impact on Christian Thought and Action in the Age of the Fathers* (Cambridge, MA: Harvard University Press, 1959).

Lampe, P., 'Iunia/Iunias: Sklavenherkunft im Kreise der vorpaulinischen Apostel [Röm 16:7]', *ZNW* 76 (1985), pp. 132–134.

————, *Die stadtrömischen Christen in den ersten beiden Jahrhunderten: Untersuchungen zur Sozialgeschichte* (WUNT 2.18; Tübingen: Mohr [Siebeck], 1987).

Lash, N., 'Performing the Scriptures', in *Theology on the Way to Emmaus* (London: SCM, 1986), pp. 37–46.

Leon, H. J., *The Jews in Ancient Rome* (1960; Peabody: Hendrickson, updated 1995).

Levick, B., *Tiberius the Politician* (London: Thames and Hudson, 1976).

Levinskaya, I., *The Book of Acts in its First Century Setting* 5: *The Book of Acts in its Diaspora Setting* (Carlisle: Paternoster; Grand Rapids: Eerdmans, 1996).

Lietzmann, H., *Die Briefe des Apostels Paulus* 1: *An die Römer* (HNT 3; Tübingen: Mohr [Siebeck], 1906).

Lightfoot, J. B., *Saint Paul's Epistle to the Galatians* (Andover: Warren F. Draper; London: Macmillan, 6th edn 1885; 10th edn 1898).

——————, *St Paul's Epistles to the Colossians and to Philemon* (London: Macmillan, rev. 1876).

——————, 'St Paul and Seneca', in *St Paul's Epistle to the Philippians* (1913; repr. Grand Rapids: Zondervan, 1956).

Lincoln, A. T., *Ephesians* (WBC 42; Dallas: Word, 1990).

Lindemann, A., 'Der Apostel Paulus im 2. Jahrhundert', in J.-M. Sevrin (ed.), *The New Testament in Early Christianity: La réception des écrits néotestamentaires dans le christianisme primitif* (Louvain: Peeters, 1989), pp. 39–67.

Lindsay, H. M., 'Characterisation in the Suetonian Life of Tiberius', in T. W. Hillard et al. (eds.), *Ancient History in a Modern University* 1: *The Ancient Near East, Greece and Rome* (Grand Rapids and Cambridge: Eerdmans, 1998), pp. 299–308.

Locher, A. (ed.), *Marii Victorini Afri commentarii in Epistulas Pauli ad Galatas, ad Philippenses, ad Ephesios* (Leipzig: Teubner, 1972).

Lohfink, G., 'Weibliche Diakone im Neuen Testament', in G. Dautzenberg et al. (eds.), *Die Frau im Urchristentum* (Freiburg: Herder, 1983), pp. 320–338.

Lohfink, N., *The Covenant Never Revoked: Biblical Reflections on Christian–Jewish Dialogue* (tr. J. J. Scullion; New York and Mahwah: Paulist, 1991 [German: *Der Niemals Gekündigte Bund*; Freiburg im Bresigau: Herder, 1989]).

Lohse, E., *Colossians and Philemon* (Hermeneia; tr. W. R. Poehlmann and R. J. Karris; Philadelphia: Fortress, 1971 [German: [14]1968]).

Long, A. A., *Hellenistic Philosophy: Classical Life and Letters* (London: Duckworth, 1974).

Longenecker, R. N., 'On the concept of development in Pauline thought', in K. S. Kantzer & S. N. Gundry (eds.), *Perspectives on Evangelical Theology* (Grand Rapids: Baker, 1979), pp. 195–207.

——————, *Galatians* (WBC 41; Dallas: Word, 1990).

Luther, M., 'Vorrede zum ersten Bande der Gesamtausgaben seiner latein-ischen Schriften', Weimar Ausgabe 54, pp. 179–187; = 'Preface to the complete edition of Luther's Latin writings', *Luther's Works* 34 (tr. L. W. Spitz; Philadelphia: Fortress, 1960), pp. 327–338.

————, 'Von den Consiliis und Kirchen', Weimar Ausgabe 50, pp. 509–653; = 'On the Councils and the Church', *Luther's Works* 41 (tr. C. M. Jacobs [1916], rev. E. W. Gritsch; Philadelphia: Fortress, 1966), pp. 9–178.

————, 'Tischreden' #394, #515, Weimar Ausgabe: *Tischreden* 1, pp. 171.4–11, 235.16 – 236.9; = 'Table Talk' #394, #515, *Luther's Works* 54 (tr. T. G. Tappert; Philadelphia: Fortress, 1967), pp. 61, 92.

Luz, U., 'Überlegungen zum Epheserbrief und seiner Paränese', in H. Merklein (ed.), *Neues Testament und Ethik* (Freiburg: Herder, 1989), pp. 376–396.

Lyons, G., *Pauline Autobiography: Toward a New Understanding* (SBLDS 73; Atlanta: Scholars, 1985).

McConville, J. G., *Judgment and Promise: An Interpretation of the Book of Jeremiah* (Leicester: Apollos; Winona Lake: Eisenbrauns, 1993).

McGrath, A. E., *The Genesis of Doctrine* (1990 Bampton Lectures; Oxford: Blackwell, 1990).

Macgregor, G. H. C., 'The concept of the wrath of God in the New Testa-ment', *NTS* 7 (1961), pp. 101–109.

Machen, J. G., *The Origin of Paul's Religion* (1925; Grand Rapids: Eerdmans, 1947).

McKane, W., *A Critical and Exegetical Commentary on Jeremiah*, 2 vols. (ICC; Edinburgh: T. and T. Clark, 1986, 1996).

McKnight, S., *A Light Among the Gentiles: Jewish Missionary Activity in the Second Temple Period* (Minneapolis: Fortress, 1991).

MacMullen, R., 'What difference did Christianity make?', *Historia* 35 (1986), pp. 322–343.

Macquarie, J., *Jesus Christ in Modern Thought* (London: SCM, 1990).

Malherbe, A. J., 'Antithenes and Odysseus, and Paul at war', in *Paul and Popular Philosophers* (Minneapolis: Fortress, 1989), pp. 91–119.

————, '"Pastoral care" in the Thessalonian church', *NTS* 36 (1990), pp. 375–391.

Malinowski, F. X., 'The brave women of Philippi', *BTB* 15 (1985), pp. 60–64.

Manson, W., *The Epistle to the Hebrews: An Historical and Theological Reconsideration* (The Baird Lecture for 1949; London: Hodder and Stoughton, 1951).

Marshall, I. H., 'Who were the evangelists?', in J. Ådna & H. Kvalbein (eds.), *The Mission of the Early Church to Jews and Gentiles* (Tübingen: Mohr [Siebeck], forthcoming).

Marshall, I. H., & D. G. Peterson (eds.), *Witness to the Gospel: The Theology of Acts* (Grand Rapids: Eerdmans, 1998).

Marshall, P. J., *Enmity at Corinth: Social Convention in Paul's Relations with the Corinthians* (WUNT 2.23; Tübingen: Mohr, 1987).

——————, 'Invective: Paul and his enemies in Corinth', in E. W. Conrad & E. G. Newing (eds.), *Perspectives on Language and Text* (*Festschrift* for F. I. Andersen; Winona Lake: Eisenbrauns, 1987), pp. 359–373.

——————, 'The enigmatic apostle: Paul and social change. Did Paul seek to transform Graeco-Roman society?', in T. W. Hillard, et al. (eds.), *Ancient History in a Modern University* 2: *Early Christianity, Late Antiquity and Beyond* (Grand Rapids and Cambridge: Eerdmans, 1998), pp. 153–174.

Martin, H. V., 'The messianic age', *ExpT* 52 (1940–41), pp. 270–275.

Martin, R. P., *The Family and the Fellowship: New Testament Images of the Church* (Exeter: Paternoster, 1979).

——————, *2 Corinthians* (WBC 40; Waco: Word, 1986).

——————, 'The setting of 2 Corinthians', *TynB* 37 (1986), pp. 3–19.

——————, 'The opponents of Paul in 2 Corinthians: an old issue revisited', in G. F. Hawthorne & O. Betz (eds.), *Tradition and Interpretation in the New Testament* (*Festschrift* for E. E. Ellis; Grand Rapids: Eerdmans, 1987), pp. 279–289.

——————, 'The Spirit in 2 Corinthians in light of the "fellowship of the Holy Spirit"', in W. H. Gloer (ed.), *Eschatology and the New Testament* (*Festschrift* for G. R. Beasley-Murray; Peabody, MA: Hendrickson, 1988), pp. 113–128.

Martin, T. W., 'Apostasy to paganism: the rhetorical stasis of the Galatian controversy', *JBL* 114 (1995), pp. 437–61.

——————, 'Whose flesh? What temptation? (Gal. 4:13–14)', *JSNT* 74 (1999), pp. 65–91.

Martyn, J. L., *Galatians: A New Translation with Introduction and Commentary* (AB 33A; New York: Doubleday, 1997).

Matthews, J., *The Roman Empire of Ammianus* (London: Duckworth, 1989).

Meeks, W. A., *The First Urban Christians: The Social World of the Apostle Paul* (New Haven and London: Yale University Press, 1983).

Merklein, H., 'Der (neue) Bund als Thema der paulinischen Theologie', *ThQ* 176 (1996), pp. 290–308.

Metzger, B. M., *A Textual Commentary on the Greek New Testament* (New York: UBS, corrected edn. 1975, rev. 1994).

Michaelis, W., '*syngenēs, syngeneia*', *TDNT* 7, pp. 736–742.

Michel, O., '*katantaō, hypantaō, hypantēsis*', *TDNT* 3, pp. 623–626.

Misch, G., *A History of Autobiography in Antiquity* (London: Routledge, 1950 [German: 1907]).

Mitchell, M. M., "'A variable and many-sided man": John Chrysostom's treatment of Pauline inconsistency', *JECS* 6.1 (1998), pp. 93–111.

Mitchell, S., *Anatolia: Land, Men, and Gods in Asia Minor* 2: *The Rise of the Church* (Oxford: Clarendon; New York: Oxford University Press, 1993).

Moles, J. L., 'Cynics', in S. Hornblower & A. Spawforth (eds.), *Oxford Classical Dictionary* (Oxford: Oxford University Press, 3rd edn 1996), pp. 418–419.

Molland, E., *Das paulinische Euangelion. Das Wort und die Sache* (Oslo: Dybwad, 1934).

Moltmann, J., *The Way of Jesus Christ: Christology in Messianic Dimension* (tr. M. Kohl; San Francisco: Harper, 1990).

Montague, G. T., *Growth in Christ A Study in Saint Paul's Theology of Progress* (Fribourg: St Paul's, 1961).

Moo, D. J., *Romans 1 – 8* (WEC; Chicago: Moody, 1991).

————, *The Epistle to the Romans* (NICNT; Grand Rapids: Eerdmans, 1996).

Morgan, R., 'The Bible and Christian theology', in J. Barton (ed.), *The Cambridge Companion to Biblical Interpretation* (Cambridge: Cambridge University Press, 1998), pp. 114–128.

Morgan-Wynne, J. E., Review of P. T. O'Brien, *Introductory Thanksgivings*, *JTS* 30 (1979), pp. 537–539.

Morris, L. L., *The New Testament and the Jewish Lectionaries* (London: Tyndale, 1964).

————, Review of P. T. O'Brien, *Introductory Thanksgivings*, *RTR* 37 (1978), pp. 85–86.

Mott, S. C., 'The power of giving and receiving: reciprocity in Hellenistic benevolence', in G. F. Hawthorne (ed.), *Current Issues in Biblical and Patristic Interpretation* (*Festschrift* for M. C. Tenney; Grand Rapids: Eerdmans, 1975), pp. 60–72.

Moule, C. F. D., *An Idiom Book of New Testament Greek* (Cambridge: University Press, 1953).

————, *Essays in New Testament Interpretation* (Cambridge: Cambridge University Press, 1982).

Munck, J., *Paul and the Salvation of Mankind* (tr. F. Clarke; London: SCM, 1959 [German: 1954]).

Murphy-O'Connor, J., *Paul: A Critical Life* (Oxford: Clarendon, 1996).

Musurillo, H., *The Acts of the Christian Martyrs* (Oxford: Clarendon, 1972).

Mussner, F., *Der Galaterbrief* (HTKNT 9; Freiburg, Basel and Wien: Herder, 1974).

Nauck, A., *Tragicorum graecorum fragmenta* (2nd edn 1889); now see B. Snell, *Tragicorum graecorum fragmenta* (Göttingen: Vandenhoeck und Ruprecht, 1971).

Neri, V., *Ammiano e il cristianesimo: religione e politica nelle Res Gestae di Ammiano Marcellino* (Bologna: CLUEB, 1985).

Neuer, W., *Man and Woman in Christian Perspective* (tr. G. J. Wenham; Wheaton, IL: Crossway, 1991 [German: 1981]).

Niccacci, A., *The Syntax of the Verb in Classical Hebrew* (JSOTSup 86; tr. W. G. E. Watson; Sheffield: Sheffield Academic Press, 1990 [*Sintassi del verbo ebraico nella prosa biblica classica*; Jerusalem: Franciscan Printing Press, 1986]).

Nixon, R. E., 'Silas', in *New Bible Dictionary*, ed. I. H. Marshall et al. (Leicester and Downers Grove: IVP, 3rd edn 1996), p. 1101.

Nolland, J., 'Proselytism or politics in Horace *Satires* i.4.138–143?', *VC* 33 (1979), pp. 347–355.

————, *Luke 1 – 9:20* (WBC 35A; Dallas: Word, 1989).

Noormann, R., *Irenäus als Paulusinterpret* (Tübingen: Mohr, 1994).

North, R., '*ḥāḏāš*', *TDOT* 4, pp. 225–244.

Norwood, M. T., Jr, Review of P. T. O'Brien, *Introductory Thanksgivings*, *JAAR* 46 (1978), p. 582.

Noy, D., *Jewish Inscriptions of Western Europe 2: The City of Rome* (Cambridge: Cambridge University Press, 1995).

Nussbaum, M., *The Therapy of Desire: Theory and Practice in Hellenistic Ethics* (Princeton: Princeton University Press, 1994).

O'Brien, P. T., 'Thanksgiving and the gospel in Paul', *NTS* 21 (1974–5), pp. 144–155.

————, *Introductory Thanksgivings in the Letters of Paul* (NovTSup 9; Leiden: Brill, 1977).

————, 'Thanksgiving within the structure of Pauline theology', in D. Hagner (ed.), *Pauline Studies* (*Festschrift* for F. F. Bruce; Exeter: Paternoster, 1980), pp. 50–66.

————, *Colossians, Philemon* (WBC 44; Waco: Word, 1982).

————, 'The church as a heavenly and eschatological entity', in D. A. Carson (ed.), *The Church in the Bible and the World* (Exeter: Paternoster, 1987), pp. 88–119, 307–311.

————, *The Epistle to the Philippians: A Commentary on the Greek Text* (NIGTC; Grand Rapids: Eerdmans, 1991).

————, 'The gospel and godly models in Philippians', in M. J. Wilkins & T. Paige (eds.), *Worship, Theology and Ministry in the Early Church: Essays in Honor of Professor Ralph Martin* (Sheffield: Sheffield Academic Press, 1992), pp. 273–284.

—————, 'Paul's missionary calling within the purposes of God', in D. G. Peterson & J. Pryor (eds.), *In the Fullness of Time: Biblical Studies in Honour of Archbishop Donald Robinson* (Homebush West, NSW: Lancer, 1992), pp. 131–148.

—————, *Gospel and Mission in the Writings of Paul: An Exegetical and Theological Analysis* (Carlisle: Paternoster; Grand Rapids: Baker, 1995); originally published as *Consumed by Passion: Paul and the Dynamic of the Gospel* (Homebush West, NSW: Lancer, 1993).

—————(ed.), *God's Mission and Ours: The Challenge of Telling the Nations* (Sydney: CMS, 1999).

Oden, T. C., *The Word of Life: Systematic Theology* 2 (San Francisco: Harper & Row, 1989).

O'Donovan, O., *Resurrection and Moral Order: An Outline for Evangelical Ethics* (1986; Leicester: Apollos; Grand Rapids: Eerdmans, 2nd edn 1994).

Ollrog, W.-H., *Paulus und seine Mitarbeiter: Untersuchungen zu Theorie und Praxis der paulinischen Mission* (WMANT 50; Neukirchen-Vluyn: Neukirchener, 1979).

—————, 'Die Abfassungsverhältnisse von Röm 16', in D. Lührmann & G. Strecker (eds.), *Kirche: Festschrift für Günther Bornkamm zum 75. Geburtstag* (Tübingen: Mohr [Siebeck], 1980), pp. 221–244.

Ortlund, R. C., Jr, 'Male–female equality and male headship', in J. Piper & W. Grudem (eds.), *Recovering Biblical Manhood and Womanhood* (Wheaton, IL: Crossway, 1991), pp. 95–112.

Ovey, M. J., 'Augustine and the skeptics: is *Si fallor* worth revisiting?', *RTR* 55.3 (1996), pp. 134–148.

Pagels, E. H., *The Gnostic Paul: Gnostic Exegesis of the Pauline Letters* (Philadelphia: Fortress, 1975).

Paget, J. C., 'Jewish proselytism at the time of Christian origins: chimera or reality?', *JSNT* 62 (1996), pp. 65–103.

Pannenberg, W., *Basic Questions in Theology*, 3 vols. (tr. G. H. Kehm & R. A. Wilson; London: SCM, 1970–73).

—————, 'The crisis of the Scripture principle', in *Basic Questions in Theology* (see above), pp. 1–14.

—————, *Systematic Theology* (tr. G. W. Bromiley; Edinburgh and Grand Rapids: T. & T. Clark and Eerdmans, 3 vols 1991, 1994, 1998 [German: 1988, 1991, 1993]).

Parsons, M., 'Being precedes act: indicative and imperative in Paul's writings', in B. S. Rosner (ed.), *Understanding Paul's Ethics: Twentieth Century Approaches* (Grand Rapids: Eerdmans, 1995), pp. 217–247. Originally published in *EQ* 88.2 (1988), pp. 99–127.

Parunak, H. van D., 'Some discourse functions of prophetic quotation formulas in Jeremiah', in R. D. Bergen (ed.), *Biblical Hebrew and Discourse Linguistics* (Dallas: Summer Institute of Linguistics; Winona Lake: Eisenbrauns, 1994), pp. 489–519.

Penney, J. M., *The Missionary Emphasis of Lukan Pneumatology* (Sheffield: Sheffield Academic Press, 1997).

Perriman, A., *Speaking of Women: Interpreting Paul* (Leicester: Apollos, 1998).

Pesch, R., *Die Apostelgeschichte (Apg 13–28)* (Zürich: Benziger; Neukirchen: Neukirchener, 1986).

Peterson, D. G., *Hebrews and Perfection: An Examination of the Concept of Perfection in the 'Epistle to the Hebrews'* (SNTSMS 47; Cambridge: Cambridge University, 1982).

—————, *Engaging with God: A Biblical Theology of Worship* (Leicester: Apollos; Grand Rapids: Eerdmans, 1992).

Pfitzner, V. C., *Paul and the Agon Motif* (Leiden: Brill, 1967).

Pierce, C. A., *Conscience in the New Testament* (London: SCM, 1955).

Pietersma, A., *The Acts of Phileas, Bishop of Thmuis* (Geneva: Cramer, 1984).

Piper, J., & W. Grudem, 'An overview of central concerns: questions and answers', in J. Piper & W. Grudem (eds.), *Recovering Biblical Manhood and Womanhood: A Response to Evangelical Feminism* (Wheaton, IL: Crossway, 1991), pp. 60–92.

Pohlenz, M., *Die Stoa: Geschichte einer Geistigen Bewegung*, 2 vols. (Göttingen: Vandenhoeck und Ruprecht, 1959, 1970).

Polkinghorne, J., *Science and Providence: God's Interaction within the World* (London: SPCK, 1989).

Poythress, V. S., 'The church as family: why male leadership in the family requires male leadership in the church', in J. Piper & W. Grudem (eds.), *Recovering Biblical Manhood and Womanhood: A Response to Evangelical Feminism* (Wheaton, IL: Crossway, 1991), pp. 233–247.

Rakotoharintsifa, A., 'Jérémie en action à Corinthe: citations et allusions jérémiennes dans 1 Corinthiens', in A. H. W. Curtis et al. (eds.), *The Book of Jeremiah and its Reception* (BETL 128; Leuven: Leuven University Press, 1997), pp. 207–216.

Räisänen, H., *Paul and the Law* (Philadelphia: Fortress, 1986).

Ramsay, W. M., 'Historical commentary on the epistles to the Corinthians', *Exp*, 6th series (1898–99).

—————, *A Historical Commentary on St. Paul's Epistle to the Galatians* (London: Hodder and Stoughton, 2nd edn 1900).

—————, *The Cities of St Paul* (London, 1907).

Rapske, B., *The Book of Acts in its First Century Setting* 3: *The Book of Acts and Paul in Roman Custody* (Carlisle: Paternoster; Grand Rapids: Eerdmans, 1994).

Reed, J. T., 'Are Paul's thanksgivings "epistolary"?', *JSNT* 61 (1996), pp. 87–99.

Rendtorff, R., 'What is new in the new covenant?', *Canon and Theology: Overtures to an Old Testament Theology* (tr. M. Kohl; Edinburgh: T. and T. Clark, 1993 [German: *Kanon und Theologie: Vorarbeiten zu einer Theologie des Alten Testaments*; Neukirchen: Neukirchener, 1991]), pp. 196–206.

——————, *Die 'Bundesformel': Eine exegetisch-theologische Untersuchung* (SB 160; Stuttgart: Katholisches Bibelwerk, 1995).

Rengstorf, K. H., 'hypēretēs, hypēreteō', *TDNT* 8, pp. 530–544.

Richardson, P., 'From apostles to virgins: Romans 16 and the roles of women in the early church', *TJT* 2 (1986), pp. 232–261.

——————, *Herod King of the Jews and Friend of the Romans* (Columbia: University of South Carolina, 1997).

Rickman, G., *The Corn Supply of Ancient Rome* (Oxford: Clarendon, 1980).

Ridderbos, H., *Paul: An Outline of his Theology* (tr. J. R. de Witt; Grand Rapids: Eerdmans, 1975 [Dutch: 1966]).

Riesner, R., *Jesus als Lehrer* (Tübingen: Mohr, 1984).

——————, 'Jesus as preacher and teacher', in H. Wansbrough (ed.), *Jesus and the Oral Gospel Tradition* (Sheffield: Sheffield Academic Press, 1991), pp. 185–210.

Rike, R. L., *Apex omnium: Religion in the* Res Gestae *of Ammianus* (Berkeley: University of California Press, 1987).

Rinaldi, G., *Biblia Gentium* (Rome: Sacre Scritture, 1989).

Ringgren, H., *Israelite Religion* (tr. D. Green; London: SPCK, 1966 [German: 1963]).

Robert, L., *Documents de l'Asie Mineure méridionale* (Geneva and Paris: Droz, 1966).

Robinson, D. W. B., 'Who were "the saints"?', *RTR* 22.2 (1963), pp. 45–53.

——————, 'The salvation of Israel in Romans 9 – 11', *RTR* 26.3 (1967), pp. 81–96.

——————, *Faith's Framework: The Structure of New Testament Theology* (Sutherland, NSW: Albatross, 1985).

——————, '"The church" revisited: an autobiographical fragment', *RTR* 48.1 (1989), pp. 4–14.

——————, 'Biblical understanding of Israel – the geographical entity: some prolegomena', *St Mark's Review* 159 (1994), pp. 24–29.

————, 'Origins and unresolved tensions', in R. J. Gibson (ed.), *Interpreting God's Plan: Biblical Theology and the Pastor* (Explorations 11; Adelaide: Openbook, 1997; Carlisle: Paternoster, 1998), pp. 1–17.

————, 'Ministry-service in the Bible: human and divine, secular and sacred', in *Forward in Faith? Proceedings of the 1996 Conference of the Association for the Apostolic Ministry (Australia)* (Enmore, NSW: Aquila Books, 1998), pp. 51–64.

Robinson, J. A. T., *Redating the New Testament* (London: SCM, 1976).

Robinson, O. F., *The Criminal Law of Ancient Rome* (London: Duckworth, 1995).

Römer, T., 'Les "anciens" pères (Jér 11,10) et la "nouvelle" alliance (Jér 31,31)', *Biblische Notizen* 59 (1991), pp. 23–27.

Rowland, C. C., *Christian Origins* (London: SPCK, 1985).

Rubenson, S., *The Letters of St Antony: Monasticism and the Making of a Saint* (Minneapolis: Fortress, 1995).

Rudolph, W., *Jeremia* (HAT 12; Tübingen: Mohr [Siebeck], 3rd edn 1967).

Russell, D. A., 'Plutarch', in S. Hornblower & A. Spawforth (eds.), *Oxford Classical Dictionary* (Oxford: Oxford University Press, 3rd edn 1996), pp. 1200–1201.

————, *Plutarch* (London: Duckworth, 1973).

Sanday, W., & A. C. Headlam, *A Critical and Exegetical Commentary on the Epistle to the Romans* (1895; ICC; Edinburgh: T. and T. Clark, 5th edn 1902).

Sandbach, F. H., *Plutarch's Moralia XV* (LCL; Cambridge, MA: Harvard University Press; London: Heinemann, 1969).

————, *The Stoics* (New York: Norton, 1975).

Sanders, E. P., *Paul, the Law and the Jewish People* (London: SCM, 1985).

Sandnes, K. O., 'Paul and Socrates: the aim of Paul's Areopagus speech', *JSNT* 50 (1993), pp. 13–26.

Sarason, R. S., 'The interpretation of Jeremiah 31:31–34 in Judaism', in J. J. Petuchowski (ed.), *When Jews and Christians Meet* (Albany: State University of New York Press, 1988), pp. 99–123.

Savage, T. B., *Power through Weakness: Paul's Understanding of the Christian Ministry in 2 Corinthians* (SNTSMS 86: Cambridge: Cambridge University Press, 1996).

Schenk, W., Review of P. T. O'Brien, *Introductory Thanksgivings*, *ThLZ* 104 (1979), pp. 823–825.

Schlier, H., '*ekptyō*', *TDNT* 2, pp. 448–449.

————, *Der Brief an die Galater* (KEK 7; Göttingen: Vandenhoeck und Ruprecht, 14th edn 1971).

408   *The gospel to the nations*

Schmidt, T. E., *Straight and Narrow? Compassion and Clarity in the Homo-sexual Debate* (Leicester: IVP, 1995).

Schmithals, W., *Paul and James* (London: SCM, 1965).

Schnabel, E. J., *Law and Wisdom from Ben Sira to Paul* (Tübingen: Mohr [Siebeck], 1985).

Schnackenburg, R., 'Apostles before and during Paul's time', in W. W. Gasque & R. P. Martin (eds.), *Apostolic History and the Gospel: Biblical and Historical Essays Presented to F. F. Bruce* (Exeter: Paternoster; Grand Rapids: Eerdmans, 1970), pp. 287–303.

Schneemelcher, W., *New Testament Apocrypha* 2 (tr. R. McL. Wilson; Cambridge: Clarke, 6th edn 1992).

Schnider F., & W. Stenger, *Studien zum neutestamentlichen Briefformular* (NTTS 11; Leiden: Brill, 1987).

Schniewind, J., '*angelia, angellō, ktl.*, *TDNT* 2, pp. 56–73.

Schreiner, T. R., 'Is perfect obedience to the law possible? A re-examination of Galatians 3:10', *JETS* 27 (1984), pp. 151–160.

————, 'The valuable ministries of women in the context of male lead-ership: a survey of Old and New Testament examples and teaching', in J. Piper & W. Grudem (eds.), *Recovering Biblical Manhood and Woman-hood: A Response to Evangelical Feminism* (Wheaton, IL: Crossway, 1991), pp. 209–224.

————, *The Law and Its Fulfillment: A Pauline Theology of Law* (Grand Rapids: Baker, 1993).

————, *Romans* (BECNT; Grand Rapids: Baker, 1998).

Schröter, J., *Der versöhnte Versöhner: Paulus als unentbehrlicher Mittler im Heilsvorgang zwischen Gott und Gemeinde nach 2 Kor 2:14 – 7:4* (Tübingen: Francke Verlag, 1993).

Schubert, P., *Form and Function of the Pauline Thanksgivings* (BZNW 20; Berlin: Alfred Töpelmann, 1939).

Schulz, R. R., 'Romans 16:7: Junia or Junias?', *ExpT* 98 (1986–87), pp. 108–110.

————, 'A case for "President" Phoebe in Romans 16:2', *LTJ* 24 (1990), pp. 124–127.

Schürer, E., *The History of the Jewish People in the Age of Jesus Christ*, rev. and ed. G. Vermes, F. Millar & M. Goodman, 3 vols. in 4 (tr. T. A. Burkill et al.; Edinburgh: T. and T. Clark, 1986).

Schüssler Fiorenza, E., 'Missionaries, apostles, co-workers: Romans 16 and the reconstruction of women's early Christian history', *WW* 6 (1986), pp. 420–433.

————, *In Memory of Her* (New York: Crossroads, 1987).

Schweiker, W., & M. Welker, 'A new paradigm of theological and biblical inquiry', in C. L. Rigby (ed.), *Power, Powerlessness and the Divine: New Inquiries in Bible and Theology* (Atlanta: Scholars, 1997), pp. 3–20.

Schweizer, E., 'The testimony of Jesus in the early Christian community', *HBT* 7.1 (1985), pp. 77–98.

Scott, J. M., '"For as many as are of works of the law are under a curse" (Galatians 3:10)', in C. A. Evans & J. A. Sanders (eds.), *Paul and the Scriptures of Israel* (*JSNT*Sup 83; Sheffield: Sheffield Academic Press, 1993), pp. 187–221.

————, 'Luke's geographical horizon', in D. W. J. Gill & C. Gempf (eds.), *The Book of Acts in its First-Century Setting* 2: *Graeco-Roman Setting* (Grand Rapids: Eerdmans; Carlisle: Paternoster, 1994), pp. 483–544.

————, 'The triumph of God in 2 Cor. 2:14: additional evidence of Merkabah mysticism in Paul', *NTS* 42 (1996), pp. 260–281.

Scroggs, R., 'Women in the New Testament', *IDB*Sup, pp. 966–968.

Searle, J., *Speech Acts: An Essay in the Philosophy of Language* (Cambridge: Cambridge University Press, 1969).

Seccombe, D. P., *Jesus and the New Age: Investigating the Puzzles of Jesus' Career* (Cape Town: White Horse Books, forthcoming).

Sevenster, J. N., *Paul and Seneca* (Leiden: Brill, 1961).

Sherwin-White, A. N., *Roman Society and Roman Law in the New Testament* (Oxford: Clarendon, 1963).

————, *The Roman Citizenship* (Oxford: Clarendon, 2nd edn 1973 [1939]).

Sieben, H. J., *Kirchenväterhomilien zum Neuen Testament mit einem Anhang der Kirchenväterkommentare* (The Hague: Nijhoff, 1991).

Silva, M., *Biblical Words and Their Meaning: An Introduction to Lexical Semantics* (Grand Rapids: Zondervan, 1983, rev. 1994).

————, *Philippians* (BECNT; Grand Rapids: Baker, 1992).

————, 'Systematic theology and the apostle to the Gentiles', *TrinJ* 15 (1994), pp. 3–26.

————, *Explorations in Exegetical Method: Galatians as a Test Case* (Grand Rapids: Baker, 1996).

Skarsaune, O., 'Mission to the Jews – a closed chapter? Some patristic reflections on the Great Commission', in J. Ådna & H. Kvalbein (eds.), *The Mission of the Early Church to Jews and Gentiles* (Tübingen: Mohr [Siebeck], forthcoming).

Smallwood, E. M., 'The alleged Jewish tendencies of Poppaea Sabina', *JTS* 10 (1959), pp. 329–335.

Smith, R. B. E., *Julian's Gods: Religion and Philosophy in the Thought and Action of Julian the Apostate* (London: Routledge, 1995).

Sohn, S.-T., "'I will be your God and you will be my people": the origin and background of the covenant formula', in R. Chazan et al. (eds.), *Ki Baruch Hu: Ancient Near Eastern, Biblical and Judaic Studies in Honor of Baruch A. Levine* (Winona Lake: Eisenbrauns, 1999), pp. 355–372.

Souter, A., *The Earliest Latin Commentaries on the Epistles of St Paul* (Oxford: Clarendon, 1927).

Squires, J., 'The plan of God in the Acts of the Apostles', in I. H. Marshall and D. G. Peterson (eds.), *Witness to the Gospel: The Theology of Acts* (Grand Rapids: Eerdmans, 1998), pp. 19–39.

Stählin, G., 'orgē E. The wrath of man and the wrath of God in the New Testament', *TDNT* 5, pp. 19–447.

Stuehrenberg, P. F., 'Proselyte', *ABD* 5, pp. 503–505.

Swain, S., 'Character change in Plutarch', *Phoenix* 43 (1989), pp. 62–68.

Tajra, H. W., *The Martyrdom of St Paul: Historical and Judicial Context, Traditions and Legends* (Tübingen: Mohr [Siebeck], 1994).

Talbert, C. H., *Reading Luke: A Literary and Theological Commentary on the Third Gospel* (New York: Crossroad, 1982).

————, *Reading Corinthians: A Literary and Theological Commentary on 1 and 2 Corinthians* (New York: Crossroad, 1987).

Tannehill, R. C., *Dying and Rising with Christ* (BZNW 32; Berlin: A. Töpelmann, 1967).

————, 'Rejection by Jews and turning to Gentiles: the pattern of Paul's mission in Acts', in J. B. Tyson (ed.), *Luke-Acts and the Jewish People: Eight Critical Perspectives* (Minneapolis: Augsburg, 1988), pp. 83–101.

Tatum, J. (ed.), *The Search for the Ancient Novel* (Baltimore: Johns Hopkins University Press, 1994).

Taylor, N., *Paul, Antioch and Jerusalem: A Study in Relationships and Authority in Earliest Christianity* (Sheffield: Sheffield Academic Press, 1992).

Theissen, G., *The Social Setting of Pauline Christianity: Essays on Corinth* (ed. and tr. J. H. Schütz; Philadelphia: Fortress, 1982 [German: various dates]).

Thiessen, W., *Christen in Ephesus: Die historische und theologische Situation in vorpaulinischer und paulinischer Zeit und zur Zeit der Apostelgeschichte und der Pastoralbriefe* (Tübingen: Francke, 1995).

Thrall, M. E., *II Corinthians* (ICC; Edinburgh: T. and T. Clark, 1994).

Tomes, R., 'The reception of Jeremiah in rabbinic literature and in the Targum', in A. H. W. Curtis et al. (eds.), *The Book of Jeremiah and its Reception* (BETL 128; Leuven: Leuven University Press, 1997), pp. 233–253.

Torrance, T. F., *Theological Science* (Oxford: Oxford University Press, 1969).

——————, *The Mediation of Christ* (Edinburgh: T. and T. Clark, 1982, rev. 1992).

——————, *The Trinitarian Faith: The Evangelical Theology of the Ancient Catholic Church* (Edinburgh: T. and T. Clark, 1993).

——————, *Preaching Christ Today: The Gospel and Scientific Thinking* (Grand Rapids: Eerdmans, 1994).

——————, *Divine Meaning: Studies in Patristic Hermeneutics* (Edinburgh: T. and T. Clark, 1995).

Travis, S. H., 'Wrath of God (NT)', in *ABD* 6, pp. 996–998.

Trench, R. C., *Plutarch: His Life, his Parallel Lives and his Moral. Five Lectures* (London: Macmillan, 1874).

van Unnik, W. C., *Tarsus or Jerusalem? The City of Paul's Youth* (tr. G. Ogg; London: Epworth, 1962).

Vanhoozer, K. J., 'From canon to concept: "same" and "other" in the relation between biblical and systematic theology', *SBET* 12 (1994), pp. 96–124.

——————, 'God's mighty speech-acts: the doctrine of Scripture today', in P. E. Satterthwaite & D. F. Wright (eds.), *A Pathway into the Holy Scripture* (Grand Rapids: Eerdmans, 1994), pp. 143–181.

—————— (ed.), *The Trinity in a Pluralistic Age: Theological Essays on Culture and Religion* (Grand Rapids: Eerdmans, 1997).

——————, *Is There a Meaning in this Text? The Bible, the Reader, and the Morality of Literary Knowledge* (Grand Rapids: Zondervan; Leicester: Apollos, 1998).

Verhoef, P. A., '*ḥdš*', in *NIDOTTE* 2, pp. 30–37.

Vermes, G., *Jesus the Jew* (London: Collins, 1973).

——————, *Jesus and the World of Judaism* (London: SCM, 1983).

——————, *The Religion of Jesus the Jew* (London: SCM, 1993).

Vernière, Y., 'Le Léthé de Plutarque', *RÉA* 66 (1964), pp. 22–32.

Wallis, W., 'Irony in Jeremiah's prophecy of a new covenant', *BETS* 12 (1969), pp. 107–110.

Walton, S. J., *Paul in Acts and Epistles: The Miletus speech and 1 Thessalonians as a test case* (unpublished PhD thesis; Sheffield University, 1997).

Watson, W. G. E., *Classical Hebrew Poetry: A Guide to its Techniques* (JSOTSup 26; Sheffield: Sheffield Academic Press, 1984, rev. 1986).

Watt, I., *The Rise of the Novel* (London: Chatto and Windus, 1957).

Weaver, P. R. C., *Familia Caesaris: A Social Study of the Emperor's Freedmen and Slaves* (Cambridge: Cambridge University Press, 1972).

Webster, J. B., 'Hermeneutics in modern theology: some doctrinal reflections', *SJT* 51.3 (1998), pp. 307–341.

Wedderburn, A. J. M., *The Reasons for Romans* (Edingurgh: T. and T. Clark, 1998).

Weippert, H., 'Das Wort vom neuen Bund in Jeremia xxxi 31–34', *VT* 29 (1979), pp. 336–351.

Wenham, D., 'Acts and the Pauline corpus II: the evidence of parallels', in B. W. Winter & A. D. Clarke (eds.), *The Book of Acts in its First Century Setting* 1: *The Book of Acts in Its Ancient Literary Setting* (Grand Rapids: Eerdmans; Carlisle: Paternoster, 1993), pp. 215–258.

——————, *Paul: Follower of Jesus or Founder of Christianity?* (Grand Rapids: Eerdmans, 1995).

——————, 'The enigma of John's Gospel', *TynB* 48 (1997), pp. 149–178.

Wenham, J., *Redating Matthew, Mark and Luke* (London: Hodder and Stoughton, 1991).

Westerholm, S., *Israel's Law and the Church's Faith: Paul and his Recent Interpreters* (Grand Rapids: Eerdmans, 1988).

White, J. L., 'New Testament epistolary literature in the framework of ancient epistolography', in W. Haase (ed.), *ANRW* 2.2 (Berlin: de Gruyter, 1984), pp. 1730–1756.

White, J. R., '"Baptized on account of the dead": the meaning of 1 Corinthians 15:29 in its context', *JBL* 116 (1997), pp. 487–499.

Wiles, G. P., *Paul's Intercessory Prayers: The Significance of the Intercessory Prayer Passages in the Letters of Paul* (SNTSMS 24; Cambridge: Cambridge University Press, 1974).

Wiles, M., *The Divine Apostle: The Interpretation of St Paul's Epistles in the Early Church* (Cambridge: Cambridge University Press, 1967).

——————, 'Does Christology rest on a mistake?', *Working Papers in Doctrine* (London: SCM, 1976), pp. 122–131. Originally published in *RS* 6 (1970), pp. 69–76.

——————, 'Scriptural authority and theological construction: the limitations of narrative interpretation', in G. Green (ed.), *Scriptural Authority and Narrative Interpretation* (Philadelphia: Fortress, 1987), pp. 42–58.

Wilken, R. L., *The Christians as the Romans Saw Them* (New Haven: Yale University Press, 1984).

——————, Review of W. Kinzig, *Novitas christiana: die Idee des Fortschritts in der alten Kirche bis Eusebius* (Göttingen: Vandenhoeck und Ruprecht, 1994), in *JTS* 47 (1996), pp. 271–274.

Williams, M. H., *Theosebēs gar ēn*: The Jewish tendencies of Poppaea Sabina', *JTS* 39 (1988), pp. 97–111.

Williams, R., *The Wound of Knowledge: Christian Spirituality from the New Testament to St John of the Cross* (London: Darton, Longman and Todd, 1979).

Williams, T. F., '*prr*', in *NIDOTTE* 3, pp. 695–698.

Wilson, S. G., *Gentiles and the Gentile Mission in Luke-Acts* (Cambridge: Cambridge University Press, 1973).

——————, 'From Jesus to Paul: the contours and consequences of a debate', in P. Richardson & J. C. Hurd (eds.), *From Jesus to Paul* (Waterloo, Ontario: Wilfred Laurier University Press, 1984), pp. 1–21.

Wimbush, V. L. (ed.), *Ascetic Behaviour in Greco-Roman Antiquity: A Sourcebook* (Minneapolis: Fortress, 1990).

Winter, B. W., 'The role of the *captatio benevolentia* in the speeches of Tertullus and Paul in Acts 24', *JTS* 42.2 (1991), pp. 505–531.

——————, 'In public and private: early Christians and religious pluralism', in A. D. Clarke & B. W. Winter (eds.), *One God, One Lord: Christianity in a World of Religious Pluralism* (Exeter: Paternoster, 1992), pp. 125–148.

——————, 'The problem with "church" for the early church', in D. G. Peterson and J. Pryor (eds.), *In the Fullness of Time: Biblical Studies in Honour of Archbishop Robinson* (Sydney: Lancer, 1992), pp. 203–217.

——————, 'Official proceedings and forensic speeches in Acts 24–26', in A. D. Clarke and B. W. Winter (eds.), *The Book of Acts in its First Century Setting* 1: *The Book of Acts in its Ancient Literary Setting* (Grand Rapids: Eerdmans; Carlisle: Paternoster, 1993), pp. 305–336.

——————, *Seek the Welfare of the City: Christians as Benefactors and Citizens* (Carlisle: Paternoster; Grand Rapids: Eerdmans, 1994).

——————, 'On introducing gods to Athens: an alternative reading of Acts 17:18–20', *TynB* 47.1 (1996), pp. 71–90.

——————, 'Gallio's ruling on the legal status of early Christianity (Acts 18:14–15)', *TynB* 50.2 (1999), pp. 213–24.

Witherington III, B., 'On the road with Mary Magdalene, Joanna, Susanna, and other disciples – Luke 8:1–3', *ZNW* 70 (1979), pp. 243–248.

——————, *Women in the Earliest Churches* (SNTSMS 59; Cambridge: Cambridge University Press, 1988).

——————, *The Acts of the Apostles: A Socio-Rhetorical Commentary* (Grand Rapids: Eerdmans, 1998).

——————, *Grace in Galatia: A Commentary on Paul's Letter to the Galatians* (Grand Rapids: Eerdmans, 1998).

Wolff, C., *Jeremia im Frühjudentum und Urchristentum* (TUGAL 118; Berlin: Akademie-Verlag, 1976).

Wolff, H. W., 'What is new in the new covenant? A contribution to the Jewish–Christian dialogue according to Jer. 31:31–34', *Confrontations With Prophets: Discovering the Old Testament's New and Contemporary Significance* (tr. M. Kohl et al.; Philadelphia: Fortress, 1983 [German: *Prophetische Alternativen: Entdeckungen des Neuen im Alten Testament*; München: Kaiser, 1982]), pp. 49–62.

Wolterstorff, N., *Divine Discourse: Philosophical Reflections on the Claim that God Speaks* (Cambridge: Cambridge University Press, 1995).

Wood, C., *The Formation of Christian Understanding: An Essay in Theological Hermeneutics* (Philadelphia: Westminster, 1981).

Wright, A., *The Composition of the Four Gospels* (London: Macmillan, 1890).

Wright, N. T., 'Reflected glory: 2 Corinthians 3:18', in L. D. Hurst & N. T. Wright (eds.), *The Glory of Christ in the New Testament: Studies in Christology in Memory of George Bradford Caird* (Oxford: Oxford University Press, 1987), pp. 139–150.

————, 'Curse and covenant: Galatians 3: 10–14', in *The Climax of the Covenant: Christ and the Law in Pauline Theology* (Edinburgh: T. and T. Clark, 1991).

————, 'How can the Bible be authoritative?', *VoxEv* 21 (1991), pp. 7–32.

————, 'Jerusalem in the New Testament', in P. W. L. Walker (ed.), *Jerusalem Past and Present in the Purposes of God* (Grand Rapids: Eerdmans, 1992), pp. 53–77.

————, *What Saint Paul Really Said: Was Paul of Tarsus the Real Founder of Christianity?* (Oxford: Lion, 1997).

Young, F. M., *Biblical Exegesis and the Formation of Christian Culture* (Cambridge: Cambridge University Press, 1997).

————, 'Note on 2 Corinthians 1:17b', *JTS* 37 (1986), pp. 404–415.

Young, F. M., & D. F. Ford, *Meaning and Truth in 2 Corinthians* (Grand Rapids: Eerdmans, 1987).

Young, F. M., *The Art of Performance: Towards a Theology of Holy Scripture* (London: Darton, Longman and Todd, 1990).

Young, M. O., 'Did some Middle Platonists deny the immortality of the soul?', *HTR* 68 (1975), pp. 58–60.

Zahn, T., *Geschichte des neutestamentlichen Kanons* (Erlangen: Deichert, 1888–90).

Zeller, E., *The Stoics, Epicureans, and Sceptics* (tr. O. J. Reichel; London: Longmans, 1870), pp. 45–46.

Index of Scripture references